Economic Sophisms and
"What Is Seen and What Is Not Seen"

The Collected Works of Frédéric Bastiat

Jacques de Guenin, General Editor

The Man and the Statesman: The Correspondence and Articles on Politics

"The Law," "The State," and Other Political Writings, 1843–1850

Economic Sophisms and "What Is Seen and What Is Not Seen"

Miscellaneous Works on Economics: From "Jacques-Bonhomme" to Le Journal des Économistes

Economic Harmonies

The Struggle against Protectionism: The English and French Free-Trade Movements

Frédéric Bastiat

Economic Sophisms and
"What Is Seen and What Is Not Seen"

FRÉDÉRIC BASTIAT

Jacques de Guenin, *General Editor*
Translated from the French by
Jane Willems and Michel Willems
with a foreword by
Robert McTeer
and an introduction and appendixes
by Academic Editor
David M. Hart

Annotations and Glossaries by
Jacques de Guenin, Jean-Claude Paul-Dejean,
and David M. Hart

Translation Editor
Dennis O'Keeffe

Liberty Fund

This book is published by Liberty Fund, Inc., a foundation established
to encourage study of the ideal of a society of free and responsible individuals.

𒂼𒄄

The cuneiform inscription that serves as our logo and as the design motif
for our endpapers is the earliest-known written appearance of the word "freedom"
(*amagi*), or "liberty." It is taken from a clay document written about 2300 B.C.
in the Sumerian city-state of Lagash.

17 22 23 24 25 C 5 4 3 2 1
22 23 24 25 26 P 6 5 4 3 2

Library of Congress Cataloging-in-Publication Data

Names: Bastiat, Frédéric, 1801–1850, author. | Guenin, Jacques de, editor.
| Bastiat, Frédéric, 1801–1850. Sophismes économiques. English. |
Bastiat, Frédéric, 1801–1850. Ce qu'on voit et ce qu'on ne voit pas.
English.
Title: Economic sophisms ; and, What is seen and what is not seen /
Frédéric Bastiat ; Jaques de Guenin, General Editor ; translated from the French by
Jane Willems and Michel Willems ; with a foreword by Robert McTeer ; and an introduction
and appendixes by Academic Editor David M. Hart
Other titles: Economic sophisms. | What is seen and what is not seen.
Description: Indianapolis, Indiana : Liberty Fund, Inc., [2016] |
Series: The collected works of Frédéric Bastiat | Includes bibliographical references and index.
Identifiers: LCCN 2016015271 (print) | LCCN 2016021940 (ebook) | ISBN 9780865978874
(hardcover : alk. paper) | ISBN 9780865978881 (pbk. : alk. paper) | ISBN 9781614876502
(Mobi) | ISBN 9781614879206 (PDF) | ISBN 9781614872740 (epub)
Subjects: LCSH: Free trade. | Free enterprise. | Protectionism. | Economics.
Classification: LCC HB105.B3 A25 2016 (print) | LCC HB105.B3 (ebook) | DDC 330—dc23
LC record available at https://lccn.loc.gov/2016015271

Liberty Fund, Inc.
11301 North Meridian St.
Carmel, Indiana 46032
libertyfund.org

Contents

———

Foreword

"The state is the great fiction by which everyone endeavors to live at the expense of everyone else."

—FROM "THE STATE" (1848), BY FRÉDÉRIC BASTIAT

Claude Frédéric Bastiat was born in France in 1801. Two hundred years later, in 2001, I was invited to speak at his birthday celebration.[1] I titled my remarks "Why Bastiat Is My Hero." That was over ten years ago, but I do not have to look back into my notes to remember the reasons why Bastiat was and still is my hero.

During his brief life of forty-nine years, Bastiat fought for individual liberty in general and free trade in particular. He fought against protectionism, mercantilism, and socialism. He wrote with a combination of clarity, wit, and wisdom unmatched to this day. He not only made his arguments easy to understand; he made them impossible to misunderstand and to forget. He used humor and satire to expose his opponents' arguments as not just wrong, but absurd, by taking them to their logical extreme. He noted that his adversaries often had to stop short in their arguments to avoid that trap.

My introduction to Bastiat as a student was snippets from his "Petition by the Manufacturers of Candles" in economics textbooks. The brilliance of this text still thrills and inspires me.[2] In the petition, the candle makers call on the Chamber of Deputies to pass a law requiring the closing of all blinds and shutters to prevent sunlight from coming inside. The sun was unfair

---

1. To commemorate the two hundredth anniversary of the birth of Frédéric Bastiat an international conference was held in Dax in June 2001 under the auspices of the Cercle Frédéric Bastiat and Jacques de Guenin. It was here that Liberty Fund's project of translating the collected works of Bastiat was conceived.

2. As it did the great economic journalist Henry Hazlitt. See Henry Hazlitt's "Introduction" to *Economic Sophisms,* FEE Edition, p. xiv.

competition to the candle makers and they needed protection. Protection from the sunlight would not only benefit the candle makers and related industries competing with the sun; it would also benefit unrelated industries as spending and prosperity spread. Bastiat anticipated Keynesian multiplier analysis, although for Bastiat it was satire with a very serious intent.

Bastiat wanted *Economic Sophisms* to serve as a handbook for free traders, and, indeed, when I was president of the Federal Reserve Bank of Dallas, we used his writings in our economic education efforts. Throughout the book, Bastiat attacks protectionist sophisms, or fallacies, methodically and exhaustively; however, he identifies a major problem of persuasion, namely, that most sophisms contain some truth, usually a half-truth, but it is the half that is visible. As he writes in his introduction: "Protection brings together in one single point all the good it does and distributes among the wider mass of people the harm it inflicts. One is visible to the naked eye, the other only to the mind's eye."[3]

For example, we can see for ourselves imports and new technology destroying domestic jobs. We can see government spending creating jobs, and minimum wage laws raising wages. To get from these half-truths to the whole truth, however, requires considering what is not seen, except "in the mind's eye."

The fable of the broken window is Bastiat's most famous illustration of the seen versus the unseen.[4] The son of Jacques Bonhomme[5] broke his window, and a crowd gathered. What a shame; Jacques will have to pay for another window. But wait. There is a silver lining. The window repairman will receive additional income to spend. Some merchant will then also have new income to spend, and so on. It's a shame about the broken window, but it did set off a chain reaction of new spending, creating prosperity for many.

Hold on, cautions Bastiat. If Jacques didn't have to replace his window, he would have spent or invested his money elsewhere. Then another merchant would have new income to spend, and so on. The spending chain initiated by the broken window happens and will be seen; the spending chain that would otherwise have happened won't be seen. The broken window diverted spending; it didn't increase spending. But the stimulus from the broken window was seen, and seeing is believing.

3. ES1 Introduction, p. 4.
4. See WSWNS 1.
5. One of Bastiat's fictional stock characters, who appears frequently in *Economic Sophisms*.

The broken window fallacy sounds like a child's fairy tale, yet nothing could be more relevant today. We're told every day of the benefits of some government program or project, and most do some good. What we don't see is how taxpayers might have spent their own money for their own good. Or, if the government spending is financed by borrowing, we probably won't see the implications for the future burden of the additional debt, or for future inflation if the debt is monetized. We forget that governments can give to us only what they take from us.

Bastiat's lectures on the half-truth versus the whole truth, the short run versus the long run, the part versus the whole, and the seen versus the unseen teach us the economic way of thinking. While he was steeped in classical economics, his views were also based on what he experienced empirically. All he had to do was walk around the port city of Bayonne where he was born to see firsthand the disastrous results of "protection." The protection was protection from prosperity.

Bastiat was also influenced by the free-trade movement in England and its leader, Richard Cobden, who became a regular correspondent and firm friend for the last five years of Bastiat's life. Bastiat wanted to do for France what Cobden was doing for England, so he became an activist, establishing free-trade associations. He entered politics and was elected to the Chamber of Deputies. Many of his speeches, pamphlets, and other articles were directed specifically to statements made by his opponents in that chamber. He named names, but he was ever the gentleman in his debates, attacking the argument rather than the person.

In debate, Bastiat not only proved his opponents wrong; he showed that their positions, when stripped to the core, were absurd. Their focus on the producer rather than the consumer led them to view less output as better than more, and more work to achieve a given end as better than less. Consumers have a stake in efficiency and productivity, and their goals are in harmony with the greater good. Producers, on the other hand, find merit in inefficiency and obstacles to productivity. They wanted to count jobs, while Bastiat wanted to make jobs count. He exposed the absurdity of the fallacy when he suggested allowing workers to use their left hands only and creating jobs by burning Paris.

Bastiat pointed out that the lawmakers who were also merchants or farmers held conflicting positions. Back home they value efficiency and productivity, trying to get the most output and income from the least labor. Yet, as legislators, they tried to make work by creating obstacles and inefficiency.

They built roads and bridges to facilitate transportation and commerce, then put customs agents on the roads to do the opposite. He pointed out that if they farmed the way they legislated, they would use only hoes and mattocks to till the earth and eschew the plow.

The obvious question is, if Bastiat's rhetoric was so effective, why didn't he prevail in the Chamber? His opponents' answer then, as now, is that these fancy notions may work in theory, but not in practice. "Go write your books, Mr. Intellectual; we are men of practical affairs." We might, however, answer on behalf of Bastiat that, in the short term at least, the fight against protectionism was sidetracked by the outbreak of the 1848 Revolution and the rise of socialism during the Second Republic. Bastiat, like many of his free market colleagues, had other matters to attend to during this period. In the medium term, we might say that Bastiat's free trade ideas did in fact have an impact. The signing of the Cobden-Chevalier Trade Treaty between England and France in 1860 is one important measure of the success of free trade ideas, at least in the middle of the nineteenth century. In the longer term, unfortunately, he, as do we today, underestimated the power that economic sophisms have over the popular mind in general and even over most of our legislators in particular. This confirms the importance of returning to Bastiat's ideas, for the power of his economic arguments as well as for the enjoyment of his inimitable brilliant style. So, even after more than ten years, Bastiat remains "my intellectual hero."

Robert McTeer

General Editor's Note

The Collected Works of Frédéric Bastiat will be the most complete edition of Bastiat's works published to date, in any country or in any language. The main source for this translation is the *Œuvres complètes de Frédéric Bastiat,* published by Guillaumin in the 1850s and 1860s.[1]

Although the Guillaumin edition was generally chronological, the volumes in this series have been arranged thematically:

*The Man and the Statesman: The Correspondence and Articles on
    Politics*
"The Law," "The State," and Other Political Writings, 1843–1850
Economic Sophisms and "What Is Seen and What Is Not Seen"
Miscellaneous Works on Economics: From "Jacques Bonhomme" to Le
    Journal des Économistes
Economic Harmonies
*The Struggle against Protectionism: The English and French Free-Trade
    Movements*

There are three kinds of notes in this edition: footnotes by the editor of the Guillaumin edition (Prosper Paillottet), which are preceded by "(Paillottet's note)"; footnotes by Bastiat, which are preceded by "(Bastiat's note)"; and new editorial footnotes to this edition, which stand alone (unless they are commenting on Paillottet's notes, in which case they are in square brackets following Paillottet's note). Each sophism is preceded by a detailed publishing history which consists of (1) the original title, (2) the place and date of first publication, (3) the date of the first French edition as a book or a pamphlet, (4) the location in Paillottet's edition of the *Œuvres complètes* (1st ed. 1854–55), and (5) the dates of the following English translations: the first

---

1. For a more detailed description of the publication history of the *Œuvres complètes,* see Note on the Editions of the *Œuvres complètes* and the bibliography.

English (England) translation, the first American translation, and the FEE translation.

In the text, Bastiat (and Paillottet in the notes) makes many passing references to his works, for which we have provided an internal cross-reference if the work is in this volume. For those works not in this volume, we have provided the location of the orignal French version in the *Œuvres complètes* (indicated in a footnote by "*OC,*" followed by the Guillaumin volume number, beginning page number, and French title of the work).

In addition, we have made available two online sources[2] for the reader to consult. The first source is a table of contents of the seven-volume *Œuvres complètes* with links to PDF facsimiles of each volume. The second source is our "Comparative Table of Contents of the Collected Works of Frédéric Bastiat," which is a table of contents of the complete Liberty Fund series. Here the reader can find the location of the English translation of the work in its future Liberty Fund volume. These contents will be filled in and updated as the volumes come out and will eventually be the most complete comparative listing of Bastiat's works.

In order to avoid multiple footnotes and cross-references, we have provided a glossary of persons, a glossary of places, a glossary of newspapers and journals, and a glossary of subjects and terms to identify those persons, places, historical events, and terms mentioned in the text. The glossaries will also provide historical context and background for the reader as well as a greater understanding of Bastiat's work. If a name as it appears in the text is ambiguous or is in the glossary under a different name, a brief footnote has been added to identify the name as it is listed in the glossary.

Finally, original italics as they appear in the Guillaumin edition have been retained.

Jacques de Guenin
Saint-Loubouer, France

---

2. The first source is the main Bastiat page in the Online Library of Liberty, which lists all Bastiat's works we have online http://oll.libertyfund.org/people/frederic-bastiat. The second source is "A List of Bastiat's Works in Chronological Order," which lists each of Bastiat's known works with information about the original date and place of publication, its location in Paillottet's edition of the *Œuvres complètes,* and its location in Liberty Fund's edition http://oll.libertyfund.org/pages/bastiat-chrono-list.

Note on the Translation

Below we discuss some of the problems faced by translating a French work on political economy from the mid-nineteenth century into English. We begin with some general observations which are applicable to all the volumes in the Collected Works of Frédéric Bastiat. These are followed by some remarks which are specific to the matters covered in this particular volume.

TRANSLATION MATTERS OF A GENERAL NATURE IN THE COLLECTED WORKS

Throughout the translation of this series, we have made a deliberate decision not to translate Bastiat's French into modern, colloquial American English. Wherever possible we have tried to retain a flavor of the more florid, Latinate forms of expression which were common among the literate class in mid-nineteenth-century France. Bastiat liked long, flowing sentences, where idea followed upon idea in an apparently endless succession of dependent clauses. We have broken up many but not all of these thickets of expression for the sake of clarity. In those that remain, you, dear reader, will have to navigate.

Concerning the problematic issue of how to translate the French term *la liberté*—whether to use the more archaic-sounding English word "liberty" or the more modern word "freedom"—we have let the context have the final say. Bastiat was much involved with establishing a free-trade movement in France and to that end founded the Free Trade Association (L'Association pour la liberté des échanges) and its journal *Le Libre-échange* (Free Trade). In this context the word choice is clear: we must use the word "freedom," because this is intimately linked to the idea of "free trade." The English phrase "liberty of trade" would sound awkward. Another word is *pouvoir*, which we have variously translated as "power," "government," or "authority," again depending on the context.

A third example consists of the words *économie politique* and *économiste*. Throughout the eighteenth and for most of the nineteenth century, in both French and English, the term "political economy" was used to describe what we now call "economics." Toward the end of the nineteenth century, as economics became more mathematical, the adjective "political" was dropped and not replaced. We have preferred to keep the term "political economy" both because it was still current when Bastiat was writing and because it better describes the state of the discipline which proudly mixed an interest in moral philosophy, history, and political theory with the main dish, which was economic analysis. In Bastiat's day it was assumed that any *économiste* was a free-market economist, and so the noun needed no adjectival qualifier. Today one can be a free-market economist, a Marxist economist, a Keynesian economist, a mathematical economist, or an Austrian economist, to name a few. The qualifier before the noun is therefore quite important. This was not the case in Bastiat's time.

A particularly difficult word to translate is *l'industrie,* as is its related term *industriel.* In some respects it is a "false friend," as one is tempted to translate it as "industry" or "industrious" or "industrial," but this would be wrong because these terms have the more narrow modern meaning of "heavy industry" or "manufacturing" or "the result of some industrial process." The meaning in Bastiat's time was both more general and more specific to a particular social and economic theory current in his day. The word "industry" had a specific meaning which was tied to a social and economic theory developed by Jean-Baptiste Say and his followers Charles Comte and Charles Dunoyer in the 1810s and 1820s, as well as by other theorists such as the historian Augustin Thierry. According to these theorists, there were only two means of acquiring wealth, by productive activity and voluntary exchanges in the free market (i.e., *industrie*—which included agriculture, trade, factory production, services, and so on) or by coercive means (conquest, theft, taxation, subsidies, protection, transfer payments, or slavery). Anybody who acquired wealth through voluntary exchange and productive activities belonged to a class of people collectively called *les industrieux,* in contrast to those individuals or groups who acquired their wealth by force, coercion, conquest, slavery, or government privileges. The latter group was seen as a ruling class or as "parasites" who lived at the expense of *les industrieux.*

Bastiat uses the French term *la spoliation* (plunder) many times in his writings. Following from his view of "industry" as defined above, Bastiat believed that there is a distinction between two ways in which wealth can be acquired, either through peaceful and voluntary exchange (i.e., the free market) or by theft, conquest, and coercion (i.e., using the power of the state to tax, repossess, or grant special privileges). The latter he described as "plunder."

In Bastiat's time, the word "liberal" had the same meaning in France and in the English-speaking worlds of England and America. In the United States, however, the meaning of the word has shifted progressively toward the left of the political spectrum. A precise translation of the French word would be either "classical liberal" or "libertarian," depending upon the context, and indeed Bastiat is considered to be a classical liberal by present-day conservatives and a libertarian by present-day libertarians. To avoid the resulting awkwardness, we have decided to keep the word "liberal," with its nineteenth-century meaning, in the translations as well as the notes and the glossaries.

TRANSLATION MATTERS SPECIFIC TO THIS VOLUME

More specific to this volume are the words and phrases which will be discussed below. In many cases we have found it very helpful to consult the earlier translation of the first two series of *Economic Sophisms* made by the Foundation for Economic Education (FEE) in 1964.[1] Although we sometimes disagreed with their interpretation, we have found their notes and comments very informative and useful. We acknowledge in the footnotes when we have made use of their earlier work.

Sophism

The very title economic "sophisms" poses a problem. *Sophisme* can be translated directly as "sophism," preferred by the FEE translator in 1964, or as "fallacy," which is the term preferred by nineteenth-century translators. We have sided with the FEE translator here in most instances. Bastiat uses the word in a couple of different senses. The term can refer to an obvious error in economic theory; that is, a "fallacy." It can also refer to an argument that has an element of truth in which this partial truth is used speciously to make a case for one particular economic interest in a debate; that is, a piece of "sophistry." In this latter sense, which makes up the bulk of this book, the word "sophism" is the preferred translation. The word "sophism" is also

---

1. *Economic Sophisms,* FEE edition, and "What Is Seen and What Is Not Seen," in *Selected Essays on Political Economy,* FEE edition.

used to refer to Bastiat's essays in which he attacks these false or sophistical economic ideas, as in "In the sophism about the broken window Bastiat argues. . . . " We hope the meaning is clear from the context.

Humor

Bastiat enjoyed creating neologisms in order to poke fun at his adversaries. These words were sometimes based on Latin words and sometimes on French words. We have tried to find English equivalents which capture the flavor of Bastiat's originals and his intent. These are explained in the footnotes. Some examples are the two towns "Stulta" and "Puera" ("Stupidville" and "Childishtown"); the tax collector "M. Lasouche" (Mr. Blockhead); "M. Prohibant" (Mr. Prohibitor or Mr. Prohibitionist); and the two lobby groups the "Sinistrists" (the Left Handers) and the "Dexterists" (the Right Handers).

Another weapon in Bastiat's lexical armory was parody. He liked to take government institutions or documents, or well-known works of literature, and write a parody of their structure and content. A good example of this is his creation of a "Lower Council of Labor" (for ordinary shopkeepers and workers) to make fun of the protectionist and establishment "Superior Council of Commerce." Another is his mimicking of government "circulars" (or memoranda) issued in the early months of the Second Republic. As a deputy and vice president of the Finance Committee of the Chamber he would have seen many of these, and he is thus able to mimic their style wonderfully. But the supreme example of his skill as a writer is his parody of Molière's parody of seventeenth-century doctors. He takes Molière's acerbic commentary on the primitive medical practices of his day and turns it into a very sharp critique of the behavior of customs officers of his own day. These pose some difficulty for a modern translator; indeed, much has to be explained in the footnotes in order for these parodies to make sense, as he wrote his parody in "dog Latin" for which we have used the excellent translation made by FEE.[2]

Of all the challenges facing a translator, one of the hardest is explaining puns, which are usually unique to a given language. Bastiat liked to pun, as the footnotes will make clear. A good example is from the sophism "The Right Hand and the Left Hand" (ES2 16) in which the king is asked to expand the amount of work in the country (and thus increase "prosperity") by forbidding people to use their right hands. Bastiat has a field day creating a

---

2. See *Economic Sophisms,* FEE edition, p. 194.

new lobby group, the "Dexterists," who campaign for the freedom to work with one's right hand, and the "Sinistrists," who lobby for the use of the left hand only. In Bastiat's mind, all this is so much *"gaucherie."* Another good example is the case of the customs barrier across the Bidassoa River, on the border with Spain, which legally permits trade (which is taxed) "over the river," but which drives the black market in untaxed goods "under the river" (or "underground" as it were).[3] He also puns on the names of the streets on which various lobby groups were located. For example, the main protectionist lobby group, the Association for the Defense of National Employment, had its headquarters on the rue de Hautville (Highville Street) and thus is an open target for puns on whether or not they are in favor of high prices or low prices.

Some of Bastiat's funniest moments come with his frequent wordplay, which is especially hard for a translator to convey. We have attempted to do this without intruding too much on the reader's patience. England was seen as both a real military enemy because of its role in the war against the French Republic and then Napoléon's Empire, and as an economic enemy because of its advocacy of free trade. England was known as "Perfidious Albion" (Deceitful England), and so to show the absurdity of this idea Bastiat invents the notion of "Perfidious Normandy,"[4] which threatens Paris because it can produce butter more cheaply.

French word order is also used to make a political point. In French an adjective can precede a noun or follow it without too much difference in meaning. In English this makes no sense. Bastiat has a protagonist argue with an opponent of free trade (*libre-échange*) who despises the very idea because it is English, but quite likes the idea of being free to buy and sell things because this is an example of *échange libre* (trade which is free).[5]

Plain Speaking

Bastiat was torn between using a more lighthearted style which used humor, puns, wordplay, and satire to make his important economic and political points, or using a more serious and sober style. He made a name for himself as a witty and clever economic journalist when he wrote for the free trade journal *Le Libre-échange,* which he edited between 1846 and early 1848, in

3. See ES3 10.
4. See the entry for "Perfidious Albion," in the Glossary of Subjects and Terms.
5. See ES3 13.

which he pilloried his opponents.[6] However, as the political and economic situation got worse in France, he seemed unable to make up his mind which was the best strategy and flip-flopped on the matter. A good example of this self-doubt appears in "Theft by Subsidy" (ES2 9), in which he called for an "explosion of plain speaking" and the avoidance of circumlocutions and euphemisms when describing government policies and their impact on ordinary taxpayers and consumers. We have tried to capture his outrage, anger, and sense of injustice at protectionism and government interventionism in our choice of words by not toning down his language, which is at times very harsh, even extending to curses. In this sophism Bastiat uses a variety of words in his attempt to speak plainly and brutally. Here is a list with our preferred translation for each: *dépouiller* (to dispossess), *spolier* (to plunder), *voler* (to steal), *piller* (to loot or pillage), *raviser* (to ravish or rape), *filouter* (filching), and variants, such as *le vol de grand chemin* (highway robbery).

There was also some debate in Bastiat's time about what to call the compulsory conscription of young men into the French Army. It was called *requisition* in 1793, *conscription* in 1798, and, more euphemistically, *recrutement*, during the Restoration and the July Monarchy. Bastiat rejected the euphemism used during the 1840s, preferring to see it as a violation of individual liberty, and hence *conscription* was his preferred term.

The theory of plunder which Bastiat was working on in the last couple of years of his life, most notably in "The Physiology of Plunder" (ES2 1) and "Two Moral Philosophies" (ES2 2), is a good example of the application of his more brutal style to an analysis of how the state goes about extracting the revenue it needs to carry out its activities. Bastiat described taxation as nothing less than "plunder" (*la spoliation*), where the more powerful, the plunderers (*les spoliateurs*), use force to seize the property of others (the plundered) in order to provide benefits for themselves or favored vested-interest groups like the aristocracy or the church, resulting in what he termed "aristocratic" or "theocratic plunder." He uses a number of closely linked expressions to describe this process of plunder: the plunderers (*les spoliateurs*) use a combination of outright coercion (*la force*), fraud (*la ruse*), and deception (*la duperie*) to acquire resources from ordinary workers and consumers. They also resort to the use of misleading and deceptive arguments (*sophismes*) to deceive ordinary people, the dupes (*les dupes*), and to convince them that these actions are taken in their own interests and not those of the ruling elites. We have

6. See the entry for "*Le Libre-échange*," in the Glossary of Newspapers and Journals.

retained this language in our translation and have indicated in the footnotes when Bastiat is using this form of "plain speaking."

At times Bastiat resorts to cursing, which we have not hesitated to translate as accurately as we can. His best-known example of this is his essay on money titled "Maudit argent!" (Damned Money!, 1849). Other examples include the expressions *que Dieu maudisse* (what God would damn, or God-damned),[7] *malédiction sur les machines!* (a curse on machines!), *le fesse-mathieu,* which is a coarse expression for a usurer or moneylender,[8] and *où diable l'économie politique va-t-elle se nicher?* (where the devil is political economy taking us?).

Opposition to Circumlocutions and Euphemisms

The use of the words "plunder" and "dupes" is not the only example of Bastiat's attempts to avoid circumlocutions and euphemisms in describing government policies like taxation and tariff protection. In the sophism "The Tax Collector" (ES2 10), Bastiat makes a concerted effort to distinguish clearly between two types of "representation," and we have tried to follow closely the specific set of terms he uses to describe each one. In the first type of representation, an individual contracts with another party, perhaps a business representative or a lawyer with power of attorney, to act on their behalf in a strictly limited manner. For this Bastiat uses phrases such as *s'arranger directement* (to engage in an exchange directly with a supplier of a good or service) or *placer une procuration* (to appoint someone to act with one's power of attorney). He contrasts this with political *représentation,* where a voter (in the case of France before 1848 this was a very limited number of wealthy taxpayers—some 240,000 in a population of 36 million) could *nommer pour député* (nominate as one's representative) or *se faire représenter par quelqu'un* (to be represented by somebody). The latter terminology is used by Mr. Blockhead (the tax collector) to try to persuade Jacques Bonhomme that his tax money is being wisely spent by responsible political representatives in the Chamber of Deputies. Jacques Bonhomme is very skeptical and is not persuaded. We have endeavored in the translation to bring out this very different understanding of the nature of "representation," which was Bastiat's intention in choosing this very specific terminology.

The language of war and battle was something that Bastiat wanted to ban-

7. See WSWNS 7.
8. See WSWNS 11.

ish from all discussion of economic activity. In "Domination through Work" (ES2 17), he argued that it is dangerous to use metaphors drawn from war and the military to describe economic phenomena, as the former acquire wealth for a nation through violence, destruction, and killing, while the latter do it by peaceful, voluntary, and mutually beneficial exchange. He rejected such terms as invasion (of foreign goods), flood, tribute (to describe payment for foreign goods), domination (through trade), fight on equal terms, conquer, crush, be defeated (by one's trade rivals), and machines that kill off work. He uses these military expressions throughout the sophisms in order to rebut the premises which lie behind their popular usage in the press and in debates in the Chamber, and we have followed his practice. His conclusion was unmistakable: "Bannissons de l'économie politique toutes ces expressions empruntées au vocabulaire des batailles: *Lutter à armes égales, vaincre, écraser, étouffer, être battu, invasion, tribut*" (Let us banish from political economy all the following expressions borrowed from a military vocabulary: *to fight on equal terms, to conquer, to crush, to stifle, to be defeated, invasion,* or *tribute*).[9]

Use of the Familiar "Tu" Form

As Bastiat oscillated between his more popular and humorous style of writing and his more serious and plain-speaking style, he would use quite different language. In the more lighthearted vein he would have ordinary people espouse opposing views in his constructed dialogues or plays. Sometimes he would use the familiar form of the word "you," which in French is *tu*. For example, in his appeal to the workers on the streets of Paris in the early days of the 1848 Revolution, he would speak to them using *tu*, which we indicate in the footnotes.[10]

A quite interesting example is provided by the conversations between Robinson Crusoe and Friday on their island. Bastiat may have invented "Crusoe economics" as a way of making complex economic problems more understandable to ordinary readers. In their conversations about how to organize their time and labor most productively on the island, Bastiat has them address each other using *tu*, which suggests a certain friendship and equal status between the two, which is surprising given the historical context of European colonialism.[11] We indicate in the footnotes when *tu* is being used.

9. ES2 17, p. 253.
10. See ES3 21, p. 378n4.
11. See ES2 14, pp. 226–34.

It is also interesting to note that Bastiat put the free trade arguments in the mouth of the native Friday and the protectionist ideas in the mouth of the European Crusoe.

Technical Economic Terms

In a work which relies so heavily on economic theory it is not surprising to come across many technical economic terms. We have tried to translate these terms consistently, but it is not always possible. A good example is the word *travail,* which could be translated in several ways, all of which are accurate in their own way. For example, one could use the following English words, depending on the context: "work," "labor," "production," and "employment." If there is any ambiguity, we indicate this in the footnotes.

Sometimes Bastiat makes a distinction between, on the one hand, *les protectionnistes* (the advocates of protectionism) and *le régime de la protection* (the protectionist system), and on the other hand, *les prohibitionistes* (the advocates of prohibiting imports) and *le régime prohibitif* (the system of import prohibition). He does this because French tariff policy was a mixture of numerous categories of goods the importation of which was prohibited outright in order to protect French manufacturers, and a complex system of tariffs which raised the price of imported goods to raise money for the French state as well as to give some economic advantage (protection) to French manufacturers. We have preserved Bastiat's distinction wherever possible because it reveals the three-way split which existed in the French debate about tariffs between the free traders like Bastiat, the hard-core prohibitionists, and the protectionists.

Bastiat uses several terms for "money," which can be confusing at times: *numéraire* (cash or gold coins), *papier monnaie* (paper money or notes), and *argent* (money). Bastiat makes a very clear distinction between paper money and cash (*numéraire*), as the European economies of his day were based upon the gold standard, and paper money was often viewed with suspicion as a result of the hyperinflation of the "assignat" paper currency during the Revolution.

There are also several different uses of the word *prix* (price) which need to be made clear. There is *le prix d'achat* (the purchase price), *le prix de vente* (the sale price), *le prix courant* (the market price), *le prix de revient* (the cost price), and *le prix rémunérateur* (the price which covers one's costs). Very important for Bastiat is the idea of *le prix débattu* (the freely negotiated price), which is essential for the operation of the free market. This is a price which is agreed upon by two voluntary participants in an exchange who "debate" or negotiate a price which is acceptable to both parties. Both are equally free to accept or to refuse the price by concluding the bargain or walking away. Also crucial to his argument is the idea that there is a difference between real economic wealth and the accounting device (the money price) used to measure it, and thus the *prix absolus* (nominal or money price) of a good or service is not a true measure of the amount of wealth in a society.

Bastiat uses the terms *droit, tarif,* and *taxe,* sometimes interchangeably and sometimes reserving different meanings to each one. We have tried to be consistent in translating them as "duty" (*droit*), "tariff" (*tarif*), and "tax" (*taxe*) in order to preserve these sometimes subtle distinctions. It should also be kept in mind that Bastiat, like many free-market economists of the period, distinguished between a *tarif protecteur* (protectionist tariff) and a *tarif des douanes* (fiscal tariff or duty). The former, which he opposed, was designed to provide a competitive advantage to a favored manufacturer at the expense of consumers. The latter, which he supported if it was at a low rate, like 5 percent, was purely for revenue-raising purposes.

Bastiat's References to Laissez-Faire

"The Economists," as mid-nineteenth-century political economists like Bastiat called themselves, embraced the physiocrats' policy prescription of *laissez-faire,* which requires no translation. Where the term appears in this sense, of a recommended government policy, we have left it in the French. Sometimes Bastiat uses the word *laissez* (leave me free to do something) as a normal French verb but often with the intention of alluding to the free-market policy prescription; for example, *laissez-les faire* (let them do these things), *laissez-le entrer* (let it freely enter), and *laissez-passer* (leave them free to move about). Such occurrences are indicated in the footnotes.

Industry versus Plunder: The Plundered Classes, the Plundering Class, and the People[12]

The word *classe* is used sixty-five times by Bastiat in *Economic Sophisms* and *What Is Seen and What Is Not Seen* in at least four different senses, and the frequency of its use increases markedly during and after the 1848 Revolution,

---

12. See "Bastiat's Theory of Class" in appendix 1, "Further Aspects of Bastiat's Life and Thought."

as Bastiat responded to the socialist critique of French society. Bastiat had his own theory of class, but he also used the word "class" in the socialists' sense when he was engaged in rebutting their ideas. We have indicated in the footnotes the various meanings of the word "class" and Bastiat's use of them in order to keep these distinctions clear.

Bastiat uses the word *classe* in four different ways in the sophisms. First, he uses it as a neutral term to mean any group which has some aspect in common, such as *les classes riches* (the rich classes), *la classe moyenne* (the middle class), or *la classe des propriétaires* (the landowning class). His second way of using the word is in the socialist sense of class warfare. Bastiat was fighting two intellectual battles in the late 1840s, the first against the established elites who controlled the Chamber and who benefited from agricultural and manufacturing protection and subsidies, and the second against the rising socialist movement. As the socialist movement became more influential he began to confront its supporters more directly in debate and used the same expressions they did, such as *l'aristocratie* (the aristocracy), *la bourgeoisie* (the bourgeoisie), and *la classe des travailleurs* or *la classe ouvrière* (the working class) or *les prolétaires* (the proletarian class). "The people" (*le peuple*) was also becoming a more common phrase in socialist critiques of the French political system, and Bastiat uses this on occasion as well. He uses the socialists' language of class and turns it around in order to show the errors in their thinking about the nature of property rights and the free market and how they have mistaken the true nature of exploitation and class in French society.

Bastiat's third use of the word "class" is a political one, as in the expressions *la classe électorale* (the electoral class) and *la classe des protégés* (the protected class). By *la classe électorale*, Bastiat means the very restricted group of people (who had an "electoral monopoly," as he called it) who were entitled to vote during the July Monarchy. On the eve of the 1848 Revolution, which reintroduced universal male suffrage, the electoral class numbered about 240,000 taxpayers.[13] By *la classe des protégés* Bastiat meant the class of favored people given special privileges by state legislation such as tariff protection, industrial subsidies, or monopolies of a particular market. Another example of the use of "class" in a political sense is his discussion of the struggle between the aristocratic class and democracy in Britain in "Anglomania, Anglophobia"

13. Bastiat uses this term in ES3 6, p. 286. See also "The Chamber of Deputies and Elections," in appendix 2, "The French State and Politics."

(ES3 14), where he provides a lengthy analysis of the political power held by the English aristocracy.

The fourth use of the word is part of Bastiat's own theory of class, which had its origins in the theory of "industrialism" developed by two thinkers who influenced Bastiat considerably in his intellectual development: Charles Comte and Charles Dunoyer. In their theory the terms *l'industrie* (productive economic activity), *les industrieux, les classes d'industrieux,* and *l'industriel* (those engaged in productive economic activity) had very specific meanings which are not the same as their modern meanings. It would be wrong therefore to translate them always in the more narrow modern meaning of "heavy industry" or "manufacturing" or "the result of some industrial process." Bastiat sometimes does use these words in the modern sense, but he also uses them in the broader sense of Dunoyer's theory of industrialism, and we have indicated when Bastiat does this in the footnotes.

According to the theory of industrialism, the class of *industriels* played a very important role in the economy because there were only two means of acquiring wealth: by productive activity and voluntary exchanges in the free market (i.e., *l'industrie,* which included agriculture, trade, and factory production, as well as services) or by coercive means, what Bastiat called *la spoliation* (plunder), which included conquest, slavery, theft, taxation, subsidies, protection, and transfer payments. Anybody who acquired wealth through voluntary exchange and productive activities belonged to a class of people collectively called *les industrieux,* in contrast to those individuals or groups who acquired their wealth by force, coercion, conquest, slavery, or government privileges, or what Bastiat called *la classe spoliatrice* or *les spoliateurs* (the plundering class or the plunderers). The latter group was seen as "parasites" who lived at the expense of *les industrieux* (the productive class) or *les classes spoliées* (the plundered classes).

To give an idea of the importance Bastiat placed on his theory of plunder, the following frequencies of use should provide a clue: there are 55 instances of the term *la spoliation* (plunder), 12 of *parasite,* 10 of *le spoliateur* (the plunderer), 5 of *spoliée* (plundered), and 1 of *spoliatrice* (plunderous).

Bastiat's Use of the Socialist Terms "Organization" and "Association"

As with the word *classe,* there are two other words which were widely used by socialists in the 1840s (such as Louis Blanc and Charles Fourier) and which became closely associated with their criticism of the free market and their demands for government regulation and even ownership of the means of production, namely *l'organisation* (organization of labor) and *l'association* (cooperative living and working arrangements). Bastiat frequently uses these words in the socialist sense, often with a capital *O* or *A,* in order to mock or criticize them, pointing out that supporters of the free market are also firm believers in "organization" and "association," but only if they result from voluntary actions by individuals and are not the result of government coercion and legislation. A good example of this is Bastiat's disparaging term *la grande organization,*[14] by which he means the folly of believing that one individual or government could centrally plan or organize an entire economy, as many socialists of his day believed. We have indicated in the footnotes when Bastiat is using these words in this socialist sense.

The Difference between "Droit à" and "Droit de"

A third important socialist idea which emerged during the 1840s with which Bastiat had to contend was the idea of *le droit au travail* (the right to a job).[15] In English one could well translate it as "the right to work" or "the right to a job," which would miss the subtle distinction between the two. This idea of *le droit au travail* (the right to a job) came to the fore in the early days of the 1848 Revolution when the provisional government established a government unemployment relief program known as the National Workshops. It was based on the ideas of socialists like Louis Blanc and was an attempt by the government to guarantee every able-bodied French male a job paid for by the taxpayers. Bastiat warned about its economic unviability, and it eventually collapsed in June 1848, sparking rioting in Paris. In French, there is a distinction between *le droit à quelque chose* (the right to [have] something) and *le droit de quelque chose* (the right to [do] something). The Economists, including Bastiat, believed in *le droit du travail* (the right to engage in work) and not the socialist formulation. We indicate in the footnotes when this distinction is an issue.

Interestingly, Bastiat extends this distinction to the area of profits with his formulation of *le droit au profit* (the right to a [guaranteed] profit) and *le droit de profiter* (the right to seek profits). The protectionists wanted the former, meaning that the government should guarantee them a profitable

14. See ES3 24, p. 385.
15. See WSWNS 12.

return on their investments, whereas the Economists wanted the latter, that businesses should take their chances on the free market and make profits only if they adequately satisfied consumer demand.

Bastiat's Translation of Adam Smith

In "Theft by Subsidy" (ES2 9), Bastiat translates a passage from Adam Smith's *Wealth of Nations* on the tendency of businessmen to engage in conspiracies against the public whenever they get together.[16] We have taken the unusual step of retranslating Bastiat's translation back into English in order to show how much it differed from the original (which can be found in a footnote). Bastiat was often rather cavalier in his quoting from other texts, doing it from memory in many cases and sometimes getting it wrong or conflating different passages into one (as seems to have happened with the Smith quotation). We have checked as many of Bastiat's quotations against the original texts as we could and indicate in the footnotes where he strays. Sometimes he is in error, other times he slightly changes the text to better make his point, for example, by changing the name of the king in order to bring the passage up to date.

French Names, Weights, Measures, and Currency; Use of English Words

We have retained the use of French names of people (like Jacques and Jean) instead of translating them into their English equivalents (Jack and John) because we wanted to keep a French flavor to the translation and believed that this would be readily understood by readers. We have also retained the use of French terms for land area (arpent), weight (kilogram), and currency (sou), as it seemed quite artificial to convert them into English or American terms. We have explained what they mean in the footnotes and several entries in the glossary.

Finally, now and again Bastiat uses English words in his essays, such as "cheapness," "go on," "meeting," "free-trader," "drawback," and "budget." We have indicated where this occurs in the footnotes.

---

16. Adam Smith, *An Inquiry Into the Nature and Causes of the Wealth of Nations,* vol. 1, ed. R. H. Campbell and A. S. Skinner, vol. 2 of the *Glasgow Edition of the Works and Correspondence of Adam Smith* (Indianapolis: Liberty Fund, 1981). I.x.c., Part II: Inequalities occasioned by the Policy of Europe, I.x.c. 27 p. 145.

Key Terms

In addition to the longer discussion of economic terms in the Note on the Translation, we have added here a list of key terms most frequently encountered in the texts. We have provided a brief explanation of the different contexts in which Bastiat used these terms and how we translated them.

ASSOCIATION, ORGANIZATION. When used with lowercase, Bastiat means any voluntary association which free individuals might create; when used with uppercase (as in Association), he is using the word in its socialist meaning of cooperative living and working arrangements.

CLASSE. The word can be used in a descriptive fashion, as in *la classe moyenne* (the middle class), but Bastiat usually uses it to describe groups which had some kind of political privilege, such as *la classe électorale* (the electoral class, i.e., the very small group of taxpayers who were legally allowed to vote and stand for election), or *la classe spoliatrice* (the plundering class).

DUPE, DUPERIE, RUSE. Bastiat believed that individuals were deprived of their property directly by means of *la force* (coercion or force) or indirectly by means of *la ruse* (fraud or trickery) or *la duperie* (deception). The beneficiaries of this force and fraud used *les sophismes* (misleading and deceptive arguments) to deceive ordinary people, whom he referred to as *les dupes* (dupes).

ÉCONOMISTE. The Economists were the group of free-market and free-trade political economists, as in *Le Journal des économistes,* for which Bastiat wrote.

INDUSTRIE, INDUSTRIEUX. Sometimes used in the modern sense of manufacturing industry but also used to mean any productive activity which produced goods and services for exchange in the free market. Individuals who engaged in these productive activities were called *les industrieux.*

LAISSEZ-FAIRE. The policy prescription of *laissez-faire* favored by free-market economists like Bastiat requires no translation. However, Bastiat uses it in a number of ways which require careful translation, such as *laissez-les faire* (let them do these things), *laissez-le entrer* (let it freely enter), and *laissez-passer* (leave them free to move about).

LIBERTÉ, LIBÉRAL. *Liberté* is usually translated as "liberty" except in cases such as *la liberté des échanges* (free trade), where the word "free" is more commonly used. *Libéral* has been translated as "liberal," with the understanding that it should mean "classical liberal" and not "liberal" in the contemporary American sense of the word.

MONNAIE. The word "money" is used in many senses by Bastiat, such as *la numéraire* (cash or gold or silver coins), *la papier monnaie* (paper money or notes), and *l'argent* (money in a general sense).

PRIX. Bastiat uses many expressions to talk about price, such as *le prix d'achat* (the purchase price), *le prix de vente* (the sale price), *le prix courant* (the market price), *le prix de revient* (the cost price), *le prix rémunérateur* (the price which covers one's costs), *le prix débattu* (the freely negotiated price), and *le prix absolus* (nominal or money price).

PROHIBITIONISTE, PROTECTIONNISTE. *Les prohibitionistes* referred to the advocates of prohibiting imports so that domestic manufacturers had a monopoly of the home market, whereas *les protectionnistes* referred to the advocates of protectionism who wanted high tariffs in order to help domestic manufacturers compete with foreign manufacturers. The two different systems to which these policies gave rise Bastiat termed *le régime prohibitif* (the system of import prohibition) and *le régime de la protection* (the protectionist system) respectively.

RÉGIME. Often translated as "regime," "society," or "system," as in *le régime de la protection* (the protectionist system) or *le régime de la liberté* (the system of liberty or a free society).

SPOLIATION. Translated here as "plunder." There are several related terms, including *spolier* (to plunder), *les spoliateurs* (the plunderers), *les spoliées* (the plundered), *la classe spoliatrice* (the plundering class), *les classes spoliées* (the plundered classes), and the adjective *spoliatrice* (plunderous).

TAXE, TARIF, DROIT. The payments which the government imposed on various goods and services, such as *le droit* (duty), *le tarif* (tariff), and *la taxe* (tax).

TRAVAIL. Many different words are used to translate *travail,* such as "work," "labor," "production," and "employment." Related words include *le travail-*

leur (worker or laborer) and *la classe des travailleurs* (the working or laboring class). Bastiat also carefully distinguished between these two different expressions involving work or labor: *le droit au travail* (the right to work or the right to a job), which was advocated by the socialists, and *le droit du travail* (the right to engage in work), which was advocated by the free-market economists.

Note on the Editions of the Œuvres complètes

The first edition of the *Œuvres complètes* appeared in 1854–55, consisting of six volumes.[1] The second edition, which appeared in 1862–64, was an almost identical reprint of the first edition (with only minor typesetting differences) but was notable for the addition of a new, seventh volume, which contained additional essays, sketches, and correspondence.[2] In addition, the second edition contained a preface by Prosper Paillottet and a biographical essay on Bastiat by Roger de Fontenay ("Notice sur la vie et les écrits de Frédéric Bastiat"), both of which were absent in the first edition.

While the second edition of the *Œuvres complètes* was being printed, a three-volume edition of Bastiat's selected works, *Œuvres choisies,* appeared in 1863 using the same plates as the *Œuvres complètes.* Volumes 1 and 2 of the *Œuvres choisies* were reproductions of volumes 4 and 5 of the *Œuvres complètes* (containing *Economic Sophisms* First and Second Series and the *Petits pamphlets*), and volume 3 of the *Œuvres choisies* was the fourth edition of *Economic Harmonies. Economic Harmonies* appeared the following year (1864) as volume 6 of the *Œuvres complètes* and was called the fifth edition.

Another difference between the first and second editions was in the sixth volume, which contained Bastiat's magnum opus, *Economic Harmonies.* The first edition of the *Œuvres complètes* described volume 6 as the "third revised and augmented edition" of *Economic Harmonies.* This is somewhat confusing but does have some logic to it. The "first" edition of *Economic Harmonies*

---

1. *Œuvres complètes de Frédéric Bastiat, mises en ordre, revues et annotées d'après les manuscrits de l'auteur* (Paris: Guillaumin, 1854–55). 6 vols. [Edited by Prosper Paillottet with the assistance of Roger de Fontenay, but they are not credited on the title page.] A listing of the volumes are as follows: Vol. 1. *Correspondance et mélanges* (1855); Vol. 2. *Le Libre-échange* (1855); Vol. 3. *Cobden et la Ligue ou L'agitation anglaise pour la liberté des échanges* (1854); Vol. 4. *Sophismes économiques. Petits pamphlets I* (1854); Vol. 5. *Sophismes économiques. Petits pamphlets II* (1854); Vol. 6. *Harmonies économiques* (1855).

2. Vol. 7. *Essais, ébauches, correspondance* (1864).

appeared in 1850 during the last year of Bastiat's life but in an incomplete form. The "second" edition appeared in 1851, after his death, edited by "La Société des amis de Bastiat" (most probably by Prosper Paillottet and Roger de Fontenay) and included the second half of the manuscript, which Bastiat had been working on when he died. Thus the edition that appeared in the first edition of the *Œuvres complètes* was called the "third" edition on its volume's title page. As noted above, volume three of the *Œuvres choisies,* which appeared in 1863, included as volume 3 the fourth edition of the *Economic Harmonies.* When the second edition of the *Œuvres complètes* was published between 1862 and 1864, it included as volume 6 the fifth edition of *Economic Harmonies* (1864). This practice continued throughout the nineteenth century, with editions of *Economic Harmonies* staying in print as a separate volume as well as being included as volume 6 in later editions of the *Œuvres complètes;* thus, by 1870–73, when the third edition of the *Œuvres complètes* appeared, the version of *Economic Harmonies* that appeared in volume 6 was titled the "sixth" edition of the work.

Other "editions" of the *Œuvres complètes* include a fourth edition, 1878–79; a fifth edition, 1881–84; if there was a sixth edition, the date is unknown; a seventh edition, 1893; and a final edition may have appeared in 1907.[3]

---

3. For a complete listing of the editions of the *Œuvres complètes* and the *Œuvres choisies* that were used in making this translation, see the bibliography.

Abbreviations

Economic Sophisms *Second Series*

ES2 1	The Physiology of Plunder
ES2 2	Two Moral Philosophies
ES2 3	The Two Axes
ES2 4	The Lower Council of Labor
ES2 5	High Prices and Low Prices
ES2 6	To Artisans and Workers
ES2 7	A Chinese Tale
ES2 8	Post Hoc, Ergo Propter Hoc
ES2 9	Theft by Subsidy
ES2 10	The Tax Collector
ES2 11	The Utopian
ES2 12	Salt, the Mail, and the Customs Service
ES2 13	Protection, or the Three Municipal Magistrates
ES2 14	Something Else
ES2 15	The Free Trader's Little Arsenal
ES2 16	The Right Hand and the Left Hand
ES2 17	Domination through Work

Economic Sophisms *"Third Series"*

ES3 1	Recipes for Protectionism
ES3 2	Two Principles
ES3 3	M. Cunin-Gridaine's Logic
ES3 4	One Profit versus Two Losses
ES3 5	On Moderation
ES3 6	The People and the Bourgeoisie
ES3 7	Two Losses versus One Profit
ES3 8	The Political Economy of the Generals
ES3 9	A Protest
ES3 10	The Spanish Association for the Defense of National Employment and the Bidassoa Bridge
ES3 11	The Specialists
ES3 12	The Man Who Asked Embarrassing Questions
ES3 13	The Fear of a Word
ES3 14	Anglomania, Anglophobia
ES3 15	One Man's Gain Is Another Man's Loss
ES3 16	Making a Mountain Out of a Molehill

What Is Seen and What Is Not Seen

OTHER WORKS REFERRED TO IN THIS VOLUME

CW: The Collected Works of Frédéric Bastiat
  CW1: *The Man and the Statesman: The Correspondence and Articles on Politics*
  CW2: *"The Law," "The State," and Other Political Writings, 1843–1850*
DEP: *Dictionnaire de l'économie politique.* 2 vols. Paris: Librairie de Guillaumin et cie., 1852–53.
Economic Harmonies, FEE edition: *Economic Harmonies.* Translated by W. Hayden Boyers. Edited by George B. de Huszar. Introduction by Dean Russell. Irvington-on-Hudson, N.Y.: Foundation for Economic Education, 1994.
Economic Sophisms, FEE edition: *Economic Sophisms* (First and Second

Series). Translated and edited by Arthur Goddard. Introduction by Henry Hazlitt. Irvington-on-Hudson, N.Y.: Foundation for Economic Education, 1964.

JDE: Le Journal des économistes

OC: Œuvres complètes de Frédéric Bastiat

Selected Essays, FEE edition: *Selected Essays on Political Economy.* Translated by Seymour Cain. Edited by George B. de Huszar. Irvington-on-Hudson, N.Y.: Foundation for Economic Education, 1968.

WSWNS, FEE edition: *What Is Seen and What Is Not Seen.* In *Selected Essays on Political Economy,* translated by Seymour Cain and edited by George B. de Huszar; introduction by F.A. Hayek, 1–50. Irvington-on-Hudson, N.Y.: Foundation for Economic Education, 1995.

"Budget Papers" refers to the summary data on government revenue and expenditure provided by the editor in appendix 4.

Acknowledgments

In addition to the guidance of the general editor, Jacques de Guenin, this translation is the result of the efforts of a team comprising Jane and Michel Willems; Dr. Dennis O'Keeffe, Professor of Social Science at the University of Buckingham and Senior Research Fellow at the Institute of Economic Affairs in London, who carefully read the translation and made very helpful suggestions at every stage; Dr. David M. Hart, Director of the Online Library of Liberty Project and Academic Editor of the Bastiat translation series at Liberty Fund, who supplied much of the scholarly apparatus and provided the translation with the insights of a historian of nineteenth-century European political economy; Professor Aurelian Craiutu, Professor of Political Science at Indiana University, Bloomington, who read the final translation and contributed his considerable knowledge of nineteenth-century French politics to this undertaking; and Dr. Laura Goetz, senior editor at Liberty Fund, who organized and coordinated the various aspects of the project from its inception through to production. This volume thus has all the strengths and all the weaknesses of a voluntary, collaborative effort. We hope Bastiat would approve, especially as no government official was involved at any stage.

It is with great sadness that we acknowledge here the deaths of two individuals who played a large role in the publication of The Collected Works of Frédéric Bastiat, namely the General Editor Jacques de Guenin and the Translation Editor Dennis O'Keeffe.

Jacques de Guenin, a retired French businessman, passed away in October 2015. He was instrumental in getting the Bastiat translation off the ground after it was first proposed at the bicentennial Bastiat Conference held in Mugron in 2001. It was he who organized the texts, arranged for the translation to be done, and wrote many of the footnotes and glossaries which accompany each volume. Unfortunately, he lived only long enough to see the first two volumes in print. In addition to working on Liberty Fund's edition, Jacques also published the first French edition of Bastiat's works in one hundred fifty years, as well as heading the Bastiat Cercle, which meets regularly in Bastiat's home region to discuss topics which would have been of great interest to Bastiat as well. Jacques's work in reviving interest in Bastiat's economic and political ideas will be his lasting legacy.

The Translation Editor for the Bastiat project, the Anglo-Irish professor of sociology Dennis O'Keeffe, also passed away before the translation could be completed. He died in December 2014 after a long illness. Dennis translated two other works for Liberty Fund in addition to his work on Bastiat: Benjamin Constant's *Principles of Politics* (2003) and Gustave de Molinari's *Evenings on the Rue Saint-Lazare* (forthcoming). His wit and clever turn of phrase will be sorely missed.

It is with remembrance and thanks that we dedicate this volume to Jacques and Dennis.

A Chronology of Bastiat's Life and Work

1801   Born in Bayonne, 30 June.
        Grandfather establishes a trading business with his son Pierre and nephew Henri Monclar.
1808   Death of mother, 27 May.
        Trading business in Spain suffers difficulties.
        Moves to Mugron with father, grandfather, and Aunt Justine.
1810   Death of father, 1 July.
        Closing of the Bastiat-Monclar trading business.
1812   Attends school run by the Abbot Meilhan in Bayonne.
1813   Attends College of Saint-Sever for one year.
1814–18 Attends school at Sorèze. Does not graduate. Forms a close friendship with Victor Calmètes.
1819–25 Works in Bayonne for his Uncle Monclar and assists his grandfather in running a farm at Souprosse in the Landes (estate called "Sengresse").
        Joins a Masonic lodge, La Zélée. Becomes a *garde des sceaux* in 1822 and an *orateur* in 1823.
        Participates in a demonstration of young liberals in support of Jacques Laffite, September 1824.
        Gives lectures on literary, religious, philosophical, and economic topics.
1825–30 Death of grandfather, 13 August. Inherits part of his estate.
        Attempts unsuccessfully to modernize the practices of his tenants on his estate.
        Expresses a desire to write on the protectionist system in France.
1830   Participates in protests in Bayonne in favor of the new regime (the July Monarchy of Louis-Philippe), 3–5 August.
        Visits Bayonne garrison and successfully persuades the officers to support the revolution, 5 August.

1831   Marries Marie Clotilde Hiart, 7 February. Separates soon after; uses her dowry to expand his estate.

Appointed justice of the peace in the canton of Mugron, 28 May.

Unsuccessfully stands for election to the legislature of the arrondissement of Dax, 6 July.

1832   Unsuccessfully stands for election to the legislature in the arrondissement of Saint-Sever, 11 July.

1833   Elected to the General Council of the Landes, 17 November.

1837   Publishes five articles on a proposed canal next to the Ardour River.

1838   Publishes two articles on the Basque language.

1839   Reelected to the General Council of the Landes, 24 November.

1840   Travels to Spain and Portugal to explore setting up an insurance business.

1841   Has plans to create an "Association for the Defense of Viticultural Interests" and a journal to be called *Le Midi* (these do not come to fruition).

1842   Unsuccessfully stands for election to the legislature in the arrondissement of Saint-Sever, 9 July.

1843   Writes "Mémoire on the Viticulture Question," 22 January. Plans to create a school for sharecroppers.

Publishes three articles on "Free Trade. State of the Question in England" in *La Sentinelle des Pyrénées,* May/June.

1844   Publishes his first major essay in the *JDE:* "On the Influence of French and English Tariffs on the Future of the Two Peoples," October.

Begins corresponding with Richard Cobden, 24 November. Tells him he would like to start his own free-trade association in France.

1845   A dinner held in his honor by the Political Economy Society to welcome him to Paris, May.

Travels to London, where he is met with enthusiasm by members of the Anti–Corn Law League, July.

Publishes his first books: *Cobden and the League* (July 1845) and *Economic Sophisms* (First Series), November.

Supports de Larnac, the center-left candidate to the local legislature, August–September.

Joins the Society for Political Economy and begins attending their monthly meetings when in Paris.

Offered editorship of *JDE* but turns it down.

1846   Elected a corresponding member of the Academy of Moral and Political Sciences, 24 January.

Cofounder of the Free Trade Association in Bordeaux, 23 February.

10 May, National Association for Free Trade is formed in Paris, and Bastiat is made the secretary of the Advisory Board. Other Associations are established in Marseilles, Lyon, and Le Havre.

Dinner in Paris to celebrate political victory of Cobden and the Anti–Corn Law League, 18 August.

Speaks at free-trade meetings in Bordeaux (23 February) and Paris (29 September).

Appearance of first issue of the weekly journal *Le Libre-échange,* 29 November.

Resigns his position as justice of the peace in Mugron, 30 November.

Debates with Lamartine and the editors of *L'Atelier* and *Le Moniteur industriel.*

Publishes many articles on free trade in a number of journals.

1847   Chamber considers bill to liberalize tariffs and sends it to a committee dominated by protectionists, March to July.

Begins lecturing on political economy at the School of Law in Paris, 3 July.

Debates throughout the year with protectionists.

1848   Publication of *Economic Sophisms* (Second Series), 5 January.

Gives up the editorship of *Le Libre-échange* for reasons of health, 13 February.

Witnesses rioting in the streets of Paris and the killing of protesters by the army, 23–25 February.

Publication of *La République française,* 26 February.

Elected deputy in the Constituent Assembly representing the département of the Landes, 23 April. Appointed vice president of the Finance Committee.

Nominated to the Chamber's commission of inquiry into labor, May.

Speech in the Chamber on free trade and against subsidies to the textile industry, 9 June.

Publication of *Jacques Bonhomme,* 11 June.

"June Days" uprising sparked by the closure of the National Workshops, 23–26 June.

Votes against trying socialist Louis Blanc for his role in the "June Days" uprising, 26 August.

Gives a speech in the Chamber in favor of postal reform, 24 August.

Visits Cobden in England to talk about disarmament, September.

Reelected to General Council of the Landes, September.

Votes for new constitution and supports General Cavaignac for president, 4 November.

1849   Invited to banquet in Manchester to celebrate the final repeal of the Corn Laws but declines because of poor health and parliamentary duties, 9 January.

Gives a speech in the Chamber on free trade and ending restriction on the importation of salt, 11 January.

Gives a speech in the Chamber in support of legislation to prevent civil servants sitting as deputies in the Chamber, 10 March.

Supports motion opposing expedition of French troops to Rome.

Elected deputy in the Legislative Assembly representing the Landes on the "Social Democratic" list, 13 May.

Attends Peace Congress in Paris presided over by Victor Hugo and gives a speech on "Disarmament and Taxes," 22–24 August.

Debate with Proudhon on credit and interest in *La Voix du peuple,* 22 October.

Attends a Friends of Peace meeting in Bradford, England, 30 October.

Gives speech in the Chamber supporting freedom to form trade unions and other associations, 17 November.

Gives speech in the Chamber on free trade and the tax on alcohol, 12 December.

1850   Organizes campaign against the Falloux Law on education, 6 February.

Last participation in Chamber of Deputies, 9 February.

Death of wife, 10 February.

Publication of the first (incomplete) part of *Economic Harmonies,* 1 February.

Completes debate with Proudhon, which is published as *Free Credit,* 7 March.

Returns to Mugron for rest, May.

Publication of "The Law," June.

Publication of WSWNS, July.

Attends a last meeting of the Political Economy Society to say farewell to his colleagues, 10 September. Departs for Rome.

Dies in Rome, 24 December.

A list of the works of Bastiat is available on the Online Library of Liberty website, http://oll.libertyfund.org/people/25. It is kept up to date as each volume is published.

Introduction

One man's gain is another man's loss.

—MONTAIGNE

Let me speak of a standard sophism, one that is the very root of a host of sophisms, one that is like a polyp which you can cut into a thousand pieces only to see it produce a thousand more sophisms, a sophism that offends alike against humanity, Christianity, and logic, a sophism that is a Pandora's box from which have poured out all the ills of the human race, in the form of hatred, mistrust, jealousy, war, conquest, and oppression, and from which no hope can spring.

O you, Hercules, who strangled Cacus! You, Theseus, who killed the Minotaur! You, Apollo, who killed Python the serpent! I ask you all to lend me your strength, your club and your arrows, so that I can destroy the monster that has been arming men against one another for six thousand years!

Alas, there is no club capable of crushing a sophism. It is not given to arrows, nor even to bayonets, to pierce a proposition. All the cannons in Europe gathered at Waterloo could not eliminate an entrenched idea from the hearts of nations. No more could they efface an error. This task is reserved for the least weighty of all weapons, the very symbol of weightlessness, the pen.

—BASTIAT, "ONE MAN'S GAIN IS
ANOTHER MAN'S LOSS" (ES3 15)

With his pen in hand, Frédéric Bastiat burst onto the Parisian political economy scene in October 1844 with the publication of his first major article, "De l'influence des tarifs français et anglais sur l'avenir des deux peuples" (On the Influence of French and English Tariffs on the Future of the Two Peoples) in *Le Journal des économistes.*[1] This proved to be a sensation, and he was welcomed with open arms by the Parisian political economists as one of their own. This was followed soon after by Bastiat's first visit to Paris and then England in order to meet Richard Cobden and other leaders of the Anti–Corn Law League. Bastiat's book *Cobden and the League* appeared in 1845. The book was Bastiat's attempt to explain to the French people the meaning and significance of the Anti–Corn Law League by means of a lengthy introduction and his translation of key speeches and newspaper articles by members of the League.[2]

It was in this context that Bastiat wrote a series of articles explicitly called "Economic Sophisms" for the April, July, and October 1845 issues of *Le Journal des économistes.* These became the first half of what was to appear in January 1846 as *Economic Sophisms* (First Series). As articles continued to pour from Bastiat's pen during 1846 and 1847 and were published in his own free-trade journal, *Le Libre-échange* (founded 29 November 1846 and closed 16 April 1848), and in *Le Journal des économistes,* he soon amassed enough material to publish a second volume of *Economic Sophisms,* called naturally enough, *Economic Sophisms* (Second Series), in January 1848, just one month before the outbreak of the 1848 Revolution in Paris. As Bastiat's literary executor and friend Prosper Paillottet noted in a footnote in the *Œuvres complètes,* which he edited, there was even enough material for a third series compiled from the short articles which had appeared between 1846 and 1848 in various organs such as *Le Libre-échange,* had Bastiat lived long enough to get them ready for publication. We have included this material in this volume as *Economic Sophisms* "Third Series."

Thus, with Liberty Fund's edition of Bastiat's Collected Works we have been able to do what he and Paillottet were not able to do, namely, gather in one volume all seventy-five of Bastiat's actual and possible *Economic Sophisms.* The selection criteria for the additional material were similarity to the other sophisms in style (short, witty, sarcastic, sometimes in dialog form) and in seeking to debunk widely held but false economic ideas (or "fallacies" or "sophisms"). We also include in this volume the pamphlet *What Is Seen and What Is Not Seen,* which is also very much in the same style and format as the sophisms. We do not think Bastiat would mind our doing so.

---

1. "De l'influence des tarifs français et anglais sur l'avenir des deux peuples," *JDE* 9 (October 1844): 244–71. (*OC,* vol. 1, pp. 334–86.)
2. *Cobden et la ligue.* (*OC,* vol. 3, pp. 1–80.)

THE FORMAT OF THE *ECONOMIC SOPHISMS*

The *Economic Sophisms* in this volume were written over a period of five years, stretching from mid-1845 to mid-1850 (the year in which *What Is Seen and What Is Not Seen* was published a few months before Bastiat's death). In writing these essays Bastiat used a variety of formats, which are listed below:

1. Conversations, or "constructed" dialogues, between individuals who represented different points of view.
2. Stand-alone economic tales and fables.
3. Fictional letters and petitions to government officials and other documents.
4. More formal or academic prose.
5. Direct appeals to the workers and citizens of France.

These five different formats reveal the wide range of Bastiat's writing, from informal to academic, and the equally wide range of audiences he was trying to reach in presenting his ideas. Whether he was appealing to prospective members of the French Free Trade Association, manufacturers who belonged to the protectionist Association for the Defense of National Employment, or workers rioting on the streets of Paris in February 1848, Bastiat believed that all would respond to his efforts to defend free trade and individual liberty.

Bastiat was quite innovative in his use of some of these formats and may have even invented one. His use of the "constructed dialogue" between an advocate of free trade and a skeptic can be traced back to earlier writings by Harriet Martineau, and his use of the "economic tale" can be traced back to the fables of La Fontaine, although his insertion of economic principles is probably unique to him. More original are his small plays[3] in which he develops economic arguments at some length over several "acts" with characters like Jacques Bonhomme, the French "everyman," who appears frequently in his stories. However, his most original invention is the use of Robinson Crusoe[4] (and sometimes Friday) in a kind of "thought experiment," which is used to illustrate the deeper underlying principles of economic theory, or what one might call "the pure theory of choice." In these stories he discusses

---

3. See especially ES2 13, which was described as "a staged argument in four scenes."

4. The dialogues in which Robinson Crusoe appears can be found in ES2 14 and ES3 16. There is also a discussion of how a negotiation might have taken place between Robinson and Friday about exchanging game and fish. See "Property and Plunder" (CW2, p. 155).

the options facing Crusoe in choosing how to use his scarce resources and limited time, what is most urgent for him to do now, how will he survive if he wants to do something other than finding food, how does he maintain his capital stock of tools, and so on. Although this argument is standard modern textbook material today, it is possible that Bastiat used it for the first time in some of his sophisms.

The most appropriate style to use when writing the sophisms was something Bastiat could never settle on, whether he should use the amusing and satirical style for which he had a certain flair, or something more serious and formal. Bastiat was stung by a critical review of the First Series, which accused him of being too stiff and too formal, and so he was determined to make the Second Series more lighthearted and amusing. Yet during the course of 1847, when he was compiling the next collection of sophisms, which were to appear in January 1848, the defeat of the free traders in the Chamber by a better-organized protectionist lobby and the rising power of socialist groups on the eve of the Revolution of February 1848 led him to declare that the time for witty and clever stories was over and that more difficult times called for the use of "blunt" and perhaps even "brutal" language. Thus he oscillated between the two different approaches, never being able to decide which was better for his purposes. This is no better illustrated than in the turmoil he experienced when he was writing *What Is Seen and What Is Not Seen,* which he lost once and rewrote twice, tossing one draft into the fire because it was too serious in style.

THE BENTHAMITE ORIGINS OF BASTIAT'S CRITIQUE OF SOPHISMS AND FALLACIES

It is interesting to ask where Bastiat got the idea of writing short, pithy essays for a popular audience in which he debunked misconceptions ("sophisms" or "fallacies") about the operations of the free market in general and of free trade in particular.

The most likely source is Bentham's *Handbook of Political Fallacies* (1824), which had originally appeared in French, edited by Étienne Dumont, in 1816 with the title *Traité des sophismes politiques.*[5] Bastiat was an admirer of Ben-

5. Bentham, "Traité des sophismes politiques." An English version of the book appeared with the editorial assistance of the Benthamite Peregrine Bingham the Younger,

tham and chose two passages from Bentham's *Théorie des peines et des récompenses* (1811) as the opening quotation for both the First and Second Series of *Economic Sophisms*. In the opening paragraph of this work Bentham offers the following definition of "fallacy," which Bastiat shared:

> By the name of *fallacy* it is common to designate any argument employed or topic suggested for the purpose, or with the probability of producing the effect of deception, or of causing some erroneous opinion to be entertained by any person to whose mind such an argument may have been presented.[6]

Bentham's purpose in categorizing and discussing the varieties of political fallacies which he had identified was to expose "the semantics of persuasion"[7] used by conservative political groups to delay or prevent much-needed political reforms. Bentham organized his critique around the main sets of arguments which facilitated "the art of deception"[8] and which caused a "hydra of sophistries"[9] that permitted "pernicious practices and institutions to be retained."[10] "Reason," on the other hand, was the "instrument"[11] which would enable the reformer to create this new "good government" by a process of logical analysis and classification. As he stated:

> To give existence to good arguments was the object of the former work [the *Theory of Legislation*]; to provide for the exposure of bad ones is the object of the present one—to provide for the exposure of their real nature, and hence for the destruction of their pernicious force. Sophistry is a hydra of which, if all the necks could be exposed, the force would be destroyed. In

---

the *Handbook of Political Fallacies,* which appeared in 1824. See Bentham, *Handbook of Political Fallacies;* and also Bentham, "The Book of Fallacies: From Unfinished Papers of Jeremy Bentham," http://oll.libertyfund.org/titles/1921#lf0872-02_head_315. See also the entry for "Jeremy Bentham" in the Glossary of Persons and "Bastiat's Political Sophisms," in the Introduction.

6. Bentham, *Handbook of Political Fallacies,* p. 3.

7. Ibid., p. xi.

8. Ibid., p. 5.

9. Bastiat used the image of an indestructible "polyp." See the opening quotation in the Introduction, p. xlix and ES3 15, p. 341.

10. Bentham, *Handbook of Political Fallacies,* p. 6.

11. Ibid., p. 6.

this work, they have been diligently looked out for, and in the course of it the principal and most active of them have been brought in view.[12]

Bastiat shared Bentham's view of "deception" as an ideological weapon used by powerful vested interests to protect their political and economic privileges. Bastiat saw that his task in writing the *Sophisms* was to enlighten "the dupes" who had been misled by *la ruse,* or the "trickery," "fraud," and "cunning" of the powerful beneficiaries of tariff protection and state subsidies.

Bentham recognized a variety of "sophistries" (or "sophisms") which allowed pernicious government to protect itself from reform, but he believed that they all could be categorized into four classes based on the purpose or strategy the sophistry was designed to promote: the fallacies of authority, the fallacies of danger, the fallacies of delay, and the fallacies of confusion.[13] Arguments from "authority" were designed to intimidate and hence repress the individual from reasoning through things himself; arguments about "imminent danger" were designed to frighten the would-be reformer with the supposed negative consequences of any change; arguments which urged caution and "delay" were designed to postpone discussion of reform until it could be ignored or forgotten; and arguments designed to promote "confusion" in the minds of reformers and their supporters were designed to make it difficult or impossible to form a correct judgment on the matter at hand.[14]

Bastiat, on the other hand, categorized the types of sophisms he was opposing along the lines of the particular social or political class interests the sophisms were designed to protect. Thus he recognized "theocratic sophisms," "economic sophisms," "political sophisms," and "financial sophisms," which were designed to protect the interests (the "legal plunder") of the established Church; the Crown, the aristocracy, and elected political officials; the economic groups who benefited from protection and subsidies; and the bankers and debt holders of the government, respectively.[15] Bastiat planned to address this broad range of "sophisms" in a book he never completed.[16]

---

12. Bentham, *Handbook of Political Fallacies,* p. 7.

13. Ibid., p. 11.

14. Ibid., p. 9.

15. See ES1 Conclusion, pp. 103–10, especially pp. 109–10 and ES2 1.

16. See "Bastiat on Enlightening the 'Dupes' about the Nature of Plunder," in this Introduction.

What he did have time to complete were two volumes exposing one of these sets of sophisms, namely "economic sophisms."

Thus, it is quite likely that Bentham's writing was the inspiration not only for the name "sophismes" (which is how Dumont translated Bentham's term "fallacies" for the French edition) for the title of Bastiat's essays and books, but also for his adoption of a purpose similar to Bentham's, namely, to debunk "any argument employed which causes some erroneous opinion to be entertained by any person to whose mind such an argument may have been presented." Furthermore, whereas Bentham focused on "political fallacies" used by opponents of political reforms, Bastiat's interest was in exposing "economic fallacies" which were used to prevent reform of the policies of government taxation, subsidies to industry, and most especially protection of domestic industry via tariffs.[17]

Whereas Bentham uses relentless reasoning and classification to make his points, Bastiat uses other methods, such as humor, his reductio ad absurdum approach to his opponents' arguments, and his many references to classical French literature, popular song, and poetry. Nevertheless, Bastiat's modification of Bentham's rhetorical strategy seems to describe Bastiat's agenda and method in opposing the ideas of the protectionists in France in the mid-1840s quite nicely, and shows the considerable influence Bentham had on Bastiat's general approach to identifying and debunking "fallacies."

BASTIAT ON ENLIGHTENING THE "DUPES" ABOUT THE NATURE OF PLUNDER

Had Bastiat lived longer, he would have written at least two more books: the first to complete his main theoretical work on political economy, *Economic Harmonies,* which he left half-finished at his death; the second, on the history of plunder. The latter was mentioned by Paillottet as something that was very much on Bastiat's mind in his last days in Rome on the eve of his death. Paillottet quotes Bastiat:

> A very important task to be done for political economy is to write the history of plunder [*la spoliation*]. It is a long history

17. In spite of his preference for exposing economic sophisms, Bastiat did on occasion write sophisms of a more political nature. See "Bastiat's Political Sophisms," in this Introduction.

in which, from the outset, there appeared conquests, the migrations of peoples, invasions, and all the disastrous excesses of force in conflict with justice. Living traces of all this still remain today and cause great difficulty for the solution of the questions raised in our century. We will not reach this solution as long as we have not clearly noted in what and how injustice, when making a place for itself among us, has gained a foothold in our customs and our laws.[18]

Perhaps realizing that his time was limited and that it was unlikely he could achieve his ambitious goals, Bastiat inserted the few sketches he had about the theory of plunder at the end of the First Series (dated 2 November 1845) and at the beginning of the Second Series (which appeared in January 1848). These sketches sit rather awkwardly with his other sophisms and look as if they were added at a late stage in the editing,[19] as if Bastiat wanted to provide a broader theoretical framework for his sophisms which otherwise was lacking. Thus the "Conclusion" to the First Series and the first two chapters of the Second Series, "The Physiology of Plunder" (ES2 1) and "Two Moral Philosophies" (ES2 2), along with a few scattered remarks in footnotes in *Economic Harmonies,* can be seen as the theoretical excursus I think they are.[20]

In "Monita Secreta: The Secret Book of Instruction" (ES3 20), Bastiat wrote a satirical "guidebook for rulers" on how to go about deceiving (or duping) the consumers and undermining the lobbying efforts of the advocates of free trade, such as himself. There is a slight bitterness in some of his

18. ES1 Conclusion, p. 110n16 (in Paillottet's note).

19. See his apology in the last lines of ES1 Conclusion: "Good public, it is with this last thought in mind that I am addressing this first essay to you, although the preface has been strangely transposed and the dedication is somewhat belated" (p. 110).

20. See "Bastiat on Plunder and Class" in appendix 1. See also ES3 6, where Bastiat talks about the class conflict between the aristocracy, the bourgeoisie, and the people; WSWNS 3, where he talks about the conflict between taxpayers and government employees; and his letter to Mme Cheuvreux of 23 June 1850, where Bastiat talks about how history is divided into two stages of class warfare: "As long as the state is regarded in this way as a source of favors, our history will be seen as having only two phases, the periods of conflict as to who will take control of the state and the periods of truce, which will be the transitory reign of a triumphant oppression, the harbinger of a fresh conflict" (CW1, p. 252); and "Plunder and Law" (CW2, pp. 266–76) for additional thoughts on this topic. See also Paillottet's footnote at the end of chapter 10 of *Economic Harmonies* (*OC,* vol. 6, "Concurrence," p. 357), in which he relates Bastiat's plans for further work on the theory and history of plunder.

remarks, as they obviously were based on what he observed going on in the Chamber of Deputies when a free-trade bill was before the Chamber and which the advocates of protection were able to have defeated in committee between April and July 1847. This is where Bastiat's job begins. As he states at the end of the First Series, the "sophistry" used by the ruling elite to hide their plundering ways must be exposed by economists like him so that the people will no longer be duped:

> But at least in civilized nations, the men who produce the wealth have become sufficiently numerous and *strong* to defend it. Is this to say that they are no longer dispossessed? Not at all; they are just as dispossessed as ever and, what is more, they mutually dispossess each other.
>
> Only, the thing which promotes it has changed; it is no longer by force but by fraud that public wealth can be seized.
>
> In order to steal from the public, it is first necessary to deceive them. To deceive them it is necessary to persuade them that they are being robbed for their own good; it is to make them accept imaginary services and often worse in exchange for their possessions. This gives rise to *sophistry.* Theocratic sophistry, economic sophistry, political sophistry, and financial sophistry. Therefore, ever since force has been held in check, *sophistry* has been not only a source of harm, it has been the very essence of harm. It must in its turn be held in check. And to do this the public must become *cleverer* than the clever, just as it has become *stronger* than the strong.[21]

He believed it was highly unlikely that the powerful beneficiaries of state-organized "legal plunder" would give up their privileges voluntarily, so they needed to be persuaded by one or both of the "Two Moral Philosophies" (ES2 2) which were at hand. He was doubtful that "religious morality" would be strong enough for the task, but he believed that political economy had the tools required to bring the system of plunder to an end:

> Let religious morality therefore touch the hearts of the Tartuffes, the Caesars, the colonists, sinecurists, and monopolists, etc. if it can. The task of political economy is to enlighten their dupes.

21. ES1 Conclusion, pp. 109–10.

Which of these two procedures works more effectively toward social progress? Do we have to spell it out? I believe it is the second. I fear that humanity cannot escape the necessity of first learning a *defensive moral philosophy*.

No matter how much I look, whatever I read or observe and whatever the questions I ask, I cannot find any abuse carried out on anything like a wide scale that has been destroyed through the voluntary renunciation of those benefiting from it.

On the other hand, I have found many that have been overcome by the active resistance of those suffering from them.

Describing the consequences of abuse is therefore the most effective way of destroying it. And how true this is, especially when it concerns abuses like protectionism, which, while inflicting genuine harm on the masses, nurture only illusion and disappointment in those who believe they are benefiting from them.[22]

Thus it was to begin enlightening "the dupes" about the real circumstances of their oppression by the organized plunderers that Bastiat used his pen, dipped in a mixture of angry denunciation and witty satire and devastating humor.

BASTIAT'S RHETORIC OF LIBERTY: SATIRE AND THE "STING OF RIDICULE"

Bastiat's goals in organizing a French free-trade movement, engaging in popular economic journalism, and standing for election can be summarized as follows: to expose the bad effects of government intervention in the economy; to uproot preconceived and incorrect economic ideas; to arouse a sense of injustice at the immoral actions of the government and its favored elites; to create "justified mistrust among the oppressed masses" of the beneficiaries of government privilege; and to open the eyes and stiffen the resistance of "the dupes" of government policies. The problem he faced was discovering the best way to achieve this for a popular audience who were gullible about the government's professed motives in regulating the economy and who were largely ignorant of economic theory.

---

22. ES2 2, pp. 109–10.

A major problem Bastiat is acutely aware of is that political economy had a justified reputation for being "dry and dull,"[23] and it was this reputation that Bastiat wanted to overcome with the style he adopted in the *Sophisms*. The issue was how to be appealing to popular readers whom he believed had become "the dupes" of those benefiting from the system of legal plunder. The means Bastiat adopted to achieve his political goals was to write in a style which ordinary people would find appealing, amusing, and convincing, and an analysis of the devices he used in composing his *Sophisms* reveals the great pains Bastiat took in trying to do this.

The style and the rhetorical devices Bastiat used in the individual sophisms show considerable variety and skill in their construction. Bastiat has been justly recognized for his excellent style by economists such as Friedrich Hayek and the historian of economic thought Joseph Schumpeter, but his methodology has not been studied in any detail. Schumpeter described Bastiat in very mixed terms as a brilliant economic journalist but as "no theorist" at all:

> Admired by sympathizers, reviled by opponents, his name might have gone down to posterity as the most brilliant economic journalist who ever lived. . . . I do not hold that Bastiat was a bad theorist. I hold that he was no theorist.[24]

Friedrich Hayek seems to agree with Schumpeter that Bastiat was not a major theorist but that he was "a publicist of genius" who did pioneering work in exposing economic fallacies held by the general public.[25] Nevertheless, Schumpeter did acknowledge a key aspect of Bastiat's style, noting that "[a] series of *Sophismes économiques* followed, whose pleasant wit . . . has ever since been the delight of many." However, some contemporary economists reject this view and see Bastiat as fundamentally challenging the classical school of economics by attempting to go beyond its theoretical limitations, especially concerning Malthusian population theory (Bastiat believed that technological innovation and free markets would enable people to break free of the Malthusian trap) and the Ricardian theory of rent (Bastiat believed there was nothing especially productive about land and that it was just another form of an exchange of "service for service" as was profit and interest).

---

23. ES2 2, p. 135. The original French phrase is *de sécheresse et de prosaïsme*.
24. Schumpeter, *History of Economic Analysis*, p. 500.
25. Hayek, "Introduction," in *Selected Essays on Political Economy*, FEE edition, p. ix.

His innovations in a number of areas suggest that had he lived long enough to complete *Economic Harmonies* he might have taken his insights into subjective value theory (predating the Marginal Revolution of the 1870s by twenty years) and public choice theory about the behavior of political actors (predating the work of James Buchanan and others by over a hundred years), into realms that were much ahead of their time.

A list of the rhetorical devices used by Bastiat in the *Sophisms* shows the breadth and complexity of what one might call his "rhetoric of liberty," which he formulated to expose the follies of the policies of the ruling elite and their system of "legal plunder" and to undermine their authority and legitimacy with "the sting of ridicule":

1. A standard prose format which one would normally encounter in a newspaper.
2. The single authorial voice in the form of a personal conversation with the reader.
3. A serious, constructed dialogue between stock figures who represented different viewpoints (in this Bastiat was influenced by Jane Marcet and Harriet Martineau; Gustave de Molinari continued Bastiat's format in some of his writings in the late 1840s and 1850s).
4. Satirical "official" letters or petitions to government officials or ministers, and other fabricated documents written by Bastiat (in these Bastiat would usually use a reductio ad absurdum argument to mock his opponents' arguments).
5. The use of Robinson Crusoe "thought experiments" to make serious economic points or arguments in a more easily understandable format.
6. "Economic tales" modeled on the works of classic French authors, such as La Fontaine's fables and Andrieux's short stories.[26]
7. Parodies of well-known scenes from French literature, such as Molière's plays.
8. Quoting scenes of plays where the playwright mocks the pretensions of aspiring bourgeois who want to act like the nobles who disdain commerce (e.g., Molière, Beaumarchais).

26. A study of the economic ideas expressed by La Fontaine in his fables was not made until twenty-five years after Bastiat first made use of them in the *Sophisms*. See Boissonade, *La Fontaine, économiste*.

9. Quoting poems with political content, such as Horace's ode on the transience of tyrants.

10. Quoting satirical songs about the foolish or criminal behavior of kings or emperors (such as Napoléon). Bastiat seems to be familiar with the world of the *goguettiers* (political song writers, especially Béranger) and their interesting sociological world of drinking and singing clubs.

11. The use of jokes and puns (such as the names he gave to characters in his dialogues [Mr. Blockhead], or place names [Stulta and Puera], and puns on words such as Highville and *gaucherie*).

Our study of Bastiat's *Sophisms* reveals a well-read man who was familiar with classic French literature, contemporary songs and poems, and opera. The sheer number and range of materials which Bastiat was able to draw upon in his writings is very impressive. It not only includes the classics of political economy in the French, Spanish, Italian, and English languages but also a very wide collection of modern French literature which includes the following: fables and fairy tales by La Fontaine and Perrault; plays by Molière, Beaumarchais, Victor Hugo, Regnard, Désaugiers, and Collin d'Harleville; songs and poems by Béranger and Depraux, short stories by Andrieux, odes by Horace, operas by Rossini, poems by Boileau-Despréaux and Viennet, and satires by Courier de Méré. The plays of Molière were Bastiat's favorite literary source from which to quote, and he used *Le Tartuffe, ou l'imposteur* (Tartuffe, or the Imposter, 1664), *Le Misanthrope* (The Misanthrope, 1666), *L'Avare* (The Miser, 1668), *Le Bourgeois gentilhomme* (The Would-Be Gentleman, 1670), and *Le Malade imaginaire* (The Imaginary Invalid, or the Hypochondriac, 1673).

Sometimes Bastiat goes beyond quoting a famous scene from a well-known classic work and adapts it for his own purposes by rewriting it as a parody. A good example of this is Molière's parody of the granting of a degree of doctor of medicine in the last play he wrote, *Le malade imaginaire* (The Imaginary Invalid, or the Hypochondriac), from which Bastiat quotes in "Theft by Subsidy" (ES2 9). Molière is suggesting that doctors in the seventeenth century were quacks who did more harm to their patients than good, as this translation of his dog Latin clearly suggests:

> I give and grant you
> Power and authority to Practice medicine,
> Purge,

Bleed,

Stab,

Hack,

Slash,

and Kill

With impunity

Throughout the whole world.[27]

Bastiat takes Molière's Latin and writes his own pseudo-Latin, this time with the purpose of mocking French tax collectors. In his parody Bastiat is suggesting that government officials, tax collectors, and customs officials were thieves who did more harm to the economy than good, so Bastiat writes a mock "swearing in" oath which he thinks they should use to induct new officials into government service:

I give to you and I grant

virtue and power

to steal

to plunder

to filch

to swindle

to defraud

At will, along this whole

road

If a pattern emerges from the examples cited above, it is that Bastiat likes to use literary references to show his readers that economic issues need not be "dry and dull" and to help him expose the nature of politicians and the political and economic power they wield. Thus in a witty and clever way he induces readers to share his disdain for those who misuse their power and, through this unfiltered view of reality, to no longer think like "dupes."

The *Sophisms* also reveal a man who has a very good sense of humor and an understanding of how humor can be used for political purposes as well as to make political economy less "dry and dull" for average readers. Sprinkled throughout the *Sophisms* are Bastiat's own jokes, plays on words, and puns. For example, in "The Tax Collector" (ES2 10), Bastiat creates a dialogue

27. Molière, *Théâtre complet de J.-B. Poquelin de Molière,* Third Interlude, p. 286. Thanks to Arthur Goddard's excellent translation in *Economic Sophisms,* FEE edition, p. 194n (courtesy of FEE.org).

between Jacques Bonhomme (a wine producer like Bastiat himself) and a tax collector, a M. "Lasouche." Lasouche is a made-up name which Bastiat creates to poke fun at his adversaries. In the FEE edition,[28] "M. Lasouche" is translated as "Mr. Clodpate." Since "la souche" means a tree stump, log, or plant stock, we thought "Mr. Blockhead" might be appropriate in our new translation.

It is interesting to speculate whether the strategy of using irony, sarcasm, parody, mockery, puns, and other forms of humor in Bastiat's writing was an explicit and deliberate one, or one that just naturally arose out of his jovial personality. A clue comes from material written soon after the appearance of the First Series of *Economic Sophisms.* In an article in *Le Journal des économistes* of January 1846, "Theft by Subsidy" (later to become ES2 9), he opens with the following testy remarks:

> People find my small volume of Sophisms too theoretical, scientific, and metaphysical. So be it. Let us try a superficial, banal, and, if necessary, brutal style. Since I am convinced that the general public are easily taken in as far as protection is concerned, I wanted to prove it to them. They prefer to be shouted at. So let us shout:
>
> Midas, King Midas has ass's ears! [In other words, the emperor has no clothes.]
>
> An explosion of plain speaking often has more effect than the politest circumlocutions. Do you remember Oronte and the difficulty that the Misanthropist, as misanthropic as he is, has in convincing him of his folly?[29]

It seems that he was stung by some critical reviews of the First Series as "too theoretical, scientific, and metaphysical" and thus failing to achieve his major aim, which was to appeal to a broader popular audience. As a result he may well have decided deliberately to use more sarcasm, humor, and parody in future *Sophisms.* The essay "Theft by Subsidy" was unusually angry and bitter for Bastiat, as it contained some strong words about the need to call a spade a spade (or *appeller un chat un chat,* as the French would say) regardless of the sensitivities of common opinion; in this case he wanted to call most

---

28. *Economic Sophisms,* FEE edition, p. 198.
29. ES2 9, p. 170.

government policies a form of theft and the protectionist system in France a form of "mutual theft":[30]

> Frankly, my good people, *you are being robbed.* That is plain speaking, but at least it is clear.
>
> The words *theft, to steal,* and *thief* seem to many people to be in bad taste. Echoing the words of Harpagon to Elise, I ask them: Is it the word or the thing that makes you afraid?[31]

Bastiat's Invention of "Crusoe Economics"

Modern readers of economics do not find it strange when an economist uses "thought experiments" to help simplify and clarify complex economic arguments. Members of the Austrian school resort to this process as a matter of course because it helps them establish the logic of "human action" which every economic actor must face when making decisions about what to produce or what to exchange. Bastiat, too, found it helpful to offer thought experiments that used the fictional figure of Robinson Crusoe, shipwrecked on his Island of Despair, to show the obstacles he needed to overcome in order to achieve some level of prosperity, the opportunity costs of using his time on one task rather than another, the need to deprive himself of some comforts in order to accumulate some savings, and (when Friday and visitors from other islands appear on the scene) the benefits of the division of labor and the nature of comparative advantage in trade.

The relative simplicity of the choices Crusoe had to make (first just one person and then two with the arrival of Friday) makes this a useful device for economists when making "thought experiments" to illustrate basic economic principles, and Bastiat is one of the first economists (perhaps even the first) to make extensive use of "Crusoe economics" to do so. In a search of the economic works in the Online Library of Liberty[32] for references to "Robinson Crusoe" in works written before 1847, we find that there are no references at all in the works of Adam Smith, in J.-B. Say's *Treatise on Political Economy,* or in the works of David Ricardo. There are only single references scattered across the writings of economists who were writing in the 1810s, 1820s, and 1830s, such as Jeremy Bentham, Jane Marcet, Thomas Babbington

30. ES2 9, p. 177.
31. Ibid., p. 171.
32. http://oll.libertyfund.org/groups/42.

Macaulay, Richard Whately, and Thomas Hodgskin, and none of them uses the Robinson Crusoe analogy to express serious economic ideas. Whately firmly rejected the use of Crusoe in any discussion of the nature of political economy because in his view the study of economics was the study of "exchanges" and, since Crusoe did not engage in any exchanges, he was "in a situation of which Political-Economy takes no cognizance."[33] Thus, Bastiat's extensive use of "Crusoe economics" between 1847 and 1850 may well be an original contribution to economic reasoning.[34]

Bastiat may have read Daniel Defoe's novel *The Life and Strange Surprizing Adventures of Robinson Crusoe, of York, Mariner* (1719) in English, but he would also have had access to several translations into French: one in 1817, one in 1827, one in 1836, and one in 1837. One of the translations which appeared in that year was by the romantic writer Pétrus Borel, who wrote, under the nom de plume of "Wolfman," several stories published in the journal *Le Commerce,* which may have brought him to Bastiat's attention.[35] The second translation of 1837 was by the poet Mme Amable Tastu (1798–1885) and included a glowing essay on Defoe by the economist Louis Reybaud, who was known to Bastiat.[36] Reybaud did not directly discuss the economic aspects of the Crusoe story but instead focused on the political and moral aspects of Defoe's interesting and varied life. This makes Bastiat's use of the economic predicament of Robinson Crusoe as an aid to thinking about economic decision making even more remarkable for its originality.

Bastiat uses Crusoe to make his points in both *Economic Sophisms* and *Economic Harmonies.*[37] In an unpublished outline or sketch written some-

33. Whately, *Introductory Lectures on Political Economy,* Chapter: Lecture I. "A man, for instance, in a desert island, like Alex. Selkirke, or the personage his adventures are supposed to have suggested, Robinson Crusoe, is in a situation of which Political-Economy takes no cognizance," p. 8, http://oll.libertyfund.org/titles/1377#Whately_0208_28.

34. *DEP* has a brief article on Defoe under "Foë (Daniel de)." It focuses on Defoe's minor economic writings such as his *Essay on the Treaty of Commerce with France* (1713), *Giving Alms no Charity* (1704), and *A Plan of the English Commerce* (1728), but there is no mention of Robinson Crusoe.

35. *Robinson Crusoé, par Daniel de Foë.*

36. Tastu, *Aventures de Robinson Crusoé, par Daniel de Foé,* 2:371–84.

37. References to Robinson Crusoe can be found in ES3 16, pp. 345–50, and ES2 14, pp. 227–34. In addition, there is a discussion of how a negotiation might have taken place between Robinson and Friday about exchanging game and fish in "Property and Plunder" (CW2, p. 155), and there are sixteen references to "Robinson" in *Economic Harmonies,* especially in chapter 4, "Exchange."

time in 1847, "Making a Mountain Out of a Molehill" (ES3 16), Bastiat uses Robinson Crusoe for the first time to simplify the economic arguments for free trade and provides an excellent statement of his methodology:

> Let us run off to the island to see the poor shipwrecked sailor. Let us see him in action. Let us examine the motives, the purpose, and the consequences of his actions. We will not learn everything there, in particular not those things that relate to the distribution of wealth in a society of many people, but we will glimpse the basic facts. We will observe general laws in their simplest form of action, and political economy is there in essence.
>
> Let us apply this method to just a few problems....

In "Something Else" (ES2 14), Bastiat, as he often does, has created a conversation between two intellectual opponents (in this case a protectionist and a free trader) where the protectionist asks the free trader to explain the effects of protectionism. The free trader replies, "That is not easy. Before moving on to complicated examples, we would have to study it in its simplest form," and launches into a discussion of how Crusoe made a plank of wood without a saw. After two weeks of intense labor chipping away at a log with an axe, Crusoe finally has his plank (and a blunt axe). The free trader then presents an alternative scenario: what if Crusoe had not commenced making his plank and saw that the tide had washed ashore a proper saw-cut plank (the new plank is an obvious reference to a cheaper overseas import which the protectionists believed would harm the national French economy). Bastiat puts some protectionist notions into Crusoe's head, and Crusoe concludes that he can make more labor for himself (and therefore be better off according to the protectionists' theory) if he pushes the plank back out to sea. The free trader exposes this economic sophism by saying that there is something that is "not seen" by the protectionist at first glance, namely, "Did Robinson not see that the time he saved he could devote to doing *something else?*"

Bastiat then raises the level of complexity in his economic arguments by introducing a second and then a third person on Crusoe's island. With the introduction of a second person, Friday, Crusoe now has someone with whom he can cooperate. They can pool their resources, plan their economic activities, develop a simple form of the division of labor, and even trade with each other. When a third person arrives from another island and proposes a trading relationship whereby Crusoe and Friday trade their vegetables for the visitor's game, Bastiat now can explore the benefits of international comparative advantage in trade. Bastiat uses this three-way conversation to make his points. Interestingly, he gives the European Crusoe the protectionist arguments; the native islander Friday is given the domestic free-trade arguments, and the visitor becomes an advocate of international free trade.

BASTIAT'S POLITICAL SOPHISMS

Bastiat also wrote what might be called "political sophisms" in order to debunk fallacies of a political nature, especially concerning electoral politics and the ability of political leaders to initiate fundamental reforms. He had hinted in the "Conclusion" to the First Series that he had more in mind than the debunking of economic sophisms. He explicitly mentions four specific types of sophistry: theocratic, economic, political, and financial sophistry. Bastiat devoted most of his efforts to exposing economic sophisms, mentioning theocratic and financial sophisms only in passing if at all. He did, however, write a number of political sophisms which will be briefly discussed here.

The "economic" and "political" sophisms are closely related in Bastiat's mind because the advocates of protectionism were able to get special privileges only because they controlled the Chamber of Deputies and the various councils which advised the government on economic policy. Bastiat wrote five sophisms which can be categorized as political sophisms. One he explicitly called "Electoral Sophisms" (undated but probably written during 1847), which is a Benthamite listing of the kinds of false arguments people give for why they might prefer voting for one candidate over another. Another is called "The Elections" (also written sometime in 1847) and is a dialogue in which a "countryman" (a farmer) argues with a political writer, a parish priest, and an electoral candidate.[38]

Two of the sophisms which appear in this volume, although they focus on significant economic issues, also deal with political matters and thus can be regarded as political sophisms. In "The Tax Collector" (ES2 10, ca. 1847) an amusing and somewhat convoluted discussion about the nature of political representation takes place between Jacques Bonhomme and a tax collector, wickedly called "Mr. Blockhead." Bonhomme is merely confused by the

---

38. "Electoral Sophisms" (CW1, pp. 397–404); "The Elections" (CW1, pp. 404–9).

trickery of the tax collector's euphemisms that portray the elected deputies in the Chamber as his true representatives. The second is "The Utopian" (ES2 11, January 1847), where Bastiat discusses the problems faced by a free-market reform-minded minister who is unexpectedly put in charge of the country. In the face of the utopian reformer's many proposals, Bastiat presents the dilemmas and ultimate failure of top-down political and economic reform.

The fifth essay which might also be regarded as a political sophism is his famous essay "The State," which appeared initially as a draft in the magazine *Jacques Bonhomme* (11–15 June 1848) and then in a longer form in *Le Journal des débats* (September 1848).[39] Here he attempts to rebut the folly of the idea which was widespread during the first few months following the February Revolution that the state could and should take care of all the needs of the people by taxing everybody and giving benefits to everybody.

Bastiat the Revolutionary Journalist and Politician

With the failure of the free traders to get tariff reform successfully through committee in the Chamber of Deputies in the middle of 1847, Bastiat and his colleagues suffered a significant defeat. The outbreak of revolution in February 1848, the abdication of Louis-Philippe, and the creation of the Second Republic provided another opportunity for Bastiat to spread his ideas on free trade and free markets, which he seized with enthusiasm in spite of his rapidly failing health. This he did in part by immediately starting a magazine aimed at ordinary working people, *La République française,* which he, Hippolyte Castille, and Gustave de Molinari handed out on the streets of Paris two days after the revolution broke out.[40]

We include in this volume two short articles which appeared originally in the 12 March issue of *La République française.*[41] In the *Œuvres complètes* Paillottet called them "Petites affiches de Jacques Bonhomme" (Small Posters by Jacques Bonhomme) because they were one-page articles designed as posters which could be pasted on walls at head height around the streets of Paris

---

39. See "The State (draft)" (CW2, pp. 105–6) and "The State" (CW2, pp. 93–104).

40. Molinari has some interesting reminiscences about how the magazine came into existence. See "The Law-Abiding Revolutionary" (CW2, pp. 401–3).

41. See ES3 21 and ES3 22.

so they could be read by rioters and revolutionaries who walked the streets at all hours.[42] These posters reveal another side of Bastiat the writer trying to appeal to the working class of Paris in the middle of a revolution. He addresses the people in the familiar *tu* form as he makes his case for limited government, free markets, and low taxes.

Bastiat wrote seventeen articles for *La République française* that we know about, four of which appear in this volume and thirteen of which have been published in a previous volume.[43] He wrote on many topics which should not surprise us, such as the need for disarmament in order to lower taxes, the freedom of the press, freedom of education, the high level of taxation which fell on ordinary working people, the excessive size of the government bureaucracy, and so on. What is a bit surprising is the fervor of his republican sentiments which he expressed in a statement of principles in the first issue of the magazine.[44]

Needless to say, Bastiat was not successful. He did not manage to sway the masses to the cause of free trade and limited government in March 1848 and closed the magazine in order to concentrate on standing for the April elections, which he felt would offer him another opportunity to spread his ideas on free trade and free markets. On 23 April 1848 Bastiat was elected to the Constituent Assembly to represent the département of the Landes and served from 4 May 1848 until 27 May 1849. Given his expertise in economic matters, it is not surprising that he was chosen to serve on the Finance Committee, to which he was appointed vice president an extraordinary eight times. His job was to make periodic reports to the Chamber on Finance Committee matters. Politically, he supported General Cavaignac in the Chamber against Louis-Napoléon, but he sometimes voted with the left or the right depending on the specific issue. For example, he voted with the left on the right of citizens to form trade unions (which he saw as just another voluntary organization which individuals had the right to join or not join) but against the left when it came to taxpayer-funded unemployment relief in the National Workshops.

Bastiat's activities in the Chamber still await their historian, but a sum-

---

42. See ES3 21, pp. 377–78n3.

43. For a complete list of the articles Bastiat wrote for *La République française* and where they appear in the Collected Works, see appendix 6, "Bastiat's Revolutionary Magazines."

44. See "A Few Words about the Title of Our Journal *The French Republic*," in Addendum: Additional Material by Bastiat.

mary of some of the issues on which he voted follows: for the banishment of the royal family, against the reintroduction of caution money for publishers, for postal reform and the ending of the government monopoly, against the arrest and trial of the socialist Louis Blanc for his role in the June Days rioting, against the reintroduction of corporal punishment, against the death penalty, against the declaration of martial law in Paris, against military intervention in Rome, and against allowing public servants to also sit in the Chamber as elected representatives.

While Bastiat was working in the Constituent Assembly, he took another opportunity to become engaged in revolutionary journalism on the streets of Paris, this time in his journal *Jacques Bonhomme*. The magazine was founded by Bastiat with the assistance of Gustave de Molinari, Charles Coquelin, Alcide Fonteyraud, and Joseph Garnier. It appeared approximately weekly in four issues between 11 June and 13 July, with a break between 24 June and 9 July because of the rioting during the June Days uprising.[45] He wrote on the nature of freedom, laissez-faire economic policies, the fraudulent claims of the government to be able to give whatever the voters wanted, and most interestingly, a draft of what was to become one of his best-known essays, "The State."[46] As the June Days rioting became increasingly violent, Bastiat and his friends were forced to close the magazine.

Bastiat's experiences in working on *La République française* and *Jacques Bonhomme* during two of the most tumultuous and violent periods of the 1848 Revolution reveal a man who was not merely an armchair economic and political theorist. He saw at first hand the anger and determination of the people to change French society, and he also saw how the government was prepared to defend itself by calling out the troops to shoot down the protesters. In a couple of subdued and understated letters to friends he describes being on or near the barricades when these events took place and even taking steps to use his influence as a deputy to call the troops off long enough to drag people to safety in the side streets. The following two brief

---

45. Bastiat wrote eight articles, four of which appeared in CW1 and one in CW2. See also the list of articles Bastiat wrote for *La République française* and *Jacques Bonhomme* in appendix 6, "Bastiat's Revolutionary Magazines." The editor of the *Œuvres complètes,* Paillottet, attributed the authorship of several of these unsigned articles to Bastiat with the assistance of Bastiat's friend Molinari. We have followed Paillottet's practice.

46. The draft of "The State" and the final version which appeared in September 1848 in *Le Journal des débats* can be found in CW2, pp. 105–6, and CW2, pp. 93–104, respectively.

quotations, one from February and the other from June, should be sufficient to show how close Bastiat was to events:

27 February 1848, Paris

As you will see in the newspapers, on the 23rd everything seemed to be over. Paris had a festive air; everything was illuminated. A huge gathering moved along the boulevards singing. Flags were adorned with flowers and ribbons. When they reached the Hôtel des Capucines, the soldiers blocked their path and fired a round of musket fire at point-blank range into the crowd. I leave you to imagine the sight offered by a crowd of thirty thousand men, women, and children fleeing from the bullets, the shots, and those who fell.

An instinctive feeling prevented me from fleeing as well, and when it was all over I was on the site of a massacre with five or six workmen, facing about sixty dead and dying people. The soldiers appeared stupefied. I begged the officer to have the corpses and wounded moved in order to have the latter cared for and to avoid having the former used as flags by the people when they returned, but he had lost his head.

The workers and I then began to move the unfortunate victims onto the pavement, as doors refused to open. At last, seeing the fruitlessness of our efforts, I withdrew. But the people returned and carried the corpses to the outlying districts, and a hue and cry was heard all through the night. The following morning, as though by magic, two thousand barricades made the insurrection fearsome. Fortunately, as the troop did not wish to fire on the National Guard, the day was not as bloody as might have been expected.

All is now over. The Republic has been proclaimed. You know that this is good news for me. The people will govern themselves.[47]

29 June 1848, Paris

Cables and newspapers will have told you [Julie Marsan] all about the triumph of the republican order after four days of bitter struggle.

47. Letter to Mme Marsan, 27 February 1848 (CW1, p. 142).

I shall not give you any detail, even about me, because a single letter would not suffice.

I shall just tell you that I have done my duty without ostentation or temerity. My only role was to enter the Faubourg Saint-Antoine after the fall of the first barricade, in order to disarm the fighters. As we went on, we managed to save several insurgents whom the militia wanted to kill. One of my colleagues displayed a truly admirable energy in this situation, which he did not boast about from the rostrum.[48]

Eleven months after these events Bastiat was reelected to the Chamber, this time the newly created Legislative Assembly in which he sat from 28 May 1849 until he took a leave of absence on the grounds of ill health sometime in mid-1850. During this period he continued to work as vice president of the Finance Committee, but his activities in the Assembly were reduced because his deteriorating health meant that he was less able to speak in the Chamber. Nevertheless, he was able to write articles and pamphlets on matters before the Chamber which he distributed as pamphlets such as "Protectionism and Communism," "Peace and Freedom," "Damned Money!," "Plunder and the Law," "The Law,"[49] and his last pamphlet, which appears in this volume: *What Is Seen and What Is Not Seen*. All the while, he continued to work on his magnum opus on economic theory, *Economic Harmonies*. Although he gave fewer speeches in the Assembly, he was present to vote for the abolition of the tax on alcohol, for the right to form and join unions, for free trade in the wine industry, and against the power of the National University to set the curriculum for all schools. On 9 February 1850 Bastiat made his last appearance in the Chamber, speaking on behalf of the Finance Committee. He later sought a leave of absence on the grounds of ill health and spent his time writing, most notably *What Is Seen and What Is Not Seen* and the second part of *Economic Harmonies*. On the advice of his doctor he decided to travel to Italy, and on 10 September he bade farewell to his friends in the Political Economy Society (Société d'économie politique) before heading to Rome, where he died on Christmas Eve 1850.

Economic Sophisms and the other writings in this volume show Bastiat at his creative and journalistic best: his skill at mixing serious and amusing ways of making his arguments is unsurpassed; the quality of his insights into

48. Letter to Mme Marsan, 29 June 1848 (CW1, pp. 156–57).
49. All of these pamphlets except "Damned Money!" can be found in CW2.

profound economic issues is often exceptional and sometimes well ahead of his time; his ability to combine his political lobbying for the Free Trade Movement, his journalism, his political activities during the 1848 Revolution, and his scholarly activities is most unusual; and his humor, wit, and literary knowledge, which he scatters throughout his writings, demonstrate that he deserves his reputation as one of the most gifted writers on economic matters who still deserves our close attention today.

David M. Hart

A Note on the Publishing History of
Economic Sophisms *and* What Is
Seen and What Is Not Seen

Establishing the publishing history of what was to become *Economic Sophisms* is somewhat difficult because the work appeared in three different formats during Bastiat's lifetime and after his death (possibly four if one counts later editions and translations).

Economic Sophisms first appeared as short articles in various journals and newspapers which published Bastiat's material, such as his free-trade journal, *Le Libre-échange,*[1] and the main organ of the Parisian free-market political economists, *Le Journal des économistes.* In the second phase, some of the material was also published as stand-alone books or pamphlets, such as *Economic Sophisms* First and Second Series, which appeared in book form in early 1846 and 1848, respectively, in slightly reworked form. The third phase came after Bastiat's death, in 1850, when his friend and literary executor, Prosper Paillottet, had access to Bastiat's papers and from this and the previously mentioned published sources was able to edit and publish the first edition of Bastiat's *Œuvres complètes* (1854).

In most cases Paillottet indicated in footnotes the place and date of the original publication of the essays, but in some cases he did not. Sometimes he wrote that the piece was an "unpublished draft" (presumably one he found in Bastiat's papers), and at other times he simply said nothing, thus complicating the task of the researcher, as we no longer have access to Bastiat's original papers. We have taken Paillottet's word in every case, as he is the best and sometimes only source we have for this information, although at all times it must be recognized that he was a close friend and strong supporter of Bastiat,

---

1. Bastiat was one of the founders of the Association pour la liberté des échanges (Free Trade Association) in 1846 and edited its journal, *Le Libre-échange* (Free Trade), from 1846 to 1848.

which surely must have colored his judgment. That being said, we have not found any instance where Paillottet has been wrong (except that the journal *Jacques Bonhomme* was published in June–July 1848, not March 1848);[2] our main frustration is that his information is not as complete as we would like it to be.

Economic Sophisms, First Series

The First Series of *Economic Sophisms* was completed in November 1845 (Bastiat signed the conclusion, "Mugron, 2 November 1845") and was probably printed in late 1845 or early 1846. The Bibliothèque nationale de France does not show an edition published in 1845, but there are two listed for 1846, one of which is called the second edition. Presumably the other is the true first edition which appeared in early (possibly January) 1846.

The first eleven chapters (of an eventual twenty-two) had originally appeared as a series of three articles in *Le Journal des économistes* in April, July, and October 1845 under the name "Sophismes économiques." If chapters twelve to twenty-two were also published elsewhere, the place and date of original publication were not given by Paillottet.

The French printing history of the First Series is as follows: the first collection was published, according to Paillottet, at the end of 1845 (probably December), but all the printed copies bear the date 1846. The First Series continued to be published as a separate volume until 1851 and the appearance of a fourth edition (second edition in 1846, third edition in 1847).

Economic Sophisms, Second Series

The French printing history of *Economic Sophisms*, Second Series is as follows: it was published, according to Paillottet, at the end of January 1848 and consisted of seventeen essays, seven of which had previously appeared in the newspaper *Le Libre-échange* (between December 1846 and July 1847), two in *Le Journal des économistes* (in January and May 1846), and one in *Le Courrier français* (in September 1846). For the other seven articles no previous publication details were given. Only one edition of the Second Series appeared as a separate volume, in 1848.

2. We have checked Paillottet's claims against the sources to which we do have access, in particular *Le Journal des économistes.*

The first edition to combine both the First and Second Series in a single volume was an edition of 1851, which appeared simultaneously in Paris and Belgium. Thereafter, the Second Series always appeared in print with the First Series.

ECONOMIC SOPHISMS, "THIRD SERIES"

We have collected together in this volume a number of other writings by Bastiat which might well have been drawn upon had he lived long enough to compile a third series of *Economic Sophisms.* This was also the thinking of Paillottet, who collected twenty-two pieces of what he called a *nouvelle série de sophismes économiques* (a new series of economic sophisms) for volume 2 of the *Œuvres complètes.*[3] We decided to include them as well in this volume. Sixteen aticles come from Bastiat's free-trade journal, *Le Libre-échange* (published between December 1846 and its closure in March 1848), two articles from Bastiat's revolutionary magazine *La République française* (March 1848), one from *Le Journal des économistes* (March 1848); for the remaining five articles, no sources were given.

WHAT IS SEEN AND WHAT IS NOT SEEN, OR POLITICAL ECONOMY IN ONE LESSON

There is also another pamphlet which we think deserves to be included in our expanded collection of *Economic Sophisms* because of its similarities of style and content, namely, *What Is Seen and What Is Not Seen.*[4] This is the last work (other than letters) which Bastiat wrote before his death, in 1850. In a footnote Paillottet provides us with these fascinating details.[5]

The importance which Bastiat must have placed on getting this work published is revealed by the enormous effort he expended in rewriting it

---

3. See the footnote on page 1 of *OC,* vol. 2, "Le Libre-échange." Paillottet explains his selection criteria for the volume: "In putting together this volume from articles almost exclusively drawn from a weekly journal, which the author himself did not plan to do, we have attempted to classify them in the following order: (1) exposition of the aims, principles, and operation of the free-trade association, (2) articles on the subsistence question, (3) polemical pieces against other journals, and other diverse topics, (4) public speeches, (5) various other matters and a new series of economic sophisms."

4. *Ce qu'on voit et ce qu'on ne voit pas, ou l'Économie politique en une leçon* (1850).

5. See Paillottet's note at the beginning of WSWNS, p. 402n1.

from scratch twice at a time when his health was rapidly failing and when he was under considerable pressure to complete *Economic Harmonies,* which remained unfinished at his death. *What Is Seen and What Is Not Seen* was eventually published as a small stand-alone pamphlet of seventy-nine pages in July 1850 by Guillaumin. Another edition appeared in 1854 (possibly the second edition) in volume 5 of Paillottet's *Œuvres complètes;* another two in 1863 (possibly the third edition) in volume 5 of *Œuvres complètes,* as well as in volume 2 of *Œuvres choisies* (pp. 336–92). The fourth edition of 1869 and the fifth edition of 1879 were both stand-alone books.

THE POST-1850 PUBLISHING AND TRANSLATION HISTORY OF *ECONOMIC SOPHISMS* AND *WHAT IS SEEN AND WHAT IS NOT SEEN*

In French, *Economic Sophisms* and *What Is Seen and What Is Not Seen* remained in print throughout the nineteenth century as part of Bastiat's *Œuvres complètes.* Once the *Œuvres complètes* appeared in 1854, it does not seem that *Economic Sophisms* was ever printed again in French as a separate title. The same is not true for *What Is Seen and What Is Not Seen,* which was printed as a separate book by Guillaumin and by other publishers as well. In Paris, Henri Bellaire issued an edition with a biographical introduction and numerous notes (1873).[6] In Belgium an edition even appeared (which also included the essay "The State") on the eve of the outbreak of World War I (1914).[7]

The international interest in Bastiat's work can be partially gauged by the speed with which it was translated and the variety of languages in which it was published. For example, an English translation of *Economic Sophisms* appeared in 1846;[8] in 1847 German, Dutch, Spanish, and Italian translations appeared;[9] 1848 saw a Danish edition[10] as well as an American edition with an introduction by Francis Lieber.[11] The Francis Lieber edition contained both the First and Second Series. Another American edition of *Economic*

---

6. *Ce qu'on voit et ce qu'on ne voit pas* (1873).

7. *Ce qu'on voit et ce qu'on ne voit pas* (1914).

8. *Popular Fallacies Regarding General Interests.*

9. *Die Trugschlüsse der Schutzzöllner gegenüber der gesunden Handels-politik; Staats-huishoudkundige drogredenen; Sofismas económicos; Sofismi economici.*

10. *Falske Sætninger.*

11. *Sophisms of the Protective Policy.*

Sophisms (which also included both series) appeared in Chicago in 1869 as part of a movement against the post–Civil War tariffs which resulted from the Morrill tariff of 1861.[12] The first British edition containing both series appeared in 1873 in Edinburgh.[13]

When the debate about protective tariffs resurfaced in Britain and America in the late nineteenth and early twentieth centuries, Bastiat's essays were again used in the intellectual battle, with several reissues being made by groups such as the Cobden Club, which used titles that made it very clear on what side of the fence they stood.[14] In North America the American Free Trade League issued two editions (in 1870 and 1873),[15] and an "adaptation designed for the American reader" appeared in 1867 and 1874.[16]

The translation history of *What Is Seen and What Is Not Seen* is similar to that of *Economic Sophisms*. It was translated very quickly into other languages soon after it appeared in French in 1850, with a Dutch translation appearing in 1850, Danish in 1852, and German in 1853.[17] The first English translation, in 1852 by William Hodgson, appeared in the Manchester *Examiner and Times* before being published as a pamphlet in the same year.[18] Another edition appeared in the *Newcastle Weekly Chronicle* a short time later.[19] Of considerable interest is the "People's Edition" by an unnamed translator, which was intended to be distributed among working people.[20] It went through at least four editions between 1853 and the late 1870s.

Until the Foundation for Economic Education published new translations of some of Bastiat's major works in the mid 1960s, there was very little interest in Bastiat's free-trade ideas after the First World War. From this period we have been able to find only two editions of his *Economic Sophisms*, a 1921 reprint of an English edition from 1909[21] and an American edition which appeared toward the close of World War II, in 1944. The latter is noteworthy because of the introduction by the American libertarian author Rose Wilder Lane.

12. *Essays on Political Economy* (1869).
13. *Economic Sophisms* (1873).
14. *Economic Sophisms; Or, Fallacies of Protection.*
15. *Sophisms of the Protectionists.*
16. *What Is Free Trade?*
17. *Wat men ziet en wat men niet ziet; Hvad man ser og hvad man ikke ser; Was man sieht und was man nicht sieht.*
18. *What Is Seen and What Is Not Seen* (1852).
19. *Things Seen and Not Seen.*
20. *Essays on Political Economy* (1853).
21. *Economic Sophisms* (1909).

This edition was published by Raymond Cyrus "R. C." Hoiles, who had moved from Ohio to run a daily newspaper in California, the Santa Ana *Register*, in 1935. Around this time he discovered the work of Bastiat and used his newspaper's printing presses to publish a series of works by Bastiat using the nineteenth-century English translations by Patrick James Stirling, which had been published in the 1860s and 1870s.[22] Hoiles adapted them for an American audience by commissioning new forewords or by making his own compilations of Bastiat's writings to be used in his battle against the New Deal.

The new foreword to what was now called *Social Fallacies* was by the libertarian journalist and writer Rose Wilder Lane, who described Bastiat as "one of the leaders of the revolution whose work and fame, like Aristotle's, belong to the ages. . . . What modern science owes to Aristotle, a free world will someday owe to Bastiat."[23] Hoiles in his "Publisher's Statement," which introduces the *Social Fallacies*, explained why he thought reprinting Bastiat in 1944 was warranted:

> The reason for republishing Bastiat's "Economic Sophisms" (which we have called "Social Fallacies") is that we believe Bastiat shows the fallacy of government planning better than any other writer of any period. Since he wrote a century ago, his work cannot be regarded as party-policies now. It deals with fundamental principles of political economy which out-last all parties.[24]

In the years immediately following the end of the Second World War, Bastiat's ideas found an American supporter in the economic journalist Henry Hazlitt (1894–1993), who wrote for the *Wall Street Journal* and the *New York Times*. In 1946 Hazlitt published a popular defense of free-market ideas titled *Economics in One Lesson* in which he acknowledged the influence of Bastiat by taking Bastiat's subtitle for *What Is Seen and What Is Not Seen* as the title for his own book. He noted in his introduction that, like Bastiat, he wanted to debunk the economic sophisms he saw around him:

> My greatest debt, with respect to the kind of expository framework on which the present argument is being hung, is to

22. Stirling translated the *Economic Sophisms* (*Social Fallacies*) in 1873 and the *Economic Harmonies* over a period between 1860 and 1880.
23. *Social Fallacies by Frederic Bastiat*, p. 3
24. *Social Fallacies by Frederic Bastiat*, p. 1

Frédéric Bastiat's essay *Ce qu'on voit et ce qu'on ne voit pas,* now nearly a century old. The present work may, in fact, be regarded as a modernization, extension, and generalization of the approach found in Bastiat's pamphlet.[25]

In postwar America Bastiat's works were made available to a new generation of readers with new translations of his key works published by the Foundation for Economic Education in Irvington-on-Hudson, New York, under the direction of Leonard Reed. The project began with the translation and publication of Bastiat's pamphlet "The Law" in 1950, exactly one hundred years after its first appearance in June 1850. Other works were translated with the assistance of the William Volker Fund, and these appeared in 1964 along with a new biography of Bastiat written by Dean Russell in 1965.[26] The trilogy of works which the Foundation for Economic Education published in 1964—*Selected Essays on Political Economy* (including "What Is Seen and What Is Not Seen"), *Economic Sophisms,* and *Economic Harmonies*—have remained the backbone of Bastiat studies in America ever since.[27]

With regard to French-language editions of Bastiat's work, after a hiatus of nearly seventy years since the appearance of the Belgian edition of *Ce qu'on voit et ce qu'on ne voit pas* in 1914, a revival of interest in Bastiat in the early 1980s led to the reprinting of a number of his works, beginning in 1983 with a reissue of two of his pamphlets, "Property and Law" (*Propriété et loi*) and "The State" (*L'état*), by the Economic Institute of Paris,[28] as well as a collection of Bastiat's economic writings edited by Florin Aftalion (which included excerpts from *Economic Sophisms*).[29] This was followed in 1994 by the reissue of *Ce qu'on voit et ce qu'on ne voit pas* by Alain Madelin[30] and another in 2004 by Jacques Garello.[31] Michel Leter has edited two volumes of Bastiat's writings for the publisher Les Belles Lettres in a series called La bibliothèque classique de la liberté (The Classic Library of Liberty). Leter's

25. Hazlitt, *Economics in One Lesson,* p. 9.

26. Russell, *Frédéric Bastiat: Ideas and Influence.* This began as a doctoral thesis which Russell wrote under Wilhelm Röpke at the Graduate Institute of International Studies in Geneva.

27. WSWNS, FEE edition; *Economic Sophisms,* FEE edition; *Economic Harmonies,* FEE edition.

28. *Propriété et loi, L'État.*

29. In *Œuvres économiques.*

30. *Ce qu'on voit et ce qu'on ne voit pas* (1994).

31. *Ce qu'on voit et ce qu'on ne voit pas* (2004).

edition of *Economic Sophisms* appeared in 2005,[32] and his collection of Bastiat's pamphlets, which included *What Is Seen and What Is Not Seen,* was published in 2009.[33]

To commemorate the two hundredth anniversary of the birth of Bastiat, an international conference was held in Bayonne in June 2001 under the auspices of the Cercle Frédéric Bastiat and M. Jacques de Guenin. It was here that Liberty Fund's project of translating the collected works of Bastiat was conceived. Concurrent with Liberty Fund's publishing project, Jacques de Guenin and the Institut Charles Coquelin are publishing a seven-volume French-language edition, the first volume of which appeared in late 2009.

David M. Hart

---

32. *Sophismes économiques* (2005).
33. *Pamphlets* (2009).

Map of France Showing Cities Mentioned by Bastiat

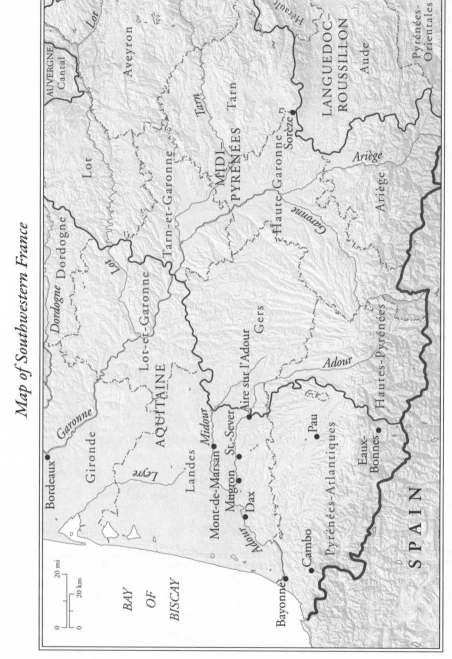

Map of Southwestern France

Cartography by Mapping Specialists, Madison, Wisconsin.

Economic Sophisms
First Series[1]

1. (Paillottet's note) The small volume containing the first series of *Economic Sophisms* was published at the end of 1845. Several of the chapters it contained had already been published by *Le Journal des économistes* in issues that appeared in April, July, and October of the same year.

Author's Introduction to *Economic Sophisms*

PUBLISHING HISTORY:

Original title: No title given.
Place and date of first publication: *Economic Sophisms* (First
   Series) (1846).
First French edition as book or pamphlet: *Economic Sophisms*
   (First Series) (1846).
Location in Paillottet's edition of *OC:* Vol. 4. *Sophismes
   économiques. Petits pamphlets I,* pp. 1–5.
Previous translations: 1st English ed., 1846; 1st American ed.,
   1848; FEE ed., 1964.

In political economy there is a lot to learn and very little to do.
(Bentham)[2]

In this small volume, I have sought to refute a few of the arguments against
the deregulation of trade.

This is not a conflict that I am entering into against protectionists. It is a
principle that I am attempting to instill into the minds of sincere men who
hesitate because they doubt.

I am not one of those who say: "Protection is based on interests." I believe
that it is based on error or, if you prefer, on *half-truths*. Too many people fear
freedom for this apprehension not to be sincere.

This is setting my sights high, but I must admit that I would like this
small work to become in some way a *manual* for men called upon to decide
between the two principles. When you do not possess a long-standing familiarity with the doctrine of freedom, protectionist sophisms will constantly

---

2. Bastiat chose two passages from Bentham's *Théorie des peines et des récompenses* as
the opening for both the First and Second Series of *Economic Sophisms.* The quotation
above comes from Dumont's translation, p. 270. It is possible that Bentham was the inspiration behind Bastiat's choice of words for the title of this series of articles known as
"Economic Sophisms." See the *Traité des sophismes politiques*, which appeared in 1816.
An English version of the book appeared as *The Handbook of Political Fallacies* in 1824.

come to one's mind in one form or another. To release it from them, a long effort of analysis is required on each occasion, and not everyone has the time to carry out this task, least of all the legislators. This is why I have tried to do it all at once.

But, people will say, are the benefits of freedom so hidden that they are apparent only to professional economists?

Yes, we agree that our opponents in the debate have a clear advantage over us. They can set out a half-truth in a few words, and to show that it is a *half-truth* we need long and arid dissertations.

This is in the nature of things. Protection brings together in one single point all the good it does and distributes among the wider mass of people the harm it inflicts. One is visible to the naked eye, the other only to the mind's eye.[3] It is exactly the opposite for freedom.

This is so for almost all economic matters.

If you say: Here is a machine that has thrown thirty workers out into the street;

Or else: Here is a spendthrift who will stimulate all forms of industry;

Or yet again: The conquest of Algiers[4] has doubled Marseilles's trade;

Or lastly: The budget assures the livelihood of one hundred thousand families.

You will be understood by everyone, and your statements are clear, simple, and true in themselves. You may deduce the following principles from them:

Machines are harmful;

Luxury, conquest, and heavy taxes are a blessing;

And your theory will have all the more success in that you will be able to support it with irrefutable facts.

We, on the other hand, cannot stick to one cause and its immediate effect. We know that this effect itself becomes a cause in its turn. To judge a measure, it is therefore necessary for us to follow it through a sequence of results up to its final effect. And, since we must give utterance to the key word, we are reduced to *reasoning.*

---

3. (Paillottet's note) This glimpse gave rise later to the pamphlet titled *What Is Seen and What Is Not Seen,* which is included in this volume.

4. Algeria was invaded and conquered by France in 1830, and the occupied parts were annexed to France in 1834. The new constitution of the Second Republic (1848) declared that Algeria was no longer a colony but an integral part of France (with three départements) and that the emigration of French settlers would be officially encouraged and subsidized by the government. These policies were vigorously opposed by Bastiat.

But right away here we are, assailed by these cries: "You are theorists, metaphysicians, ideologues, utopians, and in thrall to rigid principles," and all the prejudices of the public are turned against us.

What are we to do, therefore? Call for patience and good faith in the reader and, if we are capable of this, cast into our deductions such vivid clarity that the truth and falsehood stand out starkly in order for victory to be won either by restriction or freedom, once and for all.

I must make an essential observation at this point.

A few extracts from this small volume have appeared in the *Journal des économistes*.

In a criticism that was incidentally very benevolent, published by the Vicomte de Romanet[5] (see the issues of *Le Moniteur industriel* dated 15 and 18 May 1845),[6] he assumed that I was asking for *customs dues to be abolished*. M. de Romanet is mistaken. What I am asking for is the abolition of the protectionist regime. We do not refuse taxes to the government; what we would like, if possible, is to dissuade those being governed from taxing each other. Napoléon said: "Customs dues ought not to be a fiscal instrument, but a means of protecting industry."[7] We plead the contrary and say: "Customs dues must not be an instrument of mutual plunder in the hands of workers, but it can be a fiscal instrument that is as good as any other." We are so far, or

5. Auguste, Vicomte de Romanet (n.d.), was a staunch protectionist who served on the Conseil général de l'agriculture, du commerce, et des manufactures.

6. See the entry for "*Le Moniteur industriel*," in the Glossary of Newspapers and Journals and the entries for "Mimerel Committee" and "Association pour la défense du travail national," in the Glossary of Subjects and Terms. *Le Moniteur industriel* was the journal of the protectionist "Association pour la défense du travail national" (Association for the Defense of National Employment) founded by Mimerel de Roubaix in 1846.

7. Remarks about tariffs and protection for French industry are scattered throughout the *Mémoires* of Napoléon. His most direct comments come in a discussion of the Continental System (also called the Contintal Blockade) that he introduced in November 1806 to weaken the British economy by preventing the sale of British goods in Europe. In the *Mémoires* Napoléon is very proud of his economic accomplishments, believing that the system of protection he introduced stimulated French industry enormously. "Experience showed that each day the continental system was good, because the State prospered in spite of the burden of the war.... The spirit of improvement was shown in agriculture as well as in the factories. New villages were built, as were the streets of Paris. Roads and canals made interior movement much easier. Each week some new improvement was invented: I made it possible to make sugar out of turnips, and soda out of salt. The development of science was at the front along with that of industry" (*Mémoires de Napoléon Bonaparte*, pp. 95–99).

to involve only me in the conflict, I am so far from demanding the abolition of customs dues that I see in them a lifeline for our finances.[8] I believe that they are likely to produce huge revenues for the Treasury, and if my idea is to be expressed in its entirety, at the snail's pace that sound economic doctrine takes to circulate, I am counting more on the needs of the Treasury than on the force of enlightened public opinion for trade reform to be accomplished.

But finally what are your conclusions, I am asked.

I have no need of conclusions. I am opposing sophisms, that is all.

But, people continue, it is not enough to destroy, you have to build. My view is that in the destruction of an error the truth is created.

After that, I have no hesitation in expressing my hope. I would like public opinion to be persuaded to ratify a customs law that lays down terms of approximately this order:

Objects of prime necessity shall pay an
    ad valorem duty of   5 percent
Objects of normal usefulness   10 percent
Luxury objects   15 or 20 percent

Furthermore, these distinctions are taken from an order of ideas that is totally foreign to political economy as such, and I am far from thinking that they are as useful and just as they are commonly supposed to be. However, that is another story.

8. Free traders like Bastiat and Cobden distinguished between two kinds of tariffs—"fiscal tariffs," which were solely designed to raise revenue for the government (it should be noted that income taxes did not exist at this time), and "protectionist tariffs," which were designed to provide government favors to particular vested-interest groups. In ES2 11 Bastiat says he would like to reduce tariffs to 5 percent across the board (for both imports and exports) in order to achieve the former goal.

1. Abundance and Scarcity

PUBLISHING HISTORY:

Original title: "Abondance, disette."
Place and date of first publication: *JDE* 11 (April 1845): 1–8.
First French edition as book or pamphlet: *Economic Sophisms*
    (First Series) (1846).
Location in Paillottet's edition of *OC:* Vol. 4. *Sophismes*
    économiques. Petits pamphlets I, pp. 5–14.
Previous translations: 1st English ed., 1846; 1st American ed.,
    1848; FEE ed., 1964.

What is better for mankind and society, abundance or scarcity?

What, people will exclaim, is that a question to ask? Has it ever been stated or is it possible to assert that scarcity is the basis of man's well-being?

Yes, that has been claimed; yes, it has been asserted. It is asserted every day, and I have no fear in saying that the *theory of scarcity* is by far the more popular. It is the subject of conversation in the journals, books, and on the rostrum, and although this may appear extraordinary, it is clear that political economy will have fulfilled its task and its practical mission when it has popularized and made irrefutable this very simple proposition: "Mankind's wealth lies in the abundance of things."

Do we not hear this every day: "Foreigners are going to swamp us with their products"? We therefore fear abundance.

Has M. de Saint-Cricq[1] not said: "Production is too high"? He therefore feared abundance.

Do workers not smash machines? They are therefore terrified of excess production or, in other words, abundance.

Has M. Bugeaud[2] not pronounced these words: "Let bread become ex-

---

1. Pierre Laurent Barthélemy, comte de Saint Cricq (1772–1854), was a protectionist deputy who became Director General of Customs (1815), president of the Trade Council, and then Minister of Trade and Colonies (1828–29).

2. Bugeaud, Thomas, marquess de Piconnerie, duc d'Isly (1784–1849), became a conservative deputy after the 1830 Revolution (Dordogne 1831–48) and supported a pol-

pensive and farmers will be rich!"? Well, bread can become expensive only if it becomes scarce; therefore M. Bugeaud was recommending scarcity.

Has not M. d'Argout[3] used the very fact of the productive capacity of the sugar industry as an argument against it? Has he not said: "Beetroot has no future, and its cultivation could not be expanded, since if just a few hectares per département were allocated to it this would meet the entire consumption needs of France." Therefore, in his eyes, good lies in lack of production, or scarcity, and harm in fertility and abundance.

Do *La Presse, Le Commerce,* and the majority of daily newspapers[4] not publish one or more articles each morning to demonstrate to the Chambers and the government that it would be sound policy to raise the price of everything by law through the operation of tariffs? Do the three powers of state[5] not comply every day with this injunction from the regular press? Now tariffs raise the price of things only because they decrease the quantity *offered* in the marketplace! Therefore the papers, the Chambers, and the government put into practice the theory of scarcity, and I was right to say that this theory is by far the most popular one.

How has it come about that in the eyes of workers, political writers, and statesmen abundance is shown as something to be feared and scarcity as being advantageous? I propose to go back to the source of this illusion.

We note that men become rich to the extent that they earn a good return from their work, that is to say, from what *they sell at the highest price.* They sell at the highest price in proportion to the rarity, that is to say, the relative shortage, of the type of good their efforts produce. We conclude from this that, as far as they are concerned at least, scarcity makes them rich. When this reasoning is applied successively to all people who work, *the theory of scarcity* is thereby deduced. From this we move to its application, and in order to benefit all these people, high prices and the scarcity of all goods are provoked artificially by means of prohibition, restriction, the suppression of machines, and other similar means.

This is also true for abundance. We observe that when a product is plenti-

---

icy of protection for agriculture. In 1840 he was appointed the Governor of Algeria by Thiers.

3. Antoine Maurice Appolinaire, Comte d'Argout (1782–1858), was the Minister for the Navy and Colonies, then Commerce, and Public Works during the July Monarchy. In 1834 he was appointed Governor of the Bank of France.

4. See the Glossary of Newspapers and Journals.

5. The king, the Chamber of Peers, and the Chamber of Deputies.

ful it is sold at a low price and therefore producers earn less. If all producers are in this situation, they all become poor, and it is therefore abundance that ruins society. And, since all beliefs attempt to become reality, in a great many countries, we see laws made by men combating the abundance of things.

This sophism, expressed as a general statement, would perhaps have little effect; but when it is applied to a particular order of facts, to such and such a branch of production, or to a given class of workers, it is extremely specious, and this can be explained. It is a syllogism that is not *false* but *incomplete*. Now, whatever *truth* there is in a syllogism is always and necessarily available to cognitive inspection. But the *incomplete* element is a negative phenomenon, a missing component which is very possible and even very easy not to take into account.

Man produces in order to consume. He is both producer and consumer. The reasoning that I have just set out considers him only from the first of these points of view. From the second, the opposite conclusion would have been reached. Could we not say in fact:

The consumer is all the richer when he *buys* everything cheaply. He buys things cheaply the more abundant they are; therefore abundance makes him rich. This reasoning, when extended to all consumers, would lead to the *theory of abundance!*

It is the way in which the concept of *trade* is imperfectly understood that produces these illusions. If we look to our own personal interest, we will recognize immediately that it has a twin nature. As *sellers,* our interest is in things being expensive and consequently that things should be scarce; as *buyers,* what counts is low prices or what comes to the same thing, that things should be abundant. We cannot therefore base a line of reasoning on one or the other of these interests without having established which of the two coincides and is identified with the general and constant interest of the human race.

If man were a solitary animal,[6] if he worked exclusively for himself, if he consumed the fruit of his labor directly, in a word, *if he did not trade,* the theory of scarcity would never have been able to infiltrate the world. It is only too obvious that abundance would be advantageous to him, from wherever it arose, either as the result of his industry or the ingenious tools or

---

6. Without mentioning him by name, Bastiat is referring here to the activities of Robinson Crusoe, which he used several times in *Economic Sophisms* and the *Economic Harmonies* as a thought experiment to explore the nature of economic action. See "Bastiat's Invention of Crusoe Economics," in the Introduction.

powerful machines that he had invented or through the fertility of the soil, the generosity of nature, or even a mysterious *invasion* of products which the waves brought from elsewhere and washed up on the beach. Never would a solitary man, seeking to spur on his own work or to secure some support for it, envisage breaking tools that spared him effort or neutralizing the fertility of the soil or throwing back into the sea any of the advantageous goods it had brought him. He would easily understand that work is not an aim but a means, and that it would be absurd to reject the aim for fear of damaging the means. He would understand that if he devotes two hours a day to providing for his needs, any circumstance (machine, fertility, free gift, or anything else) that spares him one hour of this work, the result remaining the same, makes this hour available to him, and that he may devote it to increasing his well-being. In a word, he would understand that *sparing people work* is nothing other than *progress*.

But *trade* clouds our vision of such a simple truth. In a social state, with the division of labor it generates, the production and the consumption of an object are not combined in the same individual. Each person is led to consider his work no longer as a means but as an end. With regard to each object, trade creates two interests, that of the producer and that of the consumer, and these two interests are always in direct opposition to each other.

It is essential to analyze them and study their nature.

Let us take a producer, any producer; what is his immediate interest? It lies in these two things, 1. that the smallest possible number of people should devote themselves to the same work as him; 2. that the greatest possible number of people should seek the product of this work; political economy explains this more succinctly in these terms: supply should be very restricted and demand very high, or in yet other terms: that there should be limited competition with limitless markets.

What is the immediate interest of the consumer? That the supply of the product in question should be extensive and demand restrained.

Since these two interests are contradictory, one of them has of necessity to coincide with the social or general interest while the other runs counter to it.

But which should legislation favor as being the expression of public good, if indeed it has to favor one?

To know this, you need only examine what would happen if the secret desires of men were accomplished.

As producers, it must be agreed, each of us has antisocial desires. Are we vine growers? We would be little displeased if all the vines in the world froze, except for ours: *that is the theory of scarcity*. Are we the owners of foundries? We would want there to be no other iron on the market than what we brought to it, whatever the needs of the public might be, and with the deliberate intention that this public need, keenly felt and inadequately met, would result in our receiving a high price: *that is also the theory of scarcity.* Are we farm workers? We would say, with M. Bugeaud, "Let bread become expensive, that is to say, scarce, and the farmers will get on with their business": *this is the same theory of scarcity.*

Are we doctors? We could not stop ourselves from seeing that certain physical improvements, such as the improvement in a country's health, the development of certain moral virtues such as moderation and temperance, the progress of enlightenment to the point that each person was able to take care of his own health, the discovery of certain simple drugs that were easy to use, would be so many mortal blows to our profession. Given that we are doctors, our secret desires are antisocial. I do not mean to say that doctors formulate such desires. I prefer to believe that they would joyfully welcome a universal panacea; but this sentiment reveals not the doctor but the man or Christian who, in self-denial, puts himself in the situation of the consumer. As one who exercises a profession and who draws his well-being from this profession, his consideration and even the means of existence of his family make it impossible for his desires, or if you prefer, his interests not to be antisocial.

Do we manufacture cotton cloth? We would like to sell it at a price most advantageous *to us.* We would readily agree that all rival factories should be prohibited, and while we do not dare to express this wish publicly or pursue its total achievement with any chance of success, we nevertheless succeed to a certain extent through devious means, for example, by excluding foreign fabrics in order to reduce the *quantity on offer,* and thus produce, through the use of force, a scarcity of clothing to our advantage.

We could go through all forms of industry in this way, and we would always find that producers as such have antisocial views. "Merchants," says Montaigne, "do good business only when young people are led astray; farm workers when wheat is expensive; architects when houses are ruined; and officers of justice when court cases and quarrels between men occur. The very honor and practice of ministers of religion are drawn from our death and vices. No doctor takes pleasure in the health even of his friends nor soldiers in peace in the town, and so on."[7]

7. Montaigne, "Le profit d'un est dommage de l'autre," pp. 130–31. Sometime in 1847 Bastiat wrote an introduction to a chapter on this very topic. He called this phrase "a standard sophism, one that is the very root of a host of sophisms" (ES3 15, p. 342).

It follows from this that if the secret wishes of each producer were realized the world would regress rapidly into barbarism. Sail would outlaw steam, oars would outlaw sail and would soon have to give up transport in favor of carts, carts would yield to mules, and mules to human carriers of bales. Wool would exclude cotton and cotton exclude wool and so on, until a scarcity of everything had made man himself disappear from the face of the earth.

Let us suppose for a moment that legislative power and public force were put at the disposal of the Mimerel Committee,[8] and that each of the members making up this association had the right to require it to propose and sanction one little law: is it very difficult to guess to what codes of production the public would be subjected?

If we now consider the immediate interest of the consumer we will find that it is in perfect harmony with the general interest and with what the well-being of humanity demands. When a buyer enters the market, he wants to find it with an abundance of products. That the seasons are propitious to all harvests, that increasingly wonderful inventions bring a greater number of products and satisfactions within reach, that time and work are saved, that distance dissolves, that a spirit of peace and justice allows the burden of taxes to be reduced, and that barriers of all sorts fall: in all this the immediate interest of the consumer runs parallel with the public interest properly understood. He may elevate his secret desires to the level of illusion or absurdity without his desires ceasing to be humanitarian. He may want bed and board, hearth and home, education and the moral code, security and peace, and strength and health to be obtained effortlessly, without work or measure, like dust in the road, water in the stream, the air or the light that surrounds us, without the achievement of such desires being contrary to the good of society.

---

8. There are two protectionist bodies which are referred to as the "Mimerel Committee." Pierre Mimerel de Roubaix was a textile manufacturer and politician from Roubaix who was a vigorous advocate of protectionism. In 1842 he founded the protariff Comité de l'industrie (Committee of Industry) in his hometown to lobby the government for protection and subsidies. This committee, known as the Mimerel Committee, was expanded in 1846 into a national body called the Association pour la défense du travail national (Association for the Defense of National Employment) in order to better counter the growing interest in Bastiat's Free Trade Association, which had also been established in that year. Mimerel and Antoine Odier sat on the Association's Central Committee, which was commonly referred to as the "Mimerel Committee" or the "Odier Committee." See the entries for "Mimerel de Roubaix, Auguste Pierre," and "Odier, Antoine," in the Glossary of Persons and the entries for "Mimerel Committee" and the "Association pour la défense du travail national," in the Glossary of Subjects and Terms.

Perhaps people will say that if these desires were granted, the work of the producer would be increasingly restricted and would end by ceasing for lack of sustenance. Why, though? Because, in this extreme supposition, all imaginable needs and all desires would be completely satisfied. Man, like the Almighty, would create everything by a single act of will. Would someone like to tell me, on such an assumption, what would there be to complain about in productive economic activity?

I imagined just now a legislative assembly made up of workers,[9] of which each member would formulate into law his *secret desire* as a producer, and I said that the code that would emerge from this assembly would be systematic monopoly, the theory of scarcity put into practice.

In the same way, a Chamber in which each person consults only his immediate interest as a consumer would lead to the systematic establishment of freedom, the suppression of all restrictive measures, and the overturning of all artificial barriers, in a word, the realization of the theory of abundance.

From this it follows:

That to consult the immediate interest of production alone is to consult an antisocial interest;

That to make the immediate interest of consumption the exclusive criterion is to adopt the general interest.

May I be allowed to stress this point of view once more at the risk of repeating myself?

There is radical antagonism between sellers and buyers.[10]

Sellers want the object of the sale to be *scarce,* in short supply and at a high price;

Buyers want it to be *abundant,* available everywhere at a low price.

The laws, which ought at least to be neutral, take the side of sellers against buyers, of producers against consumers, of high prices against low prices,[11] and of scarcity against abundance.

---

9. In ES2 4 Bastiat satirizes the Superior Council of Commerce, which was a body within the Ministry of Trade which served the interests of producers, by inventing a "Lower (or Inferior) Council of Labor" which would serve the interests of "proper workers." They of course came to a very different conclusion concerning the merits of protectionism.

10. Bastiat would modify this view later in *Economic Harmonies,* where he believed there was a harmony of interests between consumers and producers. See chapter 11 "Producers—Consumers," CW5 (forthcoming).

11. (Bastiat's note) In French we do not have a noun that expresses the opposite concept to *expensiveness* (cheapness [in English in the original]). It is rather remarkable that popular instinct expresses this concept by the following paraphrase: "marché avantageux,

They act, if not intentionally, at least in terms of their logic, according to this given assumption: *A nation is rich when it lacks everything.*

For they say: "It is the producer we should favor by ensuring him a proper market for his product. To do this, we have to raise its price. To raise its price, the supply has to be restricted, and to restrict the supply is to create scarcity." And look: let me suppose that right now when these laws are in full force a detailed inventory is taken, not in value but in weight, measures, volumes, and quantities of all the objects existing in France that are likely to satisfy the needs and tastes of her inhabitants, such as wheat, meat, cloth, canvas, fuel, colonial goods, etc.

Let me further suppose that on the following day all the barriers that prevent the introduction into France of foreign products are overturned.

Lastly, in order to assess the result of this reform, let me suppose that three months later, a new inventory is taken.

Is it not true that we would find in France more wheat, cattle, cloth, canvas, iron, coal, sugar, etc. on the second inventory than at the time of the first?

This is so true that our protective customs duties have no other aim than to prevent all of these things from reaching us, to restrict their supply and to prevent a decrease in their price and therefore their abundance.

Now, I ask you, are the people better fed under the empire of our laws because there is *less* bread, meat, and sugar in the country? Are they better clad because there is *less* yarn, canvas, and cloth? Are they better heated because there is *less* coal? Are they better assisted in their work because there is *less* iron and copper, *fewer* tools and machines?

But people will say: if foreigners swamp us with their products, they will carry off our money.

What does it matter? Men do not eat money; they do not clothe themselves with gold, nor heat themselves with silver. What does it matter if there is more or less money in the country, if there is more bread on the sideboard, more meat on the hook, more linen in the cupboards, and more wood in the woodshed?[12]

I will continue to confront restrictive laws with this dilemma:

Either you agree that you cause scarcity or you do not agree.

---

bon marché" (an advantageous market, a cheap market). Prohibitionists should change this expression. It implies an economic system that is quite contrary to theirs.

12. See ESi 11, pp. 60–63, for a more detailed discussion of this topic.

If you agree, you are admitting by this very fact that you are doing the people as much harm as you can. If you do not agree, then you are denying that you have restricted supply and caused prices to rise, and consequently you are denying that you have favored producers.

You are either disastrous or ineffective. You cannot be useful.[13]

2. Obstacle and Cause

PUBLISHING HISTORY:

Original title: "Obstacle, cause."
Place and date of first publication: *JDE* 11 (April 1845): 8–10.
First French edition as book or pamphlet: *Economic Sophisms* (First Series) (1846).
Location in Paillottet's edition of *OC:* Vol. 4. *Sophismes économiques. Petits pamphlets I,* pp. 15–18.
Previous translations: 1st English ed., 1846; 1st American ed., 1848; FEE ed., 1964.

The obstacle taken for the cause—scarcity taken for abundance: this is the same sophism under another guise. It is a good thing to examine it from all sides.

Man originally lacks everything.

Between his destitution and the satisfaction of his needs there is a host of *obstacles,* which it is the purpose of work to overcome. It is an intriguing business trying to find how and why these same obstacles to his well-being have become in his eyes the cause of his well-being.

I need to transport myself a hundred leagues away. But between the points of departure and arrival there are mountains, rivers, marshes, impenetrable forests, evildoers, in a word, *obstacles,* and in order to overcome these obstacles I have to make a great deal of effort or, what comes to the same thing, others have to make a great deal of effort and have me pay the price for this. It is clear that in this respect I would have been in a better situation if these obstacles did not exist.

13. (Paillottet's note) The author has dealt with this subject in greater detail in chapter XI of the *Economic Harmonies* and also in another form in the article titled *Abundance,* written for the *Dictionary of Political Economy,* which we have included at the end of the fifth volume. [Bastiat's article "Abondance" appeared in *DEP* 1:2–4.]

To go through life and travel along the long succession of days that separates the cradle from the tomb, man needs to assimilate a prodigious quantity of food, protect himself against the inclemency of the seasons, and preserve himself from or cure himself of a host of ills. Hunger, thirst, illness, heat, and cold are so many obstacles that lie along his way. In his solitary state, he will have to combat them all by means of hunting, fishing, growing crops, spinning, weaving, and building houses, and it is clear that it would be better for him if there were fewer of these obstacles, or even none at all. In society, he does not have to confront each of these obstacles personally; others do this for him, and in return he removes one of the obstacles surrounding his fellow men.

It is also clear that, taking things as a whole, it would be better for men as a group, that is, for society, that the obstacles should be as insignificant and as few as possible.

However, if we examine social phenomena in detail, and the sentiments of men as they have been altered by trade, we soon see how they have managed to confuse needs with wealth and obstacles with causes.

The division of labor, a result of the ability to trade, has meant that each person, instead of combating on his own all the obstacles that surround him, combats only *one,* and this, not for himself but for the benefit of all his fellow men, who in turn render him the same service.

Now, the result of this is that this person sees the immediate cause of his wealth in the obstacle that it is his job to combat on other people's account. The greater, more serious, more keenly felt this obstacle is, the more his fellow men will be ready to pay him for removing it, that is to say, to remove on his behalf the obstacles that stand in his way.

A doctor, for example, does not occupy himself in baking his bread, manufacturing his instruments, weaving, or making his clothes. Others do this for him, and in return he does battle with the illnesses that afflict his patients. The more numerous, severe, and recurrent these illnesses are, the more willing or even obliged people are to work for his personal advantage. From his point of view, illness, that is to say, a general obstacle to people's well-being, is a cause of individual well-being. All producers reason in the same way with regard to things that concern them. Shipowners make their profit from the obstacle known as *distance,* farmers from that known as *hunger,* cloth manufacturers from that known as *cold.* Teachers live on *ignorance,* gem cutters on *vanity,* lawyers on *greed,* notaries on the possibility of *dishonesty,* just as doctors depend on the *illnesses* suffered by men. It is thus very true that each occupation has an immediate interest in the continuation or even the extension of the particular obstacle that is the object of its efforts.

Seeing this, theoreticians come along and develop a theory based on these individual sentiments. They say: "Need is wealth, work is wealth; obstacles to well-being are well-being. Increasing the number of obstacles is to give sustenance to production."

Next, statesmen come along. They have the coercive power of the state at their disposal, and what is more natural than for them to make use of it to develop and propagate obstacles, since this is also to develop and propagate wealth? For example, they say: "If we prevent iron from coming from those places in which it is plentiful, we will create an obstacle at home to our procuring it. This obstacle will be keenly felt and will make people ready to pay to be relieved of it. A certain number of our fellow citizens will devote themselves to combating it, and this obstacle will make their fortune. The greater it is, the scarcer the mineral or the more it is inaccessible, difficult to transport, and far from the centers of consumption, the more all this activity, with all its ramifications, will employ men. Let us keep out foreign iron, therefore; let us create the obstacle in order to create the work of combating it."

The same reasoning will lead to machines being forbidden.

People will say: "Here are men who need to store their wine. This is an obstacle; here are other men whose occupation is to remove it by manufacturing barrels. It is thus a good thing that this obstacle exists, since it supplies a part of national work and enriches a certain number of our fellow citizens. However, here comes an ingenious machine that fells oak trees, squares them and divides them into a host of staves, assembles these and transforms them into containers for wine. The obstacle has become much less and with it the wealth of coopers. Let us maintain both through a law. Let us forbid the machine."

In order to get to the bottom of this sophism you need only say to yourself that human work is not an *aim* but a *means. It never remains unused.* If it lacks one obstacle, it turns to another, and the human race is freed from two obstacles by the same amount of work that removed a single one. If ever the work of coopers became superfluous, they would turn to something else. "But with what," people will ask, "would it be paid?" Precisely with what it is paid right now, for when one quantity of labor becomes available following the removal of an obstacle, a corresponding quantity of money also becomes available. To say that human labor will be brought to an end for lack of employment you would have to prove that the human race will cease to encounter obstacles. If that happened, work would not only be impossible, it would be superfluous. We would have nothing left to do because we would be all-powerful and we would just have to utter a *fiat* for all our needs and desires to be satisfied.[1]

3. Effort and Result

PUBLISHING HISTORY:

Original title: "Effort, résultat."
Place and date of first publication: *JDE* 11 (April 1845): 10–16.
First French edition as book or pamphlet: *Economic Sophisms*
(First Series) (1846).
Location in Paillottet's edition of *OC:* Vol. 4. *Sophismes
économiques. Petits pamphlets I,* pp. 19–27.
Previous translations: 1st English ed., 1846; 1st American ed.,
1848; FEE ed., 1964.

We have just seen that there are obstacles between our needs and their satisfaction. We manage to overcome them or to reduce them by using our various faculties. In a very general way, we may say that production is an effort followed by a result.

But against what is our well-being or wealth measured? Is it on the result of the effort? Is it on the effort itself? There is always a ratio between the effort employed and the result obtained. Does progress consist in the relative increase of the second or of the first term of this relationship?

Both of these theses have been advocated; in political economy, they divide the field of opinion.

According to the first thesis, wealth is the result of output. It increases in accordance with the increase in the *ratio of the result to the effort*. Absolute perfection, of which the exemplar is God, consists in the infinite distancing of two terms, in this instance: effort nil; result infinite.

The second thesis claims that it is the effort itself that constitutes and measures wealth. To progress is to increase the *ratio of the effort to the result*.

---

1. See ES2 14 and in *Economic Harmonies* chapters 3 "On the Needs of Man" and 11 "Producers—Consumers" in CW5 (forthcoming).

Its ideal may be represented by the effort, at once eternal and sterile, of Sisyphus.[1,2]

Naturally, the first welcomes everything that tends to decrease the difficulties involved and increase the product: the powerful machines that add to human powers, the trade that enables better advantage to be drawn from the natural resources spread to a greater or lesser extent over the face of the earth, the intelligence that makes discoveries, the experience that verifies these discoveries, the competition that stimulates production, etc.

Logically, by the same token, the second willfully summons up everything whose effect is to increase the difficulties of production and decrease the output: privileges, monopolies, restrictions, prohibitions, the banning of machines, sterility, etc.

It is fair to note that the *universal practice* of men is always directed by the principle of the first doctrine. Nobody has ever seen and nobody will ever see anyone working, whether he be a farmer, manufacturer, trader, artisan, soldier, writer, or scholar, who does not devote the entire force of his intelligence to doing things better, faster, and more economically, in a word, *to doing more with less*.

The opposite doctrine is practiced by theoreticians, deputies, journalists, statesmen, and ministers, in a word, men whose role in this world is to carry out experiments on society.

Again it should be noted that, with regard to things that concern them personally, they, like everybody else in the world, act on the principle of obtaining from work the greatest number of useful results possible.

You may think I am exaggerating, and that there are no real *Sisyphists*.

If you mean that, in practice, the principle is not pushed to the limit of its consequences, I would readily agree with you. Actually, this is always the case when people start from a false principle. It soon leads to results that are so absurd and harmful that one is simply forced to abandon it. For this reason, very practical productive activity never accepts *Sisyphism:* punishment would follow errors too closely for them not to be revealed. However, with regard to speculative theories of industrial activity, such as those developed

---

1. (Bastiat's note) For this reason we ask the reader to excuse us for using the name *Sisyphism* as an abbreviation for this thesis hereafter.

2. In Greek myth Sisyphus was the king of Corinth who was notorious for his mistreatment of travelers. He also angered Zeus by revealing details of his amorous exploits. For this he was punished by being forced to roll a large boulder up a hill every day only to have it roll down the hill every night.

by theoreticians and statesmen, a false principle may be followed for a long time before people are made aware of its falsity by complicated consequences of which moreover they are ignorant, and when at last they are revealed, and action is taken in accordance with the opposing principle, people contradict themselves and seek justification in this incomparably absurd modern axiom: in political economy there is no absolute principle.[3]

Let us thus see whether the two opposing principles that I have just established do not hold sway in turn, one in actual production and the other in the legislation regulating production.

I have already recalled something M. Bugeaud has said; however, in M. Bugeaud there are two men, one a farmer and the other a legislator.

As a farmer, M. Bugeaud tends to devote all his efforts to this twin aim: to save on work and to obtain bread cheaply. When he prefers a good cart to a bad one, when he improves the quality of fertilizer, when in order to break up his soil he substitutes the action of the atmosphere for that of the harrow or the hoe as far as he can, when he calls to his assistance all the procedures in which science and experiment have shown their effectiveness, he has and can have one single goal: *to reduce the ratio of the effort to the result.* Actually, we have no other way of recognizing the skill of the farmer and the quality of the procedure other than measuring what they have saved in effort and added to the result. And since all the farmers around the world act according to this principle, it may be said that the entire human race aspires, doubtless to its advantage, to obtaining bread or any other product more cheaply and to reducing the effort required to have a given quantity available.

Once account has been taken of this incontrovertible tendency in human beings, it ought to be enough to show legislators the real principle of the matter, that is, show them how they should be supporting productive economic activity (as far as it lies within their mission to support it), for it would be absurd to say that human laws ought to act in opposition to the laws of providence.

Nevertheless, the deputy, M. Bugeaud, has been heard to exclaim, "I do not understand the theory of low prices; I would prefer to see bread more expensive and work more plentiful." And as a result, the deputy for the Dordogne has voted for legislative measures whose effect has been to hamper trade precisely because it indirectly procures us what direct production can supply us only at a higher cost.

Well, it is very clear that M. Bugeaud's principle as a deputy is diametrically

3. This is a topic taken up again in ES1 18.

opposed to that of M. Bugeaud as a farmer. If he were consistent with himself, he would vote against any restriction in the Chamber or else he would carry onto his farm the principles he proclaims from the rostrum. He would then be seen to sow his wheat on the most infertile of his fields, since he would then succeed in *working a great deal for little return.* He would be seen to forbid the use of the plough, since cultivation using his nails would satisfy his double desire of making bread more expensive and work more plentiful.

The avowed aim and acknowledged effect of restriction is to increase work.

It also has the avowed aim and acknowledged effect of raising prices, which is nothing other than making products scarce. Thus, when taken to its limit, it is pure Sisyphism as we have defined it: *infinite work, product nil.*

Baron Charles Dupin,[4] said to be a leading light among the peers in economic science, accuses the railway of *harming shipping,* and it is clear that it is the nature of a more perfect means to restrict the use of a means that is comparatively rougher. However, the railway can harm shipping only by diverting transport to itself; it can do so only by carrying it out more cheaply, and it can carry it out more cheaply only by *reducing the ratio of the effort used to the result obtained,* since this is what constitutes the lower cost. When, therefore, Baron Dupin deplores this reduction of work for a given result, he is following the lines of the doctrine of *Sisyphism.* Logically, since he prefers ships to rail, he ought to prefer carts to ships, packhorses to carts, and backpacks to all other known means of transport, since this is the means that requires the greatest amount of work for the least result.

"Work constitutes the wealth of a people," said M. de Saint-Cricq, this minister of trade who imposed so many impediments to trade. It should not be believed that this was an elliptical proposition which meant: "The results of work constitute the wealth of a people." No, this economist genuinely meant to say that it is the *intensity* of labor that measures wealth, and proof of this is that, from one inference to another, one restriction to another, he led France and considered he was doing a good thing in this, to devote twice as much work to acquire the same amount of iron, for example. In England, iron then cost 8 fr.; in France it cost 16 fr. If we take a day's work to cost 1 fr., it is clear that France could, through trade, procure a quintal[5] of iron for eight days taken from national work as a whole. Thanks to M. de Saint-

4. Charles Dupin (1784–1873) was a pioneer in mathematical economics and worked for the statistical office of France. In 1828 he was elected deputy for Tarn, was made a Peer in 1830, and served in the Constituent and then the National Assemblies during the Second Republic.

5. A quintal weighs 100 kilograms.

Cricq's restrictive measures, France needed sixteen days of work to obtain a quintal of iron through direct production. Double labor for identical satisfaction, therefore double wealth; here again wealth is measured not by outcomes but by the intensity of the work. Is this not *Sisyphism* in all its glory?

And so that there is no possible misunderstanding, the minister is careful to take his idea further, and in the same way as he has just called the intensity of labor *wealth,* he is heard calling the abundance resulting from production, or things likely to satisfy our needs, *poverty.* "Everywhere," he says, "machines have taken the place of manpower; everywhere, there is an overabundance of production; everywhere the balance between the ability to produce and the means of consumption has been destroyed." We see that, according to M. de Saint-Cricq, if France was in a critical situation it was because it produced too much and its production was too intelligent and fruitful. We were too well fed, too well clothed, too well provided for in every way. Production was too fast and exceeded all our desires. An end had to be put to this scourge, and to this end we had to force ourselves, through restrictions, to work more to produce less.

I have also recalled the opinion of another minister of trade, M. d'Argout. It is worth our spending a little time on it. As he wished to deliver a terrible blow to sugar beet, he said,

> Growing sugar beet is doubtless useful, but *its usefulness is limited.* It does not involve the gigantic developments that people were happy to forecast for it. To be convinced of this, you just have to note that this crop will of necessity be restricted to the limits of consumption. Double or triple current consumption in France if you want, *you will always find that a very minimal portion of the land would be enough to meet the needs of this consumption.* (This is certainly a strange complaint!) Do you want proof of this? How many hectares[6] were planted with sugar beet in 1828? There were 3,130, which is equivalent to 1/10540 of the cultivatable land. How many are there now that indigenous sugar[7] has taken over one-third of consumption? There are 16,700 hectares, or 1/1978 of the cultivatable land, or 45 square meters [*centiares*] per commune. If we suppose that indigenous

---

6. A hectare is 10,000 square meters, or approximately 2 1/2 acres.

7. Growing sugar beet (or beetroot) for sugar as a substitute for imported cane sugar had been encouraged at the time of the Continental Blockade. Normally, cane sugar was imported from overseas or from the slave colonies.

sugar had already taken over the entire consumption, we would have only 48,000 hectares planted with beetroot, or 1/680 of the cultivatable land.[8,9]

There are two things in this quotation: facts and doctrine. The facts tend to establish that little land, capital, and labor is needed to produce a great deal of sugar and that each commune in France would be abundantly provided with it if it devoted one hectare of its territory to its cultivation. The doctrine consists in seeing this situation as disastrous and seeing in the very power and fruitfulness of the new industry the *limit of its usefulness.*

I have no need to make myself the defender of sugar beet or the judge of the strange facts put forward by M. d'Argout,[10] but it is worth examining in detail the doctrine of a statesman to whom France entrusted for many years the fate of its agriculture and trade.

I said at the beginning that there was a variable ratio between productive effort and its result; that absolute imperfection consists in an infinite effort with no result: that absolute perfection consists in an unlimited result with no effort; and that perfectibility consists in a gradual reduction in the effort compared to the result.

But M. d'Argout informs us that death is where we believe we are glimpsing life and that the importance of a branch of production is a direct result of its impotence. What, for example, can we expect from sugar beet? Do you not see that 48,000 hectares of land and a proportional amount of capital and manpower will be enough to provide all of France with sugar? Therefore it is an industry *with limited usefulness,* limited, of course, with regard to the input of labor it requires, the only way, according to the former minister,

8. (Bastiat's note) It is true to say that M. d'Argout put this strange statement in the mouths of opponents of sugar beet. However, he adopted it formally and incidentally sanctioned it by the very law it served to justify.

9. Bastiat says "45 centiares" (45 square meters) when he should have said "0.45 hectares" (less than 1 acre). The FEE edition translator Arthur Goddard notes: "The centiare is 1/10,000 of the hectare, one square meter, or 1.196 square yards. The commune is the smallest administrative unit in France, averaging less than ten square miles. The error may be Argout's, Bastiat's, or the publisher's, but *centiare* here should read *are* (1/100 of a hectare): with about 35,000 communes in France, there would be about 0.45 hectare, or forty-five ares, per commune in sugar beets" (*Economic Sophisms*, FEE edition, p. 25; courtesy of FEE.org).

10. (Bastiat's note) If we suppose that 48,000 to 50,000 hectares were enough to supply current consumption, we would need 150,000 for a tripling of consumption, which M. d'Argout accepts is possible. What is more, if sugar beet were included in a six-year rotation of crops, it would occupy in turn 900,000 hectares or 1/38 of the cultivatable land.

in which an industry can be useful. This usefulness would be much more limited still if, because of the fertility of the soil or the richness of the sugar beet, we harvested from 14,000 hectares what we could obtain only from 48,000. Oh! If twenty or a hundred times more land, capital, or labor were needed *to achieve the same result,* fair enough, we might build a few hopes on this new industry and it would be worthy of the full protection of the state, since it would offer a vast opportunity for national work. But to produce a lot with a little! That would be a bad example, and it is right for the law to establish order in this regard.

But what is the truth with regard to sugar cannot be a falsehood with regard to bread. If, therefore, the *usefulness* of an industry is to be assessed, not by the satisfaction it can provide through a given quantity of work, but on the contrary through the development of the work it requires to meet a given amount of satisfaction; what we ought obviously to want is that each hectare of land should produce little wheat and each grain of wheat little food. In other words, our territory should be infertile, since then the mass of land, capital, and labor that we would need to mobilize to feed the population would be much more in comparison. It might even be said that the market open to human labor will be in direct proportion to this infertility. The desires of MM. Bugeaud, Saint-Cricq, Dupin, and d'Argout will be granted. Bread will be expensive, work plentiful, and France will be rich, rich as these men understand the term.

What we ought to want in addition is for human intelligence to grow weaker and die out, for as long as it exists, it will constantly seek to increase *the ratio of the end to the means and the product to the labor.* It is actually in that, and only in that, that it consists.

Thus, *Sisyphism* is the doctrine of all the men who have been responsible for our economic development. It would not be just to blame them for this. This principle directs the ministers only because it holds sway in the Chambers; it holds sway in the Chambers only because it is sent there by the electorate, and the electorate is imbued with it only because public opinion is saturated with it.

I think I should repeat here that I am not accusing men such as MM. Bugeaud, Saint-Cricq, Dupin, and d'Argout of being absolutely and in all circumstances, *Sisyphists.* They are certainly not that in their private transactions; each one of them certainly obtains by exchange what it would cost him more to obtain through direct production. However, I say that they are *Sisyphists* when they prevent the country from doing the same thing.

4. Equalizing the Conditions of Production

PUBLISHING HISTORY:

Original title: "Égaliser les conditions de production."
Place and date of first publication: *JDE* 11 (July 1845): 345–56.
First French edition as book or pamphlet: *Economic Sophisms*
(First Series) (1846).
Location in Paillottet's edition of *OC:* Vol. 4. *Sophismes
économiques. Petits pamphlets I,* pp. 27–45.
Previous translations: 1st English ed., 1846; 1st American ed.,
1848; FEE ed., 1964

It is said . . . but, so that I am not accused of putting sophisms into the mouths of protectionists, I will let one of their most vigorous athletes speak for himself.

It has been thought that protection in our country ought to be simply a representation of the difference that exists between the cost price of a commodity that we produce and the cost price of a similar commodity produced by our neighbors. . . . A protective duty calculated on these bases ensures nothing more than free competition. Free competition exists only where conditions and charges are equal. In a horse race, the weight that each runner has to bear is weighed and the conditions are equalized; without this, they are no longer competitors. In matters of trade, if one of the sellers is able to deliver at lower cost, he ceases to be a competitor and becomes a monopolist. If you abolish this protection that represents the difference in cost, as soon as foreigners invade your market, they have acquired a monopoly in it.[1]

Each person has to want, for himself as for the others, the production of the country to be protected against foreign competition, *wherever this can supply products at a lower price.*[2]

1. (Bastiat's note) The Vicomte de Romanet.
2. (Bastiat's note) Mathieu de Dombasle. [Joseph Alexandre Mathieu de Dombasle (1777–1843) was an agronomist who introduced the practice of triennial crop rotation (cereals, forage, vegetables) in France. He also wrote on the sugar-beet industry, *De l'impôt sur le sucre indigène: Nouvelles considerations* (1837).]

This argument recurs constantly in articles written by the protectionist school. I propose to examine it carefully, that is to say, I will be asking for the attention and even the patience of the reader. I will first deal with the inequalities that result from nature and then those that result from the differences in taxation.

Here, as elsewhere, we find the theoreticians of protection situated in the producers' camp, whereas we are taking up the cause of these unfortunate consumers whom they refuse to take into account. They compare the field of industry to the race track.[3] However, the race track is simultaneously the *means* and the *end*. The public takes no interest in the competition outside the competition itself. When you start your horses with the sole *aim* of knowing which is the best runner, I can understand that you make the weights equal. But if your *aim* is to ensure that a major and urgent item of news reaches the post, could you with impunity create obstacles for the one that might offer you the best conditions of speed? This is, however, what you are doing to economic production. You are forgetting the result sought, which is *well-being*. You leave this out of the account, and even sacrifice it through completely begging the question.

But since we cannot bring our opponents around to our point of view, let us adopt theirs and examine the question from the point of view of production.

I will seek to establish:

1. That leveling the conditions of production is to attack the very basis of trade;
2. That it is not true that production in one country is stifled by competition from more favored countries;
3. That even if this were true, protectionist duties do not make production conditions equal;
4. That freedom levels these conditions as far as they can be leveled;
5. Lastly, that it is the countries that are least favored that gain the most from trade.

I. Leveling the conditions of production is not merely hampering a few transactions; it is attacking the very principle of trade, since it is based pre-

3. It is not surprising that Romanet would compare economic competition to a horse race, as he had a great interest in horse racing, having given a paper to the Academy of Sciences on this topic in June 1843. See the lengthy summary of the *Mémoire* which he gives in his pamphlet to promote his candidature to the Academy in Romanet, *Notice sur les travaux de M. le vte de Romanet.*

cisely on this diversity, or, if you prefer, on these inequalities of fertility, aptitude, climate, or temperature that you wish to wipe out. If the Guyenne sends wine to Brittany and Brittany wheat to the Guyenne, it is because these two provinces are situated in different conditions of production.[4] Is there a different law for international trade? Once again, to hold against them the inequality of conditions that motivates and accounts for their actions is to attack their very raison d'être. If the protectionists had enough logic and power on their side, they would reduce men, like snails, to total isolation. Besides, there is not one of their sophisms that, when subjected to the test of rigorous deduction, does not end in destruction and annihilation.

II. It is not true *in fact* that the inequality in conditions between two similar productive enterprises necessarily leads to the fall of the one that is the less well endowed. At the race track, if one runner wins the prize, the other loses it, but when two horses work to produce useful commodities, each produces to the extent of its strength, and because the stronger provides the more services, it does not follow that the weaker provides none at all. Wheat is grown in all the départements of France, although there are huge differences of fertility between them and if, by chance, there is one that does not grow wheat, it is because it is not good, even for that département, to grow it. In the same way, a similar argument tells us that, under the regime of freedom, in spite of differences like these, wheat would be produced in all the kingdoms of Europe, and if there were one which had decided to abandon this crop it would be because, *in its own interest,* it had found a better use for its land, capital, and labor. And why does the fertility of a département not paralyze farmers in neighboring départements that are less favored? Because economic phenomena have a flexibility, elasticity, and, so to speak, a *capacity for leveling* that appears to escape the grasp of the protectionist school totally. The latter accuses us of being prisoners of a system, but it is its own members who are rigid to the highest degree, if the spirit of such consists in building arguments based on a single fact rather than on a set of facts. In the example above, it is the difference in the value of the land that compensates for the difference in its fertility. Your field produces three times as much as mine. Yes, but it has cost you ten times more and I can still compete with you. This is the question in a nutshell. And note that superiority in some

4. Guyenne was an old province in the southwest of France, with Bordeaux as its capital city. It covered roughly the same territory as Bastiat's homeland, the Landes. Brittany is a peninsula in the most northwestern part of France.

respects brings about inferiority in others. It is precisely because your land is more fruitful that it is more expensive, in such a way that it is not *accidental,* but *necessary* for a balance to be established or to tend to become established. And can it be denied that freedom is the regime that favors this trend the most?

I have quoted one branch of agriculture, but I could have quoted a branch of manufacturing just as well. There are tailors in Quimper,[5] and that does not prevent there being tailors in Paris, even though rent, furnishings, workers, and food cost Paris tailors much more. But they also have a very different class of customers, and this is enough not only to restore the balance but also even to tilt it in their favor.

So when we talk about balancing the conditions of work, we have at least to examine whether freedom does not do what we are asking arbitrary rule to do.

This natural leveling out of economic phenomena is so important functionally and at the same time so worthy of our admiration for the providential wisdom that presides in the egalitarian governance of our society, that I ask your permission to dwell on it for a moment.

You protectionists say that such and such a people have the advantage of cheap coal, iron, machines, and capital over us; we cannot compete with them.

This statement will be examined from other points of view. For the present I am limiting myself to the question whether, when superiority and inferiority confront one another, they do not carry within themselves, in the latter case, a natural tendency to rise and in the former to descend, such as to bring them back to a fair balance.

Here we have two countries, A and B. A has all sorts of advantages over B. You conclude from this that labor would be concentrated in A and that B is powerless to do anything. A, you say, sells a great deal more than it purchases, while B purchases much more than it sells. I might dispute this, but I align myself with your viewpoint.

In this hypothetical circumstance, the demand for labor is high in A and it soon becomes more expensive.

Iron, coal, land, food, and capital are in high demand in A and they soon become more expensive.

---

5. Quimper is a commune in Brittany in the northwest of France. In 1846 the population was about 11,000 people. It was sometimes the butt of jokes because of its remoteness from Paris, its small size, and the fact that its inhabitants spoke the Breton language.

At the same time, labor, iron, coal, land, food, capital, and everything else are in very low demand in B and soon become much cheaper.

That is not all. As A still continues to sell and B continues to purchase, money passes from B to A. It is plentiful in A and scarce in B.

But where there is an abundance of money, this means that you need a great deal to buy anything else. Therefore, in A, to the *high real prices* which result from very active demand must be added the *high nominal money prices* due to the excess supply of precious metals.[6]

Scarcity of money means that little is needed for each purchase. Therefore in B, *low nominal money prices* combine with *low real prices.*

In these circumstances, production will have all sorts of reasons, reasons that are, if I may put it this way, raised to the fourth power, to leave A and establish itself in B.

Or, to stick to literal truth, let us say that production would not have waited up to now, that sudden moves are contrary to its nature and that, from the outset under a free regime, it would have gradually divided and distributed itself between A and B in accordance with the laws of supply and demand, that is to say, in accordance with the laws of justice and usefulness.

And when I say that, if it were possible for production to concentrate at a single point, an irresistible force for decentralization would arise within it for this very reason, I am not speaking hypothetically.

Listen to what a manufacturer had to say in the chamber of commerce in Manchester (I am omitting the figures he used to support his demonstration):

> In former times we exported fabrics, then this activity gave
> way to the export of yarn, which is the raw material of fabric,
> and then to the export of machines, which are the tools of production
> for yarn, and later to the export of capital, with which
> we built our machines, and finally to the export of our workers
> and our industrial genius, which are the source of our capital.
> All these changes in production succeeded one another in
> moving to where they might be exercised to greatest advantage,
> where the cost of living was lowest and life easier, so that now
> we can see in Prussia, Austria, Saxony, Switzerland, and Italy
> huge factories established with English capital, operated using
> English workers and directed by English engineers.

6. Throughout the nineteenth century, European currencies were based on the gold or the silver standard. See ESI 11, pp. 60–63.

You can see clearly that nature, or rather providence, which is more ingenious, wise, and farsighted than your narrow and rigid theory supposes, did not want this concentration of work, this monopoly of all the forms of superiority that you argue to be an absolute and irremediable fact, to continue. It made it possible, using means that are as simple as they are infallible, for there to be dispersion, dissemination, solidarity, and simultaneous progress, all things that your restrictive laws paralyze as far as they can, since, by isolating peoples, they tend to make their differences in living conditions much more entrenched, to prevent leveling out, obstruct intermingling, neutralize counterbalancing tendencies, and entrap nations in their respective superiority or inferiority.

III. In the third place, to say that through a protectionist duty the conditions of production are equalized is to use an inaccurate turn of phrase to put across an error. It is not true that an import duty brings the conditions of production into balance. After the imposition of an import duty, these conditions remain what they were before. All that this duty balances at most are the *conditions of sale.* It will perhaps be said that I am playing with words, but I will throw this accusation back at my opponents. It is for them to prove that production and sale are synonymous, and unless they do so, I am entitled to blame them, if not for playing with words, at least for mixing them up.

Let me give an example to illustrate my idea.

Let me suppose that a few Parisian speculators have the bright idea of devoting their time to the production of oranges. They know that Portuguese oranges can be sold in Paris for 10 centimes, whereas they, in view of the conservatories and greenhouses they need because of the cold that often undermines their cultivation, cannot demand less than 1 franc in order to cover their costs. They demand that oranges from Portugal should be subject to a duty of 90 centimes. Through this duty, the *conditions of production,* as they say, will be balanced and the Chamber when giving way as usual to this line of reasoning, adds an import duty of 90 centimes for each foreign orange to the customs tariffs.

Well then, I say that the *conditions of production* have not changed in the slightest. The law has removed nothing from the heat of the sun in Lisbon nor the frequency or intensity of the frosts in Paris. Oranges will continue to mature *naturally* on the banks of the Tagus and *artificially* on the banks of the Seine, that is to say, that it will require much more human work in one country than in the other. What will be balanced are the conditions of sale: the Portuguese will have to sell us their oranges at 1 franc, including 90 centimes to pay the tax. Obviously, the tax will be paid by French consumers. And look at the oddity of the result. On each Portuguese orange consumed, our country will lose nothing, for the 90 centimes more that are paid by the consumer will go to the treasury. There will be displacement but no loss. However, on each French orange consumed, there will be 90 centimes or thereabouts of loss, since the purchaser will certainly lose this and the seller, also certainly, will not earn this since, according to the hypothesis itself, he will have earned only the cost price. I leave the protectionists to draw the right conclusion.

IV. If I have stressed this distinction between the conditions of production and the conditions of sale, one which the protectionists will doubtless find paradoxical, it is because it will lead me to afflict them once more with another paradox that is even stranger, which is this: Do you really want to balance the *conditions of production?* Then let trade be free.

Oh! people will say, that is too much at this time, and an abuse of intellectual games. Well then, if only through curiosity, I ask the protectionists to follow my line of argument to the bitter end. It will not take long. Let me go back to my example.

If you agree to suppose for a minute that the average, daily earnings of each Frenchman come to 1 franc, it will ineluctably follow that to produce one orange *directly* in France will require one day's work or its equivalent whereas to produce the exchange value of one Portuguese orange only one-tenth of a day's work is needed, which means nothing other than that the sun does in Lisbon what work does in Paris. Well, is it not obvious that, if I can produce an orange or what amounts to the same thing, the means to buy one, with one-tenth of a day's work, my position with regard to this production is subject to the same conditions as the Portuguese producer himself, except for the transport costs, which I must incur? It is therefore apparent that freedom balances the direct or indirect conditions of production, as far as they can be balanced, since it leaves only one remaining inevitable difference, that of transport.

I will add that freedom also balances the conditions of enjoyment, satisfaction, and consumption, which are never taken into account and which are nevertheless essential, since in the end consumption is the final aim of all our productive efforts. Through free trade we would enjoy the Portuguese sun just as Portugal herself does and the inhabitants of Le Havre, like those of London and under the same conditions, will have access to the advantages that nature has conferred on Newcastle with respect to its mineral resources.

V. Gentlemen of the protectionist persuasion, you think me full of paradox! Well, I want to go even further. I say, and I think this quite sincerely, that if two countries are placed in unequal conditions of production, *it is the one of the two which is less favored by nature that has the more to gain from free trade.* To prove this, I will have to digress a little from the form this article should take. I will nevertheless do this, first of all because this is the nub of the matter and also because it will give me the opportunity of setting out a law of economics of the greatest importance which, when correctly understood, seems to me to be destined to bring back into the fold of science all the sects that these days seek in the land of illusion the social harmony that they have been unable to discover in nature. I wish to speak about the law of consumption, which the majority of economists may be blamed for having too long much neglected.

Consumption is the *end,* the final purpose of all economic phenomena, in which purpose consequently lies their final, definitive solution.

Nothing favorable or unfavorable can stop permanently at the producer's door. The advantages that nature and society have heaped on him, like the disadvantages that afflict him, slide over him,[7] so to speak, and tend to be unconsciously absorbed by, mingled with, the community, understood from the point of view of consumption. We have here a law that is admirable in its cause and its effects alike, and the man who succeeds in describing it properly will have, I think, the right to say, "I have not spent time on this earth without contributing something to society."

Any circumstance that encourages production is welcomed joyfully by the producer since its *immediate effect* is to put him in a position to provide even more services to the community and to demand greater remuneration from it. Any circumstance that hampers production is received with disappointment by the producer since its *immediate effect* is to limit his services and therefore his remuneration. It was necessary for the *immediate* gains and losses resulting from fortunate or unfortunate circumstances to be the lot of the producer, so that he would be irresistibly drawn to seeking the former and avoiding the latter.

---

7. Here Bastiat is grappling with the concept which in two years' time he was to call the "ricochet effect" (or flow-on effect) to describe the interconnectedness of all economic activity and the need to be aware of immediate effects (the seen) and later indirect effects (the unseen). He uses the word "glisser" (to slide or slip) in this sentence. See a later occurrence of this word in ES3 17, p. 353n5. See "The Ricochet Effect" in appendix 1, "Further Aspects of Bastiat's Thought."

In the same way, when a worker succeeds in improving his output, he receives the *immediate* benefit of this improvement. This was necessary for him to be motivated to work intelligently; it was proper because an effort crowned with success ought to bring its reward with it.

But I hold that these good and bad effects, although permanent in themselves, are not so for producers. If this were so, a principle of gradual and subsequently infinite inequality between men would have been introduced, and this is why these favorable and unfavorable events are soon absorbed into the general fortunes of the human race.

How does this work? I will give a few examples to help it to be understood.

Let us go back to the thirteenth century.[8] The men who devoted themselves to the art of copying received for their services *payment that was governed by the general level of profits.* Among them, there happened to be one who sought and discovered the means to increase the copies of the same book rapidly. He invented printing.

In the first instance, one man became richer and many others grew poorer. At first glance, however marvelous the discovery was, people hesitated as to whether it was not more disastrous than useful. It seemed that it was introducing into the world, just as I said, an element of indefinite inequality. Gutenberg made money with his invention and extended his invention using this money, and did this ad infinitum until he had ruined all other copiers. As for the public, the consumers, they gained little, for Gutenberg took care to decrease the price for his books to no more than was necessary to undercut his rivals.

But the thought that put harmony into the movement of the heavenly bodies was also able to insert it into the internal mechanisms of society. We will see the economic advantages of the invention escape from one individual and become the common and eternal heritage of the masses.

In the event, the procedure ended up by becoming known. Gutenberg was no longer the only printer; others imitated him. Their profits were at first considerable. They were rewarded for being the first to go down the path of imitation, and this was still necessary in order to attract them and so that they could contribute to the great result we were approaching. They earned a great deal, but less than the inventor, since *competition* had begun to work. The price of books continued to decrease. The profits of the imitators decreased as

8. Bastiat is mistaken. Johannes Gutenberg (1398–1468) invented printing using movable type in the 1440s, so it should read here the "fifteenth," not the "thirteenth" century.

the date of the invention receded, that is to say, as imitation became less meritorious. Soon the new industry reached its normal state, in other words, the pay given to printers was no longer exceptional and, as for scribes in former times, it was governed only by the *general level of profitability.* Thus production, as such, returned to what it had been at the beginning. The invention was, nevertheless, no less of a boon; the saving in time, work, and effort for a given result, for a determined number of items, was nonetheless achieved. But how does it manifest itself? Through the low price of books. And for whose benefit? For the benefit of consumers, society, and the human race. Printers, who now have no exceptional merit, no longer receive exceptional remuneration. As men and consumers, they are doubtless beneficiaries of the advantages that the invention has bestowed on the community. But that is all. As printers and as producers, they are once again subject to the common conditions governing all producers in the country. Society pays them for their work, and not for the usefulness of the invention. The invention itself has become part of the common heritage and free to the entire human race.

I admit that the wisdom and beauty of these laws have struck me with admiration and respect. I see Saint-Simonist doctrines[9] in them: *To each according to his capacity, to each capacity according to his work.* I see communism in them, that is to say, the tendency for property to become the *common* heritage of men. But this is a Saint-Simonism and a communism governed by infinite farsightedness, and not in the slightest abandoned to the fragility, passions, and arbitrary rule of men.

What I have said about printing can be said about all the tools of work, from the hammer and nail to the locomotive and electric telegraph. Society benefits from everything through the abundance of the things it consumes, and *benefits from these freely,* for their effect is to reduce the price of objects; and the entire portion of the price that has been abolished and that represents fully the contribution of the invention in the production process obviously makes the product *free* to this extent. All that remains to be paid for is the human work, the work done now, and this is paid for regardless of the

---

9. Claude Henri de Rouvroy, count of Saint-Simon (1760–1825), was a writer and social reformer who founded one of the main schools of socialist thought during the Restoration which continued to be influential throughout the July Monarchy. He advocated rule by a new technocratic elite which would replace the old aristocracy and a system of state-supported industry which would replace what he thought was the injustice and chaos of the free market. See the entry for "Saint-Simon, Claude Henri de Rouvroy, comte de," in the Glossary of Persons.

resulting benefit of the invention, at least where it has gone through the cycle I have just described and which it is destined to go through. I call a workman to my home; he arrives with a saw, I pay two francs for his day's work, and he produces twenty-five planks. If the saw had not been invented, he would probably not have made a single plank and I would not have paid him any less for his day's work. The *usefulness* produced by the saw is therefore a free gift of nature to me; or rather it is a portion of the heritage I have received, in *common* with all my fellows, from the intelligence of our ancestors. I have two workers in my field. One holds the handles of a plough, the other the handle of a spade. The result of their work is very different, but their day's pay is the same since pay is not subject to the usefulness produced but to the effort or the work required.

I call upon the reader's patience and beg him to believe that I have not lost sight of commercial freedom. Let him just remember the conclusion that I have reached: *Remuneration is not in proportion to the useful contributions that the producer brings to the market but to his work.*[10]

I have taken my examples from human inventions. Let us now talk about natural advantages.

All products incorporate a contribution from both nature and man. However, the portion of usefulness contributed by nature is always free. Only that portion of usefulness resulting from human work is subject to exchange and consequently to remuneration. This doubtless varies a great deal because of the intensity of the work, the skill required, its promptness, its relevance, the need for it, the temporary absence of competition, etc., etc. But it is no less true in principle that the contribution of natural laws, which belong to everyone, does not enter into the price of the product.

We do not pay for the air we breathe, although it is so *useful* to us that we would not be able to live for two minutes without it. In spite of this, we do not pay for it because nature supplies it to us without any human intervention. If, however, we wish, for example, to separate out one of the gases that make it up to carry out an experiment, we have to make a certain effort or, if we have someone else make the effort, we will have to sacrifice to him an equivalent amount of effort that we have put into another product. In this way we see that there is an exchange in pain, effort, and work. It is not really

10. (Bastiat's note) It is true that work is not uniformly remunerated. It is more or less intense, dangerous, skillful, etc. Competition establishes a market price for each category, and I am talking here about the variable price for this kind of work.

for oxygen that I am paying, since it is available to me everywhere, but for the effort required to separate it out, work that I have been spared and which I need to compensate. Will I be told that other things, such as expenses, materials, or apparatus, need to be paid for? Once again, it is the work contained in these things that I am paying for. The price of the coal used represents the work that has needed to be done to extract and transport it.

We do not pay for sunlight since nature lavishes it on us. But we pay for the light obtained from gas, tallow, oil, or wax because this includes human work that requires remuneration. And note that the remuneration is so closely proportioned to the work done and not to its usefulness, that it may well happen that one of these sources of light, even though it is much brighter than the others, is nevertheless less expensive. For this to happen, all that is necessary is for the same quantity of human work to produce more.

When a water carrier comes to supply my house, if I paid him according to the *absolute usefulness* of the water, my entire fortune would not be enough. However, I pay him according to the trouble he has taken. If he demanded more, others would take over, and in the end, if need be, I would take the trouble myself. Water is not really the subject of our bargain, but in reality the work involved in relation to the water. This point of view is so important and the consequences I am going to draw from it so illuminating, with regard to international free trade, that I feel I have to elucidate my ideas with other examples.

The quantity of nourishment contained in potatoes does not cost us very much because we obtain a great deal with very little work. We pay more for wheat because, in order to produce it, nature requires a great deal of human work. It is obvious that, if nature behaved in the same way for one as for the other, their prices would tend to level out. It is not possible for wheat producers to earn much more on a regular basis than potato producers. The law of competition prevents this.

If, by a happy miracle, the fertility of all arable land happened to increase, it would not be the farmer but the consumer who would reap the advantage of this phenomenon, because the result would be abundance and cheap prices. There would be less labor incorporated in each hectoliter of wheat[11] and the farmer would be able to trade it only for less labor incorporated in another product. If, on the contrary, the fertility of the soil suddenly decreased, the contribution by nature to production would be less, the con-

---

11. One hectoliter is 100 liters, or about 22 U.S. gallons.

tribution of work more, and the product would be more expensive. I was therefore right to say that it is in consumption, in the human race, that all economic phenomena are resolved in the long run. As long as we have not followed their effects to this point, as long as we stop at the *immediate* effects, those that affect one man or one class of men, *as producers,* we are not being economists, any more than someone who, instead of monitoring the effects of a potion on the whole of the organism, merely limits himself to observing how it affects the palate or throat in order to judge it, is a doctor.[12]

Tropical regions are highly suited to the production of sugar and coffee. This means that nature carries out the majority of the task and leaves very little work to be done. Who then reaps the advantages of this generosity of nature? It is not at all these regions, since competition means that they receive payment only for their work; it is the human race, since the result of this generosity is called *low prices,* and they belong to everyone.

Here we have a temperate zone in which coal and iron ore are on the surface of the land and you have only to bend down to pick it up. In the first instance, the inhabitants benefit from this happy circumstance, I agree. But soon, competition will start and the price of coal and iron will decrease to the point where the gift of nature is free to everyone and human work alone is remunerated in accordance with the general level of profitability.

In this way, the generosity of nature, like the advances made in production processes, is or constantly tends to become the common and *free* heritage of consumers, the masses, and the human race, in accordance with the law of competition. Therefore the countries that do not have these advantages have everything to gain from trading with those that do, because it is work which is exchanged, setting aside the natural utilities that work encompasses; and obviously the countries that are most favored have incorporated the most of these *natural utilities* in a given amount of production. Their products, since they represent less work, fetch lower prices; in other words, they are *cheaper,* and if all the generosity of nature results in *cheapness,* obviously it is not the producing country but the consuming country that receives the benefit.

From this we see the immense absurdity of this consumer country if it

---

12. It should be noted that it was a severe throat condition (possibly cancer) which killed Bastiat at the end of 1850. As it was an extremely painful disease which hindered his work as a writer and politician, Bastiat saw his doctor many times in the last years of his life to get relief. Thus, he had some personal experience of what he is saying in this passage. See a brief discussion of Bastiat's fatal condition in "The Cause of Bastiat's Untimely Death" (CW2, pp. 413–14).

rejects a product precisely because it is cheap; it is as though it were saying: "I do not want anything that nature provides. You are asking me for an effort worth two in order to give me a product that I can create only with work worth four; you can do this because in your country nature has accomplished half of the work. Well then! I for my part will reject it and I will wait until your climate has become more inclement and forces you to require work worth four from me, so that we may trade *on an equal footing.*"

A is a favored country. B is a country ill-treated by nature. I say that trade is beneficial to both of them and especially to B since the trade is not in *utilities* for *utilities* but in *value* for *value.* Well, A includes *more utilities in the same value,* since the utility of the product encompasses what nature has contributed to it as well as what work has contributed, whereas the value corresponds only to what work has contributed. Therefore, B strikes a bargain that is wholly to its advantage. In paying the producer in A simply for his work, it receives more natural utilities that it gives over and above the trade.[13]

Let us set out the general rule.

A trade is an exchange of *values;* since the value is reduced by competition to the work involved, trade is thus an exchange of equal work. What nature has provided to the products being traded is given from one to the other *freely and over and above the trade,* from which it strictly follows that trade with the countries most favored by nature are the most advantageous.

The theory whose lines and contours I have tried to trace in this article needs to be developed more fully. I have discussed it as it relates to my subject, commercial freedom. But perhaps an attentive reader will have perceived the fertile seed, the growth and spread of which will necessarily stifle protection, along with protectionism, Fourierism,[14] Saint-Simonism, communism, and all the schools whose object is to exclude the law of COMPETITION from the governance of the world. Considered from the point of view of producers,

13. Bastiat is referring here to David Ricardo's idea of international comparative advantage, which he proposed in his *Principles of Political Economy and Taxation.* A French translation by Constancio appeared in 1818, with notes by Jean-Baptiste Say; it was republished with his *Complete Works* in 1847 with additional notes and translated material by Fonteyraud. See *Œuvres complètes de David Ricardo.* See also Donald J. Boudreaux, "Comparative Advantage," in *Concise Encyclopedia of Economics,* http://www.econlib .org/library/Enc/ComparativeAdvantage.html.

14. François-Marie Charles Fourier (1772–1837) was a socialist and founder of the phalansterian school or "Fourierism." This consisted of a utopian, communistic system for the reorganization of society in which individuals would live together as one family and hold property in common. See the entry for "Fourier, François-Marie Charles," in the Glossary of Persons.

competition doubtless upsets our individual and *immediate* interests, but if you consider it from the point of view of the general aim of all production, of universal well-being, in a word, of *consumption,* you will find that competition accomplishes the same role in a moral world as equilibrium does in a material one. Competition is the foundation of genuine communism, true socialism, and the equality of well-being and conditions, so longed for these days, and if so many sincere political writers, so many reformers of good faith, demand this equality from *arbitrary government power,* it is because they do not understand *freedom.*

5. Our Products Are Weighed Down with Taxes

PUBLISHING HISTORY:

> Original title: "Nos produits sont grevés de taxes."
> Place and date of first publication: *JDE* ıı (July 1845): 356–60.
> First French edition as book or pamphlet: *Economic Sophisms*
>   (First Series) (1846).
> Location in Paillottet's edition of *OC:* Vol. 4. *Sophismes*
>   *économiques. Petits pamphlets I,* pp. 46–52.
> Previous translations: 1st English ed., 1846; 1st American ed.,
>   1848; FEE ed., 1964.

This is the same sophism. People demand that foreign products be taxed in order to neutralize the effects of the taxation that burdens our national products. This too, then, is about equalizing the conditions of production. The only observation we would want to make is that tax is an artificial obstacle with exactly the same result as a natural obstacle: it forces prices to rise. If this rise reaches the point at which a greater loss is incurred in creating the product itself than there is in bringing it in from outside and creating a countervalue for it, *let it happen.*[1] Private interest will be fully capable of choosing the lesser of two evils. I could therefore refer the reader back to the preceding argument, but the sophism that I have to combat here recurs so often in the complaints and appeals, I might almost say the pressing claims, of the protectionist school, that it is well worth discussing it separately.

If we want to discuss one of those special taxes to which certain products

---

1. "Laissez faire" in the original. See "Bastiat's References to Laissez-Faire," in the Note on the Translation.

are subject, I will readily agree that it is reasonable to subject foreign products to these also. For example, it would be absurd to exempt foreign salt
from tax, not that from an economic point of view France loses anything, on
the contrary. Whatever we say about this, principles are constant, and France
would gain, just as she will always gain from avoiding a natural or artificial
obstacle. However, here the obstacle has been established with a fiscal aim.
This aim has to be achieved, and if foreign salt were to be sold in our market
free of duty, the treasury would not recover its hundred million and would
have to exact this amount from some other form of taxation. It would quite
evidently be contradictory to put in the way of a specific policy an obstacle
calculated to prevent it. It would have been better to address this other tax
first of all and not tax French salt.[2] These are the circumstances that I accept
for inflicting a duty that is *not protectionist* but fiscal on a foreign product.

But to claim that a nation has to protect itself through tariffs against competition from a rival because it is subject to heavier taxes than a neighboring
country, this is where the sophism lies, and this is what I intend to attack.

I have said several times that I intend only to set out a theory and go
back, as far as I am able, to the sources of the protectionists' errors. If I were
indulging in polemics, I would say to them, "Why are you aiming tariffs
principally against England and Belgium, the countries in the world that are
most burdened with taxes? Am I not entitled to see in your argument only a
pretext?" However, I am not one of those who believe that people are protectionist through interest and not through conviction. Protectionist doctrine is
too popular not to be sincere. If the majority had faith in freedom, we would
be free. Doubtless it is private interest that causes our tariffs to weigh down
on us so heavily, but this is after it has acted on our convictions. "Will," said
Pascal, "is one of the principal organs of belief."[3] However, belief is no less
real for having its roots in will and in the secret inspiration of egoism.

2. The domestic tax on salt, or "gabelle," was a much-hated tax on an item essential for
preserving food. It was abolished during the Revolution but revived during the Restoration. In 1816 it was set at 30 centimes per kilogram, and in 1847 it raised fr. 70.4 million. During the Revolution of 1848 it was reduced to 10 centimes per kilogram. According to the Budget Papers of 1848, the French state raised fr. 38.2 million from tariffs on
imported salt and fr. 13.4 million from the salt tax on internal sales. See "Gabelle," under
"French Taxation," in appendix 3, "Economic Policy and Taxation." See also E. de Parieu,
"Sel," in DEP 2:606–9.

3. Blaise Pascal (1623–62) was a French mathematician and philosopher whose best-
known work, *Pensées,* appeared only after his death. "The will is one of the chief organs
of belief, not that it forms belief, but that things are true or false according to the side
on which we view them. The will which chooses one side rather than the other turns

Let us return to the sophism derived from taxation.

The state can make good or bad use of taxes; it makes good use of them when it provides the public with services that are equivalent to the flow of revenue the public contributes to it. It makes bad use of them when it squanders these resources without giving anything in return.

In the first case, to say that taxes put the country that pays them in a less favorable position with regard to production than one that does not pay them is a sophism. We pay twenty million for law and the police,[4] it is true, but we have law and the police, the security they provide us, and the time they save us, and it is highly probable that production is neither easier nor more active in those nations, if they exist, where everyone carries out law and order for himself. We pay several hundred million for roads, bridges, ports, and railways, I agree.[5] But we have these railways, ports, and roads, and unless we claim that we are making a bad bargain in building them, nobody can say that they make us inferior to those peoples who, it is true, do not contribute to a budget for public works but do not have any public works either. And this explains why, while accusing taxes of being one of the causes of inferior industrial capacity, we aim our tariffs precisely against those nations that are the most taxed. It is because taxes, when used well, far from damaging them, have improved the *conditions of production* of these nations. So we always come to the same conclusion, that protectionist sophisms not only depart from the truth but are also contrary, are the direct opposite, to the truth.

As for taxes that are unproductive, abolish them if you can. The strangest conceivable way of neutralizing their effects, however, is surely to add specific individual taxes to public ones. Spare us any such compensation! The state has taxed us too much, you say. Well then, all the more reason for our not taxing each other any further!

A protectionist duty is a tax aimed against a foreign product but which falls, and let us never forget this, on the national consumer. Now, the con-

---

away the mind from considering the qualities of all that it does not like to see, thus the mind, moving in accord with the will, stays to look at the side it chooses, and so judges by what it sees." From "The Authenticity of Sacred Books," in Pascal, *The Thoughts of Blaise Pascal,* p. 128.

4. According to the budget papers for 1848, fr. 26 million was spent on courts and tribunals by the Ministry of Justice.

5. It is not clear where Bastiat gets these figures. According to the budget papers for 1848, the ordinary expenditure for the Ministry of Public Works was fr. 63.5 million, the extraordinary expenditure was fr. 47.4 million, and fr. 74.8 million was spent on the railways, for a total of fr. 185.7 million. Additional amounts were spent on public works in Algeria by the Ministry of War and on local public works by the départements.

sumer is a taxpayer. And is it not ludicrous to say to him: "Since taxes are heavy, we are going to raise the prices of everything to you; since the state takes a part of your income, we are going to pay another part to the monopoly"?

But let us probe further a sophism so esteemed by our legislators, although it is rather extraordinary that it is precisely those who maintain unproductive taxes (the proposition I am drawing your attention to now) who are attributing our alleged industrial inferiority to them in order to make this good subsequently through other taxes and restrictions.

It appears obvious to me that, without changing its nature and effects, protection might have taken the form of a direct tax raised by the state and distributed through indemnity subsidies to privileged industries.

Let us assume that foreign iron can be sold in our market at 8 francs and no lower and French iron at 12 francs and not below this.

Under such circumstances, the state has two ways of ensuring that the national producer retains a dominant position in the market.

The first is to subject foreign iron to a duty of 5 francs. It is clear that foreign iron would be excluded since it could now be sold only at 13 francs, 8 francs being the cost price and 5 francs the tax, and that at this price it would be chased out of the market by French iron, which we have taken to cost 12 francs. In this case, the purchaser, the consumer, will have paid all the costs of this protection.

The state might also have imposed a tax of 5 francs on the public and given it as a subsidy to ironmasters. The protectionist effect would have been the same. Foreign iron would have been equally excluded, since our ironmaster would have sold at 7 francs which, with the subsidy of 5 francs, would give him his profitable price of 12 francs. However, faced with iron at 7 francs, foreigners would not be able to deliver theirs at 8.

I can see only one difference between these two systems: the principle is the same and the effect is the same, except that in one case protection is paid for by a few and in the other by all.

I admit frankly my preference for the second system. It seems to me more just, more economic, and more straightforward. More just because if society wants to give handouts to a few of its members, everyone has to contribute; more economic because it would save a great deal in collection costs and would cause a great many restrictions to disappear; and finally, more straightforward since the public would see clearly how the operation worked and what they were being made to do.

If the protectionist system had taken this form, however, would it not be rather risible to hear it said, "We pay heavy taxes for the army, navy, law and order, public works, the university, the national debt, etc., and this exceeds a billion.[6] For this reason, it would be a good thing if the state took another billion from us to ease the situation of these poor ironmasters, these poor shareholders of Anzin,[7] these unfortunate owners of forests, and these cod fishermen who are so useful."

If you look closely, you will see that this is what the significance of the sophism I am combating is reduced to. Whatever you do, sirs, you can *give money* to some only by taking it from others. If you genuinely wish to drain taxpayers dry, go ahead, but at least do not mock them and say to them, "I am taking from you to compensate you for what I have already taken from you."

We would never reach the end of it if we wished to note everything that is false in this sophism. I will limit myself to three considerations.

You win acceptance for the fact that France is burdened with taxes in order to infer that such and such an industry ought to be protected. But we have to pay these taxes in spite of protection. If therefore an industry comes forward and says, "I contribute to the payment of taxes; this raises the cost price of my products and I demand that a protectionist duty should also raise the sales price," what else is it demanding than to discharge its tax onto the rest of the community? It claims to be recouping the increase in tax it has paid by raising the price of its products. So, as all taxes have always to be paid to the treasury, and as the masses have to bear this increase in price, they pay both their taxes and those of this industry. "But," you will say, "everyone is being protected." Firstly, this is impossible and, even if it were possible, where would the relief be? I am paying for you and you for me; but the tax still needs to be paid.

In this way, you are being fooled by an illusion. You want to pay taxes to have an army, a navy, a religion, a university, judges, roads, etc., and then you want to relieve of its share of taxes first one industry, then a second, and then a third, always by sharing the burden among the masses. But you are doing nothing other than creating interminable complications, with no other result than these complications themselves. Prove to me that the increase in price resulting from protection falls on foreigners, and I will be able to see something specious in your argument. But if it is true that the French public paid

6. The French government annual expenditure in 1848 was fr. 1.446 billion and its receipts were fr. 1.391 billion, resulting in a deficit of fr. 55 million.

7. The Compagnie des mines d'Anzin was a large coal-mining company in the north of France near the town of Anzin. It was founded in 1757 and nationalized by the French government in 1949. It was the setting for Émile Zola's novel *Germinal* (1885), where it was used as a symbol of French capitalism.

the tax before the law and that after the law it paid both the protection and the tax, then I really do not see what it gains by this.

I will even go much further; I say that the heavier our taxes are, the more we should be in a hurry to open our ports and frontiers to foreigners who are less taxed than us. Why? In order to pass on to them a greater part of our burden. Is it not an undeniable axiom in political economy that, in the long run, taxes fall on the consumer? The more our trading transactions are increased, the more foreign consumers will reimburse us the taxes included in the products we sell them, while we would have to make them in this respect only a lesser restitution, since according to our hypothesis their products are less taxed than ours.

In sum, have you never asked whether these heavy taxes that you use in argument to justify the protectionist regime are not caused by this regime itself? I would like to be told what the great standing armies and the powerful navies would be used for if trade were free[8] . . . But this is a question for politicians,

> And let us not confuse, by going too deeply,
> Their business with ours.[9]

6. The Balance of Trade

PUBLISHING HISTORY:

Original title: "Balance du commerce."
Place and date of first publication: *JDE* 12 (October 1845): 201–4.

8. See "Peace and Freedom, or the Republican Budget" (February 1849) for Bastiat's plans on how free trade could lead to peace and thus drastic cutbacks in government spending. In CW2, pp. 282–327.

9. Jean de La Fontaine (1621–95) was a poet and writer of fables which have become famous for their surface simplicity which masks much deeper moral and political insights. This quotation comes from the very end of La Fontaine's fable *La Belette entrée dans un grenier* (The Weasel That Got Caught in the Storeroom), about a weasel that was able to squeeze through a small hole in order to get into a grain-storage room. Once inside it ate so much that it got bigger and couldn't get back out through the same hole in the wall. A rat, on seeing its predicament, says that, after five or six days of not eating, "you would have then a belly that is much less full. You were thin to get in, you'll have to be thin to get out. What I'm telling you now, you've well heard from others: but let us not confuse, by going too deeply, their business with yours" (La Fontaine, *Fables de La Fontaine,* bk. 3, fable 17, p. 121).

First French edition as book or pamphlet: *Economic Sophisms*
(First Series) (1846).
Location in Paillottet's edition of *OC:* Vol. 4. *Sophismes
économiques. Petits pamphlets I,* pp. 52–57.
Previous translations: 1st English ed., 1846; 1st American ed.,
1848; FEE ed., 1964.

Our opponents have adopted a tactic which we cannot help feeling embarrassed about. Are we getting our views across? They accept them with the utmost respect. Are we attacking their fundamental approach? They abandon it with the best grace in the world. They ask for only one thing, which is that our views, which they hold to be true, should be relegated to books and that their approach, which they acknowledge to be faulty, should reign over the carrying out of business. Leave them the handling of tariffs and they will not dispute your having the domain of theory.

"Certainly", said M. Gaulthier de Rumilly[1] recently, "none of us wants to resurrect the old theories on the balance of trade." Very well, but M. Gaulthier, it is not enough just to administer a slap in the face to error as you pass by; you must also desist from reasoning immediately afterward and for two hours at a time as though this error was the truth.

Talk to me about M. Lestiboudois.[2] Here is someone who reasons consistently, a logician who can debate. There is nothing in his conclusions that is not in his premises: he asks nothing of practice that he cannot justify in theory. His basic ideas may be false, and that is indeed the dispute. But at least he has some basic ideas. He believes and proclaims loudly that if France pays ten to receive fifteen it is losing five, and he quite straightforwardly makes laws in this light.

"What is important," he says, "is that the figure for imports is constantly increasing and exceeds that for exports, that is to say, each year France purchases more foreign products and sells fewer products produced nationally. The figures are there to prove it. What do we see? In 1842, we see imports

---

1. Louis Gaulthier de Rumilly (1792–1884) was trained as a lawyer and served as a Deputy in 1830–34 and 1837–40. He was active in the Société d'encouragement pour l'industrie nationale (Society to Promote National Industry) and had a special interest in agriculture, railroads, and tariffs.

2. Thémistocle Lestiboudois (1797–1876) was a deputy from Lille (elected 1842) who supported the liberals in 1844 in wanting to end the stamp tax on periodicals but opposed them in supporting protectionism.

exceed exports by 200 million.[3] These facts appear to me to prove with utter clarity that national work *is not sufficiently protected,* that we let foreign work take care of our needs and that competition from our rivals *is beating* our industry *down.* The law currently in force appears to sanction the fact that it is not true, contrary to what economists say, that when we buy we sell of necessity a corresponding portion of goods. It is obvious that we can buy things, not with our customary products, not with our income, not with the fruit of ongoing production but with our capital, with products that have been accumulated and saved and those used for making more, that is to say, we can spend and dissipate the profits of previous savings, that we can grow poorer and march toward our ruin and that we can consume the national capital in its entirety. *This is exactly what we are doing. Each year, we give 200 million to foreigners."*

Well then, here is a man with whom we can agree. His language contains no hypocrisy. The balance of trade is set out clearly. France imports 200 million more than it exports. Therefore, France is losing 200 million a year. And the remedy? To prevent imports. The conclusion is irreproachable.

---

3. Bastiat is using figures which were much debated at the time. Under pressure from the free traders, the French government revised its method of calculating the value of traded goods. Under the system established in 1826, the value of many goods and the duty they were required to pay was fixed—this was the "valeurs officielles" (the official value). The economists argued that this underestimated the total value of trade because prices had been rising for many foods, merchants understated the value of their goods in order to avoid paying duty, and there was extensive smuggling of goods the value of which was not recorded by the government. In the late 1840s the government began revising its statistics in order to reflect this "valeur actuelle" (current or present day value). In addition, the economists were more interested in examining the total value of goods traded (the value of imports and the exports), not just the "balance" between them, or the trade deficit as the protectionists liked to focus on. Using the revised trade statistics, Horace Say calculated that France had had small trade surpluses throughout the late 1830s, but had gone into reverse in 1842–43, with large trade deficits of 202 and 195 million francs respectively. (The figures for 1842 were the following: total trade was 2,082 million francs, with exports 940 million and imports 1,142 million, which produced a trade deficit of 202 million francs.) There was another small spike in the trade deficit in 1846–47, when the harvest failed and more food had to be imported (77 million francs in 1846). French trade returned to surplus when imports collapsed in 1848 as a result of the revolution, and then after the revolution, when exports improved dramatically. In 1850 the total value of trade was 2,705 million with imports valued at 1,174 million and exports at 1,531 million, producing a trade surplus of 357 million francs. See Horace Say, "Douane," *DEP,* vol. 1, pp. 578–604. Figures on p. 602. Also "Commerce extérieur de la France pour l'année 1847. Valeurs officielles—Valeurs actuelles," in *Annuaire de l'économie politique* (1849), pp. 18–67.

It is therefore M. Lestiboudois whom we are going to attack, for how can we combat M. Gaulthier? If you say to him, "The balance of trade is a mistake," he will reply to you, "That is what I have put forward in my introductory remarks." If you exclaim, "But the balance of trade is a truth," he will reply to you, "That is what I have stated in my conclusions." The Economist School[4] will doubtless criticize me for debating with M. Lestiboudois. Combating the balance of trade, I will be told, is like tilting at windmills.

Take care, however; the balance of trade is neither as old, nor as sick, nor as dead as M. Gaulthier wishes to tell us, for the entire Chamber, including M. Gaulthier himself, aligned themselves with M. Lestiboudois's theory through their vote.

However, in order not to tire the reader, I will not go into this theory. I will content myself with subjecting it to the test of facts.

Our principles are constantly being accused of being correct only in theory. But tell me, sirs, do you believe that the account books of businessmen are correct in practice? It seems to me that, if there is anything in the world that has practical authority when it is a question of ascertaining profits and losses, it is commercial accounting. Apparently all the traders on earth have not agreed down the centuries to keep their books in such a fashion that profits are shown as losses and losses as profits. Truly, I would prefer to believe that M. Lestiboudois is a bad economist.

Well, when one of my friends, who is a trader, completed two operations with very contrasting results, I was curious to compare the accounts of the warehouse with those of the customs service, interpreted by M. Lestiboudois with the sanction of our six hundred legislators.

M.T. shipped from Le Havre to the United States a cargo of French goods, in the majority products known as *articles de Paris,*[5] for an amount of 200,000 fr. This was the figure declared to the customs. When it arrived in New Orleans, it was found that the cargo had incurred 10 percent of costs and paid 30 percent in duty, which made it worth 280,000 fr. It was sold at a profit of 20 percent, or 40,000 fr., and produced a total of 320,000 fr., which the consignee converted into cotton. These cotton goods further had to bear 10 percent costs for transport, insurance, commission, etc., so that, when it entered Le Havre, the new cargo was worth 352,000 fr., and this was the figure recorded in the registers of the customs. Lastly, M.T. made another

4. See the entry for "*Les Économistes,*" in the Glossary of Subjects and Terms.

5. *Articles de Paris* were high-priced luxury goods produced in France and included such items as leather goods, jewelry, fashion clothing, and perfume.

20 percent profit on this return shipment, or 70,400 fr.; in other words, the cotton goods were sold for 422,400 fr.

If M. Lestiboudois requires it, I will send him an excerpt from M.T.'s books. He will see there under the *credits* of the *profit and loss account,* that is to say as profits, two entries, one for 40,000, the other for 70,400 fr., and M.T. is totally convinced that in this respect his accounts are not misleading him.

However, what do the figures that the customs have recorded regarding this operation tell M. Lestiboudois? They tell him that France has exported 200,000 fr. and that it has imported 352,000 fr., from which the honorable deputy concludes *"that it has spent and dissipated the profits of previous savings, that it has impoverished itself, that it is marching toward ruin, and that it has given 152,000 fr. of capital to foreigners."*

A short time afterward, M.T. shipped another cargo of nationally produced goods worth 200,000 fr. But the unfortunate ship foundered on leaving the port, and M.T. was left with no alternative but to record in his books two short entries, as follows:

Various goods debited to X for 200,000 fr. for the purchase of various articles shipped by the boat N.

Profit and loss due to various goods 200,000 fr. for the total and final loss of the cargo.

In the meantime, the customs had recorded for its part 200,000 fr. on its *export* table, and since it will never have anything to record on the *imports* table, it follows that M. Lestiboudois and the Chamber will see in this shipwreck a *clear, net profit* of 200,000 fr. for France.

One more consequence has to be drawn from this, which is that according to the theory of the balance of trade, France has a very simple way of doubling its capital at every moment. To do this, once it has passed it through the customs, it just has to throw it into the sea. In this case, exports will be equal to the amount of its capital; imports will be nil and even impossible, and we will gain everything that the ocean has swallowed up.

This is a joke, the protectionists will say. It is impossible for us to say such absurd things. However, you are saying them and what is more, you are doing them; you are imposing them in practice on your fellow citizens, at least as far as you are able.

The truth is that the balance of trade would have to be taken *backward* and national profit in foreign trade calculated through the excess of imports over exports. This excess, with costs deducted, is the genuine profit. But this theory, which is the correct one, leads directly to free trade. I hand this theory to you, sirs, like all the others that were the subject of the previous chapters. Exaggerate it as much as you like, it has nothing to fear from such a test. Assume, if that amuses you, that foreigners swamp us with all sorts of useful goods without asking us for anything; if our imports are *infinite* and our exports *nil,* I challenge you to prove to me that we would be the poorer for this.[6]

7. Petition by the Manufacturers of Candles, Etc.

PUBLISHING HISTORY:

> Original title: "Pétition des fabricants de chandelles, etc."
> Place and date of first publication: *JDE* 12 (October 1845): 204–7.
> First French edition as book or pamphlet: *Economic Sophisms* (First Series) (1846).
> Location in Paillottet's edition of *OC:* Vol. 4. *Sophismes économiques. Petits pamphlets I,* pp. 57–62.
> Previous translations: 1st English ed., 1846; 1st American ed., 1848; FEE ed., 1964.

By the manufacturers of tallow candles, wax candles, lamps, candlesticks, street lamps, snuffers, extinguishers, and producers of tallow, oil, resin, alcohol, and in general everything that relates to lighting

To Honorable Members of the Chamber of Deputies
  Sirs,
  You are doing all right for yourselves. You are rejecting abstract theories; abundance and cheapness are of little account to you. You are concerned most of all with the fate of producers. You want them to be free from foreign competition, in a word, you want to keep the *domestic market* for *domestic labor.*
  We come to offer you a wonderful opportunity to apply your . . . what will we call it? Your theory? No, nothing is more misleading than theory. Your doctrine? Your system? Your principles? But you do not like doctrines, you

---

6. See also the essay "The Balance of Trade" (March 1850) in CW 4 (forthcoming).

have a horror of systems, and as for principles, you declare that none exists in the economic life of society. We will therefore call it your practice, your practice with no theory and no principle.

We are suffering from the intolerable competition of a foreign rival whose situation with regard to the production of light, it appears, is so far superior to ours that it is *flooding* our *national market* at a price that is astonishingly low for, as soon as he comes on the scene, our sales cease, all consumers go to him, and a sector of French industry whose ramifications are countless is suddenly afflicted with total stagnation. This rival, which is none other than the sun, is waging such a bitter war against us that we suspect that it is instigated by perfidious Albion (good diplomacy in the current climate!), especially as it treats this proud island in a way which it denies us.[1]

We ask you to be good enough to pass a law which orders the closure of all windows, gables, shades, windbreaks, shutters, curtains, skylights, fanlights, blinds, in a word, all openings, holes, slits, and cracks through which the light of the sun is accustomed to penetrate into houses to the disadvantage of the fine industries that we flatter ourselves that we have given to the country, which cannot now abandon us to such an unequal struggle without being guilty of ingratitude.

Deputies, please do not take our request for satire and do not reject it without at least listening to the reasons we have to support us.

Firstly, if you forbid as far as possible any access to natural light, if you thus create a need for artificial light, what industry in France would not bit by bit be encouraged?

If more tallow is consumed, more cattle and sheep will be needed, and consequently we will see an increase in artificial meadows, meat, wool, leather, and, above all, fertilizer, the basis of all agricultural wealth.

If more oil is consumed, we will see an expansion in the cultivation of poppies, olive trees, and rapeseed. These rich and soil-exhausting plants will

---

1. This is a dig by Bastiat at the famously bad British weather. By making it so often overcast in Britain, the sun seems to be favoring the British artificial light industry in a way that it doesn't the French industry, which has to suffer economic hardship because there is more sunny weather (at least in the south of France). The average number of hours of sunshine per year in Britain (1971–2000) was 1,457.4. For France, Lille in the northeast had 1,617 hours (1991–2010), Paris had 1,662 hours, Bordeaux (near where Bastiat lived) had 2,035 hours, and Marseille (on the Mediterranean) had 2,858. See "Sunshine duration," Wikipedia http://en.wikipedia.org/wiki/Sunshine_duration for general data and articles on individual cities for specific data.

be just the thing to take advantage of the fertility that the rearing of animals will have contributed to our land.

Our moorlands will be covered with coniferous trees. Countless swarms of bees will gather from our mountains scented treasures which now evaporate uselessly like the flowers from which they emanate. There is thus no sector of agriculture that will not experience significant development.

The same is true for shipping. Thousands of ships will go to catch whales, and in a short time we will have a navy capable of upholding the honor of France and satisfying the patriotic susceptibility of us who petition you, the sellers of tallow candles, etc.

But what have we to say about *Articles de Paris?*[2] You can already picture the gilt work, bronzes, and crystal in candlesticks, lamps, chandeliers, and candelabra shining in spacious stores compared with which today's shops are nothing but boutiques.

Even the poor resin tapper on top of his sand dune or the poor miner in the depths of his black shaft would see his earnings and well-being improved.

Think about it, sirs, and you will remain convinced that perhaps there is not one Frenchman, from the wealthy shareholder of Anzin to a humble match seller, whose fate would not be improved by the success of our request.

We anticipate your objections, sirs, but you cannot put forward a single one that you have not culled from the well-thumbed books of the supporters of free trade. We dare to challenge you to say one word against us that will not be turned instantly against yourselves and the principle that governs your entire policy.

Will you tell us that if we succeed in this protection France will gain nothing, since consumers will bear its costs?

Our reply to you is this:

You no longer have the right to invoke the interests of the consumer. When the latter was in conflict with the producers, you sacrificed him on every occasion. You did this to *stimulate* production and to *increase its domain.* For the same reason, you should do this once again.

You yourselves have forestalled the objection. When you were told: "Consumers have an interest in the free introduction of iron, coal, sesame, wheat, and cloth," you replied: "Yes, but producers have an interest in their exclusion." Well then, if consumers have an interest in the admission of natural light, producers have one in its prohibition.

2. See ES1 6, p. 47n3.

"But," you also said, "producers and consumers are one and the same. If manufacturers gain from protection, they will cause agriculture to gain. If agriculture prospers, it will provide markets for factories." Well then, if you grant us the monopoly of lighting during the day, first of all we will purchase a great deal of tallow, charcoal, oil, resin, wax, alcohol, silver, iron, bronze, and crystal to fuel our industry and, what is more, once we and our countless suppliers have become rich, we will consume a great deal and spread affluence throughout the sectors of the nation's production.

Will you say that sunlight is a free gift and that to reject free gifts would be to reject wealth itself, even under the pretext of stimulating the means of acquiring it?

Just take note that you have a fatal flaw at the heart of your policy and that up to now you have always rejected foreign products *because* they come close to being free gifts and *all the more so* to the degree that they come closer to this. You had only *a half reason* to accede to the demands of other monopolists; to accede to our request, you have a *complete reason* and to reject us precisely on the basis that we are better *founded* would be to advance the equation $+ x + = -$; in other words, it would be to pile *absurdity* on *absurdity*.

Work and nature contribute in varying proportions to the production of a product, depending on the country and climate. The portion provided by nature is always free; it is the portion which labor contributes that establishes its value and is paid for.

If an orange from Lisbon is sold at half the price of an orange from Paris, it is because natural and consequently free heat gives to one what the other owes to artificial and consequently expensive heat.

Therefore, when an orange reaches us from Portugal, it can be said that it is given to us half-free and half-paid for, or in other words, at *half the price* compared to the one from Paris.

Well, it is precisely *its being half-free* (excuse the expression) that you use as an argument to exclude it. You say, "How can domestic labor withstand the competition of foreign labor when domestic labor has to do everything and foreign labor only half of the task, with the sun accomplishing the rest?" But if this matter of things being *half-free* persuades you to reject competition, how will things being *totally free* lead you to accept competition? Either you are not logicians or, in rejecting half-free products as harmful to our domestic economy, you have to reject totally free goods *a fortiori* and with twice as much zeal.

Once again, when a product, coal, iron, wheat, or cloth, comes to us from abroad and if we can acquire it with less work than if we made it ourselves, the difference is a *free gift* bestowed on us. This gift is more or less significant depending on whether the difference is greater or lesser. It ranges from one-quarter to half or three-quarters of the value of the product if foreigners ask us only for three-quarters, half, or one-quarter of the payment. It is as total as it can be when the donor asks nothing from us, like the sun for light. The question, which we set out formally, is to know whether you want for France the benefit of free consumption or the alleged advantages of expensive production. Make your choice, but be logical, for as long as you reject, as you do, foreign coal, iron, wheat, and cloth, *the closer* their price gets to *zero,* how inconsistent would it be to accept sunlight, whose cost is *zero,* throughout the day?

8. Differential Duties

PUBLISHING HISTORY:

Original title: "Droits différentiels."
Place and date of first publication: *JDE* 12 (October 1845): 207–8.
First French edition as book or pamphlet: *Economic Sophisms* (First Series) (1846).
Location in Paillottet's edition of *OC:* Vol. 4. *Sophismes économiques. Petits pamphlets I,* pp. 62–63.
Previous translations: 1st English ed., 1846; 1st American ed., 1848; FEE ed., 1964.

A poor farmer in the Gironde had lovingly cultivated a vine. After a lot of tiring work, he finally had the joy of producing a cask of wine, and he forgot that each drop of this precious nectar had cost his forehead one drop of sweat. "I will sell it," he told his wife, "and with the money I will buy some yarn with which you will make our daughter's trousseau." The honest farmer went to town and met a Belgian and an Englishman. The Belgian said to him, "Give me your cask of wine and in exchange I will give you fifteen reels of yarn." The Englishman said, "Give me your wine and I will give you twenty reels of yarn, for we English spin more cheaply than the Belgians." However, a customs officer who happened to be there said, "My good man, trade with the Belgian if you like, but my job is to prevent you from trading with the Englishman." "What!" said the farmer, "you want me to be content with fifteen reels of yarn from Brussels when I can have twenty from Manchester?" "Certainly, do you not see that France would be the loser if you received twenty reels instead of fifteen?" "I find it difficult to understand this," said the wine producer. "And I to explain it," went on the customs officer, "but this is a fact, for all the deputies, ministers, and journalists agree on this point, that the more a people receive in exchange for a given quantity of their products, the poorer they become." He had to conclude the bargain with the Belgian. The farmer's daughter had only three-quarters of her trousseau, and these honest people still ask themselves how it can be that you are ruined by receiving four instead of three and why you are richer with three dozen napkins than with four dozen.

9. An Immense Discovery!!!

PUBLISHING HISTORY:

> Original title: "Immense découverte!!!"
> Place and date of first publication: *JDE* 12 (October 1845):
> 208–11.
> First French edition as book or pamphlet: *Economic Sophisms*
> (First Series) (1846).
> Location in Paillottet's edition of *OC:* Vol. 4. *Sophismes*
> *économiques. Petits pamphlets I,* pp. 63–67.
> Previous translations: 1st English ed., 1846; 1st American ed.,
> 1848; FEE ed., 1964.

At a time when all minds are occupied with searching for savings on various means of transport;

At a time when, in order to achieve these savings, we are leveling roads, canalizing rivers, improving steamships, and linking all our frontiers to Paris by an iron network, by traction systems that are atmospheric, hydraulic, pneumatic, electrical, etc.;[1]

---

1. In 1842 the government decided to encourage the building of a national network. Under the Railway Law of 11 June 1842 the government ruled that five main railways would be built radiating out of Paris which would be built in cooperation with private industry. The government would build and own the right of way, bridges, tunnels, and

Finally, at a time when I simply have to believe that everyone is enthusiastically and sincerely seeking the solution to the following problem:

"To ensure that the price of things at their place of consumption is as close as possible to their price at their place of production."

I would feel guilty toward my country, my century, and myself if I kept secret any longer the marvelous discovery I have just made.

For while the inventor's illusions may well be legendary, I am as certain as I can be that I have found an infallible means that ensures that products from around the world reach France and vice versa with a considerable reduction in their prices.

Infallible! This is just one of the advantages of my astonishing invention.

It requires neither a drawing, an estimate, nor preliminary studies, nor any engineers, machine operators, entrepreneurs, capital, shareholders, nor help from the government!

It offers no risk of shipwreck, explosion, shocks, fire, or derailment!

It can be put into practice in less than a day!

Lastly, and this will doubtless recommend it to the public, it will not cost the budget one centime, far from it. It will not increase the numbers of civil servants and the requirements of bureaucracy, far from it. It will not cost anyone his freedom, far from it.

It is not by chance that I have come about my discovery; it is through observation. I have to tell you now what led me to it.

This in fact was the question I had to solve:

"Why does something made in Brussels, for example, cost more when it reaches Paris?"

Well, it did not take me long to see that this is a result of the fact that there are several types of *obstacles* between Paris and Brussels. First of all, there is *distance;* we cannot cover this without a certain difficulty and loss of time, and we either have to subject ourselves to this or pay someone else to. Next come the rivers, the marshes, the lay of the land, and the mud; these are so many *difficulties* to be overcome. We do this by constructing roadways, building bridges, cutting roads, and reducing their resistance through the use

---

railway stations, while private industry would lay the tracks and build and maintain the rolling stock and the lines. The government would also set rates and regulate safety. The first railway concessions were issued by the government in 1844–45, triggering a wave of speculation and attempts to secure concessions. See "French Railways" in appendix 3, "Economic Policy and Taxation."

of cobbles, iron bands, etc. But all this has a cost, and the object being carried must bear its share of these costs. There are also thieves on the roads, which necessitates a gendarmerie, a police force, etc.

Well, among these *obstacles,* there is one that we have set up ourselves, and at great expense, between Brussels and Paris. This is the men lying in ambush all along the frontier, armed to the teeth and responsible for placing *difficulties* in the way of the transport of goods from one country to the other. We call them *customs officers.* They act in exactly the same way as mud or ruts in the road. They delay, hinder, and contribute to the difference we have noted between the cost of production and the consumer price, a difference which it is our problem to decrease as far as possible.

And now we have solved the problem. Reduce tariffs.

You will have built the Northern railway line without it having cost you a penny. Furthermore, you will save heavy expenditure and you will begin to put capital in your pocket right from the first day.

Really, I ask myself how it was possible for enough strange ideas to have gotten into our heads that we were persuaded to pay many millions with a view to destroying the *natural obstacles* lying between France and foreign countries and at the same time to pay many other millions to substitute *artificial obstacles* for them which have exactly the same effect, so that the obstacles created counteract those destroyed, things go on as before and the result of the operation is double expenditure.

A Belgian product worth 20 fr. in Brussels fetches 30 when it reaches Paris, because of transport costs. A similar product of Parisian manufacture costs 40 fr. So what do we do about it?

First, we put a duty of at least 10 fr. on the Belgian product in order to raise its cost price in Paris to 40 fr., and we pay a host of supervisors to ensure that it does not escape this duty, with the result that during the journey 10 fr. is charged for transport and 10 fr. for tax.

Having done this, we reason thus: transport from Brussels to Paris, which costs 10 fr., is very expensive. Let us spend two or three hundred million on railways, and we will reduce it by half.[2] Obviously, all that we will have obtained is that the Belgian product will be sold in Paris for 35 fr., that is to say:

2. Michel Chevalier estimates that the French government had spent over fr. 420 million on railway construction between 1841 and 1848. See Michel Chevalier, "Statistique des travaux publics sous le Gouvernement de Juillet," in *L'Annuaire de l'économie politique et de la statistique* (1849), pp. 209–37. See "Public Works" in appendix 3, "Economic Policy and Taxation."

20 fr.	its price in Brussels
10 fr.	duty
5 fr.	reduced transport by rail
35 fr.	total, or the cost price in Paris

Well, would we not have achieved the same result by lowering the tariff to 5 fr.? We would then have:

20 fr.	its price in Brussels
5 fr.	reduced duty
10 fr.	transport by ordinary road
35 fr.	total, or the cost price in Paris

And this procedure would have saved us the 200 million that the railway costs, plus the cost of customs surveillance, since these are bound to decrease as the incentive to smuggle decreases.

But, people will say, the duty is necessary to protect Parisian industry. So be it, but then do not ruin the effect with your railway.

For if you persist in wanting the Belgian product to cost 40 fr. like the Parisian one, you will have to raise the duty to 15 fr. to have:

20 fr.	its price in Brussels
15 fr.	protectionist duty
5 fr.	transport by rail
40 fr.	total with prices equalized.

Then my question is, from this point of view, what is the use of the railway?

Frankly, is it not somewhat humiliating for the nineteenth century to prepare a spectacle of childishness such as this for future ages with such imperturbable seriousness? To be fooled by others is already not very pleasant, but to use the huge system of representation in order to fool yourself is to fool yourself twice over and in a matter of arithmetic, this is something to take down the pride of the *century of enlightenment* a peg or two.

10. Reciprocity

PUBLISHING HISTORY:

Original title: "Réciprocité."
Place and date of first publication: *JDE* 12 (October 1845): 211.

First French edition as book or pamphlet: *Economic Sophisms*
(First Series) (1846).
Location in Paillottet's edition of *OC:* Vol. 4. *Sophismes
économiques. Petits pamphlets I,* pp. 67–70.
Previous translations: 1st English ed., 1846; 1st American ed.,
1848; FEE ed., 1964.

We have just seen that everything that makes transport expensive during a journey acts to encourage protection or, if you prefer, that protection acts to encourage everything that makes transport expensive.

It is therefore true to say that a tariff is a marsh, a rut or gap in the road, or a steep slope; in a word, an *obstacle* whose effect results in increasing the difference between the prices of consumption and production. Similarly, it is incontrovertible that marshes or bogs are genuine protective tariffs.

There are people (a few, it is true, but there are some) who are beginning to understand that obstacles are no less obstacles because they are artificial and that our well-being has more to gain from freedom than from protection, precisely for the same reason that makes a canal more favorable than a "sandy, steep and difficult track."[1]

But, they say, this freedom has to be mutual. If we reduced our barriers with Spain without Spain reducing hers with us, we would obviously be stupid. Let us therefore sign *commercial treaties* on the basis of an equitable reciprocity, let us make concessions in return for concessions, and let us make the *sacrifice* of buying in order to obtain the benefit of selling.

It pains me to tell people who reason thus that, whether they realize it or not, they are thinking along protectionist lines, the only difference being that they are slightly more inconsistent than pure protectionists, just as pure protectionists are more inconsistent than absolute prohibitionists.[2]

I will demonstrate this through the following fable:

---

1. Bastiat quotes the opening lines of a fable by La Fontaine, *Le Coche et la mouche* (The Coach and the Fly): "Over a hilly, sandy, and difficult road, exposed on all sides to the sun, six strong horses were pulling a coach." The original French is from La Fontaine, *Fables de La Fontaine,* pp. 269–70. The translation is taken from *Economic Sophisms,* FEE edition, p. 67n (courtesy of FEE.org).

2. On the difference between "protective" tariffs and "prohibitive" tariffs see "French Tariff Policy" in appendix 3, "Economic Policy and Taxation," and "Bastiat's Policy on Tariffs" in appendix 1, "Further Aspects of Bastiat's Life and Thought."

Stulta and Puera[3]

Once upon a time there were, somewhere or other, two towns, *Stulta* and *Puera*. At great expense, they built a road between the two. When it was completed, *Stulta* said to itself, "Now *Puera* is flooding us with its products; we had better look into it." As a result, it created and paid a Corps of Obstructors,[4] so called because their mission was to place obstacles in the path of convoys that arrived from *Puera*. Soon afterward, *Puera* also had a Corps of Obstructors.

After several centuries had passed, and enlightenment had made considerable progress, such was the growth of *Puera's* awareness that it had grasped that these reciprocal obstacles must necessarily be mutually detrimental. It sent a diplomat to *Stulta,* who, though his words were couched in official terms, effectively said: "We built a road and now we are obstructing it. This is absurd. It would have been better for us to have left things in their original state. First of all, we would not have had to pay for the road, and secondly for the obstacles. In the name of *Puera,* I have come to suggest to you, not that we suddenly abandon the setting up of mutual obstacles between us, which would be to act in accordance with a principle and we despise principles as much as you do, but to reduce these obstacles a little, taking care to balance our respective *sacrifices* in this respect equitably." This was what the diplomat said. *Stulta* asked for time to consider this. It consulted in turn its manufacturers and its farmers. Finally, after a few years, it declared that the negotiations had broken down.

At this news, the inhabitants of *Puera* held a council. An old man (who had always been suspected of being secretly bribed by *Stulta*) stood up and said: "The obstacles created by *Stulta* damage our sales, and this is terrible. The ones we have created ourselves damage our purchases, and this is

---

3. The names of the towns "Stulta" and "Puera" are plays on the Latin words *stultus* (foolish) and *puer/puera* (young boy or girl); thus one might translate them as "Stupidville" and "Childishtown."

4. Bastiat uses the expression *corps d'Enrayeurs* (body or corps of Obstructors), which we have translated as "Corps" to give it the flavor of an official government or military body, as in the "Army Corps of Engineers" in the United States, or the "Corps des ingénieurs des Mines" (Corps of Mining Engineers), or the "Corps des ingénieurs des Ponts, des Eaux et des Forêts" (Corps of Engineers for Bridges, Waterways, and Forests) in France.

also terrible. We cannot do anything about the first situation, but the second is in our power. Let us at least free ourselves of one since we cannot get rid of both. Let us abolish our Corps of Obstructors without demanding that *Stulta* do the same. One day, it will doubtless learn to do its sums better."

A second councilor, a practical man of action who had no theoretical principles and was imbued with the experience of his ancestors, replied: "Do not listen to this dreamer, this theoretician, this innovator, this utopian,[5] this economist, this *Stulta-lover*.[6] We would all be ruined if the obstacles on the road were not equal, in equitable balance between *Stulta* and *Puera*. There would be greater difficulty in *going* than in *coming* and in *exporting* than in *importing*. Compared with *Stulta*, we would be in the inferior position that Le Havre, Nantes, Bordeaux, Lisbon, London, Hamburg, and New Orleans are in compared with the towns situated at the sources of the Seine, the Loire, the Garonne, the Tagus, the Thames, the Elbe, and the Mississippi, for it is harder to go up rivers than to go down them." (A voice observed that towns at the mouths of rivers were more prosperous than those at their sources.) "That is not possible." (The same voice: But it is true.) "Well then, they have prospered *contrary to the rules*." Such conclusive reasoning shook the assembly. The speaker succeeded in convincing it by referring to national independence, national honor, national dignity, national production, the flood of products, tributes, and merciless competition; in short, he carried the day for maintaining the obstacles and, if you are interested in this, I can take you to certain countries in which you will see with your own eyes the Corps of Road Builders[7] and the Corps of Obstructors working with the best information available to them, in accordance with a decree issued by the same legislative assembly and at the expense of the same taxpayers, the former to clear the road and the latter to obstruct it.

5. See the entry for "Utopias," in the Glossary of Subjects and Terms.

6. Bastiat creates a neologism—*stultomane,* meaning Stultophile (used in *Economic Sophisms,* FEE edition, p. 69), or Stulta-lover.

7. Bastiat uses the term *cantonnier,* which refers to the workers who are employed by the local districts known as "cantons," whose responsibility it was to maintain the roads which passed through their districts. The system of *cantonniers* was formalized by a decree issued by Napoléon on 16 December 1811, and after 1816 they became permanent employees of the state. As a useful contrast to Bastiat's "Corps of Obstructors" we have translated *cantonniers* as "Corps of Road Builders."

11. Nominal Prices

PUBLISHING HISTORY:

Original title: "Prix absolus."
Place and date of first publication: *JDE* 12 (October 1845): 213–
15. This chapter was originally numbered 12 in the *JDE* but
became chapter 11 in the book version of *Economic Sophisms*
and incorporated chapter 11, "Stulta et Puera," from *JDE* 12:
211–12.
First French edition as book or pamphlet: *Economic Sophisms*
(First Series) (1846).
Location in Paillottet's edition of *OC:* Vol. 4. *Sophismes
économiques. Petits pamphlets I,* pp. 70–74.
Previous translations: 1st English ed., 1846; 1st American ed.,
1848; FEE ed., 1964.

Do you wish to assess the merits of freedom and protection? Do you wish
to understand the effects of an economic phenomenon? Then look for its
effects *on the abundance or scarcity of things* and not on *whether prices rise or
fall.* Be careful of thinking only about *nominal prices;*[1] this will lead you into
an inextricable labyrinth.

After establishing that protection makes things more expensive,
M. Mathieu de Dombasle adds:

"The increase in prices raises living expenses and *consequently* the price of
labor, (but) each person is compensated for the increase in their expenses by
the increase in prices for the things they produce. Thus, if everybody pays
more as a consumer, everybody also receives more as a producer."[2]

It is clear that this argument can be turned on its head, and we can say: "If
everybody receives more as a producer, everybody pays more as a consumer."

Well, what does that prove? Nothing other than that protection moves
wealth about uselessly and unjustly. This is just what plunder does.

---

1. Bastiat uses several terms to describe what he is getting at in this article: *prix absolus*
(nominal prices), *valeurs nominales* (nominal value), *en hausser le prix numérairement
parlant* (raising prices in purely monetary terms), and so on. He wants to make the point
that there is a difference between real economic wealth and the accounting device (the
money price) used to measure it.

2. Dombasle, *Œuvres diverses,* chapter 4, "Le régime de protection blesse-t-il les intérêts des consommateurs?" pp. 49–50.

Moreover, to accept that this vast apparatus results in simple mutual compensations, we have to agree with M. de Dombasle's word "*consequently*" and be sure that the price of labor rises in line with the price of protected products. This is a question of fact that I pass back to M. Moreau de Jonnès;[3] let him please look into whether pay rates have moved upward in line with Anzin mining shares. For my part, I do not think so, because I believe that the price of labor, like all the others, is governed by the relationship between supply and demand. Now, I can quite see that *restriction* decreases the supply of coal and consequently increases its price, but I see rather less clearly that it increases the demand for labor to the extent of increasing rates of pay. I see this all the less clearly in that the quantity of labor demanded depends on the capital available. Protection may well cause capital to move and shift from one industry to another, but it cannot increase it by an obole.[4]

Besides, this highly interesting question will be examined elsewhere. I will return to *nominal prices* and say that there are no absurdities that cannot be made plausible by reasoning like M. de Dombasle's.

Imagine that an isolated nation that had a given quantity of cash took pleasure in burning half of what it produced each year, and I will take it on myself to prove, using M. de Dombasle's theory, that it will not be a whit the less rich.

In effect, following the fire, everything will double in price and inventories taken before and after the disaster will show exactly the same *nominal* value. But in this case, who will have lost? If Jean buys cloth at a higher price, he will also sell his wheat at a higher price, and if Pierre loses on his purchase of wheat, he will make good on the sale of his cloth. "Each person is compensated (I say) for the increase in the amount of their expenses by the increase in the price for the things they produce; and if everybody pays more as a consumer, everybody receives more as a producer."

All this is a tissue of confusion rather than science. The truth expressed in its simplest form is this: whether men destroy cloth and wheat by fire or through use, the effect will be the same *with respect to the price* but not *with respect to wealth,* for it is precisely in the use of things that wealth or well-being consists.

---

3. Alexandre Moreau de Jonnès (1778–1870) was an economist and a statistician who was director of the statistical bureau in the ministry of trade (1834–42).

4. A coin of very low value. See a discussion of "obole" under "French Currency," in appendix 3, "Economic Policy and Taxation."

In the same way, restriction, while decreasing the abundance of things, may increase their price so that, if you like, *in purely monetary terms,* each person may be just as rich. But in an inventory, does a record of three hecto-liters of wheat at 20 francs or four hectoliters at 15 francs come to the same thing from the point of view of satisfying need because the result is still 60 francs?

And it is to this point of view of consumption that I will incessantly bring protectionists back, since this is the purpose of all our efforts and the solu-tion to all problems.[5] I will always say to them: "Is it not true that by ham-pering trade, by limiting the division of labor, and by forcing labor to grapple with the difficulties of location and temperature, restriction ultimately de-creases the quantity produced by a given amount of effort?" And what does it matter that the lesser quantity produced under a protectionist regime has the same *nominal value* as a larger quantity produced under the regime of freedom? Man does not live by *nominal values,* but by real products, and the more he has of these products, at whatever price, the richer he is.

When writing the foregoing, I did not expect ever to meet an anti-economist who was sufficiently good as a logician to contend explicitly that the wealth of peoples depends on the monetary value of things irrespective of their abundance. But just look what I have found in the book by M. de Saint-Chamans (page 210):[6]

"If 15 million francs worth of goods sold abroad is taken from normal pro-duction, estimated to be 50 million, the remaining 35 million worth can no longer meet normal demand and will increase in price and will reach a value of 50 million. Then the revenue of the country will be 15 million more.... There will therefore be an increase in wealth of 15 million for the country, exactly the amount of the cash which is imported."

Is that not ridiculous! If during the year a nation makes 50 million francs' worth of harvested products and goods, it just has to sell a quarter abroad

5. (Paillotet's note) This thought often recurs in the author's writings. In his eyes it was of capital importance, and four days before his death it dictated the following recom-mendation to him: "Tell de F. [Roger de Fontenay] to treat economic questions always from the point of view of the consumer, since the consumer's interest is at one with that of the human race." [Roger de Fontenay (1809–91) was a friend and intellectual ally of Bastiat's in their debates in the Political Economy Society on the nature of rent. Fontenay worked with Prosper Paillottet in editing the *Œuvres complètes* of Bastiat, for which he wrote the Preface.]

6. Bastiat quotes from Saint-Chamans's *Du système d'impôt fondé sur les principes de l'économie politique,* pp. 210–11.

to be a quarter richer! Therefore, if it sold half, it would increase its fortune by half, and if it trades for cash its last wisp of wool and last grain of wheat, it would raise its wealth to 100 million! Producing infinitely high prices through absolute scarcity is a very strange way of becoming wealthier!

Anyway, do you want to assess the merits of the two doctrines? Subject them to the exaggeration test.

According to the doctrine of M. de Saint-Chamans, the French would be just as rich, that is to say, as well provided with everything with a thousandth part of their annual output, since it would be worth a thousand times more.

According to ours, the French would be infinitely rich if their annual output was infinitely abundant and consequently was of no value at all.

12. Does Protection Increase the Rate of Pay?

PUBLISHING HISTORY:

Original title: "La protection élève-t-elle le taux des salaires?"
Place and date of first publication: No date given. First
   published in book form.
First French edition as book or pamphlet: *Economic Sophisms*
   (First Series) (1846).
Location in Paillottet's edition of *OC:* Vol. 4. *Sophismes
   économiques. Petits pamphlets I,* pp. 74–79.
Previous translations: 1st English ed., 1846; 1st American ed.,
   1848; FEE ed., 1964.

An atheist was railing against religion, against priests, and against God. "If you continue," said one of the audience, himself not very orthodox, "you are going to reconvert me."

Thus, when we hear our beardless scribblers, romantic writers, reformers, rose-scented and musky writers of serials, gorged on ice cream and champagne, clutching in their portfolios shares of *Ganneron, Nord,* and *Mackenzie*[1] or having their tirades against the egoism and individualism of the

___

1. The FEE translator provides the following very informative note: "Bastiat here refers by name to certain securities that enjoyed wide public confidence at the time: those of the Comptoir Ganneron, a bank in which, at the height of the speculation, almost four hundred million francs were invested; those of the fur-trading company founded by Sir Alexander MacKenzie and later amalgamated with the original Hudson's Bay Company;

century heaped with gold; when we hear them, as I say, railing against the harshness of our institutions, wailing about the wage-earners and the proletariat;[2] when we see them raise to the heavens eyes that mourn the sight of the destitution of the working classes, destitution that they never visit save to conjure up lucrative pictures of it, we are tempted to say to them: "If you continue in this way, you will make me indifferent to the fate of the workers."

Oh, such affectation! This is the sickening disease of our time! Workers, if a serious man, a sincere philanthropist, reveals a picture of your distress or writes a book that makes an impression, a rabble of reformers immediately seizes this prey in its claws. It is turned one way and another, exploited, exaggerated, and squeezed to the point of disgust and ridicule. All that you are thrown by way of a remedy are the high-sounding words, organization and association. You are flattered and fawned upon, and soon workers will be reduced by this to the situation of slaves: responsible men will be ashamed to take up their cause publicly, for how will they be able to introduce a few sensible ideas in the midst of such bland protestations?

But I refuse to adopt this cowardly indifference that is not justified by the affectation that triggers it!

Workers, your situation is strange! You are being robbed, as I will shortly be proving... No, I withdraw that word. Let us banish from our discourse all violent and perhaps misleading expressions, seeing that plunder, clad in the sophisms that conceal it, is carried out, we are expected to believe, against the will of the plunderer and with the consent of those being plundered. But when all is said and done, you are being robbed of the just remuneration for your work and nobody is concerned with achieving *justice* for you. Oh! If all that was needed to console you were noisy calls for philanthropy, impotent charity, and degrading alms, and if high-sounding words like *organization, communism,* and *phalanstery*[3] were enough, you would have your fill. But

---

and those of the Northern Railway of France" (*Economic Sophisms,* FEE edition, p. 74; courtesy of FEE.org).

2. This is the first time before the February Revolution of 1848 that Bastiat used the socialist term *prolétaires* (proletarians) or *prolétariat* (the proletariat). The second occurred in ES3 20, which was published on 20 February 1848 (the Revolution broke out on 23 February). Before this time he normally used the term *les ouvriers* (workers), so it seems the vocabulary of political debate was changing on the eve of the Revolution. After the Revolution he used the word "proletarian" or "proletariat" several times.

3. The "organization" of workers was urged by Louis Blanc in his influential pamphlet *Organisation du travail* (1839) as a way to overcome the "iniquities" of the system of wage labor and became a catchphrase of the socialist movement in the 1840s. The "phalanstery" was a method of socialist organization advocated by Charles Fourier and

nobody thinks of ensuring that *justice,* simple *justice,* is rendered to you. And yet, would it not be *just* for you, when you have been paid your meager salary following a long and hard day's work, to be able to exchange it for as many forms of satisfaction as you can obtain voluntarily from any man anywhere in the world?

One day, perhaps, I too will speak to you about association and organization, and we will then see what you can expect from these illusions that have led you down the garden path.[4]

In the meantime, let us see whether people are doing you an injustice when they pass laws which determine from whom you are permitted to buy the things you need, such as bread, meat, linen, and cloth, and, as it were, at what artificial price you will have to pay for them.

Is it true that protection, which, it is admitted, makes you to pay a high price for everything and thus causes you harm, raises your rate of pay proportionally?

On what do rates of pay depend?

One of your people has said this forcefully: "When two workers pursue an employer, earnings decrease; when two employers pursue one worker, they rise."[5]

Allow me, in short, to use this statement, which is more scientific but may be less clear: "Rates of pay depend on the ratio of the supply of and the demand for labor."

Well, on what does the *supply* of labor depend?

On the number in the marketplace, and on this initial element, protection has no effect.

On what does the *demand* for labor depend?

On the national capital available. But has the law that says: "We will no longer receive such and such a product from abroad, we will manufacture

---

his supporters in which people would live, own property, and work in common. See "Bastiat's Use of the Socialist Terms 'Organization' and 'Association,'" in the Note on the Translation.

4. Bastiat returned to this topic in his treatise *Economic Harmonies,* the first chapter of which was called "Natural Organization, Artificial Organization." It first appeared as an article in the *JDE* in January 1848. CW5, I (forthcoming).

5. This pithy and colorful formulation of how wages rise or fall according to demand is attributed to the English free trader and manufacturer Richard Cobden and was much quoted by French liberal economists. We have not been able to track down the original source.

it internally," increased this capital? Not in the slightest. The law has withdrawn the product from one area to place it in another, but it has not increased the product by one obole. Therefore the law does not increase the demand for labor.

A factory is shown off with pride. Has it been established and maintained with capital from the moon? No, capital has had to be withdrawn either from agriculture, shipping, or the wine-producing industry. And this is why, while there are more workers in our mineshafts and in the suburbs of our manufacturing towns since protectionist duties became law, there are fewer sailors in our ports and fewer workers and wine producers in our fields and hills.

I could continue on this theme for a long time. I prefer to try to make you understand my thought with this example.

A farmer had twenty arpents of land,[6] which he developed, with a capital of 10,000 francs. He divided his domain into four parts and established the following rotation: first, corn; second, wheat; third, clover; fourth, rye. He and his family needed only a small part of the grain, meat, and milk that the farm produced, and he sold the excess to purchase oil, flax, wine, etc. All of his capital was spent each year on wages and other payments owed to neighboring workers. This capital was returned through sales and even increased from one year to the next, and our farmer, knowing full well that capital produces nothing unless it is put to use, made the working class benefit from these annual surpluses which he used for fencing, land clearance, and improvements to his farm equipment and buildings. He even invested some savings with the banker in the neighboring town, who did not leave the money idle in his coffers but lent it to shipowners and entrepreneurs carrying out useful work, so that it continued to generate wages.

However, the farmer died, and his son, as soon as he had control of the inheritance, said: "It must be confessed that my father was a fool all his life. He purchased oil and thus paid *tribute* to Provence while our land could at a stretch grow olive trees. He bought wine, flax, and oranges and paid *tribute* to Brittany, the Médoc, and the islands of Hyères, while vines, jute, and orange trees could, more or less, provide a small crop on our land.[7] He paid *tribute* to millers and weavers while our domestic servants could well weave

6. An arpent is about 0.85 acre. See "French Weights and Measures," in appendix 3, "Economic Policy and Taxation."

7. Provence is a region in southeastern France along the Mediterranean Sea. Médoc is a wine-growing region in the département of the Gironde north of the city of Bordeaux. The Hyères Islands are located in the Mediterranean close to Provence.

our linen and grind our wheat between two stones. He ruined himself, and in addition he had foreigners earning the wages that were so easy for him to spread around him."

Using this reasoning, our scatterbrain changed the rotation of the domain. He divided it into twenty small strips of land. On one he grew olive trees, on another mulberry trees, on a third flax, on a fourth vines, on a fifth wheat, etc., etc. He thus managed to provide his family with everything and become *independent*. He took nothing from general circulation and, it is true, paid nothing into it either. Was he any richer? No, for the land was not suitable for growing vines, the climate was not conducive to the prospering of olive trees, and in the end the family was less well provided with these things than at the time when his father obtained them through trade.

As for the workers, there was no more work for them than in the past. There were indeed five times as many strips to cultivate, but they were five times smaller. Oil was produced but less wheat; flax was no longer purchased, but rye was no longer sold. Besides, the farmer could not pay more than his capital in salaries, and his capital, far from increasing through the new distribution of land, decreased constantly. The majority of it was tied up in buildings and countless items of equipment that were essential for someone who wanted to do everything. As a result, the supply of labor remained the same, but the means to pay these workers declined and there was of necessity a decrease in wages.

That is a picture of what happens in a nation that isolates itself through a prohibitionist regime. It increases the number of its industries, I know, but it decreases their size; it provides itself, so to say, with a *rotation of industries*[8] that is more complicated but not more fruitful, far from it, since the same capital and workforce have to attack the job in the face of greater natural difficulties. Fixed capital absorbs a greater portion of working capital, that is to say, a greater part of the funds intended for wages. What remains of the fund for wages may well be diversified, but that does not increase the total amount. It is like the water in a lake that people thought they had made more abundant because, having been put into many reservoirs, it touches the ground on more spots and offers a greater surface to the sun. They do not

---

8. The word Bastiat uses in these passages is *sole,* which is a small strip of land traditionally used for crop rotation (*assolement de culture*) in feudal agriculture. He coins another neologism here, namely *assolement industriel* (industrial rotation), suggesting that the protectionist regime creates a kind of "feudalization of industry."

understand that it is precisely for this reason that it is absorbed, evaporated, and lost more quickly.

With a given amount of capital and labor, a quantity of output is created that decreases in proportion to the number of obstacles it encounters. There is no doubt that, where barriers to international trade in each country force this capital and labor to overcome greater difficulties of climate and temperature, the general result is that fewer products are created or, which comes to the same thing, fewer needs of people are satisfied. Well, workers, if there is a general decrease in the number of needs satisfied, how can your share increase? I ask you, would those who are rich, those who make the law, have arranged things so that not only would they suffer their fair share of the total reduction in the needs that can be satisfied, but that even their already reduced portion would decrease still further, they say, by everything that is to be added to yours? Is that possible? Is it credible? Oh! This generosity is suspect and you would be wise to reject it.

13. Theory and Practice

PUBLISHING HISTORY:

Original title: "Théorie, pratique."
Place and date of first publication: No date given. First
    published in book form.
First French edition as book or pamphlet: *Economic Sophisms*
    (First Series) (1846).
Location in Paillottet's edition of *OC:* Vol. 4. *Sophismes
    économiques. Petits pamphlets I,* pp. 79–86.
Previous translations: 1st English ed., 1846; 1st American ed.,
    1848; FEE ed., 1964.

People accuse us, advocates of free trade, of being theoreticians and not taking sufficient account of practical aspects.

"What a terrible prejudice against M. Say,"[1] said M. Ferrier,[2] "is this long

---

[1]. Jean-Baptiste Say (1767–1832) was the leading French political economist in the first third of the nineteenth century. He had the first chair in political economy at the Collège de France. Say is best known for his *Traité d'économie politique* (1803).

[2]. (Bastiat's note) From page 5 of *De l'administration commerciale opposée à l'économie politique.* [Bastiat is quoting from pages v–viii of the second edition of Ferrier's *Du gou-*

line of distinguished administrators, this imposing line of writers, all of whom have seen things differently from him," a point M. Say does not hide from himself! Listen to him:

It has been said, in support of old errors, that it is necessary to have some foundation for the ideas so generally adopted by every nation. Should we not be suspicious of observations and reasoning that overturn what has been taken to be constant up to now, what has been taken to be certain by so many leading figures to whom their enlightenment and intentions give credence? This argument, I admit, is worthy of making a profound impression and might cast doubt on the most incontrovertible points if we had not seen in turn the most erroneous opinions, now generally acknowledged to be such, accepted and professed by everyone for many centuries. It is not so long ago that every nation, from the coarsest to the most enlightened, and all men, from street porters to the most learned philosophers, recognized four elements. Nobody thought of disputing this doctrine, which is nevertheless false, to the extent that today there is no assistant biologist who would not be decried if he considered the earth, water, and fire as elements.

At which point, M. Ferrier makes the following observation:

If M. Say thinks that he has answered the strong objection put forward, he is strangely mistaken. That men, who were nevertheless highly enlightened, have been wrong for several centuries on some point of natural history is understandable and proves nothing. Were water, air, earth, and fire, whether elements or not, any the less useful to man? Errors like this are inconsequential; they do not lead to upheavals; they do not cast doubt into people's minds and above all do not harm any interests, and for this reason they might be allowed to last for thousands of years without mishap. The physical world therefore moves forward as though they did not exist. But can this be

---

vernement considéré dans ses rapports avec le commerce (1821). Ferrier in turn is quoting from Say's *Traité d'économie politique* (Paris: Guillaumin, 1841), p. 43. François Ferrier (1777–1861) was an advocate for protectionism and served as director general of the Customs Administration during the Empire and was a member of the Chamber of Peers during the July Monarchy.]

so for errors that attack the moral world? Can we conceive of an administrative system that is totally false and consequently harmful being followed for several centuries and in several nations with the general consent of all educated men? Could we explain how a system like this could be allied to the increasingly great prosperity of nations? M. Say admits that the argument he is combating is worthy of making a profound impression. Yes, certainly, and this impression remains, for M. Say has argued more in its favor than destroyed it.

Let us listen to M. de Saint-Chamans:[3]

It was scarcely before the middle of the last century, the eighteenth century in which all subjects and every principle without exception were subject to discussion by writers, that these suppliers of *speculative* ideas, applied to everything without being applicable to anything, began to write on the subject of political economy. Before that, there was an unwritten system of political economy that was *practiced* by governments. Colbert, it was said, was its inventor, and it was the rule for all the states in Europe. The strangest thing about it is that it is still so, in spite of anathema and scorn and in spite of the discoveries of the modern school. This system, which our writers called the *mercantile system,* consisted in . . . obstructing, through prohibition or import duties, foreign products that might have ruined our factories by competing with them. . . . This system was declared by economist writers of all schools[4] to be inept, absurd, and likely to impoverish any country; it has been banished from all books, reduced to taking refuge in the *practice* of all peoples, and we cannot conceive that, with regard to the wealth of nations, governments have not drawn their counsel from schol-

---

3. Auguste Saint-Chamans (1777–1860) was a deputy (1824–27) and a Councillor of State. He advocated protectionism and a mercantilist theory of the balance of trade.

4. (Bastiat's note) Could it not be said: "It is a terrible prejudice against MM. Ferrier and Saint-Chamans that economists *of all schools,* that is to say, every man who has studied the question, should have reached the same conclusion, that after all, freedom is better than coercion and that God's laws are wiser than Colbert's." [Bastiat is no doubt thinking of at least two schools of economic thought which advocated free trade and laissez-faire policies, the French physiocrats (such as Quesnay and Turgot) and the Smithian School, which followed the ideas of Adam Smith.]

ars rather than from the *long-standing experience* of a system,
etc.... Above all we cannot conceive that the French government ... is determined to resist the progress of enlightenment
with regard to political economy and to retain the *practice* of
old errors that all of our economist writers have pointed out....
But this is dwelling too much on this mercantile system which
has *only facts* in its favor and which is supported by no writer![5]

Hearing this, will some people not say that when economists call for each
person to have the *free disposal of his property,* they have given birth, like
the followers of Fourier, to a new social order, fanciful, strange, a sort of
phalanstery that is unprecedented in the annals of the human race? It seems
to me that if there is anything in all this that has been invented, contingent,
it is not freedom, but protection; it is not the ability to trade but indeed the
customs service, which is applied to upsetting artificially the natural order
of income.

But it is not a question of comparing or judging the two systems. The
question for the moment is to know which of the two is based on experience.

Thus, you monopolists claim that *facts* are on your side and that we have
only *theories* to support us.

You even flatter yourselves that this long series of public acts, this *old experience* of Europe's that you invoke, appeared imposing to M. Say, and I agree
that he has not refuted you with his customary sagacity. For my part, I do not
yield the domain of *fact* to you, for you have in your support only exceptional
and restrained facts, while we have in opposition the universal facts, the free
and voluntary acts of all men.

What are we saying and what do you say?

We say:

"It is better to purchase from others what it would cost more to produce
ourselves."

You, on the other hand, say:

"It is better to make things ourselves even though it costs less to purchase
them from others."

Well, sirs, leaving theory, demonstration, and reasoning, all things that
appear to nauseate you, to one side, which of these two statements has the
approval of *universal practice* on its side?

5. (Bastiat's note) From page 11 of *Du système de l'impôt* by the vicomte de Saint-
Chamans. [Bastiat is quoting from pp. 11–13 of chap. 2 of this work.]

Just pay a visit to fields, workshops, factories, and stores, look upward, downward, and around you, scrutinize what is being done in your own households, observe your own everyday acts, and tell us what principle is governing all these laborers, workers, entrepreneurs, and merchants. Tell us what your personal *practice* is.

Do farmers make their own clothes? Do tailors produce the grain they consume? Does your housekeeper not stop making bread at home as soon as she finds it cheaper to purchase it from the baker? Do you mend your own boots instead of writing, in order not to pay *tribute* to the cobbler? Does the entire economy of society not rest on the separation of occupations, the division of labor, in a word, on *exchange*? And is trade anything other than this calculation that makes us all, whatever we are, cease direct production when indirect acquisition saves us both time and trouble?

You are thus not men of *practice,* since you cannot show us a single man anywhere in the world who acts in accordance with your principle.

But, you will say, we have never heard of our principle being used as a rule for individual relations. We fully understand that this would disrupt social links and force men to live like snails, each in his shell. We limit ourselves to claiming that it dominates *de facto* the relations established between groups in the human family.

As it happens, this assertion is also false. Families, communes, cantons, départements, and provinces are so many groups which all, without exception, reject *in practice* your principle and have never even given it a thought. All of these obtain by means of exchange what would cost them more to obtain by production. Every nation would do likewise if you did not prevent it *by force*.

It is therefore we who are the men of practice and experience, for in order to combat the prohibition that you have specially placed on some international trade, we base ourselves on the practice and experience of every individual and every group of individuals whose acts are voluntary and thus can be quoted as evidence. You, however, begin by *coercing* and *preventing* and then you seize upon acts that are *forced* or *prohibited* to claim: "You see, practice justifies us!"

You rise up against our *theory* and even against *theory* in general. But when you posit a principle that is antagonistic to ours, did you ever by chance imagine that you were not indulging in *theory?* No, no, cross that out of your papers. You are indulging in theory, just like us, but between yours and ours there is this difference:

Our theory consists only in observing universal *facts,* universal sentiments, universal calculations and procedures, and at the very most classifying them and coordinating them in order to understand them better.

It is so little opposed to practice that it is nothing other than *practice explained.* We watch the actions of men driven by the instinct of self-preservation and progress and what they do freely and voluntarily; it is exactly this that we call political economy or the economics of society. We constantly repeat that each man is in practice an excellent economist, producing or trading depending on whether there is more to gain from trading or producing. Each one through experience teaches himself this science, or rather, science is merely this same experience scrupulously observed and methodically set out.

You, however, make *theory* in the disparaging meaning of the word. You imagine and invent procedures that are not sanctioned by the practice of any living man under the heavens and then you call coercion and prohibition to your assistance. You have indeed to resort *to force* since, as you want men to produce what it is *more advantageous* to purchase, you want them to abandon an *advantage* and you require them to act in accordance with a doctrine that implies a contradiction even on its own terms.

Thus, I challenge you to extend, even in theory, this doctrine that you admit would be absurd in individual relationships, to transactions between families, communes, départements, or provinces. On your own admission, it is applicable only to international relations.

And this is why you are reduced to repeating each day:

"Principles are never absolute. What is *good* in individuals, families, communes, and provinces is *bad* in nations. What is *good* on a small scale, that is to say, purchasing rather than producing when a purchase is more advantageous than production, is the very thing that is *bad* on a large scale; the political economy of individuals is not that of peoples," and more nonsense *ejusdem farinae.*[6]

And what is the reason for all this? Look closer. To prove to us that we the consumers are your property! That we belong to you, body and soul! That you have an exclusive right over our stomachs and limbs! That it is up to you to feed us and clothe us at a price set by you whatever your incompetence, rapacity, or the inferiority of your situation!

---

6. A Latin phrase, *ejusdem farinae,* meaning literally "of the same flour"; in other words, "cut from the same cloth."

No, you are not men of practice; you are men of abstraction . . . and of extortion.

14. A Conflict of Principles

PUBLISHING HISTORY:

Original title: "Conflit de principes."
Place and date of first publication: No date given. First
    published in book form.
First French edition as book or pamphlet: *Economic Sophisms*
    (First Series) (1846).
Location in Paillottet's edition of *OC:* Vol. 4. *Sophismes
    économiques. Petits pamphlets I,* pp. 86–90.
Previous translations: 1st English ed., 1846; 1st American ed.,
    1848; FEE ed., 1964.

There is something that confuses me, and it is this:

Sincere political writers studying the economy of societies from the sole point of view of the producer have reached the following two policies:

"Governments ought to make the consumers who are subject to their laws favor national industry."

"They ought to make foreign consumers subject to their laws in order to make them favor national industry."

The first of these policies is called *Protectionism;* the second is called *opening up foreign markets.*

Both of them are based on the fundamental idea known as the *balance of trade:*

"A people grows poorer when it imports and wealthier when it exports."

For if any purchase from abroad is *tribute paid out* and a loss, it is very simple to restrict and even prohibit imports.

And if any sale abroad is *tribute received* and a profit, it is only natural to create *markets* for yourself, even through force.

Protectionist systems, colonial systems: these are therefore just two aspects of the same theory. *Preventing* our fellow citizens from purchasing from foreigners and *forcing* foreigners to purchase from our fellow citizens are just two consequences of an identical principle.

Well, it is impossible not to recognize that, according to this doctrine, if it is true, general interest is based on *monopoly,* or internal plunder, and on *conquest,* or external plunder.

I enter one of the chalets clinging to the slopes of our Pyrénées.

The head of the household has received only a meager wage for his work. A glacial wind makes his scantily clad children shiver, the fire is out and the table empty. There is wool, wood, and corn on the other side of the mountains, but these goods are forbidden to the family of the poor journeyman, as the other side of the mountains is no longer France. Foreign pine will not cheer the chalet's fireplace, the shepherd's children will not learn the taste of Basque *bread,*[1] and Navarre wool will not warm their frozen limbs. If this is what the general interest wants: fine! But let us agree that in this instance it is contrary to justice.

To command consumers by law, to force them to buy only in the national market, is to infringe on their freedom and to forbid them an activity, trade, that is in no way intrinsically immoral; in a word, it is to do them an *injustice.*

And yet it is necessary, people say, if we do not want national production to halt, if we do not want to deal a deathblow to public prosperity.

Writers of the protectionist school therefore reach the sorry conclusion that there is radical incompatibility between Justice and the Public Interest.

On the other hand, if every nation is interested in *selling* and not *purchasing,* a violent action and reaction will be the natural state of their mutual dealings, for each will seek to impose its products on everyone and everyone will endeavor to reject the products of everyone else.

A sale, in effect, implies a purchase, and since, according to this doctrine, selling is making a profit just as purchasing is making a loss, every international transaction implies the improvement of one nation and the deterioration of another.

On the one hand, however, men are inexorably drawn to whatever brings them a profit, while on the other they instinctively resist anything that harms them, which leads to the conclusion that every nation carries within itself a

---

1. Bastiat uses the term *la méture,* which is a kind of corn bread and is a specialty of the Landes region, where Bastiat grew up. It can also be made with pieces of ham (*la méture au jambon*). Bastiat would have known well the Spanish provinces Biscay and Navarre on the other side of the border where he lived, as he was fluent in Spanish and had once attempted to establish an insurance business in Spain. He may have witnessed personally the smuggling that took place across the border and might have known Béranger's poem "The Smugglers," about smuggling on the Franco-Spanish border. Bastiat knew Béranger and was known to have sung his drinking songs on occasion.

natural impulsion to expansion and a no less natural impulsion to resistance, both of which are equally harmful to everybody else, or in other words, antagonism and war are the *natural* condition of the human race.

Thus, the theory I am discussing can be summarized by these two axioms:

Public Interest is incompatible with Justice within the country.

Public Interest is incompatible with Peace abroad.

Well then! What astonishes and disconcerts me is that a political writer or a statesman, who has sincerely adopted an economic doctrine whose basic ideas are so violently contrary to other incontrovertible principles, can have even one instant of calm and peace of mind.

For my part, I think that, if I had gone into science through this particular door, if I had not clearly perceived that Freedom, Public Interest, Justice, and Peace are things that are not only compatible but closely linked with each other and, so to say, identical, I would endeavor to forget everything I had learnt and tell myself:

"How could God have wished men to achieve prosperity only through injustice and war? How could He have decreed that they should renounce war and injustice only by renouncing their well-being?

"Is the science that has led me to the horrible blasphemy implied by this alternative not misleading me with false flashes of insight, and do I dare to take it on myself to make it the basis for the legislation of a great nation? And when a long line of illustrious scholars has gathered more reassuring results from this same science, to which they have devoted their entire life, when they state that freedom and public interest can be reconciled with justice and peace; that all these great principles follow infinite parallel paths without conflicting with each other for all eternity; do they not have on their side the presumption that results from everything we know of the goodness and wisdom of God as shown in the sublime harmony of physical creation? Am I casually to believe, faced with such beliefs and on the part of so many imposing authorities, that this same God took pleasure in instilling antagonism and discord in the laws governing the moral world? No, no, before holding as certain that all social principles conflict with each other, crash into and neutralize each other, and are locked in an anarchical, eternal, and irremediable struggle; before imposing on my fellow citizens the impious system to which my reasoning has led me, I wish to review the entire chain and reassure myself that there is no point on the route at which I have gone astray."

If, after a sincere examination, redone twenty times, I continued to reach this frightful conclusion, that we have to choose between the Right and the

Good,[2] I would reject science in my discouragement, I would sink into willful ignorance, and above all I would decline any participation in the affairs of my country, leaving men of another stamp the burden and responsibility of such a painful choice.

15. More Reciprocity

PUBLISHING HISTORY:

> Original title: "Encore la réciprocité."
> Place and date of first publication: No date given. First
>   published in book form.
> First French edition as book or pamphlet: *Economic Sophisms*
>   (First Series) (1846).
> Location in Paillottet's edition of *OC:* Vol. 4. *Sophismes
>   économiques. Petits pamphlets I,* pp. 90–92.
> Previous translations: 1st English ed., 1846; 1st American ed.,
>   1848; FEE ed., 1964.

As M. de Saint-Cricq said: "Are we sure that foreigners will purchase as much from us as they sell to us?"

M. de Dombasle says: "What reason have we to believe that English producers will come to us rather than any other nation in the world in search of the products they may need and products whose value is equivalent to their exports to France?"

I am amazed that men who above all call themselves *practical* reason in a way divorced from all practicality!

In practice, is there one trading operation in a hundred, a thousand, or perhaps even ten thousand that is a direct exchange of one product for another? Since money first came into the world, has any farmer ever said to himself: "I want to buy shoes, hats, advice, and lessons only from a shoemaker, milliner, lawyer, or teacher who will buy wheat from me for exactly the equivalent value"? And why would nations impose this obstacle on themselves?

How are things really done?

Let us imagine a nation that has no foreign trade. One man has produced

2. The phrase Bastiat uses is *le Bien et le Bon,* which is difficult to translate. Given the context of what Bastiat is arguing, one might translate it as "the morally good and the materially good (or useful)."

wheat. He sells it in the national market at the highest price he can obtain and receives in exchange . . . what? Écus,[1] that is to say, money orders, goods which can be split up indefinitely, which will permit him to take from the national market the goods which he needs or wants at a time he judges suitable and up to the amount he has at hand.[2] All said and done, at the end of the operation he will have withdrawn from the total the exact equivalent of what he has put into it and in value, *his consumption will be exactly the same as his production.*

If this nation's external trade is free it is no longer in the *national* flow of goods but in the *general* flow of goods that each person places his products, and it is from that flow that he withdraws his consumption. He does not have to worry whether what he puts into this general circulation is bought by a fellow citizen or a foreigner, whether the money orders he receives come from a Frenchman or an Englishman, whether the objects for which he later trades these *money payments,* according to his needs, have been made on this or that side of the Rhine or the Pyrénées. What remains true is that there is for each individual an exact balance between what he puts in and what he takes out of the great common reservoir, and if this is true for each individual, it is also true for the nation as a whole.

The only difference between the two cases is that, in the second, each is facing a market that is wider for his sales and purchases and has consequently more opportunity to do well on both fronts.

The following objection is made: If everyone joins forces in order not to withdraw from the circulation the products of a given individual, he will not be able to withdraw anything in turn from the overall flow. This is the same for a nation.

Reply: If this nation cannot withdraw anything from the general circulation, it will not put anything into it either; it will work for its own account. It will be forced to submit to what you wish to impose on it at the outset, that is to say, *isolation.*

And that will be the ideal of the prohibitionist regime.

Is it not ludicrous that you are already inflicting this regime on the nation for fear that it will run the risk of reaching it one day without you?

1. An *écu* was a gold coin. See "French currency" in appendix 3, "Economic Policy and Taxation."

2. The technical commercial term Bastiat uses is *jusqu'à due concurrence,* which can mean in commercial transactions "proportionally" or "up to the amount of."

16. Blocked Rivers Pleading in Favor of the Prohibitionists

PUBLISHING HISTORY:

Original title: "Les fleuves obstrués plaidant pour les
prohibitionists."
Place and date of first publication: No date given. First
published in book form.
First French edition as book or pamphlet: *Economic Sophisms*
(First Series) (1846).
Location in Paillottet's edition of *OC:* Vol. 4. *Sophismes
économiques. Petits pamphlets I,* pp. 92–93.
Previous translations: 1st English ed., 1846; 1st American ed.,
1848; FEE ed., 1964.

A few years ago I was in Madrid.[1] I went to the cortès.[2] They were discussing a treaty with Portugal on improving the bed of the Douro.[3] A deputy stood up and said: "If the Douro is channeled, transport will cost less. Portuguese grain will be sold cheaper in Castile and will provide formidable competition for our *national production.* I reject the project unless the ministers undertake to raise customs duties so as to reestablish the balance." The assembly had no answer to this argument.

Three months later I was in Lisbon. The same question was put before the Senate. A noble hidalgo[4] said: "M. President, the project is absurd. You are putting guards at huge expense on the banks of the Douro to prevent the invasion of grain from Castile into Portugal and, at the same time, you want, also at huge expense, to make this invasion easier. Let the Douro be passed to our sons in the same state as our fathers left it to us."

Later, when it was a question of improving the Garonne,[5] I remembered

1. Bastiat's family had business interests in Spain. In 1840 he traveled to Spain and Portugal with the intention of setting up an insurance business. This did not come to pass.

2. The Cortes Generales are the legislative body which rules Spain. Liberal deputies enacted a new, more liberal constitution in 1812.

3. The Douro River flows across north central Spain and Portugal toward its mouth at Porto, on the Atlantic coast. It flows through a major wine-growing region.

4. A member of the lower nobility.

5. The Garonne river has its source in the Pyrénées mountains on the border between Spain and France and flows northward through the city of Toulouse before reaching Bordeaux on the coast. Before he became interested in free trade, Bastiat wrote on im-

the arguments of the Iberian speakers and said to myself: "If the deputies in Toulouse were as good economists as those from Palencia and the representatives of Bordeaux were as skilled logicians as those of Oporto,[6] the Garonne would surely be left 'to sleep to the pleasing sound of its tilting urn,'[7] for the channeling of the Garonne would encourage the *invasion* of products from Toulouse to the detriment of Bordeaux and the *flooding* of products from Bordeaux to the detriment of Toulouse."

17. A Negative Railway

PUBLISHING HISTORY:

Original title: "Un chemin de fer negative."
Place and date of first publication: No date given. First
    published in book form.
First French edition as book or pamphlet: *Economic Sophisms*
    (First Series) (1846).
Location in Paillottet's edition of *OC:* Vol. 4. *Sophismes*
    économiques. Petits pamphlets I, pp. 93–94.
Previous translations: 1st English ed., 1846; 1st American ed.,
    1848; FEE ed., 1964.

---

proving the rivers and building canals in his local area. See "The Canal beside the Adour" (1837), in CW4 (forthcoming).

6. Palencia is a Spanish city on a tributary of the Douro river; Oporto is a Portuguese city at the mouth of the Douro.

7. Bastiat misquotes some lines from Nicolas Boileau-Despréaux's (1636–1711) poem celebrating the crossing of the Rhine River by the French army in 1672: "At the foot of Mount Adule, between a thousand reeds / The tranquil Rhine, proud of the progress of its waters, / Supported with one hand on its sloping urn, / Sleeps to the flattering sounds of its new wave, / When a cry, suddenly followed by a thousand cries / Comes from a calm so soft to take its spirits away" (Boileau-Despréaux, "Au Roi," in *Œuvres de Boileau Despréaux,* p. 136). Bastiat misquotes it as "Dormir au bruit flatteur de son urne penchante," conflating two adjacent lines of the poem. This could be a mistake or it could be deliberate. The word *urne* has another meaning, namely a ballot box in which votes were deposited. Since in the previous passage he was criticizing elected politicians for their contradictory policies in wanting to both improve the transportation of goods by river by digging canals and at the same time to hamper the transportation of goods by river by setting up customs barriers, he might be having a joke at their expense by rewriting this famous poem. It might now read: "to sleep to the flattering sounds of its bent ballot box."

I have said that when, unfortunately, we took the point of view of the producers' interest, we could not fail to clash with the general interest,[1] since producers, as such, demand only effort, needs, and obstacles.

I have found a remarkable example of this in a Bordeaux journal.

M. Simiot[2] asks himself this question:

Should the Paris-to-Spain railway be offered to Bordeaux with a complete fracture in the line?[3]

He answered it in the positive with a host of reasons that it is not my place to examine but which include the following:

The railway between Paris and Bayonne should be completely broken in two[4] at Bordeaux so that goods and passengers forced to stop in the town would contribute revenue to boatmen, packmen, commission agents, shippers, hoteliers, etc.

It is clear that this is once again a case of the interest of producers being put ahead of the interest of consumers.

But if Bordeaux can be allowed to profit from this break in the line, and if this is in keeping with the public interest, Angoulême, Poitiers, Tours, Orleans, and more, all intermediary points, Ruffec, Châtellerault, etc., etc., must also demand breaks in the line in the general interest, that is of course in the

---

1. In a letter of 19 May 1846 addressed to a commission of the Chamber of Deputies which was looking into the route that should be taken by a new railway from Bordeaux to Bayonne, Bastiat argues that any political decision on routes is bound to upset somebody: the shortest route is the cheapest to build, but a winding route will serve the needs of more people. See also "On the Bordeaux to Bayonne Railway Line" (CW1, pp. 312–16).

2. Alexandre Étienne Simiot (1807–79) was a member of the Municipal Council of the Gironde and one of the leading figures in local democratic politics. He wrote *Gare du chemin de fer de Paris à Bordeaux* (impr. de Durand, 1846).

3. Bastiat here uses the medical term *La solution de la continuité,* which is used to describe, somewhat counterintuitively, a rupture, fracture, or complete break in a vessel or a bone, such as the skull. As one medical dictionary put it, the expression should really be *la dissolution de la continuité* (the rupturing or breaking of continuity). See the many references in Vidal, *Traité de pathologie externe et de médecine opératoire.*

4. Bastiat uses the term *la lacune* (break or gap) here. It is in the medical sense noted above that one should understand Bastiat's use of *la lacune* to mean not a "stop" at a station to let passengers on or off but the literal fracturing or breaking of the railway into two separate and discontinuous pieces, which would require the transshipping of passengers and luggage from one railway to the next in order for them to continue their journey. This would sometimes occur at the border between states. Fifty years after Bastiat wrote these lines, Mark Twain related his experience in traveling by train from Sydney to Melbourne in his travel book *Following the Equator* (1898). See appendix 5 for details.

interest of national production, since the more breaks there are, the more consignments, commissions, and transshipping there will be all along the line. With this system, we will have created a railway made up of consecutive segments, *a negative railway.*

Whether the protectionists want this or not, it is no less certain that the *principle of trade restriction* is the same as the *principle of breaks in the line:* the sacrifice of the consumer to the producer and of the end to the means.

18. There Are No Absolute Principles

PUBLISHING HISTORY:

Original title: "Il n'y a pas de principes absolus."
Place and date of first publication: No date given. First
   published in book form.
First French edition as book or pamphlet: *Economic Sophisms*
   (First Series) (1846).
Location in Paillottet's edition of *OC:* Vol. 4. *Sophismes*
   économiques. Petits pamphlets I, pp. 94–97.
Previous translations: 1st English ed., 1846; 1st American ed.,
   1848; FEE ed., 1964.

You cannot be too surprised at the ease with which men resign themselves to ignoring what they need most to know, and you can be sure that they are determined to fall asleep in their ignorance once they have come to the point of proclaiming this axiom: There are no absolute principles.

You enter the legislative chamber. The question before the house is to ascertain whether the law will forbid or free up international trade.

A deputy stands up and says:

"If you allow this trade, foreigners will flood you with their products, the English with cloth, the Belgians with coal, the Spanish with wool, the Italians with silk, the Swiss with cattle, the Swedish with iron, and the Prussians with wheat, so that no industry will be possible in this country."

Another replies:

"If you forbid this trade, the various benefits that nature has showered on each geographical region will be nonexistent for you. You will not share in the mechanical skills of the English, the richness of the Belgian mines, the fertility of Polish soil, the fruitfulness of Swiss pastures, the cheapness of Spanish labor, or the heat of the Italian climate, and you will have to satisfy your demand with goods produced under awkward and difficult conditions instead of with goods obtained by trading with those who can produce things more easily."

It is certain that one of these deputies is wrong. But which one? It is nevertheless worthwhile taking the trouble to find out, as it is not just a matter of opinion. You are faced with two paths and you have to choose; and one inevitably leads to *poverty*.

To escape from this quandary, people say: There are no absolute principles.

This axiom, so fashionable today, in addition to nodding to laziness, is also suited to ambition.

If the theory of prohibition won, or else if the doctrine of freedom triumphed, a very small law would encompass our entire economic code. In the first case, it would say: *All foreign trade is forbidden* and in the second: *All foreign trade is free,* and many leading figures would lose their importance.

But if trade does not have its own proper nature, if it is not governed by any natural law, if it is capriciously useful or disastrous, if it does not find its stimulus in the good it does and its limit in the good it ceases to do, and if its effects cannot be appreciated by those who carry it out; in a word, if there are no absolute principles, oh! It would then be necessary to weigh, balance, and regulate transactions, to equalize the conditions of labor, and to set the level of profits; a colossal task, but one well suited to be given to those who enjoy high remuneration and wide influence.

On entering Paris, which I had come to visit, I said to myself: Here there are a million human beings who would all die in a few days if supplies of all sorts did not flood into this huge metropolis. The mind boggles when it tries to assess the huge variety of objects that have to enter through its gates tomorrow if the lives of its inhabitants are not to be snuffed out in convulsions of famine, uprisings, and pillage. And in the meantime everyone is asleep, without their peaceful slumber being troubled for an instant by the thought of such a frightful prospect. On the other hand, eighty départements[1] have worked today without being in concert and without agreement to supply Paris. How does it happen that every day what is needed and no more or less is brought to this gigantic market? What is thus the ingenious and secret power that presides over the astonishing regularity of such complicated movements, a regularity in which everyone has such blind faith, although well-being and life depend on it? This power is an *absolute principle,* the prin-

---

1. In Bastiat's day there were eighty-six départements in France.

ciple of free commerce.[2] We have faith in this intimate light that Providence has placed in the hearts of all men to whom it has entrusted the indefinite preservation and progress of our species, *self-interest,* for we must give it its name, that is so active, vigilant, and farsighted when it is free to act. Where would you be, you inhabitants of Paris, if a minister took it into his head to substitute the arrangements he had thought up, however superior they are thought to be, for this power? Or if he took it into his head to subject this stupendous mechanism to his supreme management, to gather together all these economic activities in his own hands, to decide by whom, how, or under what conditions each object has to be produced, transported, traded, and consumed? Oh! Although there are a good many causes of suffering within your city, although destitution, despair, and perhaps starvation are causing more tears to flow than your ardent charity can stem, it is probable or, I dare to say, even certain, that the arbitrary intervention of the government would infinitely increase these sufferings and extend to you all the misfortunes that are only affecting a small number of your fellow citizens.

Well then! Why, when we have faith in a principle when it relates to domestic transactions, do we not have the same faith in this principle when it is applied to international transactions, which are certainly fewer in number and less difficult and complicated? And, if it is not necessary for the Prefecture of Paris to regulate our industries, balance our opportunities, profits, and losses, concern itself with the depletion of our money, and equalize the conditions governing our labor in domestic commerce, why is it necessary for the customs service to aspire to exercise protective action, which is beyond its fiscal mission, with regard to our foreign commerce?

19. National Independence

PUBLISHING HISTORY:

Original title; "Indépendance nationale."
Place and date of first publication: No date given. First
    published in book form.
First French edition as book or pamphlet: *Economic Sophisms*
    (First Series) (1846).

2. Bastiat uses a slightly different expression here. Instead of the usual *la liberté des échanges* (free trade), he uses *la liberté des transactions,* which could mean "freedom of commerce."

Location in Paillottet's edition of *OC:* Vol. 4. *Sophismes
économiques. Petits pamphlets I,* pp. 97–99.
Previous translations: 1st English ed., 1846; 1st American ed.,
1848; FEE ed., 1964.

Among the arguments put forward in favor of protectionism, we should not forget the one based on *national independence.*

"What will we do in case of war," people say, "if we are subject to England's discretion with regard to iron and coal?"

Monopolists in England, for their part, unfailingly proclaim:

"What would become of Great Britain in time of war if she were dependent on France for her food?"

We tend to disregard one fact, which is that this type of dependence resulting from trade and commercial transactions is *mutual.* We cannot be dependent on foreigners without these foreigners being dependent on us. This is the very essence of *society.* Breaking off natural relationships does not make us independent, but isolated.

And note this well: we isolate ourselves because of an expectation of war, but the very act of isolating ourselves is the first step to war. It makes it easier, less of a burden, and, because of this, less unpopular. If nations are constant markets for each other, if their relationships cannot be broken off without inflicting on them the twin suffering of deprivation and oversupply, they will no longer need the powerful navies that are ruining them and the massive armies now crushing them, the peace of the world will not be compromised by the caprices of M. Thiers[1] or Lord Palmerston,[2] and war will disappear for lack of incentive, resources, reasons, pretexts, and popular favor.[3]

---

1. Adolphe Thiers (1797–1877) was a lawyer, historian, politician, and journalist who served briefly as Prime Minister and Minister of Foreign Affairs in 1836 and 1840.

2. Henry John Temple, third Viscount Palmerston (1784–1860) was a British politician and leader of the Whig party. He was Minister of Foreign Affairs (1830–41 and 1846–50) and then Prime Minister during the Crimean War (1854–56).

3. These two paragraphs are a nice summary of the views held by Richard Cobden and Bastiat regarding the link between free trade and peace. Cobden and Bastiat frequently corresponded on this topic and visited each other when they attended conferences organized by the Friends of Peace. See the entry for "International Congress of the Friends of Peace (Paris, August 1849)," in the Glossary of Subjects and Terms; "Bastiat's Speech on 'Disarmament and Taxes' (August 1849)," in Addendum: Additional Material by Bastiat; and "Standing Armies, Militias, and the Utopia of Peace," in appendix 1, "Further Aspects of Bastiat's Life and Thought."

I am fully aware that I will be blamed (for this is the current fashion) for resting fraternity between nations on self-interest, vile and prosaic interest. People would prefer fraternity to be rooted in charity and love, with even a little self-sacrifice, and in hurting men's material well-being, to possess the merit of generous sacrifice.

When will we ever be rid of this puerile moralism? When will we finally banish hypocrisy from science? When will we drop this sickening contradiction between our writings and our actions? We boo at, we shout down *self-interest,* that is to say, what is useful and good (since to say that all nations are interested in a thing is to say that this thing is intrinsically good), as though self-interest was not a necessary, eternal, and indestructible motive to which Providence has entrusted human progress! As if we were all angels of disinterestedness? As if the public was not beginning to see, and with disgust, that this affected language is blackening the very pages for which the public is expected to pay so dearly? Oh, such affectation! This is really the disease of this century.

What! Because well-being and peace are closely allied, because God was pleased to establish this fine harmony in the moral world, you do not want me to admire and adore his decrees and accept with gratitude laws that make justice a condition of happiness? You do not want peace unless it is to the detriment of well-being, and freedom weighs heavy on you because it does not impose sacrifice on you? And, if self-sacrifice has such attraction for you, what stops you including it in your private actions? Society would be grateful to you if you did, for at least someone would reap the benefit from it, but to wish to impose it on humanity on principle is the height of absurdity, for the self-sacrifice of all is the sacrifice of all and constitutes misfortune raised to the status of a theory.

But thank heaven we can write and read a great number of these ranting speeches without the world ceasing to obey its driving force, which is *self-interest,* like it or not.

After all, it is rather strange to see sentiments of the most sublime self-denial invoked in support of plunder itself. This is what this ostentatious disinterestedness leads to! These men, who are so poetically delicate that they do not want peace itself if it is based on men's vile *self-interests,* are putting their hands into other people's pockets, especially those who are poor, for what article of the tariff protects the poor? Yes, sirs, do whatever you like with what belongs to you, but likewise let us do what we want with the fruit from the sweat of our brows, to use it ourselves or to trade it. Make speeches on self-renunciation, for that is fine, but at the same time at least be honest.

20. Human Labor and Domestic Labor

PUBLISHING HISTORY:

Original title: "Travail humain, travail national."
Place and date of first publication: No date given. First
published in book form.
First French edition as book or pamphlet: *Economic Sophisms*
(First Series) (1846).
Location in Paillottet's edition of *OC:* Vol. 4. *Sophismes
économiques. Petits pamphlets I,* pp. 100–105.
Previous translations: 1st English ed., 1846; 1st American ed.,
1848; FEE ed., 1964.

Smash the machines,[1] reject foreign goods; these are two acts generated by the same doctrine.

We see men who clap when a great invention is revealed to the world and who nevertheless support protectionism. Such men are very inconsistent!

What is their objection to free trade? That it results in our having things made by foreigners who are more skillful or better situated than we, which otherwise we would produce ourselves. In a word, it is accused of damaging *domestic labor.*

By the same token, should these critics not be blaming machines for accomplishing through natural agents a production, which, without them, would fall to manual effort and consequently for damaging *human labor?*

Foreign workers who are better situated than French ones are veritable economic machines that crush the latter through their competition. Similarly, a machine that carries out an operation at a lower cost than a given number of hands is, with regard to this labor, a genuine *foreign competitor* that paralyzes them with its competition.

If therefore it is appropriate to protect *domestic labor* against competition from *foreign labor,* it is no less so to protect *human labor* against competition from *mechanical labor.*

---

1. This is a reference to the Luddites, who were members of a movement in the early nineteenth century in England who protested the introduction of mechanized weaving machines, believing that they would put handloom weavers out of work. They were active during 1811–13 before being suppressed by the government in a mass trial in 1813. They took their name from a weaver named Ned Ludd, who smashed machines in 1779. See another reference to smashing machines (Luddism) in ES3 24, p. 391.

So, if he has an ounce of logic in his brain, anyone who supports a protectionist regime should not stop at forbidding foreign products; he ought to forbid even more the products of the shuttle and the plough.

And this is why I much prefer the logic of those men who, speaking out against the *invasion* of goods from far distant lands, at least have the courage to speak out as well against *overproduction* due to the inventive power of the human mind.

One of these is M. de Saint-Chamans. "One of the strongest arguments," he says, "against free trade and the overuse of machines, is that many workers are deprived of work either by foreign competition that closes factories down or by equipment that takes the place of men in the workshops." (*On the Tax System*, page 438.)[2]

M. de Saint-Chamans has accurately seen the analogy, let us go further, the identity existing between *imports* and *machines.* This is why he forbids them both; and truly, there is some pleasure in facing intrepid debaters who, even when they are wrong, take their line of reasoning to its limit.

But look at the difficulty in store for them!

While it is *a priori* true that the domains of *invention* and *labor* can expand only at the expense of one another, it is in those countries in which there are the most *machines,* for example, in Lancashire, that we ought to see the fewest *workers.* And if, on the contrary, we see *in fact* that machines and workers coexist to a greater degree in rich nations than in uncivilized ones, we have to conclude that these two forces are not mutually exclusive.

I cannot explain to myself how a thinking soul can have a moment's rest when faced with this dilemma:

Either the inventions of man do not damage his labor, as the general facts demonstrate, since there are more of both among the English and French than among the Hurons and Cherokees, and, in this case, I have gone wrong, although I do not know either where or how I have gone astray. I would be committing treason against humanity if I introduced my mistake into the legislation of my country.

Or the discoveries of the human mind reduce manual labor, as certain facts appear to indicate, since every day I see a machine being substituted for twenty or one hundred workers, in which case I am obliged to identify a flagrant, eternal, and incurable antithesis between man's intellectual and physical power, between his progress and his well-being. I cannot refrain

2. Bastiat is referring to Saint-Chamans's *Du système d'impôt.*

from saying that the author of man was bound to give him the gift of either brain or brawn, either moral strength or brute force, and that in the event he has played a trick on him by conferring on him, simultaneously, mutually destructive powers.

This is a pressing difficulty. Well, do you know how to solve it? By this strange maxim:

In political economy, there are no absolute principles.

In common, intelligible parlance, this means:

"I do not know where truth or falsehood lies and am ignorant of what constitutes general good or evil. I do not let this trouble me. The immediate effect of each measure on my personal well-being is the sole law I agree to acknowledge."

There are no principles! This is as though you were saying: "There are no facts, for principles are only formulae that sum up an entire order of well-known facts."

Machines and imports certainly have effects. These effects are either good or bad. People can have differing opinions in this respect. But whichever one you adopt is formulated using one of these two *principles:* machines are good or machines are bad. Imports are advantageous or imports are harmful. But to say *there are no principles* is certainly the lowest degree of humiliation to which the human mind can descend, and I admit that I blush for my country when I hear such a monstrous heresy enunciated before the French Chambers with their assent, that is to say, before and with the assent of the elite of our fellow citizens, and all this to justify themselves for imposing on us laws in total ignorance.

But in the end, I will be told, destroy the *sophism.* Prove that machines do not damage *human labor* and that imports do not damage *domestic labor.*

In an essay of the present kind, such proofs could not be very detailed. My aim is rather to establish the difficulties than to solve them and to arouse reflection rather than to satisfy it. No convictions are ever firmly anchored in the human mind other than those that result from its own work. I will nevertheless endeavor to set it along this path.

What misleads the opponents of imports and machines is that they judge them by their immediate and transitory effects instead of going to their general and definitive consequences.[3]

---

3. Bastiat is here stating in a more roundabout way what later he would come to call the "seen" and the "unseen," which he was to develop more explicitly in WSWNS.

The immediate effect of an ingenious machine is to render a certain amount of manual labor superfluous for a given result. However, its action does not in the slightest stop there. For the very reason that this given result is achieved with less effort, it is made available to the public at a lower price, and the sum of the savings thus realized by all purchasers enables them to satisfy other wants, that is to say, to encourage manual labor in general by precisely the amount saved by those manual laborers working in the recently improved industry. In short, the level of work has not decreased, although that of satisfaction has been increased.

Let us use an example to make this set of effects clearer.

Let us imagine that 10 million hats costing 15 francs are consumed in France. This provides the hat industry with a turnover of 150 million. A machine is invented that enables the hats to be sold at 10 francs. The turnover for this industry is reduced to 100 million, assuming that consumption does not increase. However, the 50 million is not lost to *human labor* for all that. Having been saved by the purchasers of hats, it will be used to satisfy other needs and consequently to remunerate the entire industrial system by the same figure. With the 5 francs he has saved, Jean will buy a pair of shoes, Jacques a book, Jérôme an item of furniture, etc. The human labor, taken as a whole, will thus continue to be encouraged up to a level of 150 million; this sum will provide the same number of hats as before, plus all the other satisfactions corresponding to the 50 million that the machine will have saved. These satisfactions are the net product that France would have gained from the invention. This is a free gift, a tribute that man's genius has imposed on nature. We do not deny that, during the transformation, a certain mass of labor will have been *displaced,* but we cannot agree that it has been destroyed or even diminished.

This is also true for imports. Let us return to the hypothesis.

France manufactured 10 million hats at a cost price of 15 francs. Foreigners invaded our market, supplying us with hats at 10 francs. I say that *domestic labor* will not be decreased in the slightest.

For it will have to produce up to 100 million to pay for 10 million hats at 10 francs.

And then each purchaser will have 5 francs left that he has saved on each hat, or a total of 50 million that he will pay for other pleasures, that is to say, for other things produced by labor.

Therefore the total amount of labor will remain the same as it was and the additional pleasures, representing the 50 million saved on the hats, will be the net profit from the imports or from free trade.

And people must not try to terrify us with the picture of the suffering that, according to this reasoning, will accompany the displacement of labor.

For if protectionism had never occurred, labor would have rearranged itself in line with the laws of trade and no displacement would have taken place.

If, on the other hand, protectionism has led to an artificial and unproductive structure of labor, it would be this, and not freedom, that is responsible for the inevitable displacement in the transition from bad to good.

Unless it is claimed that, because an abuse cannot be destroyed without upsetting those who benefit from it, its existence for just a moment ensures that it will last forever.

21. Raw Materials

PUBLISHING HISTORY:

Original title: "Matières premières."
Place and date of first publication: No date given. First
    published in book form.
First French edition as book or pamphlet: *Economic Sophisms*
    (First Series) (1846).
Location in Paillottet's edition of *OC:* Vol. 4. *Sophismes
    économiques. Petits pamphlets I,* pp. 105–15.
Previous translations: 1st English ed., 1846; 1st American ed.,
    1848; FEE ed., 1964.

It is said: "The most profitable of all trades is the one in which manufactured goods are exchanged for raw materials. For the raw materials supply *domestic labor.*"

And from this the following conclusion is drawn:

That the best customs law would be the one that did the most to facilitate the importation of *raw materials* and which would put the greatest number of obstacles in the path of goods which had undergone some level of manufacture.[1]

1. This was in fact the purpose of the revision of French tariff policy which took place in the first years of the French Revolution with the law of August 1791. Most prohibitions on imported goods were abolished, tariffs were abolished on the primary products used by French manufacturers and foodstuffs for consumers, and tariffs on foreign manufactured goods were lowered to 20–25 percent by value.

In political economy, there is no sophism so widespread as this one. It is the talk of not only the protectionist school but also and above all the allegedly liberal school, and this is a trying circumstance, for the worst thing for a good cause is not to be competently attacked but to be badly defended.

Commercial freedom will probably suffer the fate of all freedoms; it will be introduced into our laws only once it has gained possession of our minds. But if it is true that a reform has to be generally understood in order to be solidly established, it follows that nothing can delay it more than anything which misleads public opinion; and what is more likely to mislead it than articles that demand freedom by using the doctrines of monopoly to support them?

A few years ago, three large cities in France, Lyons, Bordeaux, and Le Havre, rose up against the protectionist regime.[2] The country and the whole of Europe were moved at seeing what they took to be the flag of freedom being raised. Alas! It was still the flag of monopoly! A monopoly that was a little more sly and a lot more absurd than the one they seemed to want to overthrow. Thanks to the *sophism* which I will attempt to unveil, the petitioners did nothing more than reproduce the doctrine on the *protection of domestic labor,* while adding one more inconsistency to it.

What in fact is protectionism? Let us listen to M. de Saint-Cricq:

"Labor constitutes the wealth of a people, since it alone creates the physical things that our needs call for, and universal prosperity consists in the abundance of such things." Such is the crux of the argument.

"But it is necessary for this abundance to be the product of the nation's activity. If it were the product of foreign activity, national output would come to a sudden stop." Here is the error. (*See the preceding sophism.*)[3]

"What therefore should an agricultural and manufacturing country do? Keep its market for the products of its own territory and industry." Here is the aim.

"And to do this, restrict through duties and prohibit if necessary the products of the territory and industry of other peoples." Here are the means.

Let us compare these arrangements with those of the petition from Bordeaux.

It divided goods into three classes.

2. This took place in 1834, and Bastiat commented on their petition in a local newspaper. See "Reflections on the Petitions from Bordeaux, Le Havre, and Lyon Relating to the Customs Service" (CW2, pp. 1–9).

3. ES1 20.

"The first covers foodstuffs and raw materials that are devoid of any human labor. In principle, a wise economy would require this class to be exempt from taxes." Here, no labor, no protection.

"The second is made up of goods which have undergone some *processing*. This processing allows us *to impose some duty on it*." Here protection starts because, according to the petitioners, here begins *domestic labor*.

"The third covers finished goods which cannot be used in any way in domestic production; we consider these to be the most liable to taxes." Here labor, and protection with it, reach their peak.

As we can see, the petitioners claimed that foreign labor damages domestic labor. This is the *error* of the protectionist regime.

They demanded that the French market be reserved for French *labor;* that is the *aim* of the protectionist regime.

They demanded that foreign labor be subject to restrictions and taxes. That is the *means* of the protectionist regime.

So what difference can we therefore discern between the petitioners from Bordeaux and the leader of the protectionist chorus?

Just one: the wider or narrower range of interpretation of the meaning of the word *labor*.

M. de Saint-Cricq extends it to everything. He therefore wants to *protect* everything.

"Labor constitutes the *entire* wealth of a nation," he says, "protecting agriculture, the *entire* agricultural sector, manufacturing, the *entire* manufacturing sector, this is the cry that will always echo around this Chamber."

The petitioners consider manufacturing alone as constituting labor; for this reason they accord only this sector the favor of protection.

"Raw materials are *devoid of any human labor*. In principle they should not be taxed. Manufactured goods can no longer be used for further productive activity in the domestic market; we consider them to be the most proper to be subject to taxes."

It is not a question here of examining whether protection for domestic labor is reasonable. M. de Saint-Cricq and the petitioners from Bordeaux agree on this point and we, as has been seen in previous chapters, differ from both in this respect.

The question is to know who is giving the proper meaning to the word *labor,* M. de Saint-Cricq or the petitioners from Bordeaux.

Well, on this terrain, it has to be said that M. de Saint-Cricq is right a thousand times, for the following is the dialogue that they might have with each other:

M. de Saint-Cricq: "You agree that domestic labor has to be protected. You agree that no foreign products can be introduced into our market without destroying an equal amount of our domestic production. The only thing is that you claim that there are a host of products that contain *value*, since they sell, and which are nevertheless *devoid of any human labor*. And you list, among other things, wheat, flour, meat, cattle, bacon, salt, iron, copper, lead, coal, wool, skins, seed, etc.

"If you prove to me that the *value* of these things is not due to labor, I will agree that they do not need to be protected.

"However, if I also demonstrate to you that there is as much labor involved in one hundred francs' worth of wool as in 100 francs' worth of cloth, you will have to admit that protection is due as much to the one as to the other.

"Now, why is this bag of wool *worth* 100 francs? Is it not because that is its cost price? And is its cost price anything other than what has to be paid in wages, earnings, and the costs of manpower, labor, and interest to all the laborers and capital providers who contributed to producing the object?"

The Petitioners: "It is true that you might be right with regard to wool. But is a sack of wheat, an ingot of iron, or a quintal[4] of coal the product of labor? Is it not nature that has created them?"

M. de Saint-Cricq: "There is no doubt that nature has created the elements of all these things, but it is labor that has created their value. I myself was mistaken when I said that labor *creates* physical objects, and this flawed expression has led me into many other errors. It is not in man's power to *create* and to make something out of nothing, any more for manufacturers than for farmers; if by *production* we meant *creation*, all of our projects would be nonproductive and yours, as traders, more so than all the others, except perhaps for mine.

"A farmer, therefore, cannot claim to have *created* wheat, but he can claim to have created its *value*, by this I mean to have transformed into wheat, through his own labor and that of his servants, cow herders, and harvesters, substances which did not resemble it in the slightest. In addition, what do the millers do who convert it into flour, or the bakers who bake it into bread?

"In order for men to be able to clothe themselves in woolen cloth, a host of operations is necessary. Before any human labor intervenes, the genuine *raw materials* of this product are air, water, heat, gaslight, and the salts that

---

4. For a description of "quintal," see "French Weights and Measures," in appendix 3, "Economic Policy and Taxation."

have to go to making it up. There are the *raw materials* that are genuinely *devoid of any human labor,* since they have no *value* and I do not envisage protecting them. However, an initial act of *labor* converts these substances into fodder, a second into wool, a third into yarn, a fourth into cloth, and a fifth into garments. Who would dare to say that everything in this operation is not *labor,* from the first cut of the plough that starts it to the last stitch that terminates it?

"And because, for greater speed and perfection in the accomplishment of the final operation, a garment, the labor is divided among several classes of industrious workers,[5] do you want to establish, through arbitrary distinction, that the order of carrying out of this labor is the sole basis for their importance, so that the first does not even merit the appellation of labor and the last, labor par excellence, is the only one worthy of the favors of protection?"

The Petitioners: "Yes, we are beginning to see that wheat is not, any more than wool, altogether *devoid of any human labor,* but at least the farmer has not, like the manufacturer, done everything himself or with the assistance of his laborers; nature has helped him and if there is labor, everything in wheat is not labor."

M. de Saint-Cricq: "But all its *value* is labor. I agree that nature has contributed to the physical forming of the grain. I even agree that this is exclusively its own work, but you must admit that I have forced it to do so through my labor, and when I sell you wheat, you have to note this clearly, I am not making you pay for *the labor of nature* but for *mine.*

"And, in your opinion, manufactured goods would not be the products of labor either. Are manufacturers not assisted by nature as well? Do they not use the weight of the atmosphere through their steam engines just as I use its humidity when plowing? Have they created the laws of gravity, the transmission of force, or the nature of chemical bonding?"

The Petitioners: "Very well, we agree for wool, but coal is certainly the work and the sole work of nature. It is truly *devoid of any human labor.*"

M. de Saint-Cricq: "Yes, nature has made coal, but *labor has created its value.* Coal had no value for millions of years when it was buried and unknown one hundred feet underground. Men had to go to look for it: that is *labor.* It had to be taken to market: that is another form of *labor,* and once

---

5. Here Bastiat uses the term, coined by Charles Dunoyer, *industrieux* in the phrase *plusieurs classes d'industrieux,* which we have translated as "several classes of industrious workers." See "Industry versus Plunder: The Plundered Classes, the Plundering Class, and the People," in the Note on the Translation.

again, the price you pay for it in the market is nothing other than payment for these jobs of extraction and transport."[6]

We can see that up to now M. de Saint-Cricq has won the argument; that the *value* of raw materials, like that of manufactured materials, represents the cost of production, that is to say, of the *labor;* that it is not possible to imagine an object that has *value* and that is *devoid of any human labor;* that the distinction made by the petitioners is futile in theory and that, as the basis of an unequal distribution of political *favors* it would be iniquitous in practice, since its result would be that one-third of French citizens who labor in factories would obtain the advantages of monopoly because they produce things *through labor,* while the other two-thirds, that is to say, the farming population, would be abandoned to face competition on the pretext that they produce things *without laboring.*

I am sure that people will insist and say that there is a greater advantage for a nation to import so-called *raw materials,* whether or not they are the product of labor, and export manufactured goods.

This is an opinion that is widely held.

"The more raw materials are abundant," says the petition from Bordeaux, "the more factories will increase in number and flourish vigorously."

"Raw materials," it says elsewhere, "leave a limitless scope for the work of the inhabitants of those countries into which they are imported."

"As raw materials," says the petition from Le Havre, "are the raw elements of labor, they have to be subjected to *a different regime* and imported *immediately at the lowest customs rate.*"

This same petition wants protection for manufactured goods to be reduced *not immediately,* but after an undetermined period and not at *the lowest rate,* but at 20 percent.

"Among other articles whose low price and abundance are a necessity," says the petition from Lyons, "manufacturers include *all raw materials.*"

All this is based on an illusion.

---

6. (Bastiat's note) I do not explicitly mention the part of the payment that relates to the entrepreneur, the capital provider, etc., for several reasons: 1. Because if you look closely, you will see that this is always payment for advances or *labor* done previously; 2. Because, under the general term of *labor,* I include not only the wages of the worker but legitimate payment for all cooperation in the work of production; 3. Lastly and above all, because the production of manufactured goods is, just like that of raw materials, subject to interest and payments other than those for *manual labor,* and the objection, which is futile in itself, would apply to the most ingenious spinning factory as much or even more than to the crudest form of agriculture.

We have seen that all *value* represents labor. Now, it is very true that the process of manufacturing multiplies by ten or sometimes a hundred the *value* of a raw product, that is to say, it spreads out ten or a hundred times more income around the nation. This being so, the reasoning goes as follows: the production of a quintal of iron earns only 15 francs for all categories of contributors. The conversion of this quintal of iron into watch springs raises their various incomes to 10,000 francs, and would you dare to say that it is not of more interest to the nation to ensure itself 10,000 francs' worth of labor than 15 francs' worth?

People forget that international trade does not function by weight or measure, any more than individual exchanges. You do not trade one quintal of iron for one quintal of watch springs, nor a pound of still greasy wool for a pound of cashmere wool, but a certain value of one of these things *for an equal value* of another. Well, to exchange equal value for equal value is to exchange equal labor for equal labor. It is therefore not true that a nation that gives 100 francs' worth of cloth or springs makes more than one that delivers 100 francs' worth of wool or iron.

In a country in which no law can be voted, no taxation imposed without the consent of those who are to be governed by this law or subjected to it, the public can be robbed only by being misled in the first place. Our ignorance is the *raw material* of any extortion that is exercised over us, and we can be certain in advance that any *sophism* is the herald of plunder. Good people, when you see a sophism in a petition, put your hand over your pocket, for it is certainly that which is being aimed at.

Shall we not therefore look at the secret thought that the shipowners of Bordeaux and Le Havre and the manufacturers of Lyons are hiding in this distinction between agricultural goods and manufactured goods?

"It is mainly in this first class (the one that includes raw materials, *devoid of any human labor*) that we find *the principal maintenance of our merchant navy*," say the petitioners of Bordeaux. "In principle, a wise economy would require this class not to be taxed. . . . The second (goods which have undergone some processing) may be *taxed*. The third (goods which require no further modification) we consider to be *the most taxable*."

The petitioners from Le Havre say, "Considering that it is essential to reduce the tax on raw materials *immediately* to the *lowest rate* so that manufacturing industry may successively put to work the *naval forces* that provide it with its primary and essential means of the employment of its labor. . . ."

The manufacturers could not be any less polite to the shipowners. For this reason, the petition from Lyon requested the free entry of raw materials "to prove," as it said, "that the interests of manufacturing towns are not always in opposition to those of those on the coast."

No, but it has to be said that both, understood as the petitioners understand them, are totally opposed to the interests of the countryside, agriculture, and consumers.

This, sirs, is what you wanted to say! This is the aim of your subtle economic distinctions! You want the law to prevent *finished* goods from crossing the ocean in order for the much more expensive transport of raw and dirty materials, including a lot of waste, to provide more cargo for your merchant navy and put your *shipping* to greater use. This is what you call a *wise economy.*

What! Why do you not also ask for Russian pines to be shipped with their branches, bark, and roots? For Mexican gold in its mineral state and leather from Buenos Aires still attached to the bones of stinking carcasses?

Soon, I expect, railway shareholders, however small their majority in the Chambers, will pass a law forbidding the production in Cognac of the brandy drunk in Paris. Would not to decree by law the transport of ten casks of wine for one cask of brandy provide the *essential income for their labor* to manufacturers in Paris and at the same time set the powers of our locomotives into action?

For how long more will people close their eyes to such a simple truth?

The purpose of manufacturing, of shipping, and of labor is the general good, the public good. Creating industries that serve no purpose, encouraging superfluous transport, and supporting unnecessary labor, not for the public good but at public expense, is to achieve a genuine contradiction in terms.[7] It is not labor that is intrinsically desirable but consumption. Any labor that yields no output represents a loss. To pay sailors to carry useless refuse across the sea is as though they were being paid to make pebbles skip across the surface of the water.[8] We therefore come to the conclusion that all

7. The term Bastiat uses is *une pétition de principe* (or in Latin, *petitio principii*), which is a philosophical expression to describe a type of logical fallacy. It means circular reasoning (literally, "begging the question").

8. The phrase Bastiat uses is *pour faire ricocher des cailloux sur la surface de l'eau* (to make stones skip, or ricochet, across the surface of the water), which is perhaps the first use of the term "ricochet," which Bastiat was to develop more fully later. He uses it here (probably written in late 1845) as a verb (*ricocher*, to skip or bounce), whereas later he uses the phrase *par ricochet* (which we have translated as the "ricochet effect") to suggest an indirect or unintended consequence of an action. In this passage he is referring to wasted labor, not the flow-on effects caused by economic activity.

economic sophisms, in spite of their infinite variety, have this in common: they confuse the *means* with the *end* and develop one at the expense of the other.

22. Metaphors

PUBLISHING HISTORY:

Original title: "Métaphores."
Place and date of first publication: No date given. First
   published in book form.
First French edition as book or pamphlet: *Economic Sophisms*
   (First Series) (1846).
Location in Paillottet's edition of *OC:* Vol. 4. *Sophismes*
   économiques. Petits pamphlets I, pp. 115–19.
Previous translations: 1st English ed., 1846; 1st American ed.,
   1848; FEE ed., 1964.

Sometimes sophisms expand and penetrate the entire fabric of a long and heavy theory. More often they contract, reduce in size, and become a principle, entirely hidden in one word.

God preserve us, Paul-Louis[1] said, from cunning men and metaphors! And in fact, it would be difficult to say which of the two causes the most harm to our planet. It is the devil, you say; he puts in all of us, such as we are, the spirit of plunder in our hearts. Yes, but he leaves the repression of abuses completely up to the resistance of those that suffer from them. It is *sophism* that paralyzes this resistance. The sword that *malice* places in the hands of attackers would be powerless if *sophism* did not shatter the shield on the arms of those under attack, and Malebranche was right in inscribing the following sentence on the frontispiece of his book: *Error is the cause of human misery.*[2]

---

1. Paul-Louis Courier de Méré (1773–1825) was a French artillery officer, translator of Greek literature, and liberal and anti-clerical polemicist during the Restoration. Bastiat quotes from Courier's *Pamphlet des pamphlets* (1824), p. 8. The complete quote is: "God, I say to myself in a low voice, God, deliver us from the devil and figurative language! Doctors plan to kill me by wanting to cool [or refresh] my blood; the latter cripple me with the fear of writing with a poison pen; others let their fields lie fallow, and we have a shortage of wheat in the marketplace. Jesus, my Savior, save us from metaphors."

2. Nicolas de Malebranche (1638–1715) was a Paris-based theologian and Cartesian philosopher. From Malebranche's "On the Senses," in *Recherche de la Vérité,* p. 1: "Error is the cause of mankind's miseries. It is wrong principles which have produced harm in the

And look at what happens. Ambitious hypocrites have a sinister interest,[3] for example, in sowing the seed of national hatred in the mind. This disastrous seed may develop and lead to general conflagration, cause civilization to stop, spill torrents of blood, and draw down the most terrible of all scourges on the country, *invasion*. In any case, before these events occur, these feelings of hatred diminish us in the eyes of other nations and reduce those people in France who have retained some vestige of a love of justice to blush for their country. These are certainly great evils, and in order for the public to be protected against the intrigues of those who want to run the risk of such events, it would be enough for them to have a clear view of the matter. How does it happen that this clear view is clouded? Through *metaphor*. The meaning of three or four words is altered, strained, and degraded, and this says it all.

Take the word *invasion* itself.

A French ironmaster says: "May we be preserved from an *invasion* of iron from England." An English landlord exclaims: "Let us reject the *invasion* of wheat from France!" And they propose that the barriers between the two peoples be raised. Barriers constitute isolation, isolation leads to hatred, hatred to war, and war to *invasion*. "What does it matter?" say the two *sophists*, "is it not better to be exposed to the risk of *invasion* than to accept certain *invasion*?" And the people believe them and the barriers remain.

And yet, what analogy is there between an exchange and an *invasion*? What similarity can be established between a warship which comes to vomit shells, fire, and devastation on our towns and a merchant ship that comes to offer us the opportunity of exchanging goods for other goods freely and voluntarily?

I would say the same for the word *flood*. This word normally has a negative meaning because the common characteristics of floods are to ravage fields and crops. If nevertheless they leave greater value on the land than they remove, as do the floods of the Nile, we ought to bless and deify them, following the example of the Egyptians. Well then, before railing against the

---

world. It has given birth and kept in our hearts all the harm which afflicts us. We ought not to hope for solid and true happiness unless we seriously work to avoid it."

3. The phrase "sinister interest" was often used by Jeremy Bentham to criticize the ruling elites who controlled British politics. Bastiat may well have been familiar with Bentham's theory of the ruling elites, as he was familiar with his writings and used quotations from Bentham as the epigraphs for both ES1 and ES2.

floods of foreign goods, before erecting obstructive and costly obstacles in their path, do people ask themselves whether these are floods that ravage or those that fertilize? What would we think of Mehemet Ali[4] if, instead of raising dams across the Nile at huge expense to extend the range of its *floods,* he spent his piastres digging a deeper bed for it so that Egypt would no longer be soiled by this *foreign* silt brought down from the Mountains of the Moon?[5] We are showing precisely this degree of wisdom and reason when, with the support of millions, we wish to preserve our country ... from what? From the benefits with which nature has endowed other climates.

Among the *metaphors* that conceal an entire and disastrous theory, there are none more commonly used than the one that uses the words *tribute, tributary.*

These words have become so commonplace that they have become synonyms of *purchase* and *purchaser* and the two sets of words are now used indiscriminately in place of one another.

However, there is as much distance between a *tribute* and a *purchase* as between a *theft* and an *exchange,* and I would as much like to hear it said that Cartouche[6] had broken into my strongbox and *purchased* a thousand écus, as to hear it said repeatedly to our deputies: "We have paid the *tribute* to Germany for a thousand horses that it has sold to us."

For what makes the action of Cartouche not a purchase is that he has not placed in my strongbox, with my consent, an equivalent value to the one he has taken.

And what makes the payment of 500,000 francs that we have made to Germany not a *tribute,* is exactly that it has not received this money for no return but because it has delivered to us in exchange one thousand horses that we ourselves estimated were worth our 500,000 francs.

Should we therefore in all seriousness bring up such abuses of language

---

4. Mehemet Ali (1769–1849), governor of Egypt, introduced reforms in order to modernize the state along European lines. He nationalized the land, created a state monopoly in foreign trade and a network of war industries, and conscripted peasants to work in the cotton factories.

5. The Nile River has two main tributaries, the White Nile and the Blue Nile. The White Nile has its origin in Lake Victoria in Uganda; the Blue Nile has its origin in Lake Tana in Ethiopia. Ancient geographers thought that the "Mountains of the Moon," located in east-central Africa, were the origins of the Nile River.

6. Louis Dominique Cartouche (1693–1721) was a notorious Parisian thief and outlaw who had the reputation of someone like Robin Hood for the English or Jesse James for the Americans.

again? Why not, since they are very seriously bandied about in both journals and books?

And let us not imagine that they slip out from a few writers whose ignorance extends to their use of language! For every one who refrains from this, I will quote you ten who indulge in it and who belong to the upper classes as well, such as Argout, Dupin, Villèle,[7] and assorted peers, deputies, ministers, that is to say, all men whose word is the law and whose most shocking sophisms are used as the basis for the country's administration.

A famous modern philosopher[8] has added to the categories of Aristotle the sophism that consists in begging the question within a single word. He quotes several examples. He might have added the word *tributary* to his list. In effect, it is a question of knowing whether purchases made abroad are useful or harmful. They are harmful, you say. Why so? Because they make us *tributaries* of foreigners. This is certainly a word that begs the question under discussion.

How has this misleading trope slipped into the monopolists' rhetoric?

Écus *leave the country* to satisfy the rapacity of a victorious enemy. Other écus also *leave the country* to pay for goods. The analogy between the two cases is established, taking account only of the circumstance that causes their resemblance and disregarding the one by which they differ.

Nevertheless this circumstance, that is to say, the nonreimbursement in the first case and the freely agreed reimbursement in the second, establishes between them a difference so great that it is actually not possible to classify them in the same category. To hand over 100 francs *as a result of force* to someone who has his hands around your neck or *voluntarily* to someone who is giving you the object of your desires are truly things that cannot be compared. It would be as true to say that throwing bread into the river is the same as eating it since the bread is in both cases *destroyed.* The fallacy of this reasoning, like that which is encompassed in the word *tribute,* would consist in establishing full similarity between two cases through their points of resemblance and disregarding what makes them differ.

---

7. Jean-Baptiste, comte de Villèle (1773–1854), was the leader of the ultra-legitimists during the Restoration. He was minister of finance in 1821 and prime minister from 1822 until his resignation in 1828.

8. Bastiat might have had in mind the work by the German philosopher Immanuel Kant (1724–1804), *Fundamental Principles of the Metaphysics of Morals* (1785), which includes a discussion of "petitio principii" (begging the question). See http://oll .libertyfund.org/titles/360#Kant_0212_300.

Conclusion

PUBLISHING HISTORY:

Original title: "Conclusion."
Place and date of first publication: Dated Mugron, 2 November
   1845. First published in book form.
First French edition as book or pamphlet: *Economic Sophisms*
   (First Series) (1846).
Location in Paillottet's edition of *OC:* Vol. 4. *Sophismes
   économiques. Petits pamphlets I,* pp. 119–26.
Previous translations: 1st English ed., 1846; 1st American ed.,
   1848; FEE ed., 1964.

All the sophisms that I have combated up to now relate to a single matter, the protectionist system; even so, out of pity for the reader, I have left out some of the best:[1] *acquired rights, inconveniences, depletion of the currency,* etc., etc.

But social economy is not limited to this narrow circle. Fourierist doctrine, Saint-Simonian doctrine, communism, mysticism, sentimentalism, bogus philanthropy, affected aspirations to illusionary equality and fraternity, questions relating to luxury, to wages, to machines, to the alleged tyranny of capital, to colonies, markets, conquests, population, association, emigration, taxes and loans: these have cluttered the field of science with a host of parasitic arguments, *sophisms* that call for the hoe and harrow of a diligent economist.

It is not that I do not acknowledge the flaw in this plan or rather the lack of a plan. To attack one by one so many incoherent sophisms that sometimes clash and most often are included in one another, is to condemn oneself to a disorganized and capricious struggle and to expose oneself to perpetual repetition.

How I would prefer to say quite simply what things *are,* without having to pay attention to a thousand aspects through which ignorance *sees them!* To present the laws according to which societies prosper or decline is *virtually* to destroy all sophisms at a stroke. When Laplace[2] described what we are able

---

1. The phrase "J'en passe, et des meilleurs" (I pass over some of the best) comes from Victor Hugo's play *Hernani, ou l'Honneur castillan* (1830). It is spoken by the Spanish grandee Don Ruy Gomez as he points out boastfully to Don Carlos some portraits of his illustrious ancestors. See "Hernani," act 3, scene 6, in *Œuvres complètes de Victor Hugo, Drame. III.* p. 127.

2. Pierre Simon, Marquis de Laplace (1794–1827), was a French astronomer, physicist, and mathematician who greatly extended the development of mathematical astronomy and statistics.

to know of the movements of the heavenly bodies up to now, he dissipated without even mentioning them by name, all the astrological musings of the Egyptians, the Greeks, and the Hindus with greater surety than he could have done if he had refuted them directly in countless volumes. Truth is unitary; the book that provides an exposition of it is an imposing and durable edifice.

> It defies greedy tyrants
> bolder than the Pyramids
> and more durable than brass.[3]

Error is multifarious and ephemeral by nature; the work that combats it does not carry within itself any principle signifying grandeur and longevity.

But if I have lacked the force and perhaps the opportunity to proceed in the same way as people such as Laplace and Say,[4] I cannot help believing that the form I have adopted also has its modest uses.[5] Above all, it seems to me to be well proportioned to the needs of the century and the fleeting moments it is able to devote to study.

A treatise doubtless has clear superiority but only on one condition, that it is to be read, reflected upon, and deepened. It addresses an elite audience only. Its mission is initially to set and then expand the circle of knowledge acquired.

The refutation of commonly held prejudices cannot have this elevated range. It aspires only to clear the way for the march of truth, to prepare men's

---

3. Bastiat quotes an imitation of an ode by Horace by the French poet Pierre-Antoine LeBrun. It is found in a polyglot edition of the works of Horace published in 1834, with the verses in the original Latin with translations and "imitations" in French, Italian, Spanish, and German. In Ode XXX Horace declares that his poetry will outlast the ravages of the elements and of political tyrants. LeBrun's version of the verse: "Grace à la Muse qui m'inspire, / Il est fini ce monument / Que jamais ne pourront détruire / Le fer ni le flot écumant. / Le ciel même, armé de la foudre, / Ne saurait le réduire en poudre: / Les siècles l'essaieraient en vain. / Il brave ces tyrans avides, / Plus hardi que les pyramides / Et plus durable que l'airain" ("Imitations en vers français. Ode XXX—Livre III," in *Œuvres complètes d'Horace*, p. 229).

4. It is not surprising that Bastiat would mention Jean-Baptiste Say in this context of key works which have exposed commonly held falsehoods. Like Adam Smith before him, whose *Wealth of Nations* (1776) debunked the sophisms of mercantilism, Say's *Treatise of Political Economy* debunked the economic sophisms which had emerged during the French Revolution and Napoléon's empire. The latter had a profound influence on the economists of Bastiat's generation.

5. See the "The Format of *Economic Sophisms*," in the Introduction, for a discussion of the changing formats Bastiat used in his economic sophisms and why he changed them.

minds, redirect the public moral sense, and destroy dangerous weapons in impure hands.

It is above all in social economy that this constant struggle and these constantly reborn battles with popular error have genuine practical use.

The sciences can be divided into two categories.

Strictly speaking, the first can be known only by scholars. These are the ones whose application occupies some specialists. Ordinary people receive the fruit of these in spite of their ignorance; although they do not know about mechanics and astronomy, they still enjoy the use of a watch, they are still transported by locomotives or steamboats given their faith in engineers or pilots. We walk in accordance with the laws of equilibrium without knowing them, just as M. Jourdain[6] spoke prose without knowing it.

But there are also sciences that exercise on the public an influence only in proportion to the enlightenment of the public itself, which draw their entire effectiveness not from the accumulated knowledge in a few exceptional heads but from the knowledge disseminated among the general public. They include morals, hygiene, social economy, and, in those countries in which men are their own masters, politics. It is of these sciences that Bentham might have said in particular: "What broadcasts them is more valuable than what advances them."[7] What does it matter that a great man, a God even, has promulgated the moral law, as long as men, imbued with false notions, take virtues for vices and vices for virtues? What does it matter if Smith, Say,[8] and, according to M. de Saint-Chamans, the economists *of all schools* proclaim, with reference to commercial transactions, that *freedom* is superior to *coercion,* if those who make the laws and for whom laws are made are convinced of the contrary?

These sciences, which have been appropriately named social, also have the particular characteristic that for the very reason that they are in common use, nobody admits to knowing nothing about them. Do we need to solve a

6. In Molière's *Le Bourgeois gentilhomme,* act 2, scene 6, the instructor of philosophy is instructing M. Jourdain on how to behave like a gentleman. Jourdain wants to woo a woman of higher social status than he is and wants to be able to write her a letter. When asked by the Philosopher if he wants to write verse or prose, M. Jourdain gets confused because he doesn't know the difference between the two. He is told that everyday speech is a form of prose, and Jourdain is astonished that for forty years he has been speaking prose without knowing it. See *Œuvres complètes de Molière* 7:138–40.

7. The quotation comes from Bentham, *Théorie des peines et des récompenses,* chapter 3, "De la diffusion des sciences," p. 249.

8. Jean-Baptiste Say.

question of chemistry or geometry? We do not pretend to be steeped in the science; we are not ashamed to call upon M. Thénard; we have no problem in opening Legendre or Bezout.[9] However, in social sciences, we acknowledge scarcely any authorities. As each of us every day acts in accordance with good or bad morals, hygiene, economy, or reasonable or absurd politics, each of us feels able to find fault with, discuss, decide, and lay down the law on these matters. Are you ill? There is no old woman who will not tell you from the outset what the cause and remedy of your ailment is: "It is because your fluids are out of sorts," she states; "you must be purged."[10] But what are these fluids? And are there such things? This is something she does not trouble herself about. I involuntarily think of this dear old woman when I hear all the social ills being explained by these banal statements: It is the overabundance of products; it is the tyranny of capital; it is too many producers and other idiocies of which it cannot even be said *verba et voces, praetereaque nihil,*[11] for they are just so many disastrous errors.

Two things result from what has gone before: 1. That the social sciences, more than the others, have to abound in *sophisms* because they are the ones in which everyone consults only his own judgment or instincts; 2. That it is in these sciences that *sophism* is particularly damaging because it misleads public opinion on a subject in which public opinion constitutes power and is taken as law.

Two sorts of books are therefore needed for these sciences: those that expound them and those that propagate them, those that reveal the truth and those that combat error.

9. Louis Jacques Thénard (1777–1857) was a chemist who became a professor at the Collège de France in 1804, discovered hydrogen peroxide, and had a significant influence on the teaching of science in nineteenth-century France; Adrien-Marie Legendre (1752–1833) was a mathematician who was elected to the Acadamy of Sciences in 1783 and is best known for his work on polynomials and the least-squares method; Étienne Bezout (1730–83) was a French mathematician who was elected to the Academy of Sciences in 1758 and is best known for his general theory of algebraic equations.

10. One of Bastiat's cleverest sophisms, ES2 9, includes a parody of Molière's parody about the primitive medical practices of the seventeenth century, including that of purging. In *The Hypochondriac* Molière creates a fictional oath of induction for new doctors in which they promise to "purge, bleed, stab" their patients to death. Bastiat does the same for tax collectors in which they pledge to "steal, plunder, filch" from all passers-by.

11. The Latin phrase *verba et voces, praetereaque nihil* (words and voices and nothing more) has been attributed to various authors such as Ovid and Quintilian, but there is no firm evidence for their authorship. It is similiar to a line from Horace, *Epistle* I.i.34, which says, "sunt verba et voces" (there are spells and sayings).

It seems to me that the inherent defect in the aesthetic form of this pamphlet, *repetition,* is what constitutes its principal usefulness.

In the subject I have discussed, each sophism doubtless has its own formula and range, but all have a common root, which is the *overlooking of men's interests as consumers.* To show that this sophism is the *originator* of a thousand paths of error[12] is to teach the general public to recognize it, understand it, and mistrust it in all circumstances.

After all, my intention is not exactly to lay the ground for deeply held convictions but to sow the seeds of doubt.

My hope is that when the reader puts the book down he will not exclaim, "I know"; please heaven, but that he might sincerely say, "I do not know!"

"I don't know, because I am beginning to fear that there might be something illusory in the alleged mild effects of scarcity." (Sophism I.)

"I am no longer so convinced of the supposed charms of obstacles to economic activity." (Sophism II.)

"The effort which produces no result seems no longer to me to be as desirable as the result which requires no effort." (Sophism III.)

"It could well be that the secret of commerce, unlike that of combat (according to the definition given by the fencing instructor in *Le Bourgeois gentilhomme*),[13] does not consist in giving and not receiving." (Sophism VI.)

"I understand that a good increases in value to the degree that it has been worked upon; but in an exchange, do two goods of equal value cease to be of equal value because one comes from a plough and the other from a Jacquard loom?"[14] (Sophism XXI.)

12. Here (circa November 1845) Bastiat argues that the *racine commune* (common root) for a thousand sophisms is "the overlooking of men's interests as consumers." In 1847 when he wrote a brief draft of a chapter on Montaigne's essay "Le Profit d'un est dommage de l'autre" (One Man's Gain Is Another Man's Loss), he called this phrase the "classical example of a sophism, the rootstock sophism from which come multitudes of sophisms." See ES3 15, p. 337.

13. The *maître d'armes* (fencing instructor) instructs M. Jourdain in the two simple secrets for success in fencing: to give and not to receive thrusts of the sword and to deflect any thrust of the sword made at you away from the line of the body. See *Le Bourgeois gentilhomme,* act 2, scene 3 (*Œuvres complètes de Molière* 7:122).

14. Joseph Marie Charles Jacquard (1752–1834), a French weaver and inventor, was a pioneer in the development of the mechanical loom which revolutionized the production of woven cloth. His contribution in 1801, the Jacquard loom, built upon the work of others and depended upon the use of punched cards with holes which controlled the pattern woven into the cloth. It was one of the earliest examples of a programmable machine.

"I admit that I am beginning to find it strange that mankind might be improved by fetters or enriched by taxes; and frankly I would be relieved of a great burden and I would feel pure joy if it could be demonstrated to me, as the author of the Sophisms assures me, that there is no contradiction between well-being and justice, between peace and liberty, between the expansion of labor and the progress of knowledge." (Sophisms XIV and XX.)

"Thus, without claiming to be satisfied with his arguments, which I don't know if I should call reasons or paradoxes, I will explore further the works of the masters of economic science."

Let us end this monograph on *sophistry* with a final and important thought:

The world is not sufficiently aware of the influence that *sophistry* exercises on it.

If I have to say what I think, when the *right of the strongest* was dethroned, *sophistry* handed empire to the *right of the most subtle,* and it would be difficult to say which of these two tyrants has been the most disastrous for the human race.

Men have an immoderate love for pleasure, influence, esteem, and power; in a word, for wealth.

And at the same time, they are driven by an immense urge to procure these things for themselves at the expense of others.

But these *others,* who are the general public, have no less an urge to keep what they have acquired, provided that they *can* and they *know how to.*

Plunder, which plays such a major role in the affairs of the world, has thus only two things which promote it: *force* and *fraud,*[15] and two things which limit it: *courage* and *enlightenment.*

Force used for plunder forms the bedrock upon which the annals of human history rest. Retracing its history would be to reproduce almost entirely the history of every nation: the Assyrians, the Babylonians, the Medes, the Persians, the Egyptians, the Greeks, the Romans, the Goths, the Francs, the Huns, the Turks, the Arabs, the Mongols, and the Tartars, not to mention the Spanish in America, the English in India, the French in Africa, the Russians in Asia, etc., etc.

But at least in civilized nations, the men who produce the wealth have become sufficiently numerous and *strong* to defend it. Is this to say that they

---

15. Bastiat uses the term *la ruse* (fraud or trickery), which is an important part of his theory of plunder. See "Bastiat on Enlightening the 'Dupes' about the Nature of Plunder," in the Introduction.

are no longer dispossessed? Not at all; they are just as dispossessed as ever and, what is more, they mutually dispossess each other.

Only the thing which promotes it has changed; it is no longer by force but by fraud that public wealth can be seized.

In order to steal from the public, it is first necessary to deceive them. To deceive them it is necessary to persuade them that they are being robbed for their own good; it is to make them accept imaginary services and often worse in exchange for their possessions. This gives rise to *sophistry*. Theocratic sophistry, economic sophistry, political sophistry, and financial sophistry. Therefore, ever since force has been held in check, *sophistry* has been not only a source of harm, it has been the very essence of harm. It must in its turn be held in check. And to do this the public must become *cleverer* than the clever, just as it has become *stronger* than the strong.

Good public, it is with this last thought in mind that I am addressing this first essay to you, although the preface has been strangely transposed and the dedication is somewhat belated.[16,17]

Mugron, 2 November 1845

END OF THE FIRST PART

16. Here Bastiat seems to be suggesting that the dedication he wrote for the volume (possibly what we have called the "Author's Introduction") was written last and in some haste, and that the "Conclusion" was meant to have been put at the beginning of the volume and thus should have been the preface. These remarks suggest that the volume was edited and published in some haste at the end of 1845, perhaps without Bastiat's full editorial control.

17. (Paillottet's note) This thought, which ends the first series of the *Sophisms*, will be taken up again and developed by the author at the start of the second series. The influence of plunder on the destiny of the human race preoccupied him greatly. After having covered this subject several times in the *Sophisms* and the *Pamphlets* (see in particular *Property and Plunder* and *Plunder and Law*) (*OC*, vol. 4, p. 394, "Propriété et spoliation"; and vol. 5, p. 1, "Spoliation et loi"), he planned a more ample place for it in the second part of the *Harmonies*, among the *disturbing factors*. Lastly, as the final evidence of the interest he took in it, he said on the eve of his death: "A very important task to be done for political economy is to write the history of plunder. It is a long history in which, from the outset, there appeared conquests, the migrations of peoples, invasions, and all the disastrous excesses of force in conflict with justice. Living traces of all this still remain today and cause great difficulty for the solution of the questions raised in our century. We will not reach this solution as long as we have not clearly noted in what and how injustice, when making a place for itself among us, has gained a foothold in our customs and our laws." ["Property and Plunder" and "Plunder and Law" appear in CW2, pp. 147–84 and 266–76, respectively.]

Economic Sophisms
Second Series[1]

What industry asks of government is as modest as the
plea of Diogenes to Alexander: "Get out of my sunlight."
(Bentham)[2]

1. (Paillottet's note) The Second Series of *Economic Sophisms*, several chapters of which had previously appeared in *Le Journal des économistes* and the journal *Le Libre-échange*, was published at the end of January 1848.

2. It is interesting that Bastiat chose two passages from Bentham's *Théorie des peines et des récompenses* (1811) as the opening for ES1 and ES2. The quotation which begins this chapter comes from *Théorie des peines et des récompenses* 2:271.

1. The Physiology of Plunder[1]

PUBLISHING HISTORY:

Original title: "Physiologie de la Spoliation."
Place and date of first publication: No date given. First
published in book form.
First French edition as book or pamphlet: *Economic Sophisms*
(Second Series) (1848). First and Second Series were
combined in one edition in 1851.
Location in Paillottet's edition: *Œuvres complètes* vol. 4.
Sophismes économiques. Petits pamphlets I, pp. 127–48.
Previous translation: 1st American ed., 1848; 1st British ed.,
1873; FEE ed., 1964.

Why should I persist in this arid science, *Political Economy?*

Why? The question is reasonable. All work is sufficiently repellent by nature for us to have the right to ask where it is leading.

So let us examine the matter.

I am not addressing the philosophers who make a profession of adoring poverty, if not in their own name, at least in the name of humanity.

I am speaking to those who consider *Wealth* as something worthwhile. Let us understand by this term, not the opulence of a few but the prosperity, well-being, security, independence, education, and the dignity of all.

---

1. (Paillottet's note) See chapters 18, 19, 22, and 24 in volume 6 for the developments projected and started by the author on the *Disturbing Factors* affecting the harmony of natural laws. [The reference is to several chapters in *Economic Harmonies:* chap. 18, "Le Mal" (Harm); chap. 19, "Guerre" (War); chap. 22, "Moteur social" (The Engine of Society); and chap. 14, "Perfectibilité" (Perfectibility). These will be in CW5 (forthcoming). Paillottet tells us in a footnote at the end of ES1 Conclusion that Bastiat planned to write a "History of Plunder" after he had finished the *Economic Harmonies* but died before he could do more than sketch out a couple of chapters. In addition, in a proposed section of *Economic Harmonies,* "Disturbing Factors," Bastiat had planned the following chapters: 16. Plunder, 17. War, 18. Slavery, 19. Theocracy, 20. Monopoly, 21. Government Exploitation, 22. False Brotherhood or Communism. Aside from the first two chapters, no notes or drafts on these proposed chapters were found among Bastiat's papers at the time of his death.]

There are only two ways of acquiring the things that are necessary for the preservation, improvement, and betterment of life: PRODUCTION and PLUNDER.

Some people say: "PLUNDER is an accident, a local and transitory abuse, stigmatized by moral philosophy, condemned by law, and unworthy of the attentions of *Political Economy.*"

But whatever the benevolence and optimism of one's heart, one is obliged to acknowledge that PLUNDER is exercised on too vast a scale in this world, that it is too universally woven into all major human events, for any social science, above all *Political Economy,* to feel justified in disregarding it.

I will go further. What separates the social order from a state of perfection (at least from the degree of perfection it can attain) is the constant effort of its members to live and progress at the expense of one another.

So that, if PLUNDER did not exist, society would be perfect and the social sciences would be superfluous.

I will go even further. When PLUNDER has become the means of existence of a large group of men mutually linked by social ties, they soon contrive to pass a law that sanctions it and a moral code that glorifies it.

You need name only a few of the most clear-cut forms of *Plunder* to show the place it occupies in human affairs.

First of all, there is WAR. Among savage peoples, the victor kills the vanquished in order to acquire a right to hunt game that is, if not incontestable, at least *uncontested.*

Then there is SLAVERY. Once man grasps that it is possible to make land fertile through work, he strikes this bargain with his fellow: "You will have the fatigue of work and I will have its product."

Next comes THEOCRACY. "Depending on whether you give me or refuse to give me your property, I will open the gates of heaven or hell to you."

Lastly, there is MONOPOLY. Its distinctive characteristic is to allow the great social law, *a service for a service,* to continue to exist, but to make force part of the negotiations and thus distort the just relationship between the *service received* and the *service rendered.*

Plunder always carries within it the deadly seed that kills it. Rarely does the majority plunder the minority.[2] In this case, the minority would imme-

2. It was this very topic that Bastiat addressed later in June 1848 in his pamphlet "The State." He had become concerned that during the Revolution the French people thought they could now plunder the entire country for their own benefit, a task which Bastiat criticized as a "fiction." A draft of this essay appeared in June in his revolutionary newspaper *Jacques Bonhomme.* See CW2, pp. 93–106.

diately be reduced to the point where it could no longer satisfy the greed of the majority, and Plunder would die for want of sustenance.

It is almost always the majority that is oppressed, and Plunder is also destined in this case as well to receive a death sentence.

For if the use of Force is Plunder's agent, as it is for War and Slavery, it is natural for Force to go over to the side of the majority in the long run.

And if the agent is Fraud, as in Theocracy and Monopoly, it is natural for the majority to become informed on this score, or intelligence would not be intelligence.

Another providential law that has planted a second deadly seed in the heart of Plunder is this:

Plunder does not only *redistribute* wealth, it always *destroys* part of it.

War annihilates many things of value.

Slavery paralyzes a great many human abilities.

Theocracy diverts a great deal of effort to puerile or disastrous purposes.

Monopoly also moves wealth from one pocket to another, but a great deal is lost in the transfer.

This law is admirable. In its absence, provided that there were a stable balance of power between the oppressors and the oppressed, Plunder would have no end. Thanks to this law, the balance always tends to be upset, either because the Plunderers become aware of the loss of so much wealth, or, where this awareness is lacking, because the harm constantly grows worse and it is in the nature of things that constantly deteriorate to come to an end.

In fact, there comes a time when, in its gradual acceleration, the loss of wealth is so great that Plunderers are less rich than they would have been if they had remained honest.

An example of this is a nation for which the cost of war is greater than the value of its booty;

A master who pays more for slave labor than for free labor;

A Theocracy that has so stupefied the people and sapped their energy that it can no longer wring anything out of them;

A Monopoly that has to increase its efforts to suck consumers dry as there is less to be sucked up, just as the effort needed to milk a cow increases as the udder dries up.[3]

---

3. Bastiat here uses the metaphor of the drying up of a cow's udder to make a point about how monopoly "swallows" or "absorbs" the property of consumers. We have extended the metaphor to that of "sucking consumers dry."

As we see, Monopoly is a Species of the Genus Plunder. There are several Varieties of it, including Sinecure, Privilege, and Trade Restriction.

Among the forms it takes, there are some that are simple and naïve. Such were feudal rights. Under this regime the masses were plundered and knew it. It involved the abuse of force and perished with it.

Others are highly complex. In this case, the masses are often plundered unaware. It may even happen that they think they owe everything to Plunder: what is left to them, as well as what is taken from them and what is lost in the operation. Further than that I would propose as time goes on, and given the highly ingenious mechanism of *custom,* many Plunderers are plunderers without knowing it and without wishing it. Monopolies of this type are generated through Fraud, and they feed on Error. They only disappear with Enlightenment.

I have said enough to show that Political Economy has an obvious practical use. It is the flame that destroys this social disorder which is Plunder, by unveiling Fraud and dissipating Error. Someone, I believe it was a woman[4] and she was perfectly right, defined political economy thus: *It is the safety lock on popular savings.*

COMMENTS

If this small volume were intended to last for three or four thousand years, to be read, reread, meditated upon, and studied sentence by sentence, word by word, and letter by letter by one generation after another like a new Koran, if it were bound to attract avalanches of annotations, explanations, and paraphrases in all the libraries around the world, I would be able to abandon to their fate the foregoing thoughts with their slightly obscure precision. But

4. We have not been able to track down the origin of this quotation. The woman Bastiat has in mind might be either Jane Haldimand Marcet (1769–1858) or Harriet Martineau (1802–76), both of whom wrote popular works on political economy which were translated into French, and both of whom were strong advocates of saving by the poorer classes as a means to get out of their poverty. Both writers had biographical articles written about them for the *DEP,* and so their works were probably know to Bastiat. It is perhaps more likely to have been Martineau to whom Bastiat was referring, as her work was the more recent and had been translated into French in the early 1830s and republished by Guillaumin sometime in the late 1840s. It was reviewed very favorably by Gustave de Molinari in April 1849 (thus after Bastiat's writing of the Second Series of *Economic Sophisms* during 1847), who said that "[s]he deserves her double reputation for being an ingenious storyteller and a learned professor of political economy."

because they need to be commented upon, I consider it prudent to do this myself.

The true and just law governing man is "*The freely negotiated exchange of one service for another.*" Plunder consists in banishing by force or fraud the freedom to negotiate in order to receive a service without offering one in return.

Plunder by force is exercised as follows: People wait for a man to produce something and then seize it from him at gunpoint.

This is formally condemned by the Ten Commandments: *Thou shalt not steal.*

When it takes place between individuals, it is called *theft* and leads to prison; when it takes place between nations, it is called *conquest* and leads to glory.

Why is there this difference? It is useful to seek its cause. It will show us an irresistible power, Opinion, which, like the atmosphere, envelops us so completely that we no longer notice it. For Rousseau never spoke a truer word than when he said, "A great deal of philosophy is needed to observe facts that are too close to us."[5]

A *thief,* by the very fact that he acts alone, has public opinion against him. He alarms everyone who surrounds him. However, if he has a few accomplices, he brags to them of his achievements and we start to see in this the force of Opinion, for he needs only the approval of his accomplices to free him of any feeling of shame for his wicked acts and even to make him proud of his ignominy.

A *warrior* lives in another environment. The Opinion that reviles him is elsewhere, in the nations that have been conquered; he does not feel pressure from them. However, the Opinion that is around him approves and supports him. His companions and he feel keenly the solidarity that binds them. The fatherland, which created enemies and dangers for itself, needs to exalt the courage of its children. It confers on the boldest of these, those who extend

5. The quote comes from Rousseau's *Discourse on Inequality,* part 1 (p. 90), but Bastiat is quoting from memory here, and it is not exactly correct. The French states: "ce n'est pas chez lui [l'homme sauvage] qu'il faut chercher la philosophie dont l'homme a besoin, pour savoir observer une fois ce qu'il a vu tous les jours" [and we should look in vain to him for that philosophy which a man needs if he is to know how to notice once what he has seen every day] (Rousseau, *Du contrat social et autres œuvres politiques,* p. 49). Bastiat was so impressed with this statement that he refers to it several times in *Economic Harmonies.*

its frontiers and bring back the most plunder to it, honors, renown, and glory. Poets sing of their exploits and women weave them wreaths. And such is the power of Opinion that it removes the idea of injustice from Plunder and strips away the very awareness of their wrongs from plunderers.

Opinion which rejects military plunder is not located among those doing the plundering but among those being plundered, and therefore exercises very little influence. However, it is not totally ineffective, and still less when nations have relations with one another and understand each other more. From this angle, we see that a study of languages and free communication between peoples tends to lead to the predominance of opinion against this type of plunder.

Unfortunately, it often happens that the nations surrounding the plundering people are themselves plunderers whenever they can be and are henceforth imbued with the same preconceived ideas.

If this is so, there is only one remedy, time. Nations have to learn by hard experience the huge disadvantage there is in plundering each other.

Another brake may be mentioned: raising moral standards. However, the aim of raising moral standards is to increase the number of virtuous actions. How then will it restrict acts of plunder when such acts are raised by Opinion to the rank of the highest virtues? Is there a more powerful means of raising the moral standards of a nation than religion? Has there ever been a Religion more disposed toward peace and more universally accepted than Christianity? And yet, what have we seen in the last eighteen centuries? We have seen men fighting, not only in spite of Religion but in the very name of Religion.

A conquering nation does not always carry out an offensive war. It also has bad times. Its soldiers then defend their homes and hearths, property, families, independence, and freedom. War takes on an aura of sanctity and greatness. The flag, blessed by the ministers of the God of Peace, represents all that there is sacred on earth; people adhere to it as to the living image of the fatherland and honor, and warlike virtues are exalted above all the other virtues. But once the danger has passed, Opinion remains, and the spirit of revenge (which is often confused with patriotism) gives rise to the natural response of people who love to parade their beloved flag from city to city. It appears that it is in this way that nature might have prepared the punishment of the aggressor.

It is the fear of this punishment and not the progress of philosophy that keeps weapons within arsenals for, it cannot be denied, the most advanced and civilized nations make war and take little notice of justice as long as they have no reprisals to fear. Examples of this are the Himalayas,[6] the Atlas mountains,[7] and the Caucasus.[8]

If religion has been powerless, if philosophy is powerless, how will we put an end to war?

Political economy shows that, even when you consider only the victors, war is always waged in the interest of a minority and at the expense of the masses. All that is needed therefore is that the masses see this truth clearly. The weight of opinion, which is still divided, will come down totally in favor of peace.[9]

Plunder exercised by force takes yet another form. People do not wait for a man to have produced something to snatch it from him. They take hold of the man himself; he is stripped of his own personality and forced to work. Nobody says to him, *"If you take this trouble on my behalf, I will take this trouble for you"* but instead, *"You will have all the fatigue of labor and I will have all the enjoyment of its products."* This is Slavery, which always involves the abuse of force.

Well, it is a profound question to ascertain whether or not it is in the na-

---

6. Bastiat may have in mind the First Anglo-Afghan War (1839–42), which was fought by the British Empire for control of Afghanistan, which is located in the western part of the Himalayan Mountains.

7. This is a possible reference to the French conquest of Algeria, which began in 1830. The Atlas Mountains stretch across the northwestern part of Africa and include what are now Morocco, Algeria, and Tunisia.

8. The Caucasus Mountains are located between the Black Sea and the Caspian Sea and are often regarded as forming the boundary between Europe and Asia. The Russian Empire fought wars in this region (1817–64) in order to expand its empire. In Bastiat's day there was fierce resistance led by Imam Shamil, who led attacks against the invading Russians with some success between 1843 and 1845.

9. (Paillottet's note) See the letter addressed to the President of the Peace Congress in Frankfurt in volume 1, p. 197. [This letter can be found in CW1, pp. 265–66. Bastiat was an active member of an international association called the Friends of Peace and took a great interest in their congresses, one of which was held in Brussels in 1848, one in Paris (chaired by Victor Hugo) in 1849, and one in Frankfurt in 1850. Because of his ill health and political commitments Bastiat was able to attend only the Paris congress in August 1849, at which he gave an address, "Disarmament, Taxes, and the Influence of Political Economy on the Peace Movement" (our title). See the entry for "International Congress of the Friends of Peace (Paris, August 1849)" in the Glossary of Subjects and Terms.]

ture of an incontestably dominating force to always take advantage of its position. As for me, I do not trust it, and would as much expect a falling stone to have the power to halt its own fall as entrust coercion to set its own limit.

I would like at least to be shown a country or an era in which Slavery has been abolished by the free and gracious will of the masters.

Slavery supplies a second and striking example of the inadequacy of religious and philanthropic sentiments in the face of a powerful sense of self-interest. This may appear a source of regret to certain modern schools that seek the reforming principle of society in self-denial. Let them begin then by reforming the nature of man.

In the Antilles,[10] the masters have professed the Christian religion from father to son from the time slavery was instituted. Several times a day, they repeat these words: "All men are brothers; loving your neighbor is to fulfill the law in its entirety." And yet they have slaves. Nothing seemed to them to be more natural and legitimate. Do modern reformers hope that their moral principles will ever be as universally accepted, as popular, with as much authority and as often heard on everyone's lips as the Gospel? And if the Gospel has been unable to pass from lips to hearts over or through the great defensive wall of self-interest, how do they hope that their moral principles will accomplish this miracle?

What then! Is Slavery therefore invulnerable? No, what founded it will destroy it; I refer to *Self-Interest,* provided that, in order to reinforce the special interests that created the wound, the general interests that have to cure it are not thwarted.

Another truth demonstrated by political economy is that free labor is essentially dynamic and slave labor is of necessity static. For this reason, the triumph of the former over the latter is inevitable. What has happened to the cultivation of indigo by black people?[11]

Free labor applied to the cultivation of sugar will make the price decrease

---

10. The French once had extensive possessions in the Caribbean, where slavery was used to produce sugar and other crops. Most of these possessions were lost as a result of the Revolution (Haiti in particular) and the defeat of Napoléon by the British. In Bastiat's day what was left included Martinique and Guadeloupe. Slavery in the French Antilles was abolished during the 1848 Revolution (27 April 1848). See Bastiat's veiled remarks about sugar production in Martinique (Saccharinique) in ES3 19, pp. 365–71.

11. The production of indigo in the French Antilles dropped as a result of the more efficient and cheaper production from Bengal, which was controlled by the British.

more and more. As this happens, slaves will be less and less profitable for their masters. Slavery would have collapsed a long time ago of its own accord in America, if the laws in Europe had not raised the price of sugar artificially. We therefore see the masters, their creditors, and delegates actively working to maintain these laws, which now form the pillars of the edifice.

Unfortunately, they still have the sympathy of the populations within which slavery has disappeared, which shows us once again that Opinion is still sovereign here.

If it is sovereign, even in the context of power, it is even more so in the world of Fraud. To tell the truth, this is its real domain. Fraud is the abuse of knowledge; the progress of Opinion is the progress of knowledge. The two powers are at least of the same nature. Fraud by a plunderer involves credulity in the person being plundered, and the natural antidote to credulity is truth. It follows that to enlighten minds is to remove the sustenance from this type of plunder.

I will review briefly a few of the forms of plunder that are exercised by Fraud on a grand scale.

The first to come forward is Plunder by theocratic fraud.

What is this about? To get people to provide real services, in the form of foodstuffs, clothing, luxury, consideration, influence, and power, in return for imaginary ones.

If I said to a man, "I am going to provide you with some immediate services," I would have to keep my word, otherwise this man would know what he was dealing with, and my fraud would be promptly unmasked.

But if I told him, "In exchange for your services, I will provide you with immense services, not in this world but in the next. After this life, you will be able to be eternally happy or unhappy, and this all depends on me; I am an intermediary between God and his creation and can, at will, open the gates of heaven or hell to you." Should this man believe me at all, he is in my power.

This type of imposture has been practiced widely since the beginning of the world, and we know what degree of total power Egyptian priests achieved.

It is easy to see how impostors behave. You have to only ask yourself what you would do in their place.

If I came, with ideas like this in mind, amongst an ignorant clan and succeeded by dint of some extraordinary act and an amazing appearance to be taken for a supernatural being, I would pass for an emissary of God with absolute discretion over the future destiny of men.

I would then forbid any examination of my titles. I would go further; since reason would be my most dangerous enemy, I would forbid the use of reason itself, at least when applied to this awesome subject. I would make this question, and all those relating to it, *taboo,* as the savages say. To solve them, discuss them, or even think of them would be an unpardonable crime.

It would certainly be the height of skill to set up a *taboo* as a barrier across all the intellectual avenues that might lead to the discovery of my deception. What better guarantee of its longevity is there than to make doubt itself a sacrilege?

However, to this fundamental guarantee I would add ancillary ones. For example, in order that enlightenment is never able to reach down to the masses, I would grant to my accomplices and myself the monopoly of all knowledge. I would hide it under the veils of a dead language and a hiero-glyphic script and, so that I would never be taken by surprise by any danger, I would take care to invent an institution which would, day after day, enable me to enter into the secret of all consciences.

It would also not be a bad thing for me to satisfy some of the genuine needs of my people, especially if, by doing so, I was able to increase my in-fluence and authority. Given that men have a great need of education and moral instruction, I would take it upon myself to dispense this. Through this, I would direct the minds and hearts of my people as I saw fit. I would weave morality and my authority into an indissoluble chain; I would rep-resent them as being unable to exist without each other, so that if a bold individual attempted to raise a question that was *taboo,* society as a whole, unable to live without a moral code, would feel the earth tremble beneath its feet and would turn in anger against this daring innovator.

Should things reach this pass, it is clear that this people would belong to me more surely than if they were my slaves. Slaves curse their chains, while my people would bless theirs, and I would have succeeded in imprinting the stamp of servitude not on their foreheads, but in the depths of their con-science.

Opinion alone is capable of tearing down an edifice of iniquity like this, but how will it set about this if each stone is *taboo?* It is a question of time and the printing press.

God forbid that I should wish to undermine here the consoling beliefs that *link* this life of trials to a life of happiness! No one, not even the head of the Christian church,[12] could deny that the irresistible urge which leads us to these beliefs has been taken advantage of. There is, it seems to me, a sign by which we can see whether a people have been duped or not. Examine Religion and priest alike; see whether the priest is the instrument of Religion or Religion the instrument of the priest.

If *the priest is the instrument of Religion,* if he thinks only of spreading its morals and benefits around the world, he will be gentle, tolerant, humble, charitable, and full of zeal. His life will reflect that of his divine model. He will preach freedom and equality among men, peace and fraternity between nations; he will reject the attractions of temporal power, not wishing to ally himself with what most needs to be restricted in this world. He will be a man of the people, a man of good counsel and gentle consolation, a man of good Opinion and a Man of the Gospel.

If, on the other hand, *Religion is the instrument of the priest,* he will treat it as some people treat an instrument that is altered, bent, and turned in many ways so as to draw the greatest benefit for themselves. He will increase the number of questions that are *taboo;* his moral principles will bend according to the climate, men, and circumstances. He will seek to impose it through studied gestures and attitudes; he will mutter words a hundred times a day whose meaning has disappeared and which are nothing other than empty *conventionalism.* He will peddle holy things, but just enough to avoid undermining faith in their sanctity, and he will take care to see that this trade is less obviously active where the people are more keen-sighted. He will involve himself in terrestrial intrigue and always be on the side of the powerful, on the sole condition that those in power ally themselves with him. In a word, in all his actions, it will be seen that he does not want to advance Religion through the clergy but the clergy through Religion, and since so much effort implies an aim and as this aim, according to our hypothesis, cannot be anything other than power and wealth, the definitive sign that the people have been duped is when priests are rich and powerful.

It is very clear that one can abuse a true Religion as well as a false one. The more its authority is respectable, the greater is the danger that it may be improperly used. But the results are very different. Abuse always revolts the healthy, enlightened, and independent sector of a nation. It is impossible for

---

12. Bastiat uses the phrase *le chef de la chrétienté,* which we have translated as "the head of the Christian church." The translator of the FEE edition translated this as "the Pope" (*Economic Sophisms,* FEE edition, p. 138).

faith not to be undermined, and the weakening of a true Religion is more of a disaster than the undermining of a false one.

Plunder using this procedure and the clear-sightedness of a people are always in inverse proportion one to the other, for it is in the nature of abuse to proceed wherever it finds a path. Not that pure and devoted priests are not to be found within the most ignorant population, but how do you prevent a swindler from putting on a cassock and having the ambition to don a miter? Plunderers obey Malthus's law: they multiply in line with the means of existence, and the means of existence of swindlers is the credulity of their dupes. It is no good searching; you always find that opinion needs to be enlightened. There is no other panacea.

Another type of Plunder by fraud is *commercial fraud,* a name that I think is too limited since not only are merchants who adulterate their goods and give short measure guilty of this, but also doctors who get paid for disastrous advice, lawyers who overcomplicate lawsuits, etc. In these exchanges of services, one is done in bad faith, but in this instance, as the service received is always agreed upon voluntarily in advance, it is clear that Plunder of this kind is bound to retreat as public clear-sightedness increases.

Next comes the abuse of *government services,* a huge field of Plunder, so huge that we can only cast a glance at it.

If God had made man to be a solitary animal, each would work for his own benefit. Individual wealth would be in proportion to the services that each person rendered to himself.

However, *as man is sociable, services are exchanged for one another,* a proposition that you can, if you like, construct in reverse.

In society, there are needs that are so general and universal that its members supply them by organizing *government services.* An example of this is the need for security. People consult with each other and agree to tax themselves in order to pay with various *services* those who supply the *service* of watching over common security.

There is nothing in this that is outside the scope of political economy: *Do this for me and I will do that for you.* The essence of the transaction is the same; the procedure of paying for it alone is different, but this difference is of far-ranging importance.

In ordinary transactions, each person remains the judge either of the service he receives or of the service he renders. He can always either refuse the exchange or make it elsewhere, which gives rise to the necessity of bringing into the market only services that will be voluntarily agreed upon.

This is not so with regard to the state, especially before the arrival of representative governments. Whether we need its services or not, whether they are good or bad quality,[13] the State always obliges us to accept them as they are supplied and pay for them at the price it sets.

Well, all men tend to see the services they render through the small end of the telescope and the services they receive through the large end,[14] and things would be in a fine state if we did not have the guarantee of a *freely negotiated price* in private transactions.

We do not have or scarcely have this guarantee in our transactions with the government. And yet the State, made up of men (although these days the contrary is insinuated), obeys the universal trend. It wants to *serve* us a great deal, indeed with more than we want, and make us accept as a *genuine* service things that are sometimes far from being so, in order to require us to supply it with *services* or taxes in return.

The state is also subject to Malthus's law. It tends to exceed the level of its means of existence, it expands in line with these means, and what keeps it in existence is whatever the people have. Woe betide those peoples who cannot limit the sphere of action of the State. Freedom, private activity, wealth, well-being, independence, and dignity will all disappear.

For there is one fact that should be noted, and it is this: of all the services we require from the State, the principal one is *security*. In order to guarantee this to us, it has to have a force capable of overcoming all other forces, whether individual or collective, internal or external, which might compromise it. If we link this thought with the unfortunate tendency we have noted in men to live at the expense of others, there is a danger here that leaps to the eye.

This being so, just look at the immense scale on which Plunder has been carried out throughout history by the abuse and excesses of the government. One might well ask what services were provided to the people and what services were exacted by governments in the Assyrian, Babylonian, Roman, Persian, Turkish, Chinese, Russian, English, Spanish, and French states! The mind boggles at this huge disparity.

Eventually, the representative system of government was invented, and

13. Bastiat uses an interesting combination of phrases to describe the compulsory services provided by the state: they may be *de bon ou mauvais aloi,* which refers to "sound or counterfeit" currency (literally, good or bad alloy). It is not surprising that Bastiat would choose the example of the government monopoly of the supply of money and its common practice of debasing the currency as a metaphor for government services in general.

14. In other words, people imagine that the services they provide other people are larger than they really are, and that the services they receive are smaller than they really are.

a priori it might have been thought that the disorder would disappear as though by magic.

In practice, the operating principle of these governments is this:

"The population itself will decide, through its representatives, on the nature and extent of the functions that it considers appropriate to establish as *government services* and the amount of revenue it intends to allocate to these *services.*"

The tendency to seize the goods of others and the tendency to defend one's own were thus brought face to face. It was bound to be thought that the latter would overcome the former.

Certainly I am convinced that in the long run this outcome will prevail. But it has to be said that up to now it has not done so.

Why? For two very simple reasons: governments have understood things only too well and the populace not well enough.

Governments are very wily. They act methodically and consistently according to a plan that has been well thought out and constantly improved by tradition and experience. They study men and their passions. If they see, for example, that they have an inclination to war, they whip up and excite this deadly tendency. They surround the nation with dangers through the actions of their diplomats, and very naturally, as a result, they require the nation to provide soldiers, sailors, arsenals, and fortifications;[15] often they have little trouble in having these supplied to them: after all, they have honors, pensions, and positions to hand out. They need a great deal of money for this, and taxes and loans exist for this purpose.

If the nation is generous, governments take it upon themselves to cure all the ills of humanity. They will revive commerce, they say; they will bring prosperity to agriculture, develop factories, encourage arts and letters, abolish poverty, etc., etc. All that is needed is to create some new government functions and pay for some new functionaries.

In a word, the tactic consists in presenting as real services things that are only hindrances; the nation then pays, not for services but for disservices. Governments take on gigantic proportions and end up absorbing half of the total revenue. And the people are surprised at having to work so hard, at hearing the announcement of astonishing inventions that will infinitely in-

---

15. Bastiat would have had in mind the fortified wall which Thiers constructed around Paris between 1841 and 1844 at a considerable cost (fr. 150 million). See the Glossary of Persons.

crease the number of products and . . . to always be like Gros-Jean and never learn.[16]

This is because, while the government is displaying such skill, the people are showing very little. Thus, when called upon to choose those who will wield authority, those who will have to determine the sphere and remuneration of government action, whom do they choose? Government officials. They make the executive power responsible for setting the limits on its own action and requirements. They imitate the *Bourgeois Gentilhomme*[17] who, in choosing the style and number of his suits, relies on the advice of . . . his tailor.[18]

Meanwhile, things go from bad to worse and the people's eyes are at last opened, not to the remedy (they have not yet reached this stage), but to the illness.

Governing is such a pleasant job that everyone aspires to it. The councilors of the people therefore constantly tell them, "We see your suffering and we deplore it. Things would be different if we were governing you."

This period, normally very long, is that of rebellion and uprising. When the people have been conquered, the cost of the war is added to their burdens. When they are the conquerors, the people in government change and the abuses remain.

And this continues until at last the people learn to recognize and defend their true interests. We therefore always reach this point: The only option lies in the progress of Public Reasoning.

16. Bastiat concludes this paragraph with a reference to the fictional character Gros-Jean (Big John), who in many respects is the opposite of Jacques Bonhomme (Jack Good-fellow), the wily French peasant everyman. Gros-Jean is quite stupid and does not learn from his mistakes. He was popularized by La Fontaine in his fable about "The Milkmaid and the Pail." After daydreaming about how she will spend the money she has not yet earned at the markets, Perrette spills her pail of milk and ends up with nothing. She concludes the story by saying, "I am Gros-Jean just like before."

17. Jean-Baptiste Poquelin (or Molière) (1622–73) was a playwright in the late seventeenth century during the classical period of French drama. Bastiat quotes Molière many times in the *Sophisms,* as he finds his comedy of manners very useful in pointing out political and economic confusions.

18. (Paillottet's note) See the letter addressed to M. Larnac in vol. 1 and the *Parliamentary Conflicts of Interest* in vol. 2. [The letter Paillottet refers to is "On Parliamentary Reform" (CW1, pp. 367–70). In the letter Bastiat objects to the practice of taxpayer-funded public servants being permitted to run for election and sitting in a Chamber which can determine their level of pay (p. 368). Bastiat likens this to allowing wig makers to create the laws which regulate hairdressing, which would result in a state where "we would soon be inordinately well groomed, indeed to the point of tyranny" (p. 370).]

Certain nations appear to be astonishingly well disposed to becoming the prey of government Plunder. They are the ones in which men, totally disregarding their own dignity and energy, think that they would be lost if they were not being *administered* and *governed* in every sphere. Although I have not traveled a great deal, I have seen countries in which it is thought that agriculture could not make any progress if the State did not keep experimental farms, that there would soon be no more horses if the State did not have a stud farm, that fathers would not bring up their children or would have them taught only immoral things if the State did not decide what was fit to be learned, etc., etc. In a country like this, revolutions may follow one another in quick succession and governments fall one after the other. But those being governed will be no less governed to within an inch of their lives (for the disposition I am pointing out here is the very stuff of which governments are made) until the point is reached at which the people finally see that it is better to leave as many *services* as possible in the category of those that interested parties exchange for a *freely negotiated price*.

We have seen that society is based on an *exchange of services*. It ought to be just an exchange of good and honest services. But we have also noted that men had a great interest and consequently an irresistible urge to exaggerate the relative value of the services they rendered. And in all truth, I cannot see any other limit to this pretension than leaving the people to whom these services are offered the freedom to accept or refuse them.

From this it results that certain men have recourse to the law to reduce the natural prerogatives of this freedom for others. This type of plunder is called Privilege or Monopoly. Note well its origin and character.

Everybody knows that the services he brings to the general marketplace will be all the more appreciated and remunerated the scarcer they are. Everyone will therefore beg for the law to intervene to remove from the marketplace all those who come to offer similar services or, what amounts to the same thing, if the use of a tool is essential for the service to be rendered, he will demand from the law its exclusive possession.[19]

Since this type of Plunder is the principal subject of this volume, I will not dwell on it here and will limit myself to one observation.

When monopoly is an isolated occurrence, it is sure to make the person empowered by the law rich. It may then happen that each class of workers

---

19. For the distinction between true monopolies and what have been called natural monopolies, see the note that accompanies the account of the doctrine of Adam Smith on *value* in chapter 5 "On Value" in *Economic Harmonies* in CW5 (forthcoming).

claims a similar monopoly for itself, instead of working toward the downfall of this monopoly. This characteristic of Plunder, reduced to a system, then becomes the most ridiculous hoax of all for everyone, and the final result is that each person thinks that he is gaining *more* from a general market that is *totally impoverished.*[20]

It is not necessary to add that this strange regime also introduces universal antagonism between all classes, professions, and peoples; that it requires constant but uncertain interference from the government; that it abounds in the abuses described in the preceding paragraph; it puts all areas of production into a position of irremediable insecurity and accustoms men to attributing the responsibility for their own existence to the law and not themselves. It would be difficult to imagine a more active cause of social unrest.[21]

Justification

People will say: "Why are you using this ugly word, Plunder? Apart from the fact that it is crude, it is upsetting, irritating, and turns calm and moderate men against you. It poisons the debate."[22]

I will declare loudly that I respect people. I believe in the sincerity of almost all the advocates of Protection, and I do not claim the right to suspect the personal probity, scrupulousness, and philanthropy of anyone at all. I repeat once more that Protection is the work, the disastrous work, of a common error of which everyone, or at least the great majority, is both victim and accomplice. After that, I cannot stop things being what they are.

20. This chapter was probably written in late 1847 and prefigures Bastiat's definition of the state as "the great fiction by which everyone endeavors to live at the expense of everyone else," which he developed during the course of 1848. A draft of the essay appeared in his revolutionary magazine *Jacques Bonhomme* in June 1848 (CW2, pp. 105–6); a larger article on "The State" appeared in *Le Journal des débats* in September 1848, and it was subsequently published as a separate booklet of the same name later that same year (CW2, pp. 93–104).

21. (Paillottet's note) The author was soon to witness the development of this cause of unrest and combat it energetically. See below "The State" (*OC*, vol. 4, p. 327, "L'État" in CW2, pp. 93–104); "Disastrous Illusions," in volume 3 [ES3 24], and the final pages of chapter 4 in volume 6 (*OC*, vol. 6, p. 94, "On Échange" in CW5). [Paillottet is incorrect when he says that "Disastrous Illusions" is in *OC*, vol. 3. It is in fact in *OC*, vol. 2, pp. 466–82.]

22. The choice of words appropriate to describe these actions is one Bastiat grappled with repeatedly. See especially ES2 9, p. 170, where Bastiat says it is time to use a more "brutal style" of language to describe things like protectionism and subsidies to businesses. See also "Plain Speaking," in the Note on the Translation.

Imagine a sort of Diogenes[23] sticking his head outside his barrel and saying: "People of Athens, you have yourselves served by slaves. Have you never thought that you are exercising over your brothers the most iniquitous type of plunder?"

Or again, a tribune in the Forum saying: "People of Rome, you have based all of your means of existence on the repeated pillage of all other peoples."

They would certainly be expressing only an incontrovertible truth. Should we then conclude that Athens and Rome were inhabited only by dishonest people? That Socrates and Plato, Cato[24] and Cincinnatus,[25] were despicable men?

Who could entertain such a thought? However, these great men lived in an environment that robbed them of any awareness of their injustice. We know that Aristotle was unable even to entertain the idea that a society could live without slavery.

In modern times, slavery has existed up to the present time without generating many scruples in the souls of plantation owners. Armies have been the instruments of great conquests, that is to say, great forms of plunder. Is this to say that they are not full of soldiers and officers who are personally just as scrupulous and perhaps more scrupulous than is generally the case in careers in industry, men whom the very thought of theft would cause to blush and who would face a thousand deaths rather than stoop to a base act?

What is condemnable are not individuals but the general milieu that carries them along and blinds them, a milieu of which society as a whole is guilty.

This is the case of monopoly. I accuse the system and not individuals, society as a whole and not any particular one of its members. If the greatest philosophers have been able to delude themselves over the iniquity of slavery, how much more reason have farmers and manufacturers to be mistaken with regard to the nature and effects of the protectionist regime?

23. Diogenes (413–327 B.C.) was a Greek philosopher who renounced wealth and lived by begging from others and sleeping in a barrel in the marketplace. His purpose was to live simply and virtuously by giving up the conventional desires for power, wealth, prestige, and fame.

24. Cato the Younger (Cato Minor) (95–46 B.C.) was a politician in the late Roman Republic and a noted defender of "Roman Liberty" and an opponent of Julius Caesar.

25. Cincinnatus (520–430 B.C.). Served as consul in 460 B.C. and briefly as Roman dictator in 458 and 439 B.C., when Rome was threatened by invasion. He was admired for his willingness to give up the powers of dictator and return to his farm after the military crisis was over.

2. Two Moral Philosophies

PUBLISHING HISTORY:

Original title: "Deux morales."
Place and date of first publication: No date given. First
    published in book form.
First French edition as book or pamphlet: *Economic Sophisms*
    (Second Series) (1848). First and Second Series were
    combined in one edition in 1851.
Location in Paillottet's edition of *OC:* Vol. 4. *Sophismes
    économiques. Petits pamphlets I,* pp. 148–56.
Previous translations: 1st American ed., 1848; 1st British ed.,
    1873; FEE ed., 1964.

At the end of the preceding chapter, if the reader has reached that far, I can well hear him cry:

"Well then! Are we mistaken in blaming economists for being dry and cold? What a picture of humanity! If they are right, plunder would be a disastrous force, one that is virtually taken for granted, taking all forms and exercised under all types of pretext, both outside the law and by the law, abusing the holiest of things, exploiting weakness and credulity in turn and advancing as these two sources of nourishment flourish around it! Can a darker picture of this world be painted?"

The question is not to know whether the picture is dark but whether it is true. History is there to tell us this.

It is rather strange that those who decry political economy (or *economism*, as they like to call this science), because it studies man and the world as they are, take pessimism very much further than it does, at least with regard to the past and present. Open their books and journals and what do you see? Bitterness, a hatred of society to the extent that the very word *civilization* is in their eyes synonymous with injustice, disorder, and anarchy. They have come to curse *freedom,* so low is their confidence in the development of the human race resulting from its natural organization. Freedom! This is what, according to them, is impelling us inexorably toward the abyss.

It is true that they are optimistic with regard to the future. For if humanity, incapable on its own, has been going the wrong way for six thousand years, a prophet has come to show it the path of salvation, and if only the flock obeys the shepherd's crook it will be led into this promised land in which well-being is achieved without effort and where order, security, and harmony are the easy prize of improvidence.

All humanity has to do is to agree to reformers' changing its *physical and moral constitution,* in the words of Rousseau.[1]

Political economy has not taken on the mission of seeking to ascertain what society would be like if God had made man otherwise than it pleased him to do. It is perhaps tedious that Providence forgot to call upon a few of our modern organizers for advice at the beginning.[2] And, as celestial mechanics would have been quite different if the Creator had consulted Alphonse the Wise,[3] and equally if he had not neglected Fourier's advice, social order would bear no resemblance to the one we are forced to breathe, live, and move in. But, since we are here, since *in eo vivimus, movemur et sumus,*[4] all we can do is to study it and learn its laws, especially since its improvement essentially depends on this knowledge.

We cannot prevent insatiable desires from springing up in the heart of man.

1. Bastiat is referring to "The Legislator" (*Social Contract* chap. 7, bk. 2, para. 3), in which Rousseau uses the following phrases: "changer pour ainsi dire la nature humaine … altérer la constitution de l'homme pour la renforcer" (to change human nature … to alter the makeup of man in order to strengthen it). This text can be found in Rousseau, *A Discourse on Inequality,* pp. 84–85; Rousseau, *Du contrat social et autres œuvres politiques,* p. 261; or Rousseau, *The Political Writings of Jean Jacques Rousseau,* http://oll.libertyfund .org/titles/711#Rousseau_0065-02c_167.

2. Bastiat here is referring to the socialist school which emerged in France during the 1830s and 1840s. Two terms that had a special meaning for its adherents were "association" and "organization," by which they meant the state organization of labor and industry, not the voluntary association and organization advocated by Bastiat and the other Economists. See "Bastiat's Use of the Socialist Terms 'Organization' and 'Association,'" in the Note on the Translation.

3. Alphonso the Wise ("El Sabio") (Alfonso X, 1221–84). King of León and Castile from 1252 to 1284 and was reputed to have said that if he had been present at the creation of the world, he would have had a few words of advice for the Creator on how better to order the universe. During his reign he attempted to reorganize the Castillian sheep industry, raised money by debasing the currency, and imposed high tariffs in order to prevent the inevitable price rises which resulted.

4. "In it we live and move and have our being." The phrase comes from the Latin Vulgate, St. Paul, Acts of the Apostles 17:18: "In ipso enim vivimus et movemur et sumus sicut et quidam vestrum poetarum dixerunt ipsius enim et genus sumus" (For in him we live and move and are: as some also of your own poets said: For we are also his offspring).

We cannot arrange things so that no work is required for these desires to be satisfied.

We cannot avoid the fact that man's reluctance to work is as strong as his desire to have his needs satisfied.

We cannot prevent the fact that, as a result of this state of affairs, there is a constant effort by men to increase their share of enjoyment while each of them tries by force or by fraud to throw the burden of labor onto the shoulders of his fellows.

It is not up to us to wipe out universal history, to stifle the voice of the past that attests that things have been like this from the outset. We cannot deny that war, slavery, serfdom, theocracy, abuse by government, privileges, frauds of all kinds, and monopolies have been the incontrovertible and terrible manifestations of these two sentiments that are intertwined in the hearts of men: *attraction to pleasure, avoidance of pain.*

"By the sweat of thy brow shalt thou eat bread." But everyone wants as much bread and as little sweat as possible. This is the conclusion of history.

Thank heaven, history also shows that the distribution of pleasures and pains among men tends to occur in an increasingly even way.

Short of denying the obvious, we have to admit that society has made some progress in this regard.

If this is so, society therefore has within it a natural and providential force, a law that increasingly causes the principle of iniquity to retreat and the principle of justice to be realized.

We state that this force is within society and that God has placed it there. If it were not there, we, like the Utopians,[5] would be reduced to seeking it in artificial means, in arrangements that require the prior alteration of the *physical and moral constitution* of man, or rather, we would believe this search to be useless and vain, since we cannot understand the action of a lever if it has no fulcrum.

Let us therefore endeavor to identify the beneficent force that tends to overcome little by little the malevolent force we have called Plunder, whose presence is only too clearly explained by reason and noted by experience.

Any malevolent action has of necessity two components, the source from which it comes and the place at which it ends; the person who carries out the action and the person on whom the action is carried out, or as one might

5. See the entry for "Utopias," in the Glossary of Subjects and Terms.

have put it in a grammar class at school, the *subject* and the *object* of the sentence.[6]

There are therefore two opportunities for a malevolent action to be eliminated: the voluntary abstention of the *active* being and the resistance of the *passive* being.

Hence there are two moral philosophies that, far from contradicting each other, work together: a morality based on religion or philosophy, or one which I will permit myself to call *economic*.

A religious moral philosophy addresses the author of a malevolent action, man *as the initiator of plunder,*[7] in order to eliminate it. It tells him, "Reform yourself, purify yourself, stop committing evil and do good. Overcome your passions, sacrifice your personal interest, cease to oppress your neighbor whom it is your duty to love and care for. Be just above all and then charitable." This moral philosophy will always be the finest, the most touching, and the one that reveals the human race in all its majesty, the one that most encourages flights of eloquence and generates the most admiration and sympathy in men.

An economic moral philosophy aspires to achieve the same result but above all addresses men *as victims of plunder.* It shows them the effects of human actions and, by this simple demonstration, stimulates them to react against the actions that hurt them and honor those that are useful to them. It endeavors to disseminate enough good sense, enlightenment, and justified mistrust in the oppressed masses to make oppression increasingly difficult and dangerous.

It should be noted that economic morality cannot help but also act on oppressors. A malevolent act has good and evil consequences: evil consequences for those who suffer it and good consequences for those who carry it out; otherwise it would not occur. But it is a long way from being compensatory. The sum of evil always outweighs the good, and this has to be so, since

---

6. Bastiat uses the technical terms "agent" and "patient," which are grammatical terms used to describe "the cause or initiator of an event" and "the target upon whom an action is carried out," respectively, which we have translated as the "subject" and "object" of a sentence.

7. Bastiat returns here and in the next paragraph to the terminology of grammar to make his point about plunder. He refers to *l'homme en tant qu'agent* (man as the initiator of the action) and *l'homme en tant que patient* (man as the object of the action). Another way of expressing this is "man as the initiator of plunder" (i.e., the plunderer) and "man as the victim of plunder" (i.e., the plundered).

the very fact of oppression leads to a depletion of strength, creates dangers, provokes retaliation, and requires costly precautions. A simple revelation of these effects is thus not limited to triggering a reaction in those oppressed; it rallies to the flag of justice all those whose hearts have not been corrupted and undermines the security of the oppressors themselves.

But it is easy to understand that this moral philosophy, which is more implicit than explicit and which is after all just a scientific demonstration; which would even lose its effectiveness if it changed character; which is not aimed at the heart, but the mind; which does not seek to persuade, but to convince; which does not give advice, but proof; whose mission is not to touch the emotions, but to enlighten and whose only victory over vice is to deprive it of sustenance: it is easy, I say, to understand that this moral philosophy has been accused of being dry and dull.

This objection is true but unjust. It amounts to saying that political economy does not state everything, does not include everything, and is not a universal science. But who has ever put forward such an exorbitant claim on its behalf?

The accusation would be well-founded only if political economy presented its procedures as being exclusive and had the effrontery, as we might say, to forbid philosophy and religion from using all their own direct means of working toward the progress of mankind.

Let us accept therefore the simultaneous action of morality proper and of political economy, with the first casting a slur on the motives and evident ugliness of malevolent acts and the second discrediting them in our beliefs by giving a picture of their effects.

Let us even admit that the triumph, when it occurs, of religious moralists is finer, more consoling, and more radical. But at the same time it is difficult not to acknowledge that the triumph of economic science is easier and more sure.

In a few lines that are worth more than a host of heavy volumes, Jean-Baptiste Say has already drawn to our attention that there are two ways of stopping the conflict introduced into an honorable family by hypocrisy: *correcting Tartuffe* or *teaching Orgon the ways of the world.*[8] Molière, a great

---

8. In Molière's play *Tartuffe, or the Imposter* (1664), Tartuffe is a scheming hypocrite and Orgon is a well-meaning dupe. With the reference in the previous sentence to the conflict between "religious moralists" and economics, and the problem of hypocrisy, Bastiat probably has in mind the following lines from J.-B. Say's *Cours complet d'économie politique pratique,* where Say discusses what he calls "one of the thorniest parts of practi-

painter of the human heart, seems to have had the second of these procedures constantly in view as being the more effective.

This is just as true on the world stage.

Tell me what Caesar did and I will tell you what the Romans of his time
were like.

Tell me what modern diplomacy is accomplishing and I will tell you what
the moral state of nations is like.

We would not be paying nearly two billion in taxes if we did not hand
over the power to vote for them to those who are gobbling them up.[9]

We would not have all the problems and expenses of the African question[10] if we were as fully convinced that *two and two are four* in political
economy just as they are in arithmetic.

M. Guizot would not have the opportunity of saying, "*France is rich
enough to pay for its glory*"[11] if France had never fallen in love with false glory.

This same Statesman would never have said, "*Freedom is sufficiently precious for France not to trade it away*" if France fully understood that a *swollen
budget* and *freedom* are incompatible.[12]

---

cal politics," namely how to keep public expenditure to a "minimum." Say warns of paying
too many public employees, having a too costly court, having an army which violates the
rights of citizens instead of protecting them, and "having a greedy and ambitious clergy
who brutalizes children, splits apart families, seizes their inheritance, makes a hypocrisy
of their honor, and supports abuses and persecutes those who tell the truth" (*Cours complet,* pt. 7, chap. 13, "De l'économie dans les dépenses de la société," p. 432).

9. The total expenditure of the French state budgeted for 1849 was fr. 1.573 billion and
the amount received in taxes and other charges was fr. 1.412 billion, creating a deficit of
fr. 160.8 million. The total amount for the Colonial Service in the Ministry of the Navy
and Colonies (which included Algeria) was fr. 20.3 million. See *L'Annuaire de l'économie
politique et de la statistique* (1850), p. 21.

10. France conquered Algiers in 1830 and began a slow process of colonization whereby
European settlement took place on the coastal plain. As resistance to the French invasion
grew, some rebels moved into neighboring Morocco, sparking a brief war between France
and Morocco in 1844 which was concluded by the signing of the Treaty of Tangiers.

11. These words have been attributed to Guizot, but a note on "Historical Phrases" in
the journal *Notes and Queries,* May 29, 1875, p. 421, disputes this. Here the author states
that "For many years M. Guizot bore with unruffled humor the burden of having said,
'La France est assez riche pour payer sa gloire.' This utterance has just been traced, however, to M. John Lemoinne, the well-known writer in the *Journal des débats* and *employé*
in the Paris financial house of Rothschild. M. Lemoinne accepts the responsibility of the
above phrase, which so enraged the economists when it was written as a justification for
the peace which France made with Morocco without asking for any indemnity whatever."

12. We have not been able to find the source of this quote.

It is not the monopolizers, as is widely believed, but those who are monopolized who keep monopolies in place.

And, where elections are concerned, it is not because there are corruptors that there are those who can be corrupted. It's the opposite; and the proof of this is that it is those who can be corrupted who pay all the costs of corruption. Would it not be up to them to put a stop to it?

Let religious morality therefore touch the hearts of the Tartuffes, the Caesars, the colonists, sinecurists, and monopolists, etc. if it can. The task of political economy is to enlighten their dupes.

Which of these two procedures works more effectively toward social progress? Do we have to spell it out? I believe it is the second. I fear that humanity cannot escape the necessity of first learning a *defensive moral philosophy*.

No matter how much I look, whatever I read or observe and whatever the questions I ask, I cannot find any abuse carried out on anything like a wide scale that has been destroyed through the voluntary renunciation of those benefiting from it.

On the other hand, I have found many that have been overcome by the active resistance of those suffering from them.

Describing the consequences of abuse is therefore the most effective way of destroying it. And how true this is, especially when it concerns abuses like protectionism, which, while inflicting genuine harm on the masses, nurture only illusion and disappointment in those who believe they are benefiting from them.

After all this, will this type of moral persuasion succeed by itself in achieving all the social progress that the attractive nature of the human soul and the noblest of its faculties gives us leave to hope for and foresee? I am far from claiming this. Let us assume the total diffusion of this *defensive moral philosophy,* which is, after all, nothing other than a recognition of well understood interests that are in accordance with the general good and with justice. A society like this, although certainly well ordered, might well fail to be very attractive, one in which there were no more rascals simply because there were no more dupes, in which vice would be constantly *latent,* numbed by famine, so to speak, and merely waiting for sustenance to revive it, and in which the prudence of each person would be governed by the vigilance of all, a society, in a word, in which reform regulating external acts would be only skin deep, not having penetrated to the depths of people's consciences. A society like this sometimes appears to us reflected in men who are strict, rigorous, just, ready to reject the slightest encroachment of their rights and skilled in avoiding being undermined in any way. You hold them in esteem and perhaps admire them; you would make them your deputy but not your friend.

Let these *two moral philosophies,* therefore, work hand in hand instead of mutually decrying one another, and attack vice in a pincer movement. While economists are doing their job, opening the eyes of the Orgons, uprooting preconceived ideas, stimulating just and essential mistrust, and studying and exposing the true nature of things and actions, let religious moralists for their part carry out their more attractive but difficult work. Let them engage in-iquity in hand-to-hand combat. Let them pursue it right into the deepest fi-bers of the heart. Let them paint the charms of benevolent action, self-denial, and self-sacrifice. Let them open the source of virtues where we can only turn off the source of vice: that is their task, and one that is noble and fine. Why then do they dispute the usefulness of the task that has fallen to us?

In a society that, while not being intrinsically virtuous, is nevertheless well ordered because of the action of *economic morality* (which is the knowledge of the *economy* which the society possesses), do the opportunities for pro-gress not open up for religious morality?

Habit, it is said, is a second nature.

A country where for a long time everyone is unaccustomed to injustice simply as a result of the resistance to this of a general public that is enlight-ened, may still be unhappy. However, in my view, it would be well placed to receive a higher and purer form of education. Being unaccustomed to evil is a great step toward good. Men cannot remain stationary. Once they have turned away from the path of vice, which no longer leads anywhere save to infamy, they would be all the more attracted to virtue.

Perhaps society has to pass through this prosaic state in which people practice virtue through calculation in order to lift itself up to that more po-etic region where they would no longer need this motive.

3. The Two Axes

PUBLISHING HISTORY:

Original title: "Les deux haches."
Place and date of first publication: No date given. First
    published in book form.
First French edition as book or pamphlet: *Economic Sophisms*

(Second Series) (1848). First and Second Series were
combined in one edition in 1851.

Location in Paillottet's edition of *OC:* Vol. 4. *Sophismes
économiques. Petits pamphlets I,* pp. 156–59.

Previous translations: 1st American ed., 1848; 1st British ed.,
1873; FEE ed., 1964.

A petition from Jacques Bonhomme,[1] *Carpenter, to M. Cunin-Gridaine,*[2]
Minister of Trade.

Minister and Manufacturer,

I am a carpenter like Jesus; I wield an axe and an adze to serve you.

Now, while chopping and hewing from dawn to dusk on the lands of our
lord the king, the idea came to me that my work is just as *national* as yours.

And this being so, I do not see why protection should not extend to my
worksite as it does to your workshop.

For, when all is said and done, if you make sheets, I make roofs. Both of us
in different ways shelter our customers from the cold and rain.

However, I pursue customers while customers pursue you. You have been
perfectly successful in forcing them to do so by preventing them from being
supplied elsewhere, whereas my customers can go where they please.

What is surprising in this? M. Cunin the Minister has remembered
M. Cunin the weaver, and that is only natural. But alas! My humble trade
has not given a minister to France, even though it gave a God to the world.

And this God, in the immortal code he bequeathed to men, has not
slipped into it the slightest little word that would authorize carpenters to
grow wealthy, as you do, at the expense of others.

Look at my position, then. I earn thirty sous a day except for when the day
is a Sunday or public holiday. If I offer you my services at the same time as a

1. This is the first use of the character "Jacques Bonhomme" in the *Economic Sophisms,*
though not the first chronologically speaking. The first occurrence appeared in an article,
"Salt, the Mail, and the Customs Service," in *JDE* (May 1846), which also appears below
as ES2.12. He also is used in ES2 10 "The Tax Collector" and ES2 13 "The Three Municipal Magistrates," which were probably written in late 1847. The main use of this character
occurs in March and June 1848 in Bastiat's revolutionary magazines, especially the one
called *Jacques Bonhomme,* which appeared in June 1848. He was next used by Bastiat in
five of the chapters of *What Is Seen and What Is Not Seen* (July 1850). See the Glossary
entry on "Jacques Bonhomme."

2. Laurent Cunin-Gridaine (1778–1859) was a very successful, self-made textile manufacturer from Sedan. As Minister for Trade from 1840 to 1848 he was a strong supporter
of protection for the textile industry.

Flemish carpenter who offered a one-sou discount, you would prefer giving him the business.

However, do I need to clothe myself? If a Belgian weaver lays out his woolen cloth side by side with yours, you throw him, and his woolen cloth, out of the country.

This means that, since I am forced to come to your shop, which is more expensive, my poor thirty sous are in effect worth only twenty-eight.

What am I saying? They are not even worth twenty-six, for instead of throwing the Belgian weaver out *at your own expense* (this would be the least you could do), you make me pay for the people who, in your interest, you order to drive them away![3]

And, since a great many of your colegislators, with whom you are in perfect collusion, all take one or two sous from me on the pretext of protecting, this one, iron, another coal, others oil or wheat, so at the end of the day I find that I have barely been able to keep fifteen sous of my thirty from being plundered.[4]

You will doubtless tell me that these small sous, which move with no compensation from my pocket to yours, provide a living for people around your chateau and enable you to live in grand style. To which I would reply, if you allowed me to do so, that they would provide a living for people around me.

Be that as it may, Minister and Manufacturer, knowing that I will receive short shrift from you, I will not come to demand, as I have every right to do, that you abandon the *restriction* that you place on your customers; I prefer to follow the common route and claim a small slice of *protection* for myself as well.

At this point you will place a difficulty in my way. "Friend," you will say, "I would like to protect you and your fellow men, but how can I confer Customs favors on the work of carpenters? Will we have to prohibit the import of houses by land and sea?"

That would be somewhat laughable, but by dint of pondering it, I have

3. According to the budget figures for 1848, the French government spent fr. 24.3 million on the salaries of workers in the Customs Service and fr. 703,000 on other administrative costs for a total of about fr. 26 million.

4. Without taking into account the increase in prices for goods protected from foreign competition, according to the budget figures for 1848 the French government spent fr. 15 million on direct subsidies to exporters and a further fr. 4.3 million on other subsidies, for a total of fr. 19.3 million. Other government expenses which might benefit the industries mentioned here are hard to determine. For example, the Ministry of Public Works spent fr. 23.2 million on the railways (iron), and the Ministry of War spent fr. 11.6 million on uniforms and housing (textiles).

discovered another way of granting favors to the sons of Saint Joseph, and you would be all the more ready to welcome this, I hope, in that it differs not a whit from the means that constitutes the privilege you vote each year in your favor.

This marvelous means is to forbid the use of sharpened axes in France.

I say that this *restriction* would be no more illogical or arbitrary than that to which we are subject with regard to your woolen cloth.

Why do you chase Belgians away? Because they sell cheaper than you. And why do they sell cheaper than you? Because as weavers, they have a superiority of some sort over you.

Between you and the Belgians, therefore, there is just about the same difference as between a dull and sharp axe.[5]

And you force me, as a carpenter, to buy the product of the dull axe!

Think of France as a worker who, through his work, wants to buy himself all sorts of things, including woolen cloth.

He has two ways of doing this:

The first is to spin and weave the wool.

The second is to manufacture clocks, wallpaper, or wine, for example, and deliver them to Belgians in return for woolen cloth.

Whichever of these two procedures gives the best result may be represented by the sharp axe and the other by the dull one.

You do not deny that we currently obtain a length of cloth from a loom in France *with more work and effort* (that is the dull axe) than from a vine (that is the sharp axe). You absolutely cannot deny it because it is exactly through consideration of this *extra effort* (which in your scheme of things constitutes wealth) that you recommend, and what is more, you *require* that we use the worse of the two axes.

Well then! Be consistent and impartial, if you wish to be just, and treat poor carpenters as you treat yourselves.

Pass a law that says:

"No one can use anything other than beams and joists produced by dull axes."

---

5. Bastiat probably got the idea of a sophism about the sharp and the blunt axes from the English free trader Thomas Perronet Thompson, who wrote a critique of the French government inquiry into tariff policy in 1834 in which he stated that "the liberty of commerce would increase the aggregate total of consumption, by all the difference of prices; in the same manner as the quantity of wood a man cuts, would be increased by the liberty of using a sharp hatchet instead of a blunt one" ("Contre-Enquête," in Thompson, *Exercises, Political and Others* 3:213).

See what would happen immediately.

Where we once gave one hundred blows of the axe, we now give three hundred. What we once could do in an hour now requires three. What a powerful incitement to work! There would no longer be enough apprentices, guild craftsmen, and masters. We would be sought after, and therefore well paid. Whoever wanted to have a roof would be obliged to submit to our demands, just as those who want cloth are obliged to submit to yours.

And if these theoreticians in favor of *free trade* ever dare to call into question the usefulness of the measure, we will know very well where to turn for a triumphant refutation. Your parliamentary inquiry of 1834[6] is there. We will beat them with it, for in it you have admirably pleaded the cause of prohibition and dull axes, which are one and the same.

4. The Lower Council of Labor

PUBLISHING HISTORY:

> Original title: "Conseil inférieur du travail."
> Place and date of first publication: No date given. First
>   published in book form.
> First French edition as book or pamphlet: *Economic Sophisms*
>   (Second Series) (1848). First and Second Series were
>   combined in one edition in 1851.
> Location in Paillottet's edition of *OC*: Vol. 4. *Sophismes
>   économiques. Petits pamphlets I*, pp. 160–63.
> Previous translations: 1st American ed., 1848; 1st British ed.,
>   1873; FEE ed., 1964.

"What! You have the nerve to demand for every citizen the right to sell, purchase, barter, exchange, and give and receive services for services and allow him to judge for himself on the sole condition that he does not infringe honesty and that he satisfies the public Treasury? You therefore want to snatch work, pay, and bread from the workers?"

6. There were two reviews of French tariff policy: one in 1822 under the Restoration, which created the modern alliance of powerful interest groups which benefited from protectionism, and a second in 1834 under the July Monarchy. The government inquiry into French tariff policy held in October 1834 raised hopes that it might lead to a reduction in the level of tariffs as the minister of commerce, Thiers, was in favor. However, the Inquiry concluded that France should continue its protection of industry.

This is what we are being told. I know what to think of this, but I wanted to find out what the workers themselves think.

I had an excellent tool available for carrying out surveys.

It was not at all one of the *Superior Councils of Industry*[1] in which large landowners who call themselves ploughmen, powerful shipowners who think they are sailors, and rich shareholders who claim to be workers carry out the sort of philanthropy we all know about.

No, these were proper workers, *serious* workers, as they are now called, joiners, carpenters, masons, tailors, shoemakers, dyers, blacksmiths, innkeepers, grocers, etc., etc., who founded a *mutual aid society*[2] in my village.

Using my own authority, I transformed this into a *Lower Council of Labor*[3] and obtained from it an inquiry which is every bit as good as any other although it is not stuffed with figures and swollen to the size of a *quarto* volume printed at State expense.[4]

It took the form of questioning these fine people on the way they are, or believe they are, affected by the protectionist regime. The Chairman pointed out to me that this was something of an infringement on the conditions for the existence of the *association*. For in France, this land of freedom, people who *form an association* give up any right to discuss politics, that is to say, any discussion of their common interest.[5] However, after much hesitation, he included the question on the agenda.

1. An ordinance of 1831 created within the ministry of commerce a "Conseil supérieur du commerce" (Superior Council of Commerce), which had the authority to conduct official inquiries into matters such as tariff policy. The first such inquiry was held in October 1834 at which the largest and most politically well-connected manufacturers, landowners, and merchants closed ranks in their opposition to any tariff reform.

2. Mutual aid societies are similar to the English "friendly societies." Their role is described by Bastiat in *Economic Harmonies,* chap. 14, "On Salaries" (*OC,* vol. 6, p. 394, "Des salaires").

3. Bastiat is making fun of the activities of the Superior Council of Commerce, the members of which were ardent supporters of protectionism. Bastiat is here imagining what would happen if smaller businessmen and artisans were able to have their say by forming an "Inferior" (or lower) Council.

4. Bastiat is referring to the detailed three-volume report issued by the Superior Council of Commerce in 1835. The list of members of the inquiry reads like a who's who of the protectionists Bastiat mentions and criticizes throughout *Economic Sophisms.* See Duchâtel, *Enquête relative à diverses prohibitions.* It was 1,459 pages in length and printed by the government printing office at taxpayers' expense.

5. Bastiat has in mind the restrictions imposed by the Le Chapelier Law of 1791. Jean Le Chapelier (1754–94) was a lawyer and politician during the early phase of the French Revolution. He was elected to the Estates General in 1789 and was a founder of the radical Jacobin Club. He is most famous for introducing the above-mentioned law, which

The assembly was divided into as many commissions as there were groups of various trades. Each one was given a chart that it had to complete after two weeks of discussion.

On the due date, the venerable Chairman took his seat on the official chair (this is a formal expression since it was just an ordinary chair) and found on the desk (another formal expression since it was a table made of poplar wood) about fifteen reports, which he read in turn.

The first was from the *tailors*. Here is a copy of it that is as accurate as if it were a facsimile.

THE EFFECTS OF PROTECTION—THE REPORT FROM THE TAILORS

Disadvantages	Advantages
1. *Because of the protectionist regime,* we pay more for bread, meat, sugar, wood, yarn, needles, etc., which amounts to a considerable reduction in earnings for us;	None[1]
2. *Because of the protectionist regime,* our customers also pay more for everything, which leaves them less to spend on clothes, from which it follows that we have less work and therefore less profit;	
3. *Because of the protectionist regime,* fabrics are expensive and people make their clothes last longer or go without. This is also a reduction in work, which forces us to offer our services at a discount.	1. No matter how we took our measurements, we found it impossible to find any way whatsoever in which the protectionist regime is advantageous to our business.

was enacted on 14 June 1791. The Assembly had abolished the privileged corporations of masters and occupations of the old regime in March, and the Le Chapelier Law was designed to do the same thing to organizations of both entrepreneurs and their workers. The law effectively banned guilds and trade unions (as well as the right to strike) until it was altered in 1864. Article 2 of the Le Chapelier Law of June 1791 states: "Citizens of the same occupation or profession, entrepreneurs, those who maintain open shop, workers, and journeymen of any craft whatsoever may not, when they are together, name either president, secretaries, or trustees, keep accounts, pass decrees or resolutions, or draft regulations concerning their alleged common interests."

Here is another table:

THE EFFECTS OF PROTECTION—THE
REPORT FROM THE BLACKSMITHS

Disadvantages	Advantages
1. The protectionist regime inflicts on us a tax, which does not go to the Treasury, each time we eat, drink, heat ourselves, or dress ourselves;	None
2. It inflicts a similar tax on our fellow citizens, who are not blacksmiths, and since they are poorer by this amount most of them make wooden nails and door latches from string, which deprives us of work;	
3. It keeps iron at such a high price that in the countryside no one uses it in carts, grills, or balconies, and our trade, which is capable of providing work for so many people who have none, is lacking work for us ourselves;	
4. What the tax authorities fail to raise on goods that are not imported is taken on our salt and letters.[6]	

All the other tables, which I will spare the reader, echoed the same refrain. Gardeners, carpenters, shoemakers, clog makers, boatmen, and millers all expressed the same complaints.

I deplored the fact that there were no farm laborers in our association. Their report would certainly have been very instructive.

But alas! In our region of the Landes,[7] the poor farm laborers, as *protected* as they are, do not have a sou, and, after they have seen to the welfare of their own cattle, they themselves cannot join any *mutual aid societies*. The

6. In 1849 the income the French government received from taxes and tariffs on salt was fr. 25.6 million and from the monopoly on mail fr. 49.8 million, out of total income of fr. 1.4 billion. The total revenue from tariffs and customs duties was fr. 156.8 million. See *L'Annuaire de l'économie politique et de la statistique* (1850), p. 24.

7. Bastiat came from the Landes, in southwest France, and represented it in the Constituent and National Assemblies after the February 1848 Revolution.

alleged favors of protection do not stop them from being the *pariahs* of our social order. What shall I say about vine growers?

What I noted above all was the common sense with which our villagers saw not only the direct harm that the protectionist regime was doing them but also the indirect harm which, as it affected their customers, ricocheted or flowed on[8] to them.

This is what, I said to myself, the economists of *Le Moniteur industriel* appear not to understand.

And perhaps those men who are dazzled by a little protection, in particular the tenant farmers, would be ready to give it up if they saw this side of the question.

Perhaps they would say to themselves, "It is better to provide for oneself surrounded by prosperous customers than to be *protected* surrounded by impoverished ones."

For wanting to enrich each industry in turn by creating an economic void around them is as vain an effort as trying to jump over your shadow.

5. High Prices and Low Prices

PUBLISHING HISTORY:

> Original title: "Cherté, bon marché."
> Place and date of first publication: *Le Libre-échange,* 25 July 1847, no. 35, pp. 273–74, with supplement from 1 August 1847.
> First French edition as book or pamphlet: *Economic Sophisms* (Second Series) (1848). First and Second Series were combined in one edition in 1851.
> Location in Paillottet's edition of *OC:* Vol. 4. *Sophismes économiques. Petits pamphlets I,* pp. 163–73.
> Previous translations: 1st American ed., 1848; 1st British ed., 1873; FEE ed., 1964.

I think I have to put forward to the reader a few remarks that are, alas, theoretical, on the illusions that arise from the words *high prices* and *low prices.*

---

8. This sophism, which is not dated but was probably written in 1847, contains one of the first instances of the phrase *par ricochet,* which we have translated as the "ricochet effect." Bastiat would later develop this into a theory of unintended consequences, or "flow on effects," caused by government intervention. See "The Ricochet Effect," in *Further Aspects.*

At first sight, I realize that these remarks will be taken to be somewhat subtle, but subtle or not, the question is to determine whether they are true. Now, I think they are perfectly true, and above all just the thing to make the many people who sincerely believe in the effectiveness of protectionism, engage in a bit of reflection.

Whether we are partisans of freedom or defenders of trade restriction, we are all reduced to using the words *high prices* and *low prices.* Partisans of freedom declare themselves in favor of *things being cheap* with an eye on the interests of consumers; defenders of restriction advocate *high prices,* taking care of producers above all. Other people intervene, saying: *"Producers and consumers are one and the same,"* which leaves up in the air the question of knowing whether the law ought to pursue low prices or high ones.

At the center of this conflict, there appears to be just one path for the law to take, and that is to allow prices to find their level naturally. However, in this case the sworn enemies of *laissez faire* appear.[1] Above all they want the law to act, even if they do not know in which direction it should act. No decision having been reached, it would seem to be up to the person who wants to use the law to generate artificially high prices or unnaturally low ones, to set out the reason for his choice and convince others of its validity. The *onus probandi*[2] is exclusively on his shoulders. From which it follows that freedom is always deemed to be good until proven otherwise, since leaving prices to establish themselves naturally constitutes freedom.

However, the roles have changed. The partisans of high prices have caused their model to triumph, and it is up to the defenders of natural prices to prove the worth of theirs. Both sides argue using just two words. It is thus essential to know what these words encompass.

Let us note first of all that there are several facts which are likely to disconcert the champions of both camps.

To make things expensive, those in favor of trade restriction obtained protective duties, and low prices, which are inexplicable to them, have come to dash their hopes.

To get cheap things, free traders have on occasion secured the triumph of freedom and, to their great astonishment, the result has been rising prices.

For example: In France, in order to stimulate agriculture, foreign wool has been subjected to a duty of 22 percent, and what has happened is that French wool has been sold at a lower price after this measure than before.

---

1. See "Bastiat's References to Laissez-Faire," in the Note on the Translation.
2. *Onus probandi* (burden of proof).

In England, to relieve consumers, foreign wool was exempted and finally freed from tax, and the result has been that local wool has been sold more expensively than ever.

And these are not isolated facts, for the price of wool does not have a nature of its own which exempts it from the general law governing prices. This same fact has recurred in all similar circumstances. Against all expectations, protection has instead led to a fall and competition to an increase in the prices of products.

This being so, confusion in the debate reached its height, with protectionists saying to their opponents: "The low prices you boasted about to us have been achieved by our system." And their opponents replied: "The high prices you found so useful have been generated by freedom."[3]

Would it not be amusing to see *low prices* becoming the watchword in rue Hauteville and *high ones* lauded in the rue Choiseul?[4]

Obviously, there is a misunderstanding in all this, an illusion that has to be destroyed. This is what I will try to do.

Let us imagine two isolated nations, each made up of one million inhabitants. Let us agree that, all other things being equal, there is in one of them double the quantity of all sorts of things as in the other, twice as much wheat, meat, iron, furniture, fuel, books, clothes, etc.

We would agree that the first of these nations would be twice as rich.

However, there is no reason to assert that *nominal prices*[5] would be different in these two nations. They might even be higher in the richer. It is possible that in the United States everything is nominally *more expensive*

---

3. (Bastiat's note) Recently, M. Duchâtel, who in the past demanded freedom with a view to cheap prices, told the Chamber: "It would not be difficult for me to prove that protection results in low prices." [Charles Marie Tanneguy, comte Duchâtel (1803–67), was a conservative with liberal sympathies who was Minister of Commerce (1834–36) during the July Monarchy.]

4. Bastiat is making a play on words here. The protectionist Association pour la défense du travail national (Association for the Defense of National Employment), led by Antoine Odier and Pierre Mimerel with their journal *Le Moniteur industriel,* had its headquarters on the rue Hauteville. The Association pour la liberté des échanges (Free Trade Association), numbering among its founders Bastiat, who edited its journal *Le Libre-échange,* had its offices on the rue Choiseul. As *haut* means "high" in French, Bastiat is saying playfully that perhaps "low" prices would become the watchword in "Highville Street" (rue Hauteville) and high prices would be lauded in the rue Choiseul.

5. Bastiat uses the term *prix absolus,* which we have translated as "nominal prices," or money prices.

than in Poland and that people there are nevertheless better supplied with everything, from which we can see that it is not the nominal price of products but their abundance that constitutes wealth. When, therefore, we want to compare trade restriction and freedom, we should not ask ourselves which of the two generates low or high prices, but which of the two brings abundance or scarcity.

For you should note this: products are traded for one another, and a relative scarcity of everything and a relative abundance of everything leave the nominal price of things exactly at the same point, but not the condition of people.

Let us go into the subject in greater detail.

When increases and decreases in duties are seen to produce such opposite effects to those expected, with lower prices often following the imposition of a tax and higher prices sometimes following the removal of a tax, political economy has had to find an explanation for a phenomenon that overturned preconceived ideas, since whatever we say, any science that is worthy of the name is only the faithful exposition and accurate explanation of facts.

Well, the one we are highlighting here is very well explained by a circumstance that should never be lost to sight.

It is that high prices have *two causes* and not one.

This is also true of low prices.

It is one of the most accepted points of political economy that price is determined by the state of Supply compared to that of Demand.

There are therefore two terms that affect price: Supply and Demand. These terms are essentially variable. They may combine in the same direction, in opposite directions, and in infinite proportions. This leads to an inexhaustible number of price combinations.

Prices rise either because Supply decreases or because Demand increases.

They drop either because Supply increases or because Demand decreases.

This shows that high prices have two natures, and so do low prices.

There is a bad sort of *high prices,* that resulting from a decrease in Supply, since this implies *scarcity* and *privation* (such as that experienced this year for wheat),[6] and there is a good sort of *high prices,* resulting from an

---

6. Crop failures in 1846–47 caused considerable hardship and a rise in food prices in 1847 across Europe. Some historians believe this was a contributing factor to the outbreak of revolution in 1848. The average price of wheat in France was 18 fr. 93 c. per hectoliter in 1845, which rose to 23 fr. 84 c. in 1846 (which had a poor harvest). Prices were even higher in the last half of 1846 and the first half of 1847, when the shortage was

increase in demand, since this presupposes an increase in the level of general wealth.

In the same way, there is a desirable sort of *low prices,* arising from abundance, and a disastrous version, resulting from a decrease in demand and the destitution of customers.

Now, note this: trade restriction tends to trigger simultaneously the bad sorts both of high and low prices; bad high prices in that it decreases Supply, and this is even its expressed aim, and the bad sort of low prices in that it also decreases Demand, since it gives a wrong direction to capital and labor and burdens customers with taxes and hindrances.

With the result that, *with regard to price,* these two trends cancel one another out, and this is why this system, by restricting Demand at the same time as Supply, does not even in the long run achieve the high prices which are its aim.

But, with regard to the condition of the people, they do not cancel one another out. On the contrary, they contribute to making it worse.

The effect of freedom is just the opposite. Its general result may not be the low prices it promised either, for it too has two trends, one toward desirable low prices through the expansion of Supply or abundance, the other toward noticeably higher prices through the increase of Demand or general wealth. These two trends cancel one another out with regard to *nominal prices,* but they combine with regard to improving the condition of men.

In a word, under protectionism and to the extent that it is put into effect, people regress to a state in which both Supply and Demand weaken; under free trade, they progress to a state in which these develop equally without the nominal price of things necessarily being affected. This price is not a good measure of wealth. It may well remain the same whether society is descending into the most abject poverty or rising toward greater prosperity.

May we be allowed to apply this doctrine in a few words?

A farmer in the South-East of France thinks that he has struck it rich

---

most acutely felt. In December 1846 wheat rose to 28 fr. 41 c. per hectoliter and reached a maximum of 37 fr. 98 c. in May 1847. The average price for the period 1832–1846 had been 19 fr. 5 c. per hectoliter. The lowest average price reached between 1800 and 1846 was 14 fr. 72 c. in 1834. See *L'Annuaire de l'économie politique et de la statistique* (1848), pp. 179–80. See the entry on "Irish Famine and the Failure of French Harvests, 1846–47," in the Glossary of Subjects and Terms.

because he is protected by duties against competition from abroad. He is as poor as Job, but this does not matter; he is no less convinced that protection will make him rich sooner or later. In these circumstances, if, as the Odier Committee has done, he is asked the following question worded thus:

"Do you or do you not wish to be subjected to foreign competition?" His instinctive reaction is to reply: "*No.*" And the Odier Committee gives this response an extremely enthusiastic reception.

However, we must delve a bit more deeply into the matter. Doubtless, foreign competition and even competition in general is always a nuisance, and if a branch of activity were able to break free of it on its own, it would do good business for a time.

But protection is not an isolated favor; it is a system. If it tends to produce scarcity of wheat and meat, to the advantage of this farmer, it also tends to produce scarcity of iron, cloth, fuel, tools, etc. to the advantage of other producers; in other words, the scarcity of everything.

Well, if the scarcity of wheat works toward making it more expensive by decreasing supply, the scarcity of all the other objects for which wheat is traded works toward lowering its price by decreasing demand, with the result, in a word, that it is by no means certain that wheat is more expensive by one centime than under a free regime. The only thing that is certain is that since there is less of everything in the country, each person must be less well provided with everything.

The farmer ought well to be asking himself whether it would not be better for him for a little wheat or meat to be imported from abroad and on the other hand for him to be surrounded by a prosperous population able to consume and pay for all sorts of agricultural products.

Imagine that there is a certain département in which men are covered in rags, live in hovels, and eat chestnuts. How do you expect farming to flourish there? What do you make the land produce in the reasonable hope of receiving a fair return? Meat? Nobody eats it. Milk? People drink only water from springs. Butter? That is a luxury. Wool? People do without it as much as they can. Does anyone think that all these objects of consumption can be abandoned by the masses without this abandonment having a downward effect on prices at the same time as trade protection acts to raise them?

What we have said with reference to a farmer can also be applied to a manufacturer. The manufacturers of cloth insist that foreign competition will decrease the price by increasing Supply. Maybe, but will these prices not be raised by an increase in Demand? Is the consumption of cloth a fixed and invariable quantity? Is each person as well provided for as he could and should be? And if general wealth increased through the abolition of all these taxes and restrictions, would not the population instinctively use it to clothe themselves better?

The question, the eternal question, is therefore not to ascertain whether protection favors this or that particular area but whether, after all costs and benefits have been calculated, restriction is, *by its very nature,* more productive than freedom.

But nobody dares to support this. This even explains the admission that we are constantly being given: "You are right in principle."

If this is so, if restriction benefits each particular activity only by doing greater harm to general wealth, let us therefore understand that prices themselves, taking only these into consideration, express a relationship between each particular productive activity and production in general, between Supply and Demand, and that in accordance with these premises, this *remunerative price,* the aim of protection, is more damaged than favored by it.

SUPPLEMENT

Under the title *High Prices and Low Prices* we published an article, which generated the following two letters. We follow them with a reply.

Dear Editor,

You are upsetting all my ideas. I was producing propaganda in favor of free trade and found it very convenient to highlight *low prices!* I went everywhere saying: "Under freedom, bread, meat, cloth, linen products, iron, and fuel will decrease in price." That displeased those who sell these things but pleased those who buy them. Now you are casting doubt on the claim that free trade will result in *low prices.* But what use will it be, then? What will the people gain if foreign competition, which might hurt their sales, does not help them in their purchases?

Dear Free Trader,

Please allow me to tell you that you have only half-read the article that generated your letter. We said that free trade acted in exactly the same way as roads, canals, and railways, and like everything that facilitates communications and destroys obstacles. Its initial tendency is to increase the abundance of the article freed from duty and consequently to lower its price. But since at the same time it increases the abundance of all the things that are traded for this article, it increases *demand* for it, and its price rises as a result of this aspect. You ask us what the people will gain. Let us suppose that they have a set of scales with several trays, in each of which they have for their own use a certain quantity of the objects you have listed. If a small quantity of wheat is added to a tray, it will go down, but if you add a little woolen cloth, a little iron, and a little fuel to the other trays, the balance will be maintained. If you look at the evil consequence only, nothing will have changed. If you look at the people, you will see that they are better fed, better clothed, and better heated.

Dear Editor,

I am a manufacturer of woolen cloth and a protectionist. I must admit that your article on *high prices* and *low prices* has given me food for thought. There is a certain plausibility there that needs only to be properly proved to achieve a conversion.

Dear Protectionist,

We say that your restrictive measures aim at an iniquitous result, *artificially high prices.* But we do not say that they always achieve the hopes of those who advance them. They certainly inflict on consumers all the harm of high prices, but it is not clear that they achieve any benefit for producers. Why? Because although they decrease *Supply,* they also decrease *Demand.*

This proves that there is a moral force in the economic arrangement of this world, a *vis medicatrix,* a healing power which ensures that in the long run unjust ambition is confronted with disappointment.

Please note, Sir, that one of the elements of the prosperity of each particular branch of production is general wealth. The *price* of a house does not depend only on what it cost but also on the number and fortune of its tenants. Do two houses that are exactly alike necessarily have the same *price?* Certainly not, if one is situated in Paris and the other in Lower Brittany. We should never talk about *price* without taking account of *location* and note well that there is no attempt that is more vain than that of wishing to base the prosperity of certain parts on the ruin of the whole. This is nevertheless to what restrictive regimes aspire.

Competition has always been and will always be unfortunate to those who suffer from it. For this reason, we have always seen, in every age and place, men striving to escape it. We know (as do you, perhaps) of a municipal authority in which resident traders wage a bitter war against peddlers. Their missiles are city taxes on the movement of goods, fees to be able to set up their stalls in the market, fees to display their goods, road and bridge tolls, etc., etc.

Just consider what would have become of Paris, for example, if this war had been successful.

Let us suppose that the first shoemaker who set up shop there had succeeded in routing all the others, and that the first tailor, the first mason, the first printer, the first watchmaker, the first hairdresser, the first doctor, or the first baker had been as successful. Paris would still be a village of 1,200 to 1,500 inhabitants today. This has not happened. Everyone (except for those you are still chasing away) has come to exploit this market, and this is exactly what has made it grow. This has been nothing but a long series of upsets for the enemies of competition and, through one upset after another, Paris has become a town of one million inhabitants. General wealth has doubtless gained from this, but has the individual wealth of shoemakers and tailors lost out? In your eyes, this is the question. As competitors arrived, you would have said: "The price of boots will decrease." Has this been so? No, for while *Supply* has increased, so has *Demand*.

This will also be true for cloth, Sir; let it come in.[7] You will have more competitors, that is true, but you will also have more customers, and above all, customers that are richer. What then! Have you never thought of this during the winter on seeing nine-tenths of your fellow citizens deprived of the cloth you make so well?

This is a very long lesson to learn. Do you want to prosper? Then let your customers prosper.

But when it has been learned, everyone will seek his own benefit in the general good. Then jealousies between individuals, towns, provinces, and nations will no longer trouble the world.

---

7. Bastiat uses the expression *laissez-le entrer* (let it enter), which is very similar to the Economists' general policy of "laissez-faire." See "Bastiat's References to Laissez-Faire," in the Note on the Translation.

6. To Artisans and Workers[1]

PUBLISHING HISTORY:

Original title: "Aux artisans et aux ouvriers."
Place and date of first publication: *Le Courrier français,*
    18 September 1846.
First French edition as book or pamphlet: *Economic Sophisms*
    (Second Series) (1848). First and Second Series were
    combined in one edition in 1851.
Location in Paillottet's edition of *OC:* Vol. 4. *Sophismes
    économiques. Petits pamphlets I,* pp. 173–82.
Previous translations: 1st American ed., 1848; 1st British ed.,
    1873; FEE ed., 1964.

Several journals have tried to lower my standing in your eyes. Would you like to read my defense?

I am a trusting soul. When a man writes or says something, I believe that his words reflect his thoughts.

Even so, however much I read and reread the journals to which I am replying, I seem to find in them some sorry tendencies.

What was it all about? To find out what you prefer, trade restriction or freedom.

I believe it is freedom. They believe it is trade restriction. Let each prove his case.

Is it necessary to insinuate that we are the agents of England, of the Midi,[2] or of the government?

1. (Paillottet's note) This chapter is taken from the issue of *Le Courrier français* dated 18 September 1846, whose columns were opened to the author to repel the attacks from *L'Atelier.* It was only two months later that the journal *Le Libre-échange* appeared. [*L'Atelier* was a respected monthly, written exclusively by workers, published from December 1840 to July 1850. In September 1846 it had been very critical of Cobden, the League, and the Free Trade Association founded by Bastiat in Bordeaux. Bastiat provided a list of the protectionist journals with which he engaged in debate, such as *Le Moniteur industriel, Le Journal des débats, Le Constitutionnel, La Presse, Le Commerce, L'Esprit public,* and *Le National.* The free-trade press included journals such as *Le Courrier français, Le Siècle, La Patrie, L'Époque, La Réforme, La Démocratie pacifique,* and *L'Atelier* (see *OC,* vol. 2, p. 92 for Bastiat's list).]

2. Le Midi is the name given to the south of France. Like the United States at this time, France was divided into an agricultural, trade-dependent south (which was sympathetic to free trade) and an industrial north, which was inclined toward protectionism.

Note how easy, if these are the grounds of debate, recrimination would be for us.

We are, they say, the agents of the English, because some of us have used the words *meeting* and *free-trader!*

But do they not themselves use the words *drawback* and *budget?*[3]

We imitate Cobden and English democracy!

But don't they parody Bentinck[4] and the British aristocracy?

We borrow the doctrine of freedom from perfidious Albion!

And they, do they not borrow from her the quibbles of protection?

We follow the impulses of Bordeaux and the Midi!

And they, do they not serve the greed of Lille and the North?

We favor the secret designs of the government, which wants to distract attention from its policy!

And they, do they not favor the views of the Civil List,[5] which gains more than anyone in the world from protectionism?

You can thus see clearly that, if we did not scorn this campaign to denigrate others, we would not lack the weapons to engage in it.

But that is not the question.

The question, and I will not lose sight of it, is this:

What is better for the working classes, to be free or not to be free to purchase from abroad?

Workers, you are being told: "If you are free to purchase things from abroad that you are now making yourselves, you will no longer be making them. You will have no work, no pay, and no bread. Your freedom is therefore being restricted for your own good."

Advocates of free trade like Bastiat were often accused of being agents of "Perfidious Albion," which was pursuing a free trade policy after the repeal of the Corn Laws in 1846.

3. The words "meeting," "free-trader," "drawback," and "budget" were in English in the original text.

4. Lord George Bentinck (1802–48) was a conservative Member of Parliament who with Benjamin Disraeli led the opposition in the House of Commons against Richard Cobden's and Sir Robert Peel's attempts to repeal the Corn Laws in 1846.

5. The Civil List was an annual grant made by the state to the monarch for the maintenance and upkeep of his estates and property. In 1791 Louis XVI received fr. 25 million; in the Restoration Louis XVIII received fr. 34 million and Charles X received fr. 32 million. Louis-Philippe, the new July Monarch after the 1830 Revolution, was granted fr. 12 million per year for himself and fr. 1 million for the prince, by the law of 2 March 1832. According to the budget of 1848 (the last before the February Revolution of 1848 overthrew the monarchy), fr. 13.3 million was set aside for the Civil List. See *L'Annuaire de l'économie politique et de la statistique* (1848), p. 29.

This objection comes under multiple forms. For example, it is said: "If we dress in English cloth, if we make our ploughs with English iron, if we slice our bread with English knives, if we wipe our hands on English napkins, what will become of French workers and *national production?*"

Workers, tell me, if a man stood in the port of Boulogne and said to each Englishman who came ashore: "If you will give me these English boots, I will give you this French hat?" Or "If you will let me have this English horse, I will give you this French Tilbury?"[6] Or "Will you trade this machine from Birmingham for this clock from Paris?" Or again: "Does it suit you to trade this coal from Newcastle for this Champagne?" I ask you, assuming that our man exerted some judgment in his proposals, can we say that our *national output,* taken overall, would be affected?

Would it be more affected if there were twenty people offering services like this in Boulogne instead of one, if one million trades were being made instead of four, and if traders and cash were brought in to facilitate them and increase their number infinitely?

Well, whether one country buys wholesale from another in order to sell retail or retail to sell wholesale, if the affair is followed right to its end, it will always be found that *commerce* is just a series of *barter exchanges, products for products and services for services.* Therefore, if one *barter exchange* does not damage *national production* since it implies an equal amount of *national work given for the foreign work received,* one hundred thousand million exchanges would not damage it to any greater extent.

But, you will say, where is the profit? The profit lies in making the best use of the resources of each country so that the same amount of work provides more satisfaction and well-being everywhere.

Some people use a strange tactic with you. They begin by agreeing that the free system is better than the prohibitive system, doubtless so as not to have to defend themselves on this subject.

Then they observe that in the transition from one system to the other there will be some *displacement* of labor.

Next, they will dwell on the suffering that this *displacement* will bring in its wake, according to them. They exaggerate it and magnify it and make it the prime subject in the matter; they present this suffering as the sole and final result of the reform and strive thus to win you over to the flag of monopoly.

Moreover, this is a tactic that has been used for all sorts of abuse, and

---

6. A tilbury is an open, two-wheeled carriage which was designed and built by the London coach builders Tilbury in the early nineteenth century.

one thing that I must acknowledge quite straightforwardly is that it always embarrasses those in favor of reform, even those reforms most useful to the people. You will soon understand why.

When an abuse exists, everything is organized around it.

Some people's lives depend on it, others depend on these lives, and still others depend on these latter ones, making a huge edifice.

If you try to lay a hand on it, everyone cries out and, note this well, those who shout loudest always appear at first sight to be right, as it is easier to show the disadvantages that accompany reform than the advantages that follow it.

Those in favor of the abuse quote specific facts; they name individuals and their suppliers and workers who will be upset, while the poor devil of a reformer can refer only to the *general good* which is due to spread gradually through the masses. This is far from having the same effect.

So, does the question of abolishing slavery arise? "You unfortunate people," the black people are told, "who will feed you in the future? The foreman distributes lashes with his whip, but he also distributes manioc."

And the slaves miss their chains and ask themselves, "Where will I obtain manioc?"

They do not see that it is not the foreman who feeds them but their own work, which also feeds the foreman.

When the monasteries were reformed in Spain,[7] the mendicants were told: "Where will you find soup and robes? The Prior is your Providence. Is it not very convenient to call upon him?"

And the mendicants said, "It is true. If the Prior goes away, we clearly see what we will be losing but not what will take his place."

They were not mindful that although monasteries distributed alms, they also lived on alms, to the extent that the people had to donate more than they received.

---

7. The dissolution of monasteries in Spain had a complex history in the nineteenth century. The Constitution of 1812 suppressed religious organizations and confiscated their property. The restored King Ferdinand reestablished them in 1814, but the Cortes in 1820 suppressed them once again with the exception of a handful which continued to provide shelter to the sick and the old. The French restored Ferdinand III to the crown in 1823, and he promptly overturned the Cortes's law. In 1835 and 1836 there was yet another dissolution of the monasteries, and their property was confiscated or sold off. This was similar to the treatment of religious institutions during the early years of the French Revolution.

Workers, in just the same way, monopoly places imperceptible taxes on all of your shoulders and then, with the product of these taxes, it gives you work.

And your false friends tell you, "If there were no monopoly, who would give you work?"

To which you answer, "That is true, very true. The work provided to us by the monopolists is certain. The promises of freedom are uncertain."

For you do not see that money is being squeezed out of you in the first instance and that subsequently you are being given back part of this money in return for your work.

You ask who will give you work? You will give each other work, for heaven's sake! With the money that will no longer be taken from you, the shoemaker will dress better and will give work to the tailor. The tailor will replace his shoes more often and give work to the shoemaker. And so on for all of the trades.

It is said that with freedom there will be fewer workers in the mines and spinning mills.

I do not think so. But if that happened, *of necessity* there would be more people working freely at home or out in the sun.

For if the mines and spinning mills are supported only, as people say, with the help of the taxes imposed for their benefit on *everyone,* once these taxes are abolished, *everyone* will be better off, and it is the prosperity of all that provides work for each person.

Forgive me if I linger awhile on this argument. I would so much like to see you on the side of freedom!

In France, the capital invested in industry produces, I suppose, 5 percent profit. But here is Mondor,[8] who has invested 100,000 fr. in a factory, which is losing 5 percent. The difference between loss and gain is 10,000 fr. What do people do? They spread among you very subtly a small tax of 10,000 fr., which they give to Mondor. You do not notice it because it is skillfully disguised. It is not the tax collector who comes to ask you for your share of the tax, but you pay it to Mondor, the ironmaster, each time you buy your axes, trowels, and planes. You are then told: "If you do not pay this tax, Mondor will not provide any work, and his workers Jean and Jacques will be unemployed." Heavens above! If you were given back the tax, would you not put yourselves to work and even start your own businesses?

And then, be reassured. When he no longer has this nice cushion of a

8. See the entry for "Girard, Antoine and Philippe," in the Glossary of Persons.

higher price through taxes, Mondor will think up ways of converting his loss into profit, and Jean and Jacques will not be dismissed. Then there will be a profit *for all*.

Perhaps you will dwell on this and say: "We understand that after the reform there will generally be more work than before, but in the meantime, Jean and Jacques will be on the street."

To which I reply:

1. When work shifts only in order to increase, anyone who is ready and willing to work does not remain on the street for very long;

2. Nothing prevents the State from having a small reserve fund to cover any unemployment during the transition, although, for my part, I do not think it will happen;

3. Lastly, if in order to get out of the rut and achieve conditions that are better for everyone and above all more just, it is absolutely essential to face up to a few difficult moments, and workers are ready for this, or I am mistaken in them. Please God, may entrepreneurs be able to do the same!

What then! Just because you are workers, are you not intelligent or morally upright? It seems that your alleged friends are forgetting this. Is it not surprising that they discuss a question like this in front of you, talking about wages and interests without once mentioning the word *justice*? They know, however, that protection is *unjust*. Why then do they lack the courage to warn you of this and say: "Workers, an iniquity is widespread in the country, but it benefits you and must be given support." Why? Because they know that your answer will be "No."

But it is not true that this iniquity benefits you. Let me have a few moments more of your attention, and see for yourselves.

What are we protecting in France? Things that are made by major entrepreneurs in huge factories: iron, coal, woolen cloth, and fabric, and you are being told that this is not in the interest of the entrepreneurs but in yours, and in order to ensure that you have work.

However, each time that *products made with foreign labor* come into our market in a form that can cause you damage but which is useful to the major entrepreneurs, are they not allowed to enter?

Are there not thirty thousand Germans in Paris making suits and shoes?[9]

---

9. As Bastiat notes, there were many Germans living and working in Paris to take advantage of the economic size of the market (Paris with about one million inhabitants was one of the largest cities in Europe at the time) and the relatively greater freedoms (such as freedom of speech) compared to many German cities, which cracked down on the radical press. Ironically, just before Bastiat moved to Paris the socialist Karl Marx moved there

Why are they allowed to set up shop next to you, when cloth is being rejected? Because cloth is made in huge factories that belong to manufacturers who are also lawmakers. But suits are made at home by outworkers. These people do not want any competition for their changing wool into cloth because it is their trade, but they are all too willing to accept competition for the converting of cloth into suits because it is yours.

When the railways were built, English rails were rejected but English workers were brought in. Why? It is very simple: because English rails compete with the major factories and English labor competes only with yours.

We for our part do not ask for the expulsion of German tailors and English diggers. What we ask for is that cloth and rails be allowed to come in. We ask for justice for all and equality for all before the law!

It is laughable that they tell us that Customs restrictions have your benefit in mind. Tailors, shoemakers, carpenters, joiners, masons, blacksmiths, merchants, grocers, watchmakers, butchers, bakers, upholsterers, and milliners, I challenge you to quote me one single instance where restriction benefits you, and whenever you want I will quote you four which cause you harm.

And, at the end of the day, see how credible is this self-sacrifice that your journals attribute to monopolists.

I believe that we can call the *natural level of wages* the one which is *naturally* established under the regime of freedom. When, therefore, you are told that trade restriction benefits you, it is as though you were being told that it adds a *supplement* to your *natural* wages. Well, an *extranatural* supplement to wages has to come from somewhere; it does not fall from the moon, and it has to be taken from those who pay it.

You are thus led to the conclusion that, according to your alleged friends, protectionism was created and brought into the world so that capitalists could be sacrificed to the workers.

Tell me, is this likely?

Where then is your seat in the Chamber of Peers? When did you take your seat in the Palais Bourbon?[10] Who has consulted you? Where did you get the idea of setting up protectionism?

I hear you reply: "It is not we who established it. Alas! We are neither

---

from Cologne to start a new radical newspaper. Between 1843 and 1845 he lived in Paris, where he met Friedrich Engels.

10. The Palais Bourbon was built by Louis XIV in 1722 for his daughter Louise Françoise. It is located on the Quai d'Orsay in Paris. It was confiscated during the revolution (1791) and has been the location for the Chamber of Deputies since the Restoration.

peers, deputies, nor Councilors of State. The capitalists were the ones who set it up."

God in Heaven! They were very well disposed that day! What! The capitalists drew up the law and established the prohibitionist regime just so that you, the workers, might gain profit at their expense?

But here is something that is stranger still.

How is it that your alleged friends, who now talk to you about the goodness, generosity, and self-denial of the capitalists, constantly plead with you not to take advantage of your political rights? From their point of view, what use could you make of them? The capitalists have the monopoly of legislation,[11] that is true. Thanks to this monopoly, it is also true that they have allocated to themselves the monopoly of iron, cloth, canvas, coal, wood, and meat. But now your alleged friends claim that by acting in this way, the capitalists have robbed themselves without being obliged to do so in order to enrich you without your having any right to this! Certainly, if you were electors and deputies you could not do a better job; you would not even do as well.

If the industrial organization that governs us is established in your interest, it is therefore deceitful to claim political rights for you, for these democrats of a new type will never extricate themselves from this dilemma: the law, drawn up by the bourgeoisie, gives you *more* or gives you *less* than your natural earnings. If it gives you *less,* they deceive you by asking you to support it. If it gives you *more,* they are still deceiving you by encouraging you to claim political rights, while the bourgeoisie are making sacrifices for you which you, in your honesty, would never dare to vote for.

Workers, please God that this article will not have the effect of sowing in your hearts the seeds of resentment against the wealthy classes! If *interests* that are badly understood or sincerely alarmed still support monopoly, let us not forget that it is rooted in the *errors* that are common to both capitalists and workers. Far from whipping them up against one another, let us work to

11. After 1839 there were 460 members of the Chamber of Deputies, who were elected for a term of five years. Suffrage was limited to those who paid an annual tax of fr. 200 and were over the age of 25; and only those who paid fr. 500 in tax and were over the age of 30 could stand for election. The taxes which determined eligibility were direct taxes on land, poll taxes, and the taxes on residences, doors, windows, and businesses. By the end of the Restoration (1830) only 89,000 taxpayers were eligible to vote. Under the July Monarchy this number rose to 166,000, and by 1846 this had risen again to 241,000. In the late 1840s France had a population of about 36 million. The February Revolution of 1848 introduced universal manhood suffrage (21 years or older), and the Constituent Assembly (April 1848) had 900 members (minimum age of 25).

bring them together. And what do we need to do to achieve this? If it is true that natural social tendencies contribute to abolishing inequality between men, all that is needed is to leave these tendencies to act, to remove the artificial obstructions that delay their effect and leave the relationships between the various classes to establish themselves on the principle of JUSTICE which, in my mind at least, is combined with the principle of freedom.

7. A Chinese Tale

PUBLISHING HISTORY:

Original title: "Conte chinois."

Place and date of first publication: No date given. First published in book form.

First French edition as book or pamphlet: *Economic Sophisms* (Second Series) (1848). First and Second Series were combined in one edition in 1851.

Location in Paillottet's edition of *OC:* Vol. 4. *Sophismes économiques. Petits pamphlets I,* pp. 182–87.

Previous translations: 1st American ed., 1848; 1st British ed., 1873; FEE ed., 1964.

People are crying out at the greed and selfishness of this century!

For my part, I see that the world, and especially Paris, is peopled with so many Deciuses.[1]

Open the thousand volumes, the thousand journals, and the thousand literary and scientific articles that publishers in Paris spew out over the country every day; is all this not the work of little saints?

What verve is used to paint the vices of our day! What touching tenderness is shown for the masses! With what liberality are the rich invited to share with the poor, if not the poor to share with the rich! How many plans for social reform, social progress, and social organizations are put forward! Is there a writer, however humble, who does not devote himself to the wellbeing of the working classes? All you need is to give them an advance of a

---

1. Publius Decius Mus was a Roman consul and a military leader. When his legion was on the verge of defeat, in 340 B.C., he invoked the gods and hurled himself into the enemy ranks. He was killed but assured the victory of the legion. His son and grandson, of the same name, followed his example in 295 and 279, respectively.

few écus for them to purchase the time to indulge in their humanitarian lucubrations.

And then we dare to speak of the selfishness and individualism of our time!

There is nothing that is not claimed to be serving the well-being and moral improvement of the people, nothing, not even the *Customs Service.* Perhaps you believe that this is a tax machine, like city tolls or like the toll booth at the end of the bridge? Not at all. It is an institution that is essentially civilizing, fraternal, and egalitarian. What can you do? It is the fashion. You have to instill or pretend to instill sentiment and sentimentalism everywhere, even in the inspection booth with its *"anything to declare?"*

But to achieve these philanthropic aspirations, the Customs Service, it must be admitted, has some strange procedures.

It sets up an army[2] of managers, deputy managers, inspectors, deputy inspectors, controllers, checkers, customs collectors, heads, deputy heads, agents, supernumeraries, aspiring supernumeraries, and those aspiring to become aspirants, not counting those on *active service,* and all of this to succeed in exercising on the productive output of the people the negative action summarized by the word *prevent.*

Note that I do not say *tax,* but quite precisely *prevent.*

And *prevent,* not those acts condemned by tradition nor those that are contrary to public order, but transactions that are agreed to be innocent and even such as to encourage peace and union between peoples.

Humanity, however, is so flexible and adaptable that, in one way or another, it always overcomes such impediments. This requires additional work.

If a people are prevented from bringing in their food from abroad, they produce it at home. This is more difficult, but they have to live. If they are prevented from crossing the valley, they go over the peaks. This takes longer, but they have to get there.

This is sad, but there is something pleasant about it too. When the law has

---

2. Horace Say also calls those who work for the Customs Service *une armée considérable* (a sizable army), which numbered 27,727 individuals (1852 figures). This army is composed of two "divisions"—one of administrative personnel (2,536) and the other of "agents on active service" (24,727). See Horace Say, "Douane," in *DEP* 1:578–604 (figures from p. 597). According to the budget papers for 1848, the Customs Service collected fr. 202 million in customs duties and salt taxes, and its administrative and collection costs totaled fr. 26.4 million or 13 percent of the amount collected.

created a certain number of obstacles in this way, and when in order to circumvent them humanity has diverted a corresponding amount of work, you have no right to demand a reform to the law, for, if you point out the *obstacle,* you will be shown the amount of work it gives rise to, and if you say: "That is not created work but *diverted* work," you will be given the answer published in *L'Esprit public:* "Impoverishment alone is certain and immediate; as for enrichment, it is more than hypothetical."[3]

This reminds me of a Chinese tale, which I will now tell you.

Once upon a time, there were two major towns in China, *Chin* and *Chan*. They were linked by a magnificent canal. The Emperor thought it a good thing to throw huge boulders into it to make it unusable.

When he saw this, Kouang, his Prime Mandarin, said to him: "Son of Heaven, you are making a mistake."

To which the Emperor replied: "Kouang, you are talking nonsense."

You will understand, of course, that I am reporting only the gist of the conversation.

Three moons later, the Heavenly Emperor called the mandarin and said to him: "Kouang, look at this."

And Kouang, opening his eyes wide, looked.

And he saw, some distance from the canal, a host of men *working.* Some were digging, others were filling, this group was leveling and that one paving, and the highly literate mandarin said to himself: "They are making a road."

After a further three moons, the Emperor called Kouang and said to him: "Look!"

And Kouang looked.

And he saw that the road had been finished, and he noted that all along the way, from one end to the other, inns had been built. A host of pedestrians, carts, and palanquins were going to and fro, and countless Chinese, worn out with fatigue, carried heavy burdens hither and thither from *Chin* to *Chan* and from *Chan* to *Chin*. And Kouang said to himself: "It is the destruction of the canal that is giving work to these poor people." However, the notion that this work had been *diverted* from other employment did not occur to him.

---

3. *L'Esprit public* was a journal founded by Guy Lesseps in 1845, which merged with *La Patrie* in 1846. *La Patrie* supported the constitutional monarchy but was a strong critic of François Guizot.

And three moons passed, and the emperor said to Kouang: "Look!"

And Kouang looked.

And he saw that the inns were constantly full of travelers and that, as these travelers were hungry, shops for butchers, bakers, pork butchers, and sellers of swallows' nests had grown up around them. And as these honest artisans could not remain unclothed, tailors, shoemakers, the sellers of parasols and fans also set up shop, and since nobody could sleep in the open, even in the Heavenly Empire, carpenters, masons, and roofers had migrated there too. Then came police officers, judges, and fakirs; in a word, a town grew up with suburbs around each hostelry.

And the Emperor said to Kouang: "What do you think of this?"

And Kouang replied: "I would never have believed that the destruction of a canal could create so much work for the people," for it never occurred to him that this was not created work but *diverted* work, that travelers ate when they journeyed along the canal just as much as they later did when forced to go by road.

However, to the great astonishment of the Chinese, the Emperor died, and this Son of Heaven was laid in the ground.

His successor summoned Kouang and said to him: "Clear the canal."

And Kouang said to the new Emperor: "Son of Heaven, you are making a mistake."

To which the Emperor replied: "Kouang, you are talking nonsense."

But Kouang persisted and said: "Sire, what is your intention?"

"My intention," said the Emperor, "is to facilitate the traffic of people and goods between *Chin* and *Chan,* to make transport less expensive so that the people obtain tea and clothing more cheaply."

But Kouang was prepared for this. He had received a few issues of *Le Moniteur industriel,* a Chinese journal, the previous day. Having learnt his lesson well, he requested permission to reply and, having received it, after bowing his forehead to the parquet floor nine times, he said:

"Sire, you are aiming, by facilitating transport, to reduce the cost of consumer products in order to make them affordable by the people, and to do this, you have begun by removing from them all the work that the destruction of the canal had generated. Sire, in political economy, nominally low prices[4] ... The Emperor interrupted: "I think you are reciting from mem-

---

4. See ES1 11 for a fuller discussion of this matter.

ory." Kouang said: "That is true. It would be easier for me to read." And, unfolding *L'Esprit public,* he read:

> In political economy, nominal cheapness of consumer products is a secondary matter. The problem lies in a balance between the price of work and that of the objects that are necessary to life. Abundance of work is the wealth of nations, and the best economic system is the one that gives them the greatest amount of work possible. Do not ask whether it is better to pay 4 cash units or 8 cash units for a cup of tea or 5 taels or 10 taels for a shirt. These are childish considerations that are unworthy of a serious mind. No one queries your proposition. The question is to determine whether it is better to pay more for products and, through the abundance and higher price of work, have more means to acquire them, or whether it is better to reduce the opportunities for work, diminish the total amount of national production,[5] transport consumer products more cheaply *by water,* admittedly at lower cost, but at the same time deny some of our workers the possibility of buying them, even at these reduced prices.

As the Emperor was not fully convinced, Kouang said to him: "Sire, deign to wait awhile. I can also quote from *Le Moniteur industriel.*"

But the Emperor cut him short:

"I have no need of your Chinese journals to know that to create *obstacles* is to shift labor from one side to another. This, however, is not my mission. Go on, clear the canal. Then we will reform the Customs Service."

And Kouang went away, tearing out his beard and crying: "Oh Fô! Oh Pê! Oh Lî! And all the monosyllabic and circumflexed gods in Cathay, take pity on your people, for we have been given an Emperor of the *English School,*[6] and I can see that, in a little while, we will be short of everything, because we will no longer have any need to make anything."

---

5. Bastiat uses the word "population" here but this is obviously an error. The word should be "production."

6. It is not certain when this sophism was written, but Bastiat is referring here to the free-trading English school of politicians and political economists who successfully abolished the protectionist Corn Laws in England in May 1846. See the entries for "Anti–Corn Law League" and "Corn Laws," in the Glossary of Subjects and Terms.

8. Post Hoc, Ergo Propter Hoc[1]

PUBLISHING HISTORY:

Original title: "Post hoc, ergo propter hoc."

Place and date of first publication: *Le Libre-échange,* 6 December 1846, no. 2, p. 11.

First French edition as book or pamphlet: *Economic Sophisms* (Second Series) (1848). First and Second Series were combined in one edition in 1851.

Location in Paillottet's edition of *OC:* Vol. 4. *Sophismes économiques. Petits pamphlets I,* pp. 187–89.

Previous translations: 1st American ed., 1848; 1st British ed., 1873; FEE ed., 1964.

The most common and most erroneous lines of reasoning.

Genuine suffering is appearing in England.

This fact follows two others:

1. The reform of tariffs;[2]
2. The loss of two successive harvests.[3]

To which of these last two circumstances should the first be attributed?

Protectionists do not fail to cry: "It is this cursed freedom that is doing all the harm. It promised us milk and honey; we welcomed it, and see how the factories are closing and the people are suffering: *Cum hoc, ergo propter hoc.*

Commercial freedom distributes the fruit provided by Providence for the work of man in the most uniform and equitable way possible. If this fruit is removed in part by a plague, it no less governs the proper distribution of what remains. People are doubtless less well provided for, but should freedom be blamed for this or the plague?

---

1. The Latin phrase *post hoc, ergo propter hoc* (after this, therefore because of this) is a kind of logical fallacy relating to causation. It represents the assertion that because some event A happened after event B, event B caused event A.

2. Richard Cobden and other free-trade reformers in the Anti–Corn Law League were successful in June 1846 in getting the British Parliament to repeal the protectionist Corn Laws. This repeal was to take effect gradually over a period of three years.

3. This is a reference to the failure of the potato crop in Ireland, known as the Great Irish Famine of 1845–52. See the entry for "Irish Famine and the Failure of French Harvests, 1846–47" in the Glossary of Subjects and Terms.

Freedom acts on the same principle as insurance. When an accident happens, it distributes over a great number of people, over many years, damage that, without insurance, would fall on one nation and one time. Well, has anyone ever thought of saying that fire has ceased to be a plague since the advent of insurance?

In 1842, 1843, and 1844, taxes began to be reduced in England.[4] At the same time, harvests there were plentiful, and we came to think that these two circumstances contributed to the unheard-of prosperity observed in this country during this period.

In 1845 there was a bad harvest; in 1846, it was worse still.

The price of food increased; the people spent their savings to feed themselves and restricted their other expenditures. Clothing was in less demand, the factories less busy, and pay showed a tendency to decrease. Happily, in this same year, as restrictive barriers had once again been lowered, an enormous mass of foodstuffs was able to come onto the English market. Without this circumstance, it is almost certain that a terrible revolution would have spilled blood in Great Britain.

And yet people come forward to accuse freedom of the disasters that it prevents and puts right, at least in part!

A poor leper lived in solitude. Whatever he touched, nobody else wanted to touch. Reduced to meeting his own needs, he led a miserable existence in this world. A great doctor cured him. Here now, we have our hermit in full possession of *freedom to trade*. What fine prospects opened out before him! He delighted in calculating the fine share that, thanks to his relationships with other men, he would be able to earn through his strong arms. He then broke both of them. Alas! His fate was even more terrible. The journalists in this country who witnessed his misery, said: "See what the freedom to trade has done to him! Truly, he was less to be pitied when he lived alone." "What!" exclaimed the doctor. "Do you not take any account of his two broken arms? Have they had no part to play in his sad fate? His misfortune is to have lost his arms, and not to have been cured of leprosy. He would be much more to be pitied if he were armless and a leper to crown it all."

Post hoc, ergo propter hoc: be suspicious of this sophism.

---

4. Sir Robert Peel was the British prime minister in 1841 and introduced a series of economic reforms (he cut the rate of tariff on hundreds of items after 1842) which led to the abolition of the protectionist Corn Laws in May 1846. See the entry for "Peel, Sir Robert," in the Glossary of Persons and the entries for "Anti–Corn Law League" and "Corn Laws," in the Glossary of Subjects and Terms.

9. Theft by Subsidy

PUBLISHING HISTORY:

Original title: "Le vol à la prime."

Place and date of first publication: *JDE* 13 (January 1846): 115–20.

First French edition as book or pamphlet: *Economic Sophisms* (Second Series) (1848). First and Second Series were combined in one edition in 1851.

Location in Paillottet's edition of *OC:* Vol. 4. *Sophismes économiques. Petits pamphlets I,* pp. 189–98.

Previous translations: 1st American ed., 1848; 1st British ed., 1873; FEE ed., 1964.

People find my small volume of *Sophisms* too theoretical, scientific, and metaphysical. So be it. Let us try a mundane, banal, and, if necessary, brutal style. Since I am convinced that the general public are easily taken in as far as protection is concerned, I wanted to prove it to them. They prefer to be shouted at. So let us shout:

Midas, King Midas has ass's ears![1]

An explosion of plain speaking often has more effect than the politest circumlocutions. Do you remember Oronte and the difficulty that the Misanthropist,[2] as misanthropic as he is, has in convincing him of his folly?

---

1. This might also be translated as "The emperor has no clothes!" King Midas was ruler of the Greek kingdom of Phrygia (in modern-day Turkey) sometime in the eighteenth century B.C. According to legend, after he had been granted the power to turn anything he touched into gold, he became disillusioned and retired to the country, where he fell in love with Pan's flute music. In a competition between Pan and Apollo to see who played the best music, King Midas chose Pan's flute over Apollo's lyre. Apollo was so incensed at the tin ears of Midas that he turned them into the ears of a donkey.

2. This is a scene, in highly truncated form, from Molière's play *The Misanthrope* (1666), act 1, scene 2. Alceste is a misanthrope who is trying to tell Oronte, a foolish nobleman, that his verse is poorly written and worthless. After many attempts at avoiding the answer with circumlocutions, Alceste finally says, "Franchement, il est bon à metre au cabinet" (Frankly, it is only good to be thrown into the toilet) (Molière, *Théâtre complet de Molière* 4:86).

ALCESTE: We risk playing the wrong character.

ORONTE: Are you trying to tell me by that that I am wrong in wanting . . .

ALCESTE: I am not saying that, but . . .

ORONTE: Do I write badly?

ALCESTE: I am not saying that, but in the end . . .

ORONTE: But can I not know what there is in my sonnet . . . ?

ALCESTE: Frankly, it is fit to be flushed away.

Frankly, my good people, *you are being robbed.* That is plain speaking, but at least it is clear.

The words *theft, to steal,* and *thief* seem to many people to be in bad taste.[3] Echoing the words of Harpagon to Elise,[4] I ask them: Is it the word or the thing that makes you afraid?

"Whosoever has fraudulently taken something that does not belong to him is guilty of theft" (*Penal Code, Article 379*).

To steal: To take something furtively or by force (*The Dictionary of the Academy*).

Thief: A person who exacts more than is due to him (*Ditto*).[5]

Well, is not a monopolist who, through a law he has drafted, obliges me to pay him 20 fr. for something I can buy elsewhere for 15, fraudulently taking away 5 fr. that belongs to me?

3. Bastiat uses a variety of words in his attempt to speak plainly and brutally in this chapter. See "Plain Speaking," in the Note on the Translation.

4. From act 1, scene 4, of Molière's play *L'Avare* (*The Miser*). The miserly moneylender, Harpagon, asks his daughter, Elise, who wishes to get away from the family by marrying Valère, whether she fears the fact of marriage or the word "marriage." She is more concerned about her father not taking into account their love for each other but only financial concerns (Molière, *Théatre complet de Molière* 6:23).

5. Bastiat provides an accurate but somewhat truncated definition from the sixth edition, of 1835, of the *Dictionnaire de l'Académie française*. The full definition of "to steal" is "prendre furtivement ou par force la chose d'autrui, pour se l'approprier" (to take furtively or by force something belonging to another in order to appropriate it for oneself); and of "thief," the first definition (not quoted by Bastiat) is "celui, celle qui a volé, ou qui vole habituellement" (someone who has stolen or who steals habitually); the second definition is "celui qui exige plus qu'il ne devrait demander" (someone who demands more than he ought to demand). See *Dictionnaire de l'Académie française*; online at http://portail.atilf.fr/dictionnaires/onelook.htm.

Is he not taking it furtively or by force?

Is he not exacting more than is due to him?

He withdraws, takes, or exacts, people will say, but not *furtively* or *by force,* which is what characterizes theft.

When our tax forms show a charge of 5 fr. for the subsidy that is with-drawn, taken, or exacted by the monopolist, what can be more *furtive,* since so few of us suspect it? And for those who are not taken in by it, what can be more *forced,* since at the first refusal we have the bailiffs at our heels?

Anyway, let monopolists rest assured. Theft by *subsidy* or *tariff* does not violate the law, although it transgresses equity as much as highway robbery does; this type of theft, on the contrary, is carried out by law. This makes it worse but does not lead to the *magistrate's court.*

Besides, whether we like it or not, we are all *robbers* and *robbed* in this connection. It is useless for the author of this volume to cry *thief* when he makes a purchase; the same could be shouted at him when he sells;[6] if he differs considerably from his fellow countrymen, it is only in this respect: he knows that he loses more than he gains in this game, and they do not know this; if they did, the game would cease in a very short time.

What is more, I do not boast that I am the first to give this situation its real name. More than sixty years ago, Smith said:[7]

"When businessmen get together, we can expect a conspiracy to be woven against the pockets of the general public."[8] Should we be surprised at this, since the general public pays no attention to it?

---

6. (Bastiat's note) Since he owns some land, which provides him with a living, he be-longs to the class of the *protected.* This circumstance should disarm critics. It shows that, where he uses harsh expressions, it is against the thing itself and not against people's in-tentions. [In letter 197 to Paillottet (11 October 1850) Bastiat states that, as a landholder, he benefited from tariffs but nevertheless was trying to abolish them. CW1, p. 280.]

7. See the entry for "Smith, Adam," in the Glossary of Persons.

8. This is a colorful but not accurate translation by Bastiat of Smith's well-known com-ment about what people in the same business do when they get together: "People of the same trade seldom meet together, even for merriment and diversion, but the conversation ends in a conspiracy against the publick, or in some contrivance to raise prices" (Smith, *An Inquiry into the Nature and Causes of the Wealth of Nations,* vol. 1, bk. 1, chap. 10, part 2: "Inequalities Occasioned by the Policy of Europe," p. 145, http://oll.libertyfund .org/titles/237#Smith_0206-01_446. However, Smith on a couple of occasions did refer to governments taking money out of the pockets of taxpayers, as the following quotation shows: "Those modes of taxation, by stamp-duties and by duties upon registration, are of very modern invention. In the course of little more than a century, however, stamp-duties have, in Europe, become almost universal, and duties upon registration extremely

Well then, an assembly of businessmen officially has discussions under the authority of the General Councils.[9] What goes on there and what is decided upon?

Here is a highly abridged version of the minutes of a meeting.

A SHIPOWNER: Our fleet is on the ropes (aggressive interruption). This is not surprising because I cannot build without iron. I can certainly find it at 10 fr. *on the world market* but, according to the law, French ironmasters force me to pay them 15 fr.; therefore 5 fr. is being taken from me. I demand the freedom to buy wherever I like.

AN IRONMASTER: *On the world market,* I can find transport at 20 fr. By law, shipowners demand 30 for this; they are therefore *taking* 10 fr. from me. They are looting me, so I loot them, and everything is just fine.

A STATESMAN: The shipowner's conclusion is very rash. Oh! Let us cultivate the touching unity which gives us our strength; if we remove one iota of the theory of protectionism, the entire theory will go by the board.

THE SHIPOWNER: But protection has failed us; I repeat that the fleet is on the ropes.

A SAILOR: Well then! Let us raise a *surtax* and let shipowners who take 30 from the public for freight take 40.

A MINISTER: The government will push the excellent device of the *surtax* to the limit, but I am afraid that it will not be enough.[10]

---

common. There is no art which one government sooner learns of another than that of draining money from the pockets of the people" (Smith, *An Inquiry into the Nature and Causes of the Wealth of Nations,* vol. 2, bk. 5, chap. 2, "Appendix to Articles i and ii: Taxes upon the Capital Value of Lands, Houses, and Stock," p. 861, http://oll.libertyfund.org /titles/119#Smith_0206-02_811. This might be another example of Bastiat quoting from memory and conflating two different passages by Smith.

9. The General Councils for Commerce (1802), Manufacturing (1810), and Agriculture (1819) were set up within the Ministry of the Interior to bring together commercial, manufacturing, and agricultural elites to advise the government and to comment on legislation. Their membership came from either members of the chambers of commerce and industry or by appointment by the minister concerned.

10. (Bastiat's note) Here is the text: "I will again quote the customs laws dated 9 and 11 June last, whose object is in the main to encourage long-distance shipping by increas-

A CIVIL SERVANT: You are all worrying about nothing. Does our salvation lie only in tariffs, and are you forgetting taxation? If consumers are generous, taxpayers are no less so. Let us burden them with taxes, and let shipowners be satisfied. I propose a subsidy of 5 fr. to be taken from public taxes to be handed over to builders for each quintal of iron they use.

Mixed cries: Hear! Hear! *A farmer:* Let me have a subsidy of 3 fr. per hectoliter of wheat! *A weaver:* Let me have a subsidy of 2 fr. per meter of cloth! etc., etc.

THE CHAIRMAN: This is what has been agreed. Our meeting has given birth to the system of subsidies, and this will be its eternal glory. What industry will be able to make a loss in the future, since we have two very simple means of changing losses into profits: Tariffs and subsidies? The meeting is at an end.

Some supernatural vision must have shown me in a dream the next apparition of the *subsidy* (who knows even whether I had not put the thought into the mind of M. Dupin) when I wrote the following words a few months ago:

> It appears obvious to me that, without changing its nature
> and effects, protection might have taken the form of a direct tax
> raised by the state and distributed through indemnity subsidies
> to privileged industries.

And, after comparing protectionist duties with subsidies:

> I admit frankly my preference for the second system. It seems
> to me more just, more economic, and more straightforward.
> More just because if society wants to give handouts to a few
> of its members, everyone has to contribute; more economic
> because it would save a great deal in collection costs and would

---

ing the *surtaxes* attached to foreign flags on several articles. Our customs laws, as you know, are generally aimed at this object and gradually, the *surtax* of 10 francs, established by the law dated 28 April 1816 and often inadequate, is *disappearing* to give way to ... more effective protection, which is in closer harmony with the relatively *high cost* of our shipping." This word *disappearing* is priceless. (*The opening speech* of M. Cunin-Gridaine, in the meeting on 15 December 1845). [We have not been able to find the source of this reference.]

cause a great many restrictions to disappear; and finally, more straightforward since the public would see clearly how the operation worked and what they were being made to do."[11]

Since the opportunity has so kindly been offered to us, let us examine *theft by subsidy.* What can be said of it applies just as well to *theft by tariffs,* and while theft by tariffs is slightly better disguised, direct filching[12] will help us understand indirect filching. The mind moves forward in this way from the simple to the compound.

What then! Is there no type of theft that is simpler still? Oh, yes, there is *highway robbery:* all it needs is to be legalized, monopolized, or, as we say nowadays, *organized.*[13]

Well, this is what I have read in a traveler's account:

> When we arrived in the kingdom of A., all branches of production claimed to be in difficulty. Agriculture wailed, manufacturing complained, commerce grumbled, shipping groused, and the government did not know whom to listen to. First of all, it thought of levying heavy taxes on all those who were discontented and handing out the product of these taxes to them after taking its share: that would have been a lottery, just as in our beloved Spain. There are a thousand of you, the State will take one piastre from each of you; it then subtly pilfers 250 piastres and distributes 750 in lots that vary in size between the players. Forgetting that he has given a whole piastre, the upright Hidalgo who receives three-quarters of a piastre cannot contain his joy and runs off to spend his fifteen reals in the bar. This would have been similar to what is happening in France. Be that as it may, as barbarous as this country was, the government did not think that its inhabitants were stupid enough to accept

11. (Bastiat's note) Chapter 5 of the first series of *Economic Sophisms,* pages 49 and 50. [ES1 5, p. 41 and p. 42.]

12. Here Bastiat uses more of a slang term, *le filoutage,* from the verb *filouter* (to filch, swipe, or rob). We translate it here as "filching."

13. Bastiat is referring to one of the commonly used socialist slogans of the mid-1840s, namely "organization" (the organization of labor advocated by Blanc) and "association" (cooperative living and working arrangements advocated by Fourier). See "Bastiat's Use of the Socialist Terms 'Organization' and 'Association,'" in the Note on the Translation.

such strange forms of protection, so it thought up the following scheme.

The country was criss-crossed with roads. The government measured them accurately and said to the farmers: "Everything that you can steal from passers-by between these two posts is yours; let it serve as a *subsidy,* protection, and motivation for you." It then assigned to each manufacturer and shipowner a section of road to exploit in accordance with this formula:

Dono tibi et concedo[14] [I give to you and I grant]
Virtutem et puissantiam [virtue and power]
Volandi [to steal]
Pillandi [to plunder]
Derobandi [to filch]
Filoutandi [to swindle]
Et escroquandi [to defraud]
Impune per totam istam [at will, along this whole]
Viam [road][15]

Well, it so happened that the natives of the kingdom of A. are now so familiar with this regime and so accustomed to take account only of what they steal and not of what is stolen from them, so essentially inclined to regarding pillage only from the point of view of the pillager, that they see the tally of all individual thefts as *profits to the nation* and refuse to abandon a system of *protection* outside of which, they say, there is no form of production capable of surviving.

14. This pseudo-Latin is partly made from French words. We provide a translation in brackets.

15. In this account, Bastiat is making a parody of Molière's parody of the granting of a degree of doctor of medicine in the last play he wrote, *Le Malade imaginaire* (*The Imaginary Invalid,* or *The Hypochondriac*). Most of the dialogue is in Latin, including the swearing-in of the new doctor (Bachelierus) by Praeses, who says: "Ego, cum isto boneto / Venerabili et doctor, / Don tibi et concedo / Virtutem et puissanciam / Medicandi, / Purgandi, / Seignandi, / Perçandi, / Taillandi, / Coupandi, / Et occidendi / Impune per total terram." This might be loosely translated as (thanks to Arthur Goddard's excellent translation in the FEE edition, p. 194): "I give and grant you / Power and authority to / Practice medicine, / Purge, / Bleed, / Stab, / Hack, / Slash, / and Kill / With impunity / Throughout the whole world" (courtesy of FEE.org). (Molière, *Théâtre complet de Molière* 8:286.)

Are you astounded? It is not possible, you say, that an entire nation should agree to see what the inhabitants steal from one another as an *increase in wealth*.

Why not? We are certainly convinced of this in France, and every day we organize and perfect here the *mutual theft* that goes under the name of subsidies and protective tariffs.

Even so, let us not exaggerate. Let us agree that viewed from the angle of the *method of collection* and taking account of the collateral circumstances, the system in the kingdom of A. might be worse than ours, but let us also say that as far as the principles and necessary effects are concerned, there is not an atom of difference between all these types of theft that are legally organized to provide additional profit to producers.

Note that if *highway robbery* has several disadvantages as to its execution, it also has advantages that are absent from *theft by tariffs*.

For example: with highway robbery, an equitable share can be given to all the producers. This is not so for customs duties. These by their very nature are powerless to protect certain sectors of society, such as artisans, merchants, men of letters, lawyers, soldiers, odd-job men, etc., etc.

It is true that *theft by subsidy* also provides opportunities for an infinite number of subdivisions, and from this angle it is no less perfect than *highway robbery*. On the other hand, however, it often leads to such strange, idiotic results that the native inhabitants of the kingdom of A. might very justifiably laugh at them.

What the person robbed loses in highway robbery is gained by the robber. At least the object stolen remains in the country. However, under the sway of *theft by subsidy*, what is taken from the French is often given to the Chinese, the Hottentots, the Kaffirs, or the Algonquins, in the following way:

A piece of cloth is worth *one hundred francs* in Bordeaux. It is impossible to sell it below this price without making a loss. It is impossible to sell it for more because *competition* between merchants prevents this. In these circumstances, if a Frenchman comes forward to obtain this cloth, he has to pay *one hundred francs* or do without it. But if an Englishman comes along, then the government intervenes and says to the seller: "Sell your cloth and I will see that you are given *twenty francs* by the taxpayers." The merchant, who does not want nor is able to obtain more than one hundred francs for his cloth, hands it over to the Englishman for 80 francs. This sum, added to the 20 francs, produced from the *theft by subsidy*, makes his price exactly. It is exactly as though taxpayers had given 20 francs to the Englishman on condition that he buy French cloth at a discount of 20 francs, at 20 francs below production cost and 20 francs below what it costs us ourselves. Therefore, *theft by subsidy* has this particular characteristic, that *those robbed* are in the country that tolerates it and the *robbers* are spread out over the surface of the globe.

It is truly miraculous that the following proposition continues to be held as proven: *Anything that an individual steals from the whole is a general profit.* Perpetual motion, the philosopher's stone, or the squaring of the circle have fallen into oblivion, but the theory of *Advancement through theft* is still in fashion. However, *a priori,* we might have thought that of all forms of child-ishness, this is the least viable.

There are some who tell us: "Are you then in favor of *laissez passer?*[16] Economists of the outdated school of Smith and Say? Do you therefore not want *work to be organized?*"[17] Well, Sirs, organize work as much as you like. We, for our part, will see that you do not organize *theft.*

A greater number repeat: "*Subsidies and tariffs* have all been used exces-sively. They have to be used without being abused. Wise freedom combined with a moderate form of protection is what is being claimed by *serious* and practical men.[18] Let us beware of *absolute principles.*"[19]

According to the Spanish traveler, this is precisely what was being said in the kingdom of A. "Highway robbery," said the wise men, "is neither good nor bad; it all depends on the circumstances. It is just a question of *weighting* things correctly and paying us, the civil servants, for the work involved in this moderation. Perhaps too much latitude has been given to pillage and perhaps not enough. Let us look at, examine, and weigh in the balance the accounts of each worker. To those who do not earn enough, we will give an extra length of road to exploit. To those who earn too much, we will reduce the hours, days, or months of pillage."

Those who said these things acquired a great reputation for moderation, prudence, and wisdom. They never failed to attain the highest positions in the state.

As for those who said: "Let us repress all injustices as well as the lesser

16. This is the second half of the physiocrats' policy advice to the government, "laissez-faire, laissez-passer" (let us be free to do what we will and be free to go wherever we will). See "Bastiat's References to Laissez-Faire," in the Note on the Translation.

17. The rallying cry of many socialists in the 1840s was that workers and factories be "organized" by the state and not be left to the uncertainties of the free market.

18. See also ES3 11, pp. 305–8.

19. See also ES1 18, pp. 82–84.

forms of injustice. Let us not tolerate *theft, half-theft,* or *quarter-theft,*" these were taken for ideologues, boring dreamers always repeating the same thing. The people, in any case, find their reasoning too easy to understand. How can you believe what is so simple?

10. The Tax Collector

PUBLISHING HISTORY:

Original title: "Le Percepteur."
Place and date of first publication: No date given. First
    published in book form.
First French edition as book or pamphlet: *Economic Sophisms*
    (Second Series) (1848). First and Second Series were
    combined in one edition in 1851.
Location in Paillottet's edition: *OC:* Vol. 4. *Sophismes*
    économiques. Petits pamphlets I, pp. 198–203.
Previous translation: 1st American ed., 1848; 1st British ed.,
    1873; FEE ed., 1964.

Jacques Bonhomme, Wine Producer
Mr. Blockhead,[1] Tax Collector

BLOCKHEAD:[2] You have harvested twenty barrels[3] of wine?

BONHOMME: Yes, with much trouble and sweat.

BLOCKHEAD: Be so good as to deliver six of the best ones.

---

1. Bastiat again uses a made-up word to poke fun at his adversaries, in this case the tax collector. He calls him "Monsieur Lasouche," which the FEE translator translated as "Mr. Clodpate" (*Economic Sophisms,* FEE edition, p. 198). Since *la souche* means a tree stump, log, or stock, we thought "Mr. Blockhead" might be appropriate here. This is also the translation used in Roche, *Frédéric Bastiat: A Man Alone,* p. 60. Bastiat used the word *souche* in another context in 1847, when he wrote a brief draft of a chapter on Montaigne's essay "Le Profit d'un est dommage de l'autre" (One Man's Gain Is Another Man's Loss). He called this phrase "a standard sophism, one that is the very root of a host of sophisms" (*Sophisme type, sophisme souche, d'où sortent des multitudes de sophismes*). See ES3 15, p. 341.

2. We have added the names of the speakers in order to assist the reader. When the protagonists refer to each other by name we have followed what was used in the original French.

3. Bastiat uses a number of terms to express the volume measurement of wine, some of which are regional and not exactly defined.

BONHOMME: Six barrels out of twenty! Good heavens! Do you want to ruin me? To what use are you going to put them, if you please?

BLOCKHEAD: The first will be sent to the creditors of the State. When we have debts, the least we can do is to pay them interest.[4]

BONHOMME: And where has the capital gone?

BLOCKHEAD: It would take too long to tell you. Part in the past was placed into cartridges that produced the finest smoke in the world. Another part paid the men who were crippled on foreign soil after having ravaged it. Then, when this expenditure had attracted to our country our friends the enemy, they refused to leave without taking money, which had to be borrowed.

BONHOMME: And what is my share today?

BLOCKHEAD: The satisfaction of saying:

How proud I am of being French
When I look at the column![5]

4. Total debt held by the French government in 1848 amounted to fr. 5.2 billion. According to the Budget Papers for 1848, total government spending was fr. 1,446,210,170 (with a deficit of fr. 54,933,660). Of this, fr. 384,346,191 was spent to service the public debt, making up 26.6 percent of the total budget. Given the fact that military expenditure was a very high proportion of overall government expenditure in the nineteenth century, the vast bulk of the consolidated debt had been incurred in funding previous military activity. There is also debt which had been incurred in providing military pensions (fr. 39.3 million). Total military spending in 1848 amounted to fr. 460.5 million (31.8 percent), of which fr. 322 million was for the Ministry of War and fr. 138.5 million was for the Ministry of the Navy and Colonies. Thus the total for the repayment of past debt and current military expenditure was fr. 844.8 million, which was 58.4 percent of total government spending for the year. See appendix 4 "French Government Budgets. . . ."

5. These lines come from a song called "La Colonne" (The Column, 1818), written by the *goguettier* (a member of a social club where political, patriotic, and drinking songs were sung) Paul Émile Debraux (1796–1831). Debraux was an archsupporter of Napoléon and wrote many songs extolling his virtues. "The Column" is one of these and is a tribute to the building of the Colonne Vendôme by Napoléon in 1810 to celebrate the French victory at the Battle of Austerlitz in 1805. The Colonne Vendôme is forty-four meters high, made from the melted bronze cannons taken from the enemy. Bastiat misremembers the exact words, which read, "Ah! Qu'on est fier d'être Français / Quand on regarde la calonne!" (How proud one is to be French when one looks at the column) (Béranger, *Choix de chansons nationales anciennes, nouvelles et inédites*, p. 56). See also the entry for "Béranger, Pierre-Jean de," in the Glossary of Persons and the entry for *Goguettes* and *Goguettiers*," in the Glossary of Subjects and Terms.

BONHOMME: And the humiliation of leaving my heirs an estate encumbered by rent in perpetuity. In the end, we have to pay what we owe whatever crazy use has been made of it. I agree to give one barrel, what about the five others?

BLOCKHEAD: One must pay for public services, the Civil List, the judges who restore to you the field that your neighbor wants to take possession of, the gendarmes who hunt thieves while you sleep, the road mender[6] who maintains the road that takes you to town, the parish priest who baptizes your children, the teacher who raises them, and my good self, none of whom works for nothing.[7]

BONHOMME: That is fair—a service for a service. I have no objection to that. I would rather sort things out directly with my parish priest and schoolteacher,[8] but I will not insist on this. I agree to give another barrel, but there is a long way to go to six.

BLOCKHEAD: Do you think it is asking too much for two barrels as your contribution to the cost of the army and navy?

BONHOMME: Alas, it is not much in comparison with what they are costing me already, for they have already taken from me two sons that I loved dearly.

BLOCKHEAD: We have to maintain the balance of power in Europe.

BONHOMME: My God! The balance would be the same if these forces were reduced everywhere by half or three-quarters. We would preserve both our children and our revenue. All we need to do is agree on this.

BLOCKHEAD: Yes, but we do not agree.

6. Bastiat uses the word *cantonnier* here. See ES1 10, p. 60n7.

7. According to the Budget Papers for 1848, the following amounts were spent: the Civil List (upkeep of the Monarch) fr. 13.3 million; justice within the Ministry of Justice and Religion fr. 26.7 million; police in the Ministry of the Interior fr. 22.8 million; prisons in the Ministry of the Interior fr. 7.2 million; the Ministry of Public Works fr. 63.5 million; religion within the Ministry of Justice and Religion fr. 39.6 million; Part IV of the Budget Papers lists the costs of administration and collecting taxes (includes personnel) fr. 156.9 million.

8. Bastiat uses the phrase *s'arranger directement* (to engage in an exchange directly with a supplier of a good or service). See also the entry for "Representation," in the Glossary of Subjects and Terms.

BONHOMME: That is what astonishes me. For in the end everyone suffers.

BLOCKHEAD: You wanted this, Jacques Bonhomme.

BONHOMME: You are joking, Mr. Tax Collector. Do I have a say in the matter?

BLOCKHEAD: Who have you voted for as your deputy?[9,10]

BONHOMME: An upright army general who will shortly become a marshal if God gives him a long enough life.[11]

BLOCKHEAD: And on what does this good general live?

BONHOMME: On my barrels, I imagine.

BLOCKHEAD: And what would happen if he voted for a reduction in the army and your contribution?

BONHOMME: Instead of becoming a marshal, he would be retired.

BLOCKHEAD: Do you now understand that you have yourself...

BONHOMME: Let us move on to the fifth barrel, if you please.

BLOCKHEAD: That goes to Algeria.[12]

BONHOMME: To Algeria! And we are assured that all Muslims are wine-haters, what barbarians! I have often asked myself whether they know nothing of Médoc because they are infidels or infidels because they know nothing of Médoc.[13] Besides, what services do they do me in return for this ambrosia that has cost me so much work?

---

9. Bastiat uses the phrase *nommer pour député* (nominate as one's representative).

10. Since Jacques is able to vote, he must have been part of that wealthy minority of about 240,000 people who were entitled to vote because they paid more than fr. 300 per annum in direct taxes. From this point on, the sophism turns to the nature of representative politics.

11. Bastiat may have in mind General Lamoricière (1806–65), who was a general, an elected deputy, minister of war under Cavaignac (1848) and who took part in the military suppression of rioting during the June Days of 1848.

12. France invaded and conquered Algeria in 1830. In 1848 parts of French Algeria were established as three départements within the French government, and an official program to encourage French settlers to move there was begun. Two justifications given in favor of colonization were that France's "surplus population" could be settled in Algeria and that Algeria would become a profitable market for French goods.

13. Médoc is a wine-growing region in the département of Gironde near Bordeaux, a little to the north of the Landes where Bastiat lived. According to the 1855 official classification of Bordeaux wines, the red wines from this region are called "médoc."

BLOCKHEAD: None. For the reason that it is not intended for Muslims but for the good Christians who spend their time in Barbary.

BONHOMME: And what are they going to do there that will be useful to me?

BLOCKHEAD: Carry out incursions and be subjected to them; kill and be killed; catch dysentery and return for treatment; excavate ports, construct roads, build villages, and people them with Maltese, Italians, Spanish, and Swiss nationals who will live off your barrel and many other barrels which I will come to ask you for later.

BONHOMME: Mercy on us! This is too much and I refuse outright to give you a barrel. A wine producer who indulged in such folly would be sent to Bicêtre.[14] Driving roads through the Atlas! Good heavens! And to think I cannot leave my own home! Excavating ports in Barbary when the Garonne is silting up more every day! Taking the children I love from me in order to torment the Kabyls![15] Having me pay for the houses, seed, and horses that are delivered to Greeks and Maltese when there are so many poor people around us!

BLOCKHEAD: Poor people, that is the point! The country is being relieved of this *surplus population.*

BONHOMME: Thank you very much! By keeping them alive in Algeria on capital that would enable them to live here.[16]

14. Bicêtre Hospital on the southern outskirts of Paris was built by Louis XIII in 1633 to care for old and injured soldiers. Under Louis XIV (1656) it was used to house the insane and other political and social "undesirables." It was here during the Revolution that the guillotine was tested on live sheep and the cadavers of prisoners. Victor Hugo's novel opposing the death penalty, *Le Dernier Jour d'un condamné* (The Last Day of a Condemned Man, 1829), was set in Bicêtre.

15. The Kabyls are a Berber tribal community who live in Algeria and Tunisia. They were subject to French conquest when the French took Algeria in 1830.

16. Bastiat may have written this sophism in 1847, before the government began to actively subsidize the colonization of Algeria in 1848. *Le Journal des économistes* gives a figure of fr. 120 million spent in Algeria in 1847 and makes a very similar argument to that of Bastiat, that the money is taken from French taxpayers and then given to the troops and then into the hands of the merchants who service the needs of those troops. It goes further to argue that the civilian population of Algeria is 113,000, of which 6,000 live in administration towns and are paid by the French civilian administration out of taxpayers'

BLOCKHEAD: And then you are establishing the bases for a *great empire;* you are bringing *civilization* to Africa and bedecking your country in immortal glory.[17]

BONHOMME: You are a poet, Mr. Tax Collector, but I am a wine producer and I refuse.

BLOCKHEAD: Just think that in a few thousand years, you will be repaid your advances a hundredfold. This is what those in charge of the enterprise tell us.

BONHOMME: And in the meantime, they used only at first to ask for one cask of wine to meet the costs, then it was two, then three, and here I am being taxed a whole barrel. I continue to refuse.

BLOCKHEAD: You no longer have any time to do this. Your *political delegate*[18] has stipulated a toll[19] for you of one barrel or four full casks.

BONHOMME: That is only too true. Cursed be my weakness! I also thought that by giving him my mandate[20] I was being rash, for what is there in common between an army general and a poor wine producer?

BLOCKHEAD: You can see clearly that there is something in common between you, if only the wine that you produce and that he votes for himself in your name.

BONHOMME: Make fun of me, I deserve it, Mr. Tax Collector. But be reasonable with it; leave me at least the sixth barrel. The interest on the debts has been paid, the Civil List provided for, public

---

funds, leaving 107,000 who are paid by the army out of taxpayers' funds. In WSWNS 10, Bastiat states that fr. 8,000 was spent by the state for each colonist it subsidized to settle in Algeria. He believes that French workers at home could live well on half that amount of capital. See "Chronique," in *JDE* 19 (February 1848): 315.

17. See Bastiat's comments on Algeria and colonization in his address "To the Electors of the District of Saint-Sever," where he describes the colonial system as "the most disastrous illusion ever to have led nations astray" (*CW*1, pp. 363–65).

18. Bastiat uses the phrase *votre chargé de pouvoirs* (the person you have appointed to exercise political powers).

19. The "octroi," or the tax on goods brought into a town or city, was imposed on consumer goods which had to pass through tollgates which had been built on the outskirts of the town or city where they could be inspected and taxed. They were used to fund city expenses such as infrastructure.

20. Bastiat uses the phrase *donner ma procuration à quelqu'un* (to grant someone my power of attorney).

services assured, and the war in Africa perpetuated. What more do you want?

BLOCKHEAD: You cannot bargain with me. You should have made your intentions clear to the general. Now he has disposed of your harvest.

BONHOMME: Damned Bonapartist Guardsman![21] But in the end, what are you going to do with this poor barrel, the flower of my cellars? Here, taste this wine. See how smooth, strong, full-bodied, velvety, and what a fine color . . .

BLOCKHEAD: Excellent! Delicious! Just the job for M. D . . .[22] the cloth manufacturer.

BONHOMME: M. D . . . the cloth manufacturer! What do you mean?

BLOCKHEAD: That he will get a good share of it.

BONHOMME: How? What is all this? I am blowed if I understand you!

BLOCKHEAD: Do you not know that M. D . . . has set up an enterprise that is very useful to the country, and which, in the end, makes a considerable loss each year?

BONHOMME: I pity him wholeheartedly. But what can I do?

BLOCKHEAD: The Chamber has understood that if this continued M. D . . . would face the choice of either having to operate his factory better or closing it.

BONHOMME: But what is the connection between faulty business dealings on M. D's part . . . and my barrel?

BLOCKHEAD: The Chamber considers that if it delivered to M. D . . . some of the wine from your cellar, a few hectoliters of wheat from your neighbors, and a few sous subtracted from the earnings of the workers, his losses would be transformed into profits.

BONHOMME: The recipe is as infallible as it is ingenious. But, heavens above, it is terribly iniquitous! What! M. D . . . is to cover his debts by taking my wine from me?

21. Bastiat uses the word *Grognard* (*grogner* means to groan with pain), which was the name given to soldiers of the Old Guard of Napoléon, who were his most devoted and committed soldiers and who were often expected to fight in extreme conditions, hence their reputation for groaning and grumbling about their circumstances.

22. We have not been able to identify who "M. D . . ." the textile manufacturer might be.

BLOCKHEAD: No, not exactly your wine but its cost. This is what we call *incentive subsidies*. But you are totally speechless! Do you not see what a great service you are rendering to the country?

BONHOMME: You mean to M. D . . . ?

BLOCKHEAD: To the country. M. D . . . ensures that his industry prospers, thanks to this arrangement, and in this way, he says, the country gets richer. This is what he told the Chamber of which he is a member, in the last few days.

BONHOMME: This is rank dishonesty! What! An ignoramus sets up an idiotic enterprise and loses his money, and if he extorts enough wine or wheat to cover his losses and even achieve some profit this will be seen as a gain for the entire country!

BLOCKHEAD: As your *authorized representative*[23] has judged this to be so, you have no option but to hand over to me your six barrels of wine and sell as best you can the fourteen barrels I am leaving you.

BONHOMME: That is my business.

BLOCKHEAD: You see, it would be very unfortunate if you did not get a high price for them.

BONHOMME: I will see to it.

BLOCKHEAD: For there are a lot of things that this price has to cover.

BONHOMME: I know, Sir, I know.

BLOCKHEAD: First of all, if you purchase iron to replace your shovels and ploughs, a law has decided that you will pay twice as much as it is worth to the ironmaster.

BONHOMME: Is that so? We must be in the Black Forest![24]

BLOCKHEAD: Then, if you need oil, meat, canvas, coal, wool, or sugar, each of these, according to the law, will cost you double their worth.

BONHOMME: But this is terrible, frightful, and abominable!

---

23. Bastiat uses the phrase *votre fondé de pouvoirs* (the person you have set up to wield political power over you).

24. The Black Forest was notorious for having highwaymen who would rob travelers.

BLOCKHEAD: What is the use of complaining? You yourself, through your *authorized representative*,[25] ...

BONHOMME: Leave my mandate[26] alone! I have given it in an odd way, it is true. But I will no longer be hoodwinked and will have myself represented[27] by a good, upright member of the peasantry.

BLOCKHEAD: Nonsense! You will reelect[28] the good general.

BONHOMME: I! I will reelect the general to distribute my wine to Africans and manufacturers?

BLOCKHEAD: You will reelect him, I tell you.

BONHOMME: That is going a bit far. I will not reelect him if I do not wish to do so.

BLOCKHEAD: But you will want to and you will reelect him.

BONHOMME: Just let him come here looking for trouble. He will see with whom he has to deal.

BLOCKHEAD: We will see. Good-bye. I will take your six barrels and divide them up in accordance with the general's decision.

11. The Utopian[1,2]

PUBLISHING HISTORY:

Original title: "L'Utopiste."
Place and date of first publication: *Le Libre-échange,* 17 January 1847, pp. 63–64.

25. Bastiat uses the phrase *votre chargé de procuration* (the person you have appointed with power of attorney over your affairs).

26. Bastiat uses the word *procuration* (power of attorney or proxy vote).

27. Bastiat uses the phrase *se faire représenter par quelqu'un* (to be represented by somebody).

28. Bastiat uses the word *renommer* (reelect).

1. "The Utopian" is what might be called a "political sophism." For a discussion of this genre see "Bastiat's Political Sophisms," in the Introduction.

2. Molinari, under the nom de plume of "le Rêveur" (the Dreamer), wrote an appeal to socialists for solidarity in their joint struggle for prosperity and justice. He published this only a few days before the June Days rioting in 1848 under the title "L'Utopie de la liberté. Lettres aux socialistes" (The Utopia of Liberty. Letters to the Socialists). This work was ignored in the chaos of the aftermath of the crackdown by Cavaignac's troops. See Molinari, "L'Utopie de la liberté. Lettres aux socialistes," *JDE* 20 (15 June 1848): 328–32.

First French edition as book or pamphlet: *Economic Sophisms*
   (Second Series) (1848). First and Second Series were
   combined in one edition in 1851.
Location in Paillottet's edition of *OC*: Vol. 4. *Sophismes
   économiques. Petits pamphlets I*, pp. 203–12.
Previous translations: 1st American ed., 1848; 1st British ed.,
   1873; FEE ed., 1964.

"If only I were one of His Majesty's Ministers! ..."

"Well, what would you do?"[3]

"I would begin by ... by ... goodness me, by being highly embarrassed.
For when it comes down to it, I would be minister only because I had a
majority; I would have a majority only because I had made myself one,
and I would have made myself one, honestly at least, only by governing in
accordance with their ideas. ... Therefore, if I undertook to ensure that
my ideas prevailed by thwarting theirs, I would no longer have a majority, and if I did not have a majority I would not be one of His Majesty's
Ministers."

"Let me suppose that you are a minister and that consequently having a
majority is not an obstacle for you; what would you do?"

"I would seek to establish on which side *justice* was to be found."

"And then?"

"I would seek to establish on which side *utility* was to be found."

"And next?"

"I would seek to find out whether they were in agreement or in conflict
with one another."

"And if you found that they were not in agreement?"

> "I would say to King Philip:
> Take back your portfolio.
> The rhyme is not rich and the style outdated.
> But do you not see that that is much better

3. Fifteen months after this article was written, Bastiat was elected to the Constituent
Assembly of the Second Republic after the Revolution of February 1848. He was subsequently appointed vice president of the Chamber's Finance Committee where he, as
the resident "utopian" on the committee, attempted to enact his tax-cutting measures
proposed here. See ES3 23 for an example of Bastiat's sarcastic comments about the usefulness of the provisional government in the days immediately following the Revolution
in February 1848.

Than the *transactions* whose common sense is just a murmur,
And that *honesty* speaks these in its purest form?[4]

"But if you acknowledge that *justice* and *utility* are one and the same?"
"Then I would go right ahead."
"Very well. But to achieve utility through justice, a third element is needed."
"Which is?"
"Opportunity."
"You have given it to me."
"When?"
"A short time ago."
"How?"
"By granting me a majority."
"No wonder it seemed to me that this concession was highly risky, since in the end it implies that the majority clearly sees what is just and what is useful and clearly sees that they are in perfect harmony."

"And if it saw all these things clearly, good would be done, so to speak, automatically."

"This is where you are constantly leading me: to see the possibility of reform only through the general progress of reason."

"Which is like saying that as a result of this progress all reform is certain."

"Perfectly put. However, this preliminary progress takes rather a long time to be implemented. Let us suppose it has been accomplished. What would you do? The fact is, I cannot wait to see you at work, doing things, involved in the actual practice."

"Firstly, I would reduce the postage tax to 10 centimes."[5]
"I had heard you mention before 5 centimes."[6]

---

4. Bastiat again parodies a scene from Molière's play *Le Misanthrope* (see ES2 9, pp. 170–71 esp. n2). Here Bastiat replaces "King Henry" with "King Louis-Philippe," "Paris" with "portfolio," the word *colifichets* (trinkets or baubles) with "transactions," and the word "Passion" with "honesty" (*Molière, Théâtre complet de Molière*, p. 86). See also the entry for "Molière," in the Glossary of Persons.

5. The old system of charging by distance was abolished during the Revolution (24 August 1848). The year before, in 1847, 125 million letters were sent at an average cost of 43 centimes. The new fixed tax for mail in 1849 was reduced to 20 centimes. Thus Bastiat's proposal for a cut to 10 centimes in January 1847 was a radical one.

6. (Paillottet's note) The author had indeed mentioned 5 centimes in May 1846 in an article in *Le Journal des économistes*, which became chapter 12 of the Second Series of the *Sophisms*. [ES2 12 "Salt, the Mail, and the Customs Service"]

"Yes, but since I have other reforms in view, I must advance prudently in order to avoid a deficit."

"Good heavens! What prudence! You are already in deficit to the tune of 30 million!"

"Then I would reduce the salt tax to 10 fr."[7]

"Good! Here you are now, with a deficit of 30 million more. Doubtless you have invented a new tax?"

"God forbid! Besides, I do not flatter myself that I have a sufficiently inventive mind."

"But you need one ... Ah! I am with you! What was I thinking of? You will simply reduce expenditure. I did not think of that."

"You are not the only one—I will come to that, but for the moment that is not what I am counting on."

"Oh yes! You are reducing revenue without reducing expenditure and you will avoid a deficit?"

"Yes, by reducing other taxes at the same time."

(Here the questioner, placing his index finger on the side of his forehead, nods his head, which may be translated thus: He is off his head.)

"I do believe that this is an ingenious maneuver! I pay 100 francs to the Treasury, you save me 5 francs on salt and 5 francs on postage, and in order for the Treasury to receive no less than 100 francs, you are saving me 10 francs on some other tax?"

"Shake my hand, you have understood me."

"The devil take me if I have! I am not even sure I have heard you correctly."

"I repeat that I will balance one reduction in tax with another."

"Heavens above! I have a few minutes to spare; I might as well listen to your development of this paradox."

"This is the entire mystery. I know of a tax that costs you 20 francs and of which not a sou comes into the Treasury. I save you half of it and direct the other half to the rue de Rivoli."[8]

---

7. The tax on salt, or "gabelle," was abolished during the Revolution but revived during the Restoration. In 1816 it was set at 30 centimes per kilogram (or 30 fr. per 100 kilos), and in 1847 it raised fr. 70.4 million. During the Revolution of 1848, it was reduced to 10 centimes per kilogram (or 10 fr. per 100 kilos). Bastiat's proposed cut to 10 centimes in January 1847 was the same level adopted by the new government in 1848. See "French Taxation," in appendix 3, "Economic Policy and Taxation." See also E. de Parieu, "Sel," in *DEP* 2:606–9.

8. The Ministry of Finance was located in rue de Rivoli.

"Really! You are a financier of a rare variety. There is only one problem. On what, may I ask, am I paying a tax that does not reach the Treasury?"

"How much has this suit cost you?"

"One hundred francs."

"And if you had brought in the cloth from Verviers,[9] how much would it have cost you?"

"Eighty francs."

"Why then did you not order it from Verviers?"

"Because it is forbidden."[10]

"And why is this forbidden?"

"In order for the suit to cost me 100 francs instead of 80."

"This prohibition will therefore cost you 20 francs?"

"Without doubt."

"And where do these 20 francs go?"

"Where do they go? To the cloth manufacturer."

"Well then! Give me 10 francs for the Treasury, I will lift the prohibition, and you will still save 10 francs."

"Oh, oh! I now begin to see. Here is the Treasury account: it loses 5 francs on the post, 5 francs on salt, and gains 10 francs on woolen cloth. It is thus quits."

"And here is your account: you save 5 francs on salt, 5 francs on the post, and 10 francs on woolen cloth."

"A total of 20 francs. I quite like this plan. But what will become of the poor manufacturer of cloth?"

"Oh! I have thought of him. I am arranging compensation for him, still through tax reductions that provide profit for the Treasury, and what I have done for you with regard to cloth, I will do for him with regard to wool, coal, machines, etc., so that he will be able to reduce his price without losing out."

"But are you sure that things will remain in balance?"

"The balance will be in his favor. The 20 francs I save you on cloth will be

---

9. Verviers is a textile-manufacturing city in eastern Belgium in the province of Liège. Its textile industry dates from the fifteenth century. It suffered a serious decline when Liège was annexed to France in 1795. It revived after the Restoration and became one of the major industrial cities producing woolen cloth in the nineteenth century.

10. French tariffs on manufactured goods such as textiles were very complex. In the case of textiles, many goods were prohibited outright in order to protect French manufacturers. See Horace Say, "Douanes," in *DEP* 1:578–604. See also "French Tariff Policy," in appendix 3, "Economic Policy and Taxation."

increased by the sums I will also save you on wheat, meat, fuel, etc. This will become quite considerable, and savings like this will be made by the thirty-five million of your fellow citizens. There will be enough there to buy out the supplies of cloth from Verviers and Elbeuf[11] alike. The nation will be better dressed, that is all."

"I will think about this, as it is becoming quite confused in my mind."

"After all, with regard to clothing, the essential thing is to be clothed. Your limbs are your own property and not the property of the manufacturer. Protecting them from freezing is your business and not his! If the law takes his side against you, the law is unjust, and you have allowed me to reason on the premise that anything that is unjust is harmful."

"Perhaps I have been too bold, but please continue to set out your financial plan."

"I will therefore promulgate a law on Customs duties."

"In two folio volumes?"[12]

"No, in two articles."

"This time, no one will be able to say that the well-known saying, 'No one is supposed to be ignorant of the law,' is a fiction. Let us see what your tariffs will be."

"Here they are:

"'Article 1. All goods imported will pay a tax of 5 percent on their value.'"[13]

"Even raw materials?

"Unless they have no *value*."

"But all of them have some value, more or *less*."

"In this case they will pay more or *less*."

"How do you expect our factories to compete with foreign factories that have *raw materials* duty free?"

---

11. Elbeuf is an industrial town in northern France on the Seine River to the south of Rouen.

12. This is a snide reference by Bastiat to the three very large volumes on French tariffs which were produced by the inquiry conducted by the protectionist Conseil supérieur du commerce (Superior Council of Commerce) in 1835.

13. For Bastiat and other nineteenth-century free traders, the figure of 5 percent was regarded as a kind of magic number, below which tariffs were acceptable for revenue-raising purposes only (since there were no income taxes at this time), and above which tariffs were unacceptable as they were then regarded as "protectionist," giving advantages to politically well-connected manufacturers at the expense of the consuming public. See "Bastiat's Policy on Tariffs," in appendix 1; and "Further Aspects of Bastiat's Life and Work" and "French Tariff Policy," in appendix 3.

"Given the expenditure of the State, if we close down this source of revenue, another will have to be opened up; this will not reduce the relative inferiority of our factories, and there will be one more administrative department to create and pay for."

"That is true. I was reasoning as though it was a question of abolishing the tax and not of displacing it. I will think about this. Let us have your second article . . ."

"'Article 2. All goods exported will pay a tax of 5 percent of their value.'"

"Good heavens, Mr. Utopian! You are going to be stoned, and if necessary I will throw the first stone."

"We have agreed that the majority is enlightened."

"Enlightened! Do you maintain that an *export duty* will not be a burden?"

"Any tax is a burden, but this is less of a burden than others."

"A great deal of eccentric behavior is to be expected at carnival time.[14] Be so good as to make this new paradox plausible, if you can."

"How much have you paid for this wine?"

"One franc a liter."

"How much would you have paid for it outside the tollgates?"[15]

"Fifty centimes."[16]

"Why is there this difference?"

"Ask the city tolls, which have levied 10 sous on it."

"And who set up the city tolls?"

"The Commune of Paris, in order to pave and light the streets."

"It is therefore an import duty. But if the bordering communes had set up the city tolls for their benefit, what would have happened?"

---

14. Carnival is a festive season which occurs in many Catholic countries in February (or late December in the case of France), with public parades, the wearing of masks and costumes, and revelry which often expresses the temporary overturning of traditional authority (or at least the mocking of it). In Paris the carnival is called *la fête des fous* (feast of fools) and dates back to at least the sixteenth century. It was memorably described in Victor Hugo's novel *The Hunchback of Notre Dame* (1831), in which Quasimodo is appointed the King of Fools.

15. Louis XVI had fifty-seven *barrières d'octroi* (tollgates) built around the outskirts of Paris where goods coming into the city could be inspected and taxed.

16. In 1845 the city of Paris imposed an *octroi* (entry tax) on all goods which entered the city. The tax on wine was the heaviest as a proportion of total value and the most unequally applied. Cheap table wine was taxed at 80–100 percent by value while superior-quality wine was taxed at 5–6 percent by value. For a further discussion of *octroi*, see "French Taxation," in appendix 3, "Economic Policy and Taxation."

"I would still pay 1 franc for my 50-centime wine, and the other 50 centimes would pave and light Montmartre and the Batignoles."[17]

"So that in the end, it is the consumer who pays the tax."

"There is no doubt about this."

"Therefore, by imposing an export tax, you make foreigners pay for your expenditure.

"I have caught you out. That is no longer *justice*."

"Why not? For a product to be made, the country has to have education, security, and roads, things that cost money. Why should foreigners not pay for the charges generated by this product since they, in the long run, are the ones who will be consuming it?"

"This runs counter to established ideas."

"Not in the slightest. The final purchaser has to reimburse all the direct or indirect production costs."

"Whatever you say, it is crystal clear that a measure like this would paralyze commerce and close off our markets."

"That is an illusion. If you paid this tax on top of all the others, you would be right. But if the 100 million raised by this avenue saved them from paying as much by way of other taxes, you would reappear on foreign markets with all your previous advantages, and even more, if this tax generated fewer restrictions and less expenditure."

"I will think about this. So, now we have settled salt, the postal services, and customs duties. Is this all?"

"I have scarcely begun."

"I beg you, let me into your other Utopian plans."[18]

"I have lost 60 million on salt and the postal services. I have recovered them on Customs duties, which have given me something even more precious."

"And what is that, if you please?"

"International relationships based on justice, and the likelihood of peace, which is almost a certainty. I would disband the army."[19]

17. Montmartre and Les Batignoles were independent communes at the time. They were incorporated into Paris in 1860.

18. See the entry for "Utopias," in the Glossary of Subjects and Terms.

19. In WSWNS 2 Bastiat proposed to cut the size of the French Army immediately by 100,000 men from its total in 1849 of about 390,000 men (a reduction of 25.6 percent). The expenditure on the army in 1849 was fr. 346,319,558. Total government expenditure in 1849 was fr. 1.573 billion, with expenditure on the armed forces making up 29.6 percent of the total budget. Bastiat roughly estimates that 100,000 soldiers cost the French state

"The entire army?"

"Except for some specialized divisions, which would recruit voluntarily just like any other profession. And as you can see, conscription would be abolished."[20]

"Sir, you should say recruitment."

"Ah, I was forgetting! I admire the ease with which in certain countries it is possible to perpetuate the most unpopular things by giving them a different name."[21]

"It is just like *combined duties* which have become *indirect contributions.*"[22]

"And *gendarmes* who have adopted the name *municipal guards.*"

"In short, you are disarming the country based on a Utopian faith."

"I said that I was disbanding the army and not that I was disarming the country.[23] On the contrary, I intend to give it an invincible force."

"How are you going to sort out this heap of contradictions?"

---

fr. 100 million. See "The French Army and Conscription," in appendix 2, "The French State and Politics."

20. Some 80,000 new recruits were needed each year to maintain the size of the French Army (Armée de terre) at its full strength of about 400,000 men in the late 1840s. This consisted of a mixture of volunteers and conscripts who served for seven years. See A. Legoyt, "Recrutement," in *DEP* 2:498–503; and "Conscription," in *Dictionnaire de l'armée de terre* 3:1539–42.

21. This is a reference to the different names given to the forced enlistment of men in the French Army. It was called *requisition* in 1793, *conscription* in 1798, and more euphemistically, *recrutement* during the Restoration and the July Monarchy. During the 1848 Revolution there was a pamphlet war calling for the abolition of conscription, but this was unsuccessful. See Allyre, *Plus de conscription!* and Girardin, *Abolition de l'esclavage militaire.*

22. Many indirect taxes on consumer goods were abolished in the early years of the Revolution only to be reintroduced by Napoléon, who centralized their collection in 1804 by a single administrative body under the name of *droits réunis* (combined duties). For a discussion of *droits réunis,* see "French Taxation," in appendix 3, "Economic Policy and Taxation." See also Charles Coquelin, "Droits réunis," in *DEP* 1:619; and H. Passy, "Impôt," in *DEP* 1:898–914.

23. Bastiat called for simultaneous disarmament of all nations and a corresponding reduction of taxation in his speech at the Second General Peace Congress held in Paris on 22, 23, and 24 August 1849. Émile de Girardin summarized the resolutions of the 1849 Paris Peace Congress as follows: "reduction of armies to 1/200 the size of the population of each state, the abolition of compulsory military service, the freedom of [choosing one's] vocation, the reduction of taxes, and balanced budgets" (title page, *Les 52: Abolition de l'esclavage militaire*). Since France's population in 1849 was about 36 million, this would mean a maximum size of the French armed forces of 180,000. See Bastiat's speech at the Congress in the Addendum.

"I will call on the services of all citizens."[24]

"It is really not worth the trouble of discharging a few of them in order to call up everyone."

"You did not make me a Minister for me to leave things as they are. Therefore, when I come to power I will say, like Richelieu:[25] 'The maxims of the State have changed.' And my first maxim, which will form the basis of my administration, will be this: 'Every citizen must know two things: how to provide for his own existence and how to defend his country.'"

"At first sight, I really think that there is a spark of common sense in this."

"Following this, I would base national defense on a law with two articles:

"'Article 1. All eligible citizens, without exception, will remain under the flag for four years, from the ages of 21 to 25, in order to receive military instruction.'"

"That is a fine saving! You dismiss 400,000 soldiers and you make 10 million of them!"

"Wait for my second article.

"'Article 2. Unless they can prove at the age of 21 that they have successfully attended a training unit.'"

"I was not expecting this outcome. It is quite certain that, to avoid four years of military service, there would be a terrific rush in our youth to learn *by the right, quick march* and *in double quick time, charge.* The idea is very odd."

"It is better than that. For finally, without causing grief to families and without upsetting the principle of equality, would it not simply and cheaply ensure the country 10 million defenders capable of meeting a coalition of all the standing armies in the world?"

"Truly, if I were not on my guard, I would end up by being interested in your fantasies."

24. Bastiat probably has in mind here local militias or something like the National Guard.

25. Jean Armand Duplessis, Cardinal de Richelieu (1585–1642), was the chief minister to Louis XIII and played an important role in centralizing the power of the French state in the first half of the seventeenth century. It is not clear what maxim by Richelieu Bastiat had in mind. One that refers explicitly to the question of war and peace is his "Discours de Monseigneur sur la paix lors de la venue de M. Légat" (1625), where Richelieu recommends in Machiavellian fashion that the king not accept an offer of peace, concluding that he should "choose what will be most suitable for his reputation, for the good and advantage of his State, and for the preservation of his allies" (Richelieu, *Maximes d'état et fragments politiques,* p. 91).

The Utopian becomes excited: "Thank heavens; my budget has been reduced by 200 million![26] I will abolish city tolls, I will reform indirect taxes, I . . ."

"Just a minute, Mr. Utopian!"

The Utopian becomes increasingly excited: "I will proclaim the freedom of religion[27] and freedom of education.[28] New projects: I will purchase the railways,[29] I will reimburse the debt,[30] and I will starve stockjobbing of its profits."[31]

26. In the FEE edition of this essay (*Economic Sophisms,* FEE edition, p. 212), there is a mistranslation. Bastiat clearly says his proposed savings in these areas would amount to "200 millions," not the "two millions" stated in the FEE edition. This error seriously understates the radicalism of Bastiat's tax-cutting proposals.

27. In the 1848 budget a total of fr. 39.6 million was set aside for expenditure by the state on religion. Of this, 38 million went to the Catholic Church, 1.3 million went to Protestant churches, and 122,883 went to Jewish groups.

28. The notion of *"la liberté d'enseignement"* (freedom of education) meant different things to different political groups. For many, it meant breaking the control of the central government and transferring it to the départements, and reducing the influence of the Catholic church. For classical liberals like Bastiat, it meant taking education completely out of the state sector and letting private groups provide educational services in the market.

29. The Economists were frustrated by the state of the French railways in January 1847, when this article was written. They were excited by the possibilities railways offered for drastically lowering the price of transport, but what had begun as a private initiative of coal-mining companies had turned into a hybrid of state and favored private groups, which had serious problems. Perhaps Bastiat had in mind the state buying the entire network and starting again. See also "The French Railways," in appendix 3, "Economic Policy and Taxation."

30. Total debt held by the French government in 1848 amounted to fr. 5.2 billion, which required annual payments of fr. 384 million to service or 26.6 percent of the total budget. Since total annual income for the government in 1848 was fr. 1.4 billion, the outstanding debt was 3.7 times receipts. See Gustave du Puynode, "Crédit public," in *DEP* 1:508–25.

31. Bastiat uses the expression *affamer l'agiotage* (to starve stockjobbing of its profits). The Economists drew a distinction between *la spéculation commerciale* (commercial speculation) and *agiotage* (stockjobbing). According to Horace Say, the former was a normal part of doing business where investors took risks in trying to discover which line of economic activity was profitable and which was not. Thus it was "useful and helpful to society." *Agiotage,* on the other hand, was harmful and even "immoral" because it usually involved speculation in government-regulated stocks and bonds, such as mining leases, railway concessions, and government bonds. Since the number of stocks and bonds traded on the Paris Bourse was very small (198 in 1847), the proportion of government-regulated or -issued stocks and bonds played an exaggerated role. Say notes that in such

"Mr. Utopian!"

"Freed from responsibilities which are too numerous to mention, I will concentrate all of the forces of government on repressing fraud and distributing prompt and fair justice to all, I . . ."

"Mr. Utopian, you are taking on too much, the nation will not follow you!"

"You have given me a majority."

"I withdraw it."

"About time, too! So I am no longer a Minister, and my plans remain what they are, just so many UTOPIAS."

12. Salt, the Mail, and the Customs Service

PUBLISHING HISTORY:

> Original title: "Le Sel, la poste, et la douane."
> Place and date of first publication: *JDE* 14 (May 1846): 142–52.
> First French edition as book or pamphlet: *Economic Sophisms* (Second Series) (1848). First and Second Series were combined in one edition in 1851.
> Location in Paillottet's edition of *OC*: Vol. 4. *Sophismes économiques. Petits pamphlets I,* pp. 213–29.
> Previous translations: 1st American ed., 1848; 1st British ed., 1873; FEE ed., 1964.

A few days ago,[1] people expected to see the machine of representative government give birth to a totally new product, one that its cogwheels had not yet managed to churn out: *the relief of taxpayers.*

---

an "interventionist country" (*un pays d'intervention gouvernementale*) as France, the best way to reduce stockjobbing was to cut government expenditure, put an end to budget deficits, and reduce government borrowing. See Horace Say, "Agiotage," in *DEP* 1:27–31.

1. This article was published in May 1846, when the abolition of the protectionist Corn Laws in England was very close to being achieved (the abolition was announced by Peel in January, the House of Commons passed the legislation in May, and the House of Lords agreed in June 1846). Bastiat held out great hope that the Chamber of Deputies would reduce French tariffs following the success of the Anti–Corn Law League in England. When the issue came up for debate in 1847 the free traders lost, and when the country was engulfed in revolution, in early 1848, the issue of free trade took second place to the problem of fighting socialism, an activity in which Bastiat was very active as a deputy during 1848–50.

Everyone was paying attention: the experiment was as interesting as it was new. No one had any doubts as to the capacity of this machine to suck up resources. From this point of view, the machine works admirably, whatever the time, the place, the season, or the circumstance.

By contrast, with regard to reforms that tend to simplify, equalize, and relieve charges on the public, nobody yet knows what it is capable of doing.

People said, "Wait and see: this is the right time. It is the work of the *fourth session*,[2] a time when popularity is worth courting; 1842 brought us the railway; 1846 is going to bring us a reduction of the tax on salt and postal services; 1850 promises us a reorganization of customs duties and indirect taxes.[3] The fourth session is the *jubilee year* of the taxpayer.

Everyone was therefore full of hope, and everything appeared to favor the experiment. *Le Moniteur*[4] had announced that from one quarter to the next the sources of revenue were constantly increasing, and what better use could we make of these unexpected inflows than to allow villagers an extra grain of salt for their warm water or one more letter from the battlefield on which their sons were risking their lives?

But what happened? Like those two sugary substances which, it is said, mutually prevent each other from crystallizing, or like the two dogs whose fight was so bitter that only two tails remained, the two reforms devoured

2. In the July Monarchy deputies were elected for a maximum of five years before a new election had to be called. Most of the governments did not see out their full term, as they were frequently dissolved early by King Louis-Philippe because of some irreconcilable conflict or the loss of a majority. The "fourth session" would have been the last session before a new election had to be held, had the governments gone their full term, and it was the period of campaigning for reelection with all the promises to the voters which this entails.

3. The fifth legislature of the July Monarchy was elected in two stages, in March and July 1839, but was dissolved early by Louis-Philippe on 16 June 1842. The sixth legislature was elected on 9 July 1842 but was dissolved in July 1846. The seventh legislature was elected on 1 August 1846 and came to an end when the regime was overthrown in the Revolution of February 1848. An election was held on 23 and 24 April 1848 to appoint a new Constituent Assembly of the Second Republic, to which Bastiat was elected to represent the Landes. Another election was held on 13 May 1849 to appoint the first National Assembly of the Republic, to which Bastiat was also elected.

4. The official newspaper of government during the July Monarchy in which laws, decrees, and parliamentary debates were published. Not to be confused with *Le Moniteur industriel,* which was the journal of the protectionist Association pour la défense du travail national (Association for the Defense of National Employment), founded by Mimerel de Roubaix in 1846.

each other. All that is left for us are the tails, that is to say, a host of draft laws, dissertations on the arguments, reports, statistics, and appendices in which we have the consolation of seeing our sufferings philanthropically appreciated and homeopathically calculated. As for the reforms themselves, they have not crystallized, nothing has emerged from the crucible, and the experiment has failed.

Soon the chemists will come before the jury to explain this misfortune, and they will say,

First chemist: "I had *put forward* a postal reform, but the Chamber wished to reduce the salt tax and I had to withdraw it."

Second chemist: "I had *voted for* the reduction of the salt tax, but the government put forward postal reform and the vote came to nothing."

And the jury, finding the reasons excellent, will start the tests on the same data again and refer the work back to the same chemists.

This proves to us that, in spite of the source, there may be something reasonable in the custom that has been introduced in the last half-century on the other side of the Channel and which consists, from the public's point of view, in pursuing only one reform at a time.[5] This is a long and boring business, but it leads to something.

We have a dozen reforms in hand; they are crowding one another like the souls of the departed at the gate of oblivion, and not one of them gets through.

> Ohimè! che lasso!
> Una a la volta, per carità.[6]

This is what *Jacques Bonhomme* said in a conversation with *John Bull*[7] on *postal reform*. It is worth quoting.

---

5. The reforms across the Channel to which Bastiat refers include the First Reform Act of 1832, which expanded the franchise to include some members of the middle class, the reform of the Post Office in 1839 led by Sir Rowland Hill, Sir Robert Peel's reduction of the tariffs on hundreds of items after 1842, and of course the repeal of the Corn Laws in 1846.

6. "Oh dear! What a pace! / One at a time, for pity's sake." These lines come from "Largo al factotum" in the first act of Gioachino Rossini's opera *The Barber of Seville* (1816), where Figaro sings "Ahimè, che furia! / Ahimè chef olla! Uno alla volta per carità! Ehì, Figaro! Son qua. / Figaro qua, Figaro là, / Figaro su, Figaro gui" (Ah, what a frenzy! Ah, what a crowd! One at a time, please! Hey, Figaro! I'm here. Figaro here. Figaro there, Figaro up, Figaro down"). The libretto was by Cesare Sterbini based upon the play *Le Barbier de Séville* by Beaumarchais from 1775.

7. In England at this time the phrase used to refer to the average Englishman was "John Bull."

JACQUES BONHOMME AND JOHN BULL

JACQUES BONHOMME: Oh! Who will deliver me from this hurricane of reforms! My head is bursting. I believe that more are being invented every day: university reforms, financial reforms, health reforms and parliamentary reforms, electoral reforms, commercial reforms and social reforms, and here we now have *postal* reform!

JOHN BULL: The latter is easy to do and so useful, as we have found over here, that I dare to recommend it to you.[8]

JACQUES: It is nevertheless said that it has gone badly in England and that it has cost your Exchequer ten million pounds.

JOHN: Which have generated one hundred million for the public.

JACQUES: Is this really certain?

JOHN: Look at all the signs of public satisfaction. See the nation, Peel and Russell[9] at their head, giving Mr. Rowland Hill substantial tokens of gratitude in the British fashion. See the ordinary people putting their letters into circulation only after they have made their feelings known in writing, in the form of seals bearing the motto: *To postal reform, a grateful people*. The leaders of the League declare in full parliamentary session that, without postal reform, they would have needed thirty years to accomplish their great enterprise to set the food of the poor free. The officers of the *Board of Trade* declare that it is unfortunate that English currency does not allow a more radical reduction still in the cost of posting letters. What more proof do you want?

JACQUES: Yes, but the Treasury?

JOHN: Are the Treasury and the general public not in the same boat?

8. In 1839 the Uniform Four Penny Post reform was introduced in England. Then in 1842 it was reduced to one penny (the Uniform Penny Post and the "Penny Black" stamp), which was prepaid by the sender and was the same regardless of distance carried. Up to then the price had depended on the distance carried and was paid by the recipient. A similar law was adopted by France in 1848. As a token of thanks the British public raised through subscription £13,360 which was presented to Hill in 1846.

9. Lord John Russell (1792–1878) was a member of Parliament, leader of the Whigs, and several times a minister. He served as prime minister from 1846 to 1852 and from 1865 to 1866.

JACQUES: Not exactly. And incidentally, is it really certain that our postal system needs to be reformed?

JOHN: That is what it needs. Let us see for a moment how things are done. What happens to letters that are posted?

JACQUES: Oh! The mechanism is admirably simple: the manager opens the box at a certain time and takes out, let us say, one hundred letters.

JOHN: And then?

JACQUES: He then inspects them one by one. With a geographical table under his gaze and a set of scales in his hand, he tries to find the category to which each one belongs from the twin considerations of distance and weight. There are only eleven zones and the same number of categories of weight.

JOHN: That makes a good 121 combinations for each letter.

JACQUES: Yes, and you have to double this number since a letter may or may not be subject to the *rural service charge.*[10]

JOHN: You therefore have to look up 24,200 possibilities for the hundred letters. What does the manager do next?

JACQUES: He writes the weight on a corner and the tax right in the middle of the address under the drawing of a hieroglyph agreed upon by the administrative department.

JOHN: And then?

JACQUES: He stamps and divides the letters into ten packets depending on the post offices to which the letters have to be sent. He adds up the total of the tax for the ten packets.

JOHN: And then?

JACQUES: Then he writes the ten amounts lengthwise in a register and crosswise in another.

JOHN: And then?

JACQUES: Then he writes a letter to each of the ten postmasters to inform them of the accounting item that concerns them.

JOHN: What if the letters are prepaid?

10. Letters sent to a village without a post office had to pay a surcharge of 10 centimes.

JACQUES: Oh! Then I admit that the service becomes a little complicated. The letter has to be received, weighed, and measured. As before, it has to be paid for and change given. A suitable stamp has to be selected from the thirty available. On the letter has to be written clearly its order number, weight, and tax. The full address has to be transcribed in one register, then another, and then a third, and then onto a separate slip. The letter is then wrapped in the slip and sent, properly tied up with string, to the postmaster, and each of these steps has to be noted in a dozen columns selected from the fifty that line the record books.

JOHN: And all that for forty centimes!

JACQUES: Yes, on average.

JOHN: I can see that in effect the *sending* is quite simple. Let us see what happens on *arrival.*

JACQUES: The postmaster opens the mail bag.

JOHN: And then?

JACQUES: He reads the ten notices from his respective postmasters.

JOHN: And then?

JACQUES: He compares the total shown for each notice with the total that results from each of the ten packets of letters.

JOHN: And then?

JACQUES: He totals the totals and knows what overall amount he will make the postmen responsible for.

JOHN: And then?

JACQUES: After this, with a table of distances and a set of scales in his hand, he checks and corrects the tax on each letter.

JOHN: And then?

JACQUES: He enters from register to register, from column to column, depending on countless factors, the *excess payments* and the *underpayments* he has found.

JOHN: And then?

JACQUES: He writes to the ten postmasters to point out the errors of ten or twenty centimes.

JOHN: And then?

JACQUES: He reorganizes all the letters received to give them to the postmen.

JOHN: And then?

JACQUES: He totals the taxes for which the postmen are responsible.

JOHN: And then?

JACQUES: The postman checks and they discuss the meaning of the hieroglyphs. The postman pays the amount in advance and leaves.

JOHN: *Go on.*[11]

JACQUES: The postman goes to the recipient. He knocks on the door and a servant comes. There are six letters for this address. The taxes are added, separately at first and then together. A total of two francs seventy centimes is calculated.

JOHN: *Go on.*

JACQUES: The servant goes to find his master who checks the hieroglyphs. He misreads the 3s for 2s and the 9s for 4s, he is not sure about the weight and distances; in short, he has the postman brought up and while waiting tries to decipher the signatory of the letters, thinking that it would be wise to refuse to accept them.

JOHN: *Go on.*

JACQUES: The postman arrives and pleads the cause of the postal service. They discuss, examine, weigh, measure, and in the end the recipient accepts five letters and *refuses* one.

JOHN: *Go on.*

JACQUES: Now it is just a matter of the payment. The servant goes to the grocer to obtain change. Finally, after twenty minutes the postman is free and runs off to start the same ritual again at each door.

JOHN: *Go on.*

JACQUES: He returns to the office. He counts and recounts with the postmaster. He hands over the letters that have been refused and is paid back his advance payments. He reports the objections of the recipients with regard to the weights and distances.

JOHN: *Go on.*

---

11. Bastiat used the English phrase "go on" in the original.

JACQUES: The manager looks for the registers, record books, and special slips in order to account for the *letters refused.*

JOHN: Go on, if you please.

JACQUES: Goodness me, I am not a postmaster. We now come to the accounts for the tenths, twentieths, and ends of the months, to the means thought up not only to establish but also to check such a detailed accounting system, one that covers fifty million francs resulting from the average taxes of forty-three centimes and 116 million letters, each of which may belong to 242 categories.[12]

JOHN: This is a very complicated simple system. It is clear that the man who has solved this problem must have had a hundred times more talent than your M. Piron[13] or our Rowland Hill.

JACQUES: Now you, who seem to be laughing at our system, explain yours.

JOHN: In England, the government sells envelopes and postal wrappers at one penny apiece in all the places it considers to be useful.

JACQUES: And then?

JOHN: You write your letter, fold it into four, put it into one of the envelopes, and drop it off or send it to the post office.

JACQUES: And then?

JOHN: Then, that is all. There are no weights, no distances, no *excess payments* nor *underpayments,* no *refusals,* no slips, no registers, no record books, no columns, no accounts, no checks, no change to be given and received, no hieroglyphs, no discussions and interpretations, no urging to accept, etc., etc.

JACQUES: That really sounds simple. But is it not too simple? A child would understand it. Reforms like this stifle the genius of

12. This sophism was published in May 1846. Government statistics for 1847 reveal that the number of letters sent through the post was 125 million at an average cost of 43 centimes, which generated fr. 53 million in revenue for the state. See C. S., "Postes," in *DEP* 2:423; and appendix 4, "French Government Finances, 1848–49."

13. Alexis Piron (1689–1773) was a poet and dramatist who became famous for his witty epigrams. He was elected to the Académie française in 1753, but Louis XV refused to ratify his election because of some scandalous verse Piron had written as a young man. Piron, however, had the last laugh, as he had written his own epitaph, which says: "Here lies Piron / who was nothing, / not even an Academician."

great administrators. For my part, I prefer the French way. What is more, your *uniform tax* has the worst of all faults; it is unjust.

JOHN: Why?

JACQUES: Because it is unjust to make people pay the same for a letter delivered to a neighboring address as for one delivered a hundred leagues away.

JOHN: In any case, you will agree that the injustice is contained within the confines of one penny.

JACQUES: What does that matter? It is still an injustice.

JOHN: It can never extend to more than a halfpenny, since the other half covers fixed costs that apply to all letters whatever their distance.

JACQUES: Whether it is a penny or a halfpenny, there is still a principle of injustice.

JOHN: In the end this injustice which, at the very most, cannot exceed a halfpenny in a particular instance, is averaged out for each citizen over all his correspondence, since everyone writes letters that are sometimes to distant addresses and sometimes local.

JACQUES: I still maintain my position. The injustice is reduced to infinity if you like; it is imperceptible, infinitesimal, and minute, but it is still there.

JOHN: Does the State make you pay more for a gram of tobacco that you buy in the rue de Clichy than for the gram you *receive* at the Quai d'Orsay?[14]

JACQUES: What is the connection between the two objects of comparison?

JOHN: It is that in either case, there have been transport costs. Mathematically, it would be fair for each dose of tobacco to be more expensive in the rue de Clichy than the Quai d'Orsay by some millionth of a centime.

JACQUES: That is true; you should want only what is possible.

JOHN: You should add that your postal system is only apparently just. Two houses are next to one another, but one is outside and the other inside the area. The first will pay ten centimes more than the

14. The sale of tobacco in France was a state monopoly. It contributed fr. 120 million to government receipts in 1848 (8.6 percent of a total of fr. 1.4 billion).

second, exactly the same as the entire delivery of the letter costs in England. You can see that, in spite of appearances, there is injustice in your system on a much larger scale.

JACQUES: That appears to be very true. My objection is not worth much, but there is still a loss of revenue.

At this point, I stopped listening to the two conversationalists. It appears, however, that Jacques Bonhomme was totally convinced for, a few days later when M. de Vuitry's report had appeared,[15] he wrote the following letter to the honorable legislator:

J. Bonhomme to Mr. de Vuitry, Deputy, Reporting Chairman of the Committee Responsible for Examining the Draft Law on Postal Taxes[16]

Sir,

Although I am fully aware of the extreme disfavor that is created around anyone who sets himself up as an advocate of an *absolute theory,* I believe that I should not abandon the cause of a *single tax that is reduced to the simple reimbursement of the service rendered.*

In addressing you, I am surely doing you a good turn. On the one hand, a hothead, a closet reformer who talks about overturning an entire system at one fell swoop with no transition, a dreamer who perhaps has never set eyes on the mountain of laws, orders, tables, appendices, and statistics that accompany your report, in a word, a *theoretician,* and on the other, a lawmaker who is serious, prudent, and moderate, who has weighed and compared, who keeps various interests happy, who rejects all *systems* or, what amounts to the same, constructs one from elements he has garnered from all the others; the outcome of the struggle could not be in any doubt.

Nevertheless, for as long as the question is pending, strongly held ideas have the right to be presented. I know that mine is sufficiently clear-cut to bring a mocking smile to the lips of readers. All that I dare to expect from them is that they produce this smile, if it is produced, as much as they like, after and not before having listened to my reasons.

---

15. Adolphe Vuitry (1813–85) was a lawyer, economist, and politician. He was the undersecretary of state for finance in 1851 in the Ministry of Léon Faucher. In 1863 he was appointed governor of the Bank of France.

16. Bastiat uses throughout the term *la taxe des lettres,* which would normally be translated as "postal rate," but both Bastiat and the French government in its annual budget regarded it as a tax which raised revenue rather than a charge for a service.

For I, too, in the end can invoke *experience.* A great nation has tested this. What is its verdict? It cannot be denied that the British handle these matters adroitly, and their judgment carries some weight.

Well then, there is not a single voice in England that does not bless *postal reform.* I have evidence of this in the open subscription in favor of Mr. Rowland Hill; I have evidence of this, from what John Bull has told me, in the novel way in which the people express their gratitude; I have evidence of this in the admission so often repeated by the League:[17] "Never would we have developed the public opinion that is now overturning the protectionist system without the *penny post.*" I have evidence of this in something I have read in a work written by an official pen:

> The tax on letters has to be set not with a fiscal aim but with the sole object of covering expenditure.

To which Mr. Mac-Gregor[18] adds:

> It is true that since the tax has been reduced to our smallest coin, it is not possible to lower it further, although it provides revenue. However, this revenue, which is constantly increasing, should be devoted to improving the service and developing our steam packets on every sea.[19]

This leads me to examine the commission's fundamental thought, which on the contrary is that the tax on letters should be a source of revenue for the State.

---

17. The Anti–Corn Law League took advantage of the penny post to spread their newspapers and leaflets opposing tariffs.

18. John MacGregor (1797–1857) was a statistician, historian, diplomat, and supporter of free trade. He was appointed one of the secretaries of the British Board of Trade in 1840.

19. We have not been able to find this quotation from MacGregor. The closest we could find is the opening two paragraphs of chapter 6, "Post Office," of *The Commercial and Financial Legislation of Europe and America,* p. 264, where he states: "We have, long before the change was made in the post-office charges, been of the opinion that, as the government should never possess a monopoly of trade, the post-office charges should be regulated, not with a view to revenue, but to the purposes of covering all the expenses required to convey letters and intelligence with security and rapidity. The tax imposed on the public by the late post-office reform is so very moderate, that while it still yields a considerable revenue, which we believe confidently will increase, no one can desire any alteration in the rate of postage."

This thought dominates your entire report, and I must admit that, under the sway of this preoccupation, you could not reach a conclusion that was either grand or comprehensive; it would be fortunate, indeed, if, by wanting to reconcile every system, you did not combine all their disadvantages.

The first question that presents itself is therefore this: Is correspondence between individuals a good *subject for taxes?*

I will not go back to abstract principles. I will not point out that, as society exists only because of the communication of ideas, the aim of every government ought to be to encourage and not hinder such communication.

I will examine the existing facts.

The total length of royal, departmental, and local roads is one million kilometers. Assuming that each has cost 100,000 francs, this makes a capital of 100 billion spent by the State to encourage the movement of goods and people.

Well, I ask you, if one of your honorable colleagues put forward to the Chamber a draft law that said:

> From 1st January 1847, the state will collect from all travelers a tax that is calculated, not only to cover the expenditure on the roads but also to generate four or five times the amount of this expenditure for its coffers. . . .

Would you not find this proposal antisocial and monstrous?

How is it that this concept of *profit,* what am I saying, of simple *remuneration,* has never occurred to anyone when it is a matter of the circulation of goods, and yet it appears so natural to you when it is a question of the circulation of ideas?

I dare to say that it is a matter of habit. If it were a question of creating the postal service, it would certainly seem monstrous to base it on the *principle of raising revenue.*

And please note that in this instance oppression is more clearly visible.

When the State opens a road, it does not force anyone to use it. (Doubtless it would do so if the use of the road were taxed.) But since the existence of the royal post, nobody can any longer write using another avenue, even if it were to his mother.

Therefore, in principle, the tax on letters should be *remunerative* only, and for this reason, *uniform.*

If this concept is used as a starting point, how can we fail to marvel at the facility, the beauty and simplicity of the reform?

Here it is in its entirety and, subject to editing, formulated as a draft law:

Article 1. From 1st January 1847, *envelopes* and *stamped postal wrappers* to the value of five (or ten) centimes will be on sale everywhere considered to be useful by the postal services.

Article 2. Any letter placed inside one of these envelopes and which does not exceed the weight of 15 grams or any *journal* or *printed matter* placed within one of these wrappers and which does not exceed . . . grams, will be carried and delivered without cost to its address.

Article 3. The accounting system of the postal services will be totally abolished.

Article 4. All criminal legislation and penalties with regard to the carriage of letters will be abolished.

This is very simple, I admit, much too simple, and I am expecting a host of objections.

While we can assume, however, that this system has disadvantages, this is not the question; we need to know whether yours does not have still more serious ones.

And in good faith, can it in any way (except for revenue) bear comparison for an instant?

Let us examine them both. Let us compare them from the points of views of ease, convenience, speed, simplicity, orderliness, economy, justice, equality, increased volume, customer satisfaction, intellectual and moral development and its civilizing effect, and then say, with our hands on our hearts, that it is possible to hesitate for a second.

I will take care not to expand on each of these considerations. I have given you the *headings* of a dozen chapters and leave the rest blank, convinced that there is nobody better placed than you to fill them in.

But since there is just one objection, *revenue,* I do have to say a word about this.

You have drawn up a table from which it is apparent that a single tax, even at 20 centimes, would constitute for the Treasury a loss of 22 million.

At 10 centimes, the loss would be 28 million, and at 5 centimes, 33 million, extrapolations so terrifying that you do not even formulate them.

But allow me to say that the figures in your report cavort with a little too much abandon. In all of your tables and calculations you imply the following words: *all other things being equal.* You assume the same costs with a simple administrative structure as with a complex one, the same number of letters with an average tax of 43 as with the single tax of 20 centimes. You limit yourself to this rule of three: 87 million letters at 42½ centimes have produced so much. Half as many have yielded such and such. Therefore at 20 centimes, they will produce so and so; accepting nevertheless some differences where these run counter to the reform.

To evaluate the real loss to the Treasury, we first need to know what would be saved by the service; next, to what extent the volume of correspondence would increase. Let us take into account just this latter information, since we may assume that the savings achieved on expenditure would come down to the fact that the current staff would be confronted with a service on a larger scale.

Doubtless it is impossible to set a figure for the increase in circulation of letters, but in this type of question, a reasonable analogy has always been accepted.

You yourself say that in England a reduction of 7/8 in the tax has led to an increase of 360 percent in correspondence.

Over here, a reduction of the tax, which is currently at an average of 43 centimes, to 5 centimes would also be a reduction of 7/8. It is therefore possible to expect the same result, that is to say, 417 million letters instead of 116 million.[20]

But let us base our calculations on 300 million.

Is it an exaggeration to agree that with a tax that is half as much, we would reach eight letters per inhabitant, where the English have reached thirteen?

Well, 300 million letters at 5 centimes give	15 million
100 million journals and printed matter at 5 centimes	5
Travelers on the mail-coaches	4
Shipments of money	4
Total receipts	28 million

20. The letter tax was reduced in 1849 to 20 centimes, which raised the number of letters sent to 157 million in that year (a 25.6 percent increase) and reduced the tax revenue to fr. 42 million (a 20.7 percent decrease). In England it took twelve years after the Postal Reform of 1839 for revenues to return to what they had been before the reform. During this time, however, the number of letters sent had increased nearly 500 percent. See C. S., "Postes," in *DEP* 2:423; and appendix 4, "French Government Finances, 1848–49."

Current expenditure (which might be reduced) is	31 million
To be deducted, expenditure on steam-packets	5
Outstanding on mail bags, travelers, and money shipments	26 million
Net result	2
Currently, the net result is	19
Loss, or rather a *reduction in profit*	17 million

Now I ask if the state, which makes a *positive sacrifice* of 800 million per year to facilitate the circulation of people *free of charge,* ought not to make a *negative sacrifice* of 17 million for *failing to make money* on the circulation of ideas?

But in the end, I know that the tax authorities are people of habit, and just as they easily adopt the habit of seeing revenue increase, by the same token they are habitually uneasy to see revenue decrease by an obole. It appears that they are provided with those admirable valves that, in our bodies, allow blood to flow in one direction but prevent it from retracing its flow. So be it. The tax man[21] is a bit old for us to be able to change its behavior. Let us not hope, therefore, to persuade it not to act. But what would its staff say if I, Jacques Bonhomme, showed them a means that was simple, easy, convenient, and essentially practical for doing considerable good to the country without it costing them a centime!

The post pays the Treasury gross	50 million
Salt	70
Customs duties	160
Total for these three services	280 million

Well then! Set the tax on letters at a uniform rate of 5 centimes.

Decrease the tax on salt to 10 francs per quintal, as voted for by the Chamber.

Give me the authority to modify the rate of tariff duties so that I WILL BE FORMALLY PROHIBITED FROM RAISING ANY DUTY, BUT THAT I WILL BE FREE TO DECREASE THEM AS I SEE FIT.

And I, Jacques Bonhomme, guarantee you not 280 but 300 million. Two hundred bankers in France will be my guarantors. As my premium, I ask only for anything in excess of 300 million that these three taxes produce.

Now, do I need to list the advantages of my proposal?

---

21. Bastiat uses a colloquial term, *le fisc,* for the taxation department (or IRS) or Treasury. We have translated it as "the tax man."

1. The people will receive all the benefits of the cheapness in the price of a product of vital necessity, salt.

2. Fathers will be able to write to their sons and mothers to their daughters. The affections, feelings, and outpourings of love and friendship will not, as they are today, be buried in the depths of people's hearts by the hand of the tax man.

3. The carriage of letters from one friend to another will no longer be recorded in our records as though it were a criminal action.

4. Trade will blossom again with freedom; our merchant navy will rise from its humiliation.

The tax man will initially gain *twenty million,* and subsequently, all the savings made by each citizen on salt, letters, and objects on which duties have been decreased, will pour into the other streams of taxation.

If my proposal is not accepted, what should I deduce from this? Provided that the company of bankers that I represent offers sufficient guarantees, on what pretext will my offer be rejected? It is impossible to invoke the *balancing of budgets.* The budget will certainly be unbalanced, but in the sense that revenue will exceed expenditure. This is not a question of theory, of a system, a statistic, a probability, or a conjecture; it is an offer, like that from a company that is asking for the concession for a railway. The tax men tell me what they take from the postal services, salt, and customs duties. I offer to give them *more.* The objection cannot therefore come from them. I offer to decrease the tariff on salt, postal services, and customs services and undertake not to raise them; the objection cannot therefore come from taxpayers. Where then does it come from? The monopolists? It remains to be seen whether their voice is to stifle that of the State and that of the people in France. To be reassured in this connection, would you be so good as to forward my proposal to the Council of Ministers.

Jacques Bonhomme.

P.S. This is the text of my offer:

"I, Jacques Bonhomme, representing a company of bankers and capitalists who are ready to give any form of guarantee and deposit all the sureties necessary;

"Having learned that the State draws only 280 million from the Customs Service, the Postal Service, and from salt by means of the duties as currently set,

"I offer to give them 300 million of gross product for these three services,

"Even though it will decrease the tax on salt from 30 francs to 10 francs;

"Even though it will decrease the tax on letters from an average of 42½ centimes to a single and uniform tax of 5 to 10 centimes;

"On the sole condition that I will be permitted, not to raise (this I will formally be prohibited from doing) but to lower customs duties as far as I choose.

"Jacques Bonhomme."

"You are crazy," I said to Jacques Bonhomme, who sent me his letter; "you have never known how to do things by halves. The other day you were shouting about the *hurricane of reforms* and here you are, asking for three, making one the condition for the two others. You will be ruined." "Do not worry," he answered. "I have done all my calculations. Please God, let them agree! But they will never do so." On this we left each other with our heads bursting, his with figures and mine with thoughts which I will spare the reader.

13. Protection, or the Three Municipal Magistrates[1]

PUBLISHING HISTORY:

Original title: "La Protection ou les trois échevins."
Place and date of first publication: No date given. First
published in book form.
First French edition as book or pamphlet: *Economic Sophisms*
(Second Series) (1848). First and Second Series were
combined in one edition in 1851. Also published as "La
Protection ou les trois échevins. Démonstration en quatre

---

1. Bastiat uses a term from the ancien régime, *échevin*, in the title of this essay. Beginning in the thirteenth century, cities like Paris had a *prévôt des marchands* (provost of merchants), whose task it was to supply the city with food, to maintain public works, to levy taxes, and to regulate river trade. He was appointed by the king and was assisted by four *échevins* (assessors or magistrates). In the eighteenth century the post of provost had been farmed out by the crown to private individuals, and it was abolished early in the Revolution (July 1789), with some of its duties being given to the mayor and the post of *échevin* being converted to one of municipal councilor. Bastiat uses the archaic-sounding title of *échevin* in order to make the point that their duties in regulating trade were more in keeping with the ancien régime than they were for modern, industrializing France.

tableaux," in *L'Annuaire de l'économie politique et de la statistique* (1847), pp. 266–70.

Location in Paillottet's edition of *OC:* Vol. 4. *Sophismes économiques. Petits pamphlets I*, pp. 229–41.

Previous translations: 1st American ed., 1848; 1st British ed., 1873; FEE ed., 1964.

A staged argument in four scenes.

SCENE 1

(The scene takes place in the townhouse of Pierre, a municipal magistrate. The window gives a view of a beautiful park; three people are sitting around a table near a good fire.)

PIERRE: I say! A fire is very welcome when the Inner Man[2] is satisfied! You must agree that it is very pleasant. But, alas! How many honest people, like *the King of Yvetot,*[3]

For lack of wood, blow
On their fingers.

What unfortunate creatures! Heaven has inspired a charitable thought in me. Do you see these beautiful trees? I want to cut them down and distribute the wood to the poor.

PAUL AND JEAN: What! Free of charge?

PIERRE: Not exactly. My good works would soon be over if I dissipated my assets in this way. I estimate that my park is worth twenty thousand livres; by cutting it down I will get even more.

---

2. Bastiat uses the term *Gaster* (Mr. Stomach).

3. Bastiat is mistaken here. He is quoting a satirical song by Béranger, who made a name for himself mocking Emperor Napoléon and then all the monarchs of the Restoration period. Bastiat thinks the verse he quotes comes from the song "Le Roi d'Yvetot" (The King of Yvetot, May 1813), which is a thinly disguised criticism of Napoléon. The verse he quotes comes from another song, "Le petit homme gris" (The Little Grey Man). The man lives in Paris and is so poor and cold he has to blow on his fingers to keep warm. See Béranger, *Œuvres complètes de Béranger* 1:29–30 (for "The Little Grey Man"); 1:1ff. (for "The King of Yvetot"); for the English translation of "The King of Yvetot," see Béranger, *Béranger, Songs of the Empire, the Peace, and the Restoration*, pp. 21–24.

PAUL: You are wrong. Your wood left standing is worth more than neighboring forests because it provides more services than they can provide. If it is cut down, like its neighbors it will just be good for heating and will be worth not a denier more for each load.[4]

PIERRE: Ha, ha! Mr. Theoretician, you have forgotten that I am a practical man. I thought that my reputation as a speculator was well enough established to protect me against being accused of stupidity. Do you think I am going to pass the time selling my wood at the low prices charged for wood floated down the Seine?[5]

PAUL: You will have to.

PIERRE: What a naive person you are! And suppose I prevent the wood floated down the river from reaching Paris?

PAUL: That would change the picture. But how will you manage this?

PIERRE: This is the whole secret. You know that wood floated down the river pays ten sous per load on entry. Tomorrow, I will persuade the Municipal Magistrates to raise this duty to 100, 200, or even 300 livres, high enough to ensure that not a single log comes through. Well, do you follow me? If the good people do not want to die of cold, they will have to come to my yard. People will fight to have my wood; I will sell it for its weight in gold, and this well-organized charity will enable me to do other good works.

PAUL: Good heavens! What a fine scheme! It makes me think of another in the same vein.

JEAN: Let us see, what is it? Is philanthropy also concerned?

PAUL: What did you think of this butter from Normandy?

JEAN: It is excellent!

PAUL: Ah ha! It seemed all right just now, but do you not find that it sticks in your throat? I want to make better butter in Paris. I will have four or five hundred cows; I will distribute milk, butter, and cheese to the poor.

4. Traditionally, the relative value of coinage before the introduction of the franc was 240 denier = 20 sol = 1 livre. An obole was a small fraction of a denier (sometimes half).
5. Wood for fuel was floated down the Seine River to be sold in Paris.

PIERRE AND PAUL: What! Free of charge?

PAUL: Bah! Let us always highlight charity! It has such a pretty face that even its mask is an excellent passport. I will give my butter to the people, and the people will give me their money. Is this known as selling?

JEAN: No, according to the *Bourgeois Gentilhomme,*[6] but call it what you like, you will ruin yourself. Can Paris compete with Normandy in raising cows?

PAUL: I will have the saving on transport in my favor.

JEAN: So be it. But even if they pay for transport, the Normans are in a position to *beat* the Parisians.[7]

PAUL: Do you call it *beating* someone to deliver goods to him at low prices?

JEAN: That is the accepted term. It is still true that you, for your part, will be beaten.

PAUL: Yes, like Don Quixote. The blows will fall upon Sancho. Jean, my friend, you are forgetting *city tolls.*

JEAN: City tolls! What have they to do with your butter?

PAUL: Right from tomorrow, I will claim *protection;* I will persuade the commune to prohibit butter from Normandy and Brittany. People will have to go without or buy mine, and at my price.

JEAN: By all that is holy, sirs, I find your philanthropy fascinating.

People learn to howl with the wolves, said someone.

My mind is made up. It will not be said that I am an unworthy Municipal Magistrate. Pierre, this crackling fire has inflamed your soul: Paul, this butter has loosened up the springs of your

6. Bastiat refers here to act 4, scene 3 of Molière's play *Le Bourgeois gentilhomme* (The Would-Be Gentleman). M. Jourdain is persuaded by the valet Covielle that his father was not a merchant who "sold" goods (which is what a bourgeois would do) but merely "gave them away for money" (as a true nobleman would do) (Molière, *Théâtre complet de Molière* 7:103).

7. As the FEE translator notes, Bastiat is punning here on the French word *battre,* which can mean "to beat" as well as "to churn" (i.e., to churn butter) (*Economic Sophisms,* FEE edition, p. 232).

mind; well then, I also feel that this salted pork is stimulating my intelligence. Tomorrow, I will vote for the exclusion of pigs, alive or dead, and get it voted for too. Once this is done, I will build superb sties in the center of Paris,

For the disgusting animal that is forbidden to Jews.

I will make myself a swineherd and pork butcher. Let us see how the good people of Lutecium[8] will avoid coming to buy from my shop.

PIERRE: Not so fast, Sirs! If you make butter and salted meat so expensive, you will eat into the profit I am expecting from my wood.

PAUL: Heavens! My speculation will not be so marvelous any more if you hold me for ransom with your logs and hams.

JEAN: And what will I gain from making you pay over the odds for my sausages if you make me do likewise for my bread and faggots of wood?

PIERRE: Well, I declare! Are we going to quarrel about this? Let us rather join forces. Let us give each other mutual concessions. Besides, it is not good to listen only to the base voice of self-interest; humanity is there, should we not ensure that the people are heated?

PAUL: That is true. And people need butter to spread on their bread.

JEAN: Without doubt. And they need bacon to put in their stew.

IN CHORUS: Charity to the fore! Long live philanthropy! Tomorrow! Tomorrow! We will make an assault on city tolls.

PIERRE: Ah, I was forgetting. Just a word, and this is essential. My friends, in this century of selfishness, the world is mistrustful and the purest intentions are often misinterpreted. Paul, plead in favor of wood; Jean, defend butter; and for my part, I will devote myself to *local* pigs. It is a good thing to anticipate nasty suspicions.

PAUL AND JEAN (*leaving*): Goodness! There is a clever man!

---

8. *Le bon peuple lutécien* is a reference to "the good people of Paris." Lutèce was a town in Gaul and the main town of a tribe known as the Parisii. The Île de la Cité in Paris is probably where these people lived.

Scene 2

The Council of Municipal Magistrates

PAUL: My dear colleagues, every day, piles of wood come into Paris,
which causes piles of cash to leave. At this rate we will all be
ruined in three years, and what will become of the poor? (*Cheers!*)
Let us prohibit foreign wood. I am not speaking for myself, since
all the wood I possess would not make a toothpick. I am therefore perfectly disinterested in this matter. (*Hear! Hear!*) But here
is Pierre, who has a stand of trees; he will ensure heating for our
fellow citizens who will no longer have to depend on the charcoal
makers of the Yonne.[9] Have you ever thought of the danger we run
of dying of cold if the owners of foreign forests took it into their
heads not to send wood to Paris? Let us therefore prohibit their
wood. In this way, we will prevent our cash from running out, create a logging industry, and create a new source of work and pay for
our workers. (*Applause*)

JEAN: I support this proposal, which is so philanthropic and, above
all, so disinterested, as the honorable gentleman who has just
spoken himself has said. It is time we stopped this insolent *laissez
passer*,[10] which has brought unfettered competition into our market, with the result that there is no province reasonably endowed
for whatever form of production it may be, that is not coming to
flood us and sell it to us at rock-bottom prices, thus destroying jobs
in Paris. It is up to the State to make production conditions level
through wisely weighted duties, to allow only those goods that
are more expensive than in Paris to enter and thus protect us from
an unequal conflict. How, for example, do people want us to be
able to produce milk and butter in Paris when faced with Brittany
and Normandy? Just think, Sirs, that Bretons have cheaper land,
hay closer to hand, and labor at more advantageous rates. Does
common sense not tell us that we have to make opportunity more
equal through a city toll set at a protective rate? I request that duty

9. Yonne is a département southeast of Paris which lies on the Yonne River, a tributary
of the Seine River.
10. See ES2 9, p. 178n16.

on milk and butter should be raised to 1,000 percent and more if necessary. People's breakfast will be slightly more expensive, but how their earnings will rise! We will see barns and dairies being built, butter churns increasing in number, and new industries be- ing established. It is not that there is the slightest self-interest in my proposal. I am not a cowherd, nor do I want to be. I am moved merely by the desire to be useful to the working classes. (*Movement of approval*)

PIERRE: I am happy to see in this assembly Statesmen that are so pure, so enlightened, and so devoted to the interests of the people. (*Cheers!*) I admire their selflessness and cannot do better than to follow such noble examples. I support their motion and add one to prohibit pigs from Poitou.[11] It is not that I wish to become a swineherd or pork butcher; in this case my conscience would make it my duty to abstain. But is it not shameful, Sirs, that we should pay *tribute* to these peasants from Poitou who have the audacity to come into our own market and take work that we could be doing ourselves and who, after swamping us with sausages and hams, perhaps take nothing in return? In any case, who tells us that the balance of trade is not in their favor and that we are not obliged to pay them a remainder in cash? Is it not clear that, if industry from Poitou was transferred to Paris, it would create guaranteed openings for Parisian jobs? And then, Sirs, is it not highly possible, as M. Lestiboudois[12] said so well, that we are buying salted meat from Poitou not with our income but with our capital? Where is this going to lead us? Let us therefore not allow avid, greedy, and perfidious rivals[13] to come here and sell goods cheaply, making it impossible for us to make them ourselves. Municipal Magistrates, Paris has given us its trust, and we should justify this. The people are without work; it is up to us to create it, and if salted meat costs them slightly more, we would at least be conscious of the fact that we have sacrificed our interests in favor of those of the masses, just as any good municipal magistrate ought to do. (*Thunderous applause*)

---

11. Poitou is a province southwest of Paris.

12. (Paillottet's note) See chapter VI of the First Series of the *Sophisms*. (*OC*, vol. 4, p. 52, "Balance du commerce.") [ES1 6, pp. 44–48.]

13. See the entry for "Perfidious Albion," in the Glossary of Subjects and Terms.

A VOICE: I hear a great deal being said about the poor, but on the pretext of giving them work, people begin by taking away from them what is worth more even than work: wood, butter, and soup.

PIERRE, PAUL, AND JEAN: Let us vote! Let us vote! Down with Utopians, theoreticians, and those who speak in generalities! Let us vote! Let us vote! (*The three proposals are approved.*)

SCENE 3

Twenty years later

THE SON: Father, you must decide, we have to leave Paris. We can no longer live here. Jobs are scarce and everything is expensive.

THE FATHER: My child, you do not know how much it costs to abandon the place where we were born.

THE SON: What is worst of all is to die of hunger.

THE FATHER: Go, my son, and find a more hospitable land. For my part, I will not leave the grave in which your mother, brothers, and sisters have been laid to rest. I am longing to find in it at last the peace at their side that has been refused me in this town of desolation.

THE SON: Take courage, good father, we will find work away from home, in Poitou, Normandy, or in Brittany. It is said that all the industries of Paris are being gradually transferred to these far-off regions.

THE FATHER: It is only natural. As they can no longer sell us wood and foodstuffs, they have ceased to produce anything over their own needs; whatever time and capital they have available, they devote to making themselves the things we used to supply them with in former times.

THE SON: In the same way that in Paris, people have ceased to make fine furniture and clothing in order to plant trees and raise pigs and cows. Although I am very young, I have seen huge warehouses, sumptuous districts, and the banks of the Seine so full of life now invaded by fields and thickets.

THE FATHER: While the provinces are becoming covered with towns, Paris is turning into a rural area. What a frightful turn-around! And it needed only three misled municipal magistrates, assisted by public ignorance, to bring this terrible calamity down on us.

THE SON: Tell me the story, Father.

THE FATHER: It is very simple. On the pretext of setting up three new industries in Paris and thus supplying jobs for workers, these men had the importing of wood, butter, and meat prohibited. They claimed for themselves the right to supply these to their fellow citizens. These objects first rose to an exorbitant price. Nobody earned enough to buy them, and the small number of those who were able to obtain them spent all their resources on them and were unable to buy anything else. For this reason, all forms of industry shut down at the same time, all the quicker since the provinces no longer provided any markets. Destitution, death, and emigration began to rob Paris of its people.

THE SON: And when will this stop?

THE FATHER: When Paris has become a forest and prairie.

THE SON: The three Municipal Magistrates must have made huge fortunes?

THE FATHER: Initially, they made huge profits, but in the long run they were overcome by the general destitution.

THE SON: How is that possible?

THE FATHER: Do you see this ruin? It was once a magnificent townhouse surrounded by a fine park. If Paris had continued to progress, Master Pierre would have obtained more rent for it than its capital value is now worth.

THE SON: How can this be, since he now has no competition?

THE FATHER: Competition to sell has disappeared, but competition to buy is also disappearing with every passing day and will continue to disappear until Paris is open country and Master Pierre's thickets have no greater value than an equal area of thicket in the Forest of Bondy.[14] This is how monopoly, like any form of injustice, carries within itself the seed of its own punishment.

---

14. A large forest in the département of Seine-Saint-Denis, about fifteen kilometers east of Paris. It was a notorious refuge for thieves and highwaymen.

THE SON: This does not seem very clear to me, but what is incontrovertible is the decadence of Paris. Is there no way of overturning this iniquitous measure that Pierre and his colleagues caused to be adopted twenty years ago?

THE FATHER: I will tell you my secret. I am remaining in Paris for this; I will call upon the people to help me. It will be up to them to restore the city tolls to their original level, to remove from them the disastrous principle that has been grafted onto them and which has vegetated like a parasitic fungus.

THE SON: You should achieve success right from the very first day!

THE FATHER: Now, hold on! On the contrary, this work is difficult and laborious. Pierre, Paul, and Jean understand each other perfectly. They are ready to do anything rather than allow wood, butter, and meat to enter Paris. They have the people themselves on their side, as they clearly see the work given to them by the three protected industries; the people know how much work these industries are giving to woodcutters and cowherds, but they cannot have as accurate an idea of the production that would develop in the fresh air of freedom.

THE SON: If that is all that is needed, you will enlighten them.

THE FATHER: Child, at your age, you have no doubts about anything. If I express my thoughts in writing, the people will not read me, since there are not enough hours in the day for them to eke out their unfortunate existence. If I speak out, the Municipal Magistrates will seal my lips. The people will therefore remain disastrously misled for a long time. The political parties who base their hopes on people's passions will spend less time dissipating their misconceptions than exploiting them.[15] I will thus have to con-

---

15. The main political groups in the late 1840s, when Bastiat was writing and becoming politically active, included the Doctrinaires, who were moderate royalists; the Legitimists (also known as the "Party of Order" in 1849), who were supporters of the descendants of Charles X; the Republicans, who were a diverse and poorly organized group; the Montagnards, who were radical socialists; the Orléanists, who were supporters of the overthrown Louis-Philippe; and the Bonapartists, who were supporters of Napoléon, both the Emperor Napoléon I and then his nephew Louis-Napoléon. All of the political groups were protectionist to one degree or another, and the socialists were both protectionist and extremely interventionist as well. Free traders like Bastiat were very much in

front simultaneously those currently in power, the people, and the political parties. Oh! I see a terrible storm ready to break on the head of anyone bold enough to rise up against such deep-rooted iniquity in the country.

THE SON: You will have justice and truth on your side.

THE FATHER: And they will have force and slander on theirs. If only I were young! But age and suffering have sapped my strength.

THE SON: Very well, Father. Devote the strength left to you to serving the country. Begin the work of emancipation and leave me as an inheritance the duty to complete it.

SCENE 4

Popular Unrest

JACQUES BONHOMME: People of Paris! Let us demand a reform of the *city tolls!* Let their original function be restored. Let each citizen be FREE to buy wood, butter, and meat wherever he pleases!

THE PEOPLE: Long live FREEDOM!

PIERRE: People of Paris! Do not be swayed by these words! What use is the freedom to buy if you lack the means? And how will you obtain the means if you lack work? Can Paris produce wood as cheaply as the Forest of Bondy? Meat at as low a price as Poitou? Butter in as favorable conditions as Normandy? If you open the door wide to these rival products, what will become of the cowherds, woodcutters, and pork butchers? They cannot do without protection.

THE PEOPLE: Long live PROTECTION!

JACQUES: Protection! Are you the workers being protected? Are you not being made to compete against one another? Let the sellers of wood in turn suffer from competition! They have no right to increase the price of their wood by law unless they also raise rates of pay by law. Are you no longer a nation that loves equality?

THE PEOPLE: Long live EQUALITY!

---

the minority and could draw upon only a few lukewarm supporters in the Doctrinaire and Bonapartist groups.

PIERRE: Do not listen to this revolutionary! It is true that we have increased the price of wood, meat, and butter, but this is in order to be able to pay good wages to the workers. We are motivated by charity.

THE PEOPLE: Long live CHARITY!

JACQUES: Use city tolls, if you can, to raise wages but not to make products more expensive. The people of Paris are not asking for charity, but justice!

THE PEOPLE: Long live JUSTICE!

PIERRE: It is precisely the high prices of products that will produce higher wages as a result of the ricochet or flow-on effect!

THE PEOPLE: Long live HIGH PRICES!

JACQUES: If butter is expensive, it is not because you are paying the workers high wages. It is not even because you are making huge profits; it is just because Paris is ill-suited to this industry and because you have wanted things to be produced in town that ought to be produced in the country and things in the country that ought to be produced in town. The people do not have more work; they merely do other work. They do not have higher pay; they merely no longer buy things as cheaply.

THE PEOPLE: Long live LOW PRICES!

PIERRE: You are being swayed by the fine words of this man! Let us put the question in simple terms. Is it not true that if we allow butter, wood, and meat to enter, we will be swamped by them? We would perish from a surfeit! There is therefore no other way of protecting ourselves from this different form of invasion than to shut our door to it and, in order to maintain the price of products, to produce a scarcity of them artificially.

A FEW SCATTERED VOICES: Long live SCARCITY!

JACQUES: Let us set the question out in all its truth! We can share out among all the people of Paris only what there is in Paris. If there is less wood, meat, and butter, each person's share will be smaller. Now there will be less if we keep these out than if we let them in. People of Paris! Each person can be abundantly supplied only if there is general abundance.

THE PEOPLE: Long live ABUNDANCE!

PIERRE: Whatever this man says, he will not prove to you that it is in your interest to be subjected to unbridled competition.

THE PEOPLE: Down with COMPETITION!

JACQUES: However eloquent this man is, he will not enable you to taste the sweetness of trade restrictions.

THE PEOPLE: Down with TRADE RESTRICTIONS!

PIERRE: For my part, I declare that if you deprive the poor cowherds and swineherds of their living, if you sacrifice them to theories, I will no longer guarantee public order. Workers, do not trust this man. He is an agent of perfidious Normandy[16] and goes abroad to seek inspiration. He is a traitor and should be hanged. (*The people are silent.*)

JACQUES: People of Paris, all that I am saying today I said twenty years ago, when Pierre chose to exploit city tolls for his benefit and your loss. I am not, then, an agent of the people of Normandy. Hang me if you like, but that will not stop oppression from being oppression. Friends, it is neither Jacques nor Pierre who ought to be killed but freedom, if you are afraid of it, or trade restriction if it hurts you.

THE PEOPLE: Let us hang nobody and emancipate everybody!

14. Something Else

PUBLISHING HISTORY:

Original title: "Autre chose."

Place and date of first publication: *Le Libre-échange,* 21 March 1847, no. 17, pp. 135–36.

First French edition as book or pamphlet: *Economic Sophisms* (Second Series) (1848). First and Second Series were combined in one edition in 1851.

Location in Paillottet's edition of *OC:* Vol. 4. *Sophismes économiques. Petits pamphlets I,* pp. 241–51.

Previous translations: 1st American ed., 1848; 1st British ed., 1873; FEE ed., 1964.

---

16. "Perfidious Normandy" is a play on words by Bastiat, since the phrase normally used is "Perfidious Albion" (faithless or deceitful England).

"What is trade restriction?"

"It is partial prohibition"

"What is prohibition?"

"It is absolute trade restriction."

"So that what you say about one applies to the other?"

"Yes, except for the degree. There is the same relationship between them as between the arc of a circle and the circle itself."

"Therefore, if prohibition is bad, restriction cannot be good?"

"No more than the arc of a circle can be straight if the circle is round."

"What is the term that is common to both restriction and prohibition?"

"Protection."

"What is the final effect of protection?"

"To require a greater amount of work from men for the same result."

"Why are people so attached to protectionist regimes?"

"Because freedom is bound to provide the same result *for less work,* this apparent reduction in work terrifies them."

"Why do you say *apparent?*"

"Because any labor saved can be devoted to *something else.*"

"What else?"

"This cannot be specified and has no need to be."

"Why?"

"Because if the total of France's current satisfactions were achievable with a reduction of one-tenth of the total of the work, no one is able to specify what new satisfactions she would want to obtain for herself with the resources that remain available. Some people would want to be better clothed, others better fed, some better educated, and some better entertained."

"Please explain the mechanism and effects of protection to me."

"That is not easy. Before moving on to complicated examples, we would have to study it in its simplest form."

"Take the simplest example you want."

"Do you remember how Robinson Crusoe[1] set about making a plank when he had no saw?"

"Yes, he felled a tree and, trimming the trunk with his axe first on its left and then on its right side, he reduced it to the thickness of a beam."

"And did that take him a great deal of work?"

---

1. In this chapter Bastiat makes several references to Robinson Crusoe and the economic choices he had to make in order to survive on his island. See "Bastiat's Invention of Crusoe Economics," in the Introduction.

"Two whole weeks."

"And what did he live on during this time?"

"His provisions."

"And what became of the axe?"[2]

"It became very blunt."

"Very well. But perhaps you did not know this. Just when he was about to give the first stroke of his axe, Robinson Crusoe saw a plank cast up by the waves on the beach."

"Oh, what a coincidence! Did he run to pick it up?"

"This was his first reaction, but then he stopped for the following reason:

"'If I pick up this plank, it will cost me only the fatigue of carrying it and the time to go down the cliff and climb it again.

"'But if I make a plank with my axe, firstly, I will give myself enough work for two weeks; secondly, I will wear out my axe, which will give me the opportunity of repairing it; and then I will eat up my provisions, a third source of work, since I will need to replace them. Now, *work is wealth*. It is clear that I will ruin myself by going to pick up the plank washed up on the beach. It is important for me to protect my *personal labor,* and now that I think of it, I can create further work for myself by going to push this plank back into the sea!'"

"But this line of reasoning is absurd!"

"So it is! It is nevertheless the one followed by any nation that *protects* itself through prohibition. It rejects the plank offered to it for little work in order to give itself more work. There is no work up to and including the work of the customs officer in which it does not see advantage. This is illustrated by the trouble taken by Robinson Crusoe to return to the sea the gift it wished to make him. Think of the nation as a collective being, and you will find not an atom of difference between its way of reasoning and that of Robinson Crusoe."

"Did Robinson not see that the time he saved he could devote to doing *something else?*"

"What else?"

"As long as you have needs and time in hand, you always have *something* to do. I cannot be expected to specify the work he might have undertaken."

"I can identify clearly the work that eluded him."

"And I maintain for my part that Robinson Crusoe, through incredible

2. See also ES2 3, pp. 138–42.

blindness, was confusing work with its result and the end with the means, and I will prove it to you."

"I will let you off that. It is nevertheless true that this is the simplest example of a restrictive or prohibitionist system. If it appears absurd to you in this form, it is because the two roles of producer and consumer are here combined in the same person."

"Let us move on to a more complicated example, then."

"With pleasure. A short time afterward, when Robinson Crusoe had met Man Friday, they became friends and started to work together. In the morning they went hunting together for six hours and brought back four baskets of game. In the evening, they gardened for six hours and obtained four baskets of vegetables.

"One day, a dugout canoe landed on the *Island of Despair*.[3] A good-looking stranger got out and was invited to the table of our two castaways. He tasted and fulsomely praised the garden products and, before taking leave of his hosts, he said to them:

"'Generous islanders, I live in a land that has much more game than this but where horticulture is unknown. It would be easy for me to bring you four baskets of game each evening if you would trade me just two baskets of vegetables.'

"At these words, Robinson and Friday went aside to confer, and their discussion is too interesting for me not to quote it here in full:

FRIDAY: What do you think, Friend?[4]

CRUSOE: If we accept, we will be ruined.

F.: Are you quite sure? Let us do the calculation.

C.: The calculation has been done. When it is crushed by the competition, hunting will be a lost industry for us.

F.: What does it matter if we have the game?

3. "The Island of Despair" was the name given by Daniel Defoe to the island on which Crusoe was shipwrecked.

4. It is interesting to note that Friday uses the familiar form of "you" (*tu*) with Crusoe, which is how members of the same family or close friends would address each other. This suggests that Bastiat intended Friday and Crusoe to regard each other as equals on the island. If Crusoe and not Friday had used the familiar *tu*, this would indicate that Crusoe regarded Friday as a child or a pet. However, Crusoe does get very angry with Friday because of his stubborn belief in the benefits of free trade, and Crusoe does call him a savage.

C.: That is only theory! It will not be the product of our labor.[5]

F.: Good heavens! Yes it will, since to have it we will have to give them vegetables!

C.: Then what will we gain?

F.: The four baskets of game cost us six hours of work. The stranger will give them to us for two baskets of vegetables, which cost us only three. We will thus have three hours at our disposal.

C.: So you should say, then, that these three hours have been deducted from our activity. That is exactly where our loss lies. *Work is wealth,* and if we lose a quarter of our time, we will be a quarter less rich.

F.: Friend, you are making a huge mistake. The same game and the same vegetables and in addition, three hours available; that is progress, or there is no progress in this world!

C.: A mere generality! What will we do with these three hours?

F.: We will do *something else.*

C.: Ah, I have caught you out! You cannot be specific. *Something else, something else,* that is easy to say.

F.: We will go fishing, improve the appearance of our cabin, read the *Bible.*

C.: Utopia! Is it certain that we will do one thing rather than another?

F.: Well then, if we have nothing to do, we will rest. Is rest worth nothing?

C.: But when we rest we die of hunger.

F.: Friend, you are in a vicious circle. I am talking about rest that takes nothing away from either our game or our vegetables. You continue to forget that through our trade with the stranger, nine hours of work will obtain for us as many provisions as twelve do now.

C.: We can see that you were not brought up in Europe. Perhaps you have never read *Le Moniteur industriel?* It would have taught you

5. It is also interesting to note that Bastiat makes the European Crusoe the advocate of protectionism and the native Friday the defender of free trade.

that: "All time saved is a net loss. It is not eating that is important, it is work. If it is not the direct product of our work, everything we consume is of no account. Do you want to know whether you are rich? Do not look at your satisfactions but at the effort your work entails." This is what *Le Moniteur industriel* would have taught you. For my part, I who am not a theoretician, all I can see is the loss of our hunting.

F.: What a strange inversion of ideas! But . . .

C.: There is no *but*. Besides, there are political reasons for rejecting self-interested proposals from perfidious foreigners.

F.: Political reasons!

C.: Yes. Firstly, he is making us these proposals only because they are of benefit to him.

F.: All the better, since they are the same to us too.

C.: Secondly, through these trades we will become dependent on him.

F.: And he on us. We will need his game and he our vegetables, and we will live as friends.

C.: Theories! Do you want me to render you speechless?

F.: That remains to be seen; I am still waiting for a good argument.

C.: Let us suppose that the stranger learns how to cultivate a garden and that his island is more fertile than ours. Do you see the result?

F.: Yes. Our relationship with the stranger will cease. He will no longer take our vegetables since he will obtain them at home for less trouble. He will no longer bring us game since we will have nothing to offer him in exchange, and we will be in exactly the same position as you want us to be today.

C.: Thoughtless savage! Do you not see that once he has killed our hunting industry by swamping us with game, he will kill our gardening industry by swamping us with vegetables?

F.: But this will never happen as long as we give him *something else,* that is to say, that we find *something else* that it is economic for us to produce.

C.: *Something else, something else!* You keep harping on about it! You are in a rut, Friend *Friday;* your ideas are not in the least practical.

"The conflict lasted a long time and left each convinced that he was right, as is often the case. However, since Robinson Crusoe had great influence over Man Friday, his views won the day, and when the stranger came for their reply Robinson Crusoe told him:

"'Stranger, for your proposal to be accepted, we would have to be sure of two things:

"'Firstly, that your island is no richer in game than ours since we want to compete only *on an equal footing.*

"'Secondly, that you will lose out in the trade. For, as there is always a winner and a loser in every exchange, we would be the dupes if you did not. What do you say?'

"'Nothing,' said the stranger, and bursting out laughing, he went back to his canoe."

The tale would not be so bad if Robinson Crusoe were not so absurd.

"He is no more absurd than the committee in the rue Hauteville."[6]

"Oh, that is very different! You are supposing on one occasion a single man and on another two men living communally, which amounts to the same thing. This is not like our world; the division of labor, the intervention of traders and money changes the matter considerably."

"That does complicate transactions, it is true, but it does not change their nature."

"What! You want to compare modern trade with simple barter?"

"Trade is just a host of barters; the intrinsic nature of a barter is identical to the intrinsic nature of trade, just as a small job is of the same nature as a large one or as the gravity that pushes an atom is of the same nature as the one that moves a world."

"Thus, in your opinion, the reasons that are so erroneous in the mouth of Robinson Crusoe are no less so in the mouths of our protectionists?"

"That's right, only the error is better hidden under the complexity of the circumstances."

"Well then! Take an example from the real world of events."

"Very well. In France, in view of the demands of climate and customs, cloth is a useful product. Is the essential factor *making it* or *having it?*"

"A fine question! To have it you have to make it."

---

6. The Association pour la défense du travail national (Association for the Defense of National Employment, also called the Odier Committee or the Mimerel Committee after two of its leading members) was located in the rue Hauteville, where it had its headquarters. See Glossary.

"That is not necessarily so. To have it, someone has to make it, that is certain, but it is not obligatory for it to be the person or the country that consumes it which produces it. You have not made the cloth that clothes you so well; France has not produced the coffee for her citizens' breakfast."

"But I have purchased my cloth and France her coffee."

"Precisely, but with what?"

"With money."

"But you have not made the money, nor has France."

"We have bought it."

"With what?"

"With our products that went to Peru."

"Therefore, in reality it is your labor that you exchange for cloth and French labor that is exchanged for coffee."

"Certainly."

"It is therefore not strictly necessary to make what you consume."

"No, if you make *something else* that you give in exchange."

"In other words, France has two ways of procuring a given quantity of cloth for herself. The first is to make it; the second is to make *something else* and trade this *something else* abroad for cloth. Which of these two means is the better?"

"I do not really know."

"Is it not the one that gives a greater quantity of cloth for a given amount of labor?"

"It would appear so."

"And which is better for a nation, to have the choice between these two means or that the law should forbid one in the hope of correctly stumbling across the better one?"

"It seems to me that it is better for it to have the choice, especially since in these matters she always chooses well."

"So, the law that prohibits foreign cloth decides that if France wants to have cloth, she has to make it directly, from her own resources and that it is forbidden to make the *something else* with which she might purchase cloth from abroad?"

"That is true."

"And since it forces France to make cloth and forbids her from making the *something else,* precisely because this something else would require less work (without which consideration the law would not need to become involved), the law therefore virtually decrees that, for a given amount of labor, France would have only one meter of cloth by making it when, for the same labor, she might have two meters by making this *something else.*"

"But, good Heavens, what something else?"

"Well, good Heavens, what does it matter? Given the choice, it would make something else only when there was something else to be made!"

"That is possible, but I am still concerned with the thought that foreigners send us cloth and do not take from us the *something else,* in which case we would be well and truly caught out. In any case, this is the objection, even from your point of view. You agree that France will make this *something else* to trade for cloth with less effort than if she made the cloth herself."

"Doubtless."

"There would therefore be a certain quantity of her labor left idle."

"Yes, but without her people's being less well clothed, an undramatic circumstance but one that underlies the whole misunderstanding. Robinson Crusoe lost sight of this; our protectionists either do not see this or they are hiding it. The plank washed ashore also brought Robinson Crusoe's work to a standstill for two weeks, as far as making a plank was concerned, but it did not deprive him of work. You therefore have to distinguish between these two types of decline in the demand for labor, the one that has *deprivation* as its effect and the one which has increased *satisfaction* as its cause. These two things are very different, and if you do not distinguish between them you are reasoning like Robinson Crusoe. In the most complex cases, as in the most simple ones, the sophism consists in this: '*Judge the usefulness of the work by its duration and its intensity and not by its results,*' which leads to the following economic policy: '*Reduce the output of work with the aim of increasing its duration and intensity.*'"

15. The Free Trader's Little Arsenal

PUBLISHING HISTORY:

Original title: "Le Petit arsenal du libre-échangiste."
Place and date of first publication: *Le Libre-échange,* 26 April 1847.
First French edition as book or pamphlet: It was published as a stand-alone pamphlet in 1847 as *Le Petit arsenal du libre-échange* (Paris: E. Crugy, 1847), then in *Economic Sophisms* (Second Series) (1848). First and Second Series were combined in one edition in 1851.
Location in Paillottet's edition of *OC:* Vol. 4. *Sophismes économiques. Petits pamphlets I,* pp. 251–57.

Previous translations: 1st American ed., 1848; 1st British ed., 1873; FEE ed., 1964.

If someone says to you: "There are no absolute principles.[1] Prohibition may be bad and restriction good."

Reply: "Restriction *prohibits* everything it prevents from entering."

If someone says to you: "Agriculture is the mother that feeds the country."

Reply: "What feeds the country is absolutely not agriculture but *wheat.*"

If someone says to you: "The basic means of feeding the people is agriculture."

Reply: "The basic means of feeding the people is *wheat.* This is why a law that causes *two* hectoliters of wheat to be obtained through agricultural labor at the expense of *four* hectoliters that the same labor applied to manufacturing would have obtained in the absence of that law, far from being a law for providing food, is a law for starvation."

If someone says to you: "Restricting the entry of foreign wheat leads to more cultivation and consequently increased production within the country."

Reply: "It leads to sowing on mountain rocks and the sands by the sea. Milking a cow over and over again gives more milk, for who can tell the moment when you will not obtain a drop more? But the drop costs a great deal."

If someone says to you: "Let bread become expensive and farmers that become rich will make industrialists rich."

Reply: "Bread is expensive when there is not much of it, which can cause only poverty, or if you prefer, *very hungry* rich people."

If they insist, saying: "When the price of bread goes up, wages also increase."

Reply by pointing out that in April 1847 five-sixths of workers were on alms.[2]

---

1. See ES1 18.

2. We have not been able to verify this. However, crop failures in 1846–47 caused considerable hardship and a rise in food prices in 1847 across Europe. Some historians believe this was a contributing factor to the outbreak of revolution in 1848. The average price of wheat in France was 18 fr. 93 c. per hectoliter in 1845, which rose to 23 fr. 84 c. in 1846 (which had a poor harvest). Prices were even higher in the last half of 1846 and the first half of 1847, when the shortage was most acutely felt. In December 1846 the price rose to 28 fr. 41 c., and it reached a maximum of 37 fr. 98 c. in May 1847. The average price for the period 1832–46 had been 19 fr. 5 c. per hectoliter. The lowest average price reached between 1800 and 1846 was 14 fr. 72 c. in 1834. See AEPS, pour 1848 (Paris: Guillaumin, 1848), pp. 179–80. See the entry for "Irish Famine and the Failure of French Harvests, 1846–47," in the Glossary of Subjects and Terms.

If someone says to you: "Workers' pay ought to follow the cost of living."

Reply: "That is the same as saying that in a ship without provisions, everyone has the same amount of biscuit whether there is any or not."

If someone says to you: "A good price has to be assured for those who sell wheat."

Reply: "So be it, but then a good wage has to be assured for those who buy it."

If someone says to you: "The landowners who establish the law have increased the price of bread without concerning themselves with wages because they know that when bread becomes expensive, wages rise *totally naturally.*"

Reply: "On this principle, when workers establish the law, you should not blame them if they set a good rate of pay without concerning themselves with protecting wheat, because they know that when earnings are high, provisions become expensive *totally naturally.*"

If someone says to you: "What then ought to be done?"

Reply: "Be just to everyone."

If someone says to you: "It is essential for a great country to have an iron industry."

Reply: "What is more essential is that this great country *has iron.*"

If someone says to you: "It is indispensable for a great country to have a cloth industry."

Reply: "What is more indispensable is that in this great country, citizens *have cloth.*"

If someone says to you: "Work is wealth."

Reply: "That is wrong."

And by way of development, add: "Bloodletting is not health,[3] and the proof that it is not health is that its aim is to provide it."

If someone says to you: "Forcing men to break rocks and produce one ounce of iron from a quintal of ore is increasing their work, and therefore their wealth."

Reply: "Forcing men to dig wells by forbidding them to take water from the river is increasing their *ineffective* work, but not their wealth."

---

3. Note that Bastiat quotes favorably Molière's parody of seventeenth-century doctors who let blood in *Le Malade imaginaire* (The Imaginary Invalid, or the Hypochondriac, 1673). Bastiat turns this into his own parody to make fun of tax collectors. See ES2 9, p. 176, esp. n15.

If someone says to you: "The sun gives its heat and light for nothing."

Reply: "All the better for me; it costs me nothing to see clearly."

And if someone replies to you: "Production in general loses out on what you would have paid for lighting."[4]

Reply: "No, since having paid nothing to the sun, I use the money I save to buy clothes, furniture, and candles."

Similarly, if someone says to you: "The rascally English have *amortized* capital."

Reply: "All the better for us; they will not make us pay interest."

If someone says to you: "The perfidious English find iron and coal in the same seam."

Reply: "All the better for us; they will not make us pay for bringing them together."

If someone says to you: "The Swiss have lush pastures that cost little."

Reply: "We have the advantage since they will demand from us a smaller amount of the labor which we use to furnish the driving force for our agriculture and to supply food for our stomachs."

If someone says to you: "The fields of Crimea have no value and do not pay taxes."

Reply: "We enjoy the profit when we buy wheat free of these charges."

If someone says to you: "Serfs in Poland work for no pay."

Reply: "They reap the misfortune and we the profit since the value of their labor is deducted from the price of the wheat their masters sell us."

Lastly, if someone says to you: "Other nations have a host of advantages over us."

Reply: "Through trade they are in fact obliged to get us to share them."

If someone says to you: "With freedom, we are going to be flooded with bread, prime cuts of beef, coal, and jackets."

Reply: "Well, we won't be hungry or cold."

If someone says to you: "With what will we pay for them?"

Reply: "Do not worry about it. If we are flooded, it is because we will be able to pay, and if we cannot pay we will not be flooded."

If someone says to you: "I would agree to free trade if foreigners took some of our products when they delivered us theirs, but they will take away our money."

Reply: "Money does not grow, any more than coffee does, in the fields

---

4. This is the witty assumption behind ES1 7.

of the Beauce and does not come from the workshops of Elbeuf.[5] For us, paying foreigners with it is like paying them with coffee."

If someone says to you: "Eat meat."

Reply: "Let it come in."

If someone says to you, as *La Presse* does: "When you do not have the means to buy bread, you have to buy beef."

Reply: "Advice that is as judicious as that given by Mr. Vulture to his tenant:

> When you do not have the means to pay your rent,
> You should have a house of your own.[6]

If someone says to you, as *La Presse* does: "The State should teach the people why and how it must eat beef."

Reply: "Let the State merely allow beef to enter and, as for eating it, the most civilized nation in the world is old enough to learn how to do so without a tutor."

If someone says to you: "The State has to know everything and anticipate everything in order to direct the nation, and the nation has only to let itself be directed."

Reply: "Is there a State outside the nation and human farsightedness outside humanity? Archimedes may have repeated: 'With a lever and a fulcrum I will move the world' every day of his life, but for all that not moved it an iota because he lacked a fulcrum and a lever. The fulcrum of the State is the nation, and there is nothing more senseless than to base so much hope on the State, that is to say, to postulate collective knowledge and farsightedness after assuming in fact individual stupidity and lack of foresight."[7]

---

5. Beauce is an important grain-growing region in north-central France. Elbeuf is an industrial town in northern France on the Seine River, to the south of Rouen.

6. These lines come from a play by Marc Antoine Madelaine Désaugiers (1772–1827) called *M. Vautour, ou le propriétaire sous le scellé* (M. Vulture, or the Owner under the Seal), first performed 13 June 1805. The name of Désaugiers's grasping tobacco store owner, "Vautour," was taken up in French slang for a stereotypical hard-hearted landlord and creditor. The original French lines can be found in Désaugiers, *M. Vautour, ou le propriétaire sous le scellé,* p. 11.

7. Here Bastiat is raising what Friedrich Hayek called the knowledge problem, namely that central planners lack the necessary local knowledge provided by free market prices to make rational economic decisions. See Hayek, "The Use of Knowledge in Society." Note also Bastiat's definition of the state as "the great fiction by which everyone endeavors to live at the expense of everyone else" (CW2, p. 97), which he developed during the course of 1848.

If someone says to you: "My God! I am not asking any favors but merely for a duty on wheat and meat which compensates for all the heavy taxes to which France is subjected; just a simple little duty that is equal to what taxes add to the cost price of my wheat."

Reply: "A thousand pardons, but I too pay taxes. Therefore, if protection, which you are voting for in your own interests, has the effect of raising the price of your wheat to me, by exactly the amount of your share of the taxes, your sweet-sounding request seems to be nothing less than the following arrangement: 'In view of the fact that our taxes are weighty, I, the seller of wheat, will pay nothing and you, my neighbor and purchaser, will pay two shares, that is to say, yours and mine.' Mr. Wheat Merchant, my neighbor, you may have force on your side, but what is absolutely certain is that you do not have right."

If someone says to you: "However, it is very hard for me, who pays taxes, to compete in my own market with foreigners who do not pay any."

Reply:

1. "Firstly, it is not *your* market but *our* market. I, who live on wheat and pay for it, ought to count for something."

2. "Few foreigners, in the current climate, are exempt from taxes."

3. "If the taxes you vote for provide you with more roads, canals, security, etc. than they cost you, you are not justified in rejecting at my expense competition from foreigners who do not pay these taxes but who equally do not have the security, roads, and canals in question. It is as good as saying: I demand a compensatory duty because I have finer clothes, stronger horses, and better ploughs than Russian laborers."

4. "If taxes do not repay what they cost, do not vote for them."

5. "And finally, once you have voted for the taxes, do you want to exempt yourself from them? Imagine a system that inflicts them on foreigners. However, tariffs make your share fall upon me, and my share is quite enough."

If someone says to you: "In Russia, they need free trade *in order to trade their products advantageously.*" (The opinion of M. Thiers, speaking to the departments, April 1847.)[8]

---

8. It is not clear where these remarks by Thiers were delivered, but his hostility to the idea of free trade can be seen in an address he gave to the National Assembly in June 1851: "Of all the chimeras which I have had to combat, there is none more vain and dangerous than that which goes by the name of free trade. For several years they [advocates of free trade] have written, spoken, dogmatized, professed without meeting any contradiction.

Reply: "Freedom is necessary everywhere and for the same reason."

If someone says to you: "Every country has its own needs. It is according to these that *it is necessary to act*" (M. Thiers).

Reply: "It is according to these that a country will act *by itself* when it is not prevented from doing so."

If someone says to you: "Since we have no sheet iron, we have to allow it to enter" (M. Thiers).

Reply: "Oh, thank you very much."

If someone says to you: "We need freight for our merchant navy. Lacking loads on the return journey makes it impossible for our shipping to compete with foreign shipping" (M. Thiers).

Reply: "When people want to do everything at home, they cannot have freight either on the inward or outward journeys. It is just as absurd to want a merchant navy under a prohibitionist regime as it would be to want carts where all forms of transport have been forbidden."

If someone says to you: "Even if we suppose that protectionism is unjust, everything has been arranged on precisely that basis; capital has been committed to it and duties established. We cannot extricate ourselves from it painlessly."

Reply: "All injustice is of benefit to someone (except, perhaps, for a policy of restrictions which in the long run benefits no one); to defend injustice on the grounds of the inconvenience that its abolition will cause the person who benefits from it, is to say that an injustice should be eternal for the sole reason that it has existed for an instant."

16. The Right Hand and the Left Hand

PUBLISHING HISTORY:

Original title: "La Main droite et la main gauche."
Place and date of first publication: *Le Libre-échange,*
   13 December 1846, no. 3, p. 24.
First French edition as book or pamphlet: *Economic Sophisms*

Once I thought it useful to stop it in its tracks, and immediately I was corrected as I deserved by the great worthies which political economy has produced. But that is not what is at issue here; I only wish to raise certain assertions in order to prove their falsity" (Thiers, *Discours de M. Thiers sur le régime commercial de la France,* p. iv).

(Second Series) (1848). First and Second Series were
combined in one edition in 1851.

Location in Paillottet's edition of *OC:* Vol. 4. *Sophismes
économiques. Petits pamphlets I,* pp. 258–65.

Previous translations: 1st American ed., 1848; 1st British ed.,
1873; FEE ed., 1964.

(A report to the King)

Sire,

When we see these men from *Le Libre-échange* boldly spreading their doctrine and claiming that the right to buy and sell is included in the right to
property (a piece of insolence that M. Billaut has pointed out in true advocate style), we may be allowed to feel serious anxiety over the fate of our
nation's production, for what will French citizens do with their hands and
minds when they are free?

The government that you have honored with your confidence has had to
devote its attention to a situation rendered serious in precisely this way, and
in its wisdom seek a form of *protection* that may be substituted for the one
which appears compromised. It suggests that YOU FORBID YOUR FAITHFUL
SUBJECTS TO USE THEIR RIGHT HAND.

Sire, do not insult us by thinking that we have lightly adopted a measure
that, at first sight, may seem strange. A detailed study of *protectionism* has
revealed to us the syllogism on which the whole thing is based:

The more you work, the richer you are;

The more difficulties you have to overcome, the more you work;

Therefore, the more difficulties you have to overcome, the richer you are.

What is protection in fact, if not the ingenious application of this formal
reasoning so closely woven that it will stand up to the subtlety of M. Billault
himself?

Let us personify the country. Let us consider it a collective being with
thirty million mouths, and as a natural consequence, sixty million arms.
Here it is, having made a clock that it hopes to barter in Belgium for ten
quintal of iron. However, we say to it: "Make the iron yourself." "I cannot,"
it replies; "that will take me too long; I would not make five quintal in the
time I take to make a clock." "Utopian!" we reply. "It is for that very reason
that we forbid you to make a clock and order you to make iron. Do you not
see that we are creating work for you?"

Sire, it will not have escaped your sagacity that this is absolutely as though we were saying to the country: "*Work with your left hand and not with your right.*"

Creating obstacles in order to give labor the opportunity of increasing, that is the principle of *restriction* that is dying. It is also the principle of *restriction* that is about to be born. Sire, making regulations like this is not to innovate, it is to continue down the same path.

As for the effectiveness of the measure, this cannot be denied. It is difficult, much more difficult than you think, to do with your left hand what you are accustomed to doing with your right. You would be convinced of this, Sire, if you deigned to try out our system on an act familiar to you, such as, for example, that of shuffling cards.[1] We can therefore pride ourselves on creating an unlimited vista for work.

When workers of all sorts are reduced to using their left hands, let us imagine, Sire, the immense number that would be needed to meet current consumption, taking it to be constant, which is what we always do when we compare opposing systems of production with each other. Such a prodigious demand for labor cannot fail to cause a considerable rise in pay, and poverty would disappear from the country as if by magic.

Sire, your fatherly heart would rejoice to think that the benefits of the decree would extend also to this interesting part of the great family whose fate elicits your total solicitude. What is the destiny of women in France? The sex that is the more fearless and more strengthened by hard work, drives them heartlessly from all forms of career.

In former times they had the resources of the lottery offices to turn to. These have been closed down through a pitiless philanthropy and on what pretext? "To save the money of the poor," this philanthropy said. Alas! Has the poor man ever obtained such pleasant and innocent enjoyment from a coin as those which Fortune's mysterious urn held for him? Cut off as he was from all the pleasures of life, when he placed a day's pay on a *clear line of four numbers*[2] once a fortnight, how many hours of delicious enjoyment did he not bring into the bosom of his family! Hope was ever present in the domestic hearth. The attic was filled with fancies: wives promised themselves that

---

1. This may be a dig at King Louis-Philippe's reputation for being a card-playing bon vivant.

2. Known as the *quaterne sec,* it was a lottery ticket that had one chance in 75,000 to pay off.

they would outshine their neighbors with their dresses, sons saw themselves as drum majors, and daughters imagined themselves walking down the aisle to the altar on the arms of their fiancés.

> There is indeed something to be said about having a beautiful dream![3]

Oh! The lottery! It was the poetry of the poor and we have let it escape!

With the lottery gone,[4] what means have we to provide for those in our care? Tobacco[5] and the post.[6]

We will deal with tobacco all in good time; it is making progress, thanks to Heaven and the fine habits that many august exemplars have cleverly been able to inculcate into our elegant young people.

But the post! We will say nothing about it, as it will be the subject of a special report.

Therefore, apart from tobacco, what will be left to your subjects? Nothing but embroidery, knitting, and sewing, sorry resources that a barbaric science, the science of machinery, is increasingly restricting.

But as soon as your decree has appeared, as soon as right hands have been cut off or tied, everything will change visibly. Twenty or thirty times more embroiderers, laundresses and ironers, linen maids, dressmakers and shirt

---

3. Jean-François Collin d'Harleville (1755–1806) was a French dramatist and poet. The lines Bastiat quotes come from his play *Les Châteaux en Espagne* (1789). M. D'Orlange is the caretaker of M. D'Orfeuil's castle in Spain and dreams he is now a sultan. The owner's valet Victor wakes D'Orlange up and he reflects upon the escape provided by dreams: "Ah well, at least everyone is happy when they are dreaming. There is something indeed to be said about having beautiful dreams. It is a useful respite from our actual grief. We have need of them, we are surrounded by woes which in the end would overwhelm us, without this happy madness which flows through our veins. Gratifying illusion! Sweet oblivion from our troubles!" (Collin-Harleville, *Œuvres de Collin-Harleville* 1:337).

4. Lotteries were banned in France in January 1836. They were used during the ancien régime as a means of raising money to build and repair churches and religious communities and even as a way for the state to pay off the national debt. Lotteries were banned during the Revolution (November 1793), relegalized in 1797, but finally abolished beginning in 1832 with a phasing-out period of four years. See Edgar Duval, "Loteries," in *DEP* 2:106–7.

5. The sale of tobacco in France was a state monopoly. It contributed fr. 120 million to government receipts in 1848 (8.6 percent of a total of fr. 1.4 billion).

6. Bastiat probably has in mind the fact that the high cost of sending letters in France (another state monopoly used to raise money) made it more difficult for families to keep in contact with each other. See ES2 12.

makers will not be enough to meet demand (*honi soit qui mal y pense*)[7] in the kingdom; always assuming that demand is constant, in accordance with our method of reasoning.

It is true that this supposition may be contested by cold theoreticians, since dresses will be more expensive, as will shirts. They say the same about the iron that France extracts from its mines, compared to the grapes it could *harvest* from our hillsides. This argument is thus no more acceptable against *left-handedness*[8] than against *protection,* for this very expensiveness is the result and the expression of the additional effort and work that is exactly the basis on which, in both cases, we claim to found the prosperity of the working class.

Yes, we paint for ourselves a touching picture of the prosperity of the dressmaking industry. What animation! What activity! What a life! Each dress will occupy a hundred fingers instead of ten. No young girl will remain idle, and we have no need, Sire, to point out to your perspicacity the moral consequences of this great revolution. Not only will there be more girls occupied, but each of them will earn more, since they will be unable to meet demand and, if competition rises still further, it will not be between the seamstresses who make the dresses but between the fine ladies who wear them.

You see, Sire, our proposal is not just in line with the economic traditions of the government; it is also essentially moral and democratic.

To appreciate its effects, let us assume that it has been achieved, let us be carried in thought into the future; let us imagine the system once it has been in action for twenty years. Idleness has been banished from the country. Prosperity and concord, contentment and morality have become imbued, along with work, in every family. There is no more destitution, no more prostitution. As left hands are very gauche to work with, there will be an overabundance of work, and pay will be satisfactory. Everything has been arranged on this basis; consequently, workers in workshops have increased in number. Is it not true, Sire, that if suddenly Utopians came to demand freedom for the right hand, they would spread panic throughout the country? Is it not true that this so-called reform would throw everybody into confusion? Our system is therefore good, since it cannot be overturned without causing pain.

---

7. *Honi soit qui mal y pense* (shame on him who thinks ill of it) is the motto of the English chivalric Order of the Garter. The order was founded and its motto was coined by King Edward III.

8. Bastiat uses the word *gaucherie* in this passage, thus making his point with a pun on the French words for left (*gauche*) and for clumsiness (*gaucherie*).

And yet we have the sorry premonition that one day an association will be formed (such is the perversity of the human race!) called the association for the freedom of right hands.[9]

We can almost hear the free right-handers speak in these terms in the Montesquieu Hall[10] already:

> People, you think you are richer because the use of one hand has been taken from you and you see only the additional work that you have received. But take a look at the high prices that have resulted and the forced reduction of all forms of consumption. This measure has not made capital, the source of wages, more abundant. The water that flows from this great reservoir is directed to other channels; its volume has not increased, and the final result is, for the nation as a whole, a loss of well-being that is equal to all the extra output that the millions of right hands can produce compared to an equal number of left hands. Let us unite, therefore, and at the cost of some inevitable inconvenience, let us conquer the right to work with both hands.

Fortunately, Sire, an *association for the defense of work with the left hand*[11] will be formed, and the *Sinistrists* will have no trouble in annihilating all

9. Bastiat is drawing a number of witty verbal parallels here between *la liberté des mains droites* (freedom for right hands) and *la liberté des échanges* (free trade); the *association pour la liberté des main droites* (the free right hand association) and the Association pour la liberté des échanges (Free Trade Association); and *les libres-dextéristes* (free right-handers) and *les libre-échangistes* (free traders). All that is missing from his list is a journal to promote the cause: *Le Libre-dextérisme* (Free Right-Handedness) and *Le Libre-échange* (Free Trade). Bastiat was of course an arch free trader and one of the founders of the Free Trade Association, as well as the editor of the journal *Le Libre-échange*.

10. The first public meeting in Paris of the Free Trade Association was held in Montesquieu Hall on 28 August 1846.

11. Bastiat continues his parallels by comparing the *association pour la défense du travail par la main gauche* (association for the defense of work with the left hand) with the protectionist Association pour la défense du travail national (Association for the Defense of National Employment), which was founded by the textile manufacturer Pierre Mimerel and which published the journal *Le Moniteur industriel*. This association will of course promote the interests of the *Sinistristes* (Sinistrists, or supporters of left-hand labor). Bastiat uses the word *sinistre* here, which is another pun, this time on the French word for left (*senestre*), which comes from the Latin *sinister* (left). The pairing for this is the word *Dextéristes* (Dextrists, or supporters of right-hand labor), from the Latin *dexter* (on the right), which he uses later in the article.

these generalities and idealisms, suppositions and abstractions, dreams and utopias. All they will have to do is to exhume the 1846 issues of *Le Moniteur industriel;* in these they will find ready-made arguments against *free trade* which will pulverize *freedom for right hands* so magnificently that all they will need to do is to substitute one word for the other.

> The Paris League for *Free Trade* had no doubt that the workers would support it. However, workers are no longer men who can be led by the nose. Their eyes have been opened, and they are more fully conversant with political economy than our qualified professors.... *Free trade,* they replied, will take away our work and work is our real, great, and sovereign property; with *work, with a great deal of work, the price of goods is never out of reach.* But without work, even if bread cost only one sou per pound, workers are forced to die of hunger. Well, your doctrines, instead of increasing the current total of work in France, will decrease it, that is to say, you will reduce us to destitution. (Issue dated 13 October 1846)
>
> When there are too many goods on sale, their price does in fact go down, but as wages fall when goods lose their value, the result is that instead of being in a position to buy them, we can no longer buy anything. It is therefore when goods are at their lowest price that workers are most unfortunate." (Gauthier de Rumilly,[12] *Le Moniteur industriel* dated 17 November)

It would be no bad thing if the *Sinistrists* included a few threats in their fine theories. This is a sample:

> What? You want to substitute work using right hands for that using left hands and thus force down, if not totally annihilate, wages, the sole resource of almost the entire nation?
>
> And this at a time when poor harvests[13] are already imposing painful sacrifices on workers, making them anxious for their

---

12. Louis Gaulthier de Rumilly (1792–1884) was trained as a lawyer and served as a deputy in 1830–34 and 1837–40. He was active in the "Société d'encouragement pour l'industrie nationale" (Society to Promote National Industry) and had a special interest in agriculture, railroads, and tariffs.

13. Crop failures in 1846–47 caused considerable hardship and a rise in food prices in 1847 across Europe.

future, more likely to listen to bad advice, and ready to abandon the sensible behavior they have been following up to now.

We are confident, Sire, that through this learned reasoning, the left hand will emerge victorious in any conflict that arises.

Perhaps a further association will be formed with the aim of finding out whether the right and left hands are both wrong and if there is not between them a third hand which will reconcile everything.

Having painted the *Sinistrists* as being won over by the *apparent liberality of a principle whose accuracy has not been verified by experience* and the *Dextrists* as being encamped on their acquired positions, will that association not say:

> And can it be denied that there is a third road to take in the center of the conflict! And is it not obvious that workers have to defend themselves, both against those who want to change nothing in the current situation because it is to their advantage and those who dream of overturning the economy and have not calculated either the extent of the change or the range of its effects! (The issue of [*Le*] *National* dated 16 October)

However, we would not wish to hide from Your Majesty, Sire, that there is a vulnerable side to our project. We might be told: "In twenty years' time, all the left hands will be as skilled as right hands are now, and you will no longer be able to count on *gaucherie* (*left-handedness*) to increase national employment."

Our answer to this is that, according to learned doctors, the left-hand side of the human body has a natural weakness, which is entirely reassuring for the future of work.

And after all, if you agree to sign the decree, Sire, a great principle will have won the day: *All wealth comes from the intensity of work.* It will be easy for us to extend it and vary its applications. For example, we will decree that only work using feet will be allowed. This is no more impossible (since it has been seen) than extracting iron from the silt of the Seine. Men have even been seen to write with their backs. You see, Sire, that we do not lack the means of increasing national employment. Should the cause become hopeless, we are left with the unlimited resource of amputation.

Finally, Sire, if this report were not intended for publication, we would call your attention to the great influence that all systems similar to the one we are submitting to you are capable of giving the men in power. But this is a subject that we are keeping for discussion in private.

17. Domination through Work

PUBLISHING HISTORY:

Original title: "Domination par le travail."
Place and date of first publication: *Le Libre-échange,*
  14 February 1847, no. 12, pp. 93–94.
First French edition as book or pamphlet: *Economic Sophisms*
  (Second Series) (1848). First and Second Series were
  combined in one edition in 1851.
Location in Paillottet's edition of *OC:* Vol. 4. *Sophismes
  économiques. Petits pamphlets I,* pp. 265–71.
Previous translations: 1st American ed., 1848; 1st British ed.,
  1873; FEE ed., 1964.

"In time of peace is it possible to achieve domination through superiority in production, in the same way as in time of war, domination is achieved through superiority in weaponry?"

This question is of the greatest interest at a time in which people do not seem to doubt that, in the field of industry as on the field of battle, *the strongest crush the weakest.*

For this to be so, people must have discovered a sorry and discouraging analogy between work exercised on things and the violence exercised on men, for how can these two types of action be identical in their effect if they are in opposition by nature?

And if it is true that, in industry as in war, domination is the necessary result of superiority, why should we be concerned with progress and social economy since we are in a world in which everything has so been arranged by Providence that the same effect, oppression, ineluctably results from principles that are totally opposed to one another?

When it comes to the entirely new politics into which free trade is drawing England,[1] a certain query is being widely raised, one which, I must agree,

---

1. After the abolition of the protectionist Corn Laws in May 1846, the Economists expected that the liberalization of the British economy would lead to much greater productivity and further liberal political and economic reforms which the rest of Europe

is preoccupying the most sincere individuals: "Is England doing anything other than pursue the same aim by another means? Does she not still aspire to universal supremacy? Now sure of her superior capital formation and labor force, is she not calling for free competition so she can stifle industry on the continent, reigning supreme, and winning the privilege of feeding and clothing economically ruined nations?"

It would be easy for me to demonstrate that these anxieties are an illusion, that our alleged inferiority has been greatly exaggerated, that there is not one of our major industries that does not just resist but is even developing under the stimulus of competition from abroad and that the infallible effect of this is to bring about an increase in general consumption which is capable of absorbing both the products coming from within and those coming from without the country.

Today, I want to attack the objection frontally, leaving it all its force and all the advantage of the terrain it has chosen. Setting aside the English and the French, I will seek to find out in general whether, even though by means of its superiority in a particular branch of industry a nation manages to stifle a similar activity in another nation, the former has taken a step toward the domination of the latter and the latter a step toward dependence. In other words, I am asking whether both of them do not benefit from the operation and whether it is not the vanquished that gains more.

If a product is seen only as the *opportunity for work,* it is certain that the anxieties of protectionists are well founded. If we considered iron, for example, merely with regard to its relationship with ironmasters, we might fear that competition from a country in which it was a free gift of nature might extinguish the furnaces in another country in which both mineral and fuel were scarce.

However, is this a comprehensive view of the subject? Has iron a relationship only with those who make it? Is it foreign to those that use it? Is its sole and final purpose that of being produced? And if it is useful, not because of the work to which it gives rise but because of the qualities it possesses and the number of services for which its hardness and malleability make it suitable, does it not follow that foreigners cannot reduce its price even to the point of preventing its production here without doing us more good in this latter respect than any harm it might do in the former?

---

would also gradually adopt. In the case of France this was true with the signing of the Cobden-Chevalier Trade Treaty in 1860.

Let us consider the host of things that foreigners prevent us from producing directly, because of the natural advantages which surround them, a situation in which we *in fact* find ourselves, in the hypothetical case of iron which we have been examining. We do not produce tea, coffee, gold, or silver in this country. Does this mean that the total amount of our work is decreased because of this? No, only that, in order to create a countervalue for these things in order to acquire them through trade, we allocate a *lesser portion* of our general work than would be needed to produce them ourselves. More is left to us to devote to other satisfactions. We are richer, and stronger, by this amount. All that external rivalry has been able to do, even in cases where it prevents us absolutely from carrying out a given form of production, is to make us economize on it and to increase our productive power. Is this, for foreigners, the road to *domination?*

If a gold mine were found in France, it would not follow that it would be in our interest to exploit it. It is actually certain that the enterprise ought to be ignored since each ounce of gold would take up more of our labor than an ounce of gold purchased from Mexico in exchange for cloth. In this case, it would be better to continue to regard our looms as our gold mines. What is true of gold is also true for iron.

The illusion arises from the fact that there is something we do not see.[2] This is that foreign superiority only ever blocks national production in a specific area and makes it redundant only in this specific area by putting at our disposal the output of the very labor which has been destroyed in this way. If men lived in bells under water and had to provide themselves with air by means of a pump, there would be a huge source of work in this. Damaging this work *while leaving men in this situation* would be to do them frightful harm. But if the work ceases only because there is no longer any need for it, because men are placed in a different milieu in which air enters effortlessly into contact with their lungs, then the loss of this work is no cause for regret, except in the eyes of those who insist on seeing the value of work only in the work itself.

It is precisely this type of work that machines, free trade, and progress of all sorts are gradually destroying; not useful work, but work that has become superfluous, redundant, pointless, and ineffectual. On the other hand, pro-

---

2. This is a reference to a key idea, "the seen" and "the unseen," which Bastiat was to develop at more length in 1850 in his pamphlet *What Is Seen and What Is Not Seen,* which is included in this volume.

tection restores it; it puts us back under the water in order to supply us with the opportunity to pump; it forces us to demand gold from our inaccessible national mine rather than from our national looms. Its entire effect is encapsulated in this term: *wasted efforts.*

It will be understood that I am speaking here of general effects, and not the temporary upsets that occur when a bad system gives way to a good one. Temporary disturbance is bound to accompany any progress. This may be a reason to soften the transition, but not one to forbid all progress systematically, and still less to fail to recognize it.

Production is represented to us as a conflict. This is not true, or it is true only if each industry is considered solely with regard to its effects on another similar industry, isolating them both mentally from the rest of humanity. However, there are other considerations: their effects on consumption and on general well-being.

This is why it is not permissible to compare production to war, as is being done.

In war, the stronger overcomes the weaker.

In production, *the stronger transmits strength to the weaker.* This completely destroys the analogy.

No matter how strong and skillful the English are, how much *amortized* capital they have, or how much iron and furnace power, the two great forces in production, all this makes products *cheap.* And who benefits from the cheapness of products? The person who buys them.

It is not in their power to wipe out completely any portion of our economy. All they can do is make it superfluous for a given result, deliver air at the same time as they are abolishing pumps, thus increasing our available productive strength and, wonder of wonders, making their alleged domination all the more impossible the more their superiority is incontestable.

In this way we reach the conclusion, through a rigorous and consoling demonstration, that production and *violence,* so contrary by nature to one another, are no less so in their effect, no matter what protectionists and socialists say in this connection.

All we have needed to do to achieve this is to distinguish between production that has been *destroyed* and resources on which the system has economized.

To have less iron *because* you work less and more iron *in spite of* working less are situations that are more than different; they are quite opposite to one another. Protectionists confuse them, but we do not. That is the difference.

One thing should be made clear. If the English put to work a great deal of activity, labor, capital, intelligence, or natural strength, it is not just for the love of us. It is to provide themselves with a great many forms of satisfaction in return for their products. They certainly want to receive at least as much as they give, and *they manufacture in their own country the payment for what they buy elsewhere.* If therefore they flood us with their products, it is because they intend to be flooded in turn with ours. In this case, the best way of having a great deal for ourselves is to be free to choose, with respect to our purchases, between the following two procedures: direct production or indirect. No amount of British Machiavellianism will cause us to make the wrong choice.

Let us therefore stop this puerile nonsense of likening industrial competition to war. This is a false comparison, which draws all its fallacy from the fact that we isolate two rival productive sectors in order to assess the effects of competition. As soon as the effect produced on general well-being is taken into account, the analogy disappears.

In a battle the person killed is well and truly killed, and the army weakened accordingly. In industry a factory founders only to the extent that the whole productive system replaces what it used to produce, *with an increase in quantity.* Let us imagine a state of affairs in which, for each man killed on the spot, two sprang up full of strength and vigor. If there is a planet on which this happens, we would have to agree that war would be waged in conditions so different from those we see down here that it would not even merit the same name.

Well, this is the distinctive character of what has been so inappropriately christened *industrial warfare.*

Let the Belgians and English decrease the price of their iron if they can, let them continue to decrease it forevermore until it is reduced to nothing. In doing this, they may well extinguish one of our blast furnaces, i.e., "kill one of our soldiers"; but I challenge them to prevent a thousand other industries from immediately rising up and becoming more profitable than the one "removed from the field of battle" as a *necessary* consequence of these same low prices.

Let us conclude that domination through work is impossible and contradictory, since any superiority that appears in a nation is translated into low prices and results only in transmitting strength to all the others. Let us banish from political economy all the following expressions borrowed from a military vocabulary: *to fight on equal terms, to conquer, to crush, to stifle, to be defeated, invasion, or tribute.* What do all these expressions mean? If you squeeze them, nothing will come out. We are mistaken, as what comes out of such thinking are absurd errors and disastrous preconceived ideas. These are the words that stop nations from coming together in a peaceful, universal, and indissoluble alliance and humanity from making progress![3]

END OF THE SECOND SERIES

---

3. (Paillottet's note) If the author had lived longer, he would probably have published a third series of *Sophisms*. The main elements of this publication seem to us to have been prepared in the columns of *Le Libre-échange*. [We have gathered these articles as Paillottet noted and present them together as *Economic Sophisms* "Third Series."]

Economic Sophisms
"Third Series"

1. Recipes for Protectionism

PUBLISHING HISTORY:

Original title: "Recettes protectionnistes."
Place and date of first publication: *Le Libre-échange*,
    27 December 1846, no. 5, p. 40.
First French edition as book or pamphlet: Not applicable.
Location in Paillottet's edition of *OC:* Vol. 2. *Le Libre-échange*,
    pp. 358–63.
Previous translation: None.

27 December 1846

Since we published a report to the King on the great advantage we might draw from the general paralysis of right hands[1] as a means of encouraging work, it appears that a great many minds are looking for new recipes for protectionism. One of our subscribers has sent us a letter on this subject, which he intends to send to the Council of Ministers. We think it contains views that are worthy of attracting the attention of Statesmen, and we therefore make haste to reproduce it.

Dear Ministers,

At a time when Customs protection appears to be compromised, a grateful nation sees with confidence that you are concerned with resuscitating it in another form. This opens a wide field to the imagination. Your system of *gaucherie* (left-handedness)[2] has good points, but I do not consider that it is radical enough, and I am taking the liberty of suggesting to you means that are more heroic but still based on this fundamental axiom: *the intensity of work, notwithstanding its results, constitutes wealth.*

What is this about? Supplying new sustenance for human activity. That is

---

1. (Paillottet's note) See vol. 4, p. 258. (*OC*, vol. 4, p. 258, "La Main droite et la main gauche.") [ES2 16]

2. See ES2 16. In this sophism Bastiat describes a proposal that the king forbid his subjects' use of their right hands in order to increase wealth by increasing the amount of labor which must be exerted in order to do anything.

what it is lacking, and to achieve this we need to clear out the current means of satisfaction and create a great demand for products.

I originally thought that we might base a great deal of hope on *fire,* without neglecting war or pestilence. To start fires at the four corners of Paris[3] with a good west wind would certainly ensure the population the two major benefits that the protectionist regime has in view: *work and high prices,* or rather, *work by means of high prices.* Do you not see what an immense impetus the burning of Paris would give to national industry? Is there a single person who would not have enough work to last him twenty years? How many houses would there be to rebuild, items of furniture to restore, tools, instruments, fabrics, books, and pictures to replace! I can see from here the work that will move step by step and increase by itself like an avalanche, for a worker who is busy will give work to others, and these employ yet others. It is not you who will come forward to defend consumers, for you know only too well that the producer and consumer are one and the same. What holds up production? Obviously, existing products. Destroy them and production will take on a new lease of life. What constitutes our wealth? Our needs, since without needs there is no wealth; without disease, no doctors; without wars, no soldiers; without court cases, no lawyers and judges. If windows did not break, glaziers would be gloomy; if houses did not crumble, if furniture was indestructible, how many trades would be held up! To destroy is to make it necessary for you to replace. To increase the number of needs is to increase wealth. Therefore, spread fire, famine, war, pestilence, vice, and ignorance, and you will see all occupations flourish, for all will have a vast field of activity. Do you not say to yourselves that the scarcity and high price of iron make the fortune of ironmasters? Do you not prevent Frenchmen from buying iron cheaply? In doing this, are you not causing the interests of production to outweigh those of consumers? Are you not creating, so to speak, disease in order to give work to doctors? Be consistent, then. Either it is consumer interest that guides you, and therefore you allow iron to enter, or it is the interest of producers, and in this case you set Paris on fire. Either you believe that wealth consists in having more while working less, and therefore you allow iron to enter, or you think that it consists in having less with more work, and in this case, you burn Paris; for to say, as some do: "We do not want absolute

---

3. See WSWNS 1, pp. 406–7n4, on the protectionist Saint-Chamans's argument that the Great Fire of London in 1666 destroyed one million pounds' worth of capital stock, which permitted rebuilding and thus was a net gain for the English nation.

principles" is to say: "We want neither truth nor error, but a combination of the two: error when it is convenient and truth when it suits us."

However, Ministers, although this system of protection is in theory in perfect harmony with a prohibitionist regime, it may well be rejected by public opinion, which has not yet been sufficiently prepared and enlightened by experience and the findings of *Le Moniteur industriel.* You will consider it prudent to delay execution to better times. As you know, *there is overproduction and a surfeit of goods everywhere, the capacity to consume falls short of the capacity to produce, and markets are too restricted,* etc., etc. All this tells us that fire will soon be regarded as an effective remedy for a great many evils.

In the meantime, I have invented a new method of protection that I think has a great potential for success.

It consists simply in substituting direct for indirect encouragement.

Double all taxes; that would create a surplus of revenue of 1,400 to 1,500 million.[4] You should then share out these funds as subsidies to all the sectors of *national production* in order to support them, assist them, and enable them to resist foreign competition.

This is what will happen.

Let us suppose that French iron can be sold only at 350 francs a ton. Belgian iron is offered at 300 francs. You quickly take 55 francs from the subsidy fund and give them to our ironmaster. He then supplies his iron at 295 francs. Belgian iron is kept out, which is what we want. French iron covers its costs at 350 francs, which is also what we want.

Is foreign wheat impertinent enough to be on offer at 17 francs where domestic wheat requires 18 francs to be profitable? You immediately give 1 franc 50 centimes for each hectoliter of our wheat, which is then sold at 16 francs 50 centimes and sees off its competitor. You take the same action for woolen cloth, canvas, coal, cattle, etc., etc. In this way, national production will be protected, foreign competition driven away, a remunerative price assured, flooding of the market prevented, and all will be well.

"Well, good heavens! That is exactly what we are doing," you will tell me. "Between your plan and our practice there is not an atom of difference. It is the same principle, with the same result. It is just the procedure that is

---

4. In 1848 the state received a total of fr. 1.391 billion in revenue from taxes and charges, which was made up of fr. 420 million from direct taxes (land, personal, door and window, licenses), fr. 308 million from indirect taxes (mainly from the tax on alcohol, tobacco, and sugar), fr. 263 million from registrations and stamp duty, fr. 202 million from customs and the salt monopoly, fr. 51 million from the post office, plus other sources.

slightly different. The burden of protection that you place on the shoulders of taxpayers, we place on those of consumers which, in the end, comes to the same thing. We pass the subsidy from the general public directly to the sector protected. You, on the other hand, make it reach the sector protected from the general public via the Treasury, which is a superfluous step, and the only difference between your invention and ours."

Just a moment, Ministers; I agree that I am suggesting nothing new. My system and yours are identical. It is still the work done by everyone that subsidizes the work of each person, a pure illusion, or the work of a few, which is brazen injustice.

But let me show you the positive side of my procedure. Your indirect protection protects only a small number of industries effectively. I am offering you the means of protecting them all. Each one would have its share of the spoils. Farmers, manufacturers, traders, lawyers, doctors, civil servants, authors, artists, artisans, and workers all put their obole into the protection money box; is it not only fair that all should take something out of it?

No doubt that would be fair, but in practice . . . I see what you mean. You are going to say to me: "How can we double or triple taxes? How can we snatch 150 million from the postal services, 300 million from salt, or a billion from land taxes?"[5]

There is nothing simpler. First of all, through tariffs: you already take them from the general public, and you will understand that my procedure will cause you no embarrassment, apart from a few bookkeeping entries, for all of this will take place on paper.

In effect, according to our public law, each person contributes to taxes in proportion to his wealth.

According to the principles of justice, the State owes everyone *equal protection*.

The result of this is that my system, with regard to the Minister of Finances, will be reduced to opening an account for each citizen that will invariably be made up of two articles, as follows:

N. owes the Subsidy Fund 100 francs for his share of taxes.

N. is owed 90 francs by the Subsidy Fund for his share of protection.

---

5. According to the budget of 1848, the tax on letters and other charges raised fr. 51.5 million; customs duties on salt raised fr. 38.2 million and the domestic consumption tax on salt raised fr. 13.3 million (for a total from salt of fr. 51.5 million); and direct taxes levied on land raised fr. 279.5 million.

"But that is the same as if we did nothing at all!"

"That is very true. And you would equally do nothing through the Customs if you were able to use it to protect *everyone* equally."

"Then let us concentrate on merely protecting *a few.*"

"You could do this very well using my procedure. All you have to do is to designate in advance the classes that will be excluded when the funds from the tontine[6] are shared out, so that the others will get a larger share."

"That would be terribly unjust."

"You are doing this right now."

"At least we do not notice it."

"Nor does the general public. That is why they go along with it."

"What ought we to do?"

"Protect everyone or no one."

2. Two Principles

PUBLISHING HISTORY:

Original title: "Deux principes."
Place and date of first publication: *Le Libre-échange,* 7 February
   1847, no. 11, p. 88.
First French edition as book or pamphlet: Not applicable.
Location in Paillottet's edition of *OC:* Vol. 2. *Le Libre-échange,*
   pp. 363–70.
Previous translation: None.

"I have just read a masterpiece on free trade."

"What did you think of it?"

"I would have thought extremely highly of it if I had not read a masterpiece on protection immediately afterward."

---

6. A tontine is a voluntary investment or insurance scheme in which a group of individuals each contribute a certain amount to a group fund from which they receive an annual payment. Upon the death of one of the contributors, that person's contribution is shared among the survivors. The fund is wound up upon the death of the second-last person, with the survivor receiving the full amount left in the fund. Tontines were used in the seventeenth and eighteenth centuries by the French and other governments to manage state debt before the invention of the financing of modern public debt, which was initiated during the Napoleonic wars by the British government. See A. Legoyt, "Tontines," in *DEP* 2:742–48.

"You prefer the latter, then?"

"Yes, if I had not read the former just before."[1]

"Well then, which of the two won you over?"

"Neither, or rather, both, for when I had finished, like Henri IV[2] on leaving a court hearing, I said: 'Upon my word, they were both right!'"

"So, you are no further forward?"

"It is fortunate that I have not gone further backward! For I have since come across a third work titled *Economic contradictions,* in which *Freedom* and *Non-Freedom, Protection* and *Non-Protection* are arranged in fine style.[3] Truly, Sir, my head is swimming.

Vo solcando un mar crudele
Senza vele
E senza sarte.[4]

"East and West, Zenith and Nadir, all are confused in my head, and I have not the smallest of compasses to find my way in the middle of this labyrinth. This reminds me of the sorry position I found myself in a few years ago."

1. This is Bastiat's amusing reference to his own work and that of his archrival, the anarchist socialist Pierre-Joseph Proudhon. Bastiat's own work debunking economic fallacies, or "sophisms" as he called them, appeared in January 1846. It is of course strongly in favor of free trade and the free market. The same liberal publisher, Guillaumin, published later in 1846 a two-volume work by Proudhon from the very opposite perspective, *Système des contradictions économiques, ou, Philosophie de la misère* (System of Economic Contradictions, or the Philosophy of Misery). Note also that in the dialogue at the end of ES2 13, pp. 224–26, the people cheer vociferously for whatever opinion they last heard.

2. Henri IV (1562–1610) was a Huguenot (French Protestant) who was active in the wars of religion before becoming king, as a precondition for which he had to convert to Catholicism. In 1598 he enacted the Edict of Nantes, which granted religious toleration to the Protestants in an attempt to end the religious wars in France. In 1610 he was assassinated by a Catholic fanatic. His edict of toleration was revoked in October 1685 by Louis XIV.

3. Bastiat might be referring here to the work of the Anti–Corn Law advocate Thomas Perronet Thompson, whose work was well known to the Economists. He wrote many best-selling "free trade catechisms," pamphlets in which he listed arguments for and against free trade and protection in well-organized columns of text.

4. This verse comes from act 1, scene 15 of the opera *Artaserse,* written by Metastasio and set to music by numerous composers in the eighteenthth century. The translation of the verse Bastiat quotes is "I sail across a cruel sea without sail or rigging" (*Opere scelte di Pietro Metastasio* 1:147).

"Tell me about it, please."

"Eugène and I[5] were hunting in the immense Landes between Bordeaux and Bayonne, on which nothing, no trees or fences, limits the view. There was a heavy mist. We made so many turns this way and that in pursuit of a hare that at length . . ."

"You caught it?"

"No, it caught us, for the rascal succeeded in disorienting us totally. In the evening, an unknown road came into view. To my great surprise, Eugène and I started in opposite directions. 'Where are you going?' I asked him. 'To Bayonne.' 'But you are going toward Bordeaux.' 'You are joking. The wind is from the North and is freezing our shoulders.' 'That is because it is blowing from the South.' 'But this morning the sun rose there.' 'No, it appeared here.' 'Do you not see the Pyrenées in front of us?' 'Those are clouds on the edge of the sea.' In short, we just could not agree."

"How did it end?"

"We sat down on the side of the road, waiting for a passer-by to save us. Soon a traveler came along; 'Sir,' I said, 'my friend here claims that Bayonne is to the left and I say it is to the right.' 'Fine Sirs,' he replied, 'both of you are a little right and a little wrong. Beware of *rigid ideas* and *dogmatic systems*. Good evening!' And he left. I was tempted to throw a stone at his back when I saw a second traveler coming toward us. I hailed him extremely politely and said: 'Good man, we are disoriented. Tell us whether we should go this way or that to return to Bayonne.' 'That is not the question,' he told us; 'the essential thing is not to cover the distance that separates you from Bayonne in a single bound *without a transition stage*. That would not be wise, and you would risk falling flat on your face.' 'Sir,' I said, 'it is you who are not answering the question. As for our faces, you are too interested in them. You can be sure that we will take care of them ourselves. However, before deciding whether to walk quickly or slowly, we have to know in which direction to walk.' Nevertheless, the rogue persisted: 'Walk steadily,' he said, 'and never

5. Bastiat mentions only one "Eugène" in his correspondence but gives no surname. It is in a letter to his childhood friend Félix Coudroy, who obviously knew whom he meant. In a letter dated Rome, 11 November 1850, Bastiat states: "What is more, I have met Eugène again and he comes to spend part of the day with me. So, if I go out, I can always give my walks an interesting aim. I would ask for one thing only, and that is to be relieved of this piercing pain in the larynx; this constant suffering distresses me" (CW1, pp. 288–89).

put one foot in front of the other without reflecting carefully on the consequences. Bon voyage!' It was fortunate for him that I had buckshot in my gun; if it had been just bird shot, frankly I would have peppered at least the rump of his horse."

"To punish the horseman! What distributive justice!"

"A third traveler came along. He appeared to be serious and staid. I took this to be a good sign and asked him my question: which was the way to Bayonne? 'Diligent hunter,' he said to me, 'you have to distinguish between theory and practice. Study the lay of the land, and if theory tells you that Bayonne is downward, go upward.'

"'Thundering heavens!' I shouted, 'Have you all sworn . . . ?'"

"Do not, yourself, swear. And tell me what decision you took."

"That of following the first half of the last piece of advice. We examined the external appearance of the heather and the direction of flow of the water. A flower made us agree. 'See,' I said to Eugène 'it normally turns toward the sun

And still seeks the gaze of Phoebus.[6]

"'Therefore, Bayonne is there.' He yielded to this gracious arbitration, and we went on our way in quite good humor. But what a surprise! Eugène found it difficult *to leave things as they were* and the universe, doing a half turn in his imagination, constantly put him back under the influence of the same error."

"What happened to your friend with regard to geography often happens to you with regard to political economy. The map turns around in your mind and you find all the dispensers of advice equally convincing."

"What should I do, then?"

"What you did: learn to *orient yourself.*"

"But in the heathlands of political economy,[7] will I find a poor little flower to guide me?"

"No, but you will find a principle."

---

6. Bastiat quotes a line from Évariste de Parny's poem "Les Fleurs" (Flowers, 1788). The full verse is: "In the hyacinth flower a beautiful child breathes; / There I recognize the son of Pierus. / He still seeks the gaze of Phoebus; / He still fears the breath of Zephyrus" (Parny, *Œuvres choisies de Parny,* "Les Fleurs," pp. 154–55).

7. Bastiat uses the phrase *les landes* of political economy to suggest that just as he and Eugène were disoriented and lost in the Landes, in southwest France, one could also get lost in the wilderness or marshlands of political economy.

"That is not as pretty. Is there really an idea that is clear and simple and which can be used as a leading thread through the labyrinth?"[8]

"Yes, there is."

"Tell it to me, please!"

"I prefer you to tell it to yourself. Tell me. What is wheat good for?"

"Heavens above! To be eaten!"

"That is a principle."

"You call that a principle? In that case, I often make principles without knowing it, just as M. Jourdain[9] spoke in prose."

"It is a principle, I tell you, and one that is most ignored, although it is the most true of all those ever included in a body of doctrine. And tell me, has wheat not another use?"

"For what else would it be useful, if not to be eaten?"

"Think hard."

"Ah! I have found it! To provide work for the ploughman."

"You have indeed found it. That is another principle."

"Good heavens! I did not know it was so easy to make principles. I am making one with each word I speak!"

"Is it not true that every imaginable product has the two types of *utility* that you have just attributed to wheat?"

"What do you mean?"

"What use is coal?"

"It supplies us with heat, light, and strength."

"Has it no other use?"

"It also provides work to miners, haulers, and sailors."

"And has woolen cloth not two types of utility?"

"Yes, indeed. It protects you from cold and rain. What is more, it gives work to shepherds, spinners, and weavers."

8. In Greek mythology the Minotaur was a creature half man and half bull which lived in a maze or labyrinth on the island of Crete. In the power struggle with his brothers for control of the throne of Crete, Minos was given a white bull as a sign of support by the god Poseidon. Instead of killing it as he promised, Minos kept it. As punishment his wife was made to fall in love with the bull, producing the Minotaur, which had to be caged in the labyrinth because of its monstrous behaviour. A yearly tribute of Athenian youths and maidens was sent to be sacrificed as food for the Minotaur. The Athenian hero Theseus was able to kill the Minotaur with the assistance of Ariadne, the oldest daughter of King Minos, who told him to use a thread to navigate his way out of the labyrinth once he had killed the beast.

9. See ES1 Conclusion, pp. 105–6n6.

"To prove to you that you have genuinely produced two principles, allow me to express them in a general form. The first says: *Products are made to be consumed,* while the second says: *Products are made to be produced.*"

"Here I am beginning to understand a little less."

"I will therefore change the theme:

"*First principle:* Men work in order to consume.

"*Second principle:* Men consume in order to work.

"*First principle:* Wheat is made for stomachs.

"*Second principle:* Stomachs are made for wheat.

"*First principle:* Means are made for an end.

"*Second principle:* The end is made for the means.

"*First principle:* Ploughmen plough so that people can eat.

"*Second principle:* People eat so that the ploughman can plough.

"*First principle:* Oxen go before the cart.

"*Second principle:* The cart goes before the oxen."

"Heavens above! When I said: *Wheat is useful because we eat it* and then: *Wheat is useful because it is cultivated,* was I putting forward, without realizing it, this torrent of principles?

> Heavens! *Sir,* I did not believe I was
> As *learned* as I am."[10]

"Hold on a little! You have merely uttered two principles, and I have played variations on a theme."[11]

"What on earth do you mean?"

"I want you to be able to tell north from south on a compass in case you ever become lost in the labyrinth of economics. Each of them will guide you

---

10. This line comes from act 2, scene 6 of Molière's play *Le Misanthrope* (1666), where the misanthrope, Alceste, is trying to explain why it is so hard to tell powerful individuals (like a king) that their poetry is badly written. He tells his friends that he could be tortured or hanged for doing so, and when they laugh, he replies, "Gracious me! Sirs, I didn't think I was as witty as I am." As Bastiat often does, he inserts his own words into a well-known poem or play to make his points, replacing *plaisant* (witty) with *savant* (learned). See *Théâtre complet de Molière* 4:108.

11. This is another reference to a play, this time by Beaumarchais. In act 4 of the *The Barber of Seville* (1775), Don Basile, a singing teacher, says to Dr. Bartholo that when he is unable to understand an argument he resorts to using proverbs such as "What is good to take, is good to keep." He then says, "Yes, I arrange several little proverbs with variations, just like that" (Beaumarchais, *Théâtre de Beaumarchais,* p. 254).

in an opposite direction, one to the temple of truth, the other to the region of error."

"Do you mean to say that the two schools, the liberal and the protectionist, that divide opinion, differ solely in that one *puts the oxen before the cart* and the other *the cart before the oxen?*"

"Exactly. I say that if we go back to the *exact point* that divides these two schools, we find it in the true or false use of the word *utility*. As you have just said yourself, each product has two types of usefulness: one relates to the consumer and consists in *satisfying needs;* the other relates to the producer and consists in *providing an opportunity for work.* We can therefore call the first of these forms of utility *fundamental* and the second *occasional.* One is the compass of true science and the other that of false science. If you are unfortunate enough, as is only too frequent, to ride a horse using the second principle to guide you, that is to say to consider products merely from the point of view of their relationship with producers, you are traveling with a compass that is back to front, and you become increasingly lost. You become enmeshed in the realms of *privileges, monopolies, antagonism, national jealousies, dissipation, regulations,* and *restrictive and invasive policies,* in a word, you introduce a series of consequences which undermine humanity, constantly mistaking the wrong for the right, and seeking in new wrongs the remedy for the wrongs that legislation has brought about. If, on the other hand, the interest of the consumer, or rather that of *general consumption,* is taken as a torch and compass right from the start, we progress toward liberty, equality, fraternity,[12] universal peace, well-being, savings, order, and all the progressive principles of the human race."

"What! These two axioms: *Wheat is made to be eaten* and *wheat is made to be grown* can lead to such opposing results?"

"Yes indeed. You know the story of the two ships that were traveling in convoy. A storm arose. When it was over, nothing had changed in the universe, except that one of the two compasses had veered to the South as a result of the electricity. But this was enough to make one ship go the wrong way for eternity, at least while it followed this false direction."

12. Bastiat is here taking the slogan of the French Revolution, *Liberté, égalité, fraternité,* which had been appropriated by the Jacobins in the 1790s and then by the socialists afterward, and turning it into his own liberal rallying cry for the 1840s, which might be phrased as follows: "Liberty, equality, fraternity, tranquility, prosperity, frugality, and stability."

"I must admit that I am a thousand leagues away from understanding the importance you attach to what you call the two principles (although I have had the honor of finding them), and I would be very relieved if you would let me know your thoughts in their entirety."

"Well then! Listen! I divide my subject into . . ."

"Mercy me! I have no time to listen to you. But next Sunday I am all yours."

"I would like, however, . . ."

"I am in a hurry. Farewell."

"While I have you here . . ."

"You do not have me any more. See you on Sunday."[13]

"On Sunday, then. My goodness, how hard listeners find it to focus!"

"Heavens! What heavy going lecturers make it!"

3. M. Cunin-Gridaine's Logic

PUBLISHING HISTORY:

> Original title: "La Logique de M. Cunin-Gridaine."
> Place and date of first publication: *Le Libre-échange,* 2 May
> 1847, no. 23, p. 184.
> First French edition as book or pamphlet: Not applicable.
> Location in Paillottet's edition of *OC:* Vol. 2. *Le Libre-échange,*
> pp. 370–73.
> Previous translation: None.

Speaking about the two associations[1] that have been formed, one to demand that the general public be held for ransom and the other to demand that the general public not be held for ransom, M. Cunin-Gridaine said the following:

"Nothing demonstrates exaggeration better than the exaggeration that opposes it. It is the best way of showing calm and disinterested minds where truth lies, since truth is never divorced from moderation."

---

13. (Paillottet's note) Sunday was the day of the week on which *Le Libre-échange* appeared.

1. L'Association pour la défense du travail national (Association for the Defense of National Employment) and L'Association pour la liberté des échanges (the Free Trade Association).

It is certain, according to Aristotle, that truth is to be found between two opposing exaggerations. The important thing is to ascertain whether two contrary statements are equally exaggerated, without which the judgment that is to be made, while appearing to be impartial, will in fact be inequitable.

Pierre and *Jean* are pleading their cause before the judge in a small town.

Pierre, the plaintiff, moved that he should beat *Jean* every day.

Jean, the defendant, moved that he should not be beaten at all.

The judge pronounced the following sentence:

"Seeing that nothing proves exaggeration better than the exaggeration that opposes it, let us cut the quarrel in half and say that Pierre will beat Jean, but only on odd days."

Jean appealed against this, as was to be expected, but having learned logic, he was careful this time not to move that his brutish adversary's case be simply *dismissed.*

Therefore, when Pierre's lawyer read the introductory plea to the court, it ended with these words: "May it please the court to allow Pierre to rain a hail of blows on Jean's shoulders."

Jean's lawyer replied with this equally conventional request: "May it please the court to allow Jean to take his revenge on Pierre's back."

The precaution was necessary. Suddenly, justice found itself placed between two forms of exaggeration. It decided that Jean would no longer be beaten by Pierre nor Pierre by Jean. Basically, Jean did not want any other result.

Let us imitate this example. Let us take our precautions against M. Cunin-Gridaine's logic.

What is involved? The *Pierres* of the rue Hauteville[2] are pleading for the right to hold the general public for ransom. The *Jeans* of the rue Choiseul are naively pleading for the general public not to be held for ransom. At which the Minister has gravely pronounced that *truth* and *moderation* are at the midpoint between these two claims.

Since the judgment has to be based on the assumption that the association for free trade is exaggerating, what this association can best do is to exaggerate in fact and place itself at the same distance from truth as the prohibitionist association, so that the exact center coincides more or less with justice.

---

2. (Paillottet's note) The offices of *Le Libre-échange* were in the rue de Choiseul and those of *Le Moniteur industriel* in the rue Hauteville.

For this reason, while one side demands a tax on consumers for the benefit of producers, the other, instead of wasting its time opposing a refusal, will formally demand a tax on producers for the benefit of consumers.

And when ironmasters say: "For each quintal of iron that I deliver to the general public, I expect them to pay me a premium of 20 francs, in addition to the price,"

The general public should be quick to reply: "For every quintal of iron that we bring in from abroad, free of duty, we expect ironmasters in France to pay us a premium of 20 francs."

Then it would be true to say that the pretensions of both parties are equally exaggerated, and the Minister would throw them out, saying, "Go away, and do not inflict taxes on one another," at least if he is faithful to his line of logic.

Faithful to his line of logic? Alas, the entire line of his logic lies in the exposition of motives; it no longer appears again in the acts themselves. After having proposed in fact that injustice and justice are two forms of exaggeration, that those who want protectionist duties to be maintained and those who demand their removal are equally far from the truth, what should the Minister[3] do to remain consistent? He should place himself at the center, and imitate the village judge who passed a sentence of half a beating;[4] in a word, reduce protectionist duties *by half.* He has not even touched them. (*See number 50.*)[5]

His dialectic, commented on by his actions, amounts to this: Pierre, you request to be allowed to give four strokes: Jean, you request not to receive any.

The *truth,* which is never divorced from *moderation,* lies between these two requests. According to my line of logic, I should authorize only two strokes; following my inclination, I will allow four, as before. And for the execution of my sentence, I will make the legal authorities available to Pierre at Jean's expense.

But the finest bit of the story is that Pierre leaves the court furious because

3. Laurent Cunin-Gridaine.

4. Bastiat uses the French *la demi-bastonnade. Bastonnade* was a form of judicial punishment where a rod was used to beat a person, usually on the back. When he was a deputy in the Constituent Assembly, Bastiat voted in September 1848 against the reintroduction of corporal punishment and for the abolition of the death penalty.

5. ES3 5.

the judge has dared openly to compare his exaggeration with that of Jean. (See *Le Moniteur industriel.*)

4. One Profit versus Two Losses

PUBLISHING HISTORY:

> Original title: "Un Profit contre deux pertes."
> Place and date of first publication: *Le Libre-échange,* 9 May 1847, no. 24, p. 192.
> First French edition as book or pamphlet: Not applicable.
> Location in Paillottet's edition of *OC:* Vol. 2. *Le Libre-échange,* pp. 377–84.
> Previous translation: None.

It is now seventeen years since a political writer, whom I will not name, directed an argument against protection by the Customs Service in an algebraic form, which he called *the double incidence of loss.*[1]

This argument made something of an impression. Those benefiting from privilege made haste to refute it, but it so happened that all they did to this end served only to elucidate the argument, to make it increasingly invincible and, what is more, make it popular, to the extent that these days, in the country in which this took place, protection no longer has any partisans.

Perhaps people will ask me why I do not mention the name of the author? Because my philosophy master taught me that this sometimes very adversely compromises the effect of the quotation.[2]

This master imposed on us a course peppered with passages some of which were taken from Voltaire and Rousseau and invariably preceded by the following formula: "A famous author said, etc." As a few volumes of these

---

1. Bastiat is referring to an idea first developed by the anti–Corn Law campaigner Thomas Perronet Thompson (1783–1869). Bastiat says here that Thompson's argument about "the double incidence of loss" appeared seventeen years earlier, in 1830, but no new work by Thompson appeared in that year. The phrase does appear in his "A running commentary on anti-commercial fallacies" which was published in 1834. See "The Double Incidence of Loss," in appendix 1, "Further Aspects of Bastiat's Life and Thought."

2. (Paillottet's note) The name that the author does not mention is that of an eminent member of the English League, Colonel Perronnet [sic] Thompson.

tiresome writers had slipped into our school, we were well aware to whom he was referring. We therefore never failed, when reciting a lesson, to replace the formula with these words: Rousseau said or Voltaire said. But instantly, the teacher, raising his arms to the sky, would cry out: "Do not mention names, friend B.; you have to learn that many people will admire the phrase but would consider it dreadful if they knew where it came from." It was at the time when opinion inspired our great songwriter,[3] or I ought rather to say, our great poet, to pen the following chorus:

> It is Voltaire's fault,
> It is Rousseau's fault.[4]

I will therefore suppress the name of the author and the algebraic form and reproduce the argument, which is limited to establishing that any advantage flowing from tariffs will of necessity bring about the following:

1. A profit for one industry;
2. An equal loss for another industry;
3. An equal loss for the consumer.

These are the *direct* and *necessary* effects of protection. In all justice, and to complete the assessment, we ought in addition to impute to it a number of *ancillary losses,* such as the cost of surveillance, expensive formalities, commercial uncertainty, fluctuations in duties, aborted operations, the increased likelihood of war, smuggling, repression, etc.

However, I will limit myself here to the *necessary* consequences of protection.

A short story will perhaps clarify the explanation of our problem.

An ironmaster needed wood for his factory. He had negotiated with a poor woodcutter who was not very educated and who had to chop wood one day a week, from morning to night, for 40 sous.[5]

This may seem curious, but it so happened that by dint of hearing talk on

---

3. Pierre-Jean de Béranger.

4. These lines come from the satirical song by Béranger "Mandement des vicaires généraux de Paris" (Pastoral from the Vicars General of Paris, 1817), which mocks the ruling elites of the early Restoration who blamed every problem of the day on the ideas of Rousseau and Voltaire. A typical verse is the following: "In order to teach children that they were born to be slaves, shackles were fitted when they first learned to move. If mankind is free in the cradle, it is the fault of Rousseau; if reason enlightens them, then it is the fault of Voltaire" (Béranger, *Chansons de Béranger,* pp. 442–47).

5. 1 franc = 20 sous.

protection, domestic industry, the superiority of foreign goods, cost prices, etc., our woodcutter became an economist in the style of *Le Moniteur industriel,* so effectively that a bright idea entered his mind at the same time as the thought of a monopoly entered his heart.

He went to find the ironmaster and said to him:

"Master, you give me 2 francs for one day of work; in the future you will give me 4 francs and I will work for 2 days."

"Friend," replied the ironmaster, "I have enough wood with the wood you split in one day."

"I know," said the woodcutter, "and so I have taken steps. Look at my axe; see how blunted and ragged it is. I assure you that I will take two full days to split the wood that I split now in one day."[6]

"I will lose 2 francs in this arrangement."

"Yes, but I, for my part, will gain them and, with regard to the wood and you, I am the producer and you are just a consumer. A consumer! Does he warrant any pity?"

"And if I proved to you that apart from the 40 sous it will cause me to lose, this agreement will also cost another worker 40 sous?"

"Then I will say that his loss balances my gain, and that the final result of my invention is that you, and consequently the nation as a whole, will suffer a clear loss of 2 francs. But who is this worker who will have something to complain about?"

"Jacques the gardener, for example, whom I will no longer give the opportunity to earn 40 sous a week as he does now, since I will have already spent the 40 sous; and if I do not deprive Jacques of this sum, I will be depriving someone else."

"That is true; I give up and will go to sharpen my axe. Incidentally, if because of my axe, work to the value of 2 francs is lost to the world, that is a loss and it has to fall on someone ... Pardon me, Master, I have just had an idea. If you allow me to earn these 2 francs, I will enable the café owner to earn them and this gain will compensate the loss to Jacques."

"My friend, you would be doing only what Jacques would do himself as long as I employed him and what he would no longer do if I dismissed him, as you are asking me to do."

"That is true; I am defeated and can clearly see that there is no profit to the nation to be had from dulling the blades of axes."

6. See a similar story in ES2 3.

However, our woodcutter went over the problem in his head, while chopping wood. He said to himself: "Nonetheless, I have heard it said to the boss a hundred times that it was beneficial to protect producers at the expense of consumers. It is true that he has pointed out here another producer whom I had not considered."

A short time later, he went to the ironmaster and said to him:

"Master, I need 20 kilograms of iron, and here is 5 francs to pay for it."

"My friend, for this price, I can give you only 10 kilograms."

"That is a shame for you since I know an Englishman who will give me the 20 kilograms I need for 5 francs."

"He is a scoundrel."

"So be it."

"An egoist, a perfidious man who acts in his own interest."

"So be it."

"An individualist, a bourgeois, a trader who does not know what self-denial, self-sacrifice, fraternity, or philanthropy are."

"So be it, but he is giving me 20 kilograms of iron for 5 francs while you, as fraternal, self-sacrificing, and philanthropic as you are, you are giving me only 10."

"That is because his machines are more advanced than mine."

"Oh! Oh! Mr. Philanthropist! So you are working with a dull axe and you want me to bear the loss?"

"My friend, you have to, so that my industry may be favored. In this world, we must not always think of ourselves and our own interests."

"But it seems to me that it is always your turn to think of your interests. In the last few days you have not wanted to pay me for using a bad axe, and today you want me to pay you for using bad machines."

"My friend, that is quite different! My industry is a national one and of great importance."

"With regard to the 5 francs in question, it is not important for you to gain them if I have to lose them."

"And do you no longer remember that when you suggested to me that my wood be split with a blunt axe I proved to you that in addition to my loss, an additional loss, equal to mine, would be suffered by poor Jacques, and each of these losses would equal your profit, which in the end would amount to a clear loss for the nation as a whole of 2 francs? For the two cases to be equal, you would have to prove that if my gain and your loss were in balance there would still be loss caused to a third party."

"I do not see that this proof is very necessary, for according to what you say, whether I buy from you or the Englishman, the nation is not bound to lose or gain anything. And in this case, I do not see why I should spend for your benefit and not mine what I have earned through the sweat of my brow. What is more, I think I can prove that if I give you 10 francs for your 20 kilograms of iron, I would lose 5 francs and someone else would lose 5 francs; you would gain only 5 francs, with the result that the entire nation would suffer a clear loss of 5 francs."

"I am intrigued at the prospect of listening to your chopping down my proof."

"And if I split it neatly, will you agree that your claim is unjust?"

"I do not promise to agree with your case, you know, because where these matters are concerned, I am a little like the gambler in the comedy,[7] and I say to political economy:

> You may well convince me, O Science, my enemy,
> But make me admit it, there I challenge you!

"But let us take a look at your argument."

"First of all, you have to know one thing. The Englishman has no intention of taking my 100-sou coin back to his own country. If we strike a bargain (the ironmaster remarks *as an aside: I'll sort that out*), he has asked me to buy two pairs of gloves for 5 francs, which I will give him in return for his iron."

"That is not important. Get on with your proof."

"Very well, let us now make the calculation. With regard to the 5 francs that represent the natural price for the iron, it is clear that French production will be neither more nor less stimulated overall whether I give this money to you to make the iron directly or whether I give it to the glove maker to supply me with the gloves the Englishman has requested in exchange for the iron."

"That sounds reasonable."

"So let us leave aside these first 100 sous. There remains the problem of the other 5 francs. You say that if I agree to lose them, you would gain them and your industry would benefit by this amount."

---

7. These lines come from act 1, scene 4, of *Le Joueur* (The Gambler, 1696), a comedy by J. F. Regnard (1685–1709). Bastiat changes the original "fortune" to "science" in order to suit his purpose in this sophism. In the original, Valère, a compulsive gambler, says, "You can make me lose, O Fortune, my enemy! But to make me pay, hell, I challenge you! Because I don't have a sou" (Regnard, *Œuvres de Regnard* 1:79).

"Doubtless."

"But if I reach agreement with the Englishman, these 100 sous would remain in my pocket. As it happens, I find that I have a pressing need for a pair of shoes. Here then is a third person, the shoemaker, who is concerned by this matter. If I deal with you, your industry would be stimulated to the extent of 5 francs; that of the shoemaker would be depressed to the extent of 5 francs, which is the exact balance. And in the end, I would not have any shoes; so that my loss would be clear and the nation, in my person, would have lost 5 francs."

"Not a bad line of reasoning for a woodcutter! But you have lost sight of one thing, and that is that the 5 francs you will cause the shoemaker to earn, if you traded with the Englishman, I would myself allow him to earn if you traded with me."

"I beg your pardon, Master, but you yourself taught me the other day that I should beware of this confusion.

"I have 10 francs.

"If I trade with you I will give them to you, and you will do what you want with them.

"If I trade with the Englishman, I will distribute them thus: 5 francs to the glove maker and 5 francs to the shoemaker, and they will do what they like with them.

"The subsequent consequences of the circulation of these 10 francs, by you in one case and by the glove maker and shoemaker in the other, are identical and cancel each other out. There should be no question of this.

"There is therefore just one difference in all this. Following the first bargain, I would not have any shoes; following the second, I *would have*."

The ironmaster goes off grumbling: "Ah, where the devil is political economy taking us? Two good laws will stop all this nonsense; a Customs law that will give me the power of the State, since I will not be in the right, and a law on education that will send all the young people to study society in Sparta or Rome.[8] It is not a good thing for the people to have such a clear view of its affairs."

---

8. Bastiat had a deep dislike of the classics and disapproved of teaching them in the schools. He thought that the Greek and Roman authors whom schoolchildren had to read had served in the army, held high political office, owned slaves, and disdained most economic activity. He regarded them as conquerors and plunderers who should not be used as models. See his many references to the classics in his correspondence (CW1, pp. 11–302).

5. On Moderation

PUBLISHING HISTORY:

Original title: "De la moderation."
Place and date of first publication: *Le Libre-échange,* 23 May
  1847, no. 26, p. 201.
First French edition as book or pamphlet: Not applicable.
Location in Paillottet's edition of *OC:* Vol. 2. *Le Libre-échange,*
  pp. 343–48.
Previous translation: None.

We are criticized for being too dogmatic and extreme, and this accusation, carefully propagated by our opponents, has been echoed by men whose talents and high position give them authority, M. Charles Dupin, a peer of France, and M. Cunin-Gridaine, a Minister.[1]

And this is because we have the audacity to think that wanting to make men wealthy by restricting them and tightening social bonds by isolating nations is a vain and foolish enterprise; that the collection of taxes cannot be established without both the freedom of commerce and freedom of work being hindered in some way. These incidental restrictions are in this instance one of the drawbacks of taxation, drawbacks which may even cause the tax itself to be abandoned. But to see in them as such a source of wealth and a cause of well-being and, on this premise, to strengthen and increase their number systematically, no longer to fill the Treasury but at the Treasury's expense, to believe that restrictions have in themselves a productive virtue and result in more intensive work, better shared out, more certain in its remuneration and more capable of equalizing returns, that is an absurd *theory,* one that could lead only to an absurd *practice.* For this reason, we are opposing both of them, not in an extreme way but with zeal and perseverance.

1. At the time Bastiat wrote this article, a debate was under way in the Chamber on a proposal to reform French tariffs in light of the abolition of the Corn Laws by Britain in May of the previous year (1846). The free traders were optimistic, as a senior minister (probably Thiers) had expressed some sympathy for the idea. Bastiat's Free Trade Association (founded in February 1846) was lobbying hard for free trade, and the Association for the Defense of National Employment (founded in October 1846) was lobbying hard to maintain the existing policy of protectionism. The latter was able to outmaneuver the free traders when a bill came before the Chamber in March 1847 by having the matter sent to Committee, which was stacked with supporters of protectionism. The Committee recommended to the Chamber in July 1847 not to change French tariff policy, thus defeating the free traders.

After all, what is moderation?

We are convinced that *two plus two makes four* and we believe that we are required to say this clearly. Do people want us to use circumlocutions? That we should say, for example: "It may be that two plus two makes approximately four. We suspect that this may be so but we are not hastening to affirm this, especially since certain leading figures believed it was in their interest to base the laws of the country on this other premise, which appears to contradict ours: *three minus one equals four*."

Accusing us of dogmatism and forbidding us from proving the truth of our thesis is to want the country never to open its eyes. We will not enter the trap.

Oh! If we were told: "It is very true that *the straight line is shortest*. But what can you do? For a long time it was believed to be the longest. The nation is accustomed to following a curved line. It spends its time and strength doing this, but we have to win over this wasted time and strength little by little and gradually," we would be considered to be very laudably moderate. What are we asking for? Just one thing: for the public to see clearly what it is losing by following a curved line. After this, and if, in the full knowledge of what the curved line was costing them in tax, privations, vexations, and wasted effort, they only wished to leave it gradually or if they even persisted in keeping to it, we could not help it. Our mission is to set out the truth. We do not believe, like the socialists, that the people are an inert mass and that the driving force is in the person who describes the phenomenon, but that it is in the person who suffers or who benefits from it. Could we be more moderate?

Other people accuse us of being extreme for another reason. They say it is because we are attacking all forms of protection at once. Why not have recourse to some guile? Why antagonize agriculture, manufacturing, the merchant navy, and the working classes all simultaneously, to say nothing of the political parties who are always ready to pay court to numbers and strength?

We consider that it is in this that we show our moderation and sincerity.

How many times have people not tried, doubtless with good intentions, to induce us to abandon the terrain of principles! We were advised to attack the abuse of the protection given to a few factories.

"You would be supported by agriculture," we were told, "and with this powerful auxiliary you would overcome the most exorbitant of the industrial monopolies and initially one of the most solid links of the chain that is wearing you down. Next, you can move against the agricultural interests in the knowledge that this time you would have the support of the manufacturing industry."[2]

Those who give us this advice are forgetting one thing, which is that we do not aspire so much to overturn the protective regime as to enlighten the general public about this regime, or rather, although the first of these tasks is the aim, the second appears to us to be the essential means.

Well, what force would our arguments have had if we had carefully removed from the argument the very principle of protection? And, by implicating it, how could we avoid arousing the susceptibilities of farmers? Do people believe that manufacturers would have left us free to choose our arguments? That they would not have brought us around to expressing our views on the question of principle and to say explicitly or implicitly that protection is wrong by its very nature? Once the word was uttered, farmers would have been on their guard and we, may we be excused the expression, would have paddled about in subtle precautions and distinctions in the midst of which our polemics would have lost all their force and our sincerity any credit it may have had.

Next, the advice itself implies that, at least in the opinion of those who give it and perhaps in ours, protection is a desirable thing, since in order to wrench it away from one of the country's productive sectors, one would have to make use of some other sector that would be led to believe that its own particular privileges would be respected, since it is suggested to use the farmers to beat the manufacturers and vice versa. Well, that is not what we want. On the contrary, we are committed to the struggle because we believe protection to be bad for everybody.

The task we have set ourselves is to make this understood and widely known. "But in that case," it will be said, "the struggle will be lengthy." All the better if it is lengthy, if that is what is needed to enlighten the public.

Let us suppose that the trick that is being suggested to us is fully successful (a success that we believe to be an illusion); let us suppose that in the first year the landowners in the two Chambers sweep away all industrial privileges and that in the second year, in order to avenge themselves, the manufacturers have all the privileges of the farmers taken away.

What would happen? In two years, free trade would be ensconced in our laws, but would it be so in our minds? Is it not clear that at the first crisis,

2. (Paillottet's note) See no. 5. (*OC,* vol. 2, p. 15, "D'un plan de campagne proposé à l'Association du libre-échange.") [In CW6 (forthcoming)]

the first uprising, the first evidence of suffering, the country would rise up against a reform that was badly understood, attribute its misfortunes to foreign competition, and invoke, and swiftly and triumphantly achieve, a return to customs protection? For how many years or centuries perhaps, would this short period of freedom accompanied by accidental suffering not dominate the arguments of protectionists? They would be careful to base their reasoning on the assumption that there is an essential link between these sufferings and freedom, just as they do today with regard to the Methuen[3] and 1786 treaties.[4]

It is a very remarkable thing that, in the middle of the crisis that is devastating England, not a single voice is raised to attribute it to the liberal reforms accomplished by Sir Robert Peel. On the contrary, everyone feels that without these measures England would be in the throes of convulsions in the face of which the imagination recoils in horror. Where does this trust in freedom come from? From the work carried out by the League[5] for many years. From the fact that it has made every intelligent mind familiar with the notions of public economy. From the fact that the reform was already germinating in people's minds and that the bills by Parliament were only sanctioning a national will that was strong and enlightened.

Finally, we have rejected this advice for reasons of justice, as tempting as the *French fury in battle*[6] might find impatience.

We are fully convinced that by relieving the pressure of a protectionist

3. The Treaty of Methuen (named after one of the negotiators, John Methuen) was a commercial treaty between England and Portugal signed in 1703 during the War of the Spanish Succession (1701–14). It allowed for the free entry of English textiles into Portugal and was thus wrongly accused of having caused a decline in the Portuguese economy. In return, Portuguese wine ("port") was subject to lower tariffs than French wine, thus creating a new market for Portuguese port in England.

4. The Treaty of 1786 was also called the Eden Treaty, after the chief British negotiator, William Eden. The treaty was strongly supported by William Pitt the Younger, who was a supporter of Adam Smith's ideas on free trade as expressed in the *Wealth of Nations* (1776). This treaty lowered all tariffs to 10–15 percent by value and ended prohibitions on imports, thus bringing to an end nearly one hundred years of economic warfare between the two nations. This rivalry was to be renewed again under Napoléon's Continental Blockade of November 1806 (also called the Continental System), which attempted to deny the entry of British goods into Europe.

5. The Anti–Corn Law League.

6. Bastiat uses the Italian phrase *furia francese* (the fury of the French in battle), which refers to the commitment of French soldiers during the revolutionary and Napoleonic wars to fighting for the principles of the Revolution.

regime as gradually as opinion will allow but in accordance with a period of transition agreed in advance and *on all points simultaneously,* all forms of economic activity will be offered compensations that will make the shocks genuinely imperceptible. If the price of wheat is held slightly below the current average, on the other hand the price of ploughs, clothing, tools, and even bread and meat will be less of a burden to farmers. In the same way, if ironmasters experience a decrease of a few francs in the cost of a ton of iron, they will have coal, wood, tools, and food on better terms. Well, we consider that once compensations like these that arise from freedom have become established, they will inevitably work steadily hand in hand with the reform itself throughout the period of transition, so that the reform remains consistent with public utility and the requirements of justice.

Is this impetuous and extreme? Is this a plan devised in the brains of hotheads? And unless people wish to make us abandon our principle, which we will never do as long as it is not proved to us to be erroneous, how can they demand more moderation and prudence from us?

Moderation does not consist in saying that we have half a conviction when we have a conviction that is whole and entire. It consists in respecting opposing opinions, refuting them without excessive emotion, refraining from personal attacks, refraining from provoking dismissals or impeachments, refraining from rousing misled workers, and refraining from threatening governments with uprisings.

Is this not how we practice moderation?

6. The People and the Bourgeoisie

PUBLISHING HISTORY:

Original title: "Peuple et Bourgeoisie."
Place and date of first publication: *Le Libre-échange,* 23 May 1847, no. 26, p. 202.
First French edition as book or pamphlet: Not applicable.
Location in Paillottet's edition of *OC:* Vol. 2. *Le Libre-échange,* pp. 348–55.
Previous translation: None.

Men are easily made dupes by intellectual systems, provided that some symmetrical arrangement makes them easy to understand.

For example, nothing is more common these days than to hear it said that the people and the bourgeoisie constitute two opposing classes with the same hostile relationships to each other that once pitted the *bourgeoisie* against the *aristocracy.*

"Initially, the *bourgeoisie* were weak," it is said. "They were oppressed, crushed, exploited, and humiliated by the *aristocracy.* They grew in stature, became wealthy and stronger to the point that, through the influence engendered by numbers and wealth, they overcame their adversaries in '89.[1]

"They then in turn became the *aristocracy.* Beneath them is the *people,* which is growing in stature, becoming stronger and, in the second act of the *social war,* is preparing to conquer."[2]

If symmetry were enough to give truth to intellectual systems, we cannot see why this one will not go further. Might we not add in effect:

"When the people have triumphed over the bourgeoisie, they will dominate and consequently become the aristocracy with regard to beggars. Beggars will grow in stature, become stronger in turn, and will prepare for the world the drama of the third *social war.*"[3]

The least of the defects in this theory, which is the talk of many of the popular journals, is to be wrong.

Between a nation and its aristocracy, we clearly see a deep dividing line, an undeniable hostility of interests, which sooner or later can only lead to strife. The aristocracy has come from outside; it has conquered its place by the sword and dominates through force. Its aim is to turn the work done by the vanquished to its own advantage. It seizes land, has armies at its disposal, and seizes the power to make laws and expedite justice. In order to master all

1. The French Revolution, which broke out in July 1789 with the storming of the Bastille prison in Paris.

2. Bastiat is referring here to the socialist notions of class, which were emerging during the 1840s. He is closely paraphrasing the socialist Victor Considérant's views on "social warfare" in "Qu'est-ce que le socialisme?" (What Is Socialism?), especially section 2: "L'affranchisement des prolétaires, ou ... la guerre sociale" (Considérant, *Le Socialisme devant le vieux monde, ou Le Vivant devant les morts,* pp. 2–3). The best-known articulation of these ideas, of course, is Karl Marx and Friedrich Engels's *The Communist Manifesto,* which appeared in February 1848.

3. In a letter to Mme Cheuvreux which he wrote two and a half years later, Bastiat continues this discussion about the class differences between the people and the bourgeoisie, which must be read in light of the revolutionary events of 1848. See Letter to Mme Cheuvreux, CW1, pp. 229–31.

the channels of influence, it has not even disdained the functions, or at least the dignities, of the church. In order not to weaken the esprit de corps that is its lifeblood, it transmits the privileges it has usurped from father to son by way of primogeniture. The aristocracy does not recruit from outside its ranks, or if it does so, it is because it is already on the slippery slope.

What similarity can we find between this arrangement and that of the bourgeoisie? In fact, can we say that there is a bourgeoisie? What does this word mean? Do we call a *bourgeois* someone who, through his activity, assiduity, and self-denial has put himself in a position to live on the accumulated value of previous work; in a word, on capital? Only an abject ignorance of political economy could suggest the idea that living on the accumulated value of work is to live off the work of others. Let those, therefore, who define the bourgeoisie in this way start by telling us what there is, in leisure time laboriously acquired, in the intellectual development that is the consequence of this, and in the accumulation of capital which forms its foundation, that is essentially opposed to the interests of humanity, the community, or even the working classes.

If these leisure activities cost nothing to anyone, do they deserve to arouse jealousy? Does this intellectual development not benefit progress, both in the moral and industrial spheres? Is not the ever-increasing amount of capital, precisely because of the advantages it confers, the basis on which those who have not yet become emancipated from manual work live? And is not the well-being of these classes, all other things being equal, exactly in proportion to the size of this capital, and consequently to the speed with which it is formed and the activities which compete for it?

Obviously, however, the word *bourgeoisie* would have a very limited meaning if it were applied solely to men of leisure. We hear it also applied to all those who are not salaried, who have an independent profession, who manage at total risk to themselves farming, manufacturing, and commercial enterprises or who devote themselves to the study of science, the exercise of the arts, or intellectual activity.[4]

But in this case it is difficult to imagine how the radical opposition be-

4. Bastiat is presenting here a slightly modified version of Charles Dunoyer's theory of industrialism and *les industrieux,* which was developed in the 1820s and 1830s. He has modified it by using the new terminology of "bourgeoisie" and social war, which socialists were using during the 1840s. See "Industry versus Plunder: The Plundered Classes, the Plundering Class, and the People," in the Note on the Translation.

tween the bourgeoisie and the people that justifies a comparison between their relationships and those of the aristocracy and democracy can be found. Has not every enterprise its opportunities? Is it not very natural and fortunate that the social mechanism allows those who may lose to take advantage of them? And besides, is it not from the ranks of the workers that the bourgeoisie is constantly and at all times being recruited? Is it not within the working class that capital, the object of so many wild denunciations, is built up? What! For the very reason that a worker has all the virtues by means of which man is emancipated from the yoke of immediate need, because he is hard-working, thrifty, well-organized, in control of his emotions, and upright, because he works with some success to leave his children in a better situation than the one he himself had, in a word, he has founded a family, it might be said that this worker is on the wrong track, a track that takes him away from the popular cause and which leads to the place of perdition which is the *bourgeoisie!* On the contrary, it will be enough for a man to have no ambition for the future, to waste his gains irresponsibly, to do nothing to warrant the trust of those who employ him or to refuse any sacrifice, for it to be true to say that he is a *man of the people* par excellence, a man who will never rise above the roughest kind of work, and a man whose own interest will, of course, always be in line with the interest of society well understood!

It is a cause of deep sadness to be faced with the frightful consequences contained in these erroneous doctrines and the way in which these ideas are propagated with such ardour. A *social war* is spoken of as being natural and inevitable, which is bound to be brought on by the alleged radical hostility between the people and the bourgeoisie and which is similar to the strife that in all countries has brought the aristocracy and democracy to blows. But, once again, is the comparison accurate? Can one assimilate wealth obtained by force to that acquired through work? And if the people consider any rise in status, even the natural rise generated by industry, thrift, and the exercise of every virtue to be an obstacle to be overturned, what motive, stimulus, or raison d'être will there be left to human activity and foresight?

It is dreadful to think that an error so pregnant with disastrous possibilities is the outcome of the profound ignorance in which modern education swaddles the current generations with regard to anything that relates to the way society works.

Let us not therefore see two nations within the same nation; there is just one. An infinite number of rungs on the ladder of wealth, each due to the same principle, is not enough to make up different classes, and still less classes that are hostile to one another.

However, it must be said that there are in our laws, principally in our financial laws, certain arrangements that seem to be maintained merely to sustain and, in a manner of speaking, justify both the mistake the public makes and its anger.

It cannot be denied that the ability to influence laws, concentrated in just a few hands, has on occasion been used with partiality. The bourgeoisie would be in a strong position with regard to the people if it were able to say, "Our contribution to common assets differs in degree but not in principle. Our interests are identical; when I defend mine, I am also defending yours. You can see proof of this in our laws; they are based on strict justice. They guarantee all property equally, whatever its size."

But is this the case? Is the property created by labor treated by our laws in the same way as property based on land or in capital? Certainly not. Setting aside the question of the allocation of taxes, one can say that the protectionist regime is a special terrain on which individual interests and classes give themselves over to the bitterest of struggles, since this regime claims to balance up the rights and sacrifices of all forms of production. Well, in this matter, how has the class that makes the law treated labor? How has it treated itself? We can state that it has done nothing and can do nothing for labor as such, although it clearly affects the faithful guardianship of *the national workforce.* What it has tried to do is to raise the price of all products, saying that wages would naturally follow such a rise. Well, if it has failed in its initial aim, as we believe it has, it has succeeded even less in its philanthropic intentions. The price of labor depends solely on the relationship between available capital and the number of workers. Now, if protectionism can do nothing to change this ratio, if it can neither increase the pool of capital nor decrease the number of workers, whatever influence it has on the price of products, it has none on rates of pay.

We will be told that we are contradicting ourselves; on the one hand we are arguing that the interests of all classes are homogeneous, and now we are identifying a point on which the wealthy class is abusing legislative power.

Let us hasten to say that the oppression exercised in this form by one class over another is not in the least intentional; it is purely an economic error, shared by the people and the bourgeoisie. We will provide two irrefutable proofs of this; the first is that protection does not benefit those who have set it up in the long run. The second is that, if it is damaging to the working classes, they are totally unaware of this, to the point where they are ill disposed to those who favor freedom.

However, it is in the nature of things that once the cause of a wrong has been pointed out, it ends by becoming generally known. With what terrible argument will the injustice of the protectionist regime not supply the recriminations of the masses! Let the electoral class[5] be on their guard! The people will not always seek the cause of its suffering in the absence of a phalanx, of an organization for work, or some other illusory combination.[6] One day it will see injustice where it really is. One day it will discover that a great deal is being done for products but nothing for wages, and that what is being done for products has no influence on wages. It will then ask itself: "How long have things been like this? When our fathers were able to approach the ballot box, were the people forbidden as they are today from exchanging their pay for iron, tools, fuel, clothing, and bread?" They will find a reply in writing in the tariffs of 1791 and 1795.[7] And what answer will you give them, you industrialists who make the law, if they add: "We can clearly see that a new form of aristocracy has taken the place of the old"?

If, therefore, the bourgeoisie wants to avoid a *social war,* whose distant rumblings are being echoed by the popular journals, let it not separate its interests from those of the masses, and let it examine and understand the

---

5. Bastiat calls the very limited number of individuals who were allowed to vote during the July Monarchy the *classe électorale.* Suffrage was limited to those who paid an annual tax of fr. 200 and were over the age of twenty-five, and only those who paid fr. 500 in tax and were over the age of thirty could stand for election.

6. The socialist Charles Fourier (1772–1837) believed that society should be organized into small communities, known as phalansteries, where living and working would be done collectively. The socialist Louis Blanc (1811–82) believed that workers should be "organized" collectively rather than employed on the market in order to avoid exploitation by the owners of businesses and factories.

7. Tariffs were completely reorganized by a law of 6–22 August 1791, which abolished most prohibitions on imported material, abolished tariffs on primary products used by French manufacturers and foodstuffs for consumers, and reduced tariffs on manufactured goods gradually down to 20–25 percent by value of the goods imported. A decree of 31 January 1795 declared decreases in the tariff of 1791 ranging from one-half to ninetenths on many articles. See "French Tariff Policy," in appendix 3, "French Economic Policy and Taxation."

solidarity that binds them. If the bourgeoisie wants universal approval to sanction its influence, let it put this influence at the service of the entire community. If it wants its power to enact laws not to arouse too much anxiety, it has to make laws just and impartial and award Customs protection to everyone or no one. It is certain that the ownership of arms and faculties is as sacred as the ownership of products. Since the law raises the price of products, let it also raise the rate of pay, and if it cannot, let it allow both to be exchanged freely for the other.

7. Two Losses versus One Profit

PUBLISHING HISTORY:

> Original title: "Deux pertes contre un profit."
> Place and date of first publication: *Le Libre-échange,* 30 May
>   1847, no. 27, pp. 216–18.
> First French edition as book or pamphlet: Not applicable.
> Location in Paillottet's edition of *OC:* Vol. 2. *Le Libre-échange,*
>   pp. 384–91.
> Previous translation: None.

To M. Arago, of the Academy of Sciences
   Sir,
   You have the secret of making the greatest scientific truths accessible to the minds of all. Oh! If only, using x's and y's, you could find a theorem that would leave no room for controversy! Simply setting it out will be enough to show the immense service you would be giving to the country and the human race. Here it is:

IF A PROTECTIONIST DUTY RAISES THE PRICE OF AN OBJECT BY A GIVEN QUANTITY, THE NATION GAINS THIS QUANTITY ONCE AND LOSES IT TWICE.[1]

---

1. The "double incidence of loss" is a theory first formulated by the Anti–Corn Law campaigner Thomas Perronet Thompson in 1834–36 and taken up by Bastiat in 1847. Bastiat lacked the mathematical skills to quantify this loss, so he appeals to the renowned mathematician François Arago for help in doing so in order to make his arguments against protectionism "invincible." François Arago (1786–1853) was the eldest of four successful Arago brothers, the youngest of whom, Étienne Arago (1802–92), may have

If this proposition is true, it follows that nations are inflicting incalculable losses on themselves. It would have to be acknowledged that there is not one of us who does not throw one-franc coins into the river each time he eats or drinks, each time he takes it into his head to touch a tool or an item of clothing.[2]

And as this way of doing things has been going on for a long time, we should not be surprised if, in spite of the advance of science and industry, a very heavy burden of destitution and suffering is still weighing on our fellow citizens.

On the other hand, everyone agrees that a protectionist regime is a source of damage, uncertainty, and danger outside this calculus of profits and losses. It feeds national animosities, postpones unity between peoples, increases the opportunities for war, and inscribes actions that are innocent in themselves as misdemeanors and crimes in our laws. We just have to submit to these inconvenient lesser outcomes of our arrangements once we come to believe that they rest on the following concept: *any increase in price is, by its very nature, a national gain.* For, Sir, I believe that I have observed, and you will perhaps have observed as I have, that in spite of the great scorn that individuals and nations display for *gain,* they have difficulty in giving it up. If it happened to be proved, however, that this alleged gain is accompanied in the first instance by an *equal loss,* which offsets it, and then by a *second loss that is also equal,* this latter one involving absolutely blatant deceit,[3] then since the horror of loss is as strongly entrenched in the human heart as the love of profit, we would be bound to assume that the protectionist regime and all its direct and indirect consequences would evaporate with the illusion that gave rise to them.

You will therefore not be surprised, Sir, that I would like to see this demonstration clad in the invincible evidence that the language of equations communicates. You will not consider it a bad thing that I have turned to you, for, among all the problems presented by the sciences that you pursue with so much renown, there is certainly none more worthy of occupying your power-

---

gone to school with Bastiat in Sorèze. François was a famous astronomer and physicist who was also active in republican politics throughout the 1830s and 1840s.

2. Perronet Thompson remarks that the French tariff laws were tantamount to an order that every Frenchman throw every "third franc into the sea." See Thompson, *Letters of a Representative to His Constituents,* p. 189.

3. Bastiat uses the word *duperie* here. See "Bastiat on Enlightening the 'Dupes' about the Nature of Plunder," in the Introduction.

ful abilities, at least for a few moments. I dare say that the man who provides an irrefutable solution to it, were it the only thing he did in this life, would have done enough for the human race and his own reputation.[4]

Allow me therefore to set out in common parlance what I would like to see put into mathematical language.

Let us suppose that an English knife is sold in France for 2 francs.

That means that it is traded for 2 francs or for any other object which itself is worth 2 francs, for example, a pair of gloves at this price.

Let us assume that a similar knife cannot be produced in this country for less than 3 francs.

Under these circumstances, a French cutler turns to the government and says to it: "Protect me. Prevent my fellow countrymen from buying English knives, and I will ensure that I will provide them for 3 francs."

I say that this increase in price of 1 franc will be *made once only,* but add that it will be *lost twice* by France, and that the same phenomenon will be seen in all similar cases.

First of all, let us put aside for a moment the 2 francs which are not relevant to increasing prices. As far as these 2 francs are concerned, it is very clear that French industry will not have gained or lost anything through this measure. Whether these 2 francs go to the cutler or the glove maker, that may suit one of these industrialists and inconvenience the other, but they have no effect on *national production.* Up to that point, there has been a change of direction, but no increase or decrease in output: 2 francs more go to cutlery and 2 francs less go to glove making, that is all. An unjust favor here, a no less unjust oppression there, is all we can see; let us therefore say no more about these 2 francs.

However, there is a third franc whose course needs to be followed; it constitutes the increase in price of the knife: it is the *given amount* by which the price of knives is raised. It is the amount that I say is gained once and lost twice by the country.

That it is gained once, there is no doubt. Obviously the cutlery industry is favored by prohibition to the amount of 1 franc that will go to pay for salaries, profits, iron, and steel. In other terms, the production of gloves is discouraged by only 2 francs and the cutlery industry is stimulated by 3 francs,

4. Bastiat is obviously quite excited at the prospect of using mathematics to demonstrate the truth of his claims about the deleterious impact of tariffs on the French economy. See note 1, above.

which certainly constitutes a surplus stimulus of 20 sous, 1 franc, or 100 centimes,[5] whatever you like to call it, for national output.

But it is just as obvious that when the person acquired the knife from England in exchange for a pair of gloves he paid only 2 francs, whereas he is now paying 3. In the first case, he had *one franc* available over and above the cost of the knife, and as we all are in the habit of using francs for something, we have to take it as certain that this franc would have been spent in some way and would have stimulated national industry just as far as a franc can be stretched.

If, for example, you were this buyer, before prohibition you would have been able to buy a pair of gloves for 2 francs, in exchange for which you would have obtained the knife from England. And what is more, you would have had 1 franc left, with which you would have bought, depending on your tastes, a few small pies or a small book.

If therefore we do the accounts of *national output,* we will instantly find an equivalent loss to counter the gain of the cutler, which is that of the pastry cook or the bookseller.

I think it is impossible to deny that in either case your 3 francs, since you had them, encouraged the industry of the country in exactly the same way. Under a regime of liberty, they would be shared between the glove maker and the bookseller; under the protectionist regime, they would go entirely to the cutler, a truth we could safely challenge the very genius of prohibition itself to try to undermine.

Thus, the franc is gained once by the cutler and lost once by the bookseller.

All that remains is to evaluate your own position, as purchaser and consumer. Does it not leap to the eye that before prohibition, for 3 francs you had both a knife and a small pocket-sized book, whereas since then, for your same 3 francs, you would just have a knife and no small pocket-sized book? You are therefore losing the pocket book in this matter, or the equivalent of *one franc.* Well, if this second loss is not offset by any gain for anyone in France, I am right in saying that this franc, gained once, is lost twice.

Do you know, Sir, what the reply to this is, for it is right that you should know the objection? It is said that your loss is offset by the profit earned by the cutler or, in general terms, that the loss suffered by the consumer is offset by the profit to the producer.

5. These are just different ways of saying the same thing, namely "1 franc": 1 franc = 100 centimes = 20 sous.

In your wisdom you would rapidly have discovered that the sleight of hand here consists in casting a shadow over the fact, already established, that profit to one producer, the cutler, is offset by the loss to another producer, the bookseller, and that your franc, by the very fact that it has gone to stimulate the cutlery industry, has not gone to stimulate the bookshop, as it ought to have done.

After all, as it is a question of equal amounts, whether you establish, if you prefer, compensation between the producer and the consumer, it does not matter, provided that the bookshop is not forgotten and that you do not make the same gain appear twice to offset it alternatively to very distinct losses.

It is also said that all this is very small-minded and cheap. It is scarcely worth the trouble of making so much noise for one small franc, one small knife, and one small pocket-sized book. I do not need to draw your attention to the fact that the franc, the knife, and the book are my algebraic symbols and that they represent the lives and substance of nations, and it is because I do not know how to use a, b, or c to generalize questions that I am placing them under your patronage.

The following is also said: the franc that the cutler receives as a supplement, thanks to trade protection, he pays to his workers. My reply is this: the franc that the bookseller would receive in addition, thanks to free trade, he would also pay to other workers, so that in this respect the balance is not upset, and it remains true that under one regime you have a book and under the other you do not. To avoid the confusion, intentional or not, that will not fail to be cast over this subject, you have to make a clear distinction between the original distribution of your 3 francs and their subsequent circulation which, in both hypotheses, follows infinite trajectories and can never affect our calculation.[6]

It seems to me that people would have to be of extremely bad faith to plead in favor of the relative importance of the two industries under comparison by saying that cutlery is worth more than glove making or bookshops. It is clear

---

6. (Paillottet's note) See number 48, page 320, on the *Sophism of ricochets,* in this volume (*OC,* vol. 2, p. 311, "Septième discours, à Paris"); pages 74, 160, and 229 in vol. 4 (*OC,* vol. 4, p. 74, "La Protection élève-t-elle le taux des salaires?"; p. 160, "Conseil inférieur du travail"; p. 229, "La Protection ou les trois échevins") and in vol. 5, independently of pages 80 to 83, pages 336 *et seq.,* containing the pamphlet *What Is Seen and What Is Not Seen* (*OC,* vol. 5, p. 336ff., "Ce qu'on voit et ce qu'on ne voit pas"). [Paillottet notes that Bastiat is grappling with the idea of the "ricochet effect," which emerges in his thinking toward the end of 1847.]

that my line of argument has nothing in common with this type of thinking. I am seeking the general effect of prohibition on production as a whole, and not to ascertain whether one sector is more important than another. It would have been enough for me to take another example to show that what in my hypothesis results in depriving someone of a book is, in many cases, deprivation of bread, clothing, education, independence, and dignity.

In the hope that you will allocate the truly radical importance that I think it merits to the solution of this problem, please allow me to underline once more some of the objections that may be made to it. People will say: "The loss will not be *one franc,* since internal competition will be enough to bring down the price of French knives to 2 francs 50 and perhaps to 2 francs 25." I agree that this may happen. In that case, my figures will have to be changed. The *two losses* would be less and *so would the gain,* but there would nonetheless be two losses for one gain for as long as protectionism protects a given producer.

Finally, the objection would doubtless be raised that national industry should at least be protected because of the taxes it has to bear. The reply to this may be deduced from my argument itself. To subject a nation to two losses for one gain is an unfortunate method of relieving its burdens. Let people assume taxes to be as high as they like, let them assume that the government takes 99 percent of our income from us; is it an admissible solution, I ask you, to grant the overtaxed cutler 1 franc taken from the overtaxed bookseller with, in addition, the loss of 1 franc to the overtaxed consumer?

I do not know, Sir, if I am deluding myself, but it appears to me that the strict proof I am asking you to provide, should you take the trouble to formulate it, will not be an object of pure scientific curiosity, but will dissipate a great many disastrous preconceived ideas.

For example, you know how intolerant we are of any *foreign competition.* This is the monster on which all business anger is vented. Well then! What do we see in the case put forward? Where is the genuine rivalry? Who is the true and dangerous competitor of the glove maker and the bookseller in France? Is it not the French cutler who is asking for the support of the law in order to take for himself alone the income of his two colleagues, even at the expense of a clear loss for the general public? And in the same way, who are the true and dangerous opponents of the French cutler? It is not the cutler from Birmingham, it is the French bookseller and glove maker who, at least if they are not blind in some way, will make constant efforts to take from the cutler customers that he has legally and unjustly snatched from them. Is it not strange to find that this monster of competition, whose roar we think we hear from across the Channel, is being nourished by us in our very midst? Other points of view, both original and true, will no doubt emerge from this equation as a result of your enlightenment and patriotism.

8. The Political Economy of the Generals

PUBLISHING HISTORY:

Original title: "L'Économie politique des généraux."
Place and date of first publication: *Le Libre-échange,* 20 June 1847, no. 30, p. 234.
First French edition as book or pamphlet: Not applicable.
Location in Paillottet's edition of *OC:* Vol. 2. *Le Libre-échange,* pp. 355–58.
Previous translation: None.

In the Chamber, if a financier, venturing into the military theories of Jomini,[1] happens to touch on the maneuvering of squadrons, he may well bring a smile to the lips of the Generals. It is equally not surprising that the Generals sometimes understand political economy in ways that are not very intelligible to men whose occupation it is to concern themselves with this branch of human knowledge.

However, there is a difference between military strategy and political economy. The first is a specific science, which it is sufficient for soldiers to know. The second, like moral philosophy or hygiene, is a general science about which it is desirable for everyone to have accurate ideas. (*See vol. IV, page 122.*)[2]

In a speech to which we will give full justice in another context, General Lamoricière has put forward a theory of markets which we cannot allow to pass without comment.

> From the point of view of *pure* political economy [said the honorable General] markets are important: at the present time we spend money *and even men* to retain markets or gain new

1. Antoine Henri Jomini (1779–1869) was a Swiss-born general who served with distinction under Napoleon and then the Russian czars. He was the author of several important works on strategy.

2. (Paillottet's note [in the text]) See vol. 4, page 122. [Paillottet is directing the reader to a discussion of the nature of the social sciences, such as political economy, in ES1 Conclusion, where Bastiat states that every individual should have some knowledge.]

ones. Now, in the situation occupied by France in the world market, is not an outlet worth 63 million for French products something notable for her? France sends fr. 17 million worth of woven cotton to Africa, fr. 7 or 8 million worth of wine, etc.[3]

It is only too true that *at the present time,* we are spending money *and even men* to conquer markets, but, and here we beg General Lamoricière's pardon, far from this being in the light of pure political economy, it is in the light of bad, indeed very bad, political economy. A market, that is to say, a sale made abroad, is meritorious only if it covers all the costs it engenders; and if in order to make it, recourse has to be made to taxpayers' money, even though the industry concerned by this sale may congratulate itself on it, the nation as a whole suffers a loss that is sometimes considerable, not to mention the immorality of the procedure and the blood that is worse than uselessly spilled.[4]

It is much worse still when, in order to create alleged markets for ourselves, we send abroad both the people who should be buying our products and the money with which they should be paying for them. We do not doubt that Algerian civil servants, whether French or Arab, to whom their monthly salaries are sent from Paris at the expense of taxpayers, spend a small part of these on buying French cottons and wines. It appears that of the 130 million that we spend in Africa,[5] 60 million are spent thus. *Pure* political economy teaches us that if things have to be carried out on this footing, the following will result:

We remove a Frenchman from useful occupations and give him 130 francs on which to live. Out of these 130 francs, he hands us back 60 francs in exchange for products that are worth exactly this amount. The total loss is: 70

---

3. We have not been able to find the source of this quote.

4. See Bastiat's comments on Algeria and colonization in his address "To the Electors of the District of Saint-Sever," where he describes the colonial system as "the most disastrous illusion ever to have led nations astray" (CW1, pp. 363–65). See also the chapter on Algeria in WSWNS.

5. *Le Journal des économistes* gives a figure of fr. 120 million spent in Algeria in 1847 and makes a very similar argument to that of Bastiat, that the money goes to the troops and then into the hands of the merchants who service the needs of those troops. It goes further to argue that the civilian population of Algeria is 113,000, of which 6,000 live in administration towns and are paid by the French civilian administration out of taxpayers' funds, leaving 107,000 who are paid by the army out of taxpayers' funds. See "Chronique," in *JDE* 19 (February 1848): 315.

francs in money, 60 francs' worth of products, and all the work that this man might have created in France for an entire year.

Thus, whatever opinion you may have of the usefulness of our conquest in Africa (a question that is not within our competence), it is certain that it is not through these illusionary markets that this usefulness can be appreciated, but through the future prosperity of our colony.

For this reason, another general, General de Trézel,[6] minister for war, thought it necessary to present not the current markets but the future products from Algeria as compensation for our sacrifices. Unfortunately, it is impossible for us not to perceive another economic error in the background of the brilliant picture painted by the Minister to the membership of the Chamber. He expressed himself thus:

> Its *good fortune* has given Africa to the country and we will certainly not through carelessness, laziness, or even the fear of spending money *and even men,* let slip from our grasp a country which will be giving us 200 leagues of Mediterranean coastline at a distance of 36 hours from our shores, one which will be giving us products for *which we are paying enormous sums of money to our neighboring countries.*
>
> For this reason, disregarding the cereals that previously, as I have already said, fed Rome, Africa is giving us the olive, which is a special product of this country. It is giving us oil *for which we pay 60 million every year to foreigners.* In Africa, we have rice and silk, which again are bought outside France, because France does not produce these. We have tobacco. *Calculate how many millions we pay abroad for this product.* It is certain that within a few years, perhaps within twenty-five years, we will be obtaining all these products from Africa, and we might then be able to consider Africa to be one of our provinces.[7]

What predominates in this passage is the idea that France loses the total *value* of the products she imports from abroad. In fact, she imports them

---

6. Camille Alphonse de Trézel (1780–1860) was a military engineer who served in the Topographical Department of the Army. He served under Napoléon in Holland and Poland and following the restoration of the monarchy he spent a considerable part of his career in the French colony of Algeria. He was Minister of War (1847–48) and retired from public life with the fall of King Louis-Philippe in 1848.

7. We have not been able to find the source of this quote.

only because she finds it profitable to produce this same *value* in the form of products she provides in exchange, in exactly the same way as General de Trézel uses his time better in administrative work than if he spent it stitching his clothes. It is on this error that the entire restrictive regime is based.

On the other hand, the wheat, oil, silk, and tobacco to be supplied to us by Africa in twenty-five years' time are shown as a gain. This depends on what these things cost, if we include, in addition to the costs of production, the costs of conquest and defense. It is evident that if with this same sum we were able to produce the same things in France or, what amounts to the same, produce the wherewithal to purchase them from abroad and even achieve a saving, it would be a bad investment for us to go to the Barbary coast to produce them. This is said while no account is taken of all the other points of view relating to the huge question of Algeria. Whatever the importance and, if you like, the superiority of considerations drawn from a higher order, this is not a reason for making a mistake from the point of view of *pure* political economy.

9. A Protest

PUBLISHING HISTORY:

Original title: "Remontrance."
Place and date of first publication: *Le Libre-échange,*
    5 September 1847, no. 41, p. 328.
First French edition as book or pamphlet: Not applicable.
Location in Paillottet's edition of *OC:* Vol. 2. *Le Libre-échange,*
    pp. 415–18.
Previous translation: None.

Auch,[1] 30 August 1847

My dear colleagues,

When fatigue or a lack of vehicles delays me in a town, I do what every conscientious traveler ought to do; I visit its monuments, churches, promenades, and museums.

---

1. Auch is the main city of the département of Le Gers, in the eastern part of the département of the Landes, where Bastiat lived and which he represented in the Chamber. It is the historical capital of the old province of Gascogny.

Today, I went to see the statue raised to M. d'Etigny,[2] the Intendant of the subdivision of Auch,[3] by the enlightened gratitude of the good inhabitants of this region. This great administrator, and I may say this great man, crisscrossed the province entrusted to his care with magnificent roads. His memory is blessed for this but not his person, since he suffered opposition that was not always expressed in verbal or written complaint. It is said that, in workshops, he was often reduced to using the extraordinary strength with which nature had endowed him. He told country folk: "You curse me, but your children will bless me." A few days before his death, he wrote the following words, which recall those of the founder of our religion, to the general controller: "I have made many enemies; God has given me the grace to pardon them, for they do not yet know the purity of my intentions."

M. d'Etigny is represented holding a scroll of paper in his right hand and another under his left arm. It is natural to think that one of these scrolls is the plan of the network of roads with which he has endowed the region. But to what can the other scroll refer? By rubbing my eyes and glasses, I thought I could read the word A PROTEST. Thinking that the maker of the statue, in a spirit of satire, or rather to give men a salutary lesson, wished to perpetuate the memory of the opposition this region had made to the creation of roads, I rushed over to the library archives and there found the document to which the artist had probably wished to allude. It is in the regional dialect; I am producing here a faithful translation for the edification of *Le Moniteur industriel* and the protectionist committee.[4] Alas! They have invented nothing. Their doctrines flourished nearly a century ago.[5]

---

2. Antoine Megret d'Etigny (1719–67) was a provincial administrator (intendant) of the region of Auch (1751–65). He is best known for his competent administration of the compulsory labor requirement (*la corvée*), which he used to improve the roads in his region. A statue of him was erected in the Allées d'Etigny.

3. A *généralité* was an administrative division of the kingdom. It was headed by an intendant, who reported to the *contrôleur général des finances,* the finance minister of the king. There were 34 such *généralités* in 1789.

4. *Le Moniteur industriel* was the journal of the protectionist Association pour la défense du travail national (Association for the Defense of National Employment) founded by Mimerel de Roubaix in 1846. The Central Committee which ran the Association had Mimerel as its vice president, so it was called the "Mimerel Committee" for short.

5. Bastiat may have in mind here another famous eighteenth-century intendant who tried to introduce economic reforms in his region, only to be opposed by vested interests and ultimately defeated, namely Anne-Robert-Jacques Turgot.

A Protest

My Lord,

The bourgeois and villagers of the subdivision of Auch have heard mention of the project you have conceived of opening communication routes in all directions. They come, with tears in their eyes, to beg you to examine closely the sorry position in which you are going to place them.

Have you thought about this, My Lord? You want to put the subdivision of Auch into communication with the surrounding regions! What you are contemplating will, however, lead to our certain ruin. We will be *flooded* with all sorts of products. What do you think will happen to our *national labor* in the face of the *invasion* of foreign products, which you will encourage by the opening of your roads? Right now, impassable mountains and precipices *protect* us. Our production has developed in the shade of this *protection*. We export scarcely anything, but at least our market is *reserved* and *assured* for us. And now you want to hand it over to greedy foreigners! Do not talk to us about our activity, our energy, our intelligence, and the fertility of our land. For, My Lord, we are in all ways and in all regards hopelessly inferior. Note that, in fact, if nature has favored us with land and a climate that allow a great variety of products to be made, there is none for which a neighboring region does not have even better conditions. Can we compete with the plains of the Garonne for the cultivation of wheat? With the Bordeaux region for the production of wine? With the Pyrénées for the raising of cattle? With the Landes of Gascony, where the land has no value, for the production of wool? You must see that if you open up communications with all these regions, we will have to endure a deluge of wine, wheat, meat, and wool. *All these things are genuine wealth, but only on condition that they are the product of national production. If they were the product of foreign production, national employment would dry up and wealth with it.*[6]

My Lord, let us not try to be wiser than our fathers. Far from creating new avenues of circulation for goods, they very advisedly blocked those that already existed. They were careful to station Customs officers around our borders to repel competition from perfidious foreigners. How irresponsible we would be to encourage this competition!

Let us not try to be wiser than nature. It has placed mountains and chasms between the various settlements of men in order for each one to be able to work peacefully, sheltered from all external rivalry. To cross this mountain

---

6. (Bastiat's note) Seventy years later, M. de Saint-Cricq reproduced these words verbatim in order to justify the advantage of interrupting communications.

range and fill in these chasms is to inflict damage that is similar to and even identical to what would result from abolishing Customs posts. Who knows but that your current plan will not someday give rise to this disastrous thought in the mind of some theoretician! Be careful, My Lord, the logic is implacable. If once you accept that ease of communication is a good thing in itself, that in any case, even if it upsets people in some way, it nevertheless has more advantages than disadvantages on the whole, if you accept this, then M. Colbert's fine system will be ruined.[7] Well, we challenge you to prove that your planned roads are based on something other than this absurd supposition.

My Lord, we are not at all theoreticians or men of principle; we do not have any pretension to genius. But we speak the language of common sense. If you open our region to all forms of external rivalry, if you facilitate the *invasion* of our markets by wheat from the Garonne, wine from Bordeaux, flax from the Béarn,[8] wool from the Landes, or steers from the Pyrénées, it is as plain as daylight to us how our cash will be exported, how our work will dry up, how our source of wages will disappear, and how our property will lose its value. And, as for the compensations you promise us, they are, allow us to say this, highly questionable; you have to rack your brains to see them.

We therefore dare to hope that you will leave the region of Auch in the happy isolation in which it is, for if we succumb to the combat against dreamers who want to establish easy commerce, we can clearly see that our sons will have to endure another form of struggle against other dreamers who would like to establish the freedom to trade as well.[9]

10. The Spanish Association for the Defense of National Employment and the Bidassoa Bridge[1]

PUBLISHING HISTORY:

Original title: "Association espagnole pour la défense du travail national."

---

7. Jean-Baptiste Colbert (1619–83) was the comptroller-general of finance under Louis XIV from 1665 to 1683. He epitomized the policy of state intervention in trade and industry known as "mercantilism."

8. Béarn is a region located at the base of the Pyrénées in southwest France in the département of Pyrénées-Atlantiques. Its capital is the city of Pau.

9. Bastiat uses the expression *la liberté du commerce,* not *le libre-échange.*

1. We have added "and the Bidassoa Bridge" to the original title used by Bastiat in order to highlight the inclusion of this economic fable in the essay.

Place and date of first publication: *Le Libre-échange,*
   7 November 1847, no. 50, p. 404.
First French edition as book or pamphlet: Not applicable.
Location in Paillottet's edition of *OC:* Vol. 2. *Le Libre-échange,*
   pp. 429–35.
Previous translation: None.

Spain too has her association for the defense of *national employment.*[2]

Its object is this:

"Given a certain amount of capital and the labor it can set to work, to take these away from uses in which they produce a profit and propel them in a direction in which they will produce a loss, unless this loss can be transferred by law onto the general public by means of a disguised tax."

Consequently, this society is demanding, among other things, the exclusion of French products, not those that are expensive for us (no laws are needed to exclude them) but those that can be provided for us cheaply. The cheaper the price at which they can be offered to us, the more reason Spain has, so people say, to protect herself from them.

This has inspired me to record a reflection that I humbly put before the reader.

One of the characteristics of truth is universality.

If you wish to ascertain whether an association is based on a good principle, you have only to see if it is in sympathy with all those who, wherever they are in the world, have adopted an identical principle.

Associations for free trade are like this. One of our colleagues can go to Madrid, Lisbon, London, New York, Saint Petersburg, Berlin, Florence, and Rome, and even Beijing; if associations for free trade exist in these towns, he will for that reason certainly be made very welcome there. What he says here he can say there in the certainty that he will not be upsetting either opinions or even interests as these associations understand them. Between free traders of all countries there is unity of faith on this question.

Is this also the case for protectionists? In spite of the community of ideas, or rather of arguments, was Lord Bentinck, who had just voted for the exclusion of French cattle, acting in accordance with the views of our breeders?

---

2. This is a veiled reference to one of Bastiat's protectionist bêtes noires, the Association pour la défense du travail national (Association for the Defense of National Employment), which was founded in October 1846 and based in Paris.

Would the man who rejected our printed cotton goods in Parliament be made welcome by the Rouen Committee?[3] Would those who will be supporting the *Navigation Act*[4] and the differential duties in India next year arouse the enthusiasm of our shipowners? Let us suppose that a member of the Odier Committee were made a member of the Spanish Association for the Defense of *National Employment;* what is he going to say? What words could he use without betraying either the interests of his country or his own convictions? Would he advise the Spanish to open their ports and borders to the products of our factories? To take no notice of the false doctrine of the *balance of trade?* To consider that the industries that are supported solely by taxes on the community are absolutely not worthwhile? Would he tell them that Customs exemptions do not create capital and work but merely displace them, and in a damaging way? Abandoning principles and personal dignity in this way may perhaps be applauded by his coreligionists in France (for we remember that, eighteen months ago in the Rouen Committee, the question was very seriously raised as to whether it was now the right time to preach free trade . . . in Spain), but it certainly will arouse the derision of a Castilian audience. Therefore, would he want to appear heroic by putting his principles above his interests? Imagine this Brutus of restriction haranguing the Spanish in these words: "You are doing the right thing in raising the height of the barriers that separate us. I approve your rejecting our ships, our suppliers of services, our traveling salesmen, our fabrics made of cotton, wool, yarn, and jute, our spinning mules, our wallpaper, our machines, our furniture, our fashions, our haberdashery, our hardware, our pottery, our clocks, our ironmongery, our perfumes, our fancy goods, our gloves, and our books. These are all things that you ought to make yourselves, however much work they demand and even all the more if they require more work. I have only one criticism to make to you, and that is that you go only halfway down this road. It is very good of you to pay us a *tribute* of ninety million and to make yourselves dependent on us. Beware of your free traders. They are ideologists,

---

3. Nearly every industrial town had its "Committee" to represent the interests of industry and manufacturing. These were brought together under a national umbrella organization called the Association pour la défense du travail national (Association for the Defense of National Employment), a protectionist organization led by Antoine Odier, which was founded by the northern textile manufacturer Pierre Mimerel de Roubaix (1786–1872) in October 1846 and was based in Paris. The "Rouen Committee" Bastiat refers to was probably the local affiliate of the national organization.

4. See the entry for "The Navigation Acts," in the Glossary of Subjects and Terms.

stupid people, traitors, etc." This fine speech would doubtless be applauded in Catalonia; would it be approved of in Lille and Rouen?

It is thus certain that protectionist associations in various countries are antagonistic toward each other, although they give themselves the same title and apparently profess the same doctrines, and to crown their oddity, if they are sympathetic to anything from one country to the other, it is with free trade associations.

The reason for this is simple. It is that they want two contradictory things at the same time: *restrictions and markets.* To give and not to receive, to sell and not to buy, to export and not to import, this is the basis of their strange doctrine. This leads them very logically to have two forms of speech that are not only different but opposed to each another, one for the country and the other for abroad, with the very remarkable fact that, were their advice to be accepted on both sides, they would not be any closer to their goal.

In effect, just taking into account the transactions between two nations, what are exports for one are imports for the other. See this fine ship that criss-crosses the sea and carries within its hold a fine cargo. Be so good as to tell me what we should call these goods. Are they *imports* or *exports?* Is it not clear that they are both simultaneously, depending on whether you are looking at the nation dispatching them or the one receiving them? If, therefore, no one wishes to be the nation receiving them, no one can be the nation dispatching them, and it is inevitable that, overall, *markets* will dry up just as much as *restrictions* tighten the noose. This is how we arrive at this odd policy: here a *premium* at public expense is allocated to encourage a cargo to leave, while there, a *tax* at public expense is imposed on it to prevent it from entering. Can you imagine a more senseless conflict? And who will emerge as the victor? The nation most disposed to pay the larger premium or the heavier tax.

No, the truth does not lie in this pile of contradictions and antagonisms. The entire arrangement is based on the idea that *exchange* is a trick[5] for the party that is on the receiving end, and apart from the fact that the very word *exchange* contradicts this idea, since it implies that both sides receive something, what person would not see the ridiculous position in which he is placing himself when all he can say when he is abroad is: "*I advise you to be duped,*" while he is above all the dupe of his own advice?

This being said, here is a small sample of protectionist propaganda abroad.

---

5. Bastiat uses the word *duperie* here. See "Bastiat on Enlightening the 'Dupes' about the Nature of Plunder," in the Introduction.

The Bidassoa[6] Bridge

A man left the rue Hauteville[7] in Paris with the aim of teaching political economy to other nations. He came to the Bidassoa. There were a great many people on the bridge, and such a large audience could not fail to tempt our teacher. He therefore leaned against the rail, with his back to the Ocean and, taking care to prove his cosmopolitan nature by aligning his spine with the imaginary line separating France and Spain, he began to speak:

"All of you who are listening to me, you would like to know what good or bad exchanges are. It would appear at first sight that I ought to have nothing to teach you in this respect, for in the end, each of you is aware of his own self-interest, at least to the extent that I know my own, but interest is a misleading sign, and I am a member of an association in which this common motive is scorned. I am bringing you another infallible rule, which is most easy to apply. Before entering into a contract with someone, get him to chat. If, when you speak to him in French he replies in Spanish, or *vice versa,* you need go no further, proof is there and the trade will be sly in nature."

A voice: "We speak neither Spanish nor French; we all speak the same language, *Escualdun,* which you call Basque."[8]

"Damn!" the orator said to himself. "I did not expect this objection. I have to change tack." "Well then, my friends, here is a rule that is just as easy: those of you who were born on this side of the line (indicating Spain) may trade with no inconvenience with all of the country to my right up to columns of Hercules,[9] but no further, while all those born on that side of the line (indicating France) may trade at will in all the region lying to my left, up to this other imaginary line that runs between Blanc-Misseron and Quiévrain,[10] but no further. Trade carried out in this way will make you

6. The Bidassoa is a short river in southwest France which forms the border between France and Spain.

7. The Association for the Defense of National Employment (see note 3, above) had its headquarters on the rue Hauteville in Paris.

8. Bastiat had some knowledge of the Basque language, as he had a Basque housemaid and lived in a part of France where Basque was spoken. See his "Two Articles on the Basque Language" (CW1, pp. 305–8).

9. The "Pillars of Hercules" was the name given in the ancient world to the two pieces of land which lay on either side of the Strait of Gibraltar. The pillar to the north is the Rock of Gibraltar on the Anglo-Spanish side of the strait. The identity of the southern pillar in Africa is disputed but lies somewhere in Morocco.

10. Blanc-Misseron and Quiévrain are two towns on the Franco-Belgian border.

wealthy. As for the trade that you carry out across the Bidassoa, this will ruin you before you can notice it."

Another voice: "If the trade carried out across the Nivelle[11] which is two leagues from here is good, how can that carried out across the Bidassoa be bad? Do the waters of the Bidassoa produce a particular gas that poisons the trade that crosses it?"

"You are very curious," replied the teacher, "my fine Basque friend; you have to take my word for it."

In the meantime our man, having reflected on the doctrine that he had just expressed, said to himself: "I have still carried out only half of the business of my country." Asking for silence, he continued his speech thus:

"Do not believe that I am a man of *principles* and that what I have just told you constitutes an ordered *system*. Heaven preserve me! My commercial arrangements are so far from being *theoretical,* so natural and so in line with your inclinations, although you do not realize this, that you will submit to them easily with a few thrusts of the bayonet. The Utopians are those who have the audacity to say that trade is good when those who carry it out find it so. A terrible, wholly modern doctrine that has been imported from England, and to which men would naturally be drawn if the armed forces did not establish proper order.

"However, to prove to you that I am neither exclusive nor absolute, I will tell you that my idea is not to condemn all the transactions that you may be tempted to make from one bank to the other of the Bidassoa. I admit that your carts cross the bridge freely, provided that they arrive there FULL from this side (indicating France) and arrive here EMPTY from that side (indicating Spain). Through this ingenious arrangement, you will all gain: You, Spaniards, because you will receive without giving, and you, Frenchmen, because you will give without receiving. Whatever you do, though, do not take this for a fully worked-out system."

The Basques have hard heads. You may repeat to them until you are blue in the face: "This is not a system, a theory, a Utopia, or a principle"; these carefully chosen words are incapable of making them understand what is unintelligible. For this reason, in spite of the fine advice from their teacher, when they are allowed to trade (and sometimes when they are not) they trade according to the old way (which is said to be new), that is to say, as

11. The Nivelle is a small river in the French Basque country.

their fathers traded; and when they cannot conduct it "over" the Bidassoa, they do it "under" the Bidassoa, so blind are they![12]

11. The Specialists

PUBLISHING HISTORY:

Original title: "Les Hommes spéciaux."
Place and date of first publication: *Le Libre-échange*,
    28 November 1847, no. 1 (2nd year), p. 7.
First French edition as book or pamphlet: Not applicable.
Location in Paillottet's edition of *OC:* Vol. 2. *Le Libre-échange*,
    pp. 373–77.
Previous translation: None.

There are people who imagine that men of learning, or those whom they call, too indulgently, *scholars,* are not competent to talk about free trade. Freedom and restriction, they say, are questions that have to be debated by *practical* men.

Thus, *Le Moniteur industriel* calls our attention to the view that in England, trade reform has been due to the efforts of manufacturers.[1]

Similarly, the Odier Committee is very proud of the procedure it has adopted, which consists of so-called *surveys* which come down to asking each favored industry in turn if it wants to give up its privileges.

In similar fashion, a member of the General Council of the Seine, a manufacturer of woolen cloth, protected by absolute prohibition, told his colleagues while discussing one of our associates: "I know him; he was a village justice of the peace.[2] He knows nothing about manufacturing."

12. Bastiat is punning here with a reference to the "underground" (or in this case "under river") economy of smuggling across the Franco-Spanish border. The legally permitted, regulated, and taxed trade takes place "aboveground" (above river) through the customs barriers at either side of the Bidassoa river, while the traditional, free, and untaxed trade takes place "underground" (under river).

1. The Anti–Corn Law League, which was successful in having the protectionist Corn Laws repealed in May 1846, was run and supported by individuals like Richard Cobden, who was a successful cotton manufacturer.

2. Bastiat was appointed justice of the peace in Mugron in May 1831. Mugron was in a remote agricultural area in the southwest of France.

Even our friends let themselves be put down by this type of prejudice. Recently, the Le Havre Chamber of Commerce, referring to our declaration of principles (which is one page long),[3] remarked that we did not mention maritime interests. It then added: "in one sense the Chamber could not complain too much about this oversight, since the names shown at the end of this declaration did not inspire it with much confidence with regard to the study of these matters."

This associate of ours, whom I have now therefore mentioned twice, starts by very solemnly declaring that he does not claim to be more familiar with nautical procedures than shipowners, more familiar with metallurgical processes than ironmasters, more familiar with farming procedures than farmers, more familiar with weaving processes than manufacturers, or more familiar with the procedures followed by the ten thousand of our industries than those who carry them out.

But frankly, is familiarity with all this necessary to the recognition that none of these industries ought to be permitted by law to hold the others for ransom? Is it necessary to have grown old in a factory that makes woolen cloth and to have had profitable materials pass through one's hands in order to be able to consider a question of common sense and justice and to decide that the debate between the person selling and the one buying ought to be free?

It is clear that we are far from ignoring the importance of the role reserved for practical men in the conflict between common rights and privilege.

It is above all through these men that public opinion will be freed from its imaginary terrors. When a man like M. Bacot from Sedan comes forward to say: "I am a manufacturer of woolen cloth, and I do not fear the risks if I am given the advantages of freedom"; when M. Bosson from Boulogne says: "I am a flax spinner, and if the restrictionist regime was not closing off my markets abroad and impoverishing my domestic customers by making my products more expensive, my spinning factory would prosper more"; when M. Dufrayer, a farmer, says: "On the pretext of protecting me, the restrictionist regime has so contrived things that the surrounding population consumes neither wheat, nor wool, nor meat, with the result that I have to engage in the type of farming that suits only poor regions," we know the full effect that these words should be having on the general public.

---

3. "The Declaration of Principles" of the Free Trade Association was published on 10 May 1846. (*OC,* vol. 2, p. 1, "Declaration de principes.") See also CW6 (forthcoming).

When, following this, the matter comes up before the Legislature, the role of practical men will acquire an importance that is almost exclusive. It will no longer be a question of principle, but of action. There will be general agreement that an unjust and artificial situation has to be overturned so that we can get back to one that is equitable and natural. But where do we start? How far shall we go? To solve these problems of execution, it is clear that practical men, or at least those who have lined up to support the principle of liberty, will most have to be consulted.

Far be it from us, therefore, to think of rejecting the contribution made by *specialists*. You would need to have lost your mind if you failed to acknowledge the value of this assistance.

It is nonetheless true that, at the base of this conflict, there are questions that are predominant and primordial, which, if they are to be solved, have no need of the universal technical knowledge that people seem to require from us.

Is it for a lawmaker to balance the profits of various types of industry?

Can he do this without compromising the general good?

Can he, without injustice, increase the profits of some while decreasing those of others?

When endeavoring to do so, will he succeed in distributing his favors equitably?

In this same instance, will this operation not result in a dissipation of *energy*, owing to an inefficient management of production?

And is the evil not worse still if it is totally impossible to favor all types of industry equally?

In sum, are we paying a government to help us damage each other or, on the contrary, to stop us from doing so?

To answer these questions, it is not in the slightest necessary to be an experienced shipowner, an ingenious mechanic, or a first-class farmer. It is even less necessary to have an in-depth knowledge of the processes of all the arts and trades, since these processes bear no relation to the matter. Will people say, for example, that you have to know the *cost price* of woolen cloth to assess whether it is possible to compete with foreigners *on equal terms*? Yes, this is certainly necessary in the view of a protectionist regime, since the aim of this regime is to establish whether an industry is making a loss in order to have this loss borne by the general public. However, it is not necessary to the philosophy of free trade, since free trade is based on the following conundrum: Either your industry is profitable, and therefore protection is no use to you, or it is making a loss, in which case protection is hurting most people.

In what way, therefore, is a specialized survey essential, since whatever the result, the conclusion is always the same?

Let us suppose that we are dealing with slavery. People will doubtless agree that the question of what is right takes precedence over the question of what to do. We can understand that, in order to ascertain the best method of emancipation, an inquiry is needed, but that implies that the question of right has been resolved. However, if it were a matter of debating the question of *right* before the public, if the majority was still favorable to the principle of slavery itself, would we be within our rights to silence an abolitionist by telling him: "You are not competent; you are not a plantation owner, nor do you own slaves"?

Why, then, are people opposed to those who combat monopolies on the grounds that they are not admissible in debate because they do not have monopolies?

Do the shipowners of Le Havre not notice that such claims of ineligibility will be turned against them?

If they are right in claiming that they have detailed knowledge of maritime matters, they doubtless do not claim to have universal knowledge. Well, according to their way of thinking, anyone who dares to speak out against a monopoly has first of all to supply proof that he has detailed knowledge of the industry on which the monopoly has been conferred. They tell us, for our part, that we are not capable of judging whether the law should become involved in making us *overpay* for transport, since we have never chartered ships. But in this case they would be responded to thus: "Have you ever operated a blast furnace, a spinning factory, a factory making woolen cloth or porcelain, or a farm? What right have you to defend yourself against the taxes that these industries are imposing on you?"

The tactics of the prohibitionists are to be admired. They ensure that, if the general public is duped, they are at least always certain of maintaining the *status quo*. If you are not part of a protected industry, they do not accept that you are competent. "You are just for fleecing; you cannot speak." If you are part of a protected industry, you will be allowed to speak, but only about your particular sector of interest, the only one with which you are deemed to be familiar. In this way, monopoly will never be opposed.

12. The Man Who Asked Embarrassing Questions

PUBLISHING HISTORY:

Original title: "L'Indiscret."
Place and date of first publication: *Le Libre-échange,*
12 December 1847, no. 3 (2nd year), p. 20, and 19 December
1847, no. 4 (2nd year), p. 28.
First French edition as book or pamphlet: Not applicable.
Location in Paillottet's edition of *OC:* Vol. 2. *Le Libre-échange,*
pp. 435–46.
Previous translation: None.

Protection for national industry! Protection for national employment! You have
to have a very warped mind and a heart that is truly perverse to decry a notion that is so fine and good.

Yes, certainly, if we were fully convinced that protection, as decreed by the
Chamber with its double vote,[1] had increased the well-being of all Frenchmen, including ourselves, if we thought that the ballot box of the Chamber
with its double vote that is more miraculous than the urn in Cana,[2] had operated the miracle of the multiplication of foodstuffs, clothing, the means
of work, transport, and education, in a word, everything that composes the
wealth of the country, we would be both foolish and perverse to demand
free trade.

And why, in this case, would we not want protection? Well, Sirs, demonstrate to us that the favors it accords to some are not given at the expense

1. The "Law of the Double Vote" was introduced on 29 June 1820 to benefit the ul-
tramonarchists, who were under threat after the assassination of the duc de Berry in
February 1820. The law was designed to give the wealthiest voters two votes so they
could dominate the Chamber of Deputies with their supporters. Between 1820 and 1848,
258 deputies were elected by a small group of individuals who qualified to vote because
they paid more than 300 francs in direct taxes (this figure varied over time from 90,000
to 240,000). One-quarter of the electors, those who paid the largest amount of taxes,
elected another 172 deputies. Therefore, those wealthier electors enjoyed the privilege of
a double vote. Bastiat called them the *classe électorale* (electoral or voting class). See ES3
6, pp. 286–87.
2. This is a reference to the first public miracle which Christ was reported to have
performed, when he turned water into wine at a wedding feast in the town of Cana. See
John 2:1–11.

of others; prove to us that it does good to everyone, to landowners, farmers, traders, manufacturers, artisans, workers, doctors, lawyers, civil servants, priests, writers, or artists. Prove this to us and we promise you that we will align ourselves under its banner for, whatever you say, we are not yet mad.

And, as far as I am concerned, to show you that it is not through caprice or thoughtlessness that I have engaged myself in the struggle, I will tell you my story.

Having read widely, meditated deeply, gathered a host of observations, followed the fluctuations in the market in my village from week to week, and carried out a lively correspondence with a number of traders, I finally arrived at the knowledge of this phenomenon:

WHEN SOMETHING IS SCARCE, ITS PRICE RISES.

From which I considered I might, without excessive boldness, draw the following conclusion:

PRICES RISE WHEN AND BECAUSE THINGS ARE SCARCE.

With this discovery in my pocket, which ought to bring me as much fame as M. Proudhon expects from his famous formula: *Property is theft,*[3] I mounted my humble steed like a new Don Quixote and went off to campaign.

First of all, I introduced myself to a wealthy landowner and asked him:

"Sir, be so good as to tell me why you are so attached to the measure taken in 1822 by the *Chamber with its double vote* with regard to cereals?"[4]

"Heavens, it is obvious! It is because it enables me to sell my wheat better."

"Therefore you think that, between 1822 and 1847, the price of wheat has on average been higher in France thanks to this law than it would have been without it?"

"Yes, certainly I think so; if not, I would not support it."

"And if the price of wheat has been higher, it must have been because there has not been as much wheat in France under this law as without it, for if it had not affected quantity it would not have affected the price."

---

3. Bastiat is referring to Proudhon's work *Qu'est-ce que la propriété? ou Recherches sur le principe du droit et du gouvernement* (1841). Proudhon answered his own question with the statement that "property is theft."

4. There were two periods when French tariff policy was discussed and regulations introduced during the Restoration and the July Monarchy. The first was in 1822 under the Restoration, which created the modern alliance of powerful interest groups which benefited from protectionism; a second, which came from a government inquiry and its subsequent report, occurred in 1834 under the July Monarchy.

"That goes without saying."

I then drew from my pocket a *notebook* on which I wrote these words:

"On the admission of the landowner, for the last twenty-nine years[5] in which the law has existed there has, in the end, been LESS WHEAT in France than there would have been without the law."

I then went to a cattle farmer.

"Sir, would you be so good as to tell me why do you support the restriction placed on the entry of foreign steers by the *Chamber with its double vote?*"

"It is because, through these means, I sell my steers for a higher price."

"But if the price of steers is higher because of this restriction, this is a certain sign that fewer steers have been sold, killed, and eaten in the country in the last twenty-seven years than would have been the case without the restriction?"

"What a question! We voted for the restriction solely for this reason."

I wrote the following words in my *notebook:*

"On the admission of the cattle-breeder, for the last twenty-seven years in which the restriction has existed, there have been FEWER STEERS in France than there would have been without the restriction."

I then hurried off to an ironmaster.

"Sir, would you be so good as to tell me why you defend the protection that the *Chamber with its double vote* has accorded to iron so valiantly?"

"Because, thanks to it, I sell my iron for a higher price."

"But then, also thanks to it, there is less iron in France than if it had not meddled in this, for if the quantity of iron on offer had been equal or greater, how would the price have been higher?"

"It is quite straightforward that the quantity is less, since the precise aim of this law was to prevent an *invasion.*"

And I wrote on my tablets:

"On the admission of the ironmaster, for twenty-seven years, France has had LESS IRON through protection than it would have had through free trade."

"It is all starting to become clear," I said to myself, and I hurried off to a woolen cloth merchant.

---

5. Bastiat is inconsistent with his counting in this article. Sometimes he says 27 years and other times he says 29 years. The tariffs were revised in 1822, so if he were counting from this point the figure should be 25 years, as this article was published in December 1847.

"Sir, would you allow me a small item of information? Twenty-seven years ago, the *Chamber with its double vote,* of which you were a member, voted for the exclusion of foreign woolen cloth. What was its and your reason for doing this?"

"Do you not understand that it is so that I can make more profit from my woolen cloth and become rich more quickly?"

"That was my guess. But are you sure that you have succeeded? Is it certain that the price of woolen cloth has been higher during this period than if the law had been rejected?"

"There can be no doubt of this. Without the law, France would have been swamped with woolen cloth and the price would have become very low; this would have been a major disaster."

"I don't yet see that it would have been a disaster, but be that as it may, you must agree that the result of the law has been to ensure that there has been less woolen cloth in France?"

"This has been not only the result of the law but its aim."

"Very well," said I, and I wrote in my notebook:

"On the admission of the manufacturer, for the last twenty-seven years there has been LESS WOOLEN CLOTH in France because of prohibition."

It would take too long and be too monotonous to go into further detail on this curious voyage of economic exploration.

Suffice it to say that I visited in succession a shepherd who sold wool, a colonial plantation owner who sold sugar, a salt manufacturer, a potter, a shareholder in coal mines, a manufacturer of machines, farm implements, and tools, and everywhere I obtained the same reply.

I returned home to review my notes and put them into order. I can do no better than to publish them here.

"For the last twenty-seven years, thanks to the laws imposed on the country by the Chamber with its double vote, there has been in France:

"Less wheat,

"Less meat,

"Less wool,

"Less coal,

"Fewer candles,

"Less iron,

"Less steel,

"Fewer machines,

"Fewer ploughs,

"Fewer tools,

"Less woolen cloth,

"Less canvas,

"Less yarn,

"Less calico,

"Less salt,

"Less sugar,

"And less of all the things that are used to feed, clothe, and house men, to furnish, heat, and light their dwellings, and to fortify their lives."

By the Good Lord in Heaven, I cried, since this is the case, FRANCE HAS BEEN LESS WEALTHY.

In my soul and conscience, before God and men, on the memory of my father, mother, and sisters, on my eternal salvation, by all that is dear, precious, sacred, and holy on this earth and in the next, I believed that my conclusion was accurate.

And if anyone proves the contrary to me, not only will I abandon any argument on these subjects, but I will abandon any argument on anything at all, for what trust might I place in any argument if I was unable to have confidence in this?

19 December 1847

"Dear reader, you will recall clearly . . ."

"I remember nothing at all."

"What! One week is enough to erase from your memory the story of this famous campaign!"

"Do you think that I am going to meditate on it for a whole week? That is a *very tactless presumption.*"

"I will start it again, then."

"That would be to heap one tactless thing on another."

"You are putting me in a difficult position. If you want the end of the tale to be intelligible, you should not lose sight of the beginning."

"Summarize it."

"Very well. I was saying that on my return from my initial economic peregrination, my notebook said the following: 'According to the statements of all the protected producers, as a result of the restrictive laws of the Chamber with its double vote, France has had less wheat, less meat, less iron, less woolen cloth, less canvas, fewer tools, less sugar, and less of everything than it would have had without these laws.'"

"You are putting me back on track. These producers even said that this was not only the result but the aim of the laws passed by the *Chamber with its double vote*. These laws aimed to raise the price of products by making them scarce."

"From which I deduced this dilemma: Either these laws have not made these products scarce, and in this case they have not made them more expensive and they have failed in their aim, or these laws have made these products more expensive, and in this case they have made them scarce and France has been less well fed, clothed, furnished, heated, and supplied with sugar."

With total faith in this line of argument, I undertook a second campaign. I went to see the wealthy landowner and asked him to glance at my notebook, which he did somewhat unwillingly.

When he had finished reading it, I said to him, "Sir, are you quite sure that, as far as you are concerned, the excellent intentions of the Chamber with its double vote have succeeded?"

"How could they fail to succeed?" he replied. "Do you not know that the better the price at which I sell my harvest, the wealthier I am?"

"That is quite likely."

"And do you not understand that the less wheat there is in the country, the better the price for my harvest?"

"That is also quite likely."

"Ergo (Therefore) . . ."

"It is this *therefore* that worries me, and this is the source of my doubts. If the Chamber with its double vote had stipulated protection for you alone, you would have become wealthy at the expense of others. However, it wanted others to become wealthy at your expense, as this notebook shows. Are you quite certain that the balance of these illicit gains is in your favor?"

"I like to think so. The Chamber with its double vote was peopled with major landowners who were not blind to their own interests."

"In any case, you will agree that, taking all these restrictive measures, not all are beneficial to you and that your share of illicit gain is sorely undermined by the illicit gain of those who sell you iron, ploughs, woolen cloth, sugar, etc."

"That goes without saying."

"What is more, I ask you to weigh this consideration attentively: If France has been less *wealthy*, as my notebook shows . . ."

"An indiscreet notebook, indeed!"

"If," I said, "France has been less wealthy, it must have eaten less. Many people who would have eaten wheat and meat have been reduced to living off potatoes and chestnuts. Is it not possible that this reduction in consumption and demand has influenced the price of wheat downward while your laws sought to influence it upward? And as this occurrence is in addition to the tribute that you pay to ironmasters, the shareholders in mines, the manufacturers of woolen cloth, etc., does it not in the end turn the result of the operation against you?"

"Sir, you are subjecting me to an interrogation that is very intrusive. I enjoy protection, and that is enough for me; your subtle arguments and generalizations will not make me change my mind."

With my tail between my legs, I mounted my horse and went to see the manufacturer of woolen cloth.

"Sir," I said to him, "what would you think of an architect who, in order to raise the height of a column, took from the base the material to add to the summit?"

"I would order for him a bed in the Bicêtre asylum."

"And what would you think of a manufacturer who, in order to increase his output, ruined his customers?"

"I would send him to keep the architect company."

"Allow me then to ask you to glance at this notebook. It contains your considered position and that of many others, from which it clearly emerges that the restrictive laws enacted by the Chamber with its double vote, of which you were a member, have made France less wealthy than it would have been without these laws. Has it never occurred to you that if monopoly hands over to you the consumer market for the entire country, it ruins consumers, and that, if it guarantees you the national market, its first effect is to prohibit you from entering the majority of your markets abroad, and secondly to restrict considerably your markets within the country because of the impoverishment of your customer base?"

"That is indeed a cause of the reduction to my profits, but the monopoly on woolen cloth, all by itself, has not been enough to impoverish my customers to the point where my loss exceeds my profit."

"I ask you to consider that your customers are impoverished not only by the monopoly on woolen cloth but also, as is shown in this notebook, by the monopoly on wheat, meat, iron, steel, sugar, cotton, etc."

"Sir, your insistence is becoming *indiscrete*. I do my business; let my customers do theirs."

"That is what I will be advising them to do."

And, thinking that the same welcome would be in store for me by all those being protected, I dispensed with further visits. "I would be more fortunate," I told myself, "with those who are *not protected*. They do not make the laws, but they do influence public opinion, since they are by far the greatest in number. I will go, therefore, to see traders, bankers, brokers, insurance agents, teachers, priests, authors, printers, joiners, roofers, wheelwrights, blacksmiths, masons, tailors, hairdressers, gardeners, millers, milliners, lawyers, attorneys, and, in particular, the countless class of men who have nothing in this world other than the strength of their arms."

As it happened luck was on my side, and I came across a group of workers.

"My friends," I said to them, "this is a valuable notebook. Would you please cast a glance on it? As you can see, according to the depositions of those who are being protected themselves, France is less wealthy as a result of the laws passed by the Chamber with its double vote than it would be without these laws."

A worker: "Are you certain that the loss falls on our shoulders?"

"I do not know," I replied; "that is what needs to be examined; what is certain is that it has to fall on someone. Well, those *protected* claim that it does not affect them and so it must, then, affect those who are *not protected.*"

Another worker: "Is this loss very large?"

"I think it must be enormous for you; since those *protected,* while admitting that the effect of these laws is to reduce the mass of wealth, claim that, although the mass is smaller, they take a larger share of it, thus incurring a loss twice."[6]

The worker: "How much do you estimate that it is?"

"I cannot assess it in figures, but I can use figures to put across my thought. Let us take the wealth that would exist in France without these laws to be 1,000 and the share taken by those protected to be 500. That of those not protected would also be 500. Since it is accepted that restrictive laws have reduced the total, we can take it to be 800, and since those protected claim that they are richer than they would have been without these laws, they take more than 500. Let us take this to be 600. What is left to you is just 200 instead of 500. This shows you that, in order to earn 1 they make you lose 3."

The worker: "Are these figures accurate?"

"I do not claim they are; all I want is to make you understand that if out of a total that is smaller, those protected take a larger share, those not pro-

6. See Bastiat's discussion of the principle of "the double incidence of loss" in ES3 4.

tected bear all the weight not only of the total decrease but also of the excess amount that those protected allocate to themselves."

The worker: "If this is so, should the distress of those *not protected* not spill over[7] onto those *protected?*"

"I think so. I am convinced that in the long run the loss tends to spread over everyone. I have tried to make *those protected* understand this but have not succeeded in doing so."

Another worker: "Although protection is not directly given to us, we are told that it reaches us, so to speak, by the ricochet or flow-on effect."

"Then all our arguments have to be turned upside down, though they must continue to start from this fixed and acknowledged point, that restriction reduces total national wealth. If, nevertheless, your share is larger, the share of those protected is all the more undermined. In this case, why are you demanding the right to vote? It is quite clear that you ought to leave to such disinterested men the burden of making the laws."

Another worker: "Are you a democrat?"

"I am in favor of democracy if what you understand by this word is: 'to each the ownership of his own work, freedom for all, equality for all, justice for all, and peace among all.'"[8]

"How is it that the leaders of the democratic party are against you?"

"I have no idea."

"Oh! They paint you in a fine light!"

"And what are they capable of saying?"

"They say that you are one of the *learned men;* they also say that you are right *in principle.*"

"What do they mean by that?"

"They simply mean that you are right, that restriction is unjust and causes damage, that it reduces general wealth, that this reduction affects everyone and in particular, as you say, the working class,[9] and that it is one of the things that prevent us and our families from increasing the level of our well-being, education, dignity, and independence. They add that it is a good thing

7. Bastiat uses a synonym for the "ricochet or flow-on effect" in this sentence—*rejaillir* (spill or splash over, cascade). This is one of several words related to the flow of water which he uses for this purpose.

8. See ES3 2, pp. 261–68, for Bastiat's list of ideals suitable for the 1840s, which might be phrased as follows: "liberty, equality, fraternity, tranquility, prosperity, frugality, and stability."

9. Bastiat uses the expression *la classe ouvrière* (the working class).

that this is the case, that it is fortunate that we suffer and are misled as to the cause of our sufferings and that the triumph of your doctrines would, by relieving our misery and dissipating our preconceived ideas, diminish the chances of a great war which they are impatiently awaiting."

"Do they align themselves thus on the side of iniquity, error, and suffering, all to have a great war?"

"They produce admirable arguments on this subject."

"In that case, my being here is rather tactless, and I withdraw."

13. The Fear of a Word

PUBLISHING HISTORY:

> Original title: "La Peur d'un mot."
> Place and date of first publication: *Le Libre-échange,* 20 June
>   1847, no. 30, pp. 239–40.
> First French edition as book or pamphlet: Not applicable.
> Location in Paillottet's edition of *OC:* Vol. 2. *Le Libre-échange,*
>   pp. 392–400.
> Previous translation: None.

I.

> AN ECONOMIST:[1] It is rather strange that a Frenchman who is so
>   full of courage and recklessness, who has no fear of the sword, or
>   of cannon or ghosts and scarcely, indeed, of the devil, should allow
>   himself on occasion to be terrified by a word. Good heavens! I will
>   try the experiment. (*He approaches an artisan and says in a loud
>   voice:* FREE TRADE!)[2]

---

1. This is another example of the "constructed dialogue" format which Bastiat used in fourteen of the seventy-three sophisms he wrote between 1845 and 1850. This was a deliberate strategy adopted by Bastiat to make his discussions of economic principles less "dull and dry."

2. For another discussion of apparently frightening words, see ES3 14. Here, Bastiat notes how easily French people go from one extreme to the other when discussing English politics and economics: "It is hardly possible in this country to judge England impartially without being accused by anglomaniacs of anglophobia and by anglophobics

THE ARTISAN (*scared stiff*): Heavens! You scared me! How can you utter such a dirty word?

E: What ideas, may I ask, do you associate with it?

A: None; but it certainly must be a terrible thing. A Mr. Big[3] often comes into our neighborhood, saying: *Run! Free Trade is coming!* Ah, if you could hear his funereal voice! Look, I still have goose-flesh.

E: And doesn't Mr. Big tell you what it is about?

A: No, but it is certainly some diabolic invention, worse than gun-cotton or the Fieschi machine,[4] or else some wild beast they have found in the Atlas Mountains, halfway between a tiger and a jackal, or else a terrible epidemic, like asiatic cholera.[5]

E: Unless it is one of the imaginary monsters used to frighten children, such as Bluebeard, Gargantua, or the bogeyman.[6]

---

of anglomania" (p. 327). Bastiat's task in this essay is to separate what is really to be feared in England (such as the domination of English politics and the military by an oligarchy of landowners and aristocrats, a phenomenon that he termed *l'oligarcophobie* [oligarchophobia, pp. 335–36]) from that which is most to be admired (the ordinary English people's entrepreneurial energy, their love of liberty, and their belief in free trade). Both anglomania and anglophobia had their own set of sophisms attached to them which Bastiat wanted to refute.

3. Bastiat has the Artisan use the phrase *un gros monsieur,* which means a rich or important man. Given the fact that Bastiat tells us he is a successful local businessman who is trying to defend the privileges the government has given his business, we have translated it colloquially as "Mr. Big."

4. Giuseppe Marco Fieschi (1790–1836) attempted to assassinate King Louis-Philippe in July 1835 with a twenty-five-barreled gun which he had designed himself. All barrels were designed to fire simultaneously, thus killing the king and his entourage as they passed by. The king was only slightly injured, but several others were killed or injured.

5. The first cholera pandemic occurred in 1816–26, having originated in Bengal. Later episodes occurred in France in 1832 (killing 20,000 people in Paris out of a population of 650,000, and 100,000 total in France as a whole) and then in 1849 (killing about 19,000 Parisians, including the young economist and colleague of Bastiat, Alcide Fonteyraud).

6. Gargantua was the creation of the French humanist writer François Rabelais (ca. 1494–1553), who wrote a series of novels about the adventures of two giants, a father and son, Gargantua and Pantagruel (*The Life of Gargantua and of Pantagruel*). The stories are very funny, outrageous, and violent, and are written in a satirical and scatological manner

A: Do you think it is funny? Well then! If you know, tell me what *free trade* is.

E: My friend, it is *trade which is free*.[7]

A: Oh? Bah! Is that all?

E: No more, no less; the right to *freely barter*[8] our services between ourselves.

A: So, *free trade* and *trade which is free* are one and the same thing?[9]

E: Exactly.

A: Well, well! All the same, I prefer *trade which is free*. I do not know whether it is a question of habit, but *free trade* still frightens me. But why didn't Mr. Big tell us what you are telling me?

E: You see, it relates to a rather strange discussion between people who want freedom for everyone and others who also want it for everyone except for their own business. Perhaps Mr. Big was one of the latter group.

A: In any case, he may congratulate himself for making me absolutely terrified, and I can see that I was duped as my late grandfather was.

E: Did your late grandfather also take *free trade* for a three-headed dragon?

A: He often told me that in his youth people had succeeded in arousing his anger against a certain *Madame Véto*.[10] It turned out that this was a law and not the ogress he took it for.

---

that offended the censors. *Croquemitaine* is a generic French word for bogeyman and was used in children's stories.

7. Bastiat is making fun of the French expressions for "free trade" (*libre-échange*) and "trade which is free" (*échange libre*) in which there is merely a swapping of word order.

8. Bastiat uses a different word here, *troquer,* which means to barter or to swap, thus implying that no money is used in the transaction.

9. The Artisan says literally, "So free trade and trade free is the same as white bonnet and bonnet white." The latter might also be translated as "six of one and half a dozen of the other." In the French translation of Lewis Carroll's *Through the Looking-Glass, and What Alice Found There* (1871) there is a similar play on words. The twins Tweedledee and Tweedledum are called "Bonnet Blanc" (Bonnet White) and "Blanc Bonnet" (White Bonnet).

10. *Madame Véto* was the nickname given to Marie Antoinette in 1792 when her husband, King Louis XIV, was using his veto powers repeatedly in order to preserve his constitutional powers in the early years of the French Revolution.

E: That proves that the people still have a lot to learn, and while they are learning it there is no lack of persons like your Mr. Big ready to take advantage of their credulity.

A: So that everything is then reduced to ascertaining whether everyone has the right to carry out his business or if this right is subject to the convenience of Mr. Big?

E: Yes, the question is to know whether, since you suffer from competition when making your sales, you should not benefit from it when making your purchases.

A: Would you please enlighten me more about this?

E: Gladly. When you make shoes, what is your aim?

A: To earn a few écus.

E: And if you were forbidden to spend these écus, what would you do?

A: I would stop making shoes.

E: So your real aim then is not to earn écus?

A: It goes without saying that I seek écus only because of the things I can procure with them: bread, wine, lodging, an overall, a prayer book, a school for my son, a trousseau for my daughter, and fine dresses for my wife.

E: Very good. Let us leave the écus to one side for a moment then and say, to keep things short, that when you make shoes it is to have bread, wine, etc. So why do you not make this bread, wine, prayer book, or these dresses yourself?

A: Mercy me! My entire life would not be long enough to make just one page of this prayer book!

E: So, although your station is fairly modest, it makes you capable of obtaining a thousand more things than you could make yourself.

A: This is quite an agreeable thought, especially when I think that it is true of all stations in society. Nevertheless, as you say, mine is not of the best and I would prefer another, that of a bishop, for example.

E: So be it. But it is still better to be a shoemaker and trade shoes for bread, wine, dresses, etc. than to want to do all these things. Keep to your station then, and try to make the best of it that you can.

A: I do my best with that in mind. Unfortunately, I have competitors who cut me down to size. Ah! If only I were the sole shoemaker in Paris for just ten years, I would not envy the lot of the king and would lay down the law in fine fashion, practically speaking.

E: But, my friend, the others say the same thing, and if there were just one ploughman, one blacksmith, and one tailor in the world, they would lay down the law for you in fine fashion as well. Since you are subject to competition, what is your interest?

A: Good heavens! That those from whom I buy my bread and clothes be subject to it just as I am.

E: For if the tailor in the rue Saint-Denis[11] is too demanding . . . ?

A: I go to the one in the rue Saint-Martin.

E: And if the one in the rue Saint-Denis succeeds in having a law passed that forced you to go to him?

A: I would call him a . . .

E: Calm down! Did you not tell me you have a prayer book?

A: The prayer book does not tell me that I ought not to take advantage of competition, since I am subject to it.

E: No, but it says that you should not mistreat anyone, and that you should always consider yourself to be the greatest sinner of all.

A: I have read it often. But all the same, I find it hard to believe that I am more dishonest than a scoundrel.

E: Continue to believe it, faith saves us. In short, you consider that competition ought to be the law for everyone or for no one?

A: Exactly.

E: And you acknowledge that it is impossible to exempt everyone from its jurisdiction?

A: Obviously, unless you leave just one man in each trade.

---

11. Rue Saint-Denis is one of oldest streets in Paris, having been laid out by the Romans in the first century. An important post horse stop was located there, which meant that it was often the point of entry for people arriving in Paris.

E: Therefore, no one should be exempted?

A: That goes without saying. Each should be free to sell, buy, bargain, barter, or exchange things, but honestly.

E: Well, my friend, that is what is known as *free trade.*

A: Is that all there is to it?

E: That's all. (*Aside:* Here is another convert.)

A: In that case, you may clear off and leave me alone with your free trade. We enjoy it fully. Let anyone who wants to give me his custom do so, and I will give mine to anyone I like.

E: That remains to be seen.

II

A: Ah! Mr. Econo . . . Econa . . . Econe . . . What the devil do you call your trade?

E: You mean *Economist?*

A: Yes, economist. What a strange trade! I bet it earns more than a shoemaker's does; but I also read magazines in which you are smartly dressed! Be that as it may, it is a good thing you have come on a Sunday. The other day, you made me waste a quarter of a day with your discussions.[12]

E: That will happen again. But here you are, dressed to the nines! Good heavens! What a fine suit! The cloth is very soft. Where did you buy it?

A: At the merchant's.

E: Yes, but where did the merchant get it?

A: From the factory, doubtless.

E: And I am sure that he made a profit on it. Why did you not go to the factory yourself?

A: It is too far, or, to tell you the truth, I do not know where it is and have not the time to find out.

---

12. Bastiat uses the word *échanges,* which could mean "the exchange of opinions" or could refer to their discussion about *libre-échange* and *échange libre.*

E: So you have dealings with merchants? People say that they are parasites that sell for a higher price than they pay, and that they have the nerve to make people pay for their services.

A: That has always seemed to me to be very hard, for in the end, they do not fashion woolen cloth as I fashion leather; they sell it to me just as they have bought it. What right have they to make a profit?

E: None. The only right they have is to leave you to go to find your own woolen cloth in Mazamet[13] and your leather in Buenos Aires.

A: Since I occasionally read *La Démocratie pacifique,*[14] I have a horror of merchants, these intermediaries, these stockjobbers,[15] these monopolists, these secondhand dealers, these parasites, and I have often tried to do without them.

E: And?

A: Well, I do not know why, but it has always turned out badly. I have had shoddy goods or ones that did not suit me, or I was made to buy too much at one time, or I did not have any choice; it cost me a great deal of expense, postage and wasted time. My wife, who has a good head on her shoulders and who knows what she wants said to me: "Jacques, get back to making shoes!"

E: And she was right, in the sense that your exchanges being made through the intermediary of merchants and traders, you do not even know from which country you get the wheat that feeds you, the coal that heats you, the leather from which you make shoes, the nails that you use to reinforce them, or the hammer that drives them in.

A: Heavens! I do not really care, provided that they arrive.

E: Others care on your behalf. Is it not fair that they are paid for their time and effort?

A: Yes, but they should not make too much.

13. Mazamet is a town in the Tarn département, then known for its woolens industry.

14. *La Démocratique pacifique* (1843–51) was the most successful of the journals which supported the socialist ideas of Charles Fourier. It was run by Victor Considérant (1808–93).

15. Note that Bastiat himself had a dislike of *agiotage* (stockjobbing) because it dealt mainly with government loans. See ES2 11, where he states his desire to "starve stockjobbing of its profits" (p. 197 esp. n30).

E: You do not need to fear that. Do they not compete with one another?

A: Ah! I had not thought of that.

E: You were telling me the other day that exchanges are perfectly free. As you do not make your trades yourself, you cannot know this.

A: Are those that make them on my behalf not free?

E: I do not think so. Often, by preventing them from entering a market in which things are at a low price, current arrangements force them to enter another in which these things are expensive.

A: That is a dreadful injustice that is being done to them!

E: Not at all! It is to you that the injustice is being done, for what they have bought at a high price, they cannot sell to you cheaply.

A: Tell me more about this, please.

E: Here we go. On occasion, woolen cloth is expensive in France and cheap in Belgium. A merchant who is looking for woolen cloth for you naturally goes where it is available cheaply. If he were free, this is what would happen. He would take with him, for example, three of the pairs of shoes you made, in exchange for which the Belgian would give him enough cloth for him to make you a frock coat. But he does not do this, knowing that, at the border, he will meet a Customs Officer who will shout: "*Not allowed*" at him. So the merchant turns to you and asks for a fourth pair of shoes, since you need four pairs to obtain the same quantity of French woolen cloth.

A: That is the catch! Who set the Customs Officer there?

E: Who could that be, other than the manufacturer of French woolen cloth?

A: And why would he do this?

E: Because he does not like competition.

A: Oh! Damn! I do not like it either, and I have to put up with it.

E: This is what makes us say that trade is not free.

A: I thought that was a matter for the merchants.

E: It concerns you, you yourself, since in the end it is you who pays four pairs of shoes instead of three in order to have a frock coat.

A: That is a nuisance, but is it worth making such a fuss about it?

E: The same operation is repeated for almost everything you buy: wheat, meat, leather, iron, or sugar, so that you obtain for four pairs of shoes just what you might have for two.

A: There is something fishy about that. All the same, I note from what you say that the only competitors that we remove are foreigners.

E: That is true.

A: Well then! The wrong is only half a wrong since, you see, I am as patriotic as any devil.

E: As you wish. But note this well; it is not a foreigner who is losing two pairs of shoes, it is you, and you are French!

A: And proud of it!

E: And then, were you not saying that competition should cover everyone or no one?

A: That would be proper justice.

E: However, Mr. Sakoski is a foreigner, and no one is preventing him from being a competitor of yours.[16]

A: And a strong competitor at that. How he polishes off a pair of boots!

E: It is difficult to cope with, is it not? But since the law allows our dandies to choose between your boots and those of a German, why does it not allow you to choose between French and Belgian woolen cloth?

A: What ought we to do, then?

E: First of all, we should not be afraid of *free trade.*

A: Call it *trade which is free,* that is less frightening. And then what?

---

16. The anomaly which Bastiat is pointing out here is that French tariff policy prohibited trading across borders, such as the Belgian or German borders, thus protecting French manufacturers from competition, but because people were free to move from one country to another, as many thousands of Germans (perhaps as many as sixty thousand) did in order to live and work in Paris, artisans like the one in this sophism were exposed to competition in the trades in which they worked. Bastiat makes this very point in ES2 6, pp. 155–64.

E: Then, you have already said it: demand liberty for all or protection for all.

A: And how the devil do you want the Customs to protect a lawyer, a doctor, an artist, or a poor worker?

E: It is because it cannot do this that it ought not to protect anyone, for to favor the sales of one person is of necessity to burden the purchases of another.

14. Anglomania, Anglophobia[1]

PUBLISHING HISTORY:

Original title: "Anglomanie, anglophobie."
Place and date of first publication: No date given.
First French edition as book or pamphlet: Not applicable.
Location in Paillottet's edition of *OC:* Vol. 7. *Essais, ébauches, correspondance,* pp. 309–27.
Previous translation: None.

These two sentiments stand face to face, and it is hardly possible in this country to judge England impartially without being accused by anglomaniacs of anglophobia and by anglophobics of anglomania. It appears that public opinion, which in France goes beyond what was an ancient Spartan law,[2] condemns us to moral death if we do not rush headlong into one of these two extremes.

However, these two sentiments exist and are already of long standing. They therefore exist justifiably, for, in the world of sympathy and antipathy, as in the material world, there is no cause without an effect.

It is easy to verify that these two sentiments coexist. The great conflict between democracy and aristocracy, between common law and privilege, is continuing, both implicitly and openly, with more or less enthusiasm, with

---

1. (Paillottet's note) This sketch dates from 1847. The author wished to use it as a chapter in the second series of *Economic Sophisms,* which appeared at the end of the year. [This essay originally appeared in volume 1 of *OC,* pp. 320–34. It is reproduced here because it was intended to be an economic sophism, and we wanted our collection of *Economic Sophisms* to be as complete as possible.]

2. In Sparta, every newborn child was examined by the elders. If he was judged fit, he was left with his mother; otherwise, he was thrown into a pit.

more or less opportunity, worldwide. However, nowhere, not even in France, does it resound as much as in England.

As I say, not even in France. Here, in fact, privilege as a social principle was extinct before our revolution. In any case, it received its coup de grace on the night of 4 August.[3] The equal sharing of property constantly undermines the existence of any leisured class. Idleness is an accident, the transitory lot of a few individuals, and whatever we may think of our political organization, it is always the case that democracy is the basis of our social order. Probably, the human heart does not change; those who achieve legislative power seek hard to create a small administrative fiefdom for themselves, whether electoral or economic, but nothing in all that takes root. From one session to another, the slightest hint of an amendment can overturn the whole fragile edifice, remove a whole raft of political appointments, eliminate protectionist measures, or change the electoral districts.

If we cast an eye on other great nations, such as Austria and Russia, we will see a very different situation. There, privilege based on brute force reigns with absolute authority. We can scarcely distinguish the dull murmur of democracy laboring away underground, like a seed that swells and grows far from all human sight.

In England, on the other hand, the two powers are full of force and vigor. I will say nothing of the monarchy, a kind of idol on which the two opposing factions have agreed to impose a sort of neutrality.[4] But let us consider a little how the elements of force with which the aristocracy and democracy do battle are constituted and what the quality of their arms is.[5]

The aristocracy has on its side legislative power. It alone can enter the House of Lords,[6] and it has taken over the House of Commons, without one's being able to say when and how it can be dislodged from it.

It has on its side the established church—all of whose positions have been taken over by the younger sons of great families—an institution unreservedly

3. On the night of 4 August 1789, the National Assembly suppressed all the privileges of the nobility and the clergy, with their agreement, in a moment of great enthusiasm.

4. When the revolution broke out, in February 1848, and the Second Republic was declared, Bastiat demonstrated his strong support for the principles of republicanism in his revolutionary journal *La République française*.

5. See a similar discussion about the struggle between the bourgeoisie and the aristocracy in ES3 6.

6. The House of Lords was composed of hereditary peers, twenty-six Anglican prelates, sixteen Scottish peers, and an indefinite number of peers appointed by the king.

English or Anglican, as its name indicates, and unreservedly a political force, having the monarch as its head.

It has on its side the hereditary ownership of land and entails, which prevent the breaking up of estates. Through this, it is assured that its power, concentrated in a small number of hands, will never be dispersed and will never lose its characteristics.

Through its legislative power, it controls taxes, and its efforts naturally tend to transfer the fiscal burden onto the people while retaining the profit from them.

We thus see it commanding the army and the navy, that is to say, still wielding brute force. And the manner in which recruitment to these bodies is carried out guarantees that it will never transfer its support to the popular cause. We may further note that in military discipline there is something that is both energetic and degrading, which aspires to efface in the soul of the army any urge to share common human feelings.

By means of the wealth and material power of the country, the English aristocracy has been able successively to conquer all parts of the globe it considered to be useful for its security and policy. In doing this, it has been wonderfully supported by popular prejudice, national pride, and the *economic sophism* which attaches so many crazy hopes to the colonial system.[7]

In a word, the entire British diplomatic corps is concentrated in the hands of the aristocracy, and as there are always sympathetic links between all the privileged groups and all the aristocratic classes around the world, since they are all based on the same social principles and what threatens one threatens the others, the result is that all the elements of the vast power I have just described are in perpetual opposition to the development of democracy, not only in England but all over the world.

This explains the War of Independence in the United States and the even more relentless war against the French Revolution,[8] a war carried out using not only steel but also and above all gold, either used to bribe alliances or spent to lead our democracy into excesses, social disorder, and civil war.

There is no need to go into further detail, to show the interest the English aristocracy might have had in stifling, at the same time as the very idea

7. See Bastiat's comments on Algeria and colonization in his address "To the Electors of the District of Saint-Sever," where he describes the colonial system as "the most disastrous illusion ever to have led nations astray" (CW1, pp. 363–65).

8. Great Britain had been at war with France from February 1793 to March 1802, at the head of two European coalitions.

of democracy, any accompanying hints of forceful action, power, or wealth, anywhere. There is no need for a historical exposition of the action it carried out with regard to peoples in this respect, a policy which became known as the *alternating balance of power,* to show that *anglophobia* is not a sentiment that is totally blind and that it has, as I explained at the beginning, its own raison d'être.

As for *anglomania,* if it can be explained as stemming from a puerile sentiment, from the sort of fascination constantly exercised on superficial minds by the spectacle of wealth, power, energy, perseverance, and success, this is not what concerns me. I wish to speak about the serious reasons for sympathy which England is able rightly to generate in other countries.

I have just listed the powerful props of the English oligarchy, the ownership of land, the House of Lords, the House of Commons, taxes, the church, the army, the navy, the colonies, and diplomacy.

The forces of democracy possess nothing so clear and firm of purpose.

Democracy has on its side the power of the spoken word, the press, associations, work, the economy itself, increasing wealth, public opinion, a good cause, and truth.

I think that the progress of democracy is manifest. Look at the major breaches it has made in the walls of the opposing camp.

The English oligarchy, as I have said, had ownership of the land. It still has. But what it no longer has is a privilege grafted on this privilege, the Corn Laws.

It had the House of Commons. It still has, but democracy has entered Parliament through the breach of the *Reform Bill,*[9] a breach which is constantly widening.

It had the established church. It still has, but it is shorn of its exclusive ascendancy by the increase in number and popularity of dissident churches[10] and the *Catholic Emancipation Bill.*[11]

It had control of taxation. It still has taxes at its disposal but, since 1815, all ministers, whether Whigs or Tories, have been constrained to go from

---

9. The Reform Bill of 1832 put an end to the most unfair rules of the previous electoral law and permitted some elements of the middle class to vote for the first time. The franchise was further extended in 1867 and 1885.

10. The Anglican faith was a national church, the Church of England, the religion of the state itself. All other churches, called dissenting, had been legally tolerated since 1689.

11. The Catholic Emancipation Act of 1829 removed many but not all restrictions on Catholics in the United Kingdom.

reform to reform, and at the first financial difficulty, the provisional *income tax* will be converted into a permanent land tax.

It had the army. It still has, but everyone knows the avid concern of the English populace to be spared the sight of red uniforms.

It had the colonies. These provided its greatest moral authority, since it was with the illusory promises of the colonial system that it carried along a populace both swollen with pride and misled. And the people are breaking this link by acknowledging the chimerical nature of the colonial system.

Finally, I have to mention here another conquest the people have made, which is probably the greatest. For the very reason that the weapons of the people are public opinion, a good cause, and the truth, and for the additional reason that they possess in all its fullness the right of defending their cause in the press, through speeches and gatherings, the people could not fail to attract, and in fact they did attract, to their banner the most intelligent and honest of the aristocrats. For it should not be thought that the English aristocracy forms a compact unity, all of like mind. We see, on the contrary, that it is divided on all the major issues and, either through fear, social adroitness, or philanthropy, certain illustrious members of the privileged class are sacrificing part of their own privilege to the needs of democracy.

If those who take an interest in the ups and downs of this great struggle and the progress of the popular cause on British soil are to be called *anglomaniacs,* I declare that I am an *anglomaniac.*

For me there is just one truth and one justice, and equality takes the same form everywhere. I also think that liberty always produces the same results everywhere and that a fraternal and friendly link should unite the weak and oppressed in all countries.

I cannot fail to see that there are two Englands, since in England there are two bodies of sentiment, two principles, and two eternally conflicting causes.[12]

I cannot forget that, although the aristocratic interest wanted to bend American independence beneath its yoke in 1776, it encountered in a few English democrats such resistance that it had to suspend freedom of the press, *habeas corpus,* and distort trial by jury.

I cannot forget that, although the aristocratic interest wanted to stifle our glorious revolution in 1791, it needed to set its army rabble on its own soil

12. Bastiat wrote about "two Englands" in an article in *Le Libre-échange,* 6 February 1848; in CW6 (forthcoming).

against the men of the people who opposed the perpetration of this crime against humanity.

I call those who admire the acts and gestures of the two parties without distinction *anglomaniacs.* I call those who envelop both in a blind, senseless disapproval, *anglophobes.*

At the risk of attracting to this little volume the hammer blows of unpopularity, I am forced to admit that this great, unending, and gigantic effort by democracy to burst the bonds of oppression and attain its rights in full, offers in my view particularly encouraging prospects in England which are not available in other countries, or at least not to the same degree.

In France, the aristocracy fell in '89, before democracy was ready to govern itself. The latter had not been able to develop and perfect in all their aspects those qualities, robustness, and political virtues which alone could keep power in its hands and constrain it to make prudent and effective use of them. The result has been that all parties, all persons even, believed that they could inherit the aristocratic mantle, and conflict thus arose between the people and M. Decazes, the people and M. de Villèle, the people and M. de Polignac, and the people and M. Guizot.[13] This conflict of petty proportions educates us on constitutional matters. On the day we become sufficiently emancipated nothing will prevent us from taking hold of the reins of management of our affairs, for the fall of our great antagonist, the aristocracy, will have preceded our political education.

The English people, on the contrary, are growing in stature and becoming proficient and enlightened through the struggle itself. Historic circumstances which it is pointless to recall here have paralyzed the use of physical force in its hands. It has to have recourse to the power of public opinion alone, and the first condition for making public opinion a power in itself was that the people should enlighten itself on each particular question until unanimity was achieved. Public opinion will not have to be formed after the conflict; it has been formed and is formed during, for, and by the conflict itself. It is

---

13. Bastiat lists here four of the most powerful political figures during the Restoration (1815–30) and the July Monarchy (1830–48). Elie Decazes, duc de Glücksberg (1780–1860), was Minister of the Interior between 1815 and 1820 and briefly Prime Minister in 1819. Auguste-Jules-Armand-Marie de Polignac (1780–1847) was an ultra-royalist politician who served in various capacities during the restoration of the Bourbon monarchy after 1815. He was appointed ambassador to England in 1823, minister of foreign affairs in 1829, and prime minister by Charles X just prior to the outbreak of the July revolution in 1830. For Jean-Baptiste Villèle, comte de (1773–1854), and François Guizot (1787–1874), see the glossary.

always in Parliament that victory is won and the aristocracy is forced to sanction it. Our philosophers and poets shone before a revolution which they prepared, but in England it is during the struggle that philosophy and poetry do their work. From within the popular party come forth great writers, powerful orators, and noble poets who are completely unknown to us. Here we imagine that Milton, Shakespeare, Young, Thompson, and Byron encompass the whole of English literature. We do not perceive that, because the struggle is ongoing, the chain of great poets is unbroken and the sacred fire inspires poets such as Burns, Campbell, Moore, Akenside, and a thousand others, who work unceasingly to strengthen democracy by enlightening it.[14]

Another result of this state of affairs is that aristocracy and democracy confront each other with regard to all questions. Nothing is more likely to perpetuate and aggravate them than this. Something that elsewhere is just an administrative or financial debate is in this instance a social war. As far as one can tell, hardly a single question has sprung up in which the two great protagonists have not been at loggerheads. Henceforth, both sides make immense efforts to form alliances, to draft petitions, and to distribute pamphlets through mass subscription, far less over the issue itself than for the ever-present and living principles involved. This was seen, not only with regard to the Corn Laws, but regarding any law that touched on taxes, the church, the army, political order, education, foreign affairs, etc.

It is easy to understand that the English people have thus had to become accustomed, with regard to any measure, to going back to first principles and to basing discussion on this wide foundation. This being so, in general the two parties are opposite and mutually exclusive. It is a case of *all or nothing,* because both sides feel that to concede something, however small, is to concede the principle. Doubtless, when it comes to voting, bargains are sometimes struck. Reforms have naturally to be adapted to the times and circumstances, but in debates no one gives way and the invariable rule of democracy is this: take everything that is given and continue to demand the rest. And it has even had occasion to learn that its most certain course is to demand *everything,* for fifty years if necessary, rather than content itself with *a little* at the end of a few sessions.

Thus, the most rabid anglophobes cannot deceive themselves that reforms

14. Bastiat lists here a selection of lesser poets and playwrights who also contributed to the development of English and Scottish literature, such as Mark Akenside (1721–70), Edward Moore (1712–57), and Thomas Campbell (1777–1844). The exception, of course, is the famous Scottish poet Robert Burns (1759–96).

in England carry a quotient of radicalism, and therefore of grandeur, which astonishes and enthralls the mind.

The abolition of slavery[15] was won in a single step. On a particular day, at a particular time, the irons fell from the arms of poor blacks in all the possessions of Great Britain. It is related that, during the night of 31st July 1838, the slaves were gathered together in the churches of Jamaica. Their thoughts and hearts, their entire life seemed to be hanging on the hands of the clock. Vainly did the priest try to fix their attention on the most imposing subjects capable of capturing the human mind. Vainly did he speak to them of the goodness of God and their future destiny. There was but a single soul in the congregation and that soul was in a fever of expectation. When the gong sounded the first chime of midnight, a cry of joy such as the human ear had never heard before shook the rafters of the church. These poor creatures did not have enough words and gestures to express the exuberance of their joy. They rushed weeping into each other's arms until, their paroxysm now calmed, they were seen to fall to their knees, raise their grateful arms to heaven, and cover with blessings the nation that had delivered them; the great men, Clarkson and Wilberforce,[16] who had embraced their cause; and the Providence that had shone a ray of justice and humanity into the heart of a great people.

While fifty years were needed to achieve absolute personal freedom, a bargain, a truce, on political and religious freedom was reached more quickly. The *Reform Bill* and the Catholic Emancipation bill, which at first were supported as principles, were delivered as matters of *expediency*. Thus, England has still two major troubles to overcome, the people's charter and the revocation of the established church as the official religion.

The campaign against protectionism is one of those that has been led by the leaders under the safeguard and authority of *principle*. The principle of freedom of trade is either true or false, and has to triumph or fall in its entirety. To strike a bargain would have been to acknowledge that property and liberty are not rights but, depending on the time and place, ancillary circumstances, whether useful or disastrous. To accept discussion on this ground would have been to deprive oneself of everything that constitutes

---

15. The slave trade was abolished in 1807. A bill abolishing slavery in the British colonies was voted in 1833, and it came into effect fully in 1838.

16. Thomas Clarkson (1760–1846) and William Wilberforce (1759–1833) were two of the leaders in the long campaign for abolishing slavery in England.

authority and strength; it would have been to renounce having on one's side the sense of justice that lives in every human heart. The principle of the freedom to trade has triumphed and has been applied to the things that are necessary to life, and it will soon be applied to everything that can be traded internationally.

This cult of the absolute has been transferred to questions of a lesser order. When it was a matter of postal reform,[17] the question was raised as to whether individual communications of thought, the expression of friendship, maternal love, or filial piety, were *taxable matters.* Public opinion replied in the negative, and from that time on a radical, absolute reform has been pursued, with no worry as to whether the treasury would be embarrassed or in deficit in any way. The cost of carrying letters has been reduced to the smallest English coin, since this is enough to pay the state for the service rendered and reimburse it for its costs. And since the post still makes a profit, there should be no doubt that the cost of carrying letters would be reduced still further if there were in England a coin smaller than a *penny.*

I admit that in this audaciousness and vigor there is a touch of greatness which causes me to follow with interest the debates in the English Parliament and, even more, the popular debates that take place in associations and meetings. This is where the future is worked out, where long discussions end up with the question "Are we hitting a fundamental principle?" And if the answer is affirmative, we may not know the day of its triumph, but we can be sure that such triumph is assured.

Before returning to the subject of this chapter, anglomania and anglophobia, I must first warn the reader against a false interpretation that may insinuate itself into his mind. Although the conflict between aristocracy and democracy, ever present and lively at the center of each question, certainly gives heat and life to debates; although by delaying the solution and pushing it further away, it contributes to the maturing of ideas and shapes the political habits of the people, it should not be concluded from this that I consider it an absolute disadvantage for my country not to have the same obstacles to overcome and consequently not to feel the same spur, not to enjoy the same mixture of vivacity and passion.

Principles are no less involved in our country than in England. The only

17. Rowland Hill (1795–1879) pioneered reform of the British postal system in 1839 and 1842 with the introduction of a cheap, prepaid system of postage—the uniform "penny post."

thing is that our debates have to be much more general and *humanitarian* (since the word is sacred), just as, in our neighbor's country, they have to be more national. The aristocratic obstacle, in their eyes, occurs in their country. For us, it is worldwide. There is nothing, of course, to prevent us from taking principles to a height that England cannot yet reach. We do not do this, and this is a result solely of our inadequate degree of respect and devotion for principles.

If *anglophobia* were only a natural reaction in us against English oligarchy, whose policy is so dangerous to the nations and in particular to France, this would no longer be anglophobia but, and may I be forgiven for such a barbarous word (which is more than apposite since it combines two barbaric ideas), *oligarcophobia*.

Unfortunately, this is not so, and the most constant occupation of our major newspapers is to arouse national sentiment against British democracy, against the working classes, who are demanding work, industry, wealth, and the development of their faculties and the strength necessary for their emancipation. It is precisely the growth of these democratic forces, the perfection of work, industrial superiority, the extension of the use of machines, commercial aptitude, and the accumulation of capital, it is precisely an increase of all of these forces, I say, that is represented to us as being dangerous, as being opposed to our own progress and implying as of necessity a proportional decrease in similar forces in our country.

This is the *economic sophism* I have to combat, and it is through this that the subject I have just dealt with is linked to the spirit of this book and which may up to now have appeared to be a pointless digression.

First of all, if what I call here a *sophism* was a truth, how sad and discouraging it would be! If the progressive movement which is making an appearance in one part of the world caused a retrograde movement in another part, if the increase in wealth in one country was achieved at the expense of a corresponding loss spread over all the others, there would obviously be no progress possible overall and, in addition, all national jealousy would be justified. Vague ideas of humanity and fraternity would certainly not be enough to lead a nation to rejoice at progress achieved elsewhere, since such progress would have been attained at its expense. The enthusiasts of fraternity do not change the human heart to that extent, and according to the hypothesis I envisage, it is not even desirable. What element of honesty or delicacy would have me rejoice at one people's elevation to having more than they need if, as a result, another people has to descend to below what they need? No, I am not bound either morally or religiously to carry out such an act of selflessness, even in the name of my country.

This is not all. If this sort of *pendulum* were the law governing nations, it would also be the law governing provinces, communes, and families. National progress is no different from individual progress, from which it can be seen that if the axiom with which I am concerned were a truth and not a sophism, there would not be a man on earth who would not constantly have to strive to stifle the progress of all the others, only to meet in others the same effort made against himself. This general conflict would be the natural state of society, and Providence, in decreeing that *one man's gain is another man's loss,*[18] would have condemned mankind to an endless war and humanity to an invariably primitive condition.

There is no proposition in social science, therefore, that it is more important to elucidate. It is the keystone of the entire edifice. It is absolutely necessary to grasp the true nature of progress and the influence that the progressive condition of one people has on the condition of other peoples. If it were demonstrated that progress in a given constituency has as its cause or effect a proportional depression in the rest of the human race, nothing would remain to us but to burn our books, abandon all hope in the general good, and enter into the universal conflict with the firm determination to be crushed as little as possible while crushing the others as much as we can. This is not an exaggeration; it is the most rigorous logic, that which is the most often applied. A political measure that is so close to the axiom that the profit of one person is the loss of another, because it is the incarnation of this, the Navigation Act of Great Britain was situated openly in the quotation of the famous words of its preamble:[19] *It is necessary for England to crush Holland or be crushed by her.* And we have seen, *La Presse* quotes the same words to have the same measure adopted in France. Nothing is simpler, as soon as there is no other alternative, for peoples, as for individuals, than to crush or be crushed, from which we can see the point at which error and atrocity achieve fusion.[20]

18. This saying is the title of one of the essays of Montaigne, "Le Profit d'un est dommage de l'autre" (One Man's Gain Is Another Man's Loss). Bastiat called this phrase "a standard sophism, one that is the very root of a host of sophisms." See ES3 15, p. 341, and *Essais de Montaigne* 1:130–31, chap. 21, "Le Profit d'un est dommage de l'autre."

19. We have not been able to find the source of this quotation.

20. Bastiat devotes an entire sophism to the inappropriate use of military metaphors in discussions about the economy in ES1 22.

But the sad saying that I mention is well worth being opposed in a special chapter.[21] It is, in effect, not a matter of opposing vague declamations on humanity, charity, fraternity, and self-sacrifice to it. It needs to be destroyed by a demonstration that is, so to speak, mathematical. While being determined to devote a few pages to this task, I will pursue what I have to say about anglophobia.

I have said that this sentiment, insofar as it is linked to this Machiavellian policy which the English oligarchy has caused to weigh for so long on Europe, was justifiable, with its own raison d'être, and should not even be labeled anglophobia.

It deserves this name only when it envelops in the same hatred both the aristocracy and that part of English society that has suffered as much as or more than we from oligarchic predominance and resisted it, the working class, which was initially weak and powerless but which grew sufficiently in wealth, strength, and influence to carry along in its wake part of the aristocracy and hold the other in check, the class to which we should be holding out a hand, whose sentiments and hopes we should share if we were not restrained by the deadly and discouraging thought that the progress it owes to work, industry, and commerce is a threat to our prosperity and independence, and threatens it in another form but as thoroughly as do the policies of the Walpoles, Pitts, etc., etc.[22]

This is how anglophobia has become generalized, and I admit that I can view only with disgust the means that have been used to maintain and arouse it. The first means is simple but no less odious; it consists in taking advantage of the diversity of languages. Advantage has been taken of the fact that English is little known in France to persuade us that all English literature and journalism consisted only of outrages, insults, and slanders perpetually vomited out against France, from which France could not fail to conclude that, on the other side of the Channel, she was the object of general and inextinguishable hatred.

In this we were marvelously served by the boundless freedom of the

21. Bastiat wrote only a very short draft of this proposed chapter. We include this short sophism as ES3 15.

22. Robert Walpole, earl of Oxford (1676–1745), became a member of Parliament in 1700 and was several times a minister. He became chancellor of the exchequer in 1721. William Pitt (the Younger, 1759–1806) became a member of Parliament in 1781 and chancellor of the exchequer in 1782; he was prime minister from 1783 to 1801 and 1804 to 1806. Pitt was a Tory and a strong opponent of the French Revolution.

press and speech which exists in this neighboring country. In England, as in France, there is no question on which opinion is not divided, so that it is always possible, on every occasion, to uncover an orator or a newspaper that has covered the question from the point of view that hurts us. The odious tactic of our newspapers has been to extract from these speeches and writings the passages most likely to humiliate our national pride and quote them as an expression of public opinion in England, taking very good care to keep under wraps everything said or written giving the opposite view, even by the most influential newspapers and the most popular orators. The result has been what it would be in Spain if the press of that entire country agreed to take all quotations from our newspapers from *La Quotidienne*.[23]

Another means, which has been employed very successfully, is silence. Each time a major question has caused organized resistance in England and was likely to reveal whatever existed in that country in the way of life, enlightenment, warmth, and sincerity, you could be sure that our newspapers would be determined to prevent the fact reaching the general public in France, by their silence, and when they have thought it necessary, they have imposed ten years of silence on themselves. As extraordinary as it may seem, English *agitation* against the protectionist regime bears this out.

Finally, another *patriotic fraud* that has been widely used is false translation, with the addition, removal, and substitution of words. This ability to alter the meaning and the spirit of the discourse has meant that there is no limit to the indignation that can be aroused in the minds of our fellow countrymen. For example, when they found *gallant French* meaning "brave Frenchmen" ("gallant" being the word *vaillant* which was transferred to England and to which the only change made was that of the initial *V* to *G*, as opposed to the inverse change made to the words *garant*, "warrant"; *guêpe*, "wasp"; *guerre*, "war"), it was enough to translate it thus: "effeminate, philandering, corrupt nation." Sometimes they went so far as to substitute the word *hatred* for the word *friendship* and so on.

On this subject, may I be allowed to relate the origin of the book I published in 1845 under the title of *Cobden and the League*.

I was living in a village in the heart of the Landes. In this village, there is a discussion group, and I would probably greatly surprise the members of the Jockey Club if I quoted here the budget of our modest association.

---

23. *La Quotidienne* (1814–47) was a very influential ultra-royalist newspaper during the Restoration.

However, I dare to believe that there reigns there an uninhibited gaiety and zest that would not dishonor the sumptuous salons of the boulevard des Italiens. Be that as it may, in our circle we do not only laugh, we also discuss politics (which is quite different), for please note that we have two newspapers there. This shows that we were strong patriots and anglophobes of the first order. As for me, as steeped in English literature as one could be in the village, I had seriously suspected that our newspapers were exaggerating somewhat the hatred that, according to them, the word *French* aroused in our neighbors, and I sometimes happened to express doubts in this regard. "I cannot understand," I said, "why the spirit that reigns in journalism in Great Britain does not reign in its books." But I was always defeated, proof in hand or no.

One day, the most anglophobic of my colleagues, with eyes alight with fury, showed me the newspaper and said, "Read this and see." I read in effect that the prime minister of England had ended a speech by saying, "We will not adopt this measure. If we adopted it, we would fall, like France, to the lowest rank of all the nations." A patriotic flush rose to my cheeks.

However, on reflection, I said to myself, "It seems very extraordinary that a minister, the leader of a cabinet, a man who because of his position has to speak with such reserve and measure, would allow himself to utter an uncalled-for insult, which nothing has motivated, provoked, or justified. Mr. Peel does not think that France has fallen to the lowest rank of all the nations and, even if he thought that, he would not say so, in open Parliament."

I wanted to be sure of my facts. The same day, I wrote to Paris to subscribe to an English newspaper,[24] asking for the subscription to be backdated one month.

A few days later, I received about thirty issues of the *Globe.* I hurriedly searched for the unfortunate statement by Mr. Peel, and I saw that it was as follows: "We could not adopt this measure without descending to the lowest rank of all the nations." The words *like France* were missing.

That put me on the right track, and I have been able to ascertain since then a number of other *pious frauds* in our journalists' method of translating.

But that is not all I learned from the *Globe.* For two years, I was able to follow the development and progress of the *League.*[25]

24. *The Globe and Traveller* was founded by an Irish journalist, Edward Quin (d. 1823), in 1803 with the aim of serving the needs of commercial travelers.
25. The Anti–Corn Law League.

At that time, I was an ardent supporter, as I am today, of the cause of free trade, but I considered it to be lost for centuries, since it is no more spoken of in our country than it probably was in China in the last century. Imagine my surprise and joy on learning that this great question *had grabbed people's attention* across the length and breadth of England and Scotland, and on reading about this uninterrupted succession of huge *meetings*,[26] and the energy, perseverance, and enlightenment of the leaders of this admirable association!

But what surprised me even more was to see that the League was spreading, growing, and spilling floods of light over England, monopolizing the attention of ministers and Parliament, without a word of mention in our newspapers!

Naturally I suspected that there was some correlation between this absolute silence on such a serious matter and the system of *pious frauds* in translation.

Naively thinking that it was sufficient for this silence to be broken just once for it not to persist any longer, I decided, trembling, to become a writer, and I sent a few articles on the League to *La Sentinelle* in Bayonne.[27] However, the Paris newspapers paid not the slightest attention to them. I set about translating a few speeches by Cobden, Bright, and Fox and sent them to Paris newspapers themselves; they did not print them. "It is not to be tolerated," I said to myself, "that the day on which free trade is proclaimed in England should surprise us in our ignorance. I have only one course, which is to write a book . . ."

15. One Man's Gain Is Another Man's Loss[1]

PUBLISHING HISTORY:

Original title: "Le Profit de l'un est le dommage de l'autre."
Place and date of first publication: No date given.
First French edition as book or pamphlet: Not applicable.

---

26. In English in the original.

27. The three articles on "Free Trade: State of the Question in England" appeared in *La Sentinelle des Pyrénées* between 18 May and 1 June 1843. Bastiat's first known writings on free trade, they will appear in CW6.

1. (Paillottet's note) Draft written in 1847. The author stopped at this short preamble to the chapter he had promised in the previous draft. He quickly realized that one chapter was not enough for the refutation he planned. A book was needed, and so he wrote the *Harmonies*. (*OC*, vol. 6, *Harmonies économiques*; in CW5 (forthcoming).)

Location in Paillottet's edition of *OC:* Vol. 7. *Essais, ébauches, correspondance,* pp. 327–28.
Previous translation: None.

Let me speak of a standard sophism, one that is the very root[2] of a host of sophisms, one that is like a polyp which you can cut into a thousand pieces only to see it produce a thousand more sophisms, a sophism that offends alike against humanity, Christianity, and logic, a sophism that is a Pandora's box from which have poured out all the ills of the human race, in the form of hatred, mistrust, jealousy, war, conquest, and oppression, and from which no hope can spring.

O you, Hercules, who strangled Cacus! You, Theseus, who killed the Minotaur! You, Apollo, who killed Python the serpent! I ask you all to lend me your strength, your club and your arrows, so that I can destroy the monster that has been arming men against one another for six thousand years!

Alas, there is no club capable of crushing a sophism. It is not given to arrows, nor even to bayonets, to pierce a proposition. All the cannons in Europe gathered at Waterloo could not eliminate an entrenched idea from the hearts of nations. No more could they efface an error. This task is reserved for the least weighty of all weapons, the very symbol of weightlessness, the pen.

For this reason, neither the gods nor the demigods of antiquity should be invoked.

If I wished to speak from the heart, I would take inspiration from the Founder of the Christian religion. Since I am speaking to people's intellects and the matter in hand is to try to produce definitive, formal argument, I will stand under the banner of Euclid[3] and Bezout, while calling for help from Turgots, Says, Tracys, and Charles Comtes of this world.[4] People will say

---

2. Bastiat uses the phrase *sophisme souche* (the rootstock of sophisms). Note that he uses the word *souche* in the made-up name he gave to the tax collector M. Lasouche in ES2 10. We translated this as "Mr. Blockhead."

3. Euclid (fourth century B.C.). Ancient Greek geometer whose book *The Elements* was the standard work on geometry for hundreds of years.

4. Anne-Robert-Jacques Turgot, baron de Laulne (1727–81), was an economist of the physiocratic school, a politician, reformist bureaucrat, and economist. He was appointed by Louis XVI as minister of finance between 1774 and 1776, during which time he attempted to reduce regulations and taxation. Jean-Baptiste Say (1767–1832) was the leading French political economist in the first third of the nineteenth century. Antoine Destutt de Tracy (1754–1836) was one of the leading intellectuals of the 1790s and early 1800s and a member of the "ideologue" school of thought. His *Treatise of Political Econ-*

that this is not very lively. What does it matter, provided that the argument advanced is successful?...

16. Making a Mountain Out of a Molehill[1]

PUBLISHING HISTORY:

Original title: "Midi à quatorze heures."
Place and date of first publication: An unpublished outline from 1847.
First French edition as book or pamphlet: Not applicable.
Location in Paillottet's edition of *OC:* Vol. 2. *Le Libre-échange,* pp. 400–409.
Previous translation: None.

People have made political economy into a science fraught with subtleties and mystery. Nothing in it happens naturally. It is despised and ridiculed as soon as it dares to give a simple answer to a simple phenomenon.

"Portugal is poor," people say. "What is the reason for this?"

"Because the Portuguese are dull, lazy, improvident, and badly governed," says political economy.

"No!" comes the reply, "it is trade that is doing all the damage. It is the Treaty of Methuen,[2] the invasion of woolen cloth from England at low prices, a scarcity of money, etc."

---

omy was translated by Thomas Jefferson in 1817. Charles Comte (1782–1837) was one of the leading liberal theorists before the 1848 revolution, who founded, with Charles Dunoyer, the journal *Le Censeur* in 1814 and *Le Censeur européen* in 1817. In 1826 he published the first part of his magnum opus, a four-volume *Traité de législation,* which very much influenced the thought of Bastiat.

1. The French title is "Midi à quatorze heures," which is part of the French expression "chercher midi à quatorze heures" (looking for midday at two o'clock), which means to look for complicated explanations when reality is simpler. The nearest English expression we could find was "to make a mountain out of a molehill."

2. The treaty of Methuen (named after one of the negotiators, John Methuen) was a commercial treaty between England and Portugal signed in 1703 during the War of Spanish Succession (1701–14). It allowed for the free entry of English textiles into Portugal and was thus wrongly accused of having caused a decline in the Portuguese economy. In return, Portuguese wine ("port") was subject to lower tariffs than French wine, thus creating a new market for Portuguese wine in England.

And people continue: "The English work hard, and yet there are a great many poor people in their country; how can this be?"

"Because what they earn through work is taken from them through taxes," political economy replies naively. "It is distributed to colonels, commodores, governors, and diplomats. In far-off places acquisition is being made of territory that is expensive to obtain and even more so to retain. Well, what is earned once cannot be spent twice, and what the English put into satisfying their love of glory cannot be devoted to their genuine needs."

"What a sorry and prosaic explanation!" comes the cry. "It is the colonies that make England rich!"

"You were just saying that it was poor, in spite of working hard."

"English workers are poor, but England is wealthy."

"That is what it is; work produces and politics destroys. That is why work has no reward."

"But it is politics that generates work, by supplying that work with colonies as tributaries."

"On the contrary, colonies are founded at the expense of work, and it is because they are used for this purpose that they are not used to feed, clothe, educate, and improve the moral code of workers."

"But here is a nation that works hard and has no colonies. According to you, it should grow wealthy."

"That is probable."

"Well then! It is not. Now extricate yourself from that!"

"Let us see," says political economy, "perhaps this nation is reckless and wasteful. Perhaps it has a mania for turning all its revenue into festivities, games, dances, shows, brilliant costumes, luxury objects, fortifications, or military parades."

"What heresy! When in fact luxury enriches nations ... However, this nation is suffering. How does it not even manage to have enough bread?"

"Probably because the harvest has failed."[3]

"That is true. But have men not the right to live? Besides, can they not bring in food from abroad?"

"Perhaps this nation has passed laws forbidding this."

"That is also true. But is this not a good thing, to stimulate the production of food within the country?"

---

3. Bastiat might have in mind the Great Famine in Ireland. See the entry for "Irish Famine and the Failure of French Harvests, 1846–47," in the Glossary of Subjects and Terms.

"When there is no food in the country, the choice has to be made, either to do without or to bring it in."

"Is this all you have to teach us? Are you not able to suggest to the State a better solution to the problem?" . . .

So, people always want to provide complicated explanations to the simplest problems and consider themselves learned only if they try *to make a mountain out of a molehill.*

As economic facts act and react on one another, in turn becoming cause and effect, it must be agreed that they present an undeniable complication. However, with reference to the general laws that govern these facts, they are admirable in their simplicity to the extent that they sometimes embarrass the person who takes on the task of setting them out, since the public's reaction is such that it is as suspicious of what is simple as it is tired of what is not. If you show them that the sources of wealth are work, order, thrift, freedom, and security, and that laziness, dissipation, rash enterprises, wars, or attacks on property bring nations to ruin, they shrug their shoulders and say: "Is that all! Is that the economics of societies? . . . The most modest housewife organizes herself in accordance with these principles. It is impossible for such trivialities to be at the basis of a science, and I will seek an answer elsewhere. Let us discuss Fourier.

> People are trying to find out what he meant after he has
> spoken;[4]

but in his pivots, aromas, and scales, in his passions in major or minor key, in his flights of fancy, postfaces, cisfaces, and transfaces, there is something that at least resembles a scientific structure."[5]

In many respects, however, collective needs, work, and prudence resemble individual needs, work, and prudence.

Therefore, if an economic question should stump us, let us go and look at Robinson Crusoe[6] on his island, and we will find the answer to it.

4. This line is spoken by Chrysale and comes from act 2, scene 7, of Molière's play *Les Femmes savantes* (The Learned Ladies; Molière, *Théâtre complet de Molière* 8:70).

5. Bastiat is making fun of the complex definitions used by Fourier in his social theory. For example, he categorizes the passions into three kinds, the Cabalist, the Papillonne (Butterfly), and the Composite. See Fourier, *Le Nouveau monde industriel et sociétaire*, p. 283. Bastiat's list also reflects Fourier's tendency to overcategorize things, such as the preface (which goes before the main text), the postface (which goes after), the cisface (which is on this side), and the transface (which goes on the other side).

6. Bastiat is referring here to the activities of Robinson Crusoe, which he did several times in *Economic Sophisms* and *Economic Harmonies* as a thought experiment to explore

Do we need to compare freedom with restriction?

To establish what constitutes labor and what capital?

To ascertain whether one is oppressing the other?

To assess the effects of machinery?

To decide between luxury and thrift?

To judge whether it is better to export than to import?

Whether production may be overabundant and consumption deficient?

Let us run off to the island to see the poor shipwrecked sailor. Let us see him in action. Let us examine the motives, the purpose, and the consequences of his actions. We will not learn everything there, in particular not those things that relate to the distribution of wealth in a society of many people, but we will glimpse the basic facts. We will observe general laws in their simplest form of action, and political economy is there in essence.

Let us apply this method to just a few problems.

"Sir, is it not machinery that is killing off work? Machines are taking the place of people; they are the reason there is an overabundance of production and why humanity is reduced to being no longer able to consume what is being produced."

"Sir, allow me to invite you to accompany me to the Island of Despair. Here is Robinson Crusoe, who is laboring to produce food for himself. He hunts and fishes all day long. He has not a minute to repair his clothes and build himself a cabin. But what is he doing now? He is gathering together bits of string and making a net, which he stretches across a river. The fish catch themselves and Robinson Crusoe now has to devote just a few hours a day to obtaining his food. Now, he will be able to deal with his clothes and house himself."

"What conclusion do you draw from this?"

"That a machine does not *kill off* work but makes it *available,* which is a totally different thing, for work *killed off,* as when a man's arm is cut off, is a loss, whereas work made available, as though we are being given a third arm, is a benefit."

"And is this true in a society?"

"Without doubt, if you accept that the needs of society are indefinite, like those of one man."

"And if they were not indefinite?"

"In this case the profit would be translated into leisure."

---

the nature of economic action. See "Bastiat's Invention of 'Crusoe Economics,'" in the Introduction.

"But you cannot deny that in a social state a new machine leaves people without work."

"Some people, temporarily, I agree, but I disagree with regard to employment as a whole. What produces the illusion is this: people fail to see that a machine cannot make a certain amount of work *available* without making a corresponding quantity of pay equally *available*."

"How is this?"

"Let us suppose that Robinson Crusoe, instead of being alone, lives in society and sells fish instead of eating it. If, having invented the fishing net, he continues to sell fish at the same price, everyone except him will have to do the same amount of work to obtain it as before. If he sells fish cheaper, all his customers will achieve a saving, which will be used to stimulate and remunerate some other work."

"You have just mentioned savings. Would you dare say that the luxury of the wealthy does not enrich merchants and workers?"

"Let us return to Robinson Crusoe's island to form an accurate idea of luxury. Here we are; what do you see?"

"I see that Robinson Crusoe has become a Sybarite.[7] He no longer eats to satisfy his hunger; he likes variety in his meals, stimulates his appetite artificially, and, what is more, he takes care to change the line and color of his clothes every day."

"He creates work for himself this way. Is he genuinely richer?"

"No, because while he makes clothes and stirs his pots, his weapons are rusting and his cabin is falling down."

"A general rule that is very simple and much overlooked is this: each piece of work gives one result and not two. The work wasted in contenting yourself with puerile fantasies cannot satisfy more genuine needs, which are of a higher order."

"Is this also true in a society?"

"Absolutely. For a nation, work required by a taste for fashion and entertainment cannot be devoted to its railways or education."

"If the tastes of this nation turned toward study and travel, what would become of its tailors and actors?"

"Teachers and engineers."

"With what would society pay more teachers and engineers?"

---

7. Sybaris was an ancient Greek city in southern Italy which was renowned in the sixth century B.C. for its wealth and the luxurious living of its inhabitants.

"With the money it did not pay to actors and dressmakers."

"Are you insinuating that in a social state people should exclude any form of entertainment and all forms of art and clothe themselves simply instead of adorning themselves?"

"That is not my idea. I say that work that is used for one purpose is taken from another, and that it is up to the common sense of the people, like that of Robinson Crusoe, to choose. Only you need to be fully aware that luxury *does not add anything* to work; it just displaces it."

"Would we also be able to study the Treaty of Methuen on the Island of Despair?"

"Why not? Let us take a walk there … Do you see, Robinson Crusoe is busy making clothes to protect himself from the rain and cold. He is regretting the time he has to spend on this, as he also needs to eat and his garden takes up all his time. But here is a canoe that has come to the island. The stranger that disembarks shows Robinson Crusoe some warm clothes, offers to trade them to him for a few vegetables, and offers to continue this exchange in the future. Robinson Crusoe first looks to see whether the stranger is armed. Seeing that he has neither arrows nor a tomahawk, he says to himself: "After all, he cannot lay claim to anything that I do not agree to; let us have a look." He examines the clothes, calculates the number of hours he would spend making them himself, and compares this with the number of hours he would have to add to his gardening work to satisfy the stranger. If he finds that the trade, while leaving him just as well fed and clothed, makes a few extra hours of his time *available,* he will accept, knowing full well that these hours saved are a net gain, whether he devotes them to work or leisure. If, on the other hand, he thinks that the bargain is not advantageous, he will refuse it. What need is there in this case for an external force to forbid it to him? He is able to refuse it himself.

"Returning to the Treaty of Methuen, I say: The Portuguese nation takes woolen cloth from the English in return for wine only because, through this procedure, a given quantity of work in the end gives it more wine and more woolen cloth. After all, it trades because it *wants to* trade. This decision did not need a treaty. Actually, it should be noted that a treaty, in the form of a trade treaty, can only result in the destruction of conflicting agreements. So much so, that if the treaty were to stipulate that trade be free, it would be stipulating nothing at all. It should limit itself to letting the parties specify their own terms. The Treaty of Methuen does not say that the Portuguese will be forced to give wine for woolen cloth; it says that the Portuguese will take woolen cloth in exchange for wine, *if they wish.*"

"Ah! Ah! Ah! Do you not know?"

"Not yet."

"I have been alone to the Island of Despair. Robinson Crusoe is ruined."

"Are you quite sure?"

"He is ruined, I tell you."

"Since when?"

"Since he started giving vegetables in exchange for clothes."

"And why does he continue to do so?"

"Do you not know the arrangement he made in the past with the neighboring islander?"

"This arrangement allowed him to take clothes in exchange for vegetables, but did not force him to do so."

"Doubtless, but this rascal of an islander has so many skins available to him and is so skilled at preparing and sewing them, in a word, he is giving *so many* clothes for *so few* vegetables that Robinson cannot resist the temptation. He is very unfortunate that there is no *state* over him to control his conduct."

"What could the State do in this instance?"

"Forbid the trade."

"In this case, Robinson Crusoe would make his clothes as before. What is stopping him, if it is to his advantage?"

"He tried, but he cannot make them as fast as he produces the vegetables asked of him in return. And this is why he continues to trade. Actually, in the absence of a State, which doesn't need to reason with him and which conducts itself by means of orders, could we not send an issue of *Le Moniteur industriel* to poor Robinson Crusoe in order to open his eyes?"

"But, according to what you are telling me, he must be much richer than he was before."

"Can you not understand that the islander is offering him an ever-increasing quantity of clothes in return for a quantity of vegetables that remains the same?"

"That is the very reason why the bargain is becoming better and better for Robinson Crusoe."

"He is ruined, I tell you. That is a fact. You surely will not take issue with the facts?"

"No, but against the cause you are assigning to him. Let us go together to the island. But what do I see! Why have you hidden this fact from me?"

"Which one?"

"See how Robinson Crusoe has changed! He has become lazy, indolent, and disorganized. Instead of using the time that his bargain has made available to him, he is wasting both this time and more. His vegetable garden is overgrown; he is now producing neither clothes nor vegetables; he is wasting or destroying what he once made. If he is ruined, what other explanation are you seeking?"

"Yes, but what about Portugal?"

"Is Portugal lazy?"

"It is, I cannot disagree with that."

"Is it disorganized?"

"To a degree that cannot be contested."

"Does it make war on itself? Does it harbor factions, sinecures, or abuses?"

"Factions are tearing it apart, sinecures are thick on the ground, and it is the very home of abuses."

"Therefore the reason for its misery is the same as for Robinson Crusoe."

"That is too simple. I cannot be satisfied with that. *Le Moniteur industriel* sees things in a quite different light. It is not among those who would explain poverty by quoting disorder and laziness. I would suggest therefore that you take the trouble to study economic science if you want to gain a proper understanding!"

17. A Little Manual for Consumers; In Other Words, for Everyone

PUBLISHING HISTORY:

> Original title: "Le Petit manuel du consommateur ou de tout le monde."
> Place and date of first publication: An unpublished outline from 1847.
> First French edition as book or pamphlet: Not applicable.
> Location in Paillottet's edition of *OC:* Vol. 2. *Le Libre-échange,* pp. 409–15.
> Previous translation: None.

Consume—Consumer—Consumption; these are ugly words that represent people as so many barflies, constantly with coffee cups or wine glasses in front of them.

But political economy is obliged to use them. (I am referring to the three words, not the wineglasses.) It does not dare to invent others, as it has found these ready-made.

Let us nevertheless set out what they mean. The aim of work, both cerebral and manual, is to satisfy one of our needs or desires. There are therefore two terms in economic evolution: effort and reward. Reward is the product of effort. It takes effort to *produce;* enjoying the reward is *to consume.*

We can therefore *consume* an intellectual work in the same way as one produced manually: a drama, a book, a lesson, a picture, a statue, or a sermon in the same way as wheat, furniture, or clothes, visually, aurally, through the mind, or through the emotions in the same way as through the mouth and the stomach. This being so, I have to agree that the word *consume* is very narrow, very commonplace, very unsuitable, and very strange. However, I do not know any other ones, and all that I can do is to repeat what I mean by the term, namely to enjoy the reward achieved by work.

There is no metric, barometric, or dynamometric scale that can give a standard measurement of effort and reward, nor will there be until the means have been found to size up distaste and to weigh a desire.

Each person is in it for himself. Since the reward and burden of effort concern me, it is up to me to compare them and see whether the one is worth the other. In this respect, coercion would be all the more absurd since there are no two men on earth who will form the same assessment in every case.[1]

Exchange does not alter the nature of things. The general rule is that it is up to the person who wants the reward to put in the effort. If he wants the reward of other people's efforts, in return he has to offer the reward of his own effort. When this happens, he compares the strength of his desire with the trouble he would have undertaken to satisfy it and says: "Who wants to go to this trouble on my behalf? I will do the same for him."

And, as each person is the sole judge of the desire he feels and the effort demanded of him, the essential character of these transactions is that they are free.

When freedom is banished, you may be sure that one of the contracting parties is either put to too much trouble or receives too small a reward.

What is more, the action of coercing his fellow man is itself an *effort,* and

---

1. This is another example of Bastiat grappling with the idea of subjective value theory, which was later to be an important part of the Austrian school of economics. The breakthrough came in the 1870s, with the near-simultaneous publication of works by Carl Menger (1840–1921), *Principles of Economics* (1871); Stanley Jevons (1835–1882), *The Theory of Political Economy* (1871); and Léon Walras (1834–1910), *Elements of Pure Economics* (1874). These works collectively brought about a change in economic thought known as the Marginal Revolution.

resistance to this action is another *effort,* both of which are entirely lost to the human race.

We must not lose sight of the fact that there is no uniform and immutable conformity between an effort and its reward. The effort required to obtain wheat is less great in Sicily than on the summit of Mont Blanc. The effort required to obtain sugar is less great in the tropics than in Kamchatka. The best distribution of effort in the places in which it is most helped by nature and the perfectibility of the human mind tend to reduce constantly the ratio between effort and reward.

Since the effort is the means, the burdensome part of the operation, and the reward is its aim, end, and fruit, and since, on the other hand, there is no invariable ratio between these two things, it is clear that, in order to know whether a nation is wealthy, it is not the effort that should be looked at, but the result. The degree of effort does not tell us anything. The extent to which needs and desires are satisfied tells us all. This is what economists understand by these words that have been so strangely commented on: "The self-interest of the consumer, or rather consumption, is the general interest." The progress of the satisfactions a nation enjoys is obviously the progress of this nation itself. This is not necessarily true of the progress of its efforts.

This is not a pointless observation, for there are eras and countries in which the increase in the duration and intensity of effort has been taken as the touchstone of progress. And what has been the result? Laws have been applied to reducing the relationship between reward and effort so that, propelled by the intensity of desire and the call of human need, men might constantly increase their efforts.

If an angel or infallible being were sent to govern the earth, he might be able to tell each person how he should act so as to ensure that all effort would be followed by the greatest possible reward. As this has not happened, this task must be entrusted to LIBERTY.

We have already said that freedom is total justice. What is more, it strongly tends to achieve the result sought: to obtain the greatest possible reward from every effort or, in order not to lose sight of our special subject, the greatest level of consumption possible.

In fact, under a free regime, each person is not only encouraged but also bound to achieve the best outcome from his efforts, his abilities, his capital, and the natural advantages that are available to him.

He is bound to do this by competition. If I decided to extract iron from the ore found in Montmartre, I would need a great deal of effort to do this for a very meager reward. If I wanted this iron for myself, I would soon see that I would obtain more through trade by orienting my work in a different direction. And if I wanted to trade my iron, I would see even more quickly that, although it had cost me a great deal of effort, people would be willing to offer me only very little effort in return.

What drives us all to reduce the ratio of effort to result is our personal interest. But, and this is a strange and wonderful thing, there is in the free play of the social mechanism something which, in this respect, causes us to proceed from disappointment to disappointment and upsets our calculations to the benefit of the human race.

This means that it is strictly true to say that others benefit more than we do from our own progress. Fortunately the benefit we draw from other people's progress unfailingly compensates for this.

This warrants a brief explanation.

Take situations however you please, from the top or the bottom, but follow them attentively and you will always recognize the following:

The advantages that benefit producers and the disadvantages that hinder them only *wash over*[2] them without being able to be stopped. In the long run these are translated into advantages or disadvantages for consumers, the general public. They can be summed up as an increase or decrease in general enjoyment. I do not want to expand on this here; that will come later, perhaps. Let us proceed through the use of examples.

I am a joiner and make planks using an axe. People pay me 4 francs per plank, as it takes me one day to make one. As I want to improve my situation, I seek a way of making them faster and am fortunate enough to invent the saw. Here I am, making 20 planks a day and earning 80 francs. Very good, but this high profit attracts attention. Everyone wants a saw, and soon no one will pay me more than 4 francs for making 20 planks. Consumers save 19/20 of their expenditure while the only advantage remaining to me, as to them, is to obtain planks with less trouble when I need them.

Another example in the opposite direction.

A huge tax is imposed on wine and paid at harvest time. This is an advance required from producers, which producers endeavor to recoup from consumers. The struggle will be long and the suffering shared for a long time.

---

2. Bastiat uses a synonym for the "ricochet or flow-on effect" in this sentence—*glisser* (to slide or slip). This is one of several words related to the flow of water which he uses for this purpose.

The wine producer will perhaps be reduced to grubbing up his vines. The value of his land will decrease. One day he will sell it at a loss, and then the new purchaser, who has included the tax in his calculations, will have no reason to complain. I do not deny all the damage inflicted on producers any more than the temporary benefits they enjoy in the previous example. However, I say that in the long run the tax becomes part of the production costs, and consumers will have to pay them all, the tax along with the rest. A century or perhaps two centuries later, the wine-producing industry will be based on this; people will have grubbed up vines, sold land, and suffered in vineyards, and in the end, consumers will bear the tax.

It must be said in passing that this proves that if we are asked which tax is the least burdensome, we would have to reply: "The oldest, the one that has given the disadvantages and inconveniences the time to run through their disastrous cycle."

The logic of what we have been saying is that, in the long run, consumers reap all of the benefits of good legislation just as they suffer the disadvantages of bad; in other words, good laws lead to an increase and bad laws to a decrease in the benefits enjoyed by the public. This is why consumers, the general public, must keep their eyes open and minds alert, and why I am addressing myself to them.

Unfortunately, consumers are hopelessly good-humored, and this is why. Since misfortunes reach them only at the end of the process and one after the other, they have to be very provident. Producers, on the other hand, receive the first shock; they are always on the lookout.

Man, as a *producer,* is burdened with the onerous part of economic development, namely the effort. It is as a *consumer* that he is rewarded.

It has been said that producers and consumers are one and the same.

If a product is considered on its own, it is certainly not true that producers and consumers are one and the same, and we can often see one exploiting the other.

If we generalize, the axiom is perfectly accurate, and this explains the immense disappointment which is felt after any injustice or any attack on liberty; producers, by wishing to hold consumers for ransom, hold themselves for ransom as well.

There are those who believe that there is compensation. No, there is no compensation; first of all because no law is capable of allocating to each person an equal share of injustice, and also because when injustice occurs there is always a loss of benefits which can be enjoyed, especially when this injustice consists, as in a restrictive regime, in displacing labor and capital and reducing the general compensation on the pretext of increasing overall production.

To sum up, if you have two laws or two systems to compare, if you consult the interest of producers you may go down the wrong path; if you consult the interest of consumers, you cannot do this. It is not always a good thing to increase effort as a whole but never a bad thing to increase the total amount of satisfaction . . .

18. The Mayor of Énios[1]

PUBLISHING HISTORY:

> Original title: "Le Maire d'Énios."
> Place and date of first publication: *Le Libre-échange,* 6 February 1848, no. 11, pp. 63–64.
> First French edition as book or pamphlet: Republished in *L'Annuaire de l'économie politique et de la statistique* (1848), pp. 348–57.
> Location in Paillottet's edition of *OC:* Vol. 2. *Le Libre-échange,* pp. 418–29.
> Previous translation: None.

The Mayor of Énios was quite a strange Mayor. Quite a character . . . But first of all, it is a good thing for the reader to know what Énios is.

Énios is a village in the Béarn[2] situated . . .

---

1. Bastiat names his fictional town after Énios (or Ænius) who was one of several Trojans killed by "terrible Achilles" in the *Iliad,* Book XXI. In Thomas Hobbes' translation it goes "Then with his sword he slew Thersilochus, And after him the stout Astypylus, And Opholostes, Mydon, Ænius, And after these, Mnesus and Thrasius, And had shed yet much more Pæonian blood . . ." This is one of the very few occasions where Bastiat used a figure from an ancient Greek or Roman work in his writings, as he despised the moral values of the ancient authors as slave owners, warriors, and plunderers. See *The English Works of Thomas Hobbes of Malmesbury; Now First Collected and Edited by Sir William Molesworth, Bart.,* (London: Bohn, 1839–45). 11 vols. Vol. 10. Homer's *Iliad,* Book XXI http://oll.libertyfund.org/titles/773#lf0051-10_head_3021.

2. Béarn is a region located at the base of the Pyrénées in southwest France in the département of Pyrénées-Atlantiques. Its capital is the city of Pau.

However, it seems more logical to introduce the Mayor first.

Well then! Here I am, in a fine tangle, right from the start. I would prefer to have algebra to prove than to tell the story of "Donkeyskin."[3]

O Balzac! O Dumas! O Suë![4] O geniuses of fiction and the modern novel, you who in volumes packed tighter than hail in August are able to divide all the threads of an interminable intrigue without mixing them up, at least tell me if it is better to paint the hero before the backdrop or the backdrop before the hero.

Perhaps you will tell me that it is neither the subject nor the place but the time that should be given priority.

Very well, then! It was at the time when asphalt mines . . .

But I think I will be better off relying on my own way of doing things.

Énios is a village which backs against a high and steep mountain to the south, so that the enemy (I am talking about *trade*), in spite of his fraud[5] and daring, cannot, as is said in strategic terms, *fall on its rearguard* nor *take it from behind.*

To the North, Énios stretches out over the rounded crest of the mountain, whose gigantic foot is bathed by the rushing torrent of the *Gave.*[6]

Protected in this way, on one side by inaccessible peaks and on the other by an impassable torrent, Énios would be totally isolated from the rest of France

3. "Peau d'âne" (Donkeyskin) was a fairy tale written by Charles Perrault in 1694. Perrault worked as an administrator serving under Jean-Baptiste Colbert during the reign of Louis XIV. After Colbert's death in 1683 he lost his position and turned to writing children's stories. "Donkeyskin" is about a princess who was desired by her own father, the king, to be his next wife after his first wife, the princess's mother, died. The princess's fairy godmother told her to wear the skin of a donkey as a disguise to avoid her father's attentions (Perrault, *Œuvres choisies de Ch. Perrault,* pp. 175–94).

4. Honoré de Balzac (1789–1850) was a prolific author who was a leading member of the realist school, noted for his detailed depiction of everyday life in France during the July Monarchy. Alexandre Dumas (1802–70) was a prolific author of plays and historical novels such as *The Three Musketeers* (*Les Trois Mousquetaires*) (1844). Eugène Suë (1804–57) was a surgeon and served in the French navy during the 1820s. He was active in the romantic and socialist movements and is best known for the novel series *Le juif errant* (*The Wandering Jew*) (1844–45).

5. Bastiat uses the term *la ruse* (fraud) here. See "Bastiat on Enlightening the 'Dupes' about the Nature of Plunder," in the Introduction.

6. *Gave* is a Gascon word for a river. It can be used generically or with reference to particular rivers. It is a word commonly used in Béarn and Chalosse. The Gave de Pau (the main city of Béarn) was a tributary of the Adour River with which Bastiat was very familiar.

if public works engineers had not built across the Gave a daring bridge of which, to conform to modern *ways of doing things,* I am tempted to give you the description and history.

This would lead me *very naturally* to give you the history of our bureaucracy; I would tell you of the war between civil and military engineering, between the town council, the General Council, the Council for Roads and Bridges, the Council for Fortifications, and a host of other councils. I would paint a picture of weapons that consist of pens and projectiles that consist of files. I would say how one wanted the bridge to be in wood and the other in stone, this one in iron, that one with iron cables; how during this conflict the bridge was not built; how subsequently, thanks to the wise contrivances of our budget, the bridge was started several years running in the depths of winter, so that not a trace of it was left in the spring; how, when the bridge was completed, they noticed that the road leading up to it had been forgotten, at which point you had the fury of the mayor, the embarrassment of the prefect, etc. Finally, I would write a *thirty years' history,* consequently three times as interesting as that written by M. Louis Blanc.[7] But what use would that be? Would I teach anyone anything?

Following this, what would stop me from writing a description half a volume long on the bridge of Énios, its abutments, piles, roadway, or railings? Would I not have at my disposition all the resources of fashionable style, especially *personification?* Instead of saying: "The bridge at Énios is swept every morning," I would say: "The bridge at Énios is a coxcomb, a dandy, a leader of fashion, a celebrity. Every morning his manservant dresses and curls his hair, for he wants to show himself to the beautiful, fierce ladies of the Béarn only once he is sure, having admired himself in the waters of the Gave, that his tie is properly knotted, his boots properly polished, and his appearance irreproachable." Who knows? Perhaps it will be said of the narrator, as Gerontius said of Damis:[8] "He is really a man of taste!"

---

7. Louis Blanc (1811–82) was a journalist and historian who was active in the socialist movement. His book *L'Organisation du travail* (1839) was an important statement of the socialist position on the exploitation of labor and much criticized by the Economists. In 1841 he published a very popular critique of the July Monarchy, *Histoire de dix ans,* 1830–40, in six volumes, which went through many editions during the 1840s.

8. Both Géronte and Damis are characters who appeared in Molière's plays, but it is not clear what play Bastiat has in mind. They do not appear in the same play together, so Bastiat may have misremembered. There is an exchange in *Le Misanthrope* (act 2, scene 4) between Célimène and Philinte, who are talking about the quality of the meals at dinner parties they have attended, and where Célimène gives an extended comment on

It is in line with these new rules that I propose to tell my tale, just as soon as I have found a benevolent editor who will agree to this. In the meantime, I will echo the style of those who have just two or three little columns of a journal at their disposal.[9]

Imagine Énios, then, with its green meadows, on the banks of a torrent and, going upward in stages, its vineyards, its fields, its pastures, its forests, and the snow-covered summits of the mountain that dominates and rounds off the picture.

Prosperity and contentment reigned in the village. The Gave provided the motive power for mills and sawmills, the herds and flocks provided milk and wool, the fields provided wheat, farmyards poultry, the vineyards a generous wine, and the forests abundant fuel. When one of the inhabitants of the village had managed to save some money, he asked himself what it would be best to spend it on, and the price of items directed his choice. If, for example, with his savings, he had the choice of making a hat or raising two sheep properly, and at the same time, on the other side of the Gave people asked for only one sheep in return for a hat, he would have thought that making the hat was an act of folly, for civilization and with it, *Le Moniteur industriel,* had not yet penetrated into this village.

The mayor of Énios was the one destined to change all that. He was not an ordinary mayor, this mayor of Énios; he was a genuine Pasha.[10]

In the past, Napoléon had tapped him on the shoulder. Since then, he was more *Napoleonist* than Roustan[11] and more *Napoleonic* than M. Thiers.

"That is a man," he said when speaking of the emperor, "who did not discuss; he acted. He did not consult; he ordered. That is how you govern a nation properly. Above all, the French need to be led with a stick."

Damis's parties. She describes him as a rather obnoxious person who tries to be witty and overly critical of everything, yet who has impeccable taste: *rien ne touche son goût* (nothing can touch his taste): "Yes; but he's always trying to be witty, / Which drives me wild; in all his talk, he labors / To be delivered of some brilliant saying. / Since he has taken a notion to be clever, / Nothing can hit his taste, he's grown so nice. / He needs must censure everything that's written, / And thinks, to praise does not become a wit, / But to find fault will prove your skill and learning, / And to admire and laugh belongs to fools."

9. Just like Bastiat had in his free-trade journal, *Le Libre-échange.*

10. The title of *pasha* was given to high-ranking officials in the Ottoman Empire.

11. Roustam (or Roustan) Raza (1782–1845) was a Georgian slave who was purchased in Constantinople by Sala-Bey, one of the governors of Egypt. He was later freed and entered the Mamelouk cavalry. He eventually came to the attention of Napoléon when he occupied Egypt. Napoléon took him back to Paris when he returned in 1799. For the next fifteen years Roustam faithfully attended upon Napoléon as his personal servant.

When he needed services in the form of compulsory labor to be provided for the roads in his district, he would summon a farmer: "How many days of compulsory labor (corvée) do you owe?" (One still uses the word "corvée" in these parts, although "prestations" [compulsory service] would be much better).[12] "Three," replied the farmer. "How many have you already carried out?" "Two." "So, you have two more to go." "But, Mr. Mayor, two and two are . . ." "Yes, elsewhere, but . . .

> In the region of Béarn
> Two and two are three";

And the farmer carried out four days of compulsory labor, I mean "service."

Little by little, the mayor grew accustomed to viewing all men as idiots who would be rendered ignorant by freedom of education, atheistic by freedom of religion, poor by freedom to trade, who would write only foolish things with freedom of the press and under electoral freedom would contrive to have government activities controlled by civil servants. "All this rabble needs to be organized and led," he often repeated. And when he was asked: "Who will do the leading?" he proudly answered, "Me."

Where he was especially brilliant was during the deliberations of the municipal council.[13] He deliberated and voted measures on his own in his room, constituting the majority, the minority, and unanimity simultaneously. He then told the council officer:

"Is it Sunday today?" "Yes, Mr. Mayor."

"Will the municipal councilors be going to sing vespers?" "Yes, Mr. Mayor."

"And from there they will go to the café?" "Yes, Mr. Mayor."

"Will they drink too much?" "Yes, Mr. Mayor."

"In that case, take this paper." "Yes, Mr. Mayor."

"You will be going to the café this evening." "Yes, Mr. Mayor."

---

12. Bastiat uses the term *par prestation* (compulsory or required service), which has a powerful connotation to the Economists, as it referred to the common eighteenth-century practice of compulsory community labor (*la corvée*). The *corvée* was abolished by Turgot in 1776, but it survived in various forms, being renamed *prestation* in 1802. It was abolished once again in 1818 only to be revived again in 1824 when an obligation to work two days a year on local roads was introduced. This was raised to three days in 1836 but with the added improvement of being able to be commuted to a cash payment in lieu of physical work. See Courcelle Seneuil, "Prestation," in *DEP* 2:428–30.

13. Bastiat was elected to the municipal council of Mugron in 1833 after the coming to power of the July Monarchy in July 1830, a post which he held until his death. He would thus have had personal experience of council meetings.

"At a time when they can still see well enough to sign their name." "Yes, Mr. Mayor."

"But when they can no longer see enough to read." "Yes, Mr. Mayor."

"You will put before my good municipal councilors this notice and a pen dipped in ink, and you will tell them from me to read it and sign it." "Yes, Mr. Mayor."

"They will sign it without reading it, and I will be in order with regard to my prefect. This is how I understand representative government."

One day, he saw in a journal this famous saying: *Legality is killing us.* "Ah!" he cried, "I will not die before I have embraced M. Viennet."[14]

It is nevertheless correct to say that, when legality suited him, he clung to it like a real mastiff. Some men are made like this; there are not many of them, but they do exist.

This is how the Mayor of Énios was. And now that I have described both the theater and the hero of my story, I will get on with it with gusto and with no digression.

Around the time when the people of Paris were going to look for asphalt mines[15] in the Pyrénées, with shares already allocated to the tune of an untold number of millions, the mayor gave hospitality to a traveler who left behind him two or three precious issues of *Le Moniteur industriel* ... He read them eagerly, and I leave you to imagine the effect that reading this was bound to have on a mind like this. "Heavens above!" he cried. "This is a journalist who knows a lot. *To forbid, prevent, reject, restrict, and prohibit,* oh! What a fine doctrine! It is as clear as daylight. I myself used to say that men would ruin themselves if they were left to barter freely! It is only too true that legality kills us sometimes, but the absence of legality often does so as well. Not enough laws are passed in France, especially ones that *prohibit*. And, a case in point, prohibition is carried out at the borders of the kingdom, so why not carry it out at the borders of the commune? Damn it all, we have to be logical!"

---

14. The phrase *la légalité nous tue* (legality will kill us) was much quoted in the nineteenth century and has been variously attributed to the novelist Flaubert and to the politician Odilon Barrot. They in turn were probably quoting Jean-Pons-Guillaume Viennet (1777–1868), who had been a soldier under Napoléon and was a well-known poet and politician during the July Monarchy. He ruffled many feathers with his satirical and sometimes flippant works, and he was harshly criticized for making this statement by Armand Carrel, who called it "sad" and "counterrevolutionary." See "Du mot de M. Viennet: La légalité nous tue," in Carrel, *Œuvres politiques et littéraires d'Armand Carrel* 3:383.

15. In the 1820s asphalt was being used in Paris and London to pave sidewalks.

Then, rereading *Le Moniteur industriel,* he applied the principles of this famous journal to his own locality. "It fits like a glove," he used to say. "There is just one word that needs to be changed; you just have to substitute the *communal* labor for the *national* labor."

The mayor of Énios boasted, like M. Chasseloup-Laubat,[16] that he was not a *theoretician;* as was the case with his model, there was no peace nor respite in the way he subjected all his population to the *theory* (for it is indeed one) of protection.

The topography of Énios suited his plans perfectly. He summoned his council (that is to say, he shut himself in his room), discussed, deliberated, voted, and passed a new tariff for crossing the bridge, a tariff that was somewhat complicated, but whose spirit may be summed up as follows:

To leave the village, *zero per person.*

To enter the village, one hundred francs per person.

Having done this, the mayor, this time genuinely, summoned the municipal council to a meeting and gave the following speech, which we quote, complete with interruptions.

"My friends, you know that the bridge cost us a great deal of money; we needed to take out a loan to do it, and we have to pay back the principal and interest. For this reason I am going to inflict on you an additional contribution."

Jérôme: "Is the toll not enough?"

"*A good toll system,*" said the mayor in a didactic tone, "*must have protection as its aim and not revenue.*[17] Up to now, the bridge has paid for itself, but I have arranged things so that it will no longer bring in anything. In effect, goods from within the commune will pass without paying anything, and those from the exterior will not pass at all."

Mathurin: "And what will we gain from this?"

"You are novices," went on the mayor and, spreading out *Le Moniteur industriel* before him so that he would be able to find an appropriate answer

---

16. This could refer to either of the sons of a famous general, François de Chasseloup-Laubat (1754–1833), who became politicians. Justin de Chasseloup-Laubat (1800–1847) was a soldier before he was elected to the Chamber in 1837, where he supported the conservatives. His brother, Prosper de Chasseloup-Laubat (1805–73) had an even more distinguished career. After the July Revolution of 1830, he joined General Lafayette's staff in the National Guard and was elected to the Chamber in 1837 like his brother, but supported the center left. His political career blossomed under Napoléon III, and he took an interest in naval matters and the colony in Algeria.

17. This is the exact opposite of Bastiat's view of tariffs.

to any objection, he started to explain the mechanics of his system in these words:

"Jacques, would you not be happy to have the cooks of Énios paying a little more for your butter?"

"That would suit me," said Jacques.

"Well then, to do this, we have to prevent foreign butter from coming in via the bridge.[18] And you, Jean, why are you not making a fast fortune with your chickens?"

"Because there are too many on the market," said Jean.

"Then you will readily see the advantage of excluding those from the neighboring regions. As for you, Guillaume, I know that you have two old oxen on your hands. Why is this?"

"Because François, with whom I was negotiating," said Guillaume, "went off and bought oxen at the neighboring market."

"So you see that if he had not been able to bring them across the bridge, you would have sold your oxen well, and Énios would have retained five hundred or six hundred francs in cash.

"My friends, what is ruining us and preventing us at least from becoming wealthy is the invasion of products from abroad.

"Is it not fair for the *communal* market to be reserved for the products of the *commune?*

"Whether we are talking about the meadows, the fields, or the vineyards, is there not somewhere a village that is more fertile than ours for one of these things? And this village will come as far as us to take away our own work! This would not be competition but a monopoly; let us take steps, by holding each other for ransom, to fight *on equal terms.*"

Pierre, the clog maker: "At the moment I need oil, and no one makes it in our village."

"Oil! The local slate deposits are full of it.[19] You have only to extract it. That is a new source of work, and work is wealth. Pierre, do you not see that this damned foreign oil has made us lose all the wealth that nature has placed in our slate deposits?"

The schoolmaster: "While Pierre is crushing his slate, he will not be making clogs. If at the same time and with the same work he is able to have more

18. In ES2 13 Bastiat makes fun of the efforts of the three magistrates of Paris to keep cheap butter from Normandy from competing with local Paris butter. Instead of the enemy being "perfidious Albion," it is now "perfidious Normandy" they have to be frightened of.

19. Slate deposits were found in the département of the Hautes Pyrénées, near Lourdes.

oil by crushing slate than making clogs, your tariff is worthless. It causes harm if, on the contrary, Pierre obtains more oil by making clogs than crushing slate. Now, he has the choice between the two procedures; your measure will reduce him to just one, and probably the worse one since no one uses it. It is not at all a question of whether there is oil in slate but whether it is worth extracting it, and what is more, whether the time spent on this cannot be better employed doing something else. What are you risking by leaving us freedom of choice?"

Here the mayor's eyes appeared to devour *Le Moniteur industriel* for a reply to the syllogism, but they did not find one, since *Le Moniteur* has always avoided this side of the question. The mayor was not left speechless for long. The most conclusive argument even came to mind: "Schoolmaster," he said, "I withdraw your right to speak and remove you from office."

A member wished to call attention to the fact that the new tariff would upset a great many interests and that at least a *transition* had to be managed. "A transition!" cried the mayor. "An excellent pretext against people who are demanding freedom, but when it is a question of taking freedom from them," he added with great sagacity, "where have you heard talk of transition?"[20]

Finally, a vote was taken and the tariff was passed with a large majority. Does that surprise you? It should not.

Note in fact that there is more art than appears at first sight in the speech made by the leading magistrate of Énios.

Did he not mention his special interest to each person? Butter to Jacques the herdsman, wine to Jean the wine producer,[21] or oxen to Guillaume the cattle farmer? Did he not constantly leave the general interest in the shadows?

Nevertheless, his efforts, municipal eloquence, administrative notions,

---

20. Bastiat recognizes that there would be an "inevitable displacement of labor" in any transition period to a system of full liberty. See ES1 20, ES2 6, ES2 17, and ES3 19. In ES2 11, the utopian minister is reminded that his radical liberal reforms will fail if the process of reform gets too far ahead of the ideas held by ordinary people: "Mr. Utopian, you are taking on too much, the nation will not follow you!" (ES2 11, p. 197). In ES2 12, Bastiat states that the best strategy is to pursue one reform at a time, as the Anti–Corn Law League had done in England, since too many reforms at once could overwhelm the public. His most extended discussion of the problem of transition to a fully free society and the strategy required to achieve this can be found in ES3 5, where he summarizes his position as follows: "We are fully convinced that by relieving the pressure of a protectionist regime as gradually as opinion will allow but in accordance with a period of transition agreed in advance and *on all points simultaneously,* all forms of economic activity will be offered compensations that will make the shocks genuinely imperceptible" (p. 281).

21. Bastiat is mistaken here. Jean was said to be a chicken producer, not a wine maker.

and deep-seated views on social economics, all were to be shattered on the stones of the Prefecture building.

The prefect bluntly, with no regard for his feelings, annulled the *protective tariff* for the bridge at Énios.

The mayor, having run to the département capital, valiantly defended his work, the noble fruit of his thought as propagated by *Le Moniteur industriel.* As a result, between the two rivals, there took place the strangest discussion in the world, the most bizarre dialogue ever heard, for you should know that the prefect was a peer of France and a fiery protectionist. So that all the benefits that the prefect attributed to Customs tariff, the mayor took to defend the tariff for the bridge at Énios, and all the disadvantages that the prefect attributed to the tariff for the bridge, the mayor turned against Customs tariff.

"What!" said the prefect. "You want to prevent woolen cloth from the surrounding areas from entering Énios!"

"You are preventing woolen cloth from surrounding countries from coming into France."

"That is very different; my aim is to protect the *national* employment."

"And mine to protect the *communal* employment."

"Is it not right for the French Chambers of Peers and Deputies to defend French factories against foreign competition?"

"Is it not right for the municipal council of Énios to defend the factories in Énios against external competition?"

"But your tariff is damaging your trade; it is crushing consumers and does not increase work, it *displaces* it. It stimulates new industries, but at the expense of the old ones. As you said to the schoolmaster, if Pierre wants oil he will crush slate, but in that case he will no longer make clogs for the surrounding communes. You are depriving yourself of all the benefits of the proper management of labor."

"That is exactly what the theoreticians of free trade say about your restrictive measures."

"Free traders are Utopians who see things only from a general point of view. If they limited themselves to considering each protected industry in isolation, without taking account of consumers or the other branches of production, they would understand the full usefulness of restrictions."

"Why are you then talking to me about the consumers in Énios?"

"But in the long run your toll will damage the very industries you want to favor, for by ruining consumers you are ruining their customers, and it is the wealth of the customers that makes each industry prosper."

"This is another thing that free traders object to you. They say that to want to develop one sector of work through measures that close off foreign markets and which, although they guarantee customers within the country for this sector, constantly impoverish these customers, is to want to build a pyramid by starting with the top."

"Mr. Mayor, you are a nuisance, I do not need to give you my reasons and I am overturning the deliberation of the municipal council of Énios."

The mayor sadly went back along the path to his village, cursing men who have double standards, who blow hot and cold and think very sincerely that what is truth and justice in a circle of five thousand hectares becomes false and iniquitous in a circle of fifty thousand square leagues. As he was a good man at heart, he said to himself: "I prefer the straight opposition of the communal schoolmaster and will revoke his dismissal."

When he reached Énios, he summoned the council to tell them in a pitiful voice about his misfortune. "My friends," he said, "we have all lost our fortune. The prefect, who votes in favor of national restrictions each year, has rejected communal restrictions. He has overturned your deliberation and delivers you defenseless to foreign competition. However, one resource remains to us. Since the flood of foreign products is stifling us, since we are not allowed to reject these goods by force, why do we not reject them voluntarily? Let all the inhabitants of Énios agree between themselves never to purchase anything from outside."

But the inhabitants of Énios continued to purchase from outside the things that cost them more to make in the village, which confirmed the mayor in the view that men naturally tend toward their ruin when they have the misfortune to be free.

19. Antediluvian Sugar[1]

PUBLISHING HISTORY:

Original title: "Le Sucre antédiluvien."
Place and date of first publication: *Le Libre-échange,*
13 February 1848, no. 12 (2nd year), p. 68.
First French edition as book or pamphlet: Not applicable.

1. "Antediluvian" (or prediluvian) refers to the period in Biblical accounts between the creation of the earth and the flood (deluge) at the time of Noah and his ark.

Location in Paillottet's edition of *OC:* Vol. 2. *Le Libre-échange,*
pp. 446–51.
Previous translation: None.

People think that sugar is a modern invention; that is a mistake. The art of making it may have been lost in the flood,[2] but it was known before this catastrophe, as is proved by a curious historical document found in the caves of Karnak and whose translation we owe to a learned multilinguist, the illustrious Cardinal Mezzofante.[3] We reproduce here this interesting document, which also confirms this saying of Solomon: *there is nothing new under the sun.*

> In those days, between the 42nd and 52nd parallel, there was a great and rich nation, powerful and of lively and courageous disposition, numbering more than thirty-six million inhabitants, all of whom loved sugar.[4] The name of this nation has been lost, so we will call them the *Welches.*[5]
>
> Since their climate did not allow *Saccharum officinarum*[6] to be grown, the *Welches* were completely at a loss at first.
>
> However, they thought up a very strange expedient, which

2. Bastiat was right when he predicted in the closing line of this article that it would take the "flood" of revolution to finally destroy the institution of slavery in France. Note that this article was published on 13 February, only nine days before the 1848 Revolution broke out on 22–24 February. As a newly elected deputy to the Constituent Assembly, Bastiat would have been able to vote for the law signed by Victor Schoelcher, the undersecretary for the navy and colonies, on 27 April 1848, abolishing slavery. This was the second time slavery had been "abolished" in France. It was first abolished in the 1790s, when a slave revolt broke out in Haiti, but it was reintroduced by Napoléon when he became first consul.

3. The historical document Bastiat refers to is fictitious. Karnak was a temple complex in Egypt near Luxor. Cardinal Giuseppe Mezzofanti (1774–1849), not "Mezzofante," as Bastiat writes, was a gifted linguist who became professor of Oriental languages at the University of Bologna.

4. This is of course a description of France: the city of Calais in the north is latitude 51 degrees north, the city of Marseille in the south is latitude 43 degrees north, and Mugron, where Bastiat lived, is also latitude 43 degrees north. The population of France in the late 1840s was about thirty-six million people.

5. "Welches" is a made-up name but may have some reference to the German word *welsch,* a derogative word for foreigner.

6. *Saccharum officinarum* is the scientific name for sugar cane.

had just one drawback, namely its essentially theoretical, that is to say, rational, character.

Because they could not create sugar naturally, they worked out a way of creating its value.

That is to say, they made wine, silk, woolen cloth, canvas, and other goods, which they sent to the other hemisphere in order to receive sugar in exchange.

An immense number of traders, shipowners, ships, and sailors were employed to carry out these transactions.

First of all, the Welches simply thought they had found the simplest method of obtaining sugar in their situation. Since they were able to choose from more than half the globe the place where they could get the most sugar for the least amount of wine or cloth, they said to themselves: "Truly, if we made sugar ourselves we would not get one-tenth for the same amount of work!

This was too simple for the Welches, as a matter of fact, and so it could not last.

One day, a great statesman (an unemployed admiral) gave them this terrible thought: "If ever we have a maritime war, how will we manage to collect our sugar?"

This judicious thought troubled people, and this is what they thought of doing.

They set themselves the task of seizing a small scrap of land in the other hemisphere where they feared trade might be interrupted, saying: "Let us own this tiny spot, and our supply of sugar is assured."

Thus, to guard against a possible war, they started a real one that lasted a hundred years. It was finally ended with a treaty that gave the Welches possession of the scrap of land they wanted, to which the name *Saccharique* was given.[7]

They imposed new taxes on themselves to pay for the cost of the war, and

---

7. "Saccharique" is a made-up name based upon *saccharum* (Latin for sugar) and "Martinique," the French sugar colony in the Caribbean. It began producing sugar in earnest with African slave labor in the 1670s. By 1700 there were about 15,000 slaves in Martinique. When slavery was abolished, on 27 April 1848, there were about 73,000 slaves out of a total population of 120,000.

then more new taxes to organize a powerful navy in order to retain the scrap of land.

Having done this, there was the question of taking advantage of the precious conquest.

This tiny corner of the antipodes was not favorable to agriculture. It needed protection. The decision was taken that commerce with half of the globe would henceforward be forbidden to the *Welches* and that not a single one of them could suck a lump of sugar that did not come from the scrap of land in question.

Having arranged everything, both taxes and restrictions, in this fashion, they rubbed their hands, saying: "This is not how it is supposed to work in the theory."

Even so, a few *Welches* crossed the Ocean and went to Saccharique to grow sugar cane, but as it turned out, they could not bear to work in this debilitating climate. People then went to another part of the world and, once they had kidnapped some men whose skins were completely black, they transported them to their small island, and there forced them with heavy blows of the whip to cultivate it.

In spite of this forceful expedient, the tiny island was unable to provide even an eighth part of the sugar required by the *Welche* nation. The price rose, as always happens when ten people seek something that is enough only for one. The richest of the Welches were the only ones to be able to obtain sugar.

The high price of sugar had another effect. It encouraged the Saccharique planters to go and abduct a greater number of black men in order to subjugate them with more heavy blows of the whip, to grow sugar cane even on the sand and the most arid of the rocks. This led to the never-before-observed sight of the inhabitants of a country doing nothing directly to procure their sustenance and clothing, and working uniquely for export.

And the *Welches* said: "It is marvelous to see how work is developing on our island in the antipodes."

However, as time went on, the poorest of them started to grumble in these terms:

"What have we done? Sugar is no longer within our reach. What is more, we are no longer making the wine, silk, and cloth that was distributed over an entire hemisphere. Our trade is reduced to what a tiny rock is able to produce and receive. Our merchant navy is in dire straits, and we are burdened with taxes."

But they were given this correct answer: "Is it not glorious for you to have a possession in the antipodes? As for the wine, drink it. As for the cotton and woolen cloth, you will have to make do with the issuing of special manufacturing licenses. And as for the taxes, nothing has been lost since the money which leaves your pockets goes into ours."

On occasion, these same dreamers asked: "What use is this great navy?" They were given this answer: "To retain the colony." And if they persisted, saying: "What use is the colony?" the reply came without hesitation: "To preserve the navy."

In this way, the poor Utopians were beaten on all fronts.

This situation, which was already highly complicated, was made more so by an unforeseen event.

The statesmen of the *Welches'* country, relying on the fact that the advantage of having a colony entailed great expenditure, considered that in all justice, this expenditure should, at least in part, be borne by those who ate sugar. Consequently, they imposed a heavy tax on sugar.

With the result that sugar, which was already very expensive, became even more so by the full amount of the tax.[8]

Well, although the *Welches'* country was not suited to the growing of sugar cane, and since there is nothing that cannot be done if sufficient work and capital is devoted to it, chemists, lured by the high prices, began to look for sugar everywhere, in the ground, in water, in the air, in milk, in grapes, in carrots, in corn, and in pumpkins, and they looked so diligently that they ended by finding a little in a modest vegetable, in a plant that hitherto had been considered so insignificant that it had been given the doubly humiliating name: *Beta vulgaris.*[9]

Sugar was therefore made in the Welches' country, and this industry, hampered by nature but supported by the intelligence of free workers, and above all by the artificially high price, made rapid progress.

Good heavens! Who could tell the tale of the confusion that this discovery injected into the economic situation of the Welches? In a short time, it jeopardized everything at once, the highly expensive production of sugar in

8. According to the budget for 1848, the French state raised fr. 38.5 million by taxing French colonial sugar and another fr. 11.3 million by taxing other foreign-produced sugar. There was also a tax of fr. 20.8 million on domestically produced sugar from sugar beets.

9. *Beta vulgaris* is the scientific name for the common beet or sugar beet (*betterave* in French).

the tiny island in the antipodes, what remained of the merchant navy occupied with the trade from this island, and even the navy itself, which could recruit sailors only from the merchant navy.

In view of this unexpected upheaval, all the Welches set about finding a reasonable solution.

Some said: "Let us gradually revert to the state of affairs that was established naturally before absurd ideas and arrangements threw us into this confusion. As in the old days, let us make sugar in the form of wine, silk, and cloth, or rather, let those who wish to have sugar create value for it in whatever form is agreeable to them. Then we will have trade with an entire hemisphere; our merchant navy will regenerate and our navy will as well, if need be. Free labor being essentially progressive will outdo slave labor, which is essentially stagnant. Slavery will die away of its own accord[10] without its being necessary for nations to have highly dangerous policies toward each other.[11] Labor and capital will take the most advantageous direction everywhere. Doubtless, during the transitional period, some people's interests will be ruffled. We will help them as much as we can. But when we have gone down the wrong road for so long, it is childish to refuse to join the right road because it will cause some discomfort."

The people who spoke thus were labeled innovators, ideologists, metaphysicians, visionaries, traitors, and disturbers of the public peace.

The statesmen said: "It is unworthy of us to seek to escape an artificial situation by returning to a natural one. We are not great men for nothing. The height of art is to manage everything without causing any fuss or bother. Let us not tinker with slavery, that would be dangerous, nor with beet sugar, that would be unjust. Let us not allow free trade with all of the other hemisphere, which would be the death of our colony. Let us not abandon the colony, that would be the death of our navy, and let us not remain in the *status quo,* as that would be the death of everyone's interests."

---

10. The French classical liberal economists like Bastiat were fascinated by the institution of slavery because it was a violation of their deeply held views about natural rights and individual liberty and also because it was a glaring example of how a powerful vested interest could use the power of the state to its own advantage. The latter aspect encompassed the use of tariffs to protect the colonial sugar industry.

11. This is a reference to the much hated policy of the British Navy, the "right of inspection," to board, search, and even seize foreign vessels on the high seas which they believed were carrying slaves. This was a bone of contention between Britain and France throughout the Restoration and July Monarchy.

These men acquired a great reputation as moderate and practical men. It was said of them: "Here are skillful administrators who know how to take account of all forms of difficulty."

Such was the situation that, while people sought a change that would change nothing, things went from bad to worse, until the supreme solution occurred, a flood that, by engulfing them, solved this question and a great many others.

20. Monita Secreta: The Secret Book of Instructions

PUBLISHING HISTORY:

Original title: "Monita secreta."
Place and date of first publication: *Le Libre-échange,*
    20 February 1848, no. 13 (2nd year), pp. 75–76.
First French edition as book or pamphlet: Not applicable.
Location in Paillottet's edition of *OC:* Vol. 2. *Le Libre-échange,*
    pp. 452–58.
Previous translation: None.

A great number of Catalan protectionist electors drew up for their deputy a sort of Notebook, a copy of which we have received.[1] Here are some rather curious excerpts from it.

Never forget that your mission is to maintain and extend our privileges. You are a Catalan first and a Spaniard second.

The minister will promise you one favor in return for another. He will tell you: "Vote for the laws that suit me and I will then extend your monopolies." Do not be taken in by this trap, and tell him: "Extend our monopolies first and I will then vote for your laws."

Do not sit on the left, on the right, or in the center. When you give your allegiance to a government, you do not obtain very much, and when you systematically oppose it, you obtain nothing. Take your seat on the center left or the center right. The intermediate places are the best. Experience has shown

---

1. This document has been invented by Bastiat for the purposes of telling this tale. The historical *Monita Secreta* was a seventeenth-century forgery which was supposed to be a secret book of instructions for Jesuits to follow in order to increase their power and influence in society. Bastiat here creates another "secret book of instructions" for protectionists to use in order to increase their power and influence.

this. There, you are to be feared by the black balls, and you are courted by the white balls.[2]

Read deeply into the mind of the minister and also into that of the leader of the party that aspires to replace him. If one is restrictionist through necessity and the other by instinct, push for a change of cabinet. The new occupant will give you two guarantees instead of one.

It is not likely that the minister will ever ask you for *sacrifices* through a love of justice, freedom, or equality, but he may be led to doing this by the requirements of the Treasury. It may happen that one day he says to you: "I cannot hold out any longer. The balance of my budget has been broken. I have to allow French products to enter to generate an opportunity to raise taxes."

Be ready for this eventuality, which is the most threatening, and even the only threatening one at this time. You have to have two strings to your bow. Get along with your corestrictionists in the *center* and threaten to have a large battalion of your supporters move over to the *left*. The minister will resort to a loan in terror, and we will gain one year or perhaps two; the interest payments will fall on the people.

If the minister nevertheless insists, have another tax to suggest to him, for example, a tax on wine. Tell him that wine is the *taxable commodity* par excellence. That is true, since wine producers are *easygoing taxpayers* par excellence.[3]

Above all, do not, through ill-advised zeal, get it into your head to try to ward off the move by making reference to the slightest reduction in expenditure. You will alienate all present and future ministers and in addition all the journalists, which is extremely serious.

You may well talk about *economies* in general, which will make you popular. Keep strictly to these. That will be enough for the electors.

We have just mentioned journalists. You know that the press is the fourth power in the State and we might say the leading one. Your diplomacy in dealing with it cannot be too great.

If by chance you came across a journalist who is willing to write on a topic

2. An allusion to the white and black balls (representing a vote of yea or nay) which the deputies dropped into an urn for voting on bills before the Chamber.

3. According to the budget for 1848, the French state raised fr. 103.6 million by taxing alcohol.

for money, pay him to write on ours. This is a very expeditious means. But it would be even better to buy silence; that costs less and is certainly more prudent. When you have reason and justice against you, the safest thing is to stifle discussion.

As for the theoretical positions you will have to support, this is the golden rule:

If there are two ways of producing something, if one of these is expensive and the other economical, impose a heavy tax on the economical method to the advantage of the expensive method. For example, if with sixty days' work devoted to producing wool, the Spanish can import from France ten *varas* [about 33 inches] of woolen cloth while it would take them a hundred days' work to obtain the same ten *varas* of woolen cloth if they made it themselves, then encourage the second option at the expense of the first. You cannot imagine the advantages that will result from this.

First of all, everyone who uses the expensive method will be grateful and devoted to you. You will receive strong support from this quarter.

Then, as the more economical method gradually disappears from the country and the expensive method constantly spreads, you will see an increase in the number of your partisans, and the number of your opponents will decrease.

Finally, since a more expensive method implies more work, all the workers and philanthropists will be on your side. Indeed, it will be easy for you to show how the work would be affected if the more economical method were allowed to revive.

Keep to this superficial appearance and do not allow people to go into the subject in depth, for what would the result be?

What would happen is that certain minds that are too keen on investigation would soon discover the deception.[4] They would see that if the production of ten *varas* of woolen cloth takes one hundred days' work, there are sixty days less that are devoted to the production of wool in return for which people used to receive ten *varas* of French woolen cloth.

Do not argue about this initial compensation; it is too clear and you will be defeated. Just continue to show the other forty days that are spent on activity using the expensive method.

---

4. Here Bastiat uses the word *supercherie* (deception, or deceit) instead of the more usual *duperie*.

People will then answer you: "If we had kept to the more economical method, the capital which has been diverted to the direct production of woolen cloth would have been available in the country; it would have produced things that were useful and would have given work to the forty workers that you claim to have rescued from idleness. And as for the products of their work, they would have been purchased precisely by the consumers of woolen cloth since, as they obtained French woolen cloth cheaper, an amount of remuneration that was enough to pay forty workers would also have remained available in their hands."

Do not be led into these subtleties. Call all those who reason in this way dreamers, ideologists, Utopians, and economists.

Never lose sight of the following notion; at the present time the public does not push the investigation this far. The surest way of opening their eyes is to discuss it. On your side you have appearances; keep to them and laugh at the rest.

It might happen that one fine day the workers will open their eyes and say:

"Since you force products to be expensive by recourse to the law, you ought also, in order to be fair, to force wages to be expensive by recourse to the law."

Let the argument drop for as long as you can. When you can no longer remain silent, answer: "The high price of products encourages us to make more of them, and in order to do this we need more workers. This increase in the demand for labor raises your wages and in this way, indirectly, our privileges extend to you *by the ricochet or flow-on effect.*"[5]

Workers will perhaps then answer you: "This would be true if the excess production stimulated by high prices was achieved with capital that had fallen from the moon. But if all that you can do is take it from other sectors of industry, there will be no increase in wages, since there has been no increase in capital. We now, accordingly, have to pay more for the things we need, and your ricochet or flow-on effect is a trick."

At this point, take a great deal of trouble to explain and confuse the mechanism of the ricochet effect.

---

5. This sophism, published in *Le Libre-échange* on 20 February 1848, contains the largest number (five) of occurrences of the phrase "ricochet effect" before the appearance of the second half of *Economic Harmonies* in 1851 (which also contains five occurrences of the phrase).

Workers may insist and say to you:

"Since you have so much confidence in these ricochet or flow-on effects, let us change our roles. Do not protect products any more, but protect wages. Set them by law at a high rate. All the proletarians[6] will become wealthy; they will purchase a great many of your products, and you will become wealthy by the ricochet or flow-on effect."

We have put words into the mouth of a worker in order to show you how dangerous it is to go deeply into questions. This is what you should take care to avoid. Fortunately, as workers work from morning to night, they do not have much time to think. Take advantage of this; arouse their emotions; rail against foreigners, competition, freedom, and capital, in order to divert their attention from the subject of *privilege*.

Attack the professors of political economy with vigor at every opportunity. If there is one point on which they do not agree, conclude that the things on which they do agree should be rejected.

Here is the syllogism that you may use:

"Economists agree that men should be equal before the law,

"But they do not agree on *the theory of rent,*[7]

"Therefore they do not agree on every point,

"Therefore it is not certain that they are right when they say that men should be equal before the law,

6. This is only the second time before the February Revolution of 1848 that Bastiat used the socialist term *prolétaires* (proletarians) or *prolétariat* (the proletariat). The first use occurred in ES1 12, in which Bastiat addresses "the workers"; the second occurred in ES3 20, which was published on 20 February (the Revolution broke out on 23 February). Before this time he normally used the term *les ouvriers* (workers), so it seems the vocabulary of political debate was changing on the eve of the Revolution. After the Revolution he used the word "proletarian" or "proletariat" in several works: ES3 24; "Justice and Fraternity" (CW2, pp. 60–81); "Property and Plunder" (CW2, pp. 147–84); "Protection and Communism" (CW2, pp. 235–65); "Plunder and Law" (CW2, pp. 266–760); and in two letters, written on 9 September and 9 December 1850.

7. The topic of rent was especially sensitive for Bastiat, as he believed one of his major theoretical innovations was a rethinking of the classical Smithian and Ricardan notion of rent. He published some essays on the topic as he was writing *Economic Harmonies,* and these provoked some harsh criticism when they were discussed at the monthly meetings of the Political Economy Society. Most of the Economists rejected his idea that there was nothing special about rent, that there was nothing particularly productive about land to merit its special treatment as a source of income. He believed that all income, including rent from land, was the result of the voluntary exchange of "service for service."

"Therefore laws ought to create privileges for us at the expense of our fellow citizens."

This line of reasoning will have a very good effect.

There is another method of argument that you may use with great success.

Observe what is happening around the world, and if any distressing accident occurs, say: "See what freedom does."

If then Madrid is burnt down and if, in order to rebuild it at a lower cost, wood and iron are allowed in from abroad, attribute the fire, or at least all the effects of the fire, to this freedom.

A certain nation has ploughed, fertilized, harrowed, sowed, and hoed its entire territory. When they are about to reap the harvest, it is carried away by a blight; this nation is thus put into the situation of either dying of hunger or importing foodstuffs from abroad.[8] If it takes the latter alternative, and it certainly will take it, its regular activities will be greatly disturbed, that is certain; it will experience a crisis, both in production and finance. Be careful to hide the fact that in the long run this is better than dying of starvation, and say: "If this nation had not had the freedom to import foodstuffs from abroad, it would not have been subjected to a crisis in production and finance."

We can assure you from experience that this line of reasoning will bring you great good fortune.

Occasionally, *principles* are invoked. Make fun of principles, ridicule principles, and scoff at principles. This will have a good effect on a skeptical nation.

You will be seen to be a *practical* man and will inspire great confidence.

What is more, you will lead the legislature in each particular case to call into question all truths, which will save us a lot of time. Think of where astronomy would be if the theorem: *The three angles of a triangle are equal to two right angles* had not been accepted, after it was demonstrated once and for all, and if it were necessary to prove it on each occasion. It would be never-ending.

In the same way, if your opponents prove that all restrictions result in *two losses for one profit*,[9] demand that they redo the demonstration for each

---

8. Crop failures in 1846, especially in Ireland with the spread of the potato blight, caused considerable hardship and a rise in food prices in 1847 across Europe. Some historians also believe this was a contributing factor to the outbreak of revolution in 1848.

9. This is another way of stating Bastiat's principle of the "double incidence of loss," which he developed in ES3 4 and further developed in WSWNS 1.

particular case and say boldly that in political economy there are no *absolute truths.*[10]

Benefit from the huge advantage of dealing with a nation that thinks that nothing is either true or false.

Always retain your current position with regard to our opponents.

What are we asking for? Privileges.

What are they asking for? Liberty.

They do not want to usurp our rights; they are content to defend theirs.

Fortunately, in their impatient ardor they are sufficiently poor tacticians to look for proof. Allow them to do this.[11] They will thus impose on themselves the role that is due to us. Pretend to believe that they are putting forward a new system that is strange, complicated, and hazardous and that the *onus probandi* [onus of proof] lies with them. Say that you, on the contrary, are not putting forward either a *theory* or a *system.* You will be relieved of having to prove anything. All moderate men will give you their support.

21. The Immediate Relief of the People[1]

PUBLISHING HISTORY:

Original title: "Soulagement immédiat du peuple."
Place and date of first publication: *La République française,*
13 March 1848.
First French edition as book or pamphlet: Not applicable.
Location in Paillottet's edition of *OC:* Vol. 2. *Le Libre-échange,*

---

10. See ES1 18, pp. 82–84, for a fuller discussion of the topic.

11. Bastiat uses the phrase *laissez-les faire,* which is an ironic thing for the protectionist to say.

1. This and the next three articles mark a break with the previous ones, as they were all written immediately after the outbreak of revolution on 22–24 February 1848. Protests and riots forced King Louis-Philippe to resign, and on the evening of 24 February a provisional government was proclaimed, followed the next day by the Second Republic. Bastiat and some of his younger friends (Gustave de Molinari and Hippolyte Castille) decided to start a magazine in order to spread their ideas about constitutional government and free markets among the workers and protesters in Paris. Thus was launched the short-lived magazine *La République française,* from which some of the following articles are taken.

pp. 459–60. Published as one of the "Small Posters of
Jacques Bonhomme."
Previous translation: None.

People,[2]

You[3] are being told: "You have not enough to live on; let the state add
what is missing." Who would not wish for this if it were possible?[4]

But alas, the tax collector's coffers are not the wine pitcher of Cana.[5]

When Our Lord put one liter of wine into this pitcher, two came out,
but when you put one hundred sous into the coffers of the tax collector,[6]
ten francs do not emerge; not even one hundred sous come out, since the
collector keeps a few for himself.

How then does this procedure increase your work or your wages?

The advice being given to you can be summed up as follows: You will give
the State five francs in return for nothing and the State will give you four
francs in return for your work. An exchange for dupes.

People, how can the state keep you alive, since it is you who are keeping
the state alive?

Here are the mechanics of charity workshops[7] presented systematically:[8]

The state takes six loaves of bread from you; it eats two and demands
work from you in order to give you back four. If now you ask it for eight
loaves, it can do nothing else but this: take twelve from you, eat four and
make you earn the rest.

People, be more alert; do as the Republicans of America do: give the State
only what is strictly necessary and *keep the rest for yourself.*

2. This and the next piece were designed as posters to be pasted on the walls lining
the streets of Paris so the rioting population could read them during the early days of the
February revolution. It is Jacques Bonhomme who is speaking.

3. In his address to the people Bastiat uses the familiar *tu* form of you. See "Use of the
Familiar 'Tu' Form," in the Note on the Translation.

4. In this and the next article Bastiat prefigures his definition of the state as "the great
fiction by which everyone endeavors to live at the expense of everyone else," which he
developed during the course of 1848.

5. See ES3 12, p. 309n2.

6. Bastiat uses the word *buraliste,* which usually refers to a tobacconist who would sell
state-monopolized and heavily taxed tobacco products. It thus has another meaning to
do with the collection of taxes and could also be used more generally to refer to any clerk
who collected taxes on behalf of the state.

7. The National Workshops. See Glossary.

8. (Bastiat's note) Jacques Bonhomme does not mean to criticize emergency measures.

Demand the abolition of useless functions, a reduction of huge salaries, the abolition of special privileges, monopolies, and deliberate obstructions and the simplification of the wheels of bureaucracy.

With these savings, insist on the abolition of city tolls, the salt tax, the tax on cattle and on wheat.

In this way, the cost of living will be cheaper, and since it will be cheaper, each person will have a small surplus of his present wages; with this small surplus multiplied by thirty-six million inhabitants, each person will be able to take on and pay for a new form of consumption. With everyone consuming a little more, we will all get a little more employment for each other and, since labor will be in greater demand in the country, wages will rise. Then, O people, you will have solved the problem, that of earning more sous and obtaining more things for each sou.

This is not as brilliant as the alleged wine pitcher of Cana of the Luxembourg Palace,[9] but it is sure, solid, practicable, immediate, and just.

22. A Disastrous Remedy

PUBLISHING HISTORY:

Original title: "Funeste remède."
Place and date of first publication: *La République française,*
    14 March 1848, no. 17, p. 1.
First French edition as book or pamphlet: Not applicable.
Location in Paillottet's edition of *OC:* Vol. 2. *Le Libre-échange,*
    pp. 460–61. Published as one of the "Small Posters of
    Jacques Bonhomme."
Previous translation: None.

When our brother suffers, we must come to his aid.

However, it is not the goodness of the intention that makes the goodness of the medicine. A mortal remedy can be given in all charity.

A poor worker was ill. The doctor arrived, took his pulse, made him stick out his tongue, and said to him: "Good man, you are undernourished." "I think so too," said the dying man; "however, I did have an old doctor who

9. The Luxembourg Palace was the headquarters of the Government Commission for the Workers. See the entry for "National Workshops," in the Glossary of Subjects and Terms.

was very skilled. He gave me three-quarters of a loaf of bread each evening. It is true that he took the whole loaf from me each morning and kept a quarter of it as his fee. I turned him away when I saw that this regime was not curing me." "My friend and colleague was an ignorant man who thought only of his own interest. He did not see that your blood was anemic. This has to be *reorganized*.[1] I am going to transfuse some new blood into your left arm, and to do this I have to take it out of your right arm. But provided that you take no account either of the blood that comes out of your right arm or the blood that will be lost during the operation, you will find *my* remedy admirable."[2]

This is the position we are in. The State tells the people: "You do not have enough bread; I will give you some. But since I do not make any, I will begin by taking it from you, and when I have satisfied my appetite, which is not small, I will make you earn the rest."

Or else: "Your earnings are not high enough; pay me more tax. I will distribute part to my agents and with the surplus, I will set you to work."

And if the people have eyes only for the bread being given to them and lose sight of the bread being taken away from them; if they can see the small wage which taxes provide but don't see the large part of their wage which taxes take away, then we can predict that their illness will become more serious.

23. Circulars from a Government That Is Nowhere to Be Found

PUBLISHING HISTORY

Original title: "Circulaires d'un ministère introuvable."
Place and date of first publication: *Le Libre-échange,* 19 March
1848, no. 16 (2nd year), p. 88.
First French edition as book or pamphlet: Not applicable.
Location in Paillottet's edition of *OC:* Vol. 2. *Le Libre-échange,*
pp. 462–65.
Previous translation: None.

1. Bastiat uses the word *réorganiser* to make reference to one of the key slogans of the socialists in February 1848, namely *l'organisation* (the organization of labor and industry by the state for the benefit of the workers). See Louis Blanc's highly influential book *Organisation du travail* (1839), which was reprinted many times.

2. Recall Bastiat's parody of Molière's parody of seventeenth-century doctors who bled their patients (ES2 9, pp. 176–77). See also "Bastiat's Rhetoric of Liberty: Satire and the 'Sting of Ridicule,'" in the Introduction.

The Minister of the Interior to the Commissioners of the Government, the Prefects, Mayors, etc.[1]

The elections are approaching.[2] You want me to indicate to you the line of conduct you ought to be following; here it is: As citizens, I have no instructions to give you other than to draw your inspiration from your conscience and love for the public good. As civil servants, respect and ensure respect for the freedoms of the citizens.

We will be asking for the opinion of the country. This is not to drag from it, either by intimidation or fraud, an untruthful reply. If the National Assembly has views that conform to ours, we will govern with immense authority thanks to this union. If the Assembly does not share our views, all that is left to us will be to withdraw and endeavor to bring it around to us through honest discussion. Experience has warned us of what it costs to wish to govern with artificial majorities.

THE MINISTER OF TRADE TO THE MERCHANTS OF THE REPUBLIC

Citizens,

My predecessors have made or appear to have made great efforts to procure business for you. They did so in a multitude of ways with no other result than this: an increase in the nation's fiscal burden and the creation of obstacles in our path. In turn they compelled exports with subsidies and restricted imports with barriers. They often acted in collusion with their colleagues in the Department of the Navy and the Department of War to seize some small island lost in the ocean and when, after many borrowings and battles, they succeeded, you as Frenchmen were given the exclusive privilege of trading with the small island on condition that you did not trade with the rest of the world.[3]

All these tentative efforts led to the acknowledgment of the following

---

1. Bastiat is making fun of the newly installed provisional government's practice of issuing sweeping declarations which may or may not have had any support from the people or the cooperation of the state bureaucracy. The titles of his "circulars" mimic closely those of the official pronouncements of the provisional government, e.g., "Circulaire du ministre de l'intérieure aux commissaires du Gouvernement provisoire." See *Actes officiels du Gouvernement provisoire,* p. 72.

2. Elections to the Constituent Assembly were announced for 23 April with universal manhood suffrage. Bastiat was to win a seat representing the département of the Landes.

3. See Bastiat's discussion of this in ES3 19, pp. 365–71.

rule, in which your own interest, the national interest, and the interest of the human race are combined: *buy and sell wherever you can do so to the greatest advantage.*

Well, since this is what you do naturally without any interference from me, I am reduced to admitting that my functions are worse than pointless; I am not even *the backseat driver.*

For this reason, I am giving you notice that my ministry is being abolished.[4] At the same time, the Republic is abolishing all the restrictions with which my predecessors have hobbled you and all the taxes that we must make the people pay to put these restrictions into operation. I beg you to forgive me for the harm I have done you, and to prove to me that you harbor no bitterness, I hope that one of you would be so good as to accept me as a clerk in your office so that I may learn about commerce, for which my short sojourn in the ministry has given me a taste.

THE MINISTER OF AGRICULTURE TO FARMERS

Citizens,

A happy chance put a thought into my head that had never occurred to my predecessors: it is that you, like me, belong to the human race. You have a mind you can use and, what is more, that true source of all progress, a desire to improve your situation.

On this basis, I ask myself how I may serve you. Will I teach you agriculture? It is more than likely that you know more about it than I do. Will I stimulate in you a desire to replace good practices for bad? This desire is in you at least as much as it is in me. Your own self-interest generates it, and I do not see how my circulars can sound louder in your ears than your own interest.

You know the price of things. You therefore have a rule that tells you what it is better to produce and what not to produce. My predecessor wanted to find manufacturing work for you to fill your days of inactivity. You could, he said, commit yourself to this work, with benefit both to you and to consumers. You are then faced with two alternatives: either this is true, in which case do you need a ministry to inform you of lucrative work within your range? You will discover this yourselves if you do not belong to an inferior race suffering from idiocy, a hypothesis on which my ministry is based and which

4. See ES2 11 for a fuller discussion of what Bastiat would like do if he were made prime minister of the country.

I do not accept. Or this is not true, and in this case how damaging would it be for the minister to impose sterile work on all of France's farmers through an administrative measure?

Up to now, my colleagues and I have been very active with no result, other than to have you pay taxes, for you should note this clearly; each of our actions has a corresponding tax. Even this circular is not free of charge. It will be the last. Henceforward, to make farming prosper you should rely on your own efforts, and not on those of my bureaucrats; turn your gaze to your fields and not to a Ministry building in the rue de Grenelle.

The Minister for Religion to Ministers of Religion

Citizens,

The object of this letter is for me to take leave of you. Freedom of religion has been proclaimed.[5] Henceforward, you, like all citizens, will have to deal only with the minister of justice. By this I mean that if, and far be it from me to think this will happen, you use your freedom to harm the freedom of others, upset public order, or outrage common decency, you will inevitably encounter that legal repression from which no one should be exempt. Other than this you may act as you see fit, and if you do this I fail to see what use I can be to you. I and all of the huge administrative body that I manage are becoming a burden to the public. This is not to say the half of it, for how can we occupy our time without infringing freedom of conscience? Obviously any civil servant who does not do a useful job does a damaging one by the very fact of taking action. By withdrawing, we are therefore fulfilling two conditions of the Republican manifesto: economy and freedom.

> *The Secretary to the government*
> *that is nowhere to be found,*
> *F.B.*

5. Bastiat is referring to a decree issued on 10 March 1848, in which the provisional government stated: "Citizens who have been detained as a result of judgments pronounced against them for matters relating to the free exercise of religion will be immediately freed, unless they are being held for another matter. All proceedings which are under way will be terminated. Fines already imposed will be refunded. The Minister of Justice and the Minister of Finance are charged with carrying out this decree" (*Actes officiels du Gouvernement provisoire*, pp. 69–70). See also Lalouette, "La politique religieuse de la Seconde République," pp. 79–94.

24. Disastrous Illusions[1]

PUBLISHING HISTORY:

Original title: "Funestes illusions."
Place and date of first publication: *Journal des économistes*
19 (March 1848): 323–33.
First French edition as book or pamphlet: Not applicable.
Location in Paillottet's edition of *OC:* Vol. 2. *Le Libre-échange,*
pp. 466–82.
Previous translation: None.

CITIZENS GIVE THE STATE LIFE
THE STATE CANNOT GIVE ITS CITIZENS LIFE

It has sometimes happened that I have combated Privilege by making fun of it. I think this was quite excusable. When a few people wish to live at the expense of all, it is totally permissible to inflict the sting of ridicule on the minority that exploits and the majority that is exploited.

Now, I am faced with another illusion. It is no longer a question of particular privileges, but of transforming privilege into a common right. The entire nation has conceived the odd idea that it could increase production indefinitely by handing it over to the State in the form of taxes in order for the State to give it back a portion in the form of work, profit, and pay.[2] The state is being requested to ensure the well-being of every citizen; and a long and sorry procession, in which every sector of the workforce is represented, from the severe banker to the humble laundress, is parading before the *organizer in chief*[3] in order to ask for financial assistance.

---

1. Issues of the *Journal des économistes* usually appeared on the fifteenth of the month. This essay was published soon after the revolution had broken out, in February (22–24). The issue at the time, which concerned the provisional government, was the creation of the National Workshops and the program to provide state-funded work relief to the unemployed.

2. One of the first things the provisional government did after King Louis-Philippe abdicated and the Second Republic was declared (22–24 February 1848) was to announce the creation of the National Workshops (26 February), limit the length of the working day to ten hours in Paris and eleven hours in the provinces (2 March), and increase by 45 percent the level of direct taxes (15 March; the *impôt des quarante-cinq centimes*).

3. Bastiat uses the term *la grande organisateur* to disparage those who, like the socialists, wanted to "organize" society from top to bottom. One might also have translated it in the twentieth-century sense of "the central planner."

I would keep quiet if it were a matter only of temporary measures that were required and to some extent justified by the upheaval of the great revolution that we have just accomplished, but what people are demanding are not exceptional remedies but the application of a system. Forgetting that citizens' purses fill that of the State, they want the state's purse to fill those of the citizens.

I do have to make it clear that it is not by using irony and sarcasm that I will be striving to dispel this disastrous illusion. In my view at least, it casts a somber shadow over the future, which I very much fear will be the rock on which our beloved Republic will founder.[4]

Besides, how will we summon up the courage to admonish the people for not knowing what they have always been forbidden to learn, and for cherishing in their hearts illusionary hopes that have assiduously been placed there?

What did those in power in this century, the major landowners and manufacturers, do in the past as they continue to do? They demanded additional profit from the law to the detriment of the masses. Is it surprising, therefore, that the masses, now in a position to make the law, are also requiring additional pay? But alas! There is no other mass beneath them from which this source of subsidy can arise. With their gaze fixed on power, businessmen transformed themselves into solicitors of the legislature. Arrange for me to sell my wheat more profitably! Arrange for me an increased profit from my meat! Raise the price of my iron, my woolen cloth, or my coal artificially! These were the cries that deafened the Chamber, the very seat of privilege. Is it surprising that the people, now that they are victorious, are becoming solicitors of the legislature in their turn? But alas! Although the law is able, at a stretch, to give handouts to a few privileged people at the expense of the nation, how can we imagine that it can give handouts to the entire nation?[5]

What example is being given at present even by the middle class? It is seen

---

4. Bastiat seems to be having some regrets here about his use of satire and humor in many of the pieces in *Economic Sophisms* which he had written over the past three years, yet he was to change his mind when writing one of his final works, *What Is Seen and What Is Not Seen*. Paillottet tells us that Bastiat rewrote it completely because he thought he had overcorrected and made it too severe.

5. This of course is exactly what led Bastiat to declare in June that a state which tried to live by this principle had become a "great fiction"; that is, that the state was "the great fiction by which everyone endeavors to live at the expense of everyone else," which he developed during the course of 1848. A draft of the essay appeared in his revolutionary magazine *Jacques Bonhomme* in June 1848 (see CW2, 105–6), and a larger article, "The State," which appeared in the *Journal des débats* in September 1848, was published as a separate booklet of the same title later that same year (see CW2, pp.93–104).

harassing the provisional government and leaping on the budget as though onto its prey. Is it surprising that the people are also displaying the very modest ambition of making a living, at least through work?

What used those who governed to say repeatedly? At the slightest gleam of prosperity, they attributed its entire merit to themselves without ceremony; they made no mention of the popular virtues that are its basis nor of the activity, order, and economy of the workers. No, they claimed the authorship of this prosperity, which incidentally is highly doubtful. Less than two months ago, I heard the minister of trade[6] say: "Thanks to the active intervention of the government, thanks to the wisdom of the king, thanks to the patronage of science, all the productive classes are flourishing." Should we be surprised that the people have ended up believing that they obtain well-being from above, like manna from heaven, and that they now turn their gaze to the regions of power? When you claim the merit for all the good that occurs, you incur responsibility for all the harm that arises.

This reminds me of a parish priest in our region. In the initial years of his residence no hail fell in the village, and he succeeded in convincing the good villagers that his prayers had the infallible virtue of chasing storms away. This was fine so long as it did not hail, but at the first onset of the calamity he was chased out of the parish. People said to him: "Is it out of ill-will, therefore, that you have allowed us to be struck by the storm?"

The Republic was inaugurated with a similar disappointment. It made this statement to the people, who were, incidentally, only too happy to hear it: "I guarantee well-being to all citizens."[7] And let us hope this statement does not attract storms to our country!

The people of Paris have gained eternal glory through their courage.

They have aroused the admiration of the entire world for their love of public order and their respect for all rights and property.

6. Laurent Cunin-Gridaine.

7. Among many similar decrees, the provisional government stated on 25 February: "The provisional government of the French Republic undertakes to guarantee the existence of the workers by means of work; it undertakes to guarantee work to all citizens; it recognizes that workers must form associations in order to enjoy the legitimate benefits of their labor. The provisional government will hand over to the workers, what belongs to them, the million francs which is due to be paid to the civil list" (*Actes officiels du Gouvernement provisoire,* p. 9). The Civil List was the grant given by the Chamber to the Crown to assist in their upkeep. In the budget for 1847 (the year before the revolution), fr. 13.3 million was set aside for this purpose. See "Budget de 1846 et 1847," in *L'Annuaire de l'économie politique et de la statistique* (1847), p. 38.

All that remains to them is to accomplish another particularly difficult task, that of rejecting the poisoned chalice that is being presented to them. I say this with conviction; the entire future of the Republic is now resting on their common sense. It is no longer a question of the honesty of their intentions, no one can fail to recognize this; it is a question of the honesty of their instincts. The glorious revolution that they have achieved through their courage and preserved through their wisdom has just one danger to face, disappointment, and against this danger there is just one lifeline, the sagacity of the people.

Yes, if friendly voices warn the people, if courageous spirits open their eyes, something tells me that the Republic will avoid the gaping abyss that is opening in front of it, and if this happens, what a magnificent sight France will present to the world![8] A people triumphing over its enemies and false friends, a people that is conquering the obsessions of others and its own illusions!

I will start by saying that the institutions that weighed us down just a few days ago have not been overturned, and that the Republic, or the government of everyone by all, has not been founded in order to leave the people (and by this term I now mean the working class: those earning wages, or what used to be called the proletariat) in the same situation as they were before.

That is the will of all, and it is their own will that their situation should change.

However, two means are open to them, and these means are not only different, they are, it has to be said, diametrically opposed to each other.

The school of thought known as the *Economist School*[9] proposes the immediate dismantling of all privileges and all monopolies, the immediate elimination of all nonuseful state functions, the immediate reduction of all excessive salaries, deep reductions in public expenditure, and the reorganization of taxes so that those that weigh heavily on the consumption of the

8. In February 1848, the day after the Revolution broke out, Bastiat declared that he was "firmly convinced that the republican form of government is the only one which is suitable for a free people, the only one which allows the full and complete development of all kinds of liberty." This quote comes from the preface to the first issue of *La République française* (see "A Few Words about the Title of Our Journal *The French Republic*," in Addendum: Additional Materials by Bastiat). He and Molinari wanted to call their revolutionary magazine just "La République" but had to settle for "La République française," as the former had already been taken. His political beliefs could be summed up as follows: in addition to "liberty, equality, and fraternity" he also believed in "property, tranquility, prosperity, frugality, and stability" (to paraphrase him slightly).

9. See the entry for *"Les Économistes,"* in the Glossary of Subjects and Terms.

people, those that hamper their movement and paralyze their work, are got rid of. For example, this school demands that city tolls, the salt tax,[10] the duties on the import of subsistence items and working tools be abolished forthwith;

It demands that the word *Liberty,* which floats on all our banners and which is engraved on all our buildings, become the truth at last.

It demands that, after paying the government what is essential for maintaining internal and external security, repressing fraud, misdemeanors, and crime, and subsidizing the major works of national utility, THE PEOPLE SHOULD KEEP THE REST FOR ITSELF.

It confidently asserts that the more the people contribute to the security of persons and property, the faster capital will grow.

And that capital will grow even faster if the people are able *to keep their wages for themselves* instead of handing them over to the state through taxes.

And that rapid capital formation necessarily implies that wages will rise rapidly, with the result that the working classes will gradually increase their level of well-being, independence, education, and dignity.

This system does not have the advantage of promising the instant achievement of universal happiness, but it appears to us to be simple, immediately practicable, in conformity with justice, faithful to freedom, and likely to encourage all human tendencies to equality and fraternity. I will return to this once I have set out in detail the views of another school, which appears right now to have the upper hand in popularity.

This school also wants the good of the people, but it claims to achieve it through a direct route. Its pretension is no less than to increase the well-being of the masses, that is to say, increase their consumption, while reducing their work, and in order to accomplish this miracle it has conceived the idea of drawing additional pay either from the common purse or from the excessive profits of business entrepreneurs.

It is the dangers of this system that I propose to point out.

Let no one misunderstand what I am saying. I do not mean here to condemn *voluntary association.*[11] I sincerely believe that *association* will enable

10. One of the first taxes to be abolished after the Revolution of 22–24 February was the much hated salt tax, on 21 April.

11. On the difference between the socialists' and the Economists' idea of association, see "Bastiat's Use of the Socialist Terms 'Organization' and "Association,'" in the Note on the Translation.

great progress to be made in every sphere of human endeavor. Tests are being carried out at this time, in particular by the management of the Northern Railway[12] and that of the journal *La Presse.*[13] Who could criticize these attempts? I myself, before I had ever heard of the *École sociétaire,*[14] had conceived a project for a farming association with the aim of improving the sharecropping system.[15] Health reasons were the only cause of my relinquishing this enterprise.

The cause of my doubts, or to put it frankly, what my strong conviction rejects with all its strength, is the clear tendency that you have doubtless noticed, and which also perhaps carries you along with it, to invoke State intervention in all matters, and in particular for the achievement of our Utopias, or our "systems" if you prefer, with *legal coercion* as the principle and *public money* as the means.

You may well emblazon *Voluntary Association* on your flag: I say that if you call upon the aid of law and taxes, the ensign is as total a lie as it can be, since in that case there is no longer *association* nor a *voluntary act.*

I will devote myself to demonstrating that the excessive intervention of the state cannot increase the well-being of the masses and that, on the contrary, it tends to decrease it;

that it deletes the first word of our Republican motto, the word *Liberty;*

that while it is erroneous in principle, it is particularly dangerous for France, and threatens to engulf, in a great and irreparable disaster, private wealth, public wealth, the fate of the working classes, our institutions, and the Republic.

In the first place, I say that the promises of this deplorable system of thought are illusory.

---

12. The first railway concessions were issued by the government in 1844–45, triggering a wave of speculation and attempts to secure concessions. The first major line was the "chemin de fer du Nord" (June 1846), followed by the "chemin de fer d'Amiens à Boulogne" (May 1848). The Northern Railway is the one Bastiat would be familiar with in this essay. See "The French Railways" in appendix 3.

13. *La Presse* was a widely circulated daily newspaper under the control of the politician and businessman Émile de Girardin (1806–81).

14. *École sociétaire* (the school of members [of society], or the social school) was the name used by Charles Fourier and his school to describe themselves. See Fourier, *Le Nouveau monde industriel et sociétaire.*

15. See "Proposition for the Creation of a School for Sons of Sharecroppers" (CW1, pp. 334–40) on Bastiat's failed attempt to start a school for his sharecroppers.

And really, this seems so obvious to me that I would be ashamed to spend time on a long demonstration of this if striking facts did not convince me that this demonstration is necessary.

For what is the sight being offered to us by the country?

At the Town Hall[16] there is a scramble for office; at the Luxembourg Palace, a scramble for wages.[17] The first leads to ignominy, the second to deep disappointment.

As for the *scramble for office,* the obvious remedy would be to abolish all useless functions and reduce the remuneration of those functions that excite greed; but this prey is left in its entirety to the avidity of the bourgeoisie, and these people rush after it madly.

What happens then? The people in turn, the people who are the workers, who witness the joys of an existence ensured by public resources, forgetting that they themselves make up this public and that the budget is made up of their flesh and blood, demand in their turn that a scramble be prepared for them.

Long delegations throng around the Luxembourg Palace, and what do they demand? An increase in pay, that is to say, in a word, an improvement in the workers' means of existence.

However, those who go to these delegations personally are not merely acting on their own account. They genuinely mean to represent the entire great confraternity of workers who people both our towns and our countryside.

Material well-being does not consist in earning more money. It consists in being better fed, clothed, housed, heated, lit, educated, etc., etc.

What they are asking for, then, when you go into the detail of things, is that from the glorious era of our revolution, each Frenchman who is a member of the working classes should have more bread, wine, meat, linen, furniture, iron, fuel, books, etc., etc.

And, something that beggars belief, at the same time some of these want

16. The Hôtel-de-Ville (the town or city hall) was the seat of the provisional government. This is a scene which Bastiat personally witnessed. According to Molinari, he, Bastiat, and Castille went "arm in arm" to the Hôtel-de-Ville on the day the revolution broke out (24 February) in order to get permission to start their journal *La République français.* This was impossible to do, as people armed with rifles and swords had invaded the building, and an enormous crowd had gathered in order to try to get jobs in the new regime. See Molinari, "Frédéric Bastiat: Lettres d'un habitant des Landes."

17. The newly established administration for the National Workshops was located in the Luxembourg Palace.

to decrease the work needed to produce these things. Some, fortunately few in number, even go so far as to demand the destruction of machines.[18]

Can a contradiction as flagrant as this ever be imagined?

Unless the miracle of the wine pitcher of Cana[19] be repeated in the coffers of the tax collector, how can the State take more out of them than the people put in? Do the people believe that for each hundred-sou coin that goes into these coffers, ten francs can be taken out? Alas, just the opposite is true. The hundred-sou coins that the people cast into them whole and entire come out again only badly clipped, since the tax collector has to keep a share of them for himself.

What is more, what does money mean? Even if it were true that you could withdraw from the public Treasury a fund of wages that was different from what the public itself had put into it, would you be better off? It is not a matter of money, but of food, clothing, housing, etc.

Well, has the *organizer* who sits in the Luxembourg Palace[20] the power to multiply these things by decree? Or, if France produces 60 million hectoliters of wheat, is he able to ensure that each of our 36 million fellow citizens receives 3 hectoliters, and the same thing for iron, woolen cloth, and fuel?

Recourse to the public Treasury as a general practice is thus deplorably mistaken. It is ensuring that a cruel disappointment is in store for the people.[21]

Doubtless it will be said: "No one is thinking of such absurdities. What is clear, however, is that some in France have too much and others not enough. What we are trying to do is to level things justly and distribute things more equitably."

Let us examine the question from this point of view.

18. This is a reference to the Luddites. See Bastiat's reference to smashing machines in ES1 20, p. 87n1.

19. See ES3 12, p. 309n2.

20. Pierre-Émile Thomas (1822–80), a civil engineer, was appointed director of the National Workshops between March and May 1848. The socialist Louis Blanc (1811–82) was the driving intellectual force behind the scheme. He was appointed minister without portfolio by the provisional government and head of the Luxembourg Commission to study labor problems, out of which emerged the National Workshops program.

21. Shortly after this article was written, Bastiat was elected to the new Constituent Assembly of the Second Republic to represent the département of the Landes on 23 April. He was nominated by the Assembly to the Finance Committee, to which he was reappointed eight times. He spent much of his time telling the members of the Committee and the Assembly much the same things as he is saying here, and with little success.

If what they mean is that, once they had removed all the taxes that could be removed, all those that remained should as far as possible be borne by the class best able to support them, our wishes could not be better expressed. But that is too simple for the *organizers;* it is good for *economists.*

What people want is for each Frenchman to be well supplied with everything. It has been announced in advance that the State would guarantee the well-being of all, and the question is to know whether it is possible to squeeze the wealthy class sufficiently in favor of the poor class to achieve this result.

Setting the question out is to solve it, for in order for everyone to have more bread, wine, meat, woolen cloth, etc., the country has to produce more of these, and how can you take from a single class, even the wealthy class, more than all the classes together produce?

Besides, you should note this clearly: it is a question here of taxes. These have already reached a billion and a half.[22] The trends I am combating, far from allowing any decreases, will lead to inevitable increases.

Allow me a rough calculation.

It is extremely difficult to put an accurate figure on the two classes, but we can come close to one.

Under the regime that has just fallen, there were 250 thousand electors.[23] Assuming four members per family, this implies one million inhabitants, and everyone knows that electors paying 200 francs of taxes were very close to belonging to the class of less well-off landowners. However, to avoid any argument, let us attribute to the wealthy class not only these million inhabitants, but sixteen times this number. This is already a reasonable concession. We therefore have sixteen million wealthy people and twenty million who are, if not poor, at least brothers who need assistance. If we assume that a very insignificant addition of 25 percent per day is essential to put into practice philanthropic views that are more benevolent than enlightened, this means

22. Total annual income for the government in 1848 was fr. 1.4 billion.

23. Between 1820 and 1848, 258 deputies were elected by a small group of individuals (the number varied over time from 90,000 to 240,000) who qualified to vote because they paid more than 300 francs in direct taxes. One-quarter of the electors, those who paid the largest amount of taxes, elected another 172 deputies. Therefore, those wealthier electors enjoyed the privilege of a double vote. Bastiat referred to this group as the *classe électorale* (the electoral class). Another term for this group which was popular at the time was *monopole électoral* (electoral monopoly). This was used by Molinari in a number of works, as it nicely captured the idea that there was a political corollary to the phenomenon of economic monopolies. Gustave de Molinari, "La réforme électorale envisagée au point de vue économique," *L'Économiste belge,* no. 5, March 1866, p. 55.

a tax of five million per day or close to two billion per year, and we can even make it two billion to include the costs of collection.

We are already paying one and a half billion. I am willing to admit that with a more economic system of administration we can reduce this figure by one-third: we would still have to levy *three billion*. Well, I ask you, can we envisage levying three billion from sixteen million of the wealthiest inhabitants in the country?

A tax like this would be confiscatory, and look at the consequences. If in fact all property was confiscated as quickly as it was created, who would take the trouble to create property? People do not work just to live from day to day. Among the most powerful incentives to work, perhaps, is the hope of acquiring a nest egg for one's old age, setting one's children up, and improving the situation of one's family. But if you organize your financial system in a way that confiscates all property as it is created, no one would be interested in either work or thrift, and capital would not be built up; it would decrease rapidly, if indeed it did not suddenly go abroad, and in this case, what would become of the very class that you wished to relieve?

I add another truth here that it is essential for the people to learn.

In a country in which tax is very moderate, it is possible to share it out in accordance with the rules of justice and collect it at little cost. Assume, for example, that France's budget did not exceed five or six hundred million. I sincerely believe that if this were so, according to this hypothesis, it would be possible to establish a *single tax* based on the property acquired (both movable and fixed).

But when the State extracts from the nation one-quarter, one-third, or half of its income, it is reduced to acting with deception,[24] increasing the number of sources of revenue, and inventing the strangest and at the same time most vexatious of taxes. It ensures that tax is combined with the price of things, so that taxpayers pay it unknowingly. This gives rise to the consumption taxes that are so disastrous for the free movement of industry. Well, anyone who has had dealings with finance is fully aware that this type of tax is productive only if it is levied on the most general of consumer products. It is no good basing your hopes on taxes on luxury articles; I call on these earnestly for reasons of equity, but they can never provide more than an insignificant contribution to a huge budget. People would be deluding themselves

---

24. Bastiat uses the word *ruse* (deception). See "Bastiat on Enlightening the 'Dupes' about the Nature of Plunder," in the Introduction.

totally if they thought it was possible, even for the most popular government, to increase public spending which is already heavy and at the same time to make the wealthy class alone responsible for bearing it.

What should be noted is that, from the moment recourse is made to consumption tax (which is the inevitable consequence of a heavy budget), the equality of the burden is destroyed, since the objects subjected to taxes form a greater part of the consumption of the poor than the consumption of the wealthy, in proportion to their respective incomes.

In addition, unless we enter into inextricable difficulties of classification, when we subject a given object, wine for example, to a uniform tax, the injustice leaps to the eye. A worker who buys one liter of wine at 50 centimes per liter that is subjected to a tax of 50 centimes, pays 100 percent. The millionaire who drinks Lafitte wine at 10 francs a bottle pays 5 percent.[25]

From every angle, therefore, it is the working class that has the most interest in seeing the budget reduced to proportions that allow taxes to be simplified and equalized. But in order to do this, they must not be dazzled by all these philanthropic projects, which have just one certain result: that of increasing nationwide charges.

If the increase in taxes is incompatible with equality between taxpayers and with the security that is essential for capital to be created and increased, it is no less incompatible with freedom.

I remember in my youth reading one of the sentences so familiar to M. Guizot, who was then a mere substitute teacher. To justify the heavy budgets that appeared to be the obligatory corollaries of constitutional monarchies, he said: *"Freedom is an asset that is so precious that a nation should never trade it away."* From that day on, I said to myself: "M. Guizot may have eminent abilities, but he would certainly be a pitiful Statesman."[26]

25. In 1845 the city of Paris imposed an octroi (entry tax) on all goods which entered the city, which raised fr. 49 million. Of this, fr. 26.1 million were levied on wine and other alcoholic drinks, which comprised 53 percent of the total. The tax on wine was the heaviest as a proportion of total value and the most unequally applied. Cheap table wine was taxed at the rate of 80–100 percent by value, while superior quality wine was taxed at the rate of 5–6 percent by value. See Say, *Paris, son octroi et ses emprunts.*

26. We have not been able to find this quotation from Guizot. It may well have originated in a passage from D'Amilaville's article on population in Diderot's *Encyclopedia,* where he states that large populations are fostered by states which are limited and where rights are respected: "The spirit of large monarchies is not conducive to having large populations. It is in gentle and limited governments, where the rights of humanity are

In fact, freedom is a very precious asset and one for which a nation cannot pay too high a price. However, the question is precisely to know whether an overtaxed nation is able to be free, and if there is not a radical incompatibility between freedom and excessive taxation.

Well, I assert that there is a radical incompatibility.

Let us note that in reality the civil service does not act on things, but on people, and it acts on them with authority. Well, the action that certain men exercise on other men with the support of the law and public coercion can never be neutral. It is essentially harmful if it is not essentially useful.

The service of a public functionary is not one whose price is negotiated or one that people are in a position to accept or refuse. By its very nature, it is *imposed.* When a nation can do no better than to entrust a *service* to public coercion, as in the instance of security, national independence, or the repression of misdemeanors and crimes, it has to create this authority and be subject to it.

But if a nation puts into the domain of public service what absolutely ought to have remained in that of private services, it denies itself the ability to negotiate the sacrifice it wishes to make in exchange for these services and deprives itself of the right to refuse them; it reduces the sphere of its freedom.

The number of state functionaries cannot be increased without increasing the number of functions they occupy. That would be too flagrant. The point is that increasing the number of functions increases the number of infringements on freedom.

How can a monarch confiscate the freedom of religion? By having the clergy on hire.[27]

How can he confiscate freedom of education? By having a university on hire.[28]

---

respected, that men become numerous. Liberty is a good so precious that, without being accompanied by anything else, they [limited governments] attract men and increase their number" (D'Amilaville, "Population," p. 95).

27. Bastiat uses the expression *un clergé à gages,* which suggests someone for hire or a mercenary. In the statement of principles which Bastiat and his colleagues published in their journal *La République française* on 26 February, just after the Revolution broke out, was a call for an end to "salaried religion" (*plus de cultes salariés!*).

28. In 1849 fr. 21.8 million was spent on public education, of which fr. 17.9 went for the university and fr. 3.3 million for "science and letters."

What is being proposed now? To have trade and transport carried out by civil servants. If this plan is put into practice, we will pay more in taxes and be less free.

You can clearly see, then, that under the guise of philanthropy, the system being recommended today is illusory, unjust, destructive of security, harmful to the formation of capital and thereby to increasing wages. In sum, it is undermining the liberty of the citizens.

I might blame it for many other things. It would be easy for me to prove that it is an insurmountable obstacle to any progress because it paralyzes the very impetus to progress, the vigilance of private interest.

What are the areas of human activity that offer the sight of the most complete stagnation? Are these not precisely those entrusted to public services? Let us take education. It is still where it was in the Middle Ages. It has not emerged from the study of two dead languages, a study that was in the past so rational and is so irrational today. Not only are the same things being taught, but the same methods are being used to teach them. What industry other than this has remained where it was five centuries ago?

I could also accuse excessive taxes and the increase in number of public functions of developing the unfettered ardor for office that in itself and in its consequences is the greatest plague of modern times.[29] But I lack space and entrust these considerations to the sagacity of the reader.

I cannot stop myself, nevertheless, from considering the question from the point of view of the particular situation in which the February Revolution has placed France.

I do not hesitate to say this: if the common sense of the people and the common sense of the workers do not exact proper and swift justice on the mad and illusionary hopes that have been cast into their midst in a reckless thirst for popularity, these disappointed hopes will be fatal to the Republic.

Certainly, they will be disappointed, because they are illusionary. I have proved this. Promises have been made that are physically impossible to honor.

---

29. See Louis Reybaud's (1799–1879) amusing critiques of French bureaucracy in *Mémoires de Jérôme Paturot,* which appeared in serial form between 1843 and 1848, where he describes the behavior of individuals within the *ruche bureaucratique* (bureaucratic hive), where appointments are solicited by the weak and powerless of the powerful and well-connected, thus creating a network of obligation and control throughout the hierarchy which radiates outward to infinity (*ces ricochets allaient à l'infini*). Reybaud was known to Bastiat and may have influenced him in the development of his theory of the ricochet effect.

What is the situation we are in? On its death, the constitutional monarchy has left us as an inheritance a debt whose interest alone is an annual burden of three hundred million on our finances,[30] apart from an equal amount of floating debt.[31]

It has left us Algeria, which will cost us one hundred million a year for a great many years.[32]

Without attacking us, without even threatening us, the absolute kings of Europe just have to maintain their current level of military forces to oblige us to retain ours. Under this heading, five to six hundred million has to be included in our budget for the army and navy.[33]

Finally, there remain all the public services, all the costs of tax collection, and all the work of national utility.[34]

Add it all up, set out the figures any way you like, and you will see that the budget for expenditure is inevitably enormous.

It has to be assumed that the ordinary sources of revenue will be less productive from the first year of the revolution. Let us assume that the deficit that they produce is compensated for by the abolition of sinecures and the retrenchment of parasitic state functions.

The inexorable result is nonetheless that it is already very difficult to give satisfaction to the taxpayers.

30. Total debt held by the French government in 1848 amounted to fr. 5.2 billion, which required annual payments of fr. 384 million to service in 1848. Since total annual income for the government in 1848 was fr. 1.391 billion, the outstanding debt was 3.7 times receipts. See the Appendix on "French Government Finances 1848–49"; and Gustave du Puynode, "Crédit public," *DEP,* vol. 1, pp. 508–25.

31. In 1848 the consolidated debt required an annual payment of fr. 293 million; the floating debt required a payment of fr. 93 million.

32. The *JDE* gives a figure of fr. 120 million spent in Algeria in 1847. See "Chronique," *JDE* 19 (February 1848): 315.

33. According to the budget passed on 15 May 1849, the size of the French army was 389,967 men and 95,687 horses. This figure rises to 459,457 men and 97,738 horses for the entire French military (including foreign and colonial forces). The expenditure on the army in 1849 was fr. 346 million and for the navy and colonies was fr. 119 million, for a combined total of fr. 466 million. Total government expenditure in 1849 was fr. 1.573 billion, with expenditure on the armed forces making up 29.6 percent of the total budget. See appendix 4 on "French Government's Budgets for Fiscal Years 1848–49." See "The French Army and Conscription" in appendix 2.

34. In 1848 the administrative costs to the government in collecting taxes such as direct taxes, stamp duty, customs, indirect taxes, and the post office amounted to fr. 157 million out of total receipts of fr. 1.391 billion, or 11 percent.

And it is at this time that into the midst of the people is cast the vain hope that they too can draw life from this same treasure, which they are feeding with their very lives!

It is at this time, when production, trade, capital, and labor need security and freedom to widen the sources of taxes and wages, it is at this very time that you are holding over their heads the threat of a host of arbitrary plans, ill-thought-out and ill-designed institutions, projects for organization that have been hatched in the brains of political writers, who for the most part know nothing about this subject!

But what will happen on the day disappointment with this occurs? And this day will surely come.

What will happen when workers perceive that work provided by the State is not work *added* to that of the country but *subtracted* through tax at one point in order to be paid by charity at another, with all the loss that the creation of new administrative authorities implies?

What will happen when you are reduced to coming forward to say to taxpayers: "We cannot touch the salt tax, city tolls, the tax on wines and spirits, or any of the most unpopular fiscal inventions; on the contrary, we are obliged to think up new ones"?[35]

What will happen when the claim to increase ineluctably the mass of wages, taking no account of a corresponding increase in capital (which implies the most blatant contradiction), will have disrupted all the workshops on the pretext of organization and perhaps forced capital to seek the bracing atmosphere of freedom elsewhere?

I do not wish to dwell on the consequences. It is enough for me to have pointed out the danger as I see it.

"What!" it will be said. "Following the great February Revolution, was there nothing left to do? Was no satisfaction to be given to the people? Should we have left things exactly where they were before? Was there no suffering that needed to be relieved?"

This is not what we think.

In our view, increasing wages does not depend on either benevolent inten-

35. An example of the Provisional Government's confusion concerning taxes is the following. The much-hated salt tax (*gabelle*) was cut on 21 April to 10 centimes per kilogram, which cost the Treasury a relatively modest fr. 71.6 million. On the other hand, on 15 March, the Provisional Government increased direct taxes by 45 percent (the so-called *impôt des quarante-cinq centimes*) on land, movable goods, doors and windows, and trading licenses, which raised fr. 421 million, or 30 percent of total receipts, for the Treasury.

tions or philanthropic decrees. It depends and depends solely on an increase in capital. In a country such as the United States, when capital is built up quickly, wages rise and the nation is happy.

Now, in order for capital to be created, two things are needed: security and freedom. In addition, it must not be pillaged by taxation as it grows.

This, we think, is where the rules of conduct and the duties of the government lie.

New schemes, agreements, organizations, and associations ought to have been left to the common sense, experience, and initiative of the citizens. Such things are not accomplished by taxes and decrees.

Providing universal security by peaceful and reassuring public servants who have been chosen in an enlightened manner, basing true freedom on the elimination of privileges and monopolies, allowing free entry of items of prime necessity and those most essential for work, creating the resources needed at no charge by means of a reduction of excessive duties and the abolition of prohibition, simplifying all administrative procedures, cutting out whole layers of bureaucracy, abolishing parasitic state functions, reducing excessive remuneration of pubic servants, negotiating immediately with foreign powers to reduce armed forces, abolishing city tolls and the salt tax, and fundamentally reorganizing the tax on wines and spirits, and creating a sumptuary tax: all these form the mission of a popular government in my view, and this is the mission of our republic.

Under a regime like this of order, security, and liberty, we would see capital being created and giving life to all branches of production, trade expanding, farming progressing, work actively being encouraged, labor sought after and well paid, wages benefiting from the competition of increasingly abundant capital, and all the living forces of the nation, currently absorbed by useless or harmful administrative bodies, turned toward furthering the physical, intellectual, and moral well-being of the entire nation.

What Is Seen and
What Is Not Seen,
or Political Economy
in One Lesson[1]

1. (Paillottet's note) This pamphlet, published in July 1850, was the last one written by Bastiat. It had been promised to the public for more than a year. The following is the reason for its delayed publication. The author lost the manuscript when he moved house from the rue de Choiseul to the rue d'Alger. After a long and fruitless search, he decided to rewrite the work completely and selected as the principal basis for his arguments speeches recently made in the National Assembly. Once he had completed this task, he blamed himself for being too serious, threw the second manuscript into the fire, and wrote the one we are publishing here. [The subtitle was part of the first edition, but it was usually dispensed with in the later editions. The rue de Choiseul was the headquarters of the French Free Trade Association.]

What Is Seen and What Is Not Seen,
or Political Economy in One Lesson

PUBLISHING HISTORY:

Original title: "Ce qu'on voit et ce qu'on ne voit pas."
Place and date of first publication: Did not appear separately
   before publication; written July 1850.
First French edition as book or pamphlet: 1850.
Location in Paillottet's edition of *OC:* Vol. 5. *Sophismes*
   économiques, pp. 336–92.
Previous translations: 1st English ed., 1852; 1st American edition
   (FEE ed.), 1964.

[The Author's Introduction]

In the sphere of economics an action, a habit, an institution, or a law engenders not just one effect but a series of effects. Of these effects only the first is immediate; it is revealed simultaneously with its cause; *it is seen.* The others merely occur successively; *they are not seen;*[1] we are lucky if we *foresee* them.

The entire difference between a bad and a good Economist is apparent here. A bad one relies on the *visible* effect, while the good one takes account both of the effect one can *see* and of those one must *foresee.*

However, the difference between these is huge, for it almost always happens that when the immediate consequence is favorable, the later consequences are disastrous and *vice versa.* From which it follows that a bad Economist will pursue a small current benefit that is followed by a large disadvantage in the future, while a true Economist will pursue a large benefit in the future at the risk of suffering a small disadvantage immediately.[2]

1. Bastiat's first use of the concept of "the seen" and "the unseen" is most likely in ES1 20, p. 90, where he contrasts "immediate and transitory effects" and "general and definitive consequences."

2. During the course of 1849, when Bastiat repeatedly rewrote this pamphlet as he could not decide on the appropriate style to use, whether serious or satirical, he had developed his thinking on two ideas which had been of great concern to him for the pre-

This distinction is also true, moreover, for hygiene and the moral code. Often, the sweeter the first fruit of a habit, the more bitter are those that follow. Examples of this are debauchery, laziness, and prodigality. So when a man, touched by some effect that *can be seen,* has not yet learned to discern those that *are not seen,* he gives way to disastrous habits, not just through inclination but deliberately.

This explains the inexorably painful evolution of the human race. Ignorance surrounds its cradle; it therefore makes up its mind with regard to its acts according to their initial consequences, the only ones it is able to see originally. It is only in the long run that it learns to take account of the others. Two masters, very different from one another, teach it this lesson: experience and foresight. Experience governs effectively but brutally. It teaches us all the effects of an action by having us feel them, and we cannot fail to end up learning that fire burns, by burning ourselves. For this rough teacher, I would like, as far as possible, to substitute a gentler one: foresight. This is why I will be seeking the consequences of certain economic phenomena by opposing those *that are not seen* to those *that are seen.*

---

vious few years. These were first, the immediately observable and obvious consequences of an economic act ("the seen") and the longer-term and less apparent consequences ("the unseen"); and second, the "ricochet" or flow-on effects of economic actions, which may or may not have positive or negative consequences. This pamphlet is an extended exploration of the former set of ideas.

1. The Broken Window[1]

Have you ever witnessed the fury of the good bourgeois Jacques Bonhomme when his dreadful son succeeded in breaking a window? If you have witnessed this sight, you will certainly have noted that all the onlookers, even if they were thirty in number, appeared to have agreed mutually to offer the unfortunate owner this uniform piece of consolation: "Good comes out of everything. Accidents like this keep production moving. Everyone has to live. What would happen to glaziers if no window panes were ever broken?"

Well, there is an entire theory in this consoling formula, which it is good to surprise *in flagrante delicto*[2] in this very simple example, since it is exactly the same as the one that unfortunately governs the majority of our economic institutions.

If you suppose that it is necessary to spend six francs to repair the damage, if you mean that the accident provides six francs to the glazing industry and stimulates the said industry to the tune of six francs, I agree, and I do not query in any way that the reasoning is accurate. The glazier will come, do his job, be paid six francs, rub his hands, and in his heart bless the dreadful child. *This is what is seen.*

But if, by way of deduction, as is often the case, the conclusion is reached that it is a good thing to break windows, that this causes money to circulate and therefore industry in general is stimulated, I am obliged to cry: "Stop!"

---

1. The American journalist Henry Hazlitt played an important role in bringing the work of Bastiat to the attention of Americans in the immediate post–World War II period. In his preface to his book *Economics in One Lesson* (1946), he acknowledged his debt to Bastiat's pamphlet *What Is Seen and What Is Not Seen:* "My greatest debt, with respect to the kind of expository framework on which the present argument is being hung, is to Frédéric Bastiat's essay *Ce qu'on voit et ce qu'on ne voit pas,* now nearly a century old. The present work may, in fact, be regarded as a modernization, extension, and generalization of the approach found in Bastiat's pamphlet" (Hazlitt, *Economics in One Lesson* [1974], p. 9). Hazlitt's first chapter was titled "The Broken Window"; thus with the very title and the first chapter he pays homage to the work of Bastiat.

2. *In flagrante delicto* is a Latin phrase which means literally "in blazing offense." It is used in legal circles to mean that someone has been caught in the act of committing an offense.

Your theory has stopped at *what is seen* and takes no account of *what is not seen.*

What is not seen is that since our bourgeois has spent six francs on one thing, he can no longer spend them on another. *What is not seen* is that if he had not had a window to replace, he might have replaced his down-at-the-heels shoes or added a book to his library. In short, he would have used his six francs for a purpose that he will no longer be able to.

Let us therefore draw up the accounts of industry *in general.*

As the window was broken, the glazing industry is stimulated to the tune of six francs; *this is what is seen.*

If the window had not been broken, the shoemaking industry (or any other) would have been stimulated to the tune of six francs; *this is what is not seen.*

And if we took into consideration *what is not seen,* because it is a negative fact, as well as *what is seen,* because it is a positive fact, we would understand that it makes no difference to national output and employment, taken as a whole, whether window panes are broken or not.

Let us now draw up Jacques Bonhomme's account.[3]

In the first case, that of the broken window, he spends six francs and enjoys the benefit of a window neither more nor less than he did before.

In the second, in which the accident had not happened, he would have spent six francs on shoes and would have had the benefit of both a pair of shoes and a window.

Well, since Jacques Bonhomme is a member of society, it has to be concluded that, taken as a whole and comparing what he has to do with his benefits, society has lost the value of the broken window.

From which, as a generalization, we reach the unexpected conclusion: "Society loses the value of objects destroyed to no purpose" and the aphorism that will raise the hackles of protectionists: "Breaking, shattering, and dissipating does not stimulate the national employment," or more succinctly: "Destruction is not profitable."

What will *Le Moniteur industriel* say, and what will the opinion be of the followers of the worthy M. de Saint-Chamans, who has so accurately calcu-

---

3. In "drawing up this account," Bastiat was keen to introduce some mathematical precision into his calculations. His first attempt to do so resulted in his theory of "the double incidence of loss," which involved only three parties. He realized that this was inadequate and appealed to the physicist François Arago for help in using mathematics to calculate the gains and losses of many more parties. See "The Double Incidence of Loss" in appendix 1, "Further Aspects of Bastiat's Life and Work."

lated what productive activity would gain from the burning of Paris because of the houses that would have to be rebuilt?[4]

It grieves me to upset his ingenious calculations, especially since he has introduced their spirit into our legislation. But I beg him to redo them, introducing into the account *what is not seen* next to *what is seen*.

The reader must take care to note clearly that there are not just two characters, but three, in the little drama that I have put before him. One, Jacques Bonhomme, represents the Consumer, reduced by the breakage to enjoying one good instead of two. The second is the Glazier, who shows us the Producer whose activity is stimulated by the accident. The third is the Shoemaker (or any other producer) whose output is reduced to the same extent for the same reason. It is this third character that is always kept in the background and who, by personifying *what is not seen,* is an essential element of the problem. He is the one who makes us understand how absurd it is to see profit in destruction. He is the one who will be teaching us shortly that it is no less absurd to see profit in a policy of trade restriction, which is, after all, nothing other than partial destruction. Therefore, go into the detail of all the arguments brought out to support it and you will merely find a paraphrase of that common saying: *"What would happen to glaziers if windows were never broken?"*

2. Dismissing Members of the Armed Forces

The same rules apply to a nation as to a single man. When a nation wishes to acquire some economic benefit or other, it is up to that nation to see whether it is worth what it costs. For a nation, Security is the greatest asset. If, in order to acquire it, one hundred thousand men have to be drafted and one hundred million spent, I have nothing to say.[1] It is a benefit purchased at the price of a sacrifice.

4. Bastiat misremembers Saint-Chamans's argument in this passage. In his *Traité d'économie publique* (1852), which was a reworking of a previous work, *Nouvel essai sur la richesse des nations* (1824), Saint-Chamans argues against the free-market economist Joseph Droz (1773–1850), who stated that a sudden loss of a large amount of accumulated capital in Europe would cause severe hardship and would take considerable time to overcome. Saint-Chamans countered this by arguing that the Great Fire of London (so not Paris), in 1666, destroyed a huge amount of the capital stock which was quickly replaced and was thus a net gain for the nation of some one million pounds sterling (or 25 million francs). See Saint-Chamans, *Traité d'économie politique* 1:339.

1. To maintain its armed forces at the level of about 400,000 with a five-year period of enlistment, the French state had to recruit or conscript about 80,000 men each year.

Let no one therefore make any mistake about the significance of my thesis.

Imagine that a deputy proposes to discharge a hundred thousand men from the army to lessen the burden on taxpayers to the tune of a hundred million.[2]

If we limit ourselves to giving him the reply that "These hundred thousand men and this hundred million francs are essential to national security; they are a sacrifice, but without this sacrifice France would be torn apart by factions or invaded by foreigners," then I have no rebuttal to make at this point to this argument, which may be true or false, but theoretically does not encompass any economic heresy. The heresy begins when you wish to represent the sacrifice itself as an advantage because it benefits someone.

Well, unless I am much mistaken, the author of the proposal will no sooner have come down from the rostrum than another speaker will leap onto it to say:

"Dismiss a hundred thousand men! Do you really mean this? What will become of them? What will they live on? Work? But do you not know that there is a shortage of work everywhere? That there are no vacancies in any trade? Do you wish to cast them into the street to increase competition and depress earnings? Just when it is so difficult to eke out a meager livelihood, is it not fortunate that the State is providing bread to these hundred thousand people? What is more, consider that the army consumes wine, clothing, and weapons, and thus provides activity for factories and in garrison towns, and that in fact it is the very salvation of its countless numbers of suppliers. Do you not tremble at the thought of abolishing this huge engine of industrial activity?"

As we can see, this speech concludes that the hundred thousand men should be retained, taking no account of the indispensability of the service, on economic grounds. It is these considerations alone that I have to refute.

One hundred thousand men who cost the taxpayer one hundred million, live and provide a living for their suppliers to the extent that one hundred million can be spread: that is *what is seen*.

But one hundred million, extracted from the pockets of taxpayers, interferes with the economic lives of these taxpayers and their suppliers to the tune of that one hundred million: that is *what is not seen*. Do the calculation, cost it, and tell me where the profit lies for the mass of the people?

As for me, I will tell you where the *loss* lies, and to keep it simple, in-

2. According to the budget passed on 15 May 1849, the size of the French army was 389,967 men, and the expenditure was fr. 346,319,558. Thus Bastiat roughly estimates that 100,000 soldiers cost the French state fr. 100 million. See *Projet de loi pour la fixation des recettes et des dépenses de l'exercice 1850,* pp. 13–14; and Courtois, "Le budget de 1849," pp. 18–28.

stead of talking about one hundred thousand men and one hundred million francs, let us base our reasoning on one man and a thousand francs.

Here we are, in the village of "A." Recruiters are doing the rounds and have carried off one man. The tax collectors are doing their rounds and have carried off one thousand francs. The man and the money are taken to Metz,[3] one intended to provide a living for the other for a year without doing anything. If you take only Metz into consideration, you are right indeed a hundredfold; the measure is very beneficial. However, if your eyes turn to the village of A, you would think otherwise, for unless you are blind you will see that this village has lost one worker and the thousand francs that rewarded his work as well as the activity which, through the expenditure of these thousand francs, he spread around him.

At first sight it would appear that there is compensation for this. The phenomenon that occurred in the village now occurs in Metz, that is all. But this is where the loss lies. In the village, one man dug and ploughed: he was a worker. At Metz, he turns his head left and right: he is a soldier. The money and its circulation are the same in both cases, but on one, there were three hundred days of productive work; in the other there are three hundred days of unproductive work, always supposing that part of the army is not essential to public security.

Now, discharge comes. You point out to me a glut of one hundred thousand workers, stimulated competition, and the pressure that it exerts on rates of pay. This is what you see.

But here is what you do not see. You do not see that discharging one hundred thousand soldiers is not to annihilate one hundred million, it is to return this sum to the taxpayers. You do not see that casting one hundred thousand workers onto the market is at the same time to cast the one hundred million intended to pay for their work onto the same market. As a result, the same measure that increases the *supply* of labor also increases the *demand,* from which it follows that your decrease in earnings is an illusion. You do not see that before, as after the discharge of the soldiers, there are in the country one hundred million francs that correspond to one hundred thousand men, and that the entire difference lies in this: before, the country paid one hundred thousand men one hundred million to do nothing; after, it pays them this sum to work. Finally, you do not see that when a taxpayer hands over his money, either to a soldier in return for nothing or to a worker in return for something, all the subsequent consequences of the circulation

3. Metz is a city in northeast France with an important army garrison.

of this money are the same in both cases, with the sole difference that in the second case, the taxpayer receives something while in the first he receives nothing. The result: a net loss for the nation.

The sophism that I am combating here does not stand up to the test of progressive application, which is the touchstone of principles. If, everything paid for, and all interests considered, there is a *benefit to the nation* in increasing the army, why do we not enroll under the flag the entire male population of the country?

3. Taxes

Have you ever happened to hear the following?

"Taxes are the best investment; they are a life-giving dew. See how many families gain a livelihood from them; work out their ricochet or flow-on effects on industry; this is beyond measure, it is life."

To combat this doctrine, I am obliged to repeat the preceding refutation. Political economy knows full well that its arguments are not amusing enough for people to say of them: *Repetita placent.* Repetitions are pleasing. For this reason, like Basile,[1] it has arranged the proverb to suit itself, fully convinced that in its mouth *Repetita docent.* Repetitions teach.

The advantages that civil servants find in drawing their salaries are *what is seen.* The benefit that results for their suppliers is *again what is seen.* It is blindingly obvious to the eyes.

However, the disadvantage felt by taxpayers in trying to free themselves is *what is not seen,* and the damage that results for their suppliers is *what is not seen either,* although it is blindingly obvious to the mind.

When a civil servant spends *one hundred sous too much* for his own benefit, this implies that a taxpayer spends *one hundred sous too little* for his own benefit. However, the expenditure of the civil servant *is seen* because it is carried out, whereas that of the taxpayer *is not seen* as, alas! he is prevented from carrying it out.

You compare the nation to an arid land and tax to bountiful rain. So be it. But you should also ask yourself where the sources of this rain are, and if it is not taxes themselves that absorb the humidity from the earth and dry it out.

You ought to ask yourself as well if it is possible for the earth to receive as much of this precious water through rain as it loses through evaporation.

1. See ES3 2, p. 266n11.

What is obvious is that, when Jacques Bonhomme counts out one hundred sous to the tax collector, he receives nothing in return. When, subsequently, a civil servant, in spending these hundred sous, gives them back to Jacques Bonhomme, it is in return for an equal value in wheat or labor. The end result is a loss of five francs for Jacques Bonhomme.

It is very true that often, or in the majority of cases, if you prefer, the civil servant renders an equivalent service to Jacques Bonhomme. In this case, there is no loss on either side; there is merely an exchange. For this reason, my line of argument is not directed against useful activity. What I say is this: if you wish to create any such activity, prove its utility. Demonstrate that the services rendered to Jacques Bonhomme are worth what they cost him. But putting on one side this intrinsic utility, do not use as an argument the advantage it gives to the civil servant, his family, and his suppliers; do not claim that it stimulates employment.

When Jacques Bonhomme gives one hundred sous to a civil servant in return for a genuinely useful service, it is exactly the same as when he gives one hundred sous to a shoemaker for a pair of shoes. Give and take, tit for tat. But when Jacques Bonhomme hands over one hundred sous to a civil servant and then receives no services or even suffers aggravation in return, it is as though he is handing this money to a thief. It is no good saying that the civil servant will spend these hundred sous for the general benefit of *national output;* the thief would have done the same with them. So would Jacques Bonhomme if he had not met on his way either the extralegal parasite or the legal one.

Let us therefore acquire the habit of not judging things merely by *what is seen,* but also by *what is not seen.*

Last year I was a member of the Finance Committee,[2] for under the Constituent Assembly, members of the opposition were not systematically excluded from all Committees; in this the Constituent Assembly acted wisely. We heard M. Thiers say: "I have spent my life combating the men of the Legitimist Party and the Priests' Party. Since the time that a common danger brought us together, since I began seeing a lot of them and became

2. Bastiat's work on the Finance Committee of the National Assembly is a topic which has scarcely been explored in any detail and needs to be more fully researched. We know that he was nominated to be its vice president and was required to present its reports officially to the Chamber of Deputies from time to time. He was reappointed to this position eight times, such was the regard his peers had for his economic knowledge. Needless to say, his advice about cutting taxes and balancing the budget was not often heeded, and he became a bit like the resident "Utopian" on the Committee. See ES2 11, pp. 187–97.

acquainted with them, and since began speaking frankly to one another, I have noticed that they are not the monsters I took them to be."

Yes, mistrust is compounded and hatred aroused between parties that do not mix, and if the majority allowed a few members of the minority to become Committee members, perhaps it would be acknowledged on both sides that their ideas are not as far apart and, in particular, their intentions not as perverse as people suppose.

Be that as it may, last year I was a member of the Finance Committee. Each time that one of our colleagues spoke of setting at a moderate level the remuneration of the President of the Republic, ministers, or ambassadors, he was told:

"For the very good of the service, certain roles have to be surrounded by an aura of brilliance and dignity. It is a means of attracting men of worth. Very many men who are short of funds seek the ear of the President of the Republic, and it would place him in an uncomfortable position if he were obliged always to refuse them. A certain presence in ministerial and diplomatic salons is part of the wheels of constitutional government, etc., etc."

Although arguments like this can be debated, they certainly warrant close examination. They are based on public interest, whether this is correctly or incorrectly appreciated, and for my part, I take more notice of them than many of our Catos,[3] who are moved by a narrow spirit of stinginess or jealousy.

However, what revolts my conscience as an economist and makes me blush for the intellectual reputation of my country is when the argument is reduced (and this invariably happens) to the following absurd banality, which is always favorably received:

"Besides, the luxurious living of high government officials encourages the arts, industry, and labor in general. The Head of State and his ministers cannot give feasts and gala evenings without making life circulate in every vein of the social body. Reducing their remuneration is to starve productive activity in Paris, and by extension throughout the nation."

Please, Sirs, show some respect at least to arithmetic, and do not stand before the National Assembly of France to say that addition produces a different sum depending on whether one adds the figures from top to bottom or from bottom to top, because you fear that this shameful Chamber will not support your measure unless you do.

What! I am going to reach an agreement with a laborer to have a ditch

3. See the entry for "Cato, Marcus Porcius," in the Glossary of Persons.

dug in my field at a cost of one hundred sous. Just when the agreement is about to be finalized, the tax collector takes my hundred sous and passes them on to the Minister of the Interior. My agreement falls apart, but the Minister will have an extra dish for his dinner. On which basis, you dare to claim that this official expenditure is an addition to national output! Do you not understand that this is just a simple *displacement* of utility and labor? A minister has a better-laden table, it is true, but a farmer has a field that is less well drained, and this is just as true. A caterer in Paris has earned one hundred sous, I grant you, but you should grant me that a laborer in the provinces has failed to earn five francs. All that can be said is that the official dish and a satisfied caterer is *what is seen;* the flooded field and the laborer with no work is *what is not seen.*

Good God! What a lot of trouble to prove that, in political economy, two and two are four and if you succeed in doing this, the cry is heard: "This is so obvious, it is boring." And then they vote as though you had proved nothing at all.

4. Theaters and the Fine Arts
Should the State subsidize the arts?[1]

There is certainly much to say both For and Against.[2]

In favor of the system of subsidies, it might be said that the arts expand and elevate the soul of a nation and make it more poetic, that they tear it away from material preoccupations, give it an appreciation of Beauty and thus have a beneficial effect on its manners, customs, habits, and even its industry. The question might be asked where music would be in France without the

1. Music, art, theater, and other forms of fine art were heavy regulated by the French state. They could be subsidized, granted a monopoly of performance, the number of venues and prices of tickets were regulated, and they were censored and often shut down for overstepping their bounds. In the 1848 budget the relatively small amount of fr. 2.6 million was spent in the category of "beaux-arts" (within the Ministry of the Interior), which included art, historical monuments, ticket subsidies, payments to authors and composers, subsidies to the royal theaters and the Conservatory of Music (out of a total budget of fr. 1.45 billion). See "Documents extraits de l'enquête sur les théâtres," *JDE* 26 (July 1850): 409–12.

2. Bastiat's friend and colleague Gustave de Molinari was a great fan of the theater and wrote extensively about it, criticizing both its subsidies from and its censorship by the state. He has an extended discussion of this question in the eighth chapter of *Les Soirées de la rue Saint-Lazare* (Conversations on Saint Lazarus Street, 1849). See also his article "Théâtres," in *DEP* 2:731–33.

Théâtre-Italien and the Conservatoire, dramatic art without the Théâtre-Français, and painting and sculpture without our collections and museums.[3] We may go even further and ask ourselves whether, without the centralization and consequent subsidization of the fine arts, that exquisite taste that is the imposing mark of French work and makes its products attractive around the world, would have developed. Faced with these results, would it not be extremely rash to abandon this modest contribution from all of its citizens who, in the end, have succeeded in establishing their superiority and shining reputation in Europe?

These reasons and many others whose validity I do not question may be countered by others that are just as powerful. First of all, it may be said, there is the question of distributive justice. Does the right of the legislator go so far as to make inroads into the earnings of artisans to supply extra income to artists? M. Lamartine[4] said: "If you remove the subsidy from a theater, how far will you go down this road, and would you not logically be led to abolishing your Universities, Museums, Institutes, and Libraries?" The answer to this might be: "If you wish to subsidize everything that is good and useful, how far will you go down this road, and would you not logically be led to establishing a civil list for farming, industry, trade, benevolent activities, and education?" Moreover, is it certain that subsidies encourage the progress of art? This is a question that is far from being answered, and we can see with our own eyes that the theaters that prosper are those that generate their own life. Finally, raising our considerations to a higher level, we can point out that needs and desires are born one from another, and rise to levels that are increasingly refined as public wealth makes it possible to satisfy them; that the government has no need to become involved in this interaction, since in a given state of current wealth it would be unable to stimulate luxurious lines of production through taxes without upsetting essential ones, thus turning upside down the natural progress of civilization. It might be pointed out that these artificial displacements of needs, taste, production, and populations

3. The Théâtre-Italien (also known as the Opéra-Comique), after several false starts in the seventeenth century, was formally reestablished in 1716 under the patronage of the duc d'Orléans. The Conservatory of Music in Paris has experienced a large number of changes over the centuries as regimes and musical tastes have changed. Louis XIV created the Académie royale de musique by royal patent in 1669, and by 1836 it was known as the Conservatoire de musique et de déclamation. The Comédie-Français (also known as the Théâtre-Français) was founded in 1680 by Louis XIV. He also founded the Opéra de Paris in 1669.

4. Alphonse de Lamartine (1790–1869) was a poet turned statesman who was a member of the provisional government and Minister of Foreign Affairs in June 1848.

put nations in a precarious and dangerous situation whose foundation is no longer solid.

These are just a few reasons put forward by those who oppose State intervention with respect to the priorities according to which citizens believe that they ought to satisfy their needs and desires and consequently direct their activity. I must admit that I am one of those who think that choice and impulse have to come from below, not above, from citizens, not the legislators, and a doctrine to the contrary seems to me to lead to the abolition of human freedom and dignity.

However, through a deduction that is as false as it is unjust, do you know what economists are accused of? It is that when we reject subsidies, we are rejecting the very thing that is to be subsidized and are the enemies of all these types of activity since we want these activities to be free and at the same time pay their own way. Thus, if we demand that the State not intervene in religious matters through taxation, we are atheists; if we demand that the State not intervene in education through taxation, we are against enlightenment. If we say that the State ought not to give an artificial value to land or a particular sector of the economy through taxation, we are enemies of property and labor. If we think that the State ought not to subsidize artists, we are barbarians who think that art is of no use.

I protest here as forcefully as I can against these deductions. Far from entertaining the absurd notion of abolishing religion, education, property, production, and the arts, when we demand that the State protect the free development of all these kinds of human activity without having them in its pay at the citizens' mutual expense, we believe on the contrary that all these life-giving forces in society would develop harmoniously under the influence of freedom, that none of them would become, as we see today, a source of unrest, abuse, tyranny, and disorder.

Our adversaries believe that an activity that is neither in the pay of the State nor regulated is an activity that has been destroyed. We believe the contrary. Their faith lies in the legislator, not in humanity; ours lies in humanity, not in the legislator.

Thus, M. Lamartine said: "In the name of this principle, we should *abolish* the public exhibitions that constitute the honor and wealth of this country."[5]

My reply to Mr. Lamartine is: "Your point of view is that *failing to sub-*

---

5. This and the following quotations come from Lamartine, "Sur la subvention du Théâtre-Italien (Discussion du Budget) Assemblée National—Séance du 16 avril 1850," pp. 163, 161, 166.

sidize is to *abolish,* since, according to this notion that nothing exists other than through the will of the State, you conclude that nothing lives outside the things kept alive through taxes. But I am turning against you the example you have chosen and point out to you that the greatest and most noble of exhibitions, the one conceived in the most liberal and universal, and I might even use the word humanitarian, thought, which is no exaggeration in this context, is the exhibition being prepared in London, the only one in which no government is involved and where no tax is being used to pay for it."[6]

To return to the Fine Arts, it is possible, I repeat, to put forward powerful reasons for and against the system of subsidies. The reader will understand that, in accordance with the particular aim of this article, my job is neither to set out these reasons nor decide between them.

But M. Lamartine has put forward an argument that I cannot allow to pass without comment, as it comes precisely within the sphere of this economic study.

He has said:

"The economic question with regard to theaters can be summed up in a single word: it is production. The nature of this production matters little; it is an activity that is as fecund and productive as any other type of project in a nation. As you know, in France theaters feed and pay no fewer than eighty thousand workers of all types, painters, masons, decorators, costume makers, architects, etc., who are the very lifeblood and dynamism of several districts of this capital city and, for this reason, should be given your sympathy."

Your sympathy! In translation, your subsidy.

And further on:

6. The Great Exhibition of the Works of Industry of all Nations (The Great Exhibition, or the Crystal Palace Exhibition) was an international trade and industry exhibition held in Hyde Park, London, between May and October 1851. The Economists were very excited about the Exhibition because of the way it showcased the achievements of the industrial revolution as well as the possibilities which could be opened up by international free trade. The Exhibition was planned and organized privately by the members of the Royal Society for the Encouragement of Arts, Manufactures and Commerce under the patronage of Prince Albert, the husband of Queen Victoria. The French had begun the practice of holding international industrial exhibitions in 1798 and held others in 1819, 1823, 1827, 1834, 1839, and 1844. It was the 1844 exhibition, in Paris, which probably inspired the London Exhibition of 1851. An exhibition was planned for Paris in 1849, but the Revolution in 1848 meant that it was only a shadow of the previous ones. See Blanqui, "Expositions," in *DEP* 1:746–51.

"The pleasures of Paris lie in the output and consumption taking place in its departments, and the luxury of the wealthy constitutes the earnings and bread of two hundred thousand workers of all sorts who earn a living from the various industries of the theaters over the entire surface of the Republic and who receive from these noble pleasures that make France illustrious, the food to keep them alive and the necessities required by their families and children. It is to them that you are giving these sixty thousand francs. (*Hear! Hear! A host of approving gestures.*)"

For my part, I am obliged to say: *No! No!* Restricting, of course, the scope of this judgment to the economic argument we are dealing with here.

Yes, it is to the workers in the theaters that these sixty thousand francs in question will go, at least in part.[7] A few trifling sums may well be lost in transit. If you give the matter close scrutiny, actually, you may discover that things work out quite differently, such that fortunate are those workers if a few scraps are left to them! However, I am willing to accept that the entire subsidy will go to the painters, decorators, costume makers, hairdressers, etc. *This is what is seen.*

But where has it come from? This is the *other side* of the question that is just as important to examine as its *face.* Where is the source of these sixty thousand francs? And *where would they go* if a legislative vote did not initially send them to the rue de Rivoli and from there to the rue de Grenelle?[8] *That is what is not seen.*

Certainly no one will dare to claim that the legislative vote has caused this sum to blossom in the voters' urn, that it is a pure addition to national wealth, and that without this miraculous vote these sixty thousand francs would have remained forever invisible and intangible. It has to be admitted that all that the majority has been able to do is to decide that they will be taken from somewhere to be sent somewhere else, and that they are given one destination only by being taken from another.

Since things are like this, it is clear that the taxpayer who has been taxed one franc will no longer have this franc available to him. It is clear that he will be deprived of satisfaction to the value of one franc and that the worker,

7. In April 1850, a deputy asked for a subsidy of sixty thousand francs for the Théâtre des Italiens. Since 1801, this theater had had a permanent troupe and had performed the masterpieces of Italian music before French audiences. Lamartine warmly supported the proposition.

8. The Ministry of Finances was located in the rue de Rivoli, and the Ministry of Education and Fine Arts in the rue de Grenelle.

whoever he may be, who would have provided it to him will be deprived of pay to the same extent.

Let us therefore not harbor this puerile illusion of believing that the vote on 16 May[9] *adds* anything at all to national well-being and work. It *displaces* enjoyment and *displaces* pay; that is all.

Will people say that for one type of expenditure and one type of production, more urgent, more moral, and more reasonable expenditure and production have been substituted? I might make a stand here. I might say: "By snatching sixty thousand francs from taxpayers, you are reducing the earnings of ploughmen, laborers, carpenters, and blacksmiths, and you are increasing the earnings of singers, hairdressers, decorators, and costume makers by the same amount. Nothing proves that this latter class is more worthy than the other. M. Lamartine does not claim this. He himself says that the work of theaters is (*just as* fertile, *just as* productive and not more) than any other, which might itself still be contested, since the best proof that the second category is not as fertile as the first is that the first is called upon to subsidize the second.

But this comparison between the value and intrinsic merit of the diverse forms of production is not part of my present subject. All that I have to do here is to show that M. Lamartine and the people who applauded his line of argument saw with one eye the earnings of the suppliers of actors and ought to have seen with the other the earnings lost by the suppliers of taxpayers. By not doing so, they exposed themselves to the nonsense of taking a *displacement* for a *gain*. If they were consistent with their doctrine, they would demand an infinite number of subsidies, for what is true for one franc and sixty thousand francs is true in identical circumstances for a billion francs.

When it is a question of taxes, gentlemen, let us prove their utility using reasons based on fundamentals, but never resort to the wretched argument that "Public expenditure provides a livelihood for the working class." This makes the mistake of concealing an essential fact, that is to say, that *public expenditure always* takes the place of *private expenditure* and that, consequently, it provides a livelihood for one workman instead of another, but adds nothing to the lot of the working class taken as a whole. Your line of argument is very fashionable, but it is too absurd for reason not to get the better of it.

9. The subsidy of sixty thousand francs for the Théâtre des Italiens was voted on 16 May and not 16 April as Bastiat mistakenly says.

5. Public Works[1]

That a nation, after having ascertained that a great enterprise will be of benefit to the community, has it carried out using resources raised by general subscription, is perfectly normal. But I have to admit that I lose patience when I hear the following glaring economic error claimed in support of a resolution of this nature: "What is more, it is a means of creating employment for the workers."

The state opens a road, constructs a palace, repairs a street, or digs a canal; in doing this it provides work for certain workmen, *that is what is seen,* but it deprives certain other workmen of employment, and *that is what is not seen.*

Here is the road in the process of being built. A thousand workmen come every morning and go home every evening, taking their pay; that is certain. If the road had not been decided upon, if the funds had not been voted for, these good people would not have found either work or pay at this place; that is also certain.

But is this all? Does the overall operation not involve something else? At the time when M. Dupin pronounces the sacramental words: "Passed by the Assembly," do the millions miraculously slide down a moonbeam into the coffers of MM. Fould[2] and Bineau?[3] In order for the change to be complete,

---

1. Bastiat probably had in mind the two biggest public works projects that were being undertaken in the 1840s, namely the construction of the fortifications of Paris (1841–44) and the government's participation in building the railroads after 1842. The first was an initiative of Thiers, who planned to build a massive military wall around the city of Paris with sixteen surrounding forts. This was completed in 1844 at a cost of fr. 150 million. The total expenditure would have been much higher if the state had not used the labor of thousands of conscripts to dig the ditches and build the wall. See Patricia O'Brien, "*L'Embastillement de Paris:* The Fortification of Paris during the July Monarchy," *French Historical Studies* 9, no. 1 (1975): 63–82. The law of 11 June 1842 authorized the French state to partner with private companies in the building of five railroad networks spreading out from Paris. Between 1842 and the end of 1847, the state had spent about fr. 420 million in subsidies, loan guarantees, and construction costs. Lobet, "Chemins de fer," *Annuaire de l'économie politique* (1848), pp. 289–311. Data on p. 294. See the Glossary entry on "Public Works."

2. Achille Fould (1800–1867) served as Minister of Finance in the Second Republic and then as Minister of State in the Second Empire. He was a personal financial advisor to Napoleon III and played an important part in the imperial household.

3. Jean Martial Bineau (1805–55) was an engineer by training and a politician who served as Minister of Public Works in 1850 and then as Minister of Finance in 1852 during the Second Empire.

as they say, does the State not need to organize the collection of taxes as well as their expenditure? Does it not need to send its tax collectors into the field and make the taxpayers pay their taxes?

Let us then examine both sides of the question. While noting the purpose intended by the State for the millions voted, let us not fail to note also the uses to which taxpayers would have put and can no longer put these same millions. You will then understand that a public enterprise is a two-sided coin. On one side, there is an employed worker with the motto "*This is what is seen*"; on the other, a worker out of work with the motto "*This is what is not seen.*"

The sophism that I am combating in this article is all the more dangerous when applied to public works if it serves to justify the wildest enterprises or excesses. When a railway or a bridge is genuinely useful, invoking this utility is enough. But if you cannot do this, what do you do? You resort to the following grossly misleading statement: "Work has to be found for the workers."

Once this is said, why not construct and demolish the terraces on the Champ de Mars?[4] As we know, the great Napoléon considered he was performing a philanthropic act by digging and filling in ditches. He also said: "What does the result matter? All you have to see is the wealth spread around the working classes."[5]

Let us go to the heart of things. Money deludes us. Requesting a contribution in the form of money from all citizens for a work of common interest is in fact asking them for a contribution in kind, for each of them through work obtains for himself the sum on which he is taxed. Now, if all the citi-

4. The Champs de Mars (Field of Mars) is a large public park in the 7th Arrondissement in Paris. Before the Revolution it had been a military parade ground, but during the Revolution it was used for a variety of purposes, including public ceremonies as well as executions. In May 1848 it was the site for a large revolutionary Festival of Concord. In the latter part of the nineteenth century it was the site for several World Exhibitions, especially that of 1889 for which the Eiffel Tower was built at its northeast corner.

5. Napoléon did not seem to have a well-thought-out economic theory, but his scattered remarks, recorded in his *Mémoires* (1821), show him to be an economic nationalist and strong protectionist. See for example "Experience showed that each day the continental system was good, because the State prospered in spite of the burdon of the war. . . . The spirit of improvement was shown in agriculture as well as in the factories. New villages were built, as were the streets of Paris. Roads and canals made interior movement much easier. Each week some new improvement was invented: I made it possible to make sugar out of turnips, and soda out of salt. The development of science was at the front along with that of industry" (pp. 95–99).

zens were brought together in order to carry out some work useful to every-body, as part of their compulsory community obligation,[6] this would be un-derstandable; their compensation would be the results of the work itself. But if, after they have been brought together, they are subjected to making roads where no one will go and palaces in which no one will live on the pretext of procuring work for them, this would be absurd, and they would certainly have reason to object: "We have no need of work like this; we would prefer to work on our own behalf."

The procedure that consists in making citizens contribute money and not work does not alter these general results one jot. The only thing is that using the second procedure the loss is shared by all, whereas using the first, those employed by the State escape their share of the loss, adding it to the loss their fellow citizens have already had to bear.

There is an article of the Constitution which says:

"Society favors and encourages the development of labor . . . through the establishment by the State, the départements and communes of public works suitable for employing idle hands."[7]

As a temporary measure in times of crisis, or during a severe winter, this intervention by the taxpayers may have good results. It acts in the same way as insurance. It adds nothing either to labor or to pay, but it takes the labor and wages earned in good times and pays them out in difficult times, admit-tedly with some loss.

As a permanent, general, and systematic measure, this is nothing less than a ruinous deception, an impossibility, a contradiction that gives the appear-ance of a little labor which has been stimulated, that *is seen,* and hides a great deal of labor which has been prevented, that *is not seen.*

---

6. Bastiat uses the term *par prestation* (compulsory or required service), which had a powerful connotation to the Economists, as it referred to the common eighteenth-century practice of compulsory community labor (*la corvée*). See "The 'Prestation' and the 'Corvée,'" in appendix 3, "Economic Policy and Taxation."

7. Chapter 2, Article 13, of the Constitution of 4 November 1848. This article raises the problem which concerned Bastiat deeply of the difference between the free-market idea of "the liberty of work and industry" (*la liberté du travail et de l'industrie*) and the socialist idea of the "right to a job" (*la liberté au travail*), which increasingly became an issue during the Revolution. The Constitution of November 1848 specifically refers to the former but also seems to advocate the latter with the phrase "public works suitable for reemploying the unemployed." The creation and then the abolition of the National Workshops is an example of this confusion. See [Bastiat], "Opinion de M. Frédéric Bas-tiat," pp. 373–76.

6. The Middlemen

Society is the set of services that men render each other, either by force or voluntarily, i.e., *public services* and *private services.*

Public services, imposed and regulated by law, which is not always easy to change when it would be advisable, may, with the help of that law, far outlive their real usefulness and retain the name of *public services,* even when they are no longer services at all or even when they are nothing more than public vexations. Private services lie in the field of voluntary action and individual responsibility. Each person renders and receives what he wants or what he can, following face-to-face discussion. They are always characterized by the presumption of genuine utility, accurately measured by their comparative value.

This is why public services are so often characterized by immobility, while private services conform to the law of progress.

While the excessive development of public services tends to constitute within society, through the wastage of energy that it entails, a disastrous form of parasitism, it is singularly notable that several modern schools of thought, attributing this tendency to free and private services, seek to transform all jobs into state functions.[1]

These thinkers savagely attack what they describe as *middlemen.* They would happily abolish capitalists, bankers, speculators, entrepreneurs, merchants, and traders, accusing them of coming between production and consumption and holding both for ransom without adding value to either. Or rather, they would like to transfer to the State the work they do, given that this work cannot be abolished.

The sophism of the socialists on this point consists in showing the public what they are paying *middlemen* in return for their services and hiding from them what they would have to pay the State. It is a constant struggle between what is obvious at a glance and what can be perceived only by the mind, between *what is seen and what is not seen.*

It was above all in 1847 and during the subsequent famine[2] that the socialist schools sought and succeeded in popularizing their disastrous the-

---

1. This was true for the followers of the socialists Louis Blanc, Charles Fourier, and the Montagnard faction in the Chamber in 1848. It was not true for the socialist anarchist Proudhon.

2. See the entry for "Irish Famine and the Failure of French Harvests, 1846–47," in the Glossary of Subjects and Terms; and Vanhaute, O'Grada, and Paping, "The European Subsistence Crisis of 1845–1850."

ory. They knew full well that the most absurd propaganda always has some chance of success with men who are suffering; *malesuada fames.*[3]

Therefore, with the aid of high-sounding words: *the exploitation of man by man, speculation on hunger, monopolies,* they set about denigrating trade and casting a veil over its benefits.

"Why," they said, "leave traders the task of importing the necessities of life from the United States and the Crimea?[4] Why do the State, the départements and districts not organize a system of procurement and some storage warehouses? They would sell at *cost price,* and the people, the poor people, would be free of the tribute they pay to free trade, that is to say, trade that is selfish, individualistic, and anarchic."

The tribute that the people pay to trade *is what is seen.* The tribute that the people would pay to the State or its agents under the socialist system is *what is not seen.*

In what does the alleged tribute that the people pay to trade consist? In this: two men render each other mutual service in total freedom under the pressure of competition and at an agreed price.

When a stomach that is hungry is in Paris and the wheat that is able to satisfy it is in Odessa, suffering will cease only when the wheat is brought to the stomach. There are three ways of bringing about this coming together: 1. The starving men can go to seek the wheat themselves; 2. They can delegate this task to those who have specialized in it; 3. They can have themselves taxed and entrust this operation to civil servants.

Of these three alternatives, which is the most advantageous?

In every age and in all countries, especially where they enjoyed greater freedom and were more enlightened and experienced, men have *voluntarily* chosen the second alternative, which I must admit is enough in my view to attribute the benefit of doubt to this choice. My mind refuses to admit that

3. The Latin phrase *malesuada fames* (ill-counseling famine) is from Virgil's *Aeneid* (VI, 276). In John Dryden's translation it is rendered as "Famine's unresisted rage" (see http://oll.libertyfund.org/titles/1175#Virgil_0555_6052).

4. Four factors led to the opening up of world trade in agricultural products after the "Hungry 1840s": the rise in European prices caused by the crop failures of the late 1840s, the freeing up of grain markets in Britain and then other European countries, the reduction in shipping costs, and the rise of large grain markets in the United States and the port of Odessa in the Crimea. From zero wheat imports from the United States to Britain in 1846, the level rose to 1,000 metric tons per annum by 1862.

humanity in the mass would make a mistake on a point that has such a direct effect on it.

Nevertheless, let us examine the question.

That thirty-six million citizens leave to go to Odessa to look for the wheat they need is obviously impracticable. The first alternative is valueless. Consumers cannot act on their own behalf; they have to resort to *intermediaries,* civil servants or traders.

However, we should note that this first alternative would be the most natural. Basically, it is up to the person who is hungry to go to find his wheat. This is a *task* that concerns him; a *service* that he owes himself. If another person, for whatever reason, renders him this *service* and undertakes this task on his behalf, this person is entitled to compensation. What I am saying here serves to emphasize that the services of middlemen involve a principle of remuneration.

Be that as it may, since it is necessary to resort to someone the socialists call a parasite, which one, a trader or a civil servant, is the less demanding parasite?

Trade (I assume it to be free, otherwise how could I reason?), trade, as I say, out of its own interest tends to examine the seasons and note on a daily basis the state of the harvest, gather information from all corners of the globe, anticipate need and take the necessary precautions beforehand. It has ships ready, correspondents everywhere, and its immediate interest is to buy at the best possible price, make savings on each detail of the operation, and achieve the best results with the least effort. It is not only French traders, but traders the world over who are involved in procurement for France against her day of need, and if self-interest drives them invariably to fulfill their task at the least cost, the competition they wage with each other leads them no less invariably to allow consumers to benefit from all the savings achieved. Once the wheat arrives, it is in the interest of trade to sell it as soon as it can to minimize its risks, realize its funds, and start again if necessary. Driven by a comparison of prices, it distributes foodstuffs around the whole country, always starting with the most expensive point, i.e., where the need is most pressing. It is therefore not possible to imagine an *organization* more in line with the interests of those who are hungry, and the beauty of such an organization, not noticed by the socialists, results precisely from the fact that it is free. In truth, consumers are obliged to reimburse trade with the cost of its transport, its transshipments, its storage and commissions, etc., but under what system does he who eats the wheat not have to reimburse the expenditure required to bring it to him? In addition, the *service rendered* has to be paid for, but with regard to its proportion, this is reduced to the *minimum* possible by competition, and, as for its justice, it would be strange for the artisans in Paris not to work for the traders in Marseilles when the traders in Marseilles work for the artisans in Paris.

What would happen if the State took the place of trade in accordance with the socialist schema? Would someone please tell me where the saving would be for the public? Would it be in the purchase price? Just picture to yourself the delegates of forty thousand communes arriving in Odessa on a given day and at a time of need; just imagine the effect on prices. Would the saving lie in the costs? Would we need, however, fewer ships, fewer sailors, less transshipment, less warehousing, or would we be relieved of having to pay for all of these things? Would it lie in the profits of the traders? Would your delegates and civil servants go to Odessa for nothing? Would they travel and work in accordance with the principle of fraternity? Do they not have to live? Does their time not need to be paid for? And do you think that this will not exceed a thousand times the 2 or 3 percent that the trader earns, a rate he is ready to work for?

And then, think of the difficulty of raising so many taxes and distributing so much food. Think of the injustice and abuse that is inseparable from an enterprise of this nature. Think of the responsibility that would weigh on the government.

The socialists, who have invented such follies and who, on days of misfortune, instill them into the minds of the masses, freely award themselves the accolade of *progressive men,* and it is not without danger that custom, that tyrant of languages, endorses the expression and the opinion it implies. *Progressive!* This implies that these fine fellows are more farsighted than the common man, that their sole error is to be too far ahead of their century, and that if the time has not yet come to abolish certain free services that are alleged to be parasitic, the fault lies with the public, which lags behind socialism. For me, both in soul and conscience, it is the contrary that is true, and I do not know to which barbaric century you would have to return to find the present level of socialist understanding in this respect.

Modern sectarians constantly contrast association[5] with the current form

---

5. Bastiat is using the word "association" in its socialist sense, as it had become a slogan used by socialist critics of the free market during the 1840s. See "Bastiat's Use of the Socialist Terms 'Organization' and 'Association,'" in the Note on the Translation.

of society. They do not appreciate that under a regime of liberty, society is a genuine association far better than all those that their fertile imagination engenders.

Let us illustrate this by an example:

In order for a man, when he gets out of bed, to be able to put on a suit of clothes, a piece of land has to have been fenced, cleared, drained, ploughed, and sown with a specific type of plant. Flocks have to have grazed there and given their wool, this wool has to have been spun, woven, dyed, and made into cloth, and this cloth has to have been cut, sewn, and made into a garment. And this series of operations implies a host of others, for it requires the use of farming machinery, sheepfolds, factories, coal, machines, vehicles, etc.

If society were not a genuine association, the man who wanted a suit of clothes would be reduced to working in isolation, that is to say, he would have to carry out himself the many tasks in this series, from the first blow of the pick that initiates it to the final stitch of the needle that completes it.

However, thanks to the sociability that is the distinctive characteristic of our species, these operations are shared out among a host of workers, and they are increasingly subdivided for the common good, until a point is reached where a single specialized task can support an entirely new industry as consumption becomes more intense. Then comes the distribution of the income generated according to whatever value each person has contributed to the total operation. If this is not association, I do not know what is.

Note that none of the workers having been able to draw even the minutest thing of substance from nothing, they have limited themselves to providing each other with mutual services, helping each other in line with a common goal, and that all may be considered as *middlemen* with regard to one another. If, for example, during an operation, transport became important enough to occupy one person, spinning another, and weaving a third, why would the first be regarded as more *parasitic* than the two others? Is transport not necessary? Does he who carries it out not devote time and trouble to it? Does he not spare his associates this time and trouble? Do his associates do more than him or simply other things? Are they not all equally subject to the law of a *freely negotiated price* with regard to their pay, that is to say, for their share of the product? Is it not in total freedom and for the common good that this separation of tasks is carried out and these arrangements made? Why then do we need a socialist to come to destroy our voluntary arrangements on the pretext of organization, stop the division of labor, substitute isolated effort for joint effort, and cause civilization to take a backward step?

Is association, as I describe it here, any less an association because each person enters into it and leaves it of his own volition, chooses his own place in it, is responsible for his own judgments and stipulations, and brings to it the stimulus and guarantee of personal interest? For it to merit this name, is it necessary for a would-be reformer to come and impose on us his formula and will and concentrate humanity, so to speak, in himself?

The more we examine these *progressive schools,* the more we are convinced that there is just one thing at their root: ignorance proclaiming itself infallible and laying claim to despotism in the name of this infallibility.

I beg the reader to excuse this digression. It is perhaps not without point at a time when declarations against Middlemen have escaped from books by the Saint-Simonians, phalansterians, and icarians,[6] and invaded journalism and the public platform, causing a serious threat to freedom of work and exchange.

7. Trade Restrictions

M. Prohibant[1] (it is not I who have given him this name, it is M. Charles Dupin who since the, . . . but then . . .) devoted his time and his capital to transforming the ore on his land into iron. As nature had been more prodigal toward the Belgians, they supplied iron to the French cheaper than M. Prohibant, which means that all Frenchmen or France herself were able to obtain a given quantity of iron *with less labor* by buying it from the honest Flemings. Driven by their self-interest, they did not fail to do so, and every day

---

6. Saint-Simonians, phalansterians, and icarians: followers of Henri de Saint-Simon, Charles Fourier, and Étienne Cabet respectively.

1. Bastiat borrows the made-up name "M. Prohibant" (from *prohiber,* to prohibit; *prohibant,* prohibiting, thus "Mr. Trade Prohibiter" or "Mr. Protectionist") from a popular work written by Charles Dupin in the late 1820s, *Le petit producteur français.* This was an early attempt to dispel economic sophisms similar to those Bastiat was addressing from 1845 onward. Dupin states in the "Dedication" to vol. 4 (titled *Le petit commerçant français*) to the "students of the Business schools of Paris, Lyon, and Bordeaux" that he was dedicating this work to them "with the aim of refuting the long-term and entrenched errors concerning the interests of commerce." Dupin uses the fictitious M. Prohibant to represent those who continue to cling to anti-free-trade and anti-free-market sentiments (pp. ix–x). It is of course interesting to note that Bastiat also dedicates his *Economic Harmonies* to the "Youth of France" for similar reasons. Dupin's work might also be compared to other attempts by free market supporters to appeal to a popular audience, such as Jane Marcet and Harriet Martineau.

you could see a host of nail makers, blacksmiths, wheelwrights, mechanics, farriers, and ploughmen going on their own account or through middlemen to obtain supplies from Belgium. This did not please M. Prohibant at all.

First of all, the idea came to him to stop this abuse using his own forces. This was certainly the least he could do, since he alone was harmed by the abuse. "I will take my rifle," he said to himself; "I will put four pistols in my belt, I will fill my cartridge pouch, I will buckle on my sword and, thus equipped, I will go to the border. There, I will kill the first blacksmith, nail maker, farrier, mechanic, or locksmith who comes to do business with them and not with me. That will teach him how to conduct himself properly."

When he was about to leave, M. Prohibant had second thoughts, which mellowed his bellicose ardor somewhat. He said to himself: "First of all, it is not totally out of the question that my fellow citizens and enemies, the purchasers of iron, will take this action badly, and instead of letting themselves be killed they will kill me first. Next, even if I marshal all my servants, we cannot guard all the border posts. Finally, this action will cost me a great deal, more than the result is worth."

M. Prohibant was about to resign himself sadly to being merely as free as anyone else when a flash of inspiration shone in his brain.

He remembered that in Paris there was a great law factory.[2] "What is a law?" he asked himself. "It is a measure with which everyone is required to comply once it has been decreed, whether it is good or bad. To ensure the execution of the aforesaid, a public force is organized, and in order to constitute the said public force, men and money are drawn from the nation.

"If, therefore, I succeeded in obtaining from the great law factory a tiny little law that said: 'Iron from Belgium is prohibited,' I would achieve the following results: the government would replace the few servants I wanted to send to the border by twenty thousand sons of my recalcitrant blacksmiths, locksmiths, nail makers, farriers, artisans, mechanics, and ploughmen. Then, in order to keep these twenty thousand customs officers[3] in good heart and health, it would distribute twenty-five million francs taken from these same blacksmiths, nail makers, artisans, and ploughmen. The security would be better done, it would cost me nothing, I would not be exposed to the brutal-

---

2. Bastiat calls the Chamber *la grande fabrique de lois* (the great law factory).

3. Horace Say, like Bastiat, calls those who work for the Customs Service *une armée considérable* (a sizable army), which numbered 27,727 individuals (1852 figures). This army is composed of two "divisions"—one of administrative personnel (2,536) and the other of "agents on active service" (24,727). See Horace Say, "Douane," in *DEP* 1:578–604 (figures from p. 597).

ity of the dealers, I would sell iron at my price, and I would enjoy the sweet recreation of seeing our great nation shamefully bamboozled. That would teach it to claim incessantly to be the precursor and promoter of all progress in Europe. Oh! That would be a smart move and is worth trying."

Therefore, M. Prohibant went to the law factory. Perhaps on another occasion I will tell you the story of his underhand dealings; right now I merely want to talk about his very visible actions. He put the following consideration to the venerable legislators:

"Belgian iron is being sold in France for ten francs, which obliges me to sell mine at the same price. I would prefer to sell it at fifteen and cannot do so because of this God-damned Belgian iron.[4] Please manufacture a law that says: 'Belgian iron will no longer come into France.' I will immediately raise my price by five francs, and the result will be:

"For each quintal of iron I deliver to the public, instead of receiving ten francs, I will receive fifteen. I will become richer faster and will expand my operation, giving work to more workmen. My workers and I will spend more money to the great benefit of our suppliers for several leagues around. As these suppliers will have more markets, they will give more orders to various other producers, and from one sector to another the entire country will increase its activity. This fortunate hundred-sou coin that you drop into my coffer will radiate outward to the far corners of the country an infinite number of concentric circles, just like a stone thrown into a lake."

Pleased to hear this speech and delighted to learn that it is so easy to increase the wealth of a nation by means of the law, the lawmakers voted for the restriction. "What do people say about work and economics?" they said. "What use are these painful means of increasing national wealth where one Decree suffices?"

And in fact, the law produced all the consequences forecast by M. Prohibant. The trouble was that it also produced others for, to do him justice, he had not reasoned *falsely* but *incompletely*. Petitioning for a privilege, he had pointed out those of its effects *that are seen,* leaving those *that are not seen* in the shadows. He presented two people only, when there are three in the cast. It is up to us to put right this involuntary or perhaps premeditated oversight.

Yes, the écu thus diverted by law to the coffers of M. Prohibant constitutes

4. Bastiat uses the expression *que Dieu maudisse* (what God would damn), which is much stronger than the other occasion where he uses the word "damned," in the title of his essay "Damned Money!" (April 1849) in CW4 (forthcoming). In the following article, "Machines," he begins with the exclamation "Malédiction sur les machines!" (a curse on machines!).

a benefit for him and for those whose work he is bound to stimulate. And if the decree had caused this écu to come down from the moon, these beneficial effects would not be counterbalanced by any compensating bad effects. Unfortunately, it is not from the moon that the mysterious hundred-sou coin comes, but rather from the pockets of a blacksmith, nail maker, wheelwright, farrier, ploughman, or builder, in short, from the pocket of Jacques Bonhomme, who will now pay it without receiving one milligram more of iron than he did at the time when he paid ten francs. At first sight you have to see that this changes the question considerably, since very clearly the *Profit* made by M. Prohibant is offset by the *Loss* made by Jacques Bonhomme, and everything that M. Prohibant is able to do with this écu to encourage national production, Jacques Bonhomme could also have done. The stone is merely cast into a particular point on the lake because it has been prevented by law from being cast into another.

Therefore, *what is not seen* offsets *what is seen,* and up to now in the remainder of the operation there remains an injustice, and what is deplorable is that it is an injustice perpetrated by the law.

Nor is this all. I have said that a third person is always left in the shadow. I must bring him forward here so that he can show us a *second loss* of five francs. Then we will have the result of the entire operation.

Jacques Bonhomme is the possessor of fifteen francs, the fruit of his labors. We are still in the period in which he is free. What does he do with his fifteen francs? He buys a fashionable article for ten francs, and with this fashionable article he pays (or the middleman pays on his behalf) for the quintal of Belgian iron. Jacques Bonhomme still has five francs left. He does not throw them into the river[5] but (and *this is what is not seen*) gives them to a businessman in one productive sector or another in exchange for a particular purchase he desires, for example, to a bookseller for the *Discourse on Universal History* by Bossuet.[6]

---

5. In the words of the English campaigner against the Corn Laws, Perronet Thompson, who influenced Bastiat in his thinking on this topic, the French tariff laws were tantamount to an order that every Frenchman throw every "third franc into the sea" (Thompson, *Letters of a Representative to His Constituents,* p. 189).

6. Jacques Bénigne Bossuet (1627–1704) was bishop of Meaux, a historian, and tutor to the son of Louis XIV. In politics he was an intransigent Gallican Catholic, an opponent of Protestantism, and a supporter of the idea of the divine right of kings. He wrote *Discours sur l'histoire universelle* (1681). Bastiat is having a joke here as this book is not what Jacques would probably buy if he had any spare cash.

Thus, with regard to *national output,* it is stimulated to the extent of fifteen francs, as follows:

10 francs for the Parisian article;
5 francs for the book.

As for Jacques Bonhomme, for his fifteen francs, he obtains two objects of his preference, as follows:

1. One quintal of iron;
2. A book.

Now the decree comes into force.

What happens to Jacques Bonhomme's situation? What happens to national production?

When Jacques Bonhomme hands over his fifteen francs down to the last centime to Mr. Prohibant for one quintal of iron, he is limited to whatever economic satisfaction is provided by this quintal of iron. He loses the benefit provided by a book or any other equivalent object. He loses five francs. We agree on this; we cannot fail to agree on this, we cannot fail to agree that, where a policy of trade restriction raises the price of things, consumers lose the difference.

But, you will say, *national production* gains this difference.

No, it does not, for, following the decree, it is merely stimulated as it was before, to the extent of fifteen francs.

The only thing is that, following the decree, Jacques Bonhomme's fifteen francs go to the iron industry, whereas before the decree they were shared between the fashionable article and the bookshop.

The violence exercised at the border by M. Prohibant himself or that which he has exercised through the law may be considered to be very different from the moral point of view. Some people think that plunder loses all its immorality when it is legal. For my part, I cannot imagine a circumstance that is worse. Be that as it may, what is certain is that the economic results are the same.

View the matter from whatever angle you wish, but keep a sagacious eye and you will see that nothing good ever comes from plunder, whether legal or illegal. We do not deny that a profit of five francs results for M. Prohibant or his industry or, if you wish, for national production. But we do claim that two losses also result, one for Jacques Bonhomme, who pays fifteen francs for what he had for ten and the other for national production, which no longer receives the balance. Choose whichever of these two losses you please to set against the profit that we acknowledge. The other will be no less of a *dead loss.*

The Moral: The use of violence is not to produce but to destroy. Oh! If the use of violence were to produce, our France would be much richer than she is.

8. Machines

"May machines be cursed! Every year their increasing power consigns to Poverty millions of workers by taking away their work, and with work their pay and with their pay their Bread! May machines be cursed!"

This is the cry of the popularly held Prejudice whose echo resounds around the journals.

But to curse machines is to curse the human mind.

What staggers me, though, is that there can be a single man who feels at ease with a doctrine like this.

For in the end, if it is true, what is the logical consequence of this? It is that there is no activity, well-being, wealth, or happiness possible other than for people who are stupid or afflicted with mental immobility, to whom God has not given the disastrous gift of thinking, observing, putting things together, inventing, or obtaining the greatest results using the least means. On the contrary, rags, dreadful hovels, poverty, and starvation are the inevitable fate of any nation that seeks and finds in iron, fire, wind, electricity, magnetism, the laws of chemistry and mechanics, in a word, in the forces of nature, a complement to its own strength, and it is therefore appropriate to say with Rousseau: "Any man who thinks is a depraved animal."[1]

That is not all. If this doctrine is true, since all men think and invent, since they all in fact from the first to the last and at every moment of their existence seek the co-operation of the forces of nature, to do more with less, to reduce either their labor or the labor for which they are paying, to achieve the greatest amount of economic satisfaction possible with the least amount

---

1. From the first part of Rousseau's *Discourse on Inequality* (1754): "Most of our ills are of our own making, and that we might have avoided nearly all of them if only we had adhered to the simple, unchanging and solitary way of life that nature ordained for us. If nature destined us to be healthy, I would almost venture to assert that the state of reflection is a state contrary to nature, and that the man who meditates is a depraved animal" (Rousseau, *A Discourse on Inequality*, p. 45).

of work, it has to be concluded that the entire human race is being drawn toward its downfall, precisely through this intelligent aspiration to progress that torments each of its members.

This being so, it ought to be verified by statistics, that the inhabitants of Lancaster are fleeing from this land of machines and are going to seek work in Ireland where machines are unknown; and by history, that barbarism darkened the eras of civilization and that civilization shines in times of ignorance and savagery.

Obviously, in this heap of contradictions there is something that stands out and warns us that the problem hides the element of a solution that has not been sufficiently clarified.

This is the entire secret: behind *what is seen* lies *what is not seen.* I will endeavor to shed light on it. My case can be only a repetition of the preceding one, since the problem involved is identical.

Men are naturally inclined, if they are not forcibly prevented from this, to seek *low prices,* that is to say, to seek that which, for an equal amount of satisfaction, saves them work, whether these low prices result from a skillful *foreign producer* or an efficient *mechanical producer.*

The theoretical objection made to this preference is the same in both cases. In both of them it is blamed for seeming to paralyze labor. In fact, what determines this preference for low prices is precisely the fact that labor is not made *idle* but more readily *available.*

And this is why in both cases the same practical obstacle is put in its way, namely violence. Legislators *prohibit* foreign competition and *forbid* mechanical competition. For what other means can there be to stop a natural preference in all men other than to deprive them of their liberty?

It is true that in many countries legislators strike just one of these two forms of competition and limit themselves to complaining about the other. This proves one single thing, which is that in these countries legislators are inconsistent.

We should not be surprised at this. When taking the wrong road, people are always inconsistent; otherwise the human race would be annihilated. An erroneous principle has never been seen and will never be seen to be taken to its logical conclusion. I have said elsewhere that inconsistency is the limit of absurdity. I might have added that it is at the same time proof of it.

Let us proceed with our argument; it will not take much time.

Jacques Bonhomme had two francs, which he paid two workers he had hired.

What does he do, however, but devise a system of ropes and weights that reduces the work by half.

He therefore obtains the same satisfaction, saves one franc, and dismisses one worker.

He dismisses one worker; *that is what is seen.*

And if this is all that is seen, it is said: "This is how poverty follows civilization, this is why freedom is fatal to equality. The human mind has made an advance and a worker immediately falls into the abyss of poverty. Alternatively, it may happen that Jacques Bonhomme continues to employ the two workers but now pays them just ten sous each, for they will compete with each other and offer their services at a discount. This is how the rich grow ever richer and the poor ever poorer. We must reform society."

What a fine conclusion and one worthy of its introduction!

Fortunately, both introduction and conclusion are entirely wrong, since behind the half of the phenomenon *that is seen* there is the other half *that is not seen.*

What is not seen is the franc saved by Jacques Bonhomme and the necessary effects of this saving.

Since Jacques Bonhomme now spends just one franc on labor in order to achieve a given level of satisfaction as a result of his invention, he still has one more franc.

If therefore there is a worker anywhere in the world who offers his idle hands, there is also somewhere in the world a capitalist who offers his unused franc. These two elements come together and join forces.

And it is as clear as daylight that between the supply and demand for work, between the supply and demand for pay, the relationship has changed not one whit.

The invention and one worker, paid for with the first franc, now carry out the work that two workers did before.

The second worker, paid with the second franc, brings into existence a new job.

What has changed in the world, then? There is now an additional nationwide satisfaction, in other words, the invention, which is a free advance and a free source of profit for the human race.

From the structure I have given my argument, this conclusion could be drawn:

"It is the capitalist who gathers all the benefits of machines. The wage-earning class, while experiencing momentary suffering, never benefits from them, since according to your own premises machines *displace* part of the national output, without *reducing* it, it is true, but also without *increasing* it."

It is not in the scope of this short article to reply to all the objections. Its sole aim is to combat a popularly held prejudice, one that is highly dangerous and very widespread. I wanted to prove that a new machine makes not only a certain number of workers available but also, and inevitably, the money needed to pay for them. These workers and this pay come together to produce what it was impossible to produce before the invention, from which it follows that *the final result it produces is an increase in the amount of satisfaction for an equal input of labor.*

Who benefits from this extra economic satisfaction?

Who? First of all, the capitalist, the inventor, the first person who successfully uses the machine which is the reward for his genius and audacity. In this case, as we have just seen, he achieves a saving on the production costs which, however it is *spent* (and it is always spent), makes use of as much labor as the machine has caused to be laid off.

However, competition soon obliges him to lower his sales price to the extent of this saving itself.

And when this happens, it is no longer the inventor who benefits from the invention, but the purchaser of the product, the consumer, the general public, including the workers, in a word, the human race.

And *what is not seen* is that the Saving procured for all consumers forms a fund from which wages are paid, replacing those eliminated by the machine.

Thus, using the above example, Jacques Bonhomme obtains a product by spending two francs on workers' wages.

Thanks to his invention, labor now costs him only one franc.

As long as he sells the product at the same price, there is one less worker employed in making this particular product; *that is what is seen.* However, there is one worker more employed using the franc that Jacques Bonhomme has saved; *that is what is not seen.*

When, in the natural progress of things, Jacques Bonhomme is reduced to lowering the price of the product by one franc, he will no longer be making any saving; he will then no longer have a franc with which to make some new demand upon national output. However, in this respect, the purchaser of Jacques's product takes his place, and this purchaser is the human race. Whoever buys the product pays one franc less for it, saves one franc, and of necessity makes this saving available to the fund which finances wages; *that is also what is not seen.*

This problem concerning machines has been given another solution based on facts.

It has been said: Machines reduce production costs and the price of the product. The reduced price of the product triggers an increase in consumption, which requires an increase in production, and in the end the employment of as many workers or more, after the invention, as were needed before. In support of this, mention is made of the printing industry, spinning, the press, etc.

This argument is not scientific.

We would need to conclude that if the consumption of a particular product remains static or nearly so, machines would damage the demand for labor. This is not so.

Let us suppose that in a particular country all men wear hats. If, using a machine, people succeeded in reducing their price by half, it would not *necessarily* result that men would buy twice as many.

Would it then be said in this instance that part of national production had been rendered inert? Yes, according to the popular argument. No, according to mine; for while in this country no one would buy a single extra hat, the entire fund for wages would remain no less safe. The reduction in the flow of funds to the hat-making industry would reappear in the Savings made by all consumers, and from there would go on to finance all the labor that the machine had made redundant, and stimulate new development across all industries.

And this is what happens. I have seen journals that used to cost 80 francs, which now cost 48. This is a saving of 32 francs for subscribers. It is not certain, or at any rate, not inevitable, that these 32 francs continue to go into journalism. What is certain and essential is that, if they do not go in this direction, they go in another. One person will use them to buy more journals, another to eat better, a third to clothe himself better, and a fourth to buy better furniture.

In this way, industries are interdependent. They form a huge entity in which every part communicates with every other part through hidden channels. What is saved in one benefits all.[2] What is important is to understand fully that never, ever, are savings made at the expense of labor and pay.

2. This a key passage in which Bastiat summarizes his thoughts on the interdependence of all industries in the economy, and how information is transmitted from one place to another via *canaux secrets* (secret or hidden channels) in a pre-Hayekian insight into how prices transmit information to dispersed economic actors. It is also another example of the water metaphor, which he often used in his discussion of the ricochet effect.

9. Credit

In all ages, but especially in the last few years, people have thought of making wealth universal by making credit universally available.[1]

I do not think I am exaggerating when I say that, since the February Revolution, presses in Paris have vomited out more than ten thousand brochures recommending this solution to the *Social Problem.*

Alas, this solution is based on a pure optical illusion, if an illusion can be said to constitute a base.

People start by confusing money with products and then they confuse paper money with cash, and then from these two forms of confusion they claim to be plucking out something real.[2]

With respect to this question, it is absolutely essential to forget money, coins, notes, and other instruments by means of which products are passed from hand to hand, in order to see just the products themselves, which are the true basis of lending.

For when a ploughman borrows fifty francs to buy a plough, he is not really being lent fifty francs but a plough.

And when a merchant borrows twenty thousand francs to buy a house, it is not twenty thousand francs that he owes; it is the house.

Money is there only to facilitate the agreement among several parties.

Pierre may not be willing to lend his plough and Jacques may be willing to lend his money. What does Guillaume do then? He borrows Jacques's money, and with this money he buys the plough from Pierre.

But in fact, no one borrows money for its own sake. One borrows money to obtain products.

Now, in no country can more products change hands than there are products available.

Whatever the sum of specie and paper in circulation, the total number

---

1. This is a reference to the debate between Bastiat and the socialist anarchist writer Proudhon on free credit, which took place in Proudhon's journal *La Voix du peuple* in thirteen parts between 22 October 1849 and 11 February 1850, when Proudhon ended the discussion. This was later published in book form by Proudhon as *Intérêt et principal* (1850) and then by Bastiat with an additional concluding chapter as *Gratuité du crédit* (1850) in CW 4 (forthcoming).

2. Bastiat makes a distinction between two types of "money" here, *numéraire* (cash or hard money backed by gold or silver) and *papier monnaie* (paper money). We have translated *numéraire* as "money" throughout the book except, as in this passage, where a clear distinction has to be made between the two.

of borrowers cannot receive more ploughs, houses, tools, provisions, or raw materials than the entire group of lenders is able to supply.

So we should get it firmly into our heads that any borrower implies a lender and any borrowing a loan.

This having been said, what good can institutions of credit do? They can facilitate the means for borrowers and lenders to locate each other and enter into agreement. But what they cannot do is to increase instantly the quantity of objects borrowed and lent.

This is what would be necessary, however, if the aims of the Reformers were to be achieved, since they aspire to nothing less than putting ploughs, houses, tools, provisions, and raw materials into the hands of all those who want them.

And what have they dreamt up to do this?

They propose the provision of a State guarantee for loans.

Let us go deeper into the question, for there is something in it *that is seen* and something *that is not seen.* Let us endeavor to see both of these.

Let us suppose that there is just one plough in the world and that two ploughmen would like to have it.

Pierre owns the only plough available in France. Jean and Jacques want to borrow it. Jean, through his probity, property, and good reputation, offers guarantees for it. He is *believed in;* he has *credit.* Jacques does not inspire confidence, or inspires less confidence. Naturally, Pierre will lend his plough to Jean.

But now, under socialist inspiration, the State intervenes and tells Pierre: "Lend your plough to Jacques and I will guarantee its repayment; this guarantee is worth more than Jean's, for he has only himself to speak for himself while I, I have nothing it is true, but I control the wealth of all the taxpayers, and it is with their money that I will pay you the principal and interest if need be."

Consequently, Pierre lends his plough to Jacques: *that is what is seen.*

And the socialists rub their hands together, saying: "See how our plan has succeeded. Through the intervention of the State, poor Jacques has a plough. He will no longer be forced to dig the earth; he is now on the road to wealth. It is an asset for him and a benefit for the nation taken as a whole."

No, Sirs! It is not a benefit for the nation, for here is *what is not seen.*

What is not seen is that the plough has been allocated to Jacques only because it has not been allocated to Jean.

What is not seen is that if Jacques ploughs instead of digging, Jean will be reduced to digging instead of ploughing.

As a result, what was desired as an *increase* in lending is merely a *displacement* of lending.

What is more, *what is not seen* is that this displacement implies two profound forms of injustice: an injustice to Jean who, after deserving and acquiring *credit* through his probity and activity, sees himself dispossessed; and an injustice to taxpayers who risk paying a debt that does not concern them.

Will it be said that the government offers Jean the same facilities as Jacques? But since there is just one plough available, two cannot be lent. The argument always returns to the claim that, thanks to the intervention of the State, more borrowing will occur than there are loans available, for the plough represents here the mass of capital available.

It is true that I have reduced the operation to its simplest level, but use the same touchstone to test the most complicated governmental institutions of credit, and you will be convinced that this is the only result they can produce: *displacing* credit and not *increasing* it. In a given country and time there is just a certain sum of capital available, and all of it is invested. By guaranteeing those that are insolvent, the State may well increase the number of borrowers, thus raising the rate of interest (always to the disadvantage of the taxpayer), but what it cannot do is to increase the number of lenders and the total amount of lending.

Let no one attribute to me, however, a conclusion from which may God preserve me. I say that the Law should not artificially favor borrowings, but I do not say that it should artificially hinder them. If, in our mortgage system or elsewhere, there are obstacles to the dissemination and application of credit, let them be removed; nothing would be better or more just. But this is all, with freedom, that should be demanded of the Law by Reformers worthy of the name.

10. Algeria[1]

But here are four speakers who struggle to control the rostrum. First of all, they all speak at the same time, then one after the other. What have they said? Certainly some very fine things on the power and grandeur of France,

---

1. See Glossary on Algeria.

on the necessity of sowing in order to reap, on the brilliant future of our gigantic colony, on the advantage of sending off to distant places our *surplus* population,[2] etc., etc. Magnificent examples of oratory which are always adorned with the following peroration:

"Vote in favor of fifty million (more or less) to build ports and roads in Algeria, in order to take settlers there, build them houses, and clear fields for them. In doing this you will bring relief to French workers, stimulate work in Africa, and expand trade in Marseilles. It is pure profit."[3]

Yes, that is true, if you consider the said fifty million only from the time that the state spends it; if you look at where this money is going, not where it came from; if you take account only of the good it will do on leaving the coffers of the tax collectors and not of the harm that has been done nor of the good that has been prevented when it entered these coffers. Yes, from this limited point of view, it is pure profit. The house built on the Barbary coast, *that is what is seen;* the port dug on the Barbary coast, *that is what is seen;* the work stimulated on the Barbary coast, *that is what is seen;* fewer workers in France, *that is what is seen;* a major flow of goods to Marseilles, *that is also what is seen.*

But there is another thing *that is not seen.* It is that the fifty million spent by the state cannot be spent, as it might have been, by taxpayers. From all the good attributed to public expenditure carried out, we must deduct all the harm done by preventing private expenditure, unless we go so far as to say that Jacques Bonhomme would have done nothing with the hundred sous he had earned and that taxes had taken from him. This is an absurd assertion, for if he took the trouble to earn them, it is because he hoped to have the satisfaction of spending them. He would have rebuilt the fence around his garden and can no longer do so, *that is what is not seen.* He would have had his field marled[4] and can no longer do so, *that is what is not seen.* He would

2. This is a reference to the Malthusian notion that there was a "surplus" population which could not be fed at the current rate of agricultural production. Thus, the population had to be "limited" in some way, in the long term by the exercise of "moral restraint" in having smaller families, or in the short term with some people having to be moved elsewhere, such as to the colonies.

3. In a debate in the National Assembly on 11 and 19 September 1848, a budget of fr. 50 million was allocated to the Ministry of War for the years 1848–51 to "establish agricultural colonies in the provinces of Algeria and for works of public utility intended to assure their prosperity" (*Compte rendu des séances de l'Assemblée Nationale,* p. 943).

4. Marl, or marlstone, is a sedimentary rock consisting of a mixture of clay and limestone which historically had been crushed and used as fertilizer.

have added a floor to his cottage and can no longer do so, *that is what is not seen.* He would have bought more tools and can no longer do so, *that is what is not seen.* He would have fed himself better, clothed himself better, educated his sons better, increased his daughter's dowry and can no longer do so, *that is what is not seen.* He would have joined the mutual aid society[5] and can no longer do so, *that is what is not seen.* On the one hand, various satisfactions are taken from him and the means of action destroyed in his very hands, and on the other, the work by the laborer, carpenter, blacksmith, tailor, or his village schoolmaster that he might have encouraged and that is now wiped out: *all this too is what is not seen.*

People count a great deal on the future prosperity of Algeria; so be it. But they should also take account of the doldrums into which, in the meantime, France is inevitably being sunk. I am being shown the trade in Marseilles, but if it is being achieved on the basis of taxes, I will always be able to show an equal volume of trade that has been destroyed in the rest of the country. It is being said: "Here is a settler who is being sent to the Barbary coast; this provides relief for the population remaining in the country." My reply is: "How can this be so if, by transporting this settler to Algiers, you are also transporting there two or three times the amount of capital which would have afforded him a living in France?"[6]

My sole aim is to make the reader understand that, in any public expenditure, behind the apparent good there is a harm that is more difficult to perceive. As far as I am able, I would like to instill in him the habit of seeing both of these and taking account of both of them.

When an item of public expenditure is put forward, it must be examined on its own merits, setting aside the resulting stimulus claimed for production, for this stimulus is an illusion. What public expenditure does in this

5. The Economists believed that *associations des secours mutuels* (mutual aid societies, or "friendly societies") were an important way in which ordinary workers could improve their economic situation without state assistance. Bastiat mentions them in an earlier sophism, ES2 4, pp. 142–46, where he points out the legal impediments to their operation. His friend and colleague Gustave de Molinari had championed the idea of labor exchanges as a way in which workers could inform themselves about the availability of jobs and rates of pay all across Europe.

6. (Bastiat's note) The Minister of War stated recently that each person transported to Algeria cost the state 8,000 francs. Well, it is a stated fact that the unfortunate people concerned would have lived very well in France on a capital of 4,000 francs. My question is, how is the population of France being relieved when it is being deprived of one man and the means of subsistence for two?

respect, private expenditure would also have done. Therefore the alleged interests of production are always irrelevant.

An appreciation for the intrinsic merit of public expenditure made for Algeria is not part of the aim of this article.

However, I cannot refrain from making a general observation. Presumption is always unfavorable to collective expenditure carried out through taxes. Why? This is why:

First of all, justice always suffers because of it. Since Jacques Bonhomme had sweated to earn his hundred-sou piece with some kind of satisfaction in mind, it is at least unfortunate that the tax authorities intervene to remove this satisfaction from Jacques Bonhomme to give it to someone else. Certainly, it is then up to the tax authorities or those who direct them to give good reasons for this. We have seen that the State gives a detestable reason when it says: "With these hundred sous I will give work to workers," since Jacques Bonhomme (as soon as he no longer entertains any blindness in this regard) will not fail to reply: "Good heavens! With one hundred sous, I will give them work myself!"

Setting aside this reason, other reasons are put forward in all their nakedness, making the argument between the tax authorities and poor Jacques Bonhomme extremely simple. If the State says to him: "I am taking one hundred sous from you to pay the gendarme who saves you from having to look after your own security, to pave the road you cross every day, to pay the magistrate who ensures respect for your property and freedom, or to pay the soldier who defends our borders," Jacques Bonhomme would pay without a word, unless I am much mistaken. But if the State tells him: "I am taking your hundred sous to give you a subsidy of one sou if you farm your field well, or in order to teach your son what you do not want him to learn, or for the cabinet minister to add the hundred and first dish to his dinner; I am taking them to build a cottage in Algeria subject to taking one hundred sous more from you each year to keep a settler there, in addition to a further hundred to keep a soldier to guard the settler and yet another hundred to keep a general to guard the soldier, etc., etc.," I can almost hear poor Jacques cry: "This legal regime bears a strong resemblance to the legal regime which prevails in the Forest of Bondy!"[7] and as the State has foreseen the objec-

---

7. The Forest of Bondy is a large forest in the département of Seine-Saint-Denis, about 15 kilometers east of Paris. It was a notorious refuge for thieves and highwaymen. Hence one might translate Bastiat's expression le régime [légal] de la forêt de Bondy as "the law of the jungle" as does the FEE translator (WSWNS, FEE edition, p. 41).

tion, what does it do? It mixes up everything; it produces this detestable argument, which should not have any influence on the matter; it talks about the effect the many hundred sous have on production; it refers to the minister's cook and supplier, a settler, a soldier, and a general all living off these five-franc coins. It shows, in a word, *what is seen,* and as long as Jacques Bonhomme has not learned to bring to the forefront *what is not seen,* he will be duped. This is why I am endeavoring to teach him to do this by means of frequent repetition.

Because public expenditure displaces production without increasing it, a second and serious presumption weighs against it. To displace production is to displace workers and upset the laws of nature that govern the distribution of the population across the country. When 50 million is left to taxpayers, since taxpayers are everywhere, this sum stimulates work in the forty thousand communes in France. This money acts as a link to keep each person in his native area; it is spread to every possible worker and over all the forms of production imaginable. If the state withdraws this 50 million, gathers it together, and spends it for a specific purpose, it attracts to this purpose a proportional quantity of displaced output, a corresponding number of uprooted workers, a floating population that has lost its position in society[8] and is, I dare to say, dangerous once funds have run out! But the following happens (and here I return to my subject): this fevered activity, blown into a restricted space, in a manner of speaking, leaps to the eye, *that is what is seen.* The people applaud and marvel at the beauty and ease of the procedure and clamor for its continuation and extension. *What is not seen* is that an equal quantity of productive activity that is probably of a more sensible kind has been consigned to idleness throughout the rest of France.

11. Thrift and Luxury

It is not only with reference to public expenditure that *what is seen* eclipses *what is not seen.* Leaving half the economic system in shadow as it does, this phenomenon ushers in a false moral code. It leads nations to consider their moral and material interests as antagonistic. Can anything be more demoralizing and sad? Let us see.

There can be no head of a household who does not see it as his duty to teach his children order, neatness, a sense of looking after things, and economy and moderation in expenditure.

8. Bastiat uses the expression *déclassée,* which literally means "declassed."

There is no religion that does not inveigh against ostentation and luxury. That is all very good, but on the other hand, what can be more popularly accepted than the following axioms:

"Hoarding dries up the veins of the people."

"The luxury of the great leads to the prosperity of the humble."

"Those who are prodigal ruin themselves but enrich the State."

"It is on the excess of the rich that the bread of the poor is sown."

Here, certainly, there is a flagrant contradiction between moral and social ideas. How many eminent minds rest in peace after having noted the conflict! This is what I have never been able to understand, as it seems to me that there is nothing more painful than to perceive two opposing tendencies in the human race. What! It is led to degradation by either of the two extremes! If it is thrifty, it falls into destitution; if it is prodigal, it ends up in the abyss of moral decay.

Fortunately, popularly accepted maxims show Thrift and Luxury in a false light as they take account only of their immediate consequences *that are seen* and not of the later effects *that are not seen*. Let us attempt to rectify this limited view of the matter.

One Mondor and his brother Ariste,[1] having shared their father's inheritance, each have an income of fifty thousand francs. Mondor exercises the fashionable kind of philanthropy. He is what is known as a veritable executioner of money. He buys new furniture several times a year and a new wardrobe every month. The ingenious ways he comes up with to get through his inheritance sooner are the talk of the town: in short, he eclipses the high-livers of Balzac and Alexandre Dumas.

This being so, you ought to hear the chorus of praise which always surrounds him! "Tell us about Mondor! Long live Mondor! He is the benefactor of the workers and the Providence of the people. It is true that he wallows in orgies and splashes mud all over passers-by;[2] his dignity and human

1. "Mondor" is based on one of the brothers Antoine and Philippe Girard, who were street jugglers and tricksters in Paris in the early seventeenth century who sold patent medicines to passers-by. Philippe Girard's character was called "Mondor." "Ariste" was one of the brothers in Molière's play *L'École des maris* (The School for Husbands, 1661) who tutored two orphaned sisters.

2. Bastiat uses the word *éclabousser,* which means to splash or splatter somebody with something, often with mud. This could be a reference to the reckless way Mondor drives about town in his carriage, splashing pedestrians with mud from the streets. In the pamphlet "Damned Money!" Bastiat refers to the profligate Croesus, who loved to drive his

dignity in general are somewhat diminished. But what does it matter! If he is not useful himself, he makes himself useful by his wealth. He keeps money in circulation; his courtyard is always full of suppliers who always go away satisfied. Is it not said that if a gold piece is round it is so that it rolls?"

Ariste has adopted a very different lifestyle. While he is not selfish, he is at least an *individualist,* since he uses reason to govern his expenditure, seeks only moderate and reasonable pleasures, thinks of the future of his children and, to use the dreaded word, he is *thrifty.*

And you ought to hear what is said of him by the populace!

"What use is this mean rich man, this evil usurer![3] Doubtless there is something imposing and touching in the simplicity of his lifestyle; besides, he is humane, benevolent, and generous, but he *calculates.* He does not consume all his income. His townhouse is not constantly splendid and buzzing with life. What gratitude does he generate among upholsterers, coach builders, horse dealers, and confectioners?"

These assessments that are damaging to the moral code are based on the fact that there is one thing that catches the eye: the expenditure of the prodigal brother, and another that escapes it: the equal and even greater expenditure of the brother who saves.

However, things are so admirably organized by the divine inventor of social order that in this as in everything, Political Economy and Morality, far from being in conflict, are in agreement with one another, and Ariste's wisdom is not only more dignified but also more *profitable* than Mondor's folly.

And when I use the term profitable, I do not just mean that it is profitable to Ariste or even to society in general, but more beneficial to the workers of today and current productive activity.

To prove this, you need cast only your mind's eye on the hidden consequences of human action that your physical eye does not see.

Yes, Mondor's prodigality has effects that are visible to all. Everyone can see his carriages, landaus, phaetons, the dainty paintings on his ceilings, his rich carpets, and the splendor that radiates from his townhouse. Everyone

---

ostentatiously decorated chariots very recklessly, splashing mud on the onlookers. He could be making a similar comment about Mondor here.

3. Bastiat uses the term *le fesse-mathieu,* which is a coarse expression for a usurer or moneylender. It is a combination of the term *la fesse* (buttock) and *Matthew,* a reference to Saint Matthew's having been a tax collector and moneylender before he became a disciple of Christ.

knows that his *thoroughbreds* run in races. The dinners he gives at his town-house in Paris draw crowds on the pavement, and people say: "Here is a good man who, far from keeping back some of his income, probably is eating into his capital." *This is what is seen.*

From the point of view of the workers' interests, it is not as easy to see what happens to Ariste's income. Let us follow it closely, however, and we will see that all of it, *right down to the last obole,* will provide work to workers, as certainly as Mondor's income does. There is just one difference: Mondor's wild expenditure is condemned to decrease constantly and come to an in-evitable end, while Ariste's wise expenditure will increase from year to year.

And if this is so, the public interest will certainly be in line with the morality.

Ariste spends twenty thousand francs a year on himself and his house-hold. If this were not enough to make him happy, he would not deserve to be called a wise man. He is touched by the misfortunes that weigh on the poor classes; he believes that in all conscience he is called upon to contribute some relief to them, and he devotes ten thousand francs to charity. Among the traders, manufacturers, and farmers, he has friends who are temporarily on hard times. He finds out about their situation in order to be able to help them prudently and effectively and allocates another ten thousand francs to this work. Finally, he does not forget that he has daughters to provide a dowry for and sons whose future he has to ensure, and consequently he sets himself the duty to save and invest ten thousand francs each year.

Here then is the way his income is used:

1. Personal expenditure   20,000 francs
2. Charity   10,000 francs
3. Help to Friends   10,000 francs
4. Savings   10,000 francs

Let us take each of these headings and we will see that not one single obole escapes the national output.

1. Personal expenditure. With regard to workers and suppliers, this has effects that are absolutely identical to an equal level of expenditure made by Mondor. This is self-evident; we will say no more about it.

2. Charity. The ten thousand francs devoted to this heading also go to stimulating productive activity: they go to the baker, the butcher, and shops that sell clothes and furniture. The point is, however, that the bread, meat, and clothing are not directly of use to Ariste, but to those he has substituted

for himself. Well, this simple substitution of one consumer for another has not the slightest effect on general production. Whether Ariste spends one hundred sous or asks an unfortunate person to spend them in his stead is just the same.

3. Help to Friends. The friend to whom Ariste lends or gives ten thousand francs does not receive them in order to bury them; this would be repugnant to the whole conception. He uses this money to pay for goods or settle debts. In the first instance, productive activity is stimulated. Would people dare to say that such activity has more to gain from the purchase by Mondor of a *thoroughbred* for ten thousand francs than from the purchase by Ariste or his friend of ten thousand francs' worth of fabrics? Or if this sum is used to pay a debt, the only thing that results is that a third person, the creditor who receives the ten thousand francs, appears on the scene; he will certainly use this money for some purpose in his trade, his factory, or his operation. It is one middleman more between Ariste and the workers. The names change but the expenditure remains, as does the stimulus given to production.

4. Savings. There remains the ten thousand francs that is *saved,* and this is where, from the point of view of encouraging the arts, industry, work, and the labor force, Mondor appears to be vastly better than Ariste, although from the moral point of view Ariste shows himself to be somewhat better than Mondor.

It is never without physical unease that borders on pain that I see the appearance of contradictions like this among the great laws of nature. If the human race was reduced to choosing between two parties, one of which injures its interests and the other its conscience, all that would be left to us would be to despair of its future. Fortunately, this is not so.[4] And, in order to see Ariste regain his economic as well as his moral superiority, you just have to understand this consoling axiom that is no less true for appearing to be paradoxical: *To save is to spend.*

What is Ariste's aim in saving ten thousand francs? Is it to bury two thousand hundred-sou pieces in a hiding place in his garden? Certainly not; he means to increase his capital and income. Consequently, this money, which

---

4. (Paillottet's note) See the note on page 369. [This is a reference to the earlier footnote, which states: This is a reference to chap. 14 "*Conflit de principes*" (Conflict of Principles) and chap. 18 "*Il n'y a pas de principes absolus*" (There Are No Absolute Principles) in *Economic Sophisms* Part I in vol. 4 *OC* (Paillottet is incorrect in stating that these are in vol. 6); and to Reflections addressed to Thiers; and to chapter 11 "*Éparges et luxe*" (Thrift and Luxury) of "What Is Seen" in vol. 5 *OC*.]

he is not using to purchase personal forms of satisfaction, he uses to buy land, a house, state bonds and shares in industry, or else he invests it with a trader or a banker. If you follow the écus in all these alternative uses, you will ascertain that, through the offices of salesmen or lenders, they will go to provide work as surely as if Ariste, following the example of his brother, had traded them for furniture, jewelry, and horses.

The whole point is that when Ariste buys land or bonds for ten thousand francs, his choice is determined by the consideration that he has no need to spend these funds on consumption goods, this being what you are criticizing him for.

But, likewise, the person who sells him the land or the bond is guided by the belief that he needs to spend the ten thousand francs in some way or another.

This means that the expenditure is made come what may, whether by Ariste or those who take his place.

From the point of view of the working classes or the stimulation of employment, there is therefore just one difference between Ariste's action and that of Mondor. As Mondor's expenditure was made directly by him and around him, *it is seen*. As Ariste's action is carried out in part by middlemen and at a distance, *it is not seen*. However, in fact, and for anyone capable of relating cause to effect, the cause that is not seen is just as certain as that which is seen. The proof of this is that in both cases the écus *circulate* and do not remain in the wise man's strongbox any more than in that of the spendthrift.

It is therefore erroneous to say that Thrift is currently causing harm to industry. Seen from this angle, it is just as beneficial as Luxury.

But how much superior it is to the latter if the train of thought, instead of limiting itself to the hour that passes, encompasses a longer period!

Ten years have gone by. What has become of Mondor, his fortune, and his great popularity? All of this has vanished; Mondor is ruined. Far from spreading sixty thousand francs[5] each year around the social body, he is perhaps a burden on it. In any case, he no longer gives joy to his suppliers; he is no longer counted as a promoter of the arts and industry; he is no longer any use to workers any more than he is to his family, which he has left in poverty.

At the end of this same ten-year period, not only has Ariste continued

---

5. Bastiat makes a mistake here. The amount he stated earlier in the article was fifty thousand francs per year.

to put his entire income into circulation, but he puts an increasing level of income into it as the years go by. He increases the capital of the nation, that is to say, the fund out of which wages are paid, and as the demand for labor is based on the size of this fund, he continues to increase the remuneration of the working class. Should he die, he will leave children whom he has made capable of carrying on this work of progress and civilization.

From a moral point of view, the Superiority of Thrift over Luxury is obvious. It is consoling to think that this is true from the economic point of view as well, at least for anyone who does not stop at the immediate effects of phenomena but is capable of extending his investigations right up to their final effects.

12. The Right to Work[1] and the Right to Profit[2]

"Brothers, tax yourselves in order to provide me with work at your price." That is the Right to Work, Elementary Socialism, or the first stage of socialism.

"Brothers, tax yourselves in order to supply me with work at my price." That is the Right to Profit, Refined Socialism, or the second stage of socialism.

---

1. The title pairs two things—"*le droit au travail*" and "*le droit au profit.*" The first right, "*le droit au travail*" (the right to a job), was a slogan of the socialists during the Second Republic. They claimed that it was the duty of the government to provide every able-bodied Frenchman with a job, and the job-creation program initiated by the Constituent Assembly in the first days of the revolution, called the National Workshops, was designed to carry this out. Bastiat and the other Economists fiercely opposed this scheme, and Bastiat used his position in the Finance Committee to argue against it. In May 1848 the Constituent Assembly formed a committee to discuss the matter, as the burden of paying for the National Workshops scheme was becoming too much for the government to bear. Bastiat was one of the speakers, and in his speech he distinguished between the right to work ("*droit au travail,*" where "work" is used as a noun and thus might be rendered as the "right to a job") and the "right to work" (*droit de travailler,* where "work" is used as a verb). He was opposed to the former but supported the latter. The government closed down the National Workshops in June, prompting riots in Paris, which were brutally put down by the army with considerable loss of life. Although he had opposed the National Workshops from the very beginning, Bastiat went out on the streets in order to stop the bloodshed and to aid the injured.

2. Although he does not go into details here, Bastiat may well have had a similar distinction in mind with regard to profit, namely that between *le droit au profit* (the right to a [guaranteed] profit) and *le droit de profiter* (the right to seek profits).

Both live as a result of effects that are *seen*. They will die as a result of the effects that are *not seen*.

What is seen is the work and profit generated by taxes levied on society. *What is not seen* are the work and profits that would be generated by this same amount if it were left in the hands of the taxpayers.

In 1848, the Right to Work was displayed for a time under both its aspects. This was enough to cause its downfall in public opinion.

One of these aspects was called the *National Workshop*. The other, the tax of *Forty-five centimes*.[3]

Millions every day moved from the rue de Rivoli[4] to the National Workshops. This was the good side of the coin.

But here is the reverse side. In order for millions to leave the coffers, they have first to enter them. This is why the organizers of the Right to Work turned to the taxpayers.

Well, peasants in the countryside said: "I have to pay forty-five centimes. I will therefore do without an item of clothing, I will not marl my field nor repair my house."

And the laborers in the countryside said: "Since our bourgeois class is depriving itself of items of clothing, there will be less work for tailors; since it is not marling its fields, there will be less work for laborers; since it is not repairing its houses, there will be less work for carpenters and masons."

It was then proved that you cannot profit twice from the same transaction and that work paid for by the government is carried out at the expense of work paid for by taxpayers. This was the death of the Right to Work, which appeared to be just as much of an illusion as it was an injustice.[5]

And yet, the Right to a Profit, which is just an exaggeration of the Right to Work, is still alive and is doing marvelously.

Is there not something shameful in the role that protectionists make society adopt?

3. In the immediate aftermath of the February Revolution a new "temporary" tax law was introduced on 16 March 1848, which increased direct taxes on things such as land, movable goods, doors and windows, and trading licenses, by 45 percent. It was known as the *taxe de quarante-cinq centimes* (the 45-centime tax) and was deeply unpopular.

4. The Ministry of Finances was located in the rue de Rivoli.

5. The National Assembly closed down the National Workshops, the government-funded unemployment relief program, on 21 June, since their exploding cost was bankrupting the government. The Workshops had been vigorously opposed by Bastiat in the Finance Committee of which he was the vice president.

Protectionists say to it:

"You have to give me work, and what is more, lucrative work. I was silly enough to choose a form of industry that leaves me with a loss of 10 percent. If you inflict a contribution of twenty francs on my fellow citizens and hand it over to me, my loss will be converted into a profit. Well, Profit is a Right, and you owe it to me."

The society that listens to this sophist, which saddles itself with taxes to satisfy him and which does not notice that the loss made by an industry is no less of a loss because others are obliged to compensate it, this society, as I say, deserves the burden inflicted on it.

Thus, this is seen in the many subjects I have dealt with: not to know Political Economy is to let oneself be blinded by the immediate effect of a phenomenon; to know Political Economy is to take into consideration all the effects, both immediate and future.[6]

I might at this point submit a host of other questions to the same proof. However, I draw back from the monotony of an endlessly repetitive argument and will close by applying to Political Economy what Chateaubriand[7] said about History:

> There are [he said] two consequences in history; one that
> is immediate and known right away, the other more distant
> and not obvious at first sight. These consequences are often
> contradictory; some come from our recently acquired wisdom,
> the others from wisdom of long standing. A providential event
> appears after a human one. God arises behind men. You may

6. (Paillottet's note) (*Unpublished note by the author*) If all the consequences of an action were visited on its author, our education would be swift. But this does not happen. Sometimes the beneficial and visible consequences are in our favor and the harmful and invisible ones are for others to face, which makes them even more invisible. We then have to wait for a reaction from those who have had to bear the harmful consequences of the act. Sometimes this takes a long time, and this is what preserves the reign of the error.

A man carries out an action that produces beneficial consequences worth ten in his favor and harmful consequences worth fifteen spread over thirty of his fellow men, so that what was borne by each of them was just half. In all, there was a loss and the reaction was bound to come. We can see, however, that it will be all the slower since the harm is more widely spread over the mass and the benefit more concentrated on a single point.

7. François-René, Vicomte de Chateaubriand (1768–1848), was a novelist, philosopher, and supporter of Charles X. He served as Minister of Foreign Affairs from December 1822 to June 1824. He refused to take the oath to King Louis-Philippe after 1830 and spent his retirement writing *Mémoires d'outre-tombe* (1849–50).

deny as much as you like the supreme counsel, refuse to accept what it has done, query its choice of words and dismiss as the mere force of things or reason, what the common folk call Providence, as much as you like. But look to the end of an accomplished deed and you will see that it has always produced the opposite of what was expected of it, when it has not initially been based on morality and justice.[8]

(CHATEAUBRIAND, *Memoirs from Beyond the Grave*)

8. Chateaubriand, "Conclusion. L'idée chrétienne est l'avenir du monde."

Appendixes

BASTIAT'S POLICY ON TARIFFS

Bastiat distinguishes between a policy of "protectionism," which imposes tariffs or duties on the importation of foreign goods in order to "protect" domestic producers from foreign competition, and a policy of "prohibition," which prevents or prohibits the importation of any foreign goods in order to prevent any competition from challenging the position of domestic producers. This should be distinguished from the modern policy of "prohibition," such as of alcohol or certain drugs, which makes it illegal for anyone, domestic or foreign, to produce, sell, or consume these products anywhere under threat of punishment by the state.

Furthermore, free traders like Bastiat and Cobden distinguished between two kinds of tariffs: "fiscal tariffs," which were solely designed to raise revenue for the government (it should be noted that income taxes did not exist at this time) and which they approved, and "protectionist tariffs," which were designed to provide government favors to particular vested-interest groups and which they fervently opposed.[1] In his essay "The Utopian" (written 17 January 1847 and published in the Second Series [ES2 11]), Bastiat says he would like to reduce tariffs to 5 percent across the board (for both imports and exports) in order to achieve the former goal.

In the introduction to the First Series, Bastiat says that he is in favor of a tariff policy which imposes a 5 percent ad valorem tariff on "objects of prime necessity," 10 percent on "objects of normal usefulness," and 15 or 20 percent on "luxury objects." However, he qualifies this recommendation by saying that these proposed rates are based on political considerations rather than "political economy as such."

1. See "French Tariff Policy," in appendix 3, "Economic Policy and Taxation."

The Double Incidence of Loss

This is a theory first formulated by the anti–Corn Law campaigner Colonel Perronet Thompson (1783–1869) in 1834–36 and taken up by Bastiat in 1847 in which it is argued that tariff protection or subsidies to industry result in a directly observable and obvious profit for one industry (and its workers) but at the expense of two other participants in the market. These other participants (or would-be participants) suffer a loss equal to the benefit gained by the first party: the consumer loses by having to pay a higher price for a good which he or she could have bought more cheaply from another supplier (often foreign), and unknown third parties also lose because the consumer who was forced to pay more for a good which is protected or subsidized has that much less to spend on other goods and services. Hence there is one party which benefits and two which lose out to the same amount, hence "the double incidence of loss."

The phrase appears in Thompson's "A Running Commentary on Anti-Commercial Fallacies," which was published in 1834, in which he observes that "the (part) of the sum gained to the monopolists and lost twice over by the rest of France,—(viz. once by a corresponding diminution of business to some other French traders, and once more by the loss to the consumers, who are the nation).... The understanding of the misery of this basis, depends upon a clear comprehension of the way in which the gain to the monopolist is lost twice over by other parties; or what in England has been called the double incidence of loss."[1]

Bastiat recognized that this was a powerful argument which could be used against defenders of tariff protection and subsidies to industry. He used it for the first time in May 1847 in "One Profit versus Two Losses" (ES3 4) and "Two Losses versus One Profit" (ES3 7). It was an early version of his theory of "the seen" and "the unseen" where the issue was simplified to cover only three parties, and hence make it more understandable to his readers. The first party, the one receiving the tariff protection or the subsidies, was immediate and obvious to all and thus "seen," while the other two parties' losses were indirect and perhaps long-term and thus "unseen" to casual observers. Thus the long-delayed pamphlet *What Is Seen and What Is Not Seen* should really be seen as an extended essay on the theory of "the double incidence of loss" first formulated by Perronet Thompson. Bastiat was to take these ideas much

---

1. See Thompson, *Letters of a Representative to His Constituents,* pp. 188–89.

further in order to cover the economic impact on more than three parties in his theory of the ricochet effect.

THE SOPHISM BASTIAT NEVER WROTE: THE SOPHISM OF THE RICOCHET EFFECT

As the Second Series of *Economic Sophisms* was being printed in January 1848, Bastiat expressed some regret in a public lecture he gave for the Free Trade Association at the Salle Montesquieu in Paris that he had never gotten around to writing a sophism explicitly about what he called *le sophisme des ricochets* (the sophism of the ricochet effect). He had used the term several times during the course of 1847, but he had never gathered his thoughts on the topic in any coherent way, and he was to continue using the term until late in 1850 when his throat condition brought his work to an end.[1] Many in the audience must have read his earlier thoughts on the matter, as they responded very positively to his comments about his plans for "the next edition" of the *Economic Sophisms*,[2] which he promised would contain such an essay. He was not able to publish a third series of the *Economic Sophisms* as he had hoped since the February Revolution of 1848 intervened, and he spent much of his time in the following two years working in the Chamber of Deputies, where he was the vice president of the Finance Committee.

In an essay he wrote soon after his January 1848 speech, "Monita secreta" (ES3 20, published in *Le Libre-Échange* of 20 February 1848), he mentioned the term "ricochet" five times, but it never saw publication in a third collection of *Sophisms* in his lifetime. His next spurt of interest came in 1849 and 1850 when he was frantically writing chapters for the *Economic Harmonies*. There was no mention of ricochet in the first part, which was published in his lifetime. However, the second half of the treatise, which Paillottet put together from the notes and fragments he left behind, and which appeared in 1851, contained five mentions of the theory of the ricochet effect. These uses may constitute a hint of the growing significance Bastiat was attaching to this new kind of economic sophism.

---

1. Bastiat makes no explicit reference to the ricochet effect in ES1; there are nine explicit references in ES2 and ES3, with a maximum of five references in ES3 18. There are four references in speeches and other writings in 1847–48, one reference in 1849, and seven in 1850 (two in other writings and five in *Economic Harmonies*), for a total of twenty-one uses of the word.

2. Appearing in this volume as "Third Series."

Bastiat does not say where he got the idea of "the ricochet effect," but the term had been used by the socialist Charles Fourier in *Le Nouveau monde industriel et sociétaire* (1829) as part of his theory of class,[3] by Pierre-Joseph Proudhon in *Qu'est-ce que la propriété?* (1841) in his critique of private property,[4] and by a fellow liberal from whom he most likely heard the term, Louis Reybaud, who used it in his amusing critiques of French society and politics, *Mémoires de Jérôme Paturot,* which appeared in serial form between 1843 and 1848.[5] Most notably, Reybaud used the term "ricochet" to satirize influence peddling within the state bureaucracy, which surely would have grabbed Bastiat's attention.

Whereas Fourier, Proudhon, and Reybaud used the term "ricochet" in a vertical sense, of waves of hatred and disdain going up and down the social hierarchy, or ties of power and influence going up and down the levels within a bureaucracy, Bastiat used the word in a horizontal sense. In fact, he seems to view it much like horizontal flows of water (or electricity) which radiate out from a central point. Thus, by "the ricochet effect" Bastiat meant the concatenation of effects caused by a single economic event which "rippled" outward from its source, causing indirect flow-on effects to third and other parties.[6] A key insight behind this term is the idea that all economic events are tied together by webs of connectivity and mutual influence. The analogies he liked to use often involved water, such as *glisser* (to slide or slip over something),[7] or flows of communication through *canaux secrets* (hidden channels),[8] or lines of force or electricity which stretched out in parallel lines to infinity.[9] What is clear from this analysis is that Bastiat had the option of using the word in its vertical sense to refer to flows of disdain or political power from a higher class to a lower class, but he chose not to. He wanted to use the word in its horizontal sense of circles of influence expanding outward from a source of economic action which affect countless other

3. Fourier, *Le Nouveau monde industriel et sociétaire* (1841), chap. 36, "Des accords transcendants, ou ralliements de seize antipathies naturelles," pp. 324–25.

4. Proudhon, *Qu'est-ce que la propriété?*, p. 203.

5. Reybaud, *Jérôme Paturot à la recherche d'une position sociale,* chap. 13, "Paturot publiciste officiel. Son ami l'homme de lettres," pp. 126–27.

6. Other words one could use for "ricochet" include ripples, trickle down, flow on, knock on, cascading, bouncing, indirect effects, and so on.

7. Bastiat also uses other words, such as *rejaillir* (to spill, cascade, or splash over). Bastiat uses *glisser* in ES1 4, p. 32n7, and ES3 17, p. 353n5; and *rejaillir* in ES3 12, p. 317n7.

8. See WSWNS 8, p. 436.

9. See ES3 7, p. 291.

actors and economic decisions throughout the economy. Thus we have translated *ricochet* as "flow on" and not "trickle down" to reflect Bastiat's choice.

Bastiat's theory of "the ricochet (or flow-on) effect" was a further development of a simpler idea, that of the double incidence of loss, which involved only three parties who were affected by some economic action. Bastiat gradually came to the realization that economic actions affected more than just three parties since the economy was so interrelated and interconnected. Thousands, perhaps millions, of economic actors were affected by some economic actions, some positively and some negatively. Another complication was that the losses to one party and gains to another might not be exactly equal, as he had first thought. Perhaps if a sufficiently large number of participants were involved, the relative gains and losses would gradually diminish (much as the concentric waves caused by a stone being thrown into water gradually dissipate) and thus have to be calculated using mathematics which he did not possess, especially as the impact became more distant and indirect over time. Hence his appeal to François Arago (1786–1853), who was one of the leading physicists of his day and active in liberal politics, to come up with some mathematics which would calculate scientifically the gains and losses to the relevant parties and thus make his theoretical arguments against tariffs and subsidies "invincible."[10] His theory of "the ricochet (or flow-on) effect" attempted to take into account these more widespread economic effects; however, he did not have time to fully develop it before his untimely death.

From what one can piece together from his scattered references, it is clear that Bastiat thought there were two different kinds of ricochet effect which made themselves felt within the economy: negative ricochet effects (NRE) and positive ricochet effects (PRE). In the work he published in 1846–48 he focused on the negative ricochet effects (NRE) because they better suited his political agenda of fighting protectionism. As he gradually turned more to economic theory, he realized that the ricochet effect could have profound positive consequences as well, but unfortunately he had less time to explore this dimension of the theory.

An example of the negative effects is a tax or tariff which raises the price of a particular commodity. It may have been designed to benefit a particular favored industry and its employees (who may have been promised higher wages as a side benefit), but it has a ricochet effect in that the higher price eventually flows through to all consumers, including the protected or sub-

10. See ES3 7, p. 289.

sidized workers, and even other producers. If many other industries also receive benefits from the state in the form of subsidies and tariffs, the cost structure of the entire economy is eventually raised as a result of similar ricochet effects. As Bastiat argues, all increased costs and taxes are eventually borne by consumers:

> In relation to the profit or loss that initially affect this or that class of producers, the consumer, the general public, is what earth is to electricity: the great common reservoir. Everything comes out of this reservoir, and after a few more or less long detours, after the generation of a more or less great variety of phenomena, everything returns to it.
>
> We have just noted that the economic results just flow over (*glisser*) producers, to put it this way, before reaching consumers, and that consequently all the major questions have to be examined from the point of view of consumers if we wish to grasp their general and permanent consequences.[11]

Examples of a positive ricochet effect include the benefits of international free trade and technological inventions such as the printing press and steam-powered transport. According to Bastiat, international free trade in the medium and long term has the effect of dramatically lowering costs and increasing choices for consumers. These lower costs and greater choice eventually flow on to all consumers, thereby improving their standard of living. Technological inventions like steam-powered locomotives or ships lower the cost of transport for every consumer and industry in an economy, thus lowering the overall cost structure and having an economy-wide PRE. Gutenberg's invention of movable type likewise had a profound impact on lowering the cost of the transmission of knowledge which all consumers could benefit from as the savings worked their way through the economy.

It is interesting to speculate how Bastiat might have written his most famous sophism, "The Broken Window" (July 1850), if François Arago had provided him with the necessary mathematics to calculate the gains and losses of all third parties to an economic action to the nth degree. How would he have calculated the spread of the "seen" gains to the glazier and all the businesses which benefited from the expenditure of the six francs he

11. *OC,* vol. 6, p. 358, "Producteur, consommateur." Quotation is found on pp. 371–72. See chap. 11 "Producer—Consumer," in CW5 (forthcoming).

made from replacing Jacques Bonhomme's broken window? How would he have calculated the "seen" and "unseen" losses to Jacques Bonhomme and all the business enterprises which did not benefit from his spending of those same six francs? How would he have compared the two amounts?

It is also interesting to speculate on what Bastiat might have done with this idea if he had lived longer. The ricochet effect seems very similar to the Keynesian notion of the multiplier effect of the positive benefits of increased government spending to stimulate demand in a time of economic recession. Bastiat might have gone on to describe PRE in terms of a "multiplier effect" of the benefits of free trade which gradually spread throughout an economy by lowering costs and increasing consumer choice, and NRE in terms of a "negative multiplier effect" (or "divider effect") of the losses and harm caused by tariffs and government subsidies which spread through an economy by raising prices and reducing consumer choice. The tragedy of Bastiat's early death means that we will never know where he would have taken many of the ideas he was developing in the last year or so of his life.

ON MALTHUS AND MALTHUSIAN LIMITS TO THE GROWTH OF THE STATE

Thomas Malthus is best known for his writings on population, in which he asserted that population growth (increasing at a geometric rate) would outstrip the growth in food production (growing at a slower arithmetic rate):

> I said that population, when unchecked, increased in a geometrical ratio; and subsistence for man in an arithmetical ratio. . . . This ratio of increase, though short of the utmost power of population, yet as the result of actual experience, we will take as our rule; and say, That population, when unchecked, goes on doubling itself every twenty-five years or increases in a geometrical ratio. . . . It may be fairly said, therefore, that the means of subsistence increase in an arithmetical ratio. Let us now bring the effects of these two ratios together. . . . No limits whatever are placed to the productions of the earth; they may increase for ever and be greater than any assignable quantity; yet still the power of population being a power of a superior order, the increase of the human species can only be kept commensurate to the increase of the means of subsistence, by the constant op-

eration of the strong law of necessity acting as a check upon the greater power.[1]

His ideas were very influential among nineteenth-century political economists, especially *An Essay on the Principle of Population*.[2] Most of the Economists were Malthusian in their views about population growth. However, Bastiat rejected the idea that individuals could not exercise "moral restraint" and thus voluntarily limit the size of their families, and that economic output could increase only at an arithmetic rate. He presented his alternate view in a series of articles and in a chapter of *Economic Harmonies* which provoked spirited opposition within the Political Economy Society between 1849 and 1851.[3]

The question of whether mankind's reproductive behavior was like that of a plant or an animal, or something quite different, was crucial in Bastiat's rethinking of Malthus's theory in the period between 1846, when he wrote an article on "Population" for *Le Journal des économistes,* and 1850, when the *Economic Harmonies* appeared.[4] Bastiat came to believe that, unlike plants and animals, humans were thinking and reasoning creatures who could change their behavior according to circumstances: "Thus, for both plants and animals, the limiting force seems to take only one form, that of *destruction*. But man is endowed with reason, with foresight; and this new factor alters the manner in which this force affects him."[5] He also came to the conclusion that there was a significant difference between the "means

1. Malthus, *An Essay on the Principle of Population* (1798), chap. 2, "The Different Ratios in Which Population and Food Increase," http://oll.libertyfund.org/titles/311#Malthus_0195_32.

2. Around the time Bastiat was writing, there were four French-language editions of Malthus's *Principles of Population* translated by P. Prévost: Geneva, 1809; Geneva, 1824; Paris (Guillaumin), 1845, with editorial matter by Pellegrino Rossi, Charles Comte, and Joseph Garnier; and a second Guillaumin edition of 1852 with additional editorial matter by Garnier in defense of Malthus against his critics.

3. Malthusian population theory was one of three topics which convulsed the regular monthly meetings of the Political Economy Society in the last years of Bastiat's life. Challenges were made to three orthodox positions held by most of their members, namely the Smithian view of the role of the state (challenged by Molinari in *JDE*, February 1849, with his article "De la production de la sécurité," and again in the 11th Soirée of *Les Soirées de la rue Saint-Lazare*); Malthus's theory of population (challenged by Bastiat in *Economic Harmonies,* chap. 16, "Population"); and Ricardo's theory of rent (also challenged by Bastiat, *Economic Harmonies,* chap. 13, "Rent").

4. Bastiat, "Population," *JDE* 15 (October 1846): 217–34.

5. *Economic Harmonies,* FEE edition, p. 426.

of subsistence" and the "means of existence," the former being fixed physio-
logically speaking (either one had sufficient food to live or one did not) and
the latter being an infinitely flexible and expanding notion which depended
upon the level of technology and the extent of the free market.[6] Malthus
focused on the former, while Jean-Baptiste Say, Bastiat, and later Molinari
focused on the latter.[7]

One of Bastiat's objections to the Chamber of Deputies' plan to subsidize
the colonization of Algeria was his rejection of the Malthusians' argument
that this was an effective way for France to dispose of its "surplus population."
Bastiat rejected this concept for a number of reasons.[8] Bastiat believed that
people constituted a valuable form of "human capital" (although he did not
use this phrase) which was very productive if left free to be so, and that the
free market and free trade could produce far more than merely "arithmetic
increases" in output.

However, there was one aspect of Malthus's theory which Bastiat did accept and adapt for his own purposes, namely that there was an upper limit
to the expansion or growth of an entity due to the fact that resources were
limited. Whereas Malthus applied this principle to argue that there was an
upper limit to human population caused by a lack of agricultural resources
to feed that population, Bastiat applied the theory of a "Malthusian limit"
to the growth of the state and the groups which lived by plundering the productive population. According to Bastiat's theory of plunder, a state would
continue to expand in size until it reached a limit imposed on it by the capacity of the taxpaying people to continue to fund the state at this level. In
"The Physiology of Plunder" (ES2 1) Bastiat states that

> Plunderers obey Malthus's law: they multiply in line with the
> means of existence, and the means of existence of swindlers is
> the credulity of their dupes. It is no good searching; you always
> find that opinion needs to be enlightened. . . .
> The state is also subject to Malthus's law. It tends to exceed
> the level of its means of existence, it expands in line with these
> means, and what keeps it in existence is whatever the people

6. *Economic Harmonies,* FEE edition, pp. 431ff.

7. See chap. 16, "Population," in the 1851 edition of *Economic Harmonies,* and Roger
de Fontenay's Addendum, pp. 454–64; in CW5 (forthcoming). The Addendum is reprinted in *Economic Harmonies,* FEE edition, pp. 557–67.

8. See WSWNS 10, pp. 439–43.

have. Woe betide those peoples who cannot limit the sphere of action of the state. Freedom, private activity, wealth, well-being, independence, and dignity will all disappear.[9]

STANDING ARMIES, MILITIAS, AND THE UTOPIA OF PEACE

Bastiat shared his suspicion of standing armies and his preference for local, decentralized militias with many of the Economists. The closest thing France had to a militia in Bastiat's lifetime was the National Guard, which had been founded in 1789 as a national armed citizens' militia in Paris and soon spread to other cities and towns in France.[1] Its function was to maintain local order, protect private property, and defend the principles of the Revolution. The Guard consisted of sixteen legions of sixty thousand men and was under the command of the Marquis de Lafayette. It was a volunteer organization, and members had to satisfy a minimum tax-paying requirement and had to purchase their own uniform and equipment. They were not paid for service, which limited its membership to the more prosperous members of the community. The Guard was closed down in 1827 for its opposition to King Charles X but was reconstituted after the 1830 Revolution and played an important role during the July Monarchy in support of the constitutional monarchy. Membership was expanded or "democratized" in a reform of 1837 and opened to all males in 1848, tripling its size to about 190,000. Since many members of the Guard supported the revolutionaries in June 1848, they refused to join the army in suppressing the rioting. The Guard gradually began to lose what cohesion it had, and further reforms in 1851 and 1852 forced it to abandon its practice of electing its officers and to give up much of its autonomy. Because of its active participation in the 1871 Paris Commune, many of its members were massacred in the postrevolutionary reprisals, and it was closed down in August 1871.

The Economists were appalled at the cost and destruction caused by the standing armies of the Napoleonic period (whether professional or conscript).[2]

---

9. ES2 1, pp. 124, 125.

1. For a history of the National Guard, see Comte, *Histoire complète de la Garde nationale.*

2. See Amboise Clément, "Armées permanentes," in *DEP* 1:70–75.

This was reflected in the writings of Jean-Baptiste Say, especially the *Cours complet d'économie politique pratique* (1828–33), where he severely criticized standing armies and argued strongly in favor of militias of citizens.[3] The following passage from Say is something Bastiat would have read and no doubt agreed with:

> I ask you, sirs, not to confuse the system of arming an entire nation with its militias, with the extravagant project of making an entire nation an army [*militaire*]; that is to say, transforming it into mobile and seasoned warrior units ready to support diplomatic intrigues and the ambition of despots. This madness has only ever been able to enter the minds of those who are total strangers to social economy. A farmer, a manufacturer, a merchant, an artisan, a worker, a doctor, and all the other useful professions work to supply society with what it needs to eat and to maintain itself. A soldier destroys what the others produce. To turn the productive classes into destructive classes, or to only give greater importance to the latter is to confuse the accessory with the principal, to give precedence to the famine which kills over the abundance which gives life. A nation of soldiers can only live by brigandage; not producing anything and unable to do anything but consuming, it must out of necessity pillage those who produce; and after having pillaged everything within reach, whether friend or foe, as a matter of course or tumultuously, it must then devour itself. History provides us with examples of this without number.[4]

Bastiat expressed his hostility to standing armies very clearly on a number of occasions.[5] In "The Utopian" (ES2 11), someone (presumably Bastiat) dreams about what he would do if appointed a minister with the power to implement any and all of the liberal reforms he had dreamed about. Among the many measures for cutting taxes and slashing the size of the government is his proposal to end conscription and to "disband the army" (*congédier,* to

---

3. See Say, *Cours complet d'économie politique pratique,* chap. 20, "De la défense de l'état par des milices," 2:291–95.

4. Ibid., 294–95.

5. See WSWNS 2.

dismiss, sack, fire)—except for "some specialized divisions" which are not specified, but possibly the artillery and similar groups—and replace it with local militias.

To put this proposal into perspective, it should be noted that according to the budget passed on 15 May 1849, the size of the French army was 389,967 men and 95,687 horses. (This figure rises to 459,457 men and 97,738 horses for the entire French military, including foreign and colonial forces.) The expenditure on the army in 1849 was fr. 346,319,558 and for the navy and colonies fr. 119,206,857 for a combined total of fr. 465,526,415. Total government expenditure in 1849 was fr. 1.573 billion, with expenditure on the armed forces making up 29.6 percent of the budget. Bastiat calculates that he can save roughly fr. 100 million for every 100,000 men in the armed forces who are dismissed. In order to maintain an army at about 400,000 men with seven-year enlistments, the French government had to recruit about 80,000 new men each year by a combination of voluntary enlistment, conscription (by drawing lots), and substitutions. The liberal journalist and anticonscription campaigner Émile de Girardin estimated that about one-quarter of the entire French Army consisted of replacements who had been paid fr. 1,800–2,400 to take the place of some young man who had been called up but did not want to serve. The schedule of payments depended on the type of service: fr. 1,800–2,000 for the infantry; 2,000–2,400 for the artillery, cavalry, and other specialized forces.[6] Only quite well-off men could afford to pay these amounts to avoid army service, thus placing a greater burden on poor agricultural workers and artisans. During the 1848 Revolution there was a pamphlet war calling for the abolition of conscription, but this was unsuccessful.

Under criticism from the other unnamed protagonist in "The Utopian," Bastiat makes a distinction between "disbanding the army" and "disarming the country." The former is run by the state using coercion to get recruits both by means of conscription and by funding from the taxpayers, whereas defense provided by the latter will be voluntary and run "just like any other profession." The Utopian states that his "maxim" for governing is that "Every citizen must know two things: how to provide for his own existence and how to defend his country." In other words, all individuals must be productive and be able to earn a living without being a burden on others, and they must

6. See Allyre, *Plus de conscription!;* and Girardin, "Le Remplacement militaire," in *Les 52: Abolition de l'esclavage militaire,* pp. 66–84 (pp. 73–74 for the cost of substitution).

be able to defend themselves and their neighbors when their life, liberty, or property is threatened by outsiders.

In order to create this decentralized, voluntary militia, the Utopian proposes two "articles," which have the flavor of decrees, although this is not spelled out.

> Article 1. All eligible citizens, without exception, will remain under the flag for four years, from the ages of 21 to 25, in order to receive military instruction.
> Article 2. Unless they can prove at the age of 21 that they have successfully attended a training unit.

The first article seems to be just another form of conscription until one realizes what a large proviso the second article entails—that as long as a young man becomes involved in a local militia and receives some military training, he is exempt from enlisting in what remains of the state-run army. The Utopian thinks that this will create a trained citizenry of some ten million men out of a total population of France of thirty-six million. He rather optimistically concludes that "finally, without causing grief to families [because their sons are conscripted] and without upsetting the principle of equality [since only the sons of the wealthy can pay for substitutes]" the citizen army of "10 million defenders [would be] capable of meeting a coalition of all the standing armies in the world."

After dreaming up fantasy after fantasy of deregulation, tax cutting, and dismissing government employees, the Utopian has his majority withdrawn and he realizes that since the nation does not share his views on these matters, his "plans remain what they are, just so many UTOPIAS."

Bastiat returned briefly to the issue of conscription in the Manifesto or statement of principles which he and Molinari drew up for their revolutionary journal *La République française,* which had a brief existence in February and March 1848. They list nine demands for change which their journal will be promoting. The seventh of these is "No more conscription; voluntary recruitment for the army."

In addition to writing about how to drastically reduce the size of the French military, Bastiat was also an active member of an international association called the Friends of Peace and took a great interest in their congresses in spite of finding it difficult to attend them because of his declining health. The first International Peace Congress was held in London in 1843 on the initiative of the American Peace Society and Joseph Sturge. Some 340 delegates attended, the bulk of which were British. The second was organized by Elihu Burritt and chaired by the Belgian lawyer Auguste Visschers and took place in Brussels in September 1848. The third Congress was held in Paris 22–24 August 1849 and was chaired by the novelist Victor Hugo.[7]

Because of his ill health and political commitments Bastiat was able to attend only the Paris congress in August 1849, at which he gave an address on "Disarmament, Taxes, and the Influence of Political Economy on the Peace Movement" (our title). Richard Cobden organized follow-up meetings in London, Birmingham, Manchester, and Bradford, all of which Bastiat attended. In his correspondence (CW, vol. 1) there are several letters to Cobden[8] in which Bastiat makes repeated pleas for Cobden to pressure the British government into reducing the size of its army and navy, a move that would encourage the French government to do likewise.

We include a contemporary translation of Bastiat's speech in this volume.[9] It has never been republished before.[10] In this speech Bastiat called for the simultaneous disarmament of all nations and a corresponding reduction of taxation. Émile de Girardin summarized on the title page of his book the resolutions of the 1849 Paris Peace Congress as follows: "reduction of armies to 1/200 of the size of the population of each state, the abolition of compulsory military service, the freedom of [choosing one's] vocation, the reduction of taxes, and balanced budgets." Since France's population in 1849 was about thirty-six million, this would mean a maximum size of 180,000 for the French armed forces. Thus, Bastiat and the other attendees at the Peace Congress were calling for a reduction of 279,457, or 61 percent, in the size of the French armed forces.

The year after he gave his speech on "Disarmament and Taxes" to the Paris Peace Congress, Bastiat returned to this topic with a more detailed treat-

7. The fourth Congress was held in Frankfurt in August 1850, with six hundred delegates, the fifth in London in July 1851, the sixth in Manchester in 1852, and the seventh in Edinburgh in 1853. The Congresses came to an end with the outbreak of the Crimean War in 1854.

8. Bastiat's forty-four letters to Cobden are listed in CW1, p. 522. See especially Letter 83 (15 October 1847), pp. 132–35; Letter 84 (9 November 1847), pp. 135–36; Letter 96 (5 April 1848), pp. 146–47; and Letter 157 (31 December 1849), pp. 226–28.

9. See "Bastiat's Speech on 'Disarmament and Taxes' (August 1849)," in Addendum: Additional Materials by Bastiat.

10. See "Speech," in Report of the Proceedings of the Second General Peace Congress, pp. 49–52.

ment in "Dismissing Members of the Armed Forces" (WSWNS 2). In this chapter Bastiat proposes immediately reducing the size of the French Army by 100,000 men from its total in 1849 of about 390,000 men (a reduction of 25.6 percent). Again, to put this in some kind of persective, an equivalent cut in the size of the U.S. armed forces would be about 373,000 men and women.[11] Bastiat spends most of the chapter attempting to disarm criticism by showing that discharging a quarter of the army is a good example of what he calls "the seen" and "the unseen." The critics see only the loss of payment to the soldiers and their families and the businesses around army towns who will lose custom; they do not see the tax money which is saved and kept by the taxpayers who now have an equivalent amount in their pockets to spend on themeselves, their families, and the businesses located where they live.

In a letter written on 17 August 1850, to the president of the 1850 Peace Congress (Frankfurt) a few months before his death, Bastiat expresses his regrets that his "ailment of the larynx" prevented his attendance, but he supports the continued promotion of the cause of peace in Europe. In the following passage he argues that the desire for peace is not the utopian wish he seemed to think it was in January 1847 when he wrote "The Utopian" but something which the expansion of free trade and industrialization was making increasingly inevitable:

> I would have joined my efforts to yours in favor of such a holy cause with zeal and enthusiasm.
>
> In truth, universal peace is considered in many places an illusion, and as a result the Congress is considered to be an honorable effort but with no far-reaching effect. Perhaps this feeling is more prevalent in France than elsewhere because this is a country in which people are more weary of utopias and where ridicule is the more to be feared.
>
> For this reason, if it had been given to me to speak at the Congress, I would have concentrated on correcting such a false assessment.
>
> There was doubtless a time when a peace congress would have had no chance of success. When men made war to acquire loot, land, or slaves, it would have been difficult to stop them by

---

11. As vice president of the National Assembly's Finance Committee in 1848–49, Bastiat had access to the most recent figures. See *Projet de loi pour la fixation des recettes et des dépenses de l'exercice 1850,* pp. 13–14; and Courtois, "Le Budget de 1849," pp. 18–28.

moral or economic considerations. Even various forms of religion have failed to do this.

But today, two circumstances have changed the question radically.

The first is that wars no longer have vested interest as their cause or even their pretext, since they are always contrary to the real interests of the masses.

The second is that they no longer depend on the whims of a leader, but on public opinion.

The result of the combination of these two circumstances is that wars are due to become increasingly rare and finally disappear through the force of events and independently of any intervention by the Congress, since an event that harms the general public and which depends on the general public is bound to cease.

What, therefore, is the role of the Congress? It is to hasten this inevitable result by showing, to those who do not yet perceive this, how and why wars and arms are harmful to the general interest.

What element of utopia is there in such a mission?[12]

BASTIAT AND CONVERSATIONS ABOUT LIBERTY

The "constructed dialogue" format was the second most common format which Bastiat used, appearing in fourteen of the seventy-five sophisms (19 percent of the total) he wrote between 1845 and 1850. The third most common format was the "economic tale or fable" (eight essays or 11 percent of the total), of which five contained substantial dialogue. These nineteen sophisms will be considered here as part of Bastiat's "conversations about liberty."[1]

The use of dialogue was a deliberate strategy adopted by Bastiat to make his discussions of economic principles less "dull and dry," especially for the

12. "Letter to the President of the Peace Congress in Frankfurt (Paris, 17 August 1850)" (CW1, pp. 265–66).

1. Essays in dialogue form (14) can be found in ES1 13, 16, 21; ES2 9, 10, 11, 12, 14, 15; ES3 2, 13, 15, 16; and WSWNS 7. Bastiat's economic tales (8) can be found in ES1 8, 10; ES2 7, 13; and ES3 4, 11, 12, 18. Of the latter group, substantial dialogue occurs in ES1 8; ES2 7, 13; and ES3 4, 12.

more popular audience he was trying to reach through journals like *Le Libre-échange* or workers rioting on the streets of Paris in February 1848. He would have the "Economist," "Friday," or "Jacques Bonhomme" present the free-market position while the protectionist position was presented by "An Artisan," "Robinson Crusoe," or a government official like the tax collector "Mr. Blockhead." In this technique he was influenced by other free-trade writers such as Jane Marcet (1769–1858), Harriet Martineau (1802–76), and Thomas Perronet Thompson (1783–1869).

Bastiat's younger friend and colleague Gustave de Molinari also used the dialogue format to good effect in three books which consisted entirely of "conversations" between various figures representing different economic points of view. It is most likely that he was greatly influenced by Bastiat's conversations and little plays which had proven to be quite popular. In *Les Soirées de la rue Saint-Lazare* (1849), which was published while Bastiat was still alive, Molinari has an Economist debate a range of economic issues with a "Socialist" and a "Conservative," with the Economist always getting the better of his opponents.[2] Shortly after Bastiat's death Molinari returned to this theme in another book made up of conversations, *Conversations familières sur le commerce des grains* (1855), which consisted of a series of conversations on free trade in wheat between a "Rioter," a "Prohibitionist," and an "Economist."[3]

Also in 1849 another very similar book appeared by Zéphirin Jouyne, a lawyer in the Customs Administration at the Court of Appeal in Aix and a member of the Agricultural Congress of Paris (1847), with five conversations between a free-trade Economist and a protectionist Manufacturer in which the Economist argued strongly for the abolition of the protectionist system.[4] Thus it seems that in free-market circles the constructed dialogue was a popular format, but it is unclear how effective it was in converting people to the free-market cause.

Of the economic sophisms which use the constructed dialogue format, the following are particularly interesting and innovative. In "Theft by Subsidy" (ES2 9) Bastiat describes a meeting of businessmen at one of the General Councils in which there is a discussion between a shipowner, a sailor, a civil servant, and a government minister (with interjections from a farmer

2. Molinari, *Les Soirées de la rue Saint-Lazare.*
3. Molinari, *Conversations familières sur le commerce des grains.*
4. Jouyne, *Abolition du système prohibitif des douanes.*

and a weaver) on whether tariffs or taxes are a better way to subsidize French industry. It is in this dialogue that Bastiat introduces his classic "Oath of Induction" for tax collectors, which is based on Molière's parody of doctors in *Le Malade imaginaire* (The Imaginary Invalid). It is one of the wittiest things Bastiat ever wrote.

Bastiat presents his most detailed list of the reforms which he would like to see introduced in French society in "The Utopian" (ES2 11). A free-trade "Utopian," obviously modeled on Bastiat, is mysteriously made a minister in the government with a majority which would allow him to introduce any reforms he likes. In a long conversation he then outlines in some detail his plans to deregulate the economy, cut taxes, eliminate protection, and disband the army. He comes to realize that all this is impossible unless he has the people on his side as well and, since they are not, he resigns. This sophism reveals Bastiat's realism about the prospects of radical reform given the prevailing climate of opinion in France and his reluctance to see top-down reforms imposed on the people by politicians.

Perhaps Bastiat's most complex conversations take place in "Protection, or the Three Municipal Magistrates" (ES2 13), which takes the form of a short play in four scenes where three magistrates, Pierre, Paul, and Jean, scheme to get the Council and the people of Paris to agree to adopt tariffs and trade prohibitions in order to benefit themselves by excluding out-of-town competition. Twenty years later Jacques's father is tired of the poverty that protectionism has brought to Paris and Jacques is determined to right the wrong. In a series of speeches to the crowd, Jacques and Pierre urge the people to either support free trade (Jacques) or protectionism (Pierre), but the people are fickle and keep changing their minds. This sophism shows Bastiat trying to expand the conversational form into a longer piece more like a play than an amusing essay. It is the only example we have of this form, as Bastiat seemed to prefer shorter and funnier essays which were less complex in structure.

Another quite complex conversation takes place in "Something Else" (ES2 14). This sophism contains a dialogue within a dialogue. It begins with a discussion between an unnamed free trader and a skeptic. In the course of the discussion the free trader introduces the economic problems faced by Robinson Crusoe on his island. There is then a brief dialogue between Crusoe and Friday in which Friday defends free trade and Crusoe defends protectionism. This sophism is very important because it is an early example of Bastiat's use of Robinson Crusoe to explain economic concepts, which I believe is one of his most significant innovations in thinking about economics.

In one of the last sophisms he wrote before the outbreak of the Revolution in February 1848, "The Mayor of Énios" (ES3 18), Bastiat tells an elaborate story about the mayor of a small village who wants to make his town richer by applying the same policies the French government does, but on a local scale. If tariffs and protection can increase the wealth of France by keeping out foreign-made goods, the mayor reasons, why can't his village increase its wealth by keeping out goods produced outside the village? After formulating a tariff (as a council of one), he convenes the municipal council to get his policy enacted. He then tells members of the council how they individually will benefit from having village tariffs, and they agree to vote the law he wants. The prefect of the département hears of his plan and summons him for a dressing-down. Although the prefect is a staunch protectionist when it come to national policy, he is very much a free trader when it comes to internal trade and therefore rescinds the mayor's law. This confuses the mayor because he truly believes protection is valid at all levels of government. This story reveals a number of aspects of Bastiat's thinking just before he was to become active in politics during the Revolution as an agitator and an elected politician. It shows Bastiat's realistic understanding of how local councils can be manipulated by unscrupulous politicians and his frustration with the national government for their intellectual inconsistency in favoring internal free trade but not international free trade.

This sampling of Bastiat's conversations about liberty shows how much effort he expended in trying to find the best way to express his ideas and to reach his readers. It was in this context that he experimented with writing short plays, making parodies of classic French plays, using fictional characters like Robinson Crusoe to explore the nature of economic reasoning, and fantasizing about what he might do if he were made one of the king's ministers. It is proof that Bastiat's creativity was not limited to economic and political theory but also extended to the literary forms his journalism would take.

BASTIAT'S THEORY OF CLASS:
THE PLUNDERERS VS. THE PLUNDERED

A recurring theme in many essays in the *Economic Sophisms* is that of plunder (*la spoliation*) of one group of people by another group. According to Bastiat, his intention in writing the sophisms was to bring to the attention of the French people the fact that they were being deceived and that wholesale plundering was going on around them under the guise of subsidies to industry, tariffs on imported goods, taxes on essential items such as salt and sugar, and high military spending (see "Bastiat on Enlightening the 'Dupes' about the Nature of Plunder" in the Introduction). A corollary of his ideas about plunder was his view of class, or the specific relationships which developed at any given historical moment between the group who benefited from institutionalized plunder and the group who were being plundered.

This was a topic Bastiat planned to discuss in much greater detail in a future book on the history of plunder, which he did not live long enough to complete. Fortunately, he left us many clues about what it would have contained, but these are scattered across a dozen or more essays and chapters, several of which are in his three collections of *Economic Sophisms* and in the booklet *WSWNS*, which constitute this volume of his Collected Works. This note attempts a partial reconstruction of Bastiat's theory of class from these fragments.

The basis for Bastiat's theory of class was the notion of *plunder*, which he defined as the taking of another person's property without their consent, by force or fraud. Those who lived by plunder constituted "*les spoliateurs*" (the plunderers) or "*la classe spoliatrice*" (the plundering class). Those whose property was taken constituted "*les spoliés*" (the plundered) or "*les classes spoliées*" (the plundered classes). Before the Revolution of February 1848, Bastiat used the pairing of "*les spoliateurs*" (the plunderers) and "*les spoliés*" (the plundered); after the Revolution he preferred the pairing of "*la classe spoliatrice*" (the plundering class) and "*les classes spoliées*" (the plundered classes), which is one indication of how deeply the events of 1848 and the rise of socialism affected his thinking.[1] The intellectual origins of this way of thinking can be traced back to the innovative ideas of Jean-Baptiste Say concerning "productive" and "unproductive" labor, which he developed in his *Treatise of Political Economy* (1803),[2] and the work of two lawyers and journalists who were inspired by Say's work during the Restoration, Charles Comte (1782–1837)[3] and Charles Dunoyer (1786–1862).[4] Comte

---

1. Bastiat's first use of the terms "*la classe spoliatrice*" and "*les classes spoliées*" occurred in "The Law" (July 1850) and then in *Economic Harmonies* 17 "*Services privés, services publiques,*" CW5 (forthcoming).

2. Say, Jean-Baptiste, *Traité d'économie politique* (1st ed. 1803).

3. Comte, Charles, *Traité de législation,* 4 vols. (1827); *Traité de la propriété,* 2 vols. (1834).

4. Dunoyer, Charles, *L'Industrie et la morale considérées dans leurs rapports avec la liberté* (1825); "*Esquisse historique des doctrines auxquelles on a donné le nom industrialisme,*"

and Dunoyer took the idea that those who were engaged in productive economic activity of any kind, or what they called "*l'industrie*," creating either goods or services, comprised a class which they called "*les industrieux*" (industrious or productive workers). Dunoyer in particular developed from these ideas an "industrialist" theory of history and class analysis which was very influential among French liberals leading up to 1848. Bastiat's reading of these three authors during the 1820s and 1830s laid the theoretical foundation of his own thinking about productive and unproductive labor, the nature of exploitation or plunder, and the system of class rule which was created when the unproductive class used their control of the state to live off the productive labor of the mass of the people.[5]

Bastiat took the ideas of Say, Comte, and Dunoyer about plunder and the plundering class which he had absorbed in his youth and developed them further during his campaign against protectionism between early 1843 and the beginning of 1848. Thus, it is not suprising that his definition originally began as an attempt to explain how an "oligarchy" of large landowners and manufacturers exploited consumers by preventing them from freely trading with foreigners and forcing them to buy from more expensive state-protected local producers. This perspective is clearly shown in Bastiat's lengthy introduction to his first book on *Cobden and the League,* which was published by Guillaumin in July 1845.[6] He wanted to apply to France his analysis of the English class system of an oligarchy protected by tariffs and to adapt the strategies used by Cobden and the Anti–Corn Law League to France, which he attempted to do, unsuccessfully as it turned out, between 1846 and early 1848. He returned to the English class system in the essay "Anglomania, Anglophobia" (c. 1847),[7] where he discusses "the great conflict between

---

c'est-à-dire, des doctrines qui fondent la société sur l'Industrie," *Revue encyclopédique,* février 1827, vol. 33, pp. 368–94; *De la liberté du travail* (1845).

5. On the rich but not well-known French liberal theory of class, see Leonard P. Liggio, "Charles Dunoyer and French Classical Liberalism" (1977); Ralph Raico, "Classical Liberal Exploitation Theory: A Comment on Professor Liggio's Paper" (1979); "Classical Liberal Roots of the Marxist Doctrine of Classes" (1992); "The Centrality of French Liberalism" (2012); David M. Hart, *Class Analysis, Slavery and the Industrialist Theory of History in French Liberal Thought, 1814–1830* (1994).

6. This will appear in CW6 (forthcoming). A shortened version of the Introduction also appeared as an article in the *JDE*: "*Situation économique de la Grande-Bretagne. Réformes financières. Agitation pour la liberté commerciale,*" *JDE,* June 1845, T. XI, no. 43, pp. 233–65.

7. ES3 14, pp. 327–41.

democracy and aristocracy, between common law and privilege" and explains how this class conflict was playing out in England. In "The People and the Bourgeoisie" (May 1847), he also analyzed the class relationship between the aristocracy and the nation in France, which he viewed as having such "an undeniable hostility of interests" that it would lead inevitably to conflict of some kind, such as "*la guerre sociale*" (class or social war).[8]

He later expanded his understanding of class and plunder to include other forms of exploitation, such as ancient slavery, medieval feudalism, oppression by the Catholic Church, and in his own day financial and banking privileges, as well as redistributive socialism, which began to emerge during 1848. We can see this clearly in the chapter "The Physiology of Plunder," which opened the second series of *Economic Sophisms,* published in January 1848 but written in late 1847, where he defined plunder in the following rather abstract way, using his terminology of any exchange as the mutual exchange of "service for service": "The true and just law governing man is 'the freely negotiated exchange of one service for another.'[9] Plunder consists in banishing by force or fraud the freedom to negotiate in order to receive a service without offering one in return."[10] Thus, the slave was plundered by the slave-owner because the violent capture and continued imprisonment of the slave did not allow any free negotiation with the slave-owner over the terms of contract for doing the labor which the slave was forced to do. Similarly, the French manufacturer protected by a tariff or ban on imported foreign goods prevented the domestic purchaser from freely negotiating with a Belgian or English manufacturer to purchase the good at a lower price.

What turned what might have been just a one-off act of violence against a slave or a domestic consumer into a system of class exploitation and rule was its regularization, systematization, and organization by the state.[11] All societies had laws which prohibited theft and fraud by some individuals against other individuals. When these laws are broken by thieves, robbers, and con-

---

8. ES3 6, "The People and the Bourgeoisie" (22 May 1847, *Le Libre-Échange*), pp. 11–12. In this volume, pp. 281–86. Bastiat first began to use the phrase "social or class war" in 1847 and used it several times in early 1849 in speeches in the Chamber of Deputies and in his campaign for re-election in April 1849.

9. In French the key phrase is "*L'échange librement débattu de service contre service.*"

10. ES2 1, p. 117.

11. On "*la Spoliation organisée*" (organized plunder) by the state, see "Justice and Fraternity," CW2, p. 78 and online http://oll.libertyfund.org/titles/2450#Bastiat_1573 -02_564.

men, we have an example of what Bastiat called "*la spoliation extra-légale*" (plunder which takes place outside the law),[12] and we expect the police authorities to attempt to apprehend and punish the wrongdoers. However, all societies have also established what Bastiat termed "*la spoliation légale*" (plunder which is done with the sanction or protection of the law) or "*la spoliation gouvernementale*" (plunder by government itself).[13] Those members of society who are able to control the activities of the state and its legal system can get laws passed which provide them with privileges and benefits at the expense of ordinary people. The state thus becomes what Bastiat termed "*la grande fabrique de lois*" (the great law factory),[14] which makes it possible for the plundering class to use the power of the state to exploit the plundered classes in a systematic and seemingly permanent fashion.[15]

We know Bastiat had plans to apply his class analysis to European history going back to the ancient Romans. When working through his papers in preparation for publishing the second part of *Economic Harmonies,* his friend and literary executor Prosper Paillottet states that Bastiat had sketched out in seven proposed chapters what would in effect have been his *History of Plunder*: Chapter 16. Plunder, 17. War, 18. Slavery, 19. Theocracy, 20. Monopoly, 21. Government Exploitation, 22. False Brotherhood or Communism. This list was included in the second expanded edition of *Economic Harmonies* (1851), which "the friends of Bastiat" (Prosper Paillottet and Roger de Fontenay) put together from his papers after his death.[16]

The historical form of plunder which Bastiat discussed in most detail in his sketches and drafts was "theocratic plunder," especially in ES2 1, "The Physiology of Plunder."[17] Bastiat believed that the era of theocratic plunder

---

12. Bastiat first used the terms "*la spoliation extra-légale*" and "*la spoliation légale*" in the essay "Justice and Fraternity" (15 June 1848, *JDE*) and CW2, pp. 60–81; and then in "The Law" (June 1850).

13. ES2 1, "The Physiology of Plunder," pp. 113–30.

14. WSWNS, chap. 7 "Trade Restrictions," pp. 427–32.

15. Bastiat used the phrase "*la spoliation permanente*" (permanent plunder) in "Property and Plunder" (July 1848), CW2, pp. 147–84 and online http://oll.libertyfund.org /titles/2450#lf1573-02_label_218.

16. See the "List of Chapters," in Frédéric Bastiat, *Harmonies économiques. 2me édition* (1851). List on p. 335. They can also be found in the FEE edition, p. 554, and online http://oll.libertyfund.org/titles/79#lf0187_head_074.

17. ES2 1, "The Physiology of Plunder," pp. 113–30; FEE, pp. 16ff. He also talks about theocratic plunder in the conclusion to ES1, ES2 2 "Two Moral Philosophies," the conclusion to part 1 of *Economic Harmonies,* and *EH* 16 "On Population."

provided a case study of how trickery and sophistic arguments could be used to ensure compliance with the demands of the plundering class. He argued that the rule of the Church in European history was one which had practiced plunder and deception "on a grand scale." The Church had developed an elaborate system of theocratic plunder through its tithing of income and production, and on top of this it created a system of *"sophisme théocratique"* (theocratic sophistry and trickery) based upon the notion that only members of the church could ensure the people's passage to an afterlife. This and other theocratic sophisms created dupes of the ordinary people, who duly handed over their property to the Church. Bastiat had no squabble with a church in which the priests were "the instrument of the religion," but for hundreds of years religion had become instead "the instrument of its priest."[18] The challenge to this theocratic plundering came through the invention of the printing press, which enabled the transmission of ideas critical of the power and intellectual claims of the Church and gradually led to the weakening of this form of organized, legal plunder. The Reformation, the Renaissance, and the Enlightenment gradually exposed the theocratic sophisms for what they really were—so many tricks, deceptions, lies, and contradictions—and many people were thus no longer willing to be the dupes of the Church.

In a similar manner, Bastiat thought, the modern bureaucratic and regulatory state of his day was, like the Church, based upon a mixture of outright violence and coercion, on the one hand, and trickery and sophisms, on the other. The violence and coercion came from the taxes, tariffs, and regulations which were imposed on taxpayers, traders, and producers; the ideological dimension which maintained the current class of plunderers came from a new set of political and economic sophisms which confused, misled, and tricked a new generation of dupes into supporting the system. The science of political economy, according to Bastiat, was to be the means by which the economic sophisms of the present would be exposed, rebutted, and finally overturned, thus depriving the current plundering class of their livelihood and power: "I have said enough to show that Political Economy has an obvious practical use. It is the flame that destroys this social disorder which is Plunder, by unveiling Fraud and dissipating Error."[19]

The outbreak of revolution in February 1848 and the coming to power of organized socialist groups forced Bastiat to modify his theory in two ways. The first was to adopt the very language of "class" used by his socialist

18. ES2 1. "The Physiology of Plunder," p. 123; FEE, pp. 20–21.
19. ES2 1. "The Physiology of Plunder," p. 116; FEE, pp. 132.

opponents, as we have seen with his change in usage from the pairing of "*les spoliateurs*" (the plunderers) and "*les spoliés*" (the plundered) before the Revolution to that of "*la classe spoliatrice*" (the plundering class) and "*les classes spoliées*" (the plundered classes) after the Revolution. The second way he changed his theory was to consider more carefully how state-organized plunder would be undertaken by a majority of the people instead of a small minority. Before the socialists became a force to be reckoned with in the Second Republic, when they introduced the National Workshops program under Louis Blanc, a small minority of powerful individuals, such as slave-owners, high Church officials, the military, or large landowners and manufacturers, used the power of the state to plunder the ordinary taxpayers and consumers. Bastiat termed this "*la spoliation partielle*" (partial plunder).[20] He believed that what the socialists were planning during 1848 was to introduce a completely new kind of plunder, which he called "*la spoliation universelle*" (universal plunder) or "*la spoliation réciproque*" (reciprocal plunder). In this system of plunder, the majority (that is to say, the ordinary taxpayers and consumers who made up the vast bulk of French society) would plunder itself, now that the minority of the old plundering class had been removed from political power. Bastiat thought that this was unsustainable in the long run, and in his famous essay on "The State" (June, September 1848) called the socialist-inspired redistributive state "the great fiction by which everyone endeavors to live at the expense of everyone else."[21]

I don't think Bastiat fully grasped at this time how the modern welfare state might evolve into a new form of class rule in the name of the people where "*les fonctionnaires*" (state bureaucrats and other functionaries), supposedly acting in the name of the people, siphoned off resources for their own needs. Bastiat gives hints that this might happen in his discussion of the "parasitical" nature of most government services[22] and his ideas about "*la spoliation gouvernementale*" (plunder by government) and "*le gouvernementalisme*" (rule by government bureaucrats),[23] which suggest the idea that government and those who work for it have their own interests which are independent of other groups in society. These are insights which Bastiat's younger friend

20. Bastiat first used the terms "partial" and "universal" plunder in "Plunder and the Law" (15 May 1850, CW2, p. 275) and then again in "The Law" (July 1850, CW2, p. 117).

21. CW2, p. 97 and online http://oll.libertyfund.org/titles/2450#Bastiat_1573-02_671.

22. See the scattered references to parasites in WSWNS 3, "Taxes," CW3, pp. 410–13; and WSWNS 6, "The Middlemen," CW3, pp. 422–27.

23. "The Law," CW2, pp. 107–46 and online http://oll.libertyfund.org/titles/2450#Bastiat_1573-02_1015.

and colleague Gustave de Molinari took up two years after Bastiat's death, in his class analysis of how Louis Napoléon came to power and brought the Second Republic to an end.[24]

In two private letters to Madame Hortense Cheuvreux, the wife of a wealthy benefactor who helped Bastiat find time to work on his economic treatise during the last two years of his life, Bastiat makes some interesting observations about the nature of the class antagonisms which were dividing France. In the first letter (January 1850), he offered Mme Cheuvreux an analysis of the conflict between the people and the bourgeoisie, based upon what he had observed during the Revolution. He concludes that French bourgeoisie had had an opportunity to bring class rule in France to an end and by not doing so had alienated a large section of the working class:

> In France, I can see two major classes, each of which can be divided into two. To use hallowed although inaccurate terms, I will call them the people and the bourgeoisie. The people consist of a host of millions of human beings who are ignorant and suffering, and consequently dangerous. As I said, they are divided into two; the vast majority are reasonably in favor of order, security, and all conservative priciples, but, because of their ignorance and suffering, are the easy prey of ambitious sophists. This mass is swayed by a few sincere fools and by a larger number of agitators and revolutionaries, people who have an inborn attaction for disruption or who count on disruption to elevate themselves to fortune and power. The bourgeoisie, it must never be forgotten, is very small in number. This class also has its ignorance and suffering, although to a different degree. It also offers dangers, but of a different nature. It too can be broken down into a large number of peaceful, undemonstrative people, partial to justice and freedom, and a small number of agitators. The bourgeoisie has governed this country, and how has it behaved? The small minority did harm and the large majority allowed them to do this, not without taking advantage of this when they could. These are the moral and social statistics of our country.[25]

24. See Gustave de Molinari, *Les Révolutions et le despotisme envisagés au point de vue des intérêts matériel* (1852).

25. "159. Letter to Mme Cheuvreux" (2 January 1850), CW1, pp. 229–31.

In the second letter (23 June 1850), he is even more pessimistic in believing that France (and perhaps all of Europe) is doomed to never-ending "*guerre sociale*" (social or class war). He talks about how history is divided into two alternating phases of "struggle" and "truce" to control the state and the plunder which flows from this:

> As long as the state is regarded in this way as a source of favors, our history will be seen as having only two phases, the periods of conflict as to who will take control of the state and the periods of truce, which will be the transitory reign of a triumphant oppression, the harbinger of a fresh conflict.[26]

Bastiat's way of looking at plunder and class did not end with his death on 24 December 1850. His ideas inspired one of his colleagues associated with the *Journal des Économistes,* Ambroise Clément,[27] to write an article "*De la spoliation légale*" (On Legal Plunder) in July 1848,[28] in which he developed some of Bastiat's ideas further with a more detailed categorization of the kinds of legal state theft or plunder, such as aristocratic theft, monarchical theft, theft by government regulation, industrial theft, theft under the guise of philanthropy, and administrative theft by the government itself.

One should also note that Bastiat's ideas on plunder and class were taken up in a few places in the *Dictionnaire de l'Économie politique* (1852), most notably in the article "La Loi" (Law), which consisted mostly of very large quotations from Bastiat's own essay, a short entry "Fonctionnaires" (civil servants) by Ambroise Clément, and a very interesting article "Parasites" by Renouard.[29]

Bastiat's ideas also probably influenced the thinking of his younger friend and colleague Gustave de Molinari, who began to develop his own ideas about class analysis in more detail after Bastiat's death in December 1850. After he left Paris in a self-imposed exile to Brussels after Louis Napoléon's coup

---

26. "176. Letter to Mme Cheuvreux" (23 June 1850), CW1, pp. 251–52.

27. Ambroise Clément (1805–86) was an economist and secretary to the mayor of Saint-Étienne for many years. In the mid-1840s he began writing on economic matters and so impressed Guillaumin that the latter asked him to assume the task of directing the publication of the important and influential *Dictionnaire de l'économie politique,* in 1850.

28. Ambroise Clément, "De la spoliation légale," *Journal des économistes,* 1 July 1848, T. 20, no. 83, pp. 363–74.

29. Bastiat, "La Loi," *DEP,* vol. 2, pp. 93–100; A. Clément, "Fonctionnaires," *DEP,* vol. 1, pp. 787–89; and Renouard, "Parasites," *DEP,* vol. 2, pp. 323–29.

d'état of December 1851, he gave a lecture in which he explored the nature of the class dynamics which had brought Louis Napoléon to power—"*Les Révolutions et le despotisme envisagés au point de vue des intérêts matériel*" (Revolutions and Despotism Seen from the Perspective of Material Interests).[30] Molinari would return to writing on class theory after a stint as editor of the prestigious *Journal des Débats* in the late 1860s and 1870s, when he published two important works of historical sociology in which the evolution of the state and market institutions, and the class relationships between producers and the state would play a very important role—*L'évolution économique du XIXe siècle: théorie du progrès* (The Economic Evolution of the 19th Century: A Theory of Progress, 1880), and *L'évolution politique et la Révolution* (Political Evolution and the Revolution, 1884).[31]

In conclusion, to show the various theoretical threads Bastiat was pursuing in formulating his theory of class, we list here in chronological order the main works where he discusses plunder and class. Note that of the fifteen items, six are from the *Economic Sophisms* and two are from *WSWNS*:

1. "Introduction" to *Cobden and the League* (July 1845),[32] in which he discusses the English "oligarchy" which benefited from the system of tariffs which Cobden and his Anti–Corn Law League were trying to get repealed.
2. ES1 "Conclusion" (November 1845), where he reflects on the use of force throughout history to oppress the majority, and the part played by "sophistry" (ideology and false economic thinking) to justify this.
3. ES2 9 "Theft by Subsidy" (*JDE,* January 1846), where he insists on the need to use "harsh language"—like the word "theft"—to describe the policies of governments which give benefits to some at the expense of others.[33]
4. ES3 6 "The People and the Bourgeoisie" (*LE,* 23 May 1847), in which he rejects the idea that there is an inevitable antagonism,

30. Gustave de Molinari, *Les Révolutions et le despotisme envisagés au point de vue des intérêts matériel* (1852).

31. Gustave de Molinari, *L'évolution économique du XIXe siècle* (1880), and *L'évolution politique et la Révolution* (1884).

32. In CW6 (forthcoming).

33. In his parody of Molière's parody of an oath of induction into the fraternity of doctors, Bastiat has a would-be customs officer promise "to steal, plunder, filch, swindle, and defraud" travellers. ES2 9, p. 176.

"*la guerre sociale*" (war between social groups or classes), between the people and the bourgeoisie, while there is one between the people and the aristocracy; he also introduces the idea of "*la classe électorale*" (the electoral class) which controls the French state by severely limiting the right to vote to the top one or two percent of the population.

5. ES2 1 "The Physiology of Plunder" (c. 1847), his first detailed discussion of the nature of plunder, which is contrasted with "production," and the historical progression of stages through which plunder has evolved from war, slavery, theocracy, and monopoly.

6. ES2 2 "Two Moral Philosophies" (c. 1847), where he distinguishes between religious moral philosophy, which attempts to persuade the men who live by plundering others (e.g., slave-owners and protectionists) to voluntarily refrain from doing so, and economic moral philosophy, which speaks to the victims of plundering and urges them to resist by understanding the true nature of their oppression and making it "increasingly difficult and dangerous" for their oppressors to continue exploiting them.

7. ES3 14 "Anglomania, Anglophobia" (c. 1847), where he discusses "the great conflict between democracy and aristocracy, between common law and privilege" and how this class conflict is playing out in England.

8. "Justice and Fraternity" (15 June 1848, *JDE*),[34] where Bastiat first used the terms "*la spoliation extra-légale*" (extra-legal plunder) and "*la spoliation légale*" (legal plunder); he describes the socialist state as "*un intermédiaire parasite et dévorant*" (a parasitic and devouring intermediary) which embodies "*la Spoliation organisée*" (organized plunder).

9. "Property and Plunder" (JDD, 24 July 1848),[35] in the "Fifth Letter" of which Bastiat talks about how transitory plunder gradually became "*la spoliation permanente*" (permanent plunder) when it became organized and entrenched by the state.

10. "Conclusion" to the first edition of *Economic Harmonies* (late

34. CW2, pp. 60–81 and online http://oll.libertyfund.org/titles/2450#lf1573-02_label_153.

35. CW2, pp. 147–84 and online http://oll.libertyfund.org/titles/2450#lf1573-02_label_218.

1849),[36] where he sketches what his unfinished book would have included, such as the opposite of the factors leading to "harmony," namely "*les dissonances sociales*" (the social disharmonies), such as plunder and oppression, or what he also calls "*les causes perturba-trices*" (disturbing factors); here he concentrates on theocratic and protectionist plunder.

11. "Plunder and Law" (*JDE,* 15 May 1850),[37] where he addresses the protectionists who have turned the law into a "sword" or "*un instrument de Spoliation*" (a tool of plunder) which the socialists will take advantage of when they get the political opportunity to do so.

12. "The Law" (June 1850),[38] Bastiat's most extended treatment of the natural law basis of property and how it has been "perverted" by the plunderers who have seized control of the state, where "*la loi a pris le caractère spoliateur*" (the law has taken on the character of the plunderer); he reminds the protectionists that the system of exploitation they had created before 1848 has been taken over, first by the socialists and soon by the Bonapartists, to be used for their own purposes, thus creating a new form of plundering by a new kind of class rule by "*gouvernementalisme*" (government bureaucrats).

13. WSWNS 3 "Taxes" (July 1850), on the conflict between the tax-payers and the payment of the salaries of civil servants, whom he likens to so many thieves, who provide no (or very little) benefit in return for the money they receive, and thus create a form of "legal parasitism."

14. WSWNS 6 "The Middlemen" (July 1850), where he describes the government's provision of some services as a form of "dreadful parasitism."

15. *Economic Harmonies,* part 2, chapter 17, "Private Services, Public Services" (published posthumously in 1851),[39] an examination of

36. In CW5 (forthcoming). See also the FEE edition online http://oll.libertyfund .org/titles/79#lf0187_head_074.

37. CW2, pp. 266–76 and online http://oll.libertyfund.org/titles/2450#lf1573-02 _label_331.

38. CW2, pp. 107–46 and online http://oll.libertyfund.org/titles/2450#lf1573-02 _label_197.

39. In CW5 (forthcoming). See also the FEE edition online http://oll.libertyfund .org/titles/79#lf0187_label_179.

the extent to which "public services" are productive or plunderous; he discusses how in the modern era "*la spoliation par l'impôt s'exerce sur une immense échelle*" (plunder by means of taxation is exercized to a high degree), but rejects the idea that they are plunderous "*par essence*" (by their very nature); beyond a very small number of limited activities (such as public security, managing public property) the actions of the state are "*autant d'instruments d'oppression et de spoliation légales*" (only so many tools of oppression and legal plunder); he warns of the danger of the state serving the private interests of "*les fonctionnaires*" (state functionaries) who become plunderers in their own right; the plundered class is deceived by sophistry into thinking that they will benefit from whatever the plundering classes seize as a result of the "ricochet" or trickle down effect[40] as they spend their ill-gotten gains.

40. This, "the trickle down effect," is the second meaning Bastiat gave to the term "ricochet effect," which he later reserved to the idea of perhaps unintended flow on effects of government intervention. See pp. 457–61.

The Chamber of Deputies and Elections

During the Restoration (1815–30) and the July Monarchy (1830–48) France was ruled by a king, an upper house of lords (Chamber of Peers), and a lower house of elected representatives (Chamber of Deputies). The Revolution of February 1848 overthrew the monarchy and suspended the Chamber of Peers, replacing them with a republic (the Second Republic) with a single elected body called the National Assembly, which for the first year (4 May 1848–27 May 1849) was known as the Constituent Assembly as a new constitution was being developed, and then the Legislative Assembly, which lasted until Louis-Napoléon's coup d'état of December 1851.

Elections to the Chamber of Deputies between 1815 and 1848 were by limited manhood suffrage. Voters were drawn from a small number of people who were at least thirty years old and who paid at least fr. 300 in direct taxes (land tax, door and window tax, tax on businesses; these requirements were lowered in 1830 to twenty-five years and fr. 200). Men could not stand for election unless they were at least forty years old and paid at least fr. 1,000 in direct taxes (these requirements were lowered in 1830 to thirty years and fr. 500). These property and tax requirements limited the electorate to a small group of wealthy individuals which numbered only 89,000 in the Restoration, 180,000 in 1831, and a maximum of about 240,000 on the eve of the 1848 Revolution. In addition, the 1820 Law of the Double Vote gave the top 25 percent of the wealthiest voters the right to vote for an additional two deputies per département. Bastiat referred to this small group as the *classe électorale* (the electoral class).[1] Deputies were elected to a term of five years; one-fifth of their number were elected each year, and they were not paid a salary, which meant that only government civil servants (who could sit in

1. See ES3 6, p. 286.

the Chamber concurrently with their government job)[2] or the wealthy could afford to run for office. Deputies could not initiate legislation; that was a prerogative of the king. The Chamber consisted of 258 Deputies in 1816, 430 in 1820, 459 in 1831, and 460 in 1839. General elections were held in July 1831, June 1834, November 1837, March 1839, July 1842, and August 1846.

The following is a summary of the elections held between 1839 and 1846:

The fifth legislature of the July Monarchy was elected in stages on 2 March and 6 July 1839. The republican and "third party" coalition won with 240 seats; the Conservative block got 199; and the Legitimists won only 20. King Louis-Philippe lacked a majority and dissolved the government on 16 June 1842.

The sixth legislature of the July Monarchy was elected on 9 July 1842. The Conservatives won with 266 seats, and the Opposition won 193. King Louis-Philippe dissolved the government on 16 July 1846.

The seventh legislature of the July Monarchy was elected on 1 August 1846. The Conservatives won with 290 seats, and the Opposition won 168. The government was dissolved when the Revolution of February 1848 broke out.

The February Revolution of 1848 introduced universal manhood suffrage (twenty-one years or older), and the Constituent Assembly (April 1848) had nine hundred members (minimum age of twenty-five). Over nine million men were eligible to vote, and 7.8 million men voted (84 percent of registered voters) in an election held on 23 and 24 April 1848. Bastiat was elected to represent the département of the Landes in the Constituent Assembly of the Second Republic. He was the second delegate elected out of seven, with a vote of 56,445. The largest block of deputies were monarchists (290), followed by moderate republicans such as Bastiat (230) and extreme republicans and socialists (55). The remainder were unaligned.

In the first and only presidential election, held on 10–11 December 1848 under the new constitution, 7.4 million people voted, making Napoléon Bonaparte's nephew, Louis-Napoléon, the president of the Second Republic. The candidate that Bastiat supported, General Cavaignac, received 1.4 million votes (19 percent) to Louis-Napoléon's 5.5 million votes (74 percent).

---

2. Bastiat campaigned to ban civil servants from also sitting in the Chamber. See "Parliamentary Conflicts of Interest" (CW1, pp. 452–57).

In the election of 13–14 May 1849 for the Legislative Assembly, 6.7 million men voted (out of 9.9 million registered voters). Bastiat was elected to the Legislative Assembly to represent the département of the Landes. He received 25,726 votes out of 49,762. The largest block in the Legislative Assembly was "the Party of Order" (monarchists and Bonapartists; 500), followed by the extreme left ("Montagnards" or democratic socialists; 200) and the moderate republicans (80). Bastiat was part of this latter group.

FRENCH POLITICAL PARTIES

The following were the main political groups in the late 1840s when Bastiat was writing and becoming politically active:

The Doctrinaires, moderate royalists who supported the Charter of 1815 and Louis XVIII. François Guizot was their leading spokesman.

The Legitimists, who were supporters of the descendants of Charles X. They were spectacularly successful in the May 1849 elections in the "Party of Order," winning two-thirds of the seats. One of their leading advocates was Odilon Barrot.

The republicans, who were relatively weak even though France became a republic three times in less than a century, in 1792, 1848, and 1870. General Lafayette was an important figure during the 1820s, but the group's supporters fractured into socialist and liberal groups who had little else in common. Bastiat was a "moderate republican" during the Second Republic and usually sat with the left in the Chamber.

The Montagnards, radical socialists who modeled themselves on the Mountain faction of the first French Revolution. Ledru-Rollin was one of their leading advocates.

The Orléanists, who were supporters of the overthrown Louis-Philippe.

The Bonapartists, who were supporters of Napoléon, both the Emperor Napoléon I and then his nephew Louis-Napoléon, who was elected president of the Second Republic in December 1848 before seizing power in a coup d'état in December 1851 and proclaiming himself Napoléon III, Emperor of the French.

The Party of Order, which originated with the Comité de la rue de Poitiers, a group of conservative politicians who came together in May 1848 on the rue de Poitiers following an unsuccessful demonstration of radicals at the National Assembly. The group (numbering between two hundred and four hundred) met weekly and was made up of a broad coalition of conservative, legitimist, Bonapartist, and liberal groups. They supported General Cavaignac's suppression of the riots in June 1848 and then Louis-Napoléon's run for president of the Republic in December. Toward the end of 1848 the group began to be called the "Party of Order," and it became increasingly monarchical and conservative. In the national election of January 1849 the Party of Order's slogan was "Order, Property, Religion," and it fought bitterly against the party of the left, the Montagnards (the Mountain) and the Democratic Socialists. The Party of Order won a majority of seats (450) to the Left's 180. Moderate republicans won 75.

All of the political groups were protectionist to one degree or another, and the socialists were both protectionist and extremely interventionist as well. Free traders like Bastiat were very much in the minority and could draw upon only a few lukewarm supporters in the Doctrinaire and Bonapartist groups.

FRENCH NEWSPAPERS

We know from his letters that Bastiat was a keen reader of the periodical press and often wrote letters to the editor and short articles for the local papers before he came to Paris. Between 1846 and 1850, when he had moved to Paris, Bastiat participated in numerous polemics in the French press where he vigorously engaged with protectionists and socialists on a variety of topics. At one point he went so far as to provide a list of the proprotectionist journals he read and debated with (*Le Moniteur industriel, Le Journal des débats, Le Constitutionnel, La Presse, Le Commerce, L'Esprit public, Le National*) and the more free-trade journals (*Le Courrier français, Le Siècle, La Patrie, L'Époque, La Réforme, La Démocratie pacifique, L'Atelier*), even though most of the latter did not meet his high expectations of free-trade rigor.

Bastiat's most famous polemic was with the anarchist and socialist Proudhon, in the latter's journal *La Voix du peuple* (The Voice of the People) on the topic of "Intérêt et principal" (Interest and Principal), which appeared in serial form between 22 October 1849 and 11 February 1850 and was then published as a booklet. The main schools of French socialism all had journals and newspapers: the Saint-Simonians published *Le Producteur, journal philosophique de l'industrie, de la science et des beaux arts* (1825–26, 5 vols.); *Le Globe, journal de la religion saint-simonienne* (1830–32); and *L'Organisateur* (1830–32). The followers of Fourier published *La Réforme industrielle ou le phalanstère* (1832–33); *La Phalange; La Démocratie pacifique* (1843–51);

Le Nouveau-monde (1839–). The "humanitarian socialists" such as Pierre Leroux published *Revue social, ou Solution pacifique du problème du prolétariat* (1845–47) and *La Revue indépendante* (1841–48). Philippe Buchez published a journal written and produced by workers, *L'Atelier* (1840–50). *Le Populaire* (1833–35, 1841–51) was a socialist and utopian newspaper which supported the ideas of Étienne Cabet. *La Ruche populaire* (1839–49), founded by the Vinçard brothers, was the first weekly journal produced and edited by workers for workers.

Liberal journals included *Le Commerce* (1837–48), edited by Arnold Scheffer and others; *Le Courrier français* (1820–46), supported by the banker Jacques Lafitte and for which Bastiat and Molinari occasionally wrote; *Le Constitutionnel* (1815–), which had been the main opposition paper of the Restoration but became a supporter of the Orléanist regime during the July Monarchy; *Le Temps* (1829–42), a liberal daily newspaper founded by François Guizot and Jacques Coste which was very critical of the regime before the 1830 Revolution and less so afterward; the main Economist journal, *Le Journal des économistes* (1842–), to which Bastiat was a frequent contributor; *Le National* (1830–51), founded by Adolphe Thiers, François-Auguste Mignet, and Armand Carrel; *La Presse* (1836–), founded by Émile de Girardin; not to forget the journals which Bastiat founded and wrote for: *Le Libre-échange* (1846–48), *La République française* (February–March 1848), and *Jacques Bonhomme* (June 1848).

Republican journals included *Le Journal du peuple* (1834–42), which had Lafayette as one of its founders but later became left-leaning in supporting the interests of workers; *La Reforme* (1843–50), edited by Ferdinand Flocon and Eugène Baune, whose staff filled many positions in the provisional government after February 1848; *La République* (1848–50), a radical republican daily newspaper edited by Eugène Bareste—its prior existence was probably the reason Bastiat and Molinari had to change the name of their revolutionary paper to *La République française,* as their first choice had already been taken.

Conservative and legitimist journals included *Le Quotidienne* (1814–47), an ultraroyalist journal founded by Joseph Michaud; *Le Journal des débats* (1789–1944), edited by François-René de Chateaubriand, one of the most prestigious journals in France which was able to survive the vicissitudes of French political change—it should be noted that Bastiat published the longer version of his famous essay "The State" in the 25 September 1848 issue of *Le Journal des débats* and that Gustave de Molinari was an editor in the 1870s;

L'Echo français (1829–47), a legitimist newspaper which eventually merged with two other journals due to falling subscriptions; *La France* (1834–47), a daily legitimist newspaper; *La Gazette de France,* a very long-lived legitimist newspaper; *La Nation* (1843–1845), a moderate newspaper which supported the July Monarchy; *La Revue des deux mondes* (1829–1944), a liberal Orléanist journal which appeared fortnightly and became the most important literary review of the nineteenth century—Economists such as Michel Chevalier and Léon Faucher published articles in this review.

The official newspaper of the French government was *Le Moniteur.*

Hard-to-classify journals included the satirical *Le Charivari* (1832–1902), founded by Charles Philipon and Louis Desnoyers, which published among others the cartoons Honoré of Daumier; and *Le Corsaire* (1822–52), a liberal satirical and literary journal which was closed down by Louis-Napoléon.

For those journals Bastiat mentions by name, we have tried to provide some details in the glossary.

FRENCH GOVERNMENT ADMINISTRATIVE REGIONS

French government administrative regions in descending order of size are the following: regions, départements, arrondissements ("districts"), cantons ("municipalities" or "counties"), and communes ("villages" or "towns").

In the eighteenth century France was divided into about 40 provinces which were replaced by the system of 83 départements in 1790, which was expanded to 130 in 1809 when Napoléon's empire had reached its furthest extent. In Bastiat's day there were 86 départements. The old provinces were divided into about 20 administrative regions which were each in turn divided into about six départements, each of which was administered by a prefect (*préfet*). Bastiat's family lived in the city of Bayonne in what had been the province of Guyenne and Gascony and which became the département of Pyrénées-Atlantiques in the region of Aquitaine (prefectural capital in Bordeaux). The départements are divided into three or four districts or arrondissements with a main city or town called a subprefecture which is administered by a subprefect (*sous-préfet*). Each arrondissement is divided into cantons, which are in turn divided into communes. The départements are administered by a *conseil général* (general council), which is an elected body responsible for maintaining local schools, roads, and other infrastructure.

The town where Bastiat lived, Mugron, was a commune in the canton of Mugron, in the arrondissement of Dax, in the département of the Landes, in the region of Aquitaine. He was appointed magistrate (justice of the peace) in the commune of Mugron in 1831, elected to the General Council of the département of the Landes in 1833 (and reelected in 1839), and on 23 April 1848 he was elected to represent the département of the Landes in the Constituent Assembly of the Second Republic. He was elected again on 1 August 1849 to represent the Landes in the first National Assembly of the Republic.

GENERAL COUNCILS (CONSEILS GÉNÉRAUX DE DÉPARTEMENT)

The general council is a chamber in each French département that deliberates on subjects concerning that département. It has one representative per county (canton): twenty-eight at the time for the Landes département, thirty-one today; this representative is elected for nine years (six years today). Its functions have varied over time. The law of 22 December 1789 created an assembly in each département consisting of thirty-six elected members. In February 1800 this was replaced by members appointed by the government. During the July Monarchy election of members of the council was again introduced in a reform of 1833, but it was limited by the property and taxpaying requirements of the electoral law (only taxpayers who paid a minimum amount of direct taxes were allowed to vote). Universal manhood suffrage for council elections was introduced under the law of 3 July 1848. Bastiat was elected general councilor in 1833 for the county of Mugron after the reform of 1833 was enacted, a post he held until his death. At that time, the council deliberations had to be approved by the prefect.

GENERAL COUNCILS OF COMMERCE, MANUFACTURING, AND AGRICULTURE

General Councils for Commerce (1802), Manufacturing (1810), and Agriculture (1819) were set up within the Ministry of the Interior to bring together commercial, manufacturing, and agricultural elites to advise the government and to comment on legislation. Their membership came from either members of the chambers of commerce and industry or by appointment by the minister concerned. An ordinance of 1831 created within the Ministry of Commerce a *Conseil supérieur* (Superior Council) which had the authority to conduct official inquiries into matters such as tariff policy. It drew its membership from twelve people nominated by the Crown and the presidents of the three General Councils of Commerce, Manufacturing, and Agriculture and remained in existence until 1850, when all the Councils were amalgamated into one. It was under the auspices of the Superior Council for Commerce that an important inquiry into tariff policy was conducted in October 1834. The Economists criticized the Councils because their members were usually ardent supporters of tariffs, and they were composed of the largest and most politically well-connected businessmen from the large manufacturing and port towns to the exclusion of smaller traders and manufacturers. Horace Say argued that as important as this inquiry was in bringing significant economic information before the public, it also served as a way for the major beneficiaries of government tariffs and subsidies to organize their opposition to any change in government policy. Say argued that this was when an organized coalition of protected industries initially emerged in France.

In February 1850 the three General Councils were amalgamated into one General Council of Agriculture, Manufacturing, and Commerce. It had 236 members: 96 for agriculture, 59 for industry, 73 for commerce, and 8 for Algeria and the colonies. Its role was to advise the government on economic matters. The first session took place from 7 April to 11 May 1850 in the Luxembourg Palace and was opened by the president of the Republic.[1]

THE FRENCH ARMY AND CONSCRIPTION

The modern mass conscript army was pioneered by the French during the Revolution. A law of August 1793 ordered a *levée en masse* (large-scale call-up) of all unmarried men aged eighteen to twenty-five with no substitution allowed — this was called a "requisition." A law of September 1798 (the Jourdan Law) made it obligatory for all males between the ages of twenty and twenty-five to serve five years in the army with no substitution allowed — this was called "conscription" or *levée forcée*. Conscription was technically abolished under the Charter of 1814, but new legislation that was enacted in 1818 filled the army with a mixture of voluntary recruits and others chosen by lot to make up any shortfall in enlistment — this was called *recrutement*. It required military service for twelve years, six in the army and six in the reserves. An unwilling conscript could buy their way out by paying a third party to take their place. There were also many categories for exemption which were decided by boards in the local cantons which were given quotas of recruits

1. See Léon Say, "Conseil général," in *DEP* 1:458 – 60; Horace Say, "Enquêtes," in *DEP* 1:701 – 6.

to fill each year. The length of service was reduced to eight years in 1824 and then seven years in 1832.[1] Some 80,000 new recruits were needed each year to maintain the size of the French army (*armée de terre*) at its full strength of about 400,000 men in the late 1840s. During the Third Republic (1872) service in the army was again made compulsory for all males. Conscription came to an end in France in 1996.[2]

It was a common practice for those conscripted by the drawing of lots (*tirage au sort*) to pay for a replacement or substitute to take their place in the ranks. The liberal publisher and journalist Émile de Girardin estimated that about one quarter of the entire French army consisted of replacements who had been paid fr. 1,800–2,400 to take the place of some young man who had been called up but did not want to serve. The schedule of payments depended on the type of service: fr. 1,800–2,000 for the infantry; 2,000–2,400 for the artillery, cavalry, and other specialized forces. This meant that only quite well-off men could afford to pay these amounts to avoid army service, thus placing a greater burden on poor agricultural workers and artisans. During the 1848 Revolution there was a pamphlet war, calling for the abolition of conscription, but this was unsuccessful.[3]

In *What Is Seen and What Is Not Seen,* Bastiat proposed immediately reducing the size of the French army by 100,000 men from its total in 1849 of about 390,000 men (a reduction of 25.6 percent). The expenditure on the army in 1849 was fr. 346,319,558. Total government expenditure in 1849 was fr. 1.573 billion, with expenditure on the armed forces making up 29.6 percent of the total budget. Bastiat estimates that 100,000 soldiers cost the French state fr. 100 million.

STATE FUNDING OF EDUCATION

Several state-run educational institutions were established by Napoléon: the École militaire (1803), the École polytéchnique (1794, 1804), the Écoles nationales des arts et métiers (1803), and a single university for France,

1. Pierre-Didier Joffres, *Études sur le recrutement de l'armée; suivies d'un Projet de loi* (Paris: J. Dumaine, 1843), pp. 55–56.

2. See A. Legoyt, "Recrutement," in *DEP* 2:498–503; "Conscription," in *Dictionnaire de l'armée de terre,* pp. 1539–42.

3. See *Plus de conscription! (Signé: Allyre Bureau, l'un des rédacteurs de "la Démocratie pacifique")* (Paris: Impr. de Lange Lévy, 1848) and Émile de Girardin, *Les 52: Abolition de l'esclavage militaire* (Paris: M. Lévy, 1849).

L'Université impériale (1808). There were also some non-state institutions, such as the École centrale des arts et manufactures (1829), the École mutuelle (1815), and the Écoles primaires protestantes (1816).

A major restructuring took place with Guizot's law on public education (1833), which stated that every commune in France with more than five hundred inhabitants would have an elementary school for boys (girls were included in 1867), every town over six thousand people would have a higher primary school, and every département would run a teaching training school. A system of state school inspectors was established and a minimum wage of fr. 200 per annum was enacted. School attendance was not compulsory (until 1881–82), fees were charged (again until 1881–82), and the education included religious instruction. Secondary and higher education was placed under the control of the state-run university. Freedom of education was hotly debated during the Second Republic, and major reforms resulted in the Falloux Law of 1850. The notion of *la liberté d'enseignement* (freedom of education) meant different things to different political groups. For many it meant breaking the control of the central government and transferring it to the départements, and reducing the influence of the Catholic Church. For classical liberals like Bastiat it meant taking eduction completely out of the state sector and letting private groups provide educational services in the market.

In 1849 fr. 21.8 million was spent on public education, of which fr. 17.9 million went for the university and fr. 3.3 million for "science and letters."

ALGERIA

Algeria was invaded and conquered by France in 1830, and the occupied parts were annexed to France in 1834. The new constitution of the Second Republic (1848) declared that Algeria was no longer a colony but an integral part of France (with three départements) and that the emigration of French settlers would be officially encouraged and subsidized by the government. Emperor Napoléon III returned Algeria to military control in 1858. In 1848 about 200,000 of the population of 2.5 million were Europeans. The deputy Amédée Desjobert[1] in *Le Journal des économistes* gives a figure of fr. 125 million which was spent by the government in Algeria in 1847 and makes a very

---

1. Amédée Desjobert, "L'Algérie," *JDE*, T. 17, no. 66, May 1847, pp. 121–41; quote p. 121.

similar argument to that of Bastiat, that the money went to the troops and then into the hands of the merchants who serviced the needs of those troops.

In a debate in the National Assembly in 1848 (11 and 19 September) a budget of fr. 50 million was allocated to the Ministry of War for the years 1848–51 to "establish agricultural colonies in the provinces of Algeria and for works of public utility intended to assure their prosperity." The exact number of colonists was not specified, although a figure of twelve thousand for the year 1848 was mentioned. This subsidy would continue for at least three years, reaching fr. 17.5 million for each of the years 1851 and 1852. Over the four-year period each colonist would have received fr. 4,167 or a family of four some fr. 16,667. Bastiat at one stage mentions the figure of fr. 100 million per year as the level of true expenditure on Algeria. The actual state subsidy granted to French colonists who wished to settle in Algeria is hard to determine. The pro-colonizer Gustave Vesian lobbied for a community of ten thousand colonists living in three towns who would get other state benefits such as irrigated land, a guaranteed market for their grain in the domestic market, seed and food (and wine) for three years to get established, and low-interest loans.[2]

Bastiat comments on Algeria and colonization in his address "To the Electors of the District of Saint-Sever":

> To me it is a proven fact, and I venture to say a scientifically proven fact, that the colonial system is the most disastrous illusion ever to have led nations astray. I make no exception for the English, in spite of the specious nature of the well-known argument post hoc, ergo propter hoc.
>
> Do you know how much Algeria is costing you? From one-third to two-fifths of your four direct taxes, including the extra cents. Whoever among you pays three hundred francs in taxes sends one hundred francs annually to evaporate into the clouds over the Atlas mountains or to sink into the sands of the Sahara.[3]

2. See *Compte rendu des séances de l'Assemblée Nationale,* vol. 3, *Du 8 Août au 13 Septembre 1848,* Séance du 11 Septembre 1848, pp. 943–44; also vol. 4, *Du 14 Septembre au 20 Octobre 1848,* p. 117; and Vesian, *De la colonisation en Algérie.*

3. CW1, pp. 363–65.

FRENCH CURRENCY

French currency in the nineteenth century was based upon names and denominations which were a mixture of three different traditions, the Roman, the medieval, and the revolutionary, thus making the names somewhat confusing. A further complication comes from the fact that one has to keep distinct the name of the coin or monetary unit (e.g., "écu" or "louis") and its denomination or value ("livres" or "sous").[1]

The Roman tradition was based on silver coins where the highest-value coin was the "libra" (French = livre; English = pound), followed by the "solidus" (French = sol or sou; English = shilling), and then the "denarius" (French = denier; English = penny), which had the following comparative values: 1 livre = 20 sous = 240 deniers. The original value of the "libra" (livre) was one pound of silver. This was a duodecimal or base 12 system.

French currency during the medieval period was based on a gold coin called the *franc à cheval* (the Frank on horseback) which was minted in order to pay the ransom of King Jean II, who had been taken prisoner by the English. Other gold coins also circulated in the medieval period. Under Louis IX (1226–70) a gold coin known as the *denier d'or à l'écu* (gold denier with a shield), or *écu* for short, was popular.

Under the ancien régime Louis XIII in 1640 replaced the old franc with a system based on three coins: the *louis d'or* (gold Louis), the *louis d'argent* (silver Louis) or "silver écu," and the *liard* (made of copper). During the ancien régime several different types of livres were in circulation, the most common being from the city of Tours, known as the *livre tournois*. After the bankruptcy of the Banque générale established by John Law as a de facto state

---

1. A useful summary is 1 franc is equivalent to 100 centimes, or 20 sous.

bank in 1720 the *livre tournois* was seriously devalued and then abandoned and a new "livre" worth 0.31 grams of gold was introduced.

Another coin used in France owes its origin to the Greek *obelos* (obole). In the medieval period the obole was a copper coin officially worth 1/2 denier. In the ancien régime deniers were often divided into eighths; an obole was worth 4/8 denier, a *pite* was 2/8, and a *semi-pite* was 1/8. Over time, monetary devaluation eroded its value, so that the word "obole" came to mean a coin of minimal worth.

French currency was decimalized (converted to a base 10 system) in 1795 with the introduction of a new French franc, which was divisible into 100 centimes. The law of 7 January 1795 decreed the issuing of paper "assignats" denominated in francs and using as security the value of the property confiscated from the church and the nobility. A full decimalization law of 7 April 1795 defined not only the meter, liter, and gram but also the new French franc, which was fixed at a value of 5 grams of silver. Another law of 14 April 1796 decreed that the *livre tournois* and the new franc were almost identical in value at about 4.5 grams of silver.

FRENCH WEIGHTS AND MEASURES

As with currency, Bastiat uses terms which are a mixture of ancien régime and revolutionary practices. The metric system was introduced into France during the Revolution as part of the application of enlightened thinking to all aspects of life. The law of 17 April 1795 mandated the use of metric weights and measures to replace those which had been used under the ancien régime. For a time the two existed side by side until Prime Minister François Guizot passed the law of 4 July 1837, making metric measurements universal and compulsory. Below is a list of some commonly used measurements.

Quintal: The term "quintal" comes from the Latin and is a unit of measurement made of 100 subunits. In the ancien régime this meant a quintal was 100 *livres* (or pounds). After the metrification introduced by the French Revolution a quintal came to mean 100 kilograms (220 modern pounds weight).

Arpent: An arpent was 220 feet (*pied-du-roi* or royal feet) or 71.9 metres.

Lieue: A *lieue* (league) had several different meanings: an "old league" (*lieue ancienne*) was 10,000 feet (3.3 km); a "Paris league" (*lieue de Paris*) was 12,000 feet (3.9 km); and a "Postal league" (*ligue des Postes*) was 13,200 feet (4.3 km).

Acre: An acre was 48,400 square feet or 5,107 square meters or 0.51 hectares.
Centiare: A centiare was 1/10,000 hectare or 1 square meter. (A square arpent is about 3,400 square meters or 0.85 acres.)

Bastiat uses a number of terms to express the volume of wine, some of which are regional and not exactly defined. The most common one is *tonneau* (barrel or butt), which is 126 gallons. Bastiat also uses the term *pièce* (cask), which some dictionaries define as equal to a *tonneau* but which Bastiat defines here as one-quarter of a barrel. Since Bastiat was a wine grower himself we will defer to his knowledge of the matter. Tariffs and taxes were levied on a hectoliter of wine, for example. One hectoliter = 100 liters = 22 U.S. gallons.

Bastiat also uses the term *sole,* which is a small strip of land traditionally used for crop rotation (*assolement de culture*) in feudal agriculture. Each *sole* would be sown with a different crop which would be changed (rotated) from year to year in order to avoid the exhaustion of the soil.

FRENCH TAXATION

The following are the different taxes levied by the French government to which Bastiat refers in his writings: the wine and spirits tax; the octroi, or tax levied on goods brought into a town; the gabelle, or tax on salt; the *taxe de quarante-cinq centimes,* or the 45-centime tax, which was introduced on 16 March 1848 and which increased direct taxes on things such as land, movable goods, doors and windows, and trading licenses, by 45 percent; the *droits réunis* or combined indirect taxes; the forced labor obligations, or *corvées,* which were later converted into a direct money payment known as a *prestation.*

Wine and Spirits Tax

The wine and spirits tax was eliminated by the revolutionary parliament of 1789 but progressively reinstated during the empire. It comprised four components: (1) a consumption tax (10 percent of the sale price); (2) a license fee paid by the vendor, depending on the number of inhabitants; (3) a tax on circulation, which depended on the département; and (4) an entry duty for towns of more than four hundred inhabitants, depending on the sale price and the number of inhabitants. Being from a wine-producing region, Bastiat had always been preoccupied by such a law, which was very hard on the local farmers. This tax raised fr. 104 million in 1848.

Octroi

The "octroi," or tax on goods brought into a town or city, was imposed on consumer goods such as wine, beer, food (except for flour, fruit, and milk), firewood, animal fodder, and construction materials. All of these products had to pass through tollgates on the outskirts of the town or city, where they could be inspected and taxed. For example, King Louis XVI had 57 *barrières d'octroi* (tollgates) built around the city of Paris for this purpose.

In 1841 it was estimated that 1,420 communes throughout France imposed the octroi upon entry into their cities and towns, raising some fr. 75 million in revenue. The money was used to pay for the maintenance of roads, drains, lighting, and other public infrastructure. Although the Economists accepted the need for towns and cities to charge for these services, they objected to the octroi because it was not uniform across the nation, it fell more heavily on poorer consumers, it was very costly to collect, and, perhaps most important, it divided France with hundreds of separate internal customs barriers, which interfered with internal free trade. Not surprisingly, the octroi were much disliked and in the early days of the French Revolution in July 1789 the tollgates of Paris were set upon and many burned to the ground. The Constituent Assembly abolished the octroi in January 1791, but they were reestablished by the Directory in October 1798. Horace Say, the businessman son of the economist Jean-Baptiste Say, fought unsuccessfully to have the octroi abolished during the 1840s.[1] They were not abolished until 1943.

In 1845 the city of Paris imposed an octroi on all goods entering the city which raised fr. 48 million. Of this amount, fr. 26.1 million (53 percent of the total) was levied on wine and other alcoholic drinks. The tax on wine was the heaviest as a proportion of total value and the most unequally applied. Cheap table wine was taxed at 80–100 percent by value, while superior quality wine was taxed at 5–6 percent by value.[2]

Gabelle

The tax on salt, or *gabelle,* as it was known under the old regime, was a much-hated tax on an item essential for preserving and flavoring food. It was abolished during the Revolution but revived during the Restoration. In 1816

1. For a useful history of the octroi tax, see Say, *Paris, son octroi et ses emprunts;* and Esquirou de Parieu, "Octrois," in *DEP* 2:284–91.
2. Say, *Paris, son octroi et ses emprunts* (p. 11 for figures).

it was set at 30 centimes per kilogram, and in 1847 it raised fr. 70.4 million. During the Revolution of 1848 it was reduced to 10 centimes per kilogram, the level proposed by Bastiat in January 1847.[3] According to the budget papers of 1848 the French state raised fr. 38.2 million from tariffs on imported salt and fr. 13.4 million from the salt tax on internal sales.

"Taxe de Quarante-Cinq Centimes" (The 45-Centime Tax)

In the immediate aftermath of the February Revolution the government faced a budget crisis brought on by the decline in tax revenues and the increased demands being placed on it by new political groups. Louis-Antoine Pagès (Garnier-Pagès, 1803–78), a member of the provisional government and soon afterward mayor of Paris, was able to pass a new "temporary" tax law on 16 March 1848, which increased direct taxes on things such as land, movable goods, doors and windows, and trading licenses, by 45 percent. It was known as the *taxe de quarante-cinq centimes* (the 45-centime tax) and was deeply unpopular, prompting revolts and protests in the southwest of France.

Indirect Taxes and the "Droits Réunis" (Combined Taxes)

Many indirect taxes on consumer goods were abolished in the early years of the Revolution only to be reintroduced by Napoléon, who centralized their collection in 1804 by a single administrative body under the name of *droits réunis* (combined duties). In the Restoration the Charter of 1814 promised to abolish both the *droits réunis* and conscription, but these promises were not kept. The old indirect taxes were simply renamed *contributions indirectes* (indirect taxes or "contributions"), although they were imposed at a slightly reduced rate. In 1848 the state received fr. 307.9 million in indirect "contributions" (taxes) out of a total of fr. 1.391 billion, or 22 percent of all revenue. These taxes were levied on drink, salt, sugar, tobacco, gunpowder, and other goods.

The Prestation and the Corvée

Under the old regime the most hated of the taxes imposed on the peasantry were the forced labor obligations or *corvées* which required local farmers to work a certain number of days (eight) every year for their local lord or on various local and national roadworks. These were repealed and reinstated

3. See ES2 11, p. 189.

repeatedly over a period of about sixty years, beginning with Turgot's ordinances of March 1776. Forced labor obligations were reintroduced by Napoléon in 1802 under a new name, *prestations,* and were limited to work on local (not national) roads. They were abolished again in 1818 only to be reintroduced in 1824 at two days per year. This was increased to three days per year in 1836 with the further refinement that some individuals were able to buy their way out of service for a money payment. Courcelle Seneuil described the *prestations* as "vicious" and "like the old debris from feudal times, like the last vestige of barbarism and of the forced communal organization of labor."[4]

FRENCH TARIFF POLICY

French tariffs on manufactured goods such as textiles were very complex. In the case of textiles, many goods were prohibited outright in order to protect French manufacturers (what Bastiat called *le régime prohibitionniste*). Some products used to manufacture other goods, such as cotton thread used to make lace or tulle, were allowed entry upon payment of a tariff of fr. 7–8 per kilogram. Most finished goods had prohibitive duties imposed upon them, such as fr. 50–100 per piece in the case of cashmere scarves and fr. 550 per 100 kilograms for wool carpets. According to the budget papers of 1848 the French state raised fr. 202.1 million from tariffs and import duties out of total receipts of fr. 1,391 million, or 14.5 percent.[1]

Tariff policy during the Revolution was a chaotic affair. In a decree of 30–31 October 1790 the Constituent Assembly abolished all internal tariffs and duties, thus creating for the first time a largely free internal market in France. External tariffs were cut to a maximum of 20 percent by value, although some goods were prohibited entry into the French market. Tariffs were completely reorganized by a law of August 1791 which abolished most prohibitions on imported material, abolished tariffs on primary products used by French manufacturers and foodstuffs for consumers, and gradually reduced tariffs on manufactured goods to 20–25 percent by value of the goods imported. The decree of 1 March 1793 annulled all foreign trade treaties and prohibited the importation of a large number of goods, such as textiles, metal goods, and

4. Courcelle Seneuil, "Prestations," in *DEP* 2:428–30.
1. Horace Say, "Douanes," in *DEP* 1:578–604.

pottery. The decree of 29 September 1793 introduced the notorious "Maximum" or price control legislation which threw the internal French economy into considerable disarray. A decree of 31 January 1795 cut the tariff of 1791 by half to nine-tenths on many articles. This was reversed by a law of 23 November 1796 in order to increase revenue for the state.

This on-again, off-again tariff regime was changed by the tariff law of 21 November 1806 (the Berlin Decree) introducing Napoléon's Continental Blockade, which was designed to deny British goods access to the European market. Thus, the debate about tariff policy had completely shifted away from any concern with protection of domestic industry and revenue raising and had become an instrument of economic warfare against the British. In some instances tariffs were raised to absurd levels, such as fr. 300 per kilo on imported sugar. During the Restoration in 1816 tariffs on imported cotton, for example, were set at fr. 22 per 100 kilos. In 1822 there was a review of tariffs which served to create a protectionist regime around the interests of large landowners and favored manufacturers.

This process continued under the July Monarchy. The October 1834 government inquiry into French tariff policy raised hopes that there might be a reduction in the level of tariffs as the minister of commerce, Thiers, was in favor. However, the inquiry concluded that France should continue its policy of protectionism for industry and resulted in a detailed three-volume report based on its findings, issued by the Superior Council of Commerce in 1835. The list of members of the inquiry reads like a who's who of the protectionists Bastiat mentions and criticizes throughout *Economic Sophisms*.[2] The English free trader and key figure in the Anti–Corn Law League Thomas Perronet Thompson wrote a critique of the French inquiry which was translated and published as *Contre-enquête par l'homme aux quarante écus* (1835).[3] The Superior Council's report consolidated the protectionist regime and set tariff rates which would last until the 1848 Revolution.

The free traders in France were inspired by the success of Richard Cobden's Anti–Corn Law League, which was founded in 1838 and had achieved its aim of abolishing protection for agricultural products by mid-1846. The Association pour la liberté des échanges (Free Trade Association) was

2. See Duchâtel, *Enquête relative à diverses prohibitions établies à l'entrée des produits étrangers* (1835). It was 1,459 pages long and was printed by the government printing office at taxpayers' expense.

3. See Fonfrède, "Du système prohibitif."

founded in February 1846 in Bordeaux with Bastiat as the secretary of the board and editor of its journal *Le Libre-échange*. A push by Bastiat and other free traders to have the French chamber pass similar legislation in 1847 failed. Léon Faucher states that the attempt by the free traders in the Chamber to revise French tariff policy in a more liberal direction failed because they were outmaneuvered by the protectionists. The opportunity arose when a bill came before the Chamber on 31 March 1847, but the committee assigned by the Chamber to write the report was stacked with protectionists, and the lobbying by the Association for the Defense of National Employment was very effective.[4] France did not begin to loosen its policy of protectionism until the Anglo-French Commercial Treaty of 1860 which was signed by Richard Cobden for the British government and Michel Chevalier for the French government (also known as the Cobden-Chevalier Trade Treaty).

In Bastiat's day a veritable army of public servants worked for the Customs Service. According to Horace Say, there were 27,727 individuals (1852 figures) employed in two "divisions"—one of administrative personnel (2,536) and the other of "agents on active service" (24,727).[5] According to the budget papers for 1848, the Customs Service collected fr. 202 million in customs duties and salt taxes and their administrative and collection costs totaled fr. 26.4 million or 13 percent of the amount collected.

Assessing the average rate of tariffs in different countries is very difficult, given the huge variety of products, the manner in which they were taxed (by weight, volume, or price), and whether the tariff was for "fiscal" purposes (to raise revenue for the state) or protectionist purposes (to favor domestic producers at the expense of foreign producers). A useful comparative study of tariff rates in Britain, France, Germany, Italy, and Spain in the nineteenth century is provided by Antonio Tena Jungito, who compares average tariff rates of all goods taxed as well as average tariff rates on protected items alone (leaving out the usually low rates on items taxed for fiscal purposes only). From his data we can conclude the following: British aggregate tariff rates (excluding fiscal goods) peaked at about 15 percent in 1836 and began dropping in 1840, reaching a low point of about 6 percent in 1847 (the abolition of the Corn Laws was announced in January 1846 and was to come into full effect in 1849), and continued to drop steadily throughout the rest of the

4. Léon Faucher, "Du projet de loi sur les douanes," *JDE* 19 (February 1848): 254–65.
5. Horace Say, "Douane," in *DEP* 1:578–604 (figures from p. 597).

century, reaching a plateau of less than 1 percent between 1880 and 1903. France had an average rate of about 12 percent in 1836 which was still around 11 percent in 1848 before it began to drop steadily, reaching 5 percent in 1857, spiking briefly to 7.5 percent in 1858, and dropping steadily again to about 1.5 percent in 1870 (the Anglo-French Commercial Treaty was signed in 1860), before again moving steadily upward to about 8 percent in 1893. In 1849 the rates were about 6 percent in Britain and 10 percent in France.[6]

As a point of comparison, in the United States tariff rates fluctuated wildly as the protectionist North and the free-trade South fought for control of the federal government before the Civil War. In 1832 the Protectionist Tariff imposed an average rate of 33 percent; the Compromise Tariff of 1833 intended to lower rates to a flat 20 percent; and the 1846 Tariff created four tariff schedules for goods which imposed 100 percent, 40 percent, 30 percent, or 20 percent depending upon the particular kind of goods. The average rate in the United States in 1849 was about 23 percent and in 1890 about 40 percent, rates that definitely constitute "protectionist" not "fiscal" tariffs according to Bastiat's definition (5 percent).[7]

THE FRENCH RAILWAYS

The first French railway was opened in 1828. It had begun as a private initiative of coal-mining companies to facilitate the transport of coal to nearby rivers but turned into a hybrid of state and favored private groups.

The first common-carrier train for both passengers and freight was opened in 1837 between Paris and LePecq. In 1842 the government decided to encourage the building of a national network. Under the Railway Law of 11 June 1842 the government ruled that five main railways radiating out of Paris would be built in cooperation with private industry. The government would build and own the rights-of-way, bridges, tunnels, and railway stations, while private industry would lay the tracks and build and maintain the rolling stock and the lines. The government would also set rates and regulate safety. The first railway concessions were issued by the government

6. See Tena-Junguito, "Assessing the Protectionist Intensity of Tariffs in Nineteenth-Century European Trade Policy."

7. See Taussig, *The Tariff History of the United States,* pp. 110–115; and Irwin, "Tariffs and Growth in Late Nineteenth Century America," pp. 15–30.

in 1844–45, triggering a wave of speculation and attempts to secure concessions. Between 1846 and 1851 the following major railway networks were inaugurated:

Chemin de fer du Nord (June 1846)
Chemin de fer d'Amiens à Boulogne (May 1848)
Chemin de fer de Compiègne à Noyon (March 1849)
Chemin de fer de Paris à Strasbourg (July 1849)
Chemin de fer de Tours à Angers (August 1849)
Chemin de fer d'Argenteuil (April 1851)

French railway companies were hamstrung by the fact that one of their biggest costs, the purchase of steel rails, remained high because of high tariffs which kept cheaper foreign steel out of the French market. In the 1850s smaller unprofitable concessions were amalgamated into six main railway companies, which enjoyed a monopoly within their geographic area. In 1859 the government guaranteed the interest on all loans made by railway companies to investors. In 1908 the government purchased the Ouest railway company and in 1937 nationalized all the others into one government railway system, the Société nationale des chemins de fer français (SNCF).[1]

SLAVERY IN FRANCE

Slavery did not have a strong presence within France, but it played a major role in the French Caribbean colonies, such as Saint-Dominique (Haiti). Under the influence of the ideas of the French Revolution, slavery was abolished in 1794, and a number of freed blacks were elected to various French legislative bodies. Napoléon reintroduced slavery in 1802 and fought a bloody but unsuccessful war in order to prevent a free black republic from emerging in Haiti.

In 1807, under pressure from such abolitionists as William Wilberforce and Thomas Clarkson, Britain passed an act that abolished the slave trade, much of which was carried in British vessels. The United States followed suit in 1808 with a similar ban. This had significant implications for the southern states of the United States and the French Caribbean, where slavery remained firmly in place. The British Navy patroled the oceans, insisting upon a "right of inspection" to look for slaves being carried from Africa to the

---

1. See Michel Chevalier, "Chemins de fer," in *DEP* 1:337–62.

Caribbean and to punish those involved in the trade as pirates. This policy was a serious bone of contention between Britain and France, as the latter viewed the British policy as interference in their sovereign right to engage in trade and shipping. Slavery was abolished in the British Caribbean in 1833, again in the French colonies during the 1848 revolution, and in the United States in 1865 (by the Thirteenth Amendment to the Constitution).

Bastiat would most certainly have voted for a bill presented by Victor Schoelcher, the undersecretary for the navy and colonies, on 27 April 1848, to abolish slavery in French colonies. In Bastiat's planned but unwritten *History of Plunder,* slavery was one of the four major stages through which the institution of organized plunder evolved: these started with war, went through slavery and theocracy, and ended with the present period of government-protected monopoly.

Public Works

During the 1840s, the July Monarchy undertook a series of expensive public works projects which concerned the economists. Traditionally the French state spent money on roads, bridges, canals, rivers, ports, monuments, and public buildings, but these expeditures were overtaken by two new spending projects, namely the construction of the fortifications of Paris (1841–44) and the government's participation in building the railroads after 1842. In the French government's budget for 1848, a sum of fr. 111 million was allocated for civilian public works, which did not include public works paid for by the army or navy (such as in Algeria). The economist Michel Chevalier provides a useful summary of expenditure on public works during the July Monarchy between 1831 and 1845.[1] He records the following totals: bridges (fr. 15 million) monuments and public buildings (fr. 80 million), rivers (fr. 152 million), ports (fr. 176 million), canals (fr. 234 million), roads (fr. 233 million), and railways (fr. 741 million), for a total of fr. 1.614 billion.

The first new spending initiative was the creation of Adolphe Thiers, who planned to build a massive military wall 33 km (21 miles) in circumference around the city of Paris with sixteen surrounding forts.[2] All people and goods

1. Michel Chevalier, "*Statistique des travaux publics, sous le Gouvernement de Juillet,*" Annuaire de l'économie politique pour 1849, pp. 209–37.
2. Patricia O'Brien, "*L'Embastillement de Paris: The Fortification of Paris during the July Monarchy,*" *French Historical Studies* 9, no. 1 (1975): 63–82.

entering or leaving the city had to pass through one of the seventeen large entry gates built into the wall. This project was budgeted to cost fr. 150 million and was completed in 1844. The total expenditure would have been much higher if the state had not used the labor of thousands of conscripts to dig the ditches and build the wall. "Thiers' Wall," as it was known, was strongly opposed by liberals, such as the astronomer François Arago and the economist Michel Chevalier, as another example of the "Bastillization of Paris."[3]

The second major public-works program undertaken at this time was the building of the railways. Government spending on railways rapidly expanded after the law of 11 June 1842 authorized the French state to partner with private companies in the building of five railroad networks spreading out from Paris. (See the Glossary on "French Railways.") According to Chevalier, annual direct out-of-pocket expenses (not counting loan guarantees to railway companies) doubled from about fr. 6 million in 1840 to about fr. 12 million in 1842, and then increased by a factor of seven to fr. 86 million by 1845. According to Lobet, between 1842 and the end of 1847, the state had spent about fr. 420 million in subsidies, loan guarantees, and construction costs.[4]

3. François Arago, *Sur les Fortifications de Paris* (Paris: Bachelier, 1841) and *Études sur les fortifications de Paris, considérées politiquement et militairement* (Paris: Pagnerre, 1845). Michel Chevalier, *Les fortifications de Paris, lettre à M. Le Comte Molé* (Paris: Charles Gosselin, 1841) and *Cours d'Économie politique fait au Collège de France par Michel Chevalier* (Bruxelles: Meline, Cans, 1851), vol. 2, "Douzième leçon. Concours de l'armée française aux travaux des fortifications de Paris," pp. 183–96. First ed. 1844.

4. Lobet, *"Chemins de fer,"* Annuaire de l'économie politique (1848), pp. 289–311. Data on p. 294.

French Government's Budgets for Fiscal Years 1848 and 1849

List of Tables:

TABLE 1. SUMMARY OF EXPENDITURE AND INCOME.

	1848	1849
Expenditure	1,446,210,170	1,572,571,069
Income	1,391,276,510	1,411,732,007
Deficit	**54,933,660**	**160,839,062**

Data were taken from the following articles and corrected where necessary:
"Budget de 1848," *Annuaire de l'Économie politique et de la statistique pour 1848,*
pp. 29–51.
"Budget de 1849," in *Annuaire de l'Économie politique et de la statistique pour 1850,*
pp. 18–28.

TABLE 2. SUMMARY OF EXPENDITURE.

	1848	1849
I. Public Debt	384,346,191	455,143,796
II. Grants to Government Bodies	14,922,150	9,608,288
III. Ministerial Services*	731,335,104	882,057,325
IV. Administrative Costs**	156,892,495	155,265,320
V. Reimbursements, Subsidies	74,185,730	70,496,340
VI. Extraordinary Items	84,528,500	
Total	**1,446,210,170**	**1,572,571,069**

"Budget de 1848" in *Annuaire de l'Économie politique et de la statistique pour 1848,*
p. 41.
"Budget de 1849" in *Annuaire de l'Économie politique et de la statistique pour 1850,*
p. 18.
* See table 3.III and table 6.
** See table 8 for details.

TABLE 3. DETAILS OF EXPENDITURE.

	1848	*1849*
I. Public Debt	*384,346,191*	**455,143,796**
Consolidated debt	*291,287,951*	300,789,006
Other		63,795,490
Loans for canals and other works	*9,110,300*	
Floating debt interest		23,000,000
Other interest payments	*29,000,000*	8,960,300
For pensions	*54,947,940*	58,599,000
II. Grants to Nat. Assembly, Executive Office	*14,922,150*	**9,608,288**
Civil List	*13,300,000*	
Chamber of Peers	*790,000*	
Chamber of Deputies	*832,150*	
National Assembly		8,362,688
Executive		1,245,600
III. Ministerial Services*	*731,335,104*	**882,057,325**
Justice	*26,739,095*	26,460,230
Religion	*39,564,833*	41,066,393
Foreign Affairs	*8,885,422*	7,241,367
Public Education	*18,038,033*	21,751,820
Interior	*116,564,738*	128,951,534
Agriculture and Commerce	*14,384,500*	17,385,823
Public Works	*110,922,050*	157,746,633
War	*322,010,382*	346,319,558
Navy and Colonies	*138,540,895*	119,206,857
Finance	*17,753,136*	15,927,110
(Less supplemental expenditure from previous years)	*82,067,980*	
IV. Administrative Costs*	*136,892,495*	**155,265,320**
V. Reimbursements, Subsidies	*74,185,730*	**70,496,340**
VI. Extraordinary Items	*84,528,500*	
Total	*1,426,210,170*	**1,572,571,069**

"Budget de 1848" in *Annuaire de l'Économie politique et de la statistique pour 1848,* p. 29–41.

"Budget de 1849" in *Annuaire de l'Économie politique et de la statistique pour 1850,* pp. 18–23.

* See table 6 for more details.

TABLE 4. SUMMARY OF REVENUE.

	1848	1849
I. Direct Taxes*	*420,669,956*	426,040,014
II. Registrations, Stamp Duty, Public Property*	*263,359,490*	234,098,296
III. Forests and Fisheries*	*38,395,700*	27,072,100
IV. Customs, Salt Monopoly*	*202,112,000*	156,823,000
V. Indirect Taxes*	*307,962,000*	287,696,000
VI. Post Office*	*51,738,000*	49,876,000
VII. Diverse Revenue	*47,053,466*	42,869,234
VIII. Diverse Products	*19,463,398*	28,423,000
IX. Extraordinary Resources	*20,298,500*	158,834,363
(adjustment for discrepancy in totals)	*20,224,000*	
Total	*1,391,276,510*	1,411,732,007

The figures for 1848 were calculated by the editor.

"Budget de 1849" in *Annuaire de l'Économie politique et de la statistique pour 1850,* p. 18.

* See table 5.

TABLE 5. DETAILS OF REVENUE.

Source of Income	*1848*	*1849*
General Total Revenue (including debt reserve)	1,371,052,010	1,411,732,007
Total Income from Taxes and Charges (my calculation differs from that in the *Annuaire* by 20,224,000)	*1,350,754,010*	
I. Direct Taxes	*420,669,956*	426,040,014
Land Tax	*279,456,080*	281,274,204
Personal & Property Tax	*59,313,060*	60,113,740
Door & Window Tax	*34,796,826*	35,655,470
Trading Licenses	*46,310,100*	48,190,340
Other Items	*793,890*	806,260
II. Registrations, Stamp Duty, Public Property	*263,359,490*	234,098,296
Registrations, fees, levies	*216,324,000*	179,424,000
Stamp duty	*40,556,000*	29,206,000
Sale of land	*3,282,300*	3,091,316
Sale of other property	*2,123,500*	2,236,500
Other	*1,073,690*	911,480
Additional stamp duty		19,229,000
III. Forests and Fishery	*38,395,700*	27,072,100
Sale of wood	*33,548,500*	16,770,100
Fishing rights	*3,069,200*	3,092,400
Fees for forest administration	*1,778,000*	1,000,000
Other		1,209,600
Additional wood sales		5,000,000
IV. Customs, Salt Monopoly	*202,112,000*	156,823,000
Import Duty	*105,888,000*	91,313,000
Import Duty Colonial Sugar	*38,458,000*	35,000,000
Import Duty Foreign Sugar	*11,270,000*	1,570,000
Export duties	*1,919,000*	2,066,000
Navigation rights	*3,591,000*	2,847,000
Other duties	*2,833,000*	2,874,000
Imported Salt Tax	*38,153,000*	21,153,000
V. Indirect Taxes	*307,962,000*	287,696,000
Alcohol Tax	*103,603,000*	90,000,000
Additional salt duties	*13,346,000*	4,657,000
Domestic Sugar Tax	*20,840,000*	29,168,000
Other duties	*43,310,000*	36,500,000
Tobacco Sales	*120,000,000*	120,000,000
Sale of gunpowder	*6,863,000*	7,371,000

continued

TABLE 5. CONTINUED.

Source of Income	*1848*	1849
VI. Post Office	*51,738,000*	49,876,000
Letter Tax	*46,542,000*	44,829,000
Money orders	*673,000*	1,000,000
Fees for transporting gold and silver	*214,000*	210,000
Mail coach fees	*2,059,000*	1,700,000
Packet boat fees	*1,096,000*	1,102,000
Foreign transit fees	*1,108,000*	1,000,000
Other fees	*46,000*	35,000
VII. Diverse Revenue	*47,053,466*	42,869,234
VIII. Various Products from the Budget	*19,463,398*	28,423,000
IX. Extraordinary Resources	*20,298,000*	158,834,363
Supplement	*20,298,000*	20,000,000
Debt reserve		138,834,363

"Budget de 1848" in *Annuaire de l'Économie politique et de la statistique pour 1848,* pp. 48–50.

"Budget de 1849" in *Annuaire de l'Économie politique et de la statistique pour 1850,* p. 23–25.

TABLE 6. DETAILS OF EXPENDITURE FOR
SECTION III: MINISTERIAL SERVICES.

Ministry	1848	1849
I. Justice	26,739,095	26,460,230
II. Foreign Affairs	8,885,422	7,241,367
III. Public Education and Religion		
Public Education	18,038,033	21,751,820
University		17,910,452
Sciences and Letters		3,343,676
Admin, etc.		497,692
Religion	39,564,833	41,066,393
Catholic		38,917,983
Non-Catholic		1,389,584
Admin		229,295
In Algeria		529,531
IV. Interior		
a. [this section is not itemized in 1849 Budget but is in the 1848 Budget. See Table below for details.]	116,564,738	128,951,534
V. Agriculture and Commerce	14,384,500	17,385,823
VI. Public Works	110,922,050	157,746,633
Roads and Bridges		37,265,000
Navigation		31,100,750
Railways		74,788,750
Admin		8,936,540
Mines		40,000
Civil Buildings		5,130,593
Other		485,000
VII. War	322,010,382	346,319,558
VIII. Navy and Colonies	138,540,895	119,206,857
Navy		98,893,647
Colonies		20,313,210
IX. Finance	17,765,136	15,927,110
(less roll-over funds from previous year)	−82,079,980	
Total	**731,335,104**	**882,057,325**

"Budget de 1848" in *Annuaire de l'Économie politique et de la statistique pour 1848,*
pp. 30–39.

"Budget de 1849" in *Annuaire de l'Économie politique et de la statistique pour 1850,*
pp. 19–21.

TABLE 7. EXPENDITURE BY THE MINISTRY
OF THE INTERIOR IN 1848.

Ministry of the Interior	1848
Central Administration	1,328,000
Diverse Services (telegraph, National Guard)	2,278,500
Fine Arts	2,614,900
Welfare & Subsidies	3,440,500
Administration of the Departments	8,527,200
Prisons	7,200,000
Royal Court	565,548
Ordinary Departmental Expenditure	32,843,040
Optional Departmental Expenditure	13,131,710
Extraordinary & Special Departmental Expenditure	43,633,300
Other	1,002,040
Total	**116,564,738**

"Budget de 1848" in *Annuaire de l'Économie politique et de la statistique pour 1848*, pp. 32–34.

TABLE 8. DETAILS OF EXPENDITURE FOR SECTION IV: COSTS
OF ADMINISTERING AND COLLECTING TAXES AND DUTIES.

Item	1848	1849
I. Direct Taxes	17,323,210	17,018,362
II. Registrations, Stamp Duty, Public Property	11,344,700	11,359,100
III. Forests	5,433,500	6,673,900
IV. Customs	26,353,650	25,790,720
V. Indirect Taxes, Gunpowder, Tobacco	61,937,258	60,331,130
VI. Post Office	34,500,177	34,092,108
Total	**156,892,495**	**155,265,320**

"Budget de 1848" in *Annuaire de l'Économie politique et de la statistique pour 1848*, pp. 39–40.

"Budget de 1849" in *Annuaire de l'Économie politique et de la statistique pour 1850*, pp. 22–23.

Appendix 5

Mark Twain and the Australian Negative Railroad

In "A Negative Railway" (ES1 17) Bastiat ridicules protectionists for wanting to increase national wealth by increasing the amount of labor needed to produce things instead of increasing the amount of goods for sale on the market at the lowest price possible. In this essay using reductio ad absurdum, one of his favorite rhetorical devices, he takes the example of building a railway from Paris to Spain. Surely, he argued, it would increase the amount of labor, and hence wealth, if the track was literally broken into two separate and discontinuous pieces at Bordeaux, which would require the transshipping of passengers and luggage from one railway to the next in order for them to continue their journey, thus providing more work for porters, hoteliers, and shipping agents. He intended this scenario as a joke, to expose the folly of the protectionists' arguments.

However, many a true word may be spoken (or written) in jest. In 1897, in *Following the Equator,* Mark Twain described traveling by train from Sydney to Melbourne. At the border town of Albury, passengers had to get up in the middle of a cold winter's night to transship themselves and their belongings from the narrow-gauge train in New South Wales to the broad-gauge train in Victoria. Twain described this as "the oddest thing, the strangest thing, the most baffling and unaccountable marvel that Australasia can show." Interestingly, Twain, like Bastiat, saw the similarity to customs barriers and discussed the cost to the west coast of America of being forced to buy higher-priced east coast steel instead of cheaper foreign steel.

> We took the train at Sydney at about four in the afternoon. It was American in one way, for we had a most rational sleeping car; also the car was clean and fine and new—nothing about it to suggest the rolling stock of the continent of Europe. But our baggage was weighed, and extra weight charged for. That was continental. Continental and troublesome. Any detail of rail-

roading that is not troublesome cannot honorably be described as continental.

The tickets were round-trip ones—to Melbourne, and clear to Adelaide in South Australia, and then all the way back to Sydney. Twelve hundred more miles than we really expected to make; but then as the round trip wouldn't cost much more than the single trip, it seemed well enough to buy as many miles as one could afford, even if one was not likely to need them. A human being has a natural desire to have more of a good thing than he needs.

Now comes a strange thing: the oddest thing, the strangest thing, the most baffling and unaccountable marvel that Australasia can show. At the frontier between New South Wales and Victoria our multitude of passengers were routed out of their snug beds by lantern-light in the morning in the biting cold of a high altitude to change cars on a road that has no break in it from Sydney to Melbourne! Think of the paralysis of intellect that gave that idea birth; imagine the boulder it emerged from on some petrified legislator's shoulders.

It is a narrow-gauge road to the frontier, and a broader gauge thence to Melbourne. The two governments were the builders of the road and are the owners of it. One or two reasons are given for this curious state of things. One is, that it represents the jealousy existing between the colonies—the two most important colonies of Australasia. What the other one is, I have forgotten. But it is of no consequence. It could be but another effort to explain the inexplicable.

All passengers fret at the double-gauge; all shippers of freight must of course fret at it; unnecessary expense, delay, and annoyance are imposed upon everybody concerned, and no one is benefited.

Each Australian colony fences itself off from its neighbor with a custom-house. Personally, I have no objection, but it must be a good deal of inconvenience to the people. We have something resembling it here and there in America, but it goes by another name. The large empire of the Pacific coast requires a world of iron machinery, and could manufacture it economically on the spot if the imposts on foreign iron were removed.

But they are not. Protection to Pennsylvania and Alabama forbids it. The result to the Pacific coast is the same as if there were several rows of custom-fences between the coast and the East. Iron carted across the American continent at luxurious railway rates would be valuable enough to be coined when it arrived.

We changed cars. This was at Albury.[1]

1. Twain, "A Paralytic Scheme," in *Following the Equator*, pp. 152–53.

LA RÉPUBLIQUE FRANÇAISE (26 FEBRUARY– 28 MARCH 1848)

According to Eugène Hatin, *La République française* was a daily journal. The articles were signed by the editors: Bastiat, Hippolyte Castille, and Gustave de Molinari.[1]

Articles by Bastiat in La République française

Some of the following articles did not have a title when first published. Paillottet gave them titles in the OC, and we will continue that practice here. In other cases we will give the opening words of the articles as a means of identifying them.

1. "A Few Words about the Title of Our Journal" (No title in original—"Quelques mots d'abord sur le titre de nos journal"), 26 February 1848, no. 1, p. 1 [CW3, Addendum].
2. "Under the Republic" (No title in original—"Nul ne peut dire") 27 February 1848, no. 2, p. 1 [OC, vol. 7, pp. 210–12; CW1, pp. 435–37].
3. "The Streets of Paris" (No title in original—"Lorsqu'on parcourt") 26 February 1848, no. 2, p. 1 [OC, vol. 7, pp. 212–13; CW1, pp. 440–41].
4. "On Disarmament" (No title in original—"*Le National* examine") 27 February 1848, no. 3, p. 1 [OC, vol. 7, pp. 215–17; CW1, pp. 437–39].
5. "A Thought in *La Presse*" (No title in original—"Nous partageons

---

1. Eugène Hatin, *Bibliographie historique et critique de la presse périodique française* (1866), pp. 491–92.

cette pensée") 28 February 1848, no. 3, p. 1 [OC, vol. 7, pp. 213–14; CW1, pp. 441–42].

6. "All our cooperation" (No title in original—"Tous notre concours") 27 February 1848, no. 3, p. 1 [OC, vol. 7, p. 218; CW1, p. 442].

7. "The General Good" (No title in original—"Le bien général") 29 February 1848, no. 4, p. 1 [OC, vol. 7, pp. 218–21; CW1, pp. 442–44].

8. "Les Rois doivent désarmer" (The Kings must disarm) 29 February 1848, no. 4, no. 1 [OC, vol. 7, p. 221–22; CW1, pp. 439–40].

9. "Les sous-préfectures" (The Sub-Prefectures) 29 February 1848, no. 4, p. 1 [OC, vol. 7, p. 223; CW3 Addendum].

10. "A Newspaper does not achieve high circulation" (No title in original—"Un journal n'atteint pas") 1 March 1848, no. 5, p. 1 [OC, vol. 7, pp. 223–26; CW1, pp. 429–30].

11. "La presse parisienne" (The Parisian Press) 1 March 1848, no. 5, p. 1 [OC, vol. 7, pp. 226–27; CW1, pp. 425–26].

12. "Pétition d'un économiste" (Petition from an Economist) 2 March 1848, no. 6, p. 2 [OC, vol. 7, pp. 227–30; CW1, pp. 426–29].

13. "Liberté d'enseignement" (Freedom of Education) 4 March 1848, no. 7, p. 1 [OC, vol. 7, pp. 231–32; CW1, pp. 419–20].

14. "Curée des places" (The Scramble for Office) 5 March 1848, no. 8, p. 1 [OC, vol. 7, pp. 232–34; CW1, pp. 431–32].

15. "Impediments and Taxes" (No title in original—"Pendant qu'une mouvement" (While a movement) 6 March 1848, no. 9, p. 1 [OC, vol. 7, pp. 234–35; CW1, pp. 432–33].

16. "Petites affiches de Jacques Bonhomme. Soulagement immédiat du peuple" (Little Posters by Jacques Bonhomme. The Immediate Relief of the People) [Paillottet states that this article appeared in the issue of 13 March, no. 16, which is missing from the BNF collection; OC, vol. 2, pp. 459–60; CW3, ES3 21].

17. "Petites affiches de Jacques Bonhomme. Funeste remède" (Little Posters by Jacques Bonhomme. A Disastrous Remedy) 14 March 1848, no. 17, p. 1 [OC, vol. 2, pp. 460–61; CW3, ES3 22].

JACQUES BONHOMME (11 JUNE–13 JULY 1848)

According to Eugène Hatin, *Jacques Bonhomme* was a weekly journal with four issues which appeared from 11 June to 13 July, with a break between 24 June and 9 July because of the rioting during the June Days uprising. The journal was founded by Bastiat, Gustave de Molinari, Charles Coquelin, Alcide Fonteyraud, and Joseph Garnier. The editor was named as "J. Lobet." The first issue was a single page only, on "papier rose" (pink paper), designed to be posted on a wall.[2]

Articles by Bastiat in Jacques Bonhomme

1. "La Liberté" (Freedom) 11–15 June 1848, no. 1, p. 1 [*OC,* vol. 7, pp. 235–36; CW1, pp. 433–34].
2. "Laissez faire" (No title in original) 11–15 June 1848, no. 1, p. 1 [*OC,* vol. 7, p. 237; CW1, pp. 434–35].
3. "L'Assemblée Nationale" (The National Assembly) 11–15 June 1848, no. 1, pp. 1–2 [*OC,* vol. 7, pp. 237–38; CW1, p. 451].
4. "L'État" (The State) 11–15 June 1848, no. 1, p. 2 [*OC,* vol. 7, pp. 238–40; CW2, pp. 105–6].
5. "Prendre cinq et rendre quatre ce n'est pas donner" (Taking Five and Returning Four Is Not Giving) 15–18 June, no. 2, p. 1 [*OC,* vol. 7, pp. 240–42; CW4, forthcoming].
6. "Une mystification" (A Hoax) 15–18 June, no. 2, p. 2 [*OC,* vol. 7, pp. 242–44; CW4, forthcoming].
7. "Aux citoyens Lamartine et Ledru-Rollin" (To Citizens Lamartine and Ledru-Rollin) 20–23 June 1848, no. 3, p. 1 [*OC,* vol. 7, pp. 246–48; CW1, pp. 444–45].
8. "Funeste gradation" (A Dreadful Escalation) 20–23 June 1848, no. 3, p. 1 [*OC,* vol. 7, pp. 244–46; CW4, forthcoming].

2. Eugène Hatin, *Bibliographie historique et critique de la presse périodique française* (1866), p. 468.

Addendum: Additional Material by Bastiat

In the course of producing this multivolume edition of The Collected Works of Frédéric Bastiat we have come across material by Bastiat which did not appear in the standard edition of the *Œuvres complètes* produced by Prosper Paillottet in the 1850s and 1860s. When we were aware of new material ahead of time (such as the volume of his letters which appeared in 1877, or other material found by one of the editors, Jean-Claude Paul-Dejean), we have incorporated it into the relevant volume. Now and again we have come across material during the process of editing these volumes which we will include in an addendum. A complete and up-to-date table of contents of the entire Collected Works in chronological order of publication is available at the Online Library of Liberty website at http://oll.libertyfund.org/people/25.

Two of the pieces in this addendum come from a small magazine, *La République française,* which Bastiat and some friends produced in February and March of 1848, immediately after the outbreak of the Revolution. This was the first of two such magazines (the second was *Jacques Bonhomme*) with which Bastiat was involved during 1848, and many of the articles which appeared in them have already appeared in previous volumes of the Collected Works. A chronological list of the articles appearing in *La République française* and *Jacques Bonhomme* can be found in appendix 6, "Bastiat's Revolutionary Magazines."

The third piece in this addendum is Bastiat's Speech on "Disarmament and Taxes," given in August 1849.

"A Few Words about the Title of Our Journal *The French Republic*" (*La République Française*, 26 February 1848)[1]

Let's begin with a few words about the title of our journal.

The provisional government wants a republic without ratification by the people. Today we have heard the people of Paris unanimously proclaim a republican government from the top of its glorious barricades, and we are of the firm conviction that the whole of France will ratify the wishes of the conquerors of February. But whatever might happen, even if this wish were to be misunderstood, we will keep the title which the voice of all the people has thrown to us. Whatever the form of government which the nation decides upon, the press ought to henceforth remain free; no longer will any impediment be imposed upon the expression of thought. This sacred liberty of human thought, previously so impudently violated, will be recognized by the people, and they will know how to keep it. Thus, whatever might happen, being firmly convinced that the republican form of government is the only one which is suitable for a free people, the only one which allows the full and complete development of all kinds of liberty, we adopt and will keep our title:

The French Republic.

Time and events are pressing; we can only devote a few lines to stating our program.

France has just gotten rid of a regime which it found odious, but it is not sufficient just to change men; it is necessary to also change things.

Now, what was the foundation of this regime?

Restriction and privilege! Not only was the monarchy, which the heroic efforts of the people of Paris have just overturned, based on an electoral monopoly, but it also depended on numerous branches of human activity from which it profited with invisible ties of privilege.

We wish that henceforth labor should be completely free, no

---

1. This statement of principles is provided by Eugène Hatin in a long quote from *La République française* from the first issue, which is dated 26 February 1848. It was probably written by Bastiat with some assistance from Gustave de Molinari, who was one of the cofounders of the journal. See Hatin, *Bibliographie historique et critique de la presse périodique française,* pp. 491–92. Translation by David M. Hart.

more laws against unions, no more regulations which prevent capitalists and workers from bringing either their money or their labor to whatever industry they find agreeable. The liberty of labor (*la liberté du travail*) proclaimed by Turgot and by the Constituent Assembly ought henceforth be the law of a democratic France.

Universal suffrage.

No more state-funded religions. Each person should pay for the religion which he uses.

The absolute freedom of education.

Freedom of commerce, to the degree that the needs of the treasury allow. The elimination of "duties on basic food" as we enjoyed under the Convention. Low prices [*la vie à bon marché*] for the people!

No more conscription; voluntary recruitment for the army.

Institutions which allow the workers to find out where jobs are available and how to discover the going rate of wages throughout the entire country.[2]

Inviolable respect for property. All property has its origin in labor: to attack property is to attack labor.

Finally, in order to crown the work of our glorious regeneration, we demand leniency within the country and peace outside. Let us forget the past, let us launch into the future with a heart without any hatred, let us fraternize with all the people of the world, and soon the day will come when liberty, equality, and fraternity will be the law of the world!

"The Subprefectures," 29 February 1848, *La République Française*[1]

What is a Subprefecture?[2] It is a letter box. The Prefect writes: "Monsieur Subprefect, here is a letter for the mayor of . . . ; send it to him without delay and send me his reply along with your opinion."

---

2. The concept of "labor exchanges" was a pet idea of Gustave de Molinari.

1. "Les sous-préfectures," 29 February 1848, *La République française* [*OC,* vol. 7, p. 223].

2. See "French Government Administrative Regions," in appendix 2, "The French State and Politics."

The Subprefect replies: "Monsieur Prefect, I have received the letter for the Mayor of . . . ; I will send it to him without delay and will send you his reply with my opinion."

For this service, there is a Subprefect in each arrondissement who earns fr. 3,000, fr. 3,000 in administrative costs, a secretary, office rental, etc., etc.

We are mistaken: the Subprefects have another real function, namely that of influencing and corrupting the elections.

For how many days will the Subprefectures be able to survive the February Revolution?

In general, we are in no hurry to call for changes in personnel, but we are adamant in demanding the abolition of useless government jobs.

BASTIAT'S SPEECH ON "DISARMAMENT AND TAXES" (AUGUST 1849)

This speech was given at the Friends of Peace Congress, which was held in Paris in August 1849.[1] It was not included in Paillottet's *Œuvres complètes,* so we include it here. We have used a contemporary English translation.[2]

Disarmament, Taxes, and the Influence of Political Economy on the Peace Movement [3]

M. Frederic Bastiat, member of the French National Assembly, spoke as follows:—

Gentlemen, our excellent and learned colleague, M. Coquerel, spoke to us a little while since, of a cruel malady with which French society is afflicted, namely, skepticism. This malady is the fruit of our long dissensions, of our revolutions which have failed to bring about the desired end, of our attempts without results, and of that torrent of visionary projects which has recently overflowed our policy. This strange evil will, I hope, be only temporary: at all events, I know of no more efficacious remedy for it, than the extraordinary spectacle which I have now before my eyes, for if I consider the number and

1. See the entry for "International Congress of the Friends of Peace (Paris, August 1849)," in the Glossary of Subjects and Terms.

2. "Speech," in *Report of the Proceedings of the Second General Peace Congress.* A shorter French version also appeared in *Congrès des amis de la paix universelle réuni à Paris en 1849,* published by Joseph Garnier.

3. This is the title we have given Bastiat's speech.

the importance of the men who now do me the honor of listening to me, if I consider that many of them do not act in their individual capacity, but in the name of large constituencies, who have delegated them to this Congress, I have no hesitation in saying that the cause of peace unites today in this assembly, more religious, intellectual, and moral force, more positive power, than could be brought together for any other imaginable cause, in any other part of the world. Yes, this is a grand and magnificent spectacle, and I do not think that the sun has often shone on one equal to it in interest and importance. Here are men who have traversed the wide Atlantic: others have left vast undertakings in England, and others have come from the disturbed land of Germany, or from the peaceful soil of Belgium or of Holland. Paris is the place of their rendezvous. And what have they come to do? Are they drawn hither by cupidity, by vanity, or by curiosity, those three motives to which are customarily attributed all the actions of the sons of Adam? No; they come, led on by the generous hope of being able to do some good to humanity, without having lost sight of the difficulties of their task, and knowing well that they are working less for themselves, than for the benefit of future generations. Thrice welcome then, ye men of faith, to the land of France. Faith is as contagious as skepticism. France will not fail you. She also will yield her tribute to your generous enterprise. At the present stage of the discussion, I shall only trespass on your time to make a few observations on the subject of disarmament. They have been suggested to me by a passage in the speech of our eloquent President, who said yesterday, that the cause of external peace was also that of internal order. He very reasonably based this assertion on the fact that a powerful military state is forced to exact heavy taxes, which engender misery, which in its turn engenders the spirit of turbulence and of revolution. I also wish to speak on the subject of taxes, and I shall consider them with regard to their distribution. That the maintenance of large military and naval forces requires heavy taxes, is a self-evident fact. But I make this additional remark: these heavy taxes, notwithstanding the best intentions on the part of the legislator, are necessarily most unfairly distributed; whence it follows that great armaments present two causes of revolution—misery in the first place, and secondly, the deep feeling that this misery is the result of injustice. The first species of military taxation that I meet with is, that which is called, according to circumstances, conscription or recruitment. The young man who belongs to a wealthy family, escapes by the payment of two or three thousand francs; the son of an artisan or a laborer, is forced to throw away the seven best years of his life. Can we imagine a more dreadful inequality? Do we not know that it caused the people to revolt even under the empire, and do we imagine that it can long survive the revolution of February?

With regard to taxes, there is one principle universally admitted in France, namely, that they ought to be proportional to the resources and capabilities of the citizens. This principle was not only proclaimed by our last constitution, but will be found in the charter of 1830, as well as in that of 1814. Now, after having given my almost undivided attention to these matters, I affirm that in order that a tax may be proportional, it must be very moderate, and if the state is under the necessity of taking a very large part of the revenues of its citizens, it can only be done by means of an indirect contribution, which is utterly at variance with proportionality, that is to say, with justice. And this is a grave matter, gentlemen. The correctness of my statement may be doubted, but if it be correct, we cannot shut our eyes to the consequences which it entails, without being guilty of the greatest folly. I only know of one country in the world where all the public expenses, with very slight exceptions, are covered by a direct and proportional taxation. I refer to the State of Massachusetts. But there also, precisely, because the taxation is direct, and everybody knows what he has to pay, the public expenditure is as limited as possible. The citizens prefer acting by themselves in a multitude of cases, in which elsewhere the intervention of the state would be required. If the government of France would be contented with asking of us five, six, or even ten percent of our income, we should consider the tax a direct and proportional one. In such a case, the tax might be levied according to the declaration of the taxpayers, care being taken that these declarations were correct, although, even if some of them were false, no very serious consequences would ensue. But suppose that the treasury had need of 1,500 or 1,800 millions of money. Does it come directly to us and ask us for a quarter, a third, or a half of our incomes? No: that would be impracticable; and consequently, to arrive at the desired end, it has recourse to a trick, and gets our money from us without our perceiving it, by subjecting us to an indirect tax laid on food. And this is why the Minister of Finance, when he proposed to renew the tax on drinks, said that this tax had one great recommendation, that it was so entirely mixed up with the price of the article, that the taxpayer, as it were, paid without knowing it. This certainly is a recommendation of taxes on articles of consumption: but they have this bad characteristic, they are unequal and unjust, and are levied just in inverse proportion to the capabilities of the taxpayer. For, whoever has studied these matters, even very superficially, knows well that these taxes are productive and valuable only when laid upon articles of universal consumption, such as salt, wine, tobacco, sugar and such like; and when we speak of universal consumption, we necessarily speak of those things on which the laboring classes spend the whole of their small incomes. From this it follows, that these classes do not make a single purchase which is not increased to a great extent by taxation, while such is not the case with the rich.

Gentlemen, I venture to call your close attention to these facts. Large armaments necessarily entail heavy taxes: heavy taxes force governments to have recourse to indirect taxation. Indirect taxation cannot possibly be proportionate, and the want of proportion in taxation is a crying injustice inflicted upon the poor to the advantage of the rich. This question, then, alone remains to be considered: Are not injustice and misery, combined together, an always imminent cause of revolutions? Gentlemen, it is no use to be willfully blind. At this moment, in France, the need which is most imperious and most universally felt, is doubtless that of order, and of security. Rich and poor, laborers and proprietors, all are disposed to make great sacrifices to secure such precious benefits, even to abandon their political affections and convictions, and, as we have seen, their liberty. But, in fine, can we reasonably hope, by the aid of this sentiment, to perpetuate, to systematize, injustice in this country? Is it not certain that injustice will, sooner or later, engender disaffection? Disaffection all the more dangerous because it is legitimate, because its complaints are well-founded, because it has reason on its side, because it is supported by all men of upright minds and generous hearts, and, at the same time, is cleverly managed by persons whose intentions are less pure, and who seek to make it an instrument for the execution of their ambitious designs. We talk about reconciling the peoples. Ah! let us pursue this object with all the more ardor, because at the same time we seek to reconcile the classes of society. In France because, in consequence of our ancient electoral law, the wealthy class had the management of public business, the people think that the inequality of the taxes is the fruit of a systematic cupidity. On the contrary, it is the necessary consequence of their exaggeration. I am convinced that if the wealthy class could, by a single blow, assess the taxes in a more equitable manner, they would do so instantly. And in doing so, they would be actuated more by motives of justice than by motives of prudence. They do not do it, because they cannot, and if those who complain were the governors of the country, they would not be able to do it any more than those now in power; for I repeat, the very nature of things has placed a radical incompatibility between the exaggeration and the equal distribution of taxes. There is, then, only one means of diverting from this country the calamities which menace it, and that is, to equalize taxation; to equalize it, we must reduce it; to reduce it, we must diminish our military force. For this reason, among others, I support with all my heart the resolution in favor of a simultaneous disarmament.

I have just uttered the word "disarmament." This subject occupies the thoughts and the wishes of all; and nevertheless, by one of those inexplicable contradictions of the human heart, there are some persons, both in France and England, who, I am sure, would be sorry to see it carried into effect. What will become, they will say, of our preponderance? Shall we allow the influence which, as a great and powerful nation, we possess, to depart from us? Oh, fatal illusion! Oh, strange misconception of the meaning of a word! What! Can great nations exert an influence only by means of cannon and bayonets? Does the influence of England consist not in her industry, her commerce, her wealth, and the exercise of her free and ancient institutions? Does it not consist, above all, in those gigantic efforts, which we have seen made there, with so much perseverance and sagacity, for obtaining the triumph of some great principle, such as the liberty of the press, the extension of the electoral franchise, Catholic emancipation, the abolition of slavery, and free trade? And as I have alluded to this last and glorious triumph of public opinion in England, as we have amongst us many valiant champions of commercial liberty, who, adopting the motto of Caesar,—

Nil actum reputans, dum quid superesset agendum,[4]

have no sooner gained one great victory than they hasten to another still greater, let me be permitted to say for how immense a moral influence England is indebted to them, less on account of the object, all glorious as it was, which they attained, than on account of the means which they employed for obtaining it, and which they thus made known to all nations. Yes! From this school the peoples may learn to ally moral force with reason; there we ought to study the strategy of those pacific agitations which possess the double advantage of rendering every dangerous innovation impossible, and every useful reform irresistible.

---

4. "Sed Caesar in omnia praeceps, nil actum credens, cum quid superesset agendum" (But Caesar, headlong in all his designs, thought nothing done while anything remained to be done). Lucan, *Pharsalia,* bk. 2, line 656.

By such examples as these, I venture to say, Great Britain will exercise that species of influence which brings no disasters, no hatreds, no reprisals in its train, but, on the contrary, awakens no feelings but those of admiration and of gratitude. And with regard to my own country, I am proud to say, it possesses other and purer sources of influence than that of arms. But even this last might be contested, if the question were pressed, and influence measured by results. But that which cannot be taken away from us, nor be contested for a moment, is the universality of our language, the incomparable brilliancy of our literature, the genius of our poets, of our philosophers, of our historians, of our novelists, and even of our feuilletonistes, and, last though not least, the devotedness of our patriots. France owes her true influence to that almost unbroken chain of great men which, beginning with Montaigne, Descartes, and Pascal, and passing on by Bossuet, Voltaire, Montesquieu, and Rousseau, has not, thanks to heaven, come to an end in the tomb of Chateaubriand. Ah! let my country fear nothing for her influence, so long as her soil is not unable to produce that noble fruit which is called Genius, and which is ever to be seen on the side of liberty and democracy. And, at this moment, my brethren, you who were born in other lands, and who speak another language, do you not behold all the illustrious men of my country uniting with you to secure the triumph of universal peace? Are we not presided over by that great and noble poet, whose glory and privilege it has been to introduce a whole generation into the path of a renovated literature? Do we not deplore the absence of that other poet-orator, of powerful intellect and noble heart, who, I am sure, will as much regret his inability to raise his voice amongst us, as you will regret not to have heard it? Have we not borrowed from the songs of our national bard the touching device,—

"Peuples, formez une sainte alliance,
Et donnez vous la main!"[5]

Do we not number in our ranks that indefatigable and courageous journalist, who did not wait for your arrival to place at the service of absolute non-intervention the immense publicity, and the immense influence which

---

5. "People, form a Holy Alliance / And take each other by the hand." This quotation comes from the refrain in Béranger's antimonarchical and pro-French poem "La Sainte alliance des peuples" (The Holy Alliance of the Peoples, 1818), in *Œuvres complètes de Béranger* 1:294–96. For a translation, see *Béranger's Songs of the Empire, the Peace, and the Restoration,* pp. 59–62. This line was also used by Molinari at the end of his 11th Soirée in *Les Soirées de la rue Saint-Lazare* (1849).

he has at his command? And have we not among us, as fellow-laborers, ministers of nearly all Christian religions? Amidst this illustrious galaxy, permit me to claim a humble place for my brethren, the political economists; for, gentlemen, I sincerely believe that no science will bring a more valorous contingent to serve under the standard of peace than political economy. Religion and morality do not endeavour to discover whether the interests of men are antagonistic or harmonious. They say to them: Live in peace, no matter whether it be profitable or hurtful to you, for it is your duty to do so. Political economy steps in and adds: Live in peace, for the interests of men are harmonious, and the apparent antagonism which leads them to take up arms is only a gross error. Doubtless, it would be a noble sight to behold men realize peace at the expense of their material interests; but for those who know the weakness of human nature, it is consoling to think that duty and interest are not here two hostile forces, and the heart rests with confidence upon this maxim: "Seek first after righteousness, and all things shall be added unto you."[6]

6. This is a slightly secularized version of Matthew 6:33: "But seek ye first the kingdom of God, and his righteousness; and all these things shall be added unto you" (King James version).

Glossary of Persons

ARAGO, ÉTIENNE VINCENT (1802–92). Youngest brother of the famous Arago family. It is possible that Bastiat knew Étienne, as they were both in Sorèze attending school at the same time (ca. 1815), though possibly different schools (Étienne attended a Benedictine school; Bastiat attended a new progressive school). While studying chemistry at the École polytechnique he came into contact with the work of Auguste Comte and formed radical and republican political views which he retained for the rest of his life. During the 1820s he was active in Carbonari circles, and in the 1830 Revolution he took part in the fighting on the barricades as an ally of Lafayette's group. He was a prolific and successful playwright throughout the 1820s and 1840s, writing very political plays such as *Mandrin, mélodrame en 3 actes* (1827), about Louis Mandrin (1725–55), the famous eighteenth-century brigand and highwayman, and *Les Aristocraties* (1847), which was a strong republican attack on the privileges of the aristocracy.

During the early days of the February Revolution he was with a group which seized control of the administrative building of the Post Office and declared himself to be the new director general of the Post Office, later being confirmed in that position by the provisional government in which his brother François played an active role. Étienne was elected to the Constituent Assembly in April 1848 (as was Bastiat) but resigned his position as director general of the Post Office when Louis-Napoléon was elected president of the Republic in December. During the brief period he was in charge of the Post Office he introduced the new system of postage stamps for letters, modeled on the English "penny post" system, a policy which Bastiat supported. For his role in leading protests against the regime in June 1849 he was convicted and sent into exile in Belgium.

ARAGO, FRANÇOIS (1786–1853). Eldest of four successful brothers. The others were Jean Arago (1788–1836), a general who saw service in Mexico; Jacques Arago (1790–1855), a writer and explorer; and Étienne Arago. François was a famous astronomer and physicist whose work was noticed by Pierre-Simon Laplace, who got him the position of secretary and librarian at the Paris Observatory. At the young age of twenty-three he was appointed to the Academy of Sciences (1809), and in 1812 he became a professor of analytical geometry at the École polytechnique. François was also active in republican politics during the July Monarchy and was an elected deputy for its entire duration. He is mentioned several times in Bastiat's correspondence. After the outbreak of the Revolution in February 1848 he became minister of War, the Navy, and Colonies, and played an important role in the abolition of slavery in the French colonies. Refusing to swear an oath to Louis-Napoléon Bonaparte, he resigned his position and was sent into exile. In addition to his theoretical scientific works, he wrote popular science books and edited the collected works of Condorcet which appeared in a multivolume collection in 1847 (*Œuvres de Condorcet*).

ARGOUT, ANTOINE MAURICE APOLLINAIRE, COMTE D' (1782–1858). A supporter of the restored monarchy, but after 1830 he supported the new regime and was rewarded with appointments as minister for the Navy and Colonies, then Commerce, and Public Works. In 1834 he was appointed governor of the Bank of France, a position he held until 1857.

BALZAC, HONORÉ DE (1789–1850). Prolific author who was a leading member of the realist school. He was known for his detailed depiction of everyday life in France during the July Monarchy. His collection of novels and stories were called "The Human Comedy" and numbered nearly ninety titles. Although he was a conservative and supporter of the monarchy, his depiction of ordinary people endeared him to readers from across the political spectrum. See especially *The Chouans* (*Les Chouans*, 1829); *Old Goriot* (*Le Père Goriot*, 1835); *The Government Clerks* (*Les Employés*, 1838); *Lost Illusions* (*Illusions perdues*, 1843); *A Man of Business* (*Un homme d'affaires*, 1846); *The Lesser Bourgeoisie* (*Les Petits Bourgeois*, 1854).

BENTHAM, JEREMY (1748–1832). Trained as a lawyer and founded the early nineteenth-century school of political thought known as "Benthamism," later called utilitarianism. It was based on the idea that governments should act so as to promote "the greatest good for the greatest number" of people. He spent much of his life attempting to draw up an ideal constitutional code, but he was also active in parliamentary reform, education, and prison reform. He influenced the thinking of James Mill and his son John Stuart Mill and the group of reformers known as the Philosophical Radicals.

It is interesting that Bastiat chose passages from Bentham's work *Théorie des peines et des récompenses* (1811) as the openings for both the First and Second Series of the *Economic Sophisms*. Bastiat may also have taken the name "sophism" from a work by Bentham, *Traité des sophismes politiques* (1816; English version, *Handbook of Political Fallacies* [1824]). His most important works included A *Fragment on Government* (1776), *Introduction to Principles of Morals and Legislation* (1780, 1789), and *Defence of Usury* (1787).

BENTINCK, LORD GEORGE (1802–48). Elected a member of Parliament in 1828. He joined the conservative and protectionist faction and with Benjamin Disraeli led the opposition in the House of Commons against Richard Cobden's and Sir Robert Peel's attempts to repeal the Corn Laws in 1846. Although he was unsuccessful in stopping repeal, he and Disraeli were able to defeat Sir Robert Peel, splitting the conservatives into two groups, a free-trade group led by Peel and a protectionist group which joined the new Conservative Party. Bentinck later became the leader of the Conservative Party.

BÉRANGER, PIERRE-JEAN DE (1780–1857). Liberal poet and songwriter who rose to prominence during the Restoration period with his funny and clever criticisms of the monarchy and the church. His antics got him into trouble with the censors, who imprisoned him for brief periods in the 1820s. His material was much in demand in the singing societies, or *goguettes,* which sprang up during the Restoration and the July Monarchy as a way of circumventing the censorship laws and the bans on political parties.

After the appearance of his second volume of songs, in 1821, Béranger was tried and convicted and sentenced to three months' imprisonment in Sainte-Pélagie, where he wrote the poem "La Liberté" (Liberty) in January 1822.

Another bout of imprisonment (this time nine months in La Force) followed in 1828, when his fourth volume was published. Many of the figures who came to power after the July revolution of 1830 were friends or acquaintances of Béranger's, and it was assumed he would be granted a sinecure in recognition of his critiques of the old monarchy. However, he refused all government appointments in a stinging poem that he wrote in late 1830 called "Le Refus" (The Refusal). In April 1848, at the age of sixty-eight, Béranger was overwhelmingly elected to the Constituent Assembly, in which he sat for a brief period before resigning.

Béranger was a particular favorite of Bastiat, who referred to his satirical poems and songs several times. Béranger mixed in liberal circles in the 1840s in Paris, when he joined Bastiat's Free Trade Society and the Political Economy Society. He was invited to attend the welcome dinner held by the latter to honor Bastiat's arrival in Paris in May 1845 but was unable to attend. In his correspondence Bastiat mentions him several times, which shows how close his personal relationship was to the poet and songwriter as well as how closely connected some artists like Béranger were to the political economists like Bastiat. In a letter to his friend Felix Coudroy (Bayonne, 5 August 1830) Bastiat relates his activities in the 1830 Revolution (27–29 July) when the garrison in Bayonne was split over whether to side with the revolution or the sitting monarch, Charles X. Bastiat visited the garrison to speak to some of the officers in order to swing them over to the revolutionary cause. In a midnight addition to his letter Bastiat relates how some good wine and the songs of Béranger helped him persuade the officers that night when "I was expecting blood but it was only wine that was spilled." Later, when Bastiat first went to Paris in 1845, Béranger was invited to the welcoming dinner put on by the Economists for Bastiat. He also tells us that he persuaded Béranger to join the Free Trade Association.

BEZOUT, ÉTIENNE (1730–83). French mathematician who was elected to the Academy of Sciences in 1758. He is best known for his general theory of algebraic equations in *Théorie générale des équations algébriques* (1779).

BILLAUT, AUGUSTE ADOLPHE MARIE (1805–63). Lawyer, economist, mayor of Nantes, and a member of the Chamber of Deputies. Billaut served as undersecretary of state for agriculture and commerce under Thiers in 1840. In 1848 he was elected to the Constituent Assembly but was not re-elected in 1849. He became a strong supporter of Louis-Napoléon's bid to become emperor and served as his minister of the interior. In his political and economic views he was anticlerical and a follower of Saint-Simon.

BINEAU, JEAN MARTIAL (1805–55). Engineer by training and a politician who served as minister of public works in 1850 and then minister of finance in 1852 during the Second Empire.

BLANC, LOUIS (1811–82). Journalist and historian who was active in the socialist movement. He founded the journal *Revue du progès* and published articles that later became the influential pamphlet *L'Organisation du travail* (1839).[1] In 1841 he published a very popular critique of the July Monarchy, *Histoire de dix ans, 1830–1840,* which went through many editions during the 1840s. During the 1848 Revolution he became a member of the pro-

---

1. "L'Organisation du travail" was republished in book form many times during the 1840s. The earliest dated edition we have is Louis Blanc, *Organisation du travail. Association universelle. Ouvriers. Chefs d'ateliers. Hommes de lettres. Par Louis Blanc* (Paris: Administration de librairie, 1841). There is also an undated edition which is probably from 1840: *Organisation du travail, par M. Louis Blanc* (Paris: Prévot, n.d.).

visional government, promoted the National Workshops, and debated Adolphe Thiers on the merits of the right to work in *Le socialisme; droit au travail, réponse à M. Thiers* (1848). In 1847 Blanc began work on a multivolume history of the French Revolution, *Histoire de la Révolution française,* two volumes of which had appeared when the February Revolution of 1848 broke out. A second edition, of fifteen volumes, appeared in 1878.

BOILEAU-DESPRÉAUX, NICOLAS (1636–1711). Trained as a lawyer but turned his hand to writing poetry, especially satires in the style of Horace and Juvenal, and literary criticism. In the debate about "the ancients and the moderns" he was firmly on the side that regarded the ancient authors as the pinnacle of achievement. A collection of his *Satires* appeared in 1666–68.

BONAPARTE, LOUIS-NAPOLÉON (1808–73). Nephew of Napoléon Bonaparte, he was raised in Italy and became active in liberal Carbonari circles. Louis-Napoléon returned to France in 1836 and 1840 to head the Bonapartist groups seeking to install him on the throne. On both occasions he was unsuccessful. In December 1848 he was elected president of the Second Republic. Bastiat voted for his opponent, the republican General Cavaignac, and predicted in a letter written in January 1849 that Louis-Napoléon would seek to seize power in a coup d'état. In 1851 he dissolved the Assembly and won a plebiscite that made him emperor of the Second Empire. Louis-Napoléon was popular for his economic reforms, which were a mixture of popularism and liberalism. In 1860, during his reign, a free-trade treaty with England was signed by Cobden and Chevalier. A socialist uprising in 1870 and a disastrous war with Prussia in 1871 led to the ignominious collapse of his regime.

BONAPARTE, NAPOLÉON (1769–1821). French general, first consul of France (1799–1804), emperor of the French (1804–15). Although Napoléon's conquests of Europe were ultimately unsuccessful (Spain 1808; Russia 1812; Waterloo, Belgium, 1815), he dramatically altered the face of Europe economically, politically, and legally (the Civil Code of 1804).

Many European countries suffered huge economic losses from Napoléon's occupation and the looting of museums and churches. Napoléon introduced a new form of economic warfare, the Continental System (under the Berlin Decree of 21 November 1806), which was designed to cripple Britain by denying its goods access to the European market. It was partly in response to these and other measures that Jean-Baptiste Say wrote his *Traité d'économie politique* (1803). Politically, Napoléon introduced harsh censorship in order to stifle his liberal critics and weakened parliamentary institutions in order to rule in his own right. Benjamin Constant and Madame de

Staël were two of his sharpest critics. See in particular the former's *Principes de politiques applicables à tous les gouvernements* (1815). Constant also wrote a devastating critique of Napoléon's militarism in *De l'esprit de conquête et de l'usurpation, dans leurs rapports à la civilisation européen* (1813).

Liberals of Bastiat's day were divided between those who admired Napoléon because of his defense of the Revolution against its monarchical enemies such as Britain (e.g., the poet Béranger) and those who saw Napoléon as the creator of a new centralized and bureaucratic state that restored many of the economic interventions of the Old Regime such as the Continental Blockade (e.g., Dunoyer, Molinari, and Bastiat). Napoléon did not seem to have a well-thought-out economic theory, but his scattered remarks recorded in his *Mémoires de Napoléon Bonaparte: Manuscrit venu de Sainte-Hélène* (1821) reveal him as an economic nationalist and strong protectionist.

BOSSUET, JACQUES BÉNIGNE (1627–1704). Bishop of Meaux, historian, and tutor to the dauphin (son of Louis XIV). Bossuet was renowned for his oratory and classical writing style, which was used as a model for generations of French schoolchildren. In politics he was an intransigent Gallican Catholic, an opponent of Protestantism, and a supporter of the idea of the divine right of kings.

BRIGHT, JOHN (1811–89). Manufacturer from Lancashire and a leading member of the Anti–Corn Law League. He was elected to Parliament in 1843, and in 1869 he became minister of the Board of Trade in the Gladstone Cabinet.

BRUTUS, MARCUS JUNIUS (CA. 85–42 B.C.). Roman senator who had been brought up in the Stoic philosophy by his uncle, Cato the Younger. Brutus participated in the assassination of Julius Caesar and because of this was regarded by many in the eighteenth and nineteenth centuries as the model of the tyrannicide.

BUGEAUD, THOMAS, MARQUESS DE PICONNERIE, DUC D'ISLY (1784–1849). Had a distinguished military career under Napoléon fighting the partisans in Spain. After the 1830 Revolution he became a conservative deputy representing Dordogne (1831–48) and supported a policy of protection for agriculture. King Louis-Philippe appointed him a marshal of France. In 1840 he was appointed the governor of Algeria by Thiers and was active in the pacification of that country. When the 1848 Revolution broke out in February he was immediately appointed commander of the French army, but this was quickly blocked by members of the National

Guard. He was elected to the Constituent Assembly, where he supported the conservatives. He died in the cholera epidemic which swept Paris in June 1849.

CABET, ÉTIENNE (1788–1856). Lawyer and utopian socialist who coined the word "communism." Between 1831 and 1834 he was a deputy in the Chamber, until he was forced into exile to Britain, where he came into contact with Robert Owen. Cabet advocated a society in which the elected representatives controlled all property that was owned in common by the community. He promoted his views in a journal called *Le Populaire* and in a book about a fictitious communist community called Icarie, *Voyage et aventures de lord William Carisdall en Icarie* (1840). In 1848 Cabet left France in order to create such a community in Texas and then at Nauvoo, Illinois, but these efforts ended in failure. The naming of his utopian community after the figure from Greek mythology, Icarus, who failed in his attempt to flee the island of Crete by flying with wax wings too close to the sun, was perhaps unfortunate.

CASTILLE, HIPPOLYTE (1820–86). Prolific French author who wrote the popular *History of the Second French Republic* (4 vols., 1854–56) and a multivolume series of *Portraits politiques au dix-neuvième siècle* (1857–62), which included several small volumes on classical liberal figures such as Madame de Staël, Benjamin Constant, Béranger, Lafayette, Garibaldi, Cavour, and Mazzini, as well as many other individuals.

He founded in 1847 a short-lived journal devoted to the recognition of intellectual property, *Le Travail intellectuel, journal des intérêts scientifiques, littéraires et artistiques,* for which Molinari wrote a number of articles. Molinari is mentioned as a "collaborator," and other leading economists were listed as "supporters" (Frédéric Bastiat, Charles Dunoyer, Horace Say, Michel Chevalier, Joseph Garnier). The journal was monthly and lasted seven months before closing in 1848. Castille's home on the rue Saint-Lazare (the old residence of Cardinal Fesch) was the meeting place for a small group of liberals (which included Bastiat, Molinari, Garnier, Fonteyraud, and Coquelin) which met regularly between 1844 and early 1848 to discuss political and economic matters. Castille's home supplied the name for Molinari's book *Les Soirées de la rue Saint-Lazare* (1849). Castille was one of the founders, with Bastiat and Molinari, of the revolutionary journal *La République française* in February 1848.

CATO, MARCUS PORCIUS, SURNAMED UTICENSIS (95–46 B.C.). Better known as Cato the Younger (Cato Minor), he was a politician in the late Roman Republic and a noted defender of "Roman liberty." He was a supporter of the Stoic school of philosophy and became renowned for his opposition to political corruption and the growing power of Julius Caesar. He was much admired in the eighteenth century, and his name was used as a nom de plume by John Trenchard and Thomas Gordon, opponents of the British Empire in the 1720s, in their book *Cato's Letters* (1720–23).

CHATEAUBRIAND, FRANÇOIS RENÉ, VICOMTE DE (1768–1848). Novelist, philosopher, and supporter of Charles X. He was minister of foreign affairs from 28 December 1822 to 6 June 1824. A defender of freedom of the press and Greek independence, he refused to take the oath to King Louis-Philippe after 1830. He spent his retirement writing his *Mémoires d'outre-tombe* (1849–50).

CLÉMENT, AMBROISE (1805–86). Economist and secretary to the mayor of Saint-Étienne for many years. In the mid-1840s, he began writing on economic matters and so impressed Guillaumin that the latter asked him to assume the task of directing the publication of the important and influential *Dictionnaire de l'économie politique,* in 1850. Clément was a member of the Société d'économie politique from 1848, was a regular writer and reviewer for the *Journal des économistes,* and was made a corresponding member of the Académie des sciences morales et politiques in 1872. He wrote an early review of Bastiat's *Economic Harmonies* for the *Journal des économistes* (1850), in which he praised Bastiat's style but criticized his position on population and the theory of value. Two works which deserve special note are the article on "spoliation" (plunder), *"De la spoliation légale,"* *Journal des économistes,* vol. 20, no. 83, 1 July 1848, which he wrote in the heat of the June Days uprising in Paris, and the two-volume work on social theory which has numerous "Austrian" insights, *Essai sur la science sociale. Économie politique—morale expérimentale—politique théorique* (Paris: Guillaumin, 1867), 2 vols.

COBDEN, RICHARD (1804–65). Founder of the Anti–Corn Law League, Cobden was born in Sussex to a poor farmer's family and was trained by an uncle to become a clerk in his warehouse. At twenty-one, he became a traveling salesman and was so successful that he was able to acquire his own business, a factory making printed cloth. Thanks to his vision of the market and his sense of organization, his company became very prosperous. Nevertheless, at the age of thirty, he left the management of the company to his brother in order to travel. He wrote some remarkable articles in which he defended two great causes: pacifism, in the form of nonintervention in foreign affairs, and free exchange.

From 1839, he devoted himself exclusively to the Anti–Corn Law League and was elected member of Parliament for Stockport in 1841. Toward the end of the 1850s, he was asked by the government to negotiate a free-trade treaty with France. His French counterpart was Michel Chevalier, a minister of Napoléon III and a friend and admirer of Bastiat. The treaty (the Cobden-Chevalier Trade Treaty) was signed by Cobden and Chevalier in 1860.

COLBERT, JEAN-BAPTISTE (1619–83). Comptroller-general of finance under Louis XIV from 1665 to 1683. He epitomized the policy of state intervention in trade and industry known as "mercantilism" whereby the state subsidized or established domestic industry in order to replace foreign imports, imposed high tariffs in order to reduce foreign imported goods, spent taxpayers' money on lavish public works, and expanded France's empire overseas.

COMTE, CHARLES (1782–1837). Comte was a lawyer, liberal critic of Napoléon and then of the restored monarchy, and son-in-law of Jean-Baptiste Say. One of the leading liberal theorists before the 1848 Revolution, he founded, with Charles Dunoyer, the journal *Le Censeur* in 1814 and *Le Censeur européen* in 1817 and was prosecuted many times for challenging the press censorship laws and criticizing the government. He encountered the ideas of Say in 1817 and discussed them at length in *Le Censeur européen*. After having spent some time in prison he escaped to Switzerland, where he was offered the Chair of Natural Law at the University of Lausanne before he was obliged to move to England. In 1826 he published the first part of his magnum opus, the four-volume *Traité de législation,* which greatly influenced the thought of Bastiat, and in 1834 he published the second part, *Traité de la propriété*. Comte was secretary of the Académie des sciences morales et politiques and was elected a deputy representing La Sarthe after the 1830 Revolution.

CONDILLAC, ÉTIENNE BONNOT, ABBÉ DE (1714–80). Priest, philosopher, economist, and member of the Académie française. Condillac was an advocate of the ideas of John Locke and a friend of the encyclopedist Denis Diderot. In his *Traité des sensations* (1754), Condillac claims that all attributes of the mind, such as judgment, reason, and even will, derive from sensations. His book *Le Commerce et le gouvernement, considérés relativement l'un à l'autre* (1776) appeared in the same year as Adam Smith's *Wealth of Nations.*

CONSIDERANT, VICTOR PROSPER (1808–93). Follower of the socialist Fourier and edited the most successful Fourierist magazine, *La Démocratie pacifique* (1843–51). He was an advocate of the "right to work," a movement which Bastiat strongly opposed. Considerant wrote *Principes du socialisme.*

Manifeste de la démocratie au XIXe siècle (1847) and *Théorie du droit de propriété et du droit au travail* (1848).

COQUELIN, CHARLES (1802–52). One of the leading figures in the political economy movement (*Les Économistes*) in Paris before his untimely death. Coquelin was selected by the publisher Guillaumin to edit the prestigious and voluminous *Dictionnaire de l'économie politique* (1852) because of his erudition and near-photographic memory. He also wrote dozens of articles for the *Dictionnaire*.

Coquelin was very active in the free-trade movement, becoming secretary of the Association pour la liberté des échanges, writing articles for Bastiat's journal *Le Libre-échange,* and later taking over the editor's role when Bastiat had to resign because of ill health. Coquelin also wrote dozens of articles and book reviews for *Le Journal des économistes.* During the Revolution of 1848 Coquelin was active in forming a debating club, the Club de la liberté du travail (The Club for the Freedom of Working), which took on the socialists before it was violently broken up by opponents. Coquelin, along with Bastiat, Fonteyraud, Garnier, and Molinari, started a small revolutionary magazine, *Jacques Bonhomme,* which was written to appeal to ordinary people. Unfortunately, it lasted only a few weeks before it, too, was forced to close. Coquelin wrote about transport, the linen industry, the law governing corporations, money, credit, and banking (especially free banking, of which he was probably the first serious advocate).

COURIER DE MÉRÉ, PAUL-LOUIS (1773–1825). French artillery officer, translator of Greek literature, and liberal and anticlerical polemicist during the Restoration. He served in the Army of the Rhine and then saw action in Italy and Germany before apparently deserting after the battle of Wagram (1809) in horror at the terrible carnage he witnessed.

After the Restoration of the monarchy he began writing political pamphlets criticizing the illiberal policies of the regime and thus became one of its most dreaded critics with his satirical and witty pamphlets. In his first, *Pétition aux deux Chambres* (1816), he protested against the government's practice of making arbitrary arrests of its opponents. In 1819–20 he wrote a series of letters to the liberal journal *Le Censeur européen,* in which he chastised the liberals for not taking as much interest in the violation of the rights of ordinary peasants and farmers. In 1821 he was fined and spent two months in prison for offending the authorities in another of his pamphlets. Courier was found shot dead in a wood near his house in April 1825. His killer was never found, although there were rumors of a political killing in order to remove one of the gadflies of the regime.

CUNIN-GRIDAINE, LAURENT (1778–1859). Began his career as an ordinary worker in a textile factory before becoming a very successful manufacturer in his own right in the town of Sedan. He was elected to represent the Ardennes region from 1827 to 1840, sitting with the liberal group in the Chamber. He was appointed minister for trade from 1840 to 1848 and was a strong supporter of protection for the textile industry.

DAIRE, EUGÈNE (1798–1847). Tax collector turned laissez-faire economist who edited the massive fifteen-volume *Collection des principaux économistes* for Guillaumin on the history of classical economic thought.

DESCARTES, RENÉ (1596–1650). French philosopher and mathematician who lived much of his life in the Dutch republic. His best-known work is *Meditations on First Philosophy* (1641).

DESTUTT DE TRACY, ANTOINE (1754–1836). One of the leading intellectuals of the 1790s and early 1800s and a member of the idéologues (a philosophical movement not unlike the objectivists, who professed that the origin of ideas was material, not spiritual). In his writings on Montesquieu, Tracy defended the institutions of the American republic, and in his writings on political economy he defended laissez-faire.

During the French Revolution he joined the third estate and renounced his aristocratic title. During the Terror he was arrested and nearly executed. Tracy continued agitating for liberal reforms as a senator during Napoléon's regime. One of his most influential works was the four-volume *Éléments d'idéologie* (first published in 1801–15); Tracy coined the term *ideology*. Volume four of *Éléments d'idéologie*, titled *Traité de la volonté*, was translated by Thomas Jefferson and appeared in English under the title *Treatise of Political Economy* in 1817. It was then republished in France in 1823 under the same title, *Traité d'économie politique*. Tracy also wrote *Commentaire sur l'esprit des lois* (1819), which Thomas Jefferson translated and brought to the United States.

DIOGENES (413–327 B.C.). Greek philosopher who renounced wealth and lived by begging from others and sleeping in a barrel in the marketplace. His purpose was to live simply and virtuously by giving up the conventional desires for power, wealth, prestige, and fame. His philosophy went under the name of Cynicism and had an important influence on the development of Stoicism.

DOMBASLE, CHRISTOPHE-JOSEPH-ALEXANDRE MATHIEU DE (1777–1843). Pioneer agronomist who helped establish the French sugar beet industry. He began a model farm (1822), a factory to produce agricultural tools (1823), and a school of agriculture (1824). He wrote a number of works on taxation and the need for protectionism: *Des impôts dans leurs rapports avec la production agricole* (1829); *De l'impôt sur le sucre indigène: Nouvelles considérations* (1837); and "Études sur le commerce international dans ses rapports avec la richesse des peuples," in *Œuvres diverses. Économie politique. Instruction publique, Haras et remonte* (1843). Inspired by British agriculture, he introduced the practice of triennial crop rotation (cereals, forage, vegetables), which Bastiat tried in vain to introduce in his own sharecropping farms.

DUCHÂTEL, CHARLES MARIE TANNEGUY, COMTE (1803–67). One of the founding editors of the liberal magazine *Le Globe* (1824) before it became an organ of the Saint-Simonians after 1830. He was a member of the conservative liberal Doctrinaire group during the July Monarchy, serving as minister of commerce (1834–36), minister of finance (1836–37), and minister of the interior (1839–40). He was regarded as economically informed and sympathetic to liberal reform. He wrote on the economics of charity: *De la charité dans ses rapports avec l'état moral et le bien-être des classes inférieures de la société* (1829).

DUMAS, ALEXANDRE (1802–70). Prolific author of plays and historical novels. Although born into poverty, his grandfather was a nobleman who served in the artillery in Haiti and had a child with an ex-slave. His father (of mixed race) was a general in Napoléon's army who fell out of favor with the regime. Dumas participated in the 1830 overthrow of the restored monarchy and was an active supporter of the July Monarchy. His first literary successes came from writing plays and then novels which were serialized in the emerging popular press of the period. He earned a great deal of money from his writing, but he was often impoverished because of his high living. He is best known for historical novels such as *The Three Musketeers* (*Les Trois Mousquetaires,* 1844) and *The Count of Monte Cristo* (*Le Comte de Monte-Cristo,* 1845–46).

DUNOYER, BARTHÉLÉMY-PIERRE-JOSEPH-CHARLES (1786–1862). Journalist; academic (a professor of political economy); politician; author of numerous works on politics, political economy, and history; founding member of the Société d'économie politique (1842); and a key figure in the French classical liberal movement of the first half of the nineteenth century, along with Jean-Baptiste Say, Benjamin Constant, Charles Comte, Augustin Thierry, and Alexis de Tocqueville. He collaborated with Comte on the journals *Le Censeur* and *Le Censeur européen* during the end of the Napoleonic empire and the restoration of the Bourbon monarchy.

Dunoyer (and Comte) combined the political liberalism of Constant (constitutional limits on the power of the state, representative government); the economic liberalism of Say (laissez-faire, free trade); and the sociological approach to history of Thierry, Constant, and Say (class analysis and a theory of historical evolution of society through stages culminating in the laissez-faire market society of "industry").

His major works include *L'Industrie et la morale considérées dans leurs rapports avec la liberté* (1825), *Nouveau traité d'économie sociale* (1830), and his three-volume magnum opus *De la liberté du travail* (1845). After the Revolution of 1830 Dunoyer was appointed a member of the Académie des sciences morales et politiques, worked as a government official (he was prefect of L'Allier and La Somme), and eventually became a member of the Council of State in 1837. He resigned his government posts in protest against the coup d'état of Louis-Napoléon in 1851. He died while writing a critique of the authoritarian Second Empire; the work was completed and published by his son Anatole in 1864.

DUPIN, CHARLES (1784–1873). Naval engineer who attended the École polytechnique and later became minister of the navy. He taught mathematics at the Conservatoire national des arts et métiers and also ran courses for ordinary working people. He is one of the founders of mathematical economics and of the statistical office of France. In 1828 he was elected deputy for Tarn, was made a peer in 1830, and served in the Constituent and then the National Assembly during the Second Republic. His major work was *Le petit producteur français* (7 vols.).

FERRIER, FRANÇOIS LOUIS AUGUSTE (1777–1861). Advocate for protectionism, served as director general of the Customs Administration during the Empire, and was a member of the Chamber of Peers during the July Monarchy. His major works include *Du gouvernement considéré dans ses rapports avec le commerce* (1804).

FIX, THÉODORE (1800–1846). Swiss by birth, he came to France to work as a land surveyor and soon moved to Paris to work as a translator of German texts. After becoming interested in economics, he and Sismondi began in 1833 a short-lived journal, *La Revue mensuelle d'économie politique,* which lasted only three years. One of the notable aspects of Fix's works was his fluency in both German and English, which allowed him to write with authority for a French-speaking audience on the economics works published in those languages. In the course of his work Fix met many well-respected French political economists, such as Pellegrino Rossi and Adolphe Blanqui; wrote several articles for *Le Journal des économistes;* and became the chief economics writer for the periodical *Le Constitutionnel.* Before he died at a young age from heart disease, he published one book, *Observations sur l'état des classes ouvrières* (1846).

FONTENAY, ROGER-ANNE-PAUL-GABRIEL DE (1809–91). Member of the Société d'économie politique and an ally of Bastiat in their debates in the Société on the nature of rent. Fontenay worked with Prosper Paillottet in editing the *Œuvres complètes* of Bastiat and was a regular contributor to *Le Journal des économistes* right up to his death. In a work published soon after Bastiat's death in 1850, *Du revenu foncier* (1854), Fontenay describes himself and Bastiat as forming a distinct "French school of political economy" tracing its roots back to Jean-Baptiste Say and including Antoine Destutt de Tracy, Charles Comte, and especially Charles Dunoyer, in contrast with the "English school" of Adam Smith, Thomas Malthus, and David Ricardo. The main difference between the two schools was on the issue of rent from land: Bastiat and Fontenay denied that there was any special "gift of nature" that made up the rents from land, instead arguing that all returns on investments (whether capital, interest, or rent) were the result of services provided by producers to consumers.

FONTEYRAUD, HENRI ALCIDE (1822–49). Born in Mauritius and became professor of history, geography, and political economy at the École supérieure de commerce de Paris. He was a member of the Société d'économie politique and one of the founders of the Association pour la liberté des échanges. Because of his knowledge of English he went to England in 1845 to study at first hand the progress of the Anti–Corn Law League. During the Revolution of 1848, he campaigned against socialist ideas with his activity in the Club de la liberté du travail and, along with Bastiat, Coquelin, and Molinari, by writing and handing out in the streets of Paris copies of the broadside pamphlet *Jacques Bonhomme.* Sadly, he died very young during the cholera epidemic of 1849. He wrote articles in *La Revue britannique* and *Le Journal des économistes,* and he edited and annotated the works of Ricardo in the multivolume *Collection des principaux économistes.* His collected works were published posthumously as *Mélanges d'économie politique,* edited by J. Garnier (1853).

FOULD, ACHILLE (1800–1867). Banker and deputy who represented the départements of Les Hautes-Pyrénées in 1842 and La Seine in 1849. He was close to Louis-Napoléon, lending him money before he became emperor, and then serving as minister of finance, first during the Second Republic and then under the Second Empire (1849–67). Fould was an important part of the imperial household, serving as an adviser to the emperor, especially on economic matters. He was an ardent free trader but was close to the Saint–Simonians on matters of banking. (For the Saint-Simonians, see the entry for "Saint-Simon, Claude Henri de Rouvroy, comte de," in this glossary.)

FOURIER, FRANÇOIS-MARIE CHARLES (1772–1837). Socialist and founder of the phalansterian school (Fourierism). Fourierism consisted of a utopian, communistic system for the reorganization of society. The population was to be grouped in "phalansteries" of about eighteen hundred persons, who would live together as one family and hold property in common. Fourier's main works include *Le Nouveau monde industriel et sociétaire* (1829) and *La Fausse industrie morcelée répugnante et mensongère et l'antidote, l'industrie naturelle, combinée, attrayante, véridique donnant quadruple produit* (1835–36). Many of Fourier's ideas appeared in his journal *Phalanstère, ou la réforme industrielle,* which ran from 1832 to 1834.

FOX, WILLIAM JOHNSON (1786–1864). Journalist and renowned orator who became one of the most popular speakers of the Anti–Corn Law League. He served in Parliament from 1847 to 1863.

GARNIER, JOSEPH (1813–81). Professor, journalist, politician, and activist for free trade and peace. He arrived in Paris in 1830 and came under the influence of Adolphe Blanqui, who introduced him to economics and who eventually became his father-in-law.

Garnier was a pupil, professor, and then director of the École supérieure de commerce de Paris, before being appointed the first professor of political economy at the École des ponts et chaussées in 1846. Garnier played a central role in the burgeoning free-market school of thought in the 1840s in Paris and was an ardent Malthusian. He was one of the founders of the Association pour la liberté des échanges; he was active in the Congrès de la paix; he was one of the founders, along with Guillaumin, of *Le Journal des économistes,* of which he became chief editor in 1846; he was one of the founders of the Société d'économie politique and was its perpetual secretary; and he was one of the founders of the 1848 liberal broadsheet *Jacques Bonhomme.*

Garnier was acknowledged for his considerable achievements by being nominated to join the Académie des sciences morales et politiques in 1873 and to become a senator in 1876. He was the author of numerous books and articles, among which are *Introduction à l'étude de l'économie politique* (1843); *Richard Cobden, les ligueurs et la ligue* (1846); and *Congrès des amis de la paix universelle réuni à Paris en 1849* (1850). He edited Malthus's *Essai sur le principe de population* (1845); *Du principe de population* (1857); and *Traité d'économie politique sociale ou industrielle* (1863).

GIRARD, ANTOINE AND PHILIPPE. Brothers who were actors, jugglers, and sellers of patent medicines in Paris in the early seventeenth century. Antoine Girard played the part of "Tabarin," and Philippe Girard played the part of his master "Mondor." They wore brightly colored costumes and entertained passers-by with witty, philosophical, seductive, and sometimes scatological songs and dialogue in order to persuade them to buy their merchandise. Their routine was much admired and copied and became known as *les tabarinades* or *coq-à-l'âne* (cock-and-bull stories). A collection of their stories was published in two volumes in 1858, under the pen name "Tabarin": *Œuvres complètes de Tabarin, avec les recontres, fantaisies et coq-à-l'âne facétieux du Baron de Gratelkard.*

GUILLAUMIN, GILBERT-URBAIN (1801–64). French editor who founded a publishing dynasty which lasted from 1835 to around 1910 and became the focal point for the classical liberal movement in France. Guillaumin was orphaned at the age of five and was brought up by his uncle. He came to Paris in 1819 and worked in a bookstore before eventually founding his own publishing firm in 1835. He became active in liberal politics during the 1830 Revolution and made contact with the economists Adolphe Blanqui and Joseph Garnier. He became a publisher in 1835 in order to popularize and promote classical liberal economic ideas, and the firm of Guillaumin eventually became the major publishing house for liberal ideas in the mid-nineteenth century.

Guillaumin helped found *Le Journal des économistes* in 1841 with Horace Say (Jean-Baptiste's son) and Joseph Garnier. The following year he helped found the Société d'économie politique, which became the main organization that brought like-minded classical liberals together for discussion and debate.

His firm published scores of books on economic issues, making its catalog a virtual who's who of the liberal movement in France. Its 1866 catalog listed 166 separate book titles, not counting journals and other periodicals. For example, he published the works of Jean-Baptiste Say, Charles Dunoyer, Frédéric Bastiat, Gustave de Molinari, and many others, including translations of works by Hugo Grotius, Adam Smith, Jeremy Bentham, John Stuart Mill, and Charles Darwin. By the mid-1840s Guillaumin's home and business had become the focal point of the classical liberal lobby in Paris, which debated and published material opposed to a number of causes that they believed threatened liberty in France: statism, protectionism, socialism, militarism, and colonialism. After his death in 1864 the firm's activities were continued by his oldest daughter, Félicité, and after her death it was handed over to his youngest daughter Pauline. The firm of Guillaumin continued in one form or another from 1835 to 1910, when it was merged with the publisher Félix Alcan.

Guillaumin also published the following key journals, collections, and encyclopedias: *Journal des économistes* (1842–1940), *L'Annuaire de l'économie politique et de la statistique* (1844–99), the multivolume *Collection des principaux économistes* (1840–48), *Bibliothèques des sciences morales et politiques* (1857–), *Dictionnaire d'économie politique* (coedited with Charles Coquelin, 1852), and *Dictionnaire universel théorique et pratique du commerce et de la navigation* (1859–61).

GUIZOT, FRANÇOIS (1787–1874). Academic and politician whose career spanned many decades. He was born to a Protestant family in Nîmes. His father was guillotined during the Terror. As a law student in Paris, the young Guizot was a vocal opponent of the Napoleonic empire. After the restoration of the monarchy Guizot was part of the "Doctrinaires," a group of conservative and moderate liberals. He was professor of history at the Sorbonne from 1812 to 1830, publishing *Essai sur l'histoire de France* (1824), *Histoire de la révolution d'Angleterre* (1826–27), *Histoire générale de la civilisation en Europe* (1828), and *Histoire de la civilisation en France* (1829–32).

In 1829 he was elected deputy and became very active in French politics after the 1830 Revolution, supporting constitutional monarchy and a limited franchise. He served as minister of the interior, minister of education (1832–37), ambassador to England in 1840, and then foreign minister and prime minister, becoming in practice the leader of the government from 1840 to 1848. He promoted peace abroad and liberal conservatism at home, but his regime, weakened by corruption and economic difficulties, collapsed with the monarchy in 1848. He retired to Normandy to spend the rest of his days writing history and his memoirs, such as *Histoire parlementaire de France* (1863–64) and *Histoire des origines du gouvernement représentatif en Europe* (1851).

HILL, SIR ROWLAND (1795–1879). Postal reformer, advocated reform of the British postal system in 1839 and 1842 with the introduction of a cheap, prepaid system of postage—the "penny post." Hill was active in the South Australian colonization project, serving as secretary of the South Australian Colonization Commission between 1833 and 1839, working with the economist Robert Torrens, who was its chairman. In 1837 he published an influential pamphlet on postal reform, *Post Office Reform; Its Importance and Practicability* (London: Charles Knight and Co., 1837). Another strong advocate of postal reform was Richard Cobden, who believed that the existing system was another example of protection given by the government to the elite which imposed an excessive cost on business. Cobden and the

Anti–Corn Law League were able to take advantage of the cheap mail rates by distributing large numbers of their pamphlets and other propaganda before they were successful in 1846 in having the Corn Laws repealed by the British Parliament. Later Hill became a member of the Political Economy Club and a member of an exclusive discussion group which called itself "Friend in Council" and which included Edwin Chadwick and John Stuart Mill among its members.

HUGO, VICTOR-MARIE (1802–85). Poet, novelist, dramatist, and politician who wrote some of the most important literary works of nineteenth-century France. His works include the novels *Notre-Dame de Paris* (*The Hunchback of Notre Dame,* 1831) and *Les Misérables* (1862). Hugo was a conservative Catholic in his youth but had become more liberal-minded by the time he was elected deputy (1848–50). During the 1848 Revolution, he became a republican and a freethinker, which contributed to his forced exile after the coup d'état of Louis-Napoléon Bonaparte (2 December 1851). Hugo went into exile in Jersey and then Guernsey, where he remained until the 1870 revolution. He could have returned to France after an amnesty in 1859 but chose to remain in Guernsey, realizing that if he returned he would have to temper his criticisms of the emperor. Soon after his return to Paris he was elected to the National Assembly and then the Senate.

JOMINI, ANTOINE HENRI (1779–1869). Swiss-born general who served with distinction under Napoléon and then the Russian Czars. He was the author of several important works on military strategy. In his later work of 1838 he did seem to stray into the area of military policy, which may have attracted Bastiat's attention: *Traité de grande tactique, ou, Relation de la guerre de sept ans, extraite de Tempelhof, commentée et comparée aux principales opérations de la derniére guerre; avec un recueil des maximes les plus importantes de l'art militaire, justifiées par ces différents événements* (1805), and *Précis de l'art de la guerre, ou Nouveau tableau analytique des principales combinaisons de la stratégie, de la grande tactique et de la politique militaire* (1838).

LA FONTAINE, JEAN DE (1621–95). Poet and writer of fables which have become famous for superficial simplicity which masks much deeper moral and political insights. He trained as a lawyer and was active in the late seventeenth century, which is the classic period of French literature. *The Fables* were well known to French people, as they were a staple of childhood reading. Bastiat was able to use his readers' knowledge of their content in order to make his points about economic matters by using them as amusing illustrations in his arguments.

LAMARTINE, ALPHONSE MARIE LOUIS DE (1790–1869). Poet and statesman. As an immensely popular romantic poet, he used his talent to promote liberal ideas. He was a member of the provisional government and minister of foreign affairs in June 1848. After he lost the presidential election of December 1848 against Louis-Napoléon, he retired from political life and went back to writing.

LAMORICIÈRE, CHRISTOPHE-LOUIS JUCHAULT DE (1806–65). General, elected deputy (elected in 1846, reelected in 1848), and minister of war under Cavaignac (1848). Lamoricière took part in the military suppression of the rioting during the June Days of 1848. He played a significant role in the colonization of Algeria and supported government plans in 1848 to subsidize its civilian colonization. He opposed Louis-Napoléon Bonaparte and was arrested after the coup d'état of 2 December 1851 and spent five years in exile in Belgium.

LAPLACE, PIERRE SIMON, MARQUIS DE (1749–1827). French astronomer, physicist, and mathematician who greatly extended the development of mathematical astronomy and statistics. His magnum opus was the five-volume *Mécanique céleste* (Celestial Mechanics; 1799–1825). One of his greatest contributions was mathematically explaining the stability of the solar system by showing that any two planets and the sun must be in mutual equilibrium.

LEGENDRE, ADRIEN-MARIE (1752–1833). Mathematician who came from a wealthy family. He was elected to the Academy of Sciences in 1783, and lost his fortune during the Revolution. He was appointed by Napoléon to head the geometry section of the new National Institute of Sciences and Arts but fell out of favor again during the Restoration for not supporting the government's candidate for the Institute. His fortunes revived again under the July Monarchy when he was reappointed and made an officer of the Legion of Honor. He is best known for his work on Legendre polynomials, Legendre transformations, and the least squares method.

LESTIBOUDOIS, THÉMISTOCLE (1797–1876). Deputy who represented Lille in the département du Nord. He was also a physician and an economist. In the latter capacity he sided with the liberals in 1844 in supporting the ending of the stamp tax on periodicals but against them in supporting protectionism. In 1847 he published the pro-tariff book *Économie pratique des nations, ou système économique applicable aux différentes contrées, et spécialement à la France* (Paris: L. Colas, 1847).

MALTHUS, THOMAS ROBERT (1766–1858). Best known for his writings on population, in which he asserted that population growth (increasing at a geometric rate) would outstrip the growth in food production (growing at a slower arithmetic rate). Malthus studied at Jesus College, Cambridge, before becoming a professor of political economy at the East India Company College (Haileybury). His ideas were very influential among nineteenth-century political economists. His best-known work was *An Essay on the Principle of Population* (1798).

MARCET, JANE HALDIMAND (1769–1858). Daughter of a Swiss businessman, she lived in London and married a Swiss doctor who had come to know her through her writings. She wrote introductory works on science and political economy which were designed to be accessible to ordinary working people. The works on political economy were highly regarded by Jean-Baptiste Say, who acknowledged that she was the first woman to have written on economic matters and in many respects wrote better than some men, and John R. MacCulloch, who regarded her works as excellent introductions to the study of economics. Two of her works were translated into French and were thus quite likely known by Bastiat: *Conversations on Political Economy* (1816) and *Johns Hopkins's Notions on Political Economy* (1833).

MARTINEAU, HARRIET (1802–76). English writer who was born in Norwich to a family of French Huguenots who had fled religious persecution after the revocation of the Edict of Nantes. Her father was a textile manufacturer, and her loss of her senses of taste, smell, and hearing turned her toward reading widely and writing. She was unusual for becoming a professional full-time writer at a time when few women were able to pursue such a career.

She was a translator, novelist, speechwriter, and journalist who wrote a popular defense of the free market. She pioneered travel writing after a trip to America, and she wrote on the woman question. She first became interested in writing about economic matters after reading about machine-breaking riots in Manchester and then reading *Conversations on Political Economy* (1816) by Jane Marcet. Her educational tales or *Illustrations of Political Economy* appeared in nine volumes and provided an introduction to economic principles written in narrative form. They were published between 1832 and 1834, sold well, and were quickly translated into French. Gustave de Molinari reviewed an edition published by the classical liberal publishing firm Guillaumin for the *Journal des économistes* in April 1849. In this review, Molinari said that "[s]he deserves her double reputation for being an ingenious storyteller and a learned professor of political economy."

MacGregor, John (1797–1857). Born in Scotland but lived the first half of his life in Canada. He was a statistician, historian, diplomat, and supporter of free trade. He was appointed one of the secretaries of the British Board of Trade in 1840. During the 1840s he published very detailed reports on tariffs in various European countries. See, for example, *Commercial Statistics. A Digest of the Productive Resources, Commercial Legislation, Customs Tariffs, Navigation, Port, and Quarantine Laws . . .* (1843) and *Commercial Tariffs and Regulations of the Several States of Europe and America . . .* (1843).

Mimerel de Roubaix, Auguste Pierre (1786–1872). Textile manufacturer and politician from Roubaix who was a vigorous advocate of protectionism. Mimerel was the president of the Conseil général des manufacturiers, which advised the government on economic policy. In 1824 he headed a textile group in Lille known as the Comité des fileurs de Lille; in 1842 he founded a protariff Comité de l'industrie (Committee of Industry) in his home town Roubaix to lobby the government for protection and subsidies against a proposed Franco-Belgian trade treaty which was under discussion; and in October 1846 he was instrumental in organizing the regional committees to form a national body based in Paris known as the Association pour la défense du travail national (Association for the Defense of National Employment) in order to better counter the growing interest in Bastiat's Free Trade Association, which had also been established in that year.

   Mimerel and Antoine Odier sat on the Association's Central Committee, serving as vice president and president respectively of what was commonly referred to as the "Mimerel Committee" or the "Odier Committee." The Mimerel Committee was a focus for Bastiat's criticisms of protectionism, and it was the Mimerel Committee that called for the firing of free-market professors of political economy and for the abolition of their chairs. The committee later moderated its demands and called for the equal teaching of protectionist and free-trade views. Mimerel was elected deputy in 1849; appointed by Napoléon III to the Advisory Council and to the General Council of Agriculture, Industry, and Trade; and named senator in 1852.

"Molière," Jean-Baptiste Poquelin (1622–73). Playwright in the late seventeenth century during the classical period of French drama. Bastiat quotes Molière many times in the Sophisms as he finds his comedy of manners very useful in pointing out political and economic confusions. One of the cleverest examples of this is Bastiat's parody of Molière's parody of doctors in *Le Malade imaginaire* (1673), which appears in "Theft by Subsidy" (ES2 9). Molière had a very low opinion of the practice of seventeenth-century medicine with its purges and use of leeches. The play ends with an elaborate dance of doctors and apothecaries (and would-be doctors) in which a new doctor is inducted into the fraternity.

MOLINARI, GUSTAVE DE (1819–1912). Born in Belgium but spent most of his working life in Paris, where he became the leading representative of the laissez-faire school of classical liberalism in France in the second half of the nineteenth century. His liberalism was based on the theory of natural rights (especially the right to property and individual liberty), and he advocated complete laissez-faire in economic policy and an ultraminimal state in politics. In the 1840s he joined the Société d'économie politique and was active in the Association pour la liberté des échanges.

During the 1848 Revolution he vigorously opposed the rise of socialism and joined Bastiat in starting two magazines directed at the workers, which they handed out on the streets of Paris in February (*La République française*) and in June (*Jacques Bonhomme*). In 1849 he published two rigorous defenses of individual liberty in which he pushed to its ultimate limits his opposition to all state intervention in the economy, including the state's monopoly on security.

During the 1850s he contributed a number of significant articles on free trade, peace, colonization, and slavery to the *Dictionnaire de l'économie politique* (1852–53) before going into exile in his native Belgium to escape the authoritarian regime of Napoléon III. He became a professor of political economy at the Musée royale de l'industrie belge and published a significant treatise on political economy (*Cours d'économie politique,* 1855) and a number of articles opposing state education. In the 1860s Molinari returned to Paris to work on *Le Journal des débats,* becoming editor from 1871 to 1876. Toward the end of his long life, Molinari was appointed editor of the leading journal of political economy in France, *Le Journal des économistes* (1881–1909). Molinari's more important works include *Les Soirées de la rue Saint-Lazare* (1849), *L'Évolution économique du dix-neuvième siècle: Théorie du progrès* (1880), and *L'Évolution politique et la Révolution* (1884).

"MONDOR" AND "TABARIN." See the entry for "Girard, Antoine and Philippe," in this glossary.

MONTAIGNE, MICHEL EYQUEM DE (1533–92). One of the best-known and most-admired writers of the Renaissance. His *Essays* (first published in 1580) were a thoughtful meditation on human nature in the form of personal anecdotes infused with deep philosophical reflections. Montaigne was brought up with Latin as his first language and went on to study law, serving in the Bordeaux parliament from 1557 to 1570 and then as mayor of Bordeaux from 1581 to 1585. He was a close friend of Étienne de la Boétie, who wrote *Discours de la servitude volontaire* (1576), in which he explores why the majority too often willingly capitulates to the demands of a tiny ruling minority. In the religious controversies of his day Montaigne was a moderate Catholic. Bastiat was particularly attracted to refuting one of Montaigne's essays, "Le Profit de l'un est dommage de l'autre" (One Man's Gain Is Another Man's Loss), which Bastiat regarded as the classic example of an economic sophism that spawned so many other sophisms.

MONTESQUIEU, CHARLES LOUIS DE SECONDAT, BARON DE (1689–1755). One of the most influential legal theorists and political philosophers of the eighteenth century. He trained as a lawyer and practiced in Bordeaux before going to Paris, where he attended an important enlightened salon. His ideas about the separation of powers and checks on the power of the executive had a profound impact on the architects of the American Constitution. His most influential works are *L'Esprit des lois* (1748), *Les Lettres persanes* (1721), and *Considérations sur les causes de la grandeur des Romains et de leur décadence* (1732).

MOREAU DE JONNÈS, ALEXANDRE (1778–1870). Economist and statistician who was director of the Statistical Bureau in the Ministry of Trade (1834–42). He served in the army of Napoléon in the artillery, the grenadiers, and as aide-de-camp to several generals and admirals. After the war he entered the administration, and from 1834 he was in charge of editing the multivolume *Statistique générale de la France*. He published a two-volume work, *Le Commerce au dix-neuvième siècle* (1827), which established his reputation as an economic statistician. Several of his books were published by the classical liberal Guillaumin publishing firm, including *Recherches statistiques sur l'esclavage et sur les moyens de le supprimer* (1841), *Éléments de statistique* (1847), *Statistique de l'agriculture de la France* (1848), and *Statistique de l'industrie de la France* (1856). He also wrote several articles for the *Journal des économistes* on statistical subjects.

ODIER, ANTOINE (1766–1853). Swiss-born banker and textile manufacturer who came to Paris to play a part in the French Revolution, siding with the liberal Girondin group. He was a deputy (1827–37) and eventually a peer of France (1837). Odier was also president of the Chamber of Commerce of Paris and a leading member of the protectionist Association pour la défense du travail national (Association for the Defense of National Employment). He was a member of its Comité central (Central Committee), which was sometimes referred to as the Odier Committee or the Mimerel Committee.

ORLÉANS, LOUIS-PHILIPPE, DUC D' (1773–1850). Last French king during the July Monarchy (1830–48), abdicating on 24 February 1848. He served in the French army before going into exile in 1793. His exile lasted until 1815, when he was able to return to France under the restoration of the monarchy (King Louis XVIII was his cousin). During his exile he visited Switzerland, Scandinavia, the United States, and Cuba before settling in England. When the July revolution overthrew King Charles X in 1830, Louis-Philippe was proclaimed the new "king of the French." Initially, he enjoyed considerable support from the middle class for his liberal policies, but he became increasingly conservative and was ousted in the February 1848 Revolution.

PAILLOTTET, PROSPER (1804–78). Businessman who was drawn to Bastiat's free-trade association, L'Association pour la liberté des échanges, in the mid-1840s, joining it in its earliest days. Paillottet eventually became a firm friend of and companion to the ailing Bastiat, caring for him when he was very ill, in Italy. Paillottet was with Bastiat during his last few days and formed the Société des amis de Bastiat (Society of the Friends of Bastiat) only five days after his death in order to preserve his papers and drafts and to edit his collected works.

Paillottet made his living in the jewelry business, and his modest wealth enabled him to devote most of his energies to philanthropic causes. He was vice president of the Labor Tribunal (Conseil des prud'hommes) and a member of the Commission for the Encouragement of Workers' Associations (Conseil de l'encouragement aux assocations ouvrières) and of the recently formed Société d'économie politique (meetings of which Bastiat also attended). Paillottet was very active in the Association pour la liberté des échanges, even learning English in order to help Bastiat translate material on or by the Anti–Corn Law League. Much of this material probably ended up in Bastiat's book on the English Anti–Corn Law League, *Cobden et la ligue, ou l'agitation anglaise pour la liberté du commerce* (1845), which consisted mostly of translations of Anti–Corn Law League pamphlets, newspaper articles, and speeches.

As Bastiat's health worsened during 1850, Paillottet became his virtual secretary, editor, and research assistant, assisting with the editing and publishing of Bastiat's pamphlet *Property and Plunder* and the second edition of *Economic Harmonies,* which was published by the Société des amis de Bastiat.

On his deathbed Bastiat authorized Paillottet to collect his manuscripts and papers and to publish them in an edition of his complete works, the first edition of which appeared in 1854–55, and a second in 1862–64.

The various volumes of the series remained in print for much of the nineteenth century. When reading Paillottet's edition, which forms the basis of our translation, one is guided by the frequent and often intriguing footnotes and comments inserted by Bastiat's close friend throughout the volumes.

Paillottet wrote several articles and book reviews of his own that appeared in *Le Journal des économistes,* two articles of which were published separately in book form (*Des Conseils de prud'hommes,* and *De l'Encouragement aux associations ouvrières*) and an essay on intellectual property rights. He translated *On the Religious Ideas* (*Des Idées religieuses*), a religious work by William Johnson Fox, who had been a popular orator in the Manchester League and a Unitarian minister.

PALMERSTON, HENRY JOHN TEMPLE, THIRD VISCOUNT (1784–1860). British politician and leader of the Whig party. He was minister of foreign affairs (1830–41 and 1846–50) and then prime minister during the Crimean War (1854–56). He was a liberal interventionist who worked to limit French influence in world affairs.

PARNY, ÉVARISTE DÉSIRÉ DE FORGES, COMTE DE (1753–1814). French poet very popular in the early nineteenth century. He was one of the handful of French aristocrats who supported the American Revolution, and he wrote "Epitre aux insurgents de Boston" (A Letter to the Insurgents in Boston, 1777). His poetry is filled with references to liberty, and his long poem on "Flowers" might be interpreted as a discussion of how plant life needs the right conditions in which to grow and flourish just as humans need liberty. He wrote many love poems, transcribed songs from Madagascar into French verse, and wrote a notorious poem, *La Guerre des dieux* (War of the Gods, 1799), which was banned during the Restoration. He was the author of *Œuvres choisies de Parny, augmentées des variantes de texte et de notes* (1827), *Poésies érotiques* (1778), and *Chansons madécasses* (1787).

PASCAL, BLAISE (1623–62). Mathematician and philosopher whose best-known work, *Pensées* (Thoughts), appeared only after his death.

PEEL, SIR ROBERT (1788–1850). Leader of the Tories, served as home secretary under the Duke of Wellington (1822–27), and as prime minister twice (1834–35, 1841–46). He is best known for creating the Metropolitan Police Force in London; the Factory Act of 1844, which regulated the working hours of women and children in the factories; and the repeal of the Corn Laws in May 1846. The latter inspired Bastiat to lobby for similar economic reforms in France.

When he was prime minister in 1841 the economy was in severe recession, and to solve his budgetary problems he introduced an income tax in 1842 (not used since the Napoleonic Wars) which also permitted him to cut the level of tariffs on many goods such as sugar. He was sympathetic to the agitation for repeal of the protectionist Corn Laws, which he successfully maneuvered through Parliament on 26 May 1846. The Tory Party, however, was irreparably divided, and on that same evening, he lost a vote of confidence on his Irish policy and had to resign.

PROUDHON, PIERRE JOSEPH (1809–65). Political theorist, considered to be the father of anarchism. Proudhon spent many years as a printer and published many pamphlets on social and economic issues, often running afoul of the censors. He was elected to the Constituent Assembly in 1848 representing La Seine. In 1848 he became editor in chief of a number of periodicals, such as *Le Peuple* and *La Voix du peuple,* which got him into trouble again with the censors and for which he spent three years in prison, between 1849 and 1852. Between October 1849 and February 1850, Proudhon engaged in a lengthy debate with Bastiat on the nature of money and the legitimacy of charging interest on loans. He is best known for *Qu'est-ce que la propriété? ou recherches sur le principe du droit et du gouvernement* (1840), *Système des contradictions économiques* (1846), and several articles published in *Le Journal des économistes.*

REYBAUD, LOUIS (1799–1879). Businessman, journalist, novelist, fervent antisocialist, politician, and writer on economic and social issues. In 1846 he was elected deputy representing Marseilles, but his strong opposition to Napoléon III and the empire forced him to retire to devote himself to political economy. He became a member of the Académie des sciences morales et politiques in 1850. His writings include the prize-winning critique of socialists, *Études sur les réformateurs contemporains ou socialistes modernes* (1840); the satirical novel *Jérôme Paturot à la recherché d'une position sociale* (1843); and *Économistes contemporains* (1861). Reybaud also wrote many articles for *Le Journal des économistes* and the *Dictionnaire de l'économie politique* (1852).

RICARDO, DAVID (1772–1823). Born in London of Dutch-Jewish parents. He joined his father's stockbroking business and made a considerable fortune on the London Stock Exchange. In 1799 he read Adam Smith's *Wealth of Nations* (1776) and developed an interest in economic theory. He met James Mill and the Philosophical Radicals in 1807, was elected to Parliament in 1819, and was active politically in trying to widen the franchise and to abolish the restrictive Corn Laws.

He wrote a number of works, including *The High Price of Bullion* (1810), on the bullion controversy. His treatise *On the Principles of Political Economy and Taxation* (1817) was translated into French by F. S. Constancio with notes by J.-B. Say in 1818. It was reprinted, with additions from the third London edition of 1821, by Alcide Fonteyraud as part of his *Œuvres complètes* published by Guillaumin in 1847 as volume 13 of the series *Collection des principaux économistes,* in which Molinari was also involved as an editor. Most of the Economists were orthodox Ricardians on the question of rent, with the exception of Bastiat.

ROMANET, AUGUSTE, VICOMTE DE. Staunch protectionist who served on the Conseil général de l'agriculture, du commerce, et des manufactures (General Council of Agriculture, Trade, and Industry). Bastiat ridiculed his idea that the activity of industry could be compared to a horse race, which, given his great interest in horse racing, seemed the natural thing for Romanet to do. Among his works are *Rapport fait au Comité central pour la défense du travail national* (1843) and *De la protection en matière d'industrie et des réformes de Sir Robert Peel: Mémoire lu à l'Académie des sciences morales et politiques, le 15 mars 1845* (1845).

ROSSI, PELLIGRINO (1787–1848). Professor of political economy at the Collège de France (since 1833). He was assassinated in Rome in 1848 while serving as the French ambassador to the Vatican.

ROUSSEAU, JEAN-JACQUES (1712–78). Swiss philosopher and novelist who was an important figure in the Enlightenment. In his novels and discourses he claimed that civilization had weakened the natural liberty of mankind and that a truly free society would be the expression of the "general will" of all members of that society. He influenced later thinkers on both ends of the political spectrum. Bastiat often criticized Rousseau as he thought he was the inspiration behind much of the interventionist legislation introduced by the revolutionaries during the 1790s (especially Robespierre) and then later in the 1848 Revolution. He is best known for his book *Du Contrat social* (The Social Contract, 1761); he was also the author of, among other works, the *Discours sur l'origine et les fondements de l'inégalité parmi les hommes* (Discourse on Inequality, 1755), the autobiographical *Les Confessions* (1783), and the novels *Julie, ou la nouvelle Héloïse* (1761) and *Emile, ou l'éducation* (1762).

RUMILLY, LOUIS GAULTHIER (OR GAUTHIER) DE, (1792–1884). Trained as a lawyer and served as deputy 1830–34 and 1837–40. He was active in the Société d'encouragement pour l'industrie nationale (Society to Promote National Industry) and had a special interest in agriculture, railroads, and tariffs. He wrote the following report critical of free trade: *Protection du travail national. Congrès agricole des 7 départements du Nord* ... (1846).

SAINT-CHAMANS, AUGUSTE, VICOMTE DE (1777–1860). Deputy (1824–27) and a councilor of state. He advocated protectionism and a mercantilist theory of the balance of trade. He is author of *Du système d'impôt fondé sur les principes de l'économie politique* (1820). Other works include *Nouvel essai sur la richesse des nations* (1821) and *Traité d'économie publique, suivi d'un aperçu sur les finances de France* (1852).

SAINT-CRICQ, PIERRE LAURENT BARTHÉLEMY, COMTE DE (1772–1854). Protectionist deputy who became director general of Customs (1815), president of the Trade Council, minister of trade and colonies (1828–29), and then appointed to the peerage (1833).

SAINT-SIMON, CLAUDE HENRI DE ROUVROY, COMTE DE (1760–1825). Writer and social reformer. Saint-Simon came from a distinguished aristocratic family and initially planned a career in the military. He served under George Washington during the American Revolution. When the French Revolution broke out in 1789, he renounced his noble status and took the simple name of Henri Saint-Simon.

Between 1817 and 1822 Saint-Simon wrote a number of books that laid the foundation for his theory of "industry," by which he meant that the old regime of war, privilege, and monopoly would gradually be replaced by peace and a new elite of creators, producers, and industrialists.

His disciples, such as Auguste Comte and Olinde Rodrigues, carried on his work with the Saint-Simonian school of thought. Saint-Simon's views developed in parallel to the more liberal ideas about "industry" espoused by Augustin Thierry, Charles Comte, and Charles Dunoyer during the same period. What distinguished the two schools of thought was that Saint-Simonians advocated rule by a technocratic elite and state-supported "industry," which verged on being a form of socialism, while the liberal school around Comte and Dunoyer advocated a completely free market without any state intervention whatsoever, which would allow the entrepreneurial and "industrial" classes to rise to a predominant position without coercion. Saint-Simon's best-known works include *Réorganisation de la société européenne* (1814), *L'Industrie* (1817), *L'Organisateur* (1819), and *Du système industriel* (1821).

SAY, HORACE ÉMILE (1794–1860). Son of Jean-Baptiste Say, he married Anne Cheuvreux, sister of Casimir Cheuvreux, whose family were friends of Bastiat's. Say was a businessman and traveled in 1813 to the United States and Brazil. A result of his trip was *Histoire des relations commerciales entre la France et le Brésil* (1839). He became president of the Chamber of Commerce of Paris in 1834, was a councilor of state (1849–51), and headed an important inquiry into the state of industry in the Paris region (1848–51). Say was also very active in liberal circles: he participated in the foundation of the Société d'économie politique, the Guillaumin publishing firm, *Le Journal des économistes,* and *Le Journal du commerce.* He was also an important collaborator in the creation of the *Dictionnaire de l'économie politique* and the *Dictionnaire du commerce et des marchandises.* In 1857 he was nominated to the Académie des sciences morales et politiques but died before he could formally join.

SAY, JEAN-BAPTISTE (1767–1832). Leading French political economist in the first third of the nineteenth century. Before becoming an academic political economist quite late in life, Say apprenticed in a commercial office, working for a life insurance company; he also worked as a journalist, soldier, politician, cotton manufacturer, and writer. During the revolution he worked on the journal of the ideologues, *La Décade philosophique, littéraire et politique,* for which he wrote articles on political economy from 1794 to 1799.

In 1814 he was asked by the government to travel to England on a fact-finding mission to discover the secret of English economic growth and to report on the impact of the revolutionary wars on the British economy. His book *De l'Angleterre et des Anglais* (1815) was the result. After the defeat of Napoléon and the restoration of the Bourbon monarchy, Say was appointed to teach economics in Paris, first at the Athénée, then as a chair in "industrial economics" at the Conservatoire national des arts et métiers, and finally as the first chair in political economy at the Collège de France.

Say is best known for his *Traité d'économie politique* (1803), which went through many editions (and revisions) during his lifetime. One of his last major works, the *Cours complet d'économie politique pratique* (1828–33), was an attempt to broaden the scope of political economy, away from the preoccupation with the production of wealth, by examining the moral, political, and sociological requirements of a free society and how they interrelated with the study of political economy.

SIMIOT, ALEXANDRE ÉTIENNE (1807–79). Member of the Municipal Council of the Gironde and one of the leading figures in local democratic politics. He wrote on matters of taxation, free trade, and protection for several local newspapers. He was elected to represent the Gironde in April

1848 in the Constituent Assembly. Because of his radical political views he was sent into exile in 1852 and not amnestied until 1863. Later Simiot successfully stood for election in the Third Republic. He wrote *Gare du chemin de fer de Paris à Bordeaux* (1846), *Chemin de fer du Médoc* (1848), and *Centralisation et démocratie* (1861).

SMITH, ADAM (1723–90). Leading figure in the Scottish Enlightenment and one of the founders of modern economic thought with his work *The Wealth of Nations* (1776). He studied at the University of Glasgow and had as one of his teachers the philosopher Francis Hutcheson. In the late 1740s Smith lectured at the University of Edinburgh on rhetoric, belles-lettres, and jurisprudence; those lectures are available to us because of detailed notes taken by one of his students. In 1751 he moved to Glasgow, where he was a professor of logic and then moral philosophy. His *Theory of Moral Sentiments* (1759, translated into French in 1774) was a product of this period of his life.

   Between 1764 and 1766 he traveled to France as the tutor to the duke of Buccleuch. While in France Smith met many of the physiocrats and visited Voltaire in Geneva. As a result of a generous pension from the duke, Smith was able to retire to Kirkaldy to work on his magnum opus, *The Wealth of Nations,* which appeared in 1776 (French edition in 1788). Smith was appointed in 1778 as commissioner of customs and was based in Edinburgh, where he spent the remainder of his life. In 1843 an important French edition of *The Wealth of Nations* was published by Guillaumin with notes and commentary by leading French economists such as Blanqui, Garnier, Sismondi, and Say. The most complete edition of Smith's works is the *Glasgow Edition of the Works and Correspondence of Adam Smith,* originally published by Oxford University Press (1960) and later by Liberty Fund in paperback (1982–87).

SUË, EUGÈNE (1804–57). Son of a surgeon in Napoléon's army and himself a surgeon in the French navy. He served in Spain in 1823 and at the Battle of Navarino in 1828. Suë was active in the romantic and socialist movements and represented the city of Paris in the Assembly of 1850. He was forced into exile for his opposition to Louis-Napoléon. He wrote many novels on social questions and is best known for his ten-volume work, *Le Juif errant* (The Wandering Jew, 1844–45).

THÉNARD, LOUIS JACQUES (1777–1857). Chemist from a humble peasant background who became a professor of chemistry at the Collège de France in 1804 and was made a baron by Charles X in 1825. Thénard was a deputy representing Yonne (1827–30). He is best known for the discovery of hydrogen peroxide and his influence on the teaching of science in France during the nineteenth century.

THIERS, ADOLPHE (1797–1877). Lawyer, historian, politician, and journalist. While he was a lawyer he contributed articles to the liberal journal *Le Constitutionnel* and published one of his most famous works, the ten-volume *Histoire de la Révolution française* (1823–27). He was instrumental in supporting Louis-Philippe in July 1830 and was the main opponent of Guizot. Thiers defended the idea of a constitutional monarchy in such journals as *Le National.*

After 1813 he became successively a deputy, undersecretary of state, minister of agriculture, and minister of the interior. He was briefly prime minister and minster of foreign affairs in 1836 and 1840, when he resisted democratization and promoted some restrictions on the freedom of the press. During the 1840s he worked on the twenty-volume *Histoire du consulat et de l'empire,* which appeared between 1845 and 1862. After the 1848 Revolution and the creation of the Second Empire he was elected a deputy representing Rouen in the Constituent Assembly.

Thiers was a strong opponent of Napoléon III's foreign policies. After Napoléon's defeat, Thiers was appointed head of the provisional government by the National Assembly and then became president of the Third Republic until 1873. Thiers wrote some essays on economic matters for *Le Journal des économistes,* but his protectionist sympathies did not endear him to the Economists. He also wrote a book on property, *De la propriété* (1848).

THOMPSON, THOMAS PERRONET (1783–1869). Soldier, politician, polymath writer, and pamphleteer and agitator for the Anti–Corn Law League. He was a member of the Philosophical Radicals, who were inspired by the utilitarian and reformist ideas of Jeremy Bentham. Thompson was active in urging Catholic emancipation, the repeal of the Corn Laws, and the abolition of slavery, and played a leading role in managing the reformist journal the *Westminster Review.* His most significant works include *The True Theory of Rent* (1829), *A Catechism on the Corn Laws; With a List of Fallacies and the Answers* (1827), and *Contre-enquête par l'homme aux quarante écus* (1835), a defense of free trade written in response to a French government inquiry. He published a collection of his essays as *Exercises, Political and Others* (1842).

TURGOT, ANNE-ROBERT-JACQUES, BARON DE LAULNE (1727–81). Economist of the physiocratic school, politician, reformist bureaucrat, and writer. During the mid-1750s Turgot came into contact with the physiocrats, such as Quesnay, du Pont de Nemours, and Vincent de Gournay (who was the free-market intendant for commerce). Turgot had two opportunities to put free-market reforms into practice: when he was appointed intendant of Limoges in 1761–74, and when Louis XVI made him minister of finance between 1774 and 1776, at which time Turgot issued his six edicts to reduce regulations and taxation. His works include *Éloge de Gournay* (1759), *Réflexions sur la formation et la distribution des richesses* (1766), and *Lettres sur la liberté du commerce des grains* (1770).

VIENNET, JEAN-PONS-GUILLAUME (1777–1868). Army officer, deputy during the July Monarchy, and a poet and playwright. In 1827 he ran afoul of the authorities by writing in verse an "Epistle to the Rag and Bone Men" in support of freedom of the press, earning himself a demotion in the army. He became a strong supporter of Louis-Philippe during the July Monarchy and was an archcritic of the republicans in the Chamber of Deputies. His poem can be found in *Épitre aux chiffonniers sur les crimes de la presse* (1827).

VILLÈLE, JEAN-BAPTISTE, COMTE DE (1773–1854). Leader of the ultra-legitimists during the Restoration. He was minister of finance in 1821 and prime minister from 1822 until his resignation in 1828. He was instrumental in getting passed in 1825 an Indemnification Law for nobles who had been dispossessed during the Revolution, and a Law of Sacrilege for affronts to the Church.

VOLTAIRE (FRANÇOIS-MARIE AROUET) (1694–1778). One of the leading figures of the French Enlightenment. He first made a name for himself as a poet and playwright before turning to political philosophy, history, religious criticism, and other literary activities. He became notorious in the 1760s for his outspoken campaign against abuses by the Catholic Church and the use of state torture in the Calas Affair. Voltaire wrote a number of popular works, including *Lettres philosophique* (1734), in which he admired the economic and religious liberties of the English; his philosophic tale *Candide* (1759); his pathbreaking work of social history, *Le Siècle de Louis XIV* (1751); his *Traité sur la tolérance* (1763); and the *Dictionnaire philosophique* (1764), which contained his criticisms of religion and superstition.

Glossary of Places

AUCH. Main city of the département of Le Gers, in the eastern part of the département of the Landes, where Bastiat lived and which he represented in the Chamber. It is the historical capital of the old province of Gascogny.

BÉARN. Region located at the base of the Pyrénées in southwest France in the département of Pyrénées-Atlantiques. Its capital is the city of Pau.

BICÊTRE HOSPITAL AND ASYLUM. Located on the southern outskirts of Paris, it was built by Louis XIII in 1633 to care for old and injured soldiers. Under Louis XIV (1656) it was used to house the insane and other political and social "undesirables." It was here during the Revolution that the guillotine was tested on live sheep and the cadavers of prisoners. Victor Hugo's novel opposing the death penalty, *Le Dernier Jour d'un condamné* (The Last Day of a Condemned Man, 1829), was set in Bicêtre.

BONDY, THE FOREST OF. Large forest in the département of Seine-Saint-Denis, about fifteen kilometers east of Paris. It was a notorious refuge for thieves and highwaymen.

BOURBON PALACE. Built by Louis XIV in 1722 for his daughter Louise Françoise. It is located on the Quai d'Orsay in Paris. It was confiscated during the Revolution (1791) and has been the location for the Chamber of Deputies since the Restoration.

GARONNE RIVER. Has its source in the Pyrénées on the border between Spain and France and flows northward through the city of Toulouse before reaching Bordeaux on the coast.

GIRONDE. Département in the Aquitaine region in southwest France, immediately north of the département of the Landes, on the Atlantic coast. The Gironde contains the port city of Bordeaux and is famous for its wines. Because a number of liberal-minded deputies were sent to Paris from this region during the French Revolution, they were given the name of *Girondins*.

GUYENNE. Old province in the southwest of France, with Bordeaux as its capital city. It covered roughly the same territory as Bastiat's homeland, the Landes.

LANDES. Département in the region of Aquitaine in southwest France, where Bastiat was born and raised, and which he represented in the Chamber of Deputies. The Landes is short for "the heathlands of the Gascons." In Bastiat's day the Landes consisted of predominantly poorly drained heathland (*la lande*) which was burned off to allow the grazing of large numbers of sheep. Later in the nineteenth century extensive pine forests were grown, thus making possible the development of a lucrative timber industry.

LUXEMBOURG PALACE. Seventeenth-century palace in the 6th Arrondissement of Paris. The palace was seized as "national property" during the Revolution (1791) and used as a prison for a period during the Terror. In 1799 it became the seat of the French Senate and after 1814 housed the Chamber of Peers. During 1848 it became the headquarters of the Government Commission for the Workers (known as the Luxembourg Commission) under the directorship of the socialist Louis Blanc and became closely associated with the National Workshops program of government funding of unemployed workers who were used on public works programs.

MÉDOC. Wine-growing region in the département of Gironde near Bordeaux a little to the north of the Landes, where Bastiat lived. According to the 1855 official classification of Bordeaux wines, the red wines from this region are called "médoc."

MUGRON. Small town in the département of the Landes overlooking the Adour River, where Bastiat lived from 1825 to 1845. Bastiat was appointed justice of the peace in Mugron in May 1831. At the time it was a significant commercial center, with a port on the Adour River and about two thousand inhabitants (fifteen hundred now). Today, Mugron has a street, a square, and a plaza named after Bastiat.

RUE DE CHOISEUL. Street in Paris where the offices of the Free Trade Association were located. Bastiat also had an apartment here.

RUE HAUTEVILLE. Street in Paris where the headquarters of the Association for the Defense of National Employment (a protectionist organization led by Antoine Odier) were located.

Glossary of Newspapers and Journals

L'ATELIER (1840–50). Worker-run monthly newspaper edited by a collective of seventy-five skilled workers, many of whom were printers. It advocated the creation of government-financed producer cooperatives, shorter working hours, compensation for industrial accidents, and old-age pensions, and urged the abolition of workers' labor books (*livrets*), child labor, and the use of labor in prisons and convents. Two of its founders, Philippe Buchez and Claude-Anthime Corbon, were elected to the National Assembly during the 1848 Revolution and were its first president and vice president respectively.

LE COMMERCE (1837–48). According to Eugène Hatin, *Le Commerce,* subtitled "Journal des progrès moraux et matériels," appeared between 10 May 1837 and 21 March 1848. It was a liberal journal whose editors included Guillemot, Lesseps, Arnold Scheffer, and Bert.

Le Commerce should not be confused with another journal, *Le Journal du commerce,* which appeared from An III (1794) to 1848, with a number of name changes, including *Le Constitutionnel,* according to the vicissitudes of the censorship laws.

LE CONSTITUTIONNEL (1815–). Begun in 1815, it was one of the more successful liberal daily newspapers during the Restoration. It had a brief name change from 1817 to 1819, when it was known as *Le Journal du commerce,* in order to avoid problems with the censors. It wielded considerable importance during the Restoration, but during the July Monarchy it sided with the policies of Thiers and had a declining circulation. The paper was taken to court several times during the 1820s because of the anticlerical articles it published.

LE COURRIER FRANÇAIS (1819–46). Liberal and anticlerical newspaper founded by the constitutional monarchist Auguste-Hilarion, comte de Kératry (1769–1859). It was suspended and threatened with legal action several times during the 1820s for its stand against the French intervention in Spain and for criticizing the established church. The banker Jacques Lafitte

(1767–1844) supported it financially. It was more popular during the July Monarchy but still remained a small-circulation paper and was forced to close in 1846. Both Bastiat and Molinari wrote for it on occasion.

LA DÉMOCRATIE PACIFIQUE: JOURNAL DES INTÉRÊTS DES GOUVERNE-MENTS ET DES PEUPLES (1843–51). One of the journals which supported the socialist ideas of Charles Fourier. It was distinguished from similar journals in that it downplayed the ultimate social solution proposed by Fourier (the formation of small communities—the phalanxes where living and production would all be done communally) and focused on critiques of the free market and incremental reforms brought about by legislation.

L'ÉCONOMISTE BELGE (1855–68). This appeared under a variety of names: L'Economiste belge, Journal des réformes économiques et administatives, publié par M. G. de Molinari (Bruxelles: Imprimerie de Korn. Verbruggen, 1855–58). From 1859 it was entitled L'Économiste belge, Organe des intérêts de l'industrie et du commerce. Directeur-gérant: M. G. de Molinari (Bruxelles: Ch. Vanderauwera, 1859–62). From 1863: L'Économiste belge, Organe des intérêts politiques et économiques des consommateurs. Directeur-gérant: M. G. de Molinari (Bruxelles et Leipzig: A. Lacroix, Verboeckhoven, 1863–68).

JACQUES BONHOMME (1848). Editor J. Lobet. (Paris: Impr. de Napoléon Chaix). Short-lived biweekly paper Bastiat launched during the 1848 Revolution. The paper was directed at working people; "Jacques Bonhomme" (literally Jack Goodfellow) is the name used by the French to refer to "everyman," sometimes with the connotation that he is the archetype of the wise French peasant.

Bastiat uses the character Jacques Bonhomme frequently in his constructed dialogues in Economic Sophisms as a foil to criticize protectionists and advocates of government regulation. Bastiat joined Gustave de Molinari, Charles Coquelin, Alcide Fonteyraud, and Joseph Garnier in editing the journal, the first issue of which appeared just before the June Days uprising (23–26 June).

Jacques Bonhomme consisted of only four issues, which appeared from 11 June to 13 July, with a break between 24 June and 9 July. The first issue was a single page only on papier rose designed to be posted on the walls of buildings. On June 21 the government decided to close the so-called National Workshops, which were a government program to provide state-subsidized employment to unemployed workers, because of out-of-control expenses. This was promptly followed by a mass uprising in Paris to protest the decision, and troops were called in to suppress the protesters, causing considerable loss of life. While this was happening, Bastiat sent Molinari and the editorial committee an article he had written calling for the dissolution of the National Workshops, which appeared on the front page of the penultimate issue of *Jacques Bonhomme* in the last week of June 1848 ("To Citizens Lamartine and Ledru-Rollin"). Bastiat and Molinari closed the journal because of the violence which broke out in the streets as the army suppressed the rioters. It was in *Jacques Bonhomme* that Bastiat published the first draft of what was to become his essay "The State."

LE JOURNAL DES DÉBATS (1789–1944). Journal founded in 1789 by the Bertin family and managed for almost forty years by Louis-François Bertin. It went through several title changes and after 1814 became *Le Journal des débats politiques et littéraires.* The journal likewise underwent several changes of political alignment: it was against Napoléon during the First Empire; under the second restoration it became conservative rather than reactionary; and under Charles X it supported the liberal stance espoused by the Doctrinaires. It should be noted that Bastiat published the longer version of his famous essay "The State" in the 25 September 1848 issue of the journal. Gustave de Molinari was an editor in the 1870s. It ceased publication in 1944.

LE JOURNAL DES ÉCONOMISTES: REVUE MENSUELLE DE L'ÉCONOMIE POLITIQUE, DES QUESTIONS AGRICOLES, MANUFACTURIÈRES ET COMMERCIALES (Paris: Guillaumin, 1841–1940). Journal of the Société d'économie politique, which appeared starting December 1841 and then roughly every month until it was forced to close following the occupation of Paris by the Nazis in 1940. It was published by the firm of Guillaumin, which also published the writings of most of the liberals of the period.

Le Journal des économistes was the leading journal of the free-market economists (known as *Les Économistes*) in France in the second half of the nineteenth century. Bastiat wrote scores of articles for the journal, including many which were republished as essays in the *Economic Sophisms.* The editors of *Le Journal des économistes* during Bastiat's life were the founding editor and publisher Gilbert-Urbain Guillaumin; Adolphe Blanqui, between 1842 and 1843; Hippolyte Dussard, from 1843 to 1845; and Joseph Garnier, from 1845 to 1855. Gustave de Molinari edited the journal between 1881 and 1909.

LE LIBRE-ÉCHANGE (1846–48). The weekly journal of the *Association pour la liberté des échanges.* It began on 29 November 1846 as *Le Libre-échange: Journal du travail agricole, industriel et commercial* but changed its name to the simpler *Libre échange* at the start of its second year of publication. It closed on 16 April 1848 as a result of the Revolution. The first sixty-four issues were published by Bastiat, the editor in chief, and Joseph Garnier; the last eight issues were published by Charles Coquelin. The journal's editorial board included Anisson-Dupéron (pair de France), Bastiat, Adolphe Blanqui, Gustave Brunet (assistant to the mayor of Bordeaux), Campan (secretary of the Chamber of Commerce of Bordeaux), Michel Chevalier, Charles Coquelin, Charles Dunoyer, Léon Faucher, Alcide Fonteyraud, Joseph Garnier, Louis Leclerc, Gustave de Molinari, Prosper Paillottet, Horace Say, and Louis Wolowski. The first fifty-two issues were republished as a book by Guillaumin under the title *Le Libre-échange, journal de l'Association pour la liberté des échanges* (1847).

LE MONITEUR INDUSTRIEL (1839–). Became the journal of the protectionist Association pour la défense du travail national (Association for the Defense of National Employment) founded by Mimerel de Roubaix in 1846. It was the intellectual stronghold of the protectionists and became one of Bastiat's bêtes noires.

LE NATIONAL (1830–51). Liberal and increasingly republican newspaper during the July Monarchy. It was founded by Adolphe Thiers, François-Auguste Mignet, and Armand Carrel to oppose the reactionary policies of the duc de Polignac, an ultraroyalist politician who was prime minister during the Restoration. The paper played a decisive role during the "three glorious days" and contributed to the success of Louis-Philippe in 1830. However, it was in constant conflict with the censors during the first half of the 1830s, with the publisher spending three months in prison and the paper being repeatedly fined.

Under the editorship of Armand Marrast, the paper subjected the ministry of François Guizot to severe criticism throughout the 1840s for its corruption and its interventionist foreign policy. *Le National* played an important role in the outbreak of the February Revolution of 1848, and many of its friends and supporters got positions in the new government. During 1848 it opposed the uprising of the June Days riots and later supported the candidature of General Cavaignac against Louis-Napoléon for the presidency, positions also taken by Bastiat. It was forced to close after Louis-Napoléon seized power in the coup d'état of December 1851.

LA PRESSE (1836–). Widely distributed daily newspaper, created in 1836 by Émile de Girardin. During the February Revolution, Girardin's paper was suspended following the June Days uprising for criticizing the prevarication of the government.

LA RÉPUBLIQUE FRANÇAISE (Paris: Impr. de Napoléon Chaix, 26 February–28 March 1848). Short-lived revolutionary magazine which appeared two days after the revolution broke out in February 1848. Edited by Bastiat,

Hippolyte Castille, and Gustave de Molinari, it appeared daily in thirty issues between 26 February and 28 March. Accessed via BNF: Bibliothèque Nationale de France. *La République française* [Texte imprimé]: journal quotidien. 26 févr.–28 mars 1848 (no. 1–30). Publication: 1848. Notice no.: FRBNF32853034.

The format of the magazine was only one or two pages, so it could be handed out on street corners or pasted to walls and read by passers-by.

TABLE ALPHABÉTIQUE GÉNÉRALE des Matières contenues dans les deux premières séries (1841–65) *du Journal des Économistes* (Paris: Guillaumin, 1883).

Glossary of Subjects and Terms

ANTI-CORN LAW LEAGUE ("CORN LEAGUE" OR "LEAGUE"). Founded in 1838 by Richard Cobden and John Bright in Manchester. The initial aim of the League was to repeal the laws restricting the import of grain (Corn Laws), but it soon called for the unilateral ending of all agricultural and industrial restrictions on the free movement of goods between Britain and the rest of the world. For seven years it organized rallies, meetings, public lectures, and debates from one end of Britain to the other and managed to have proponents of free trade elected to Parliament. The Tory government resisted for many years but eventually yielded in 1846. The abolition was announced by Peel in January, the House passed the legislation in May, and the House of Lords agreed on 25 June 1846, when unilateral free trade became the law of Great Britain. The repeal was to take effect gradually over a period of three years. The League was the model for the Free Trade Association in France.

ASSOCIATION POUR LA DÉFENSE DU TRAVAIL NATIONAL (ASSOCIATION FOR THE DEFENSE OF NATIONAL EMPLOYMENT). Protectionist group founded in 1846 to defend the interests of industrialists and manufacturers. It was led by Antoine Odier and Pierre Mimerel de Roubaix, who also served on its Comité central (Central Committee), which was sometimes called the Mimerel Committee or the Odier Committee. Its journal was *Le Moniteur industriel,* which had its office in the rue Hauteville in Paris. The Association lobbied successfully between March and July 1847 to defeat a major reform of French tariff policy. The free traders at *Le Journal des économistes* mocked the Association by calling it the "Association prohibitionniste de Paris" (the Prohibitionist Association of Paris) or the "Comité central de la prohibition" (The Central Committee for Prohibition).

ASSOCIATION POUR LA LIBERTÉ DES ÉCHANGES (FREE TRADE ASSOCIATION). Founded in February 1846 in Bordeaux. Bastiat was the secretary of the Board, which was presided over by François d'Harcourt and having among its members Michel Chevalier, Auguste Blanqui, Joseph Garnier, Gustave de Molinari, and Horace Say. The first public meeting of the Paris Free Trade Association was held in Montesquieu Hall on 28 August 1846. The journal of the Association was called *Le Libre-échange* and was edited and largely written by Bastiat. The first issue appeared on 29 November 1846, and the journal closed on 16 April 1848 after seventy-two issues, most of which (sixty-four) were written by Bastiat. The offices of *Le Libre-échange* were in the rue de Choiseul in Paris.

COMITÉ POUR LA DÉFENSE DU TRAVAIL NATIONAL (COMMITTEE FOR THE DEFENSE OF NATIONAL EMPLOYMENT). See "Mimerel Committee," in this glossary.

CORN LAWS. Legislation introduced by Parliament in the seventeenth century to maintain a high price for corn (in the British context "corn" meant grain, especially wheat) by preventing the importation of cheaper foreign grain altogether or by imposing a duty on it in order to protect domestic producers from competition. The laws were revised in 1815 following the collapse of wheat prices at the end of the Napoleonic Wars. The artificially high prices which resulted led to rioting in London and Manchester. The laws were again amended in 1828 and 1842 to introduce a more flexible sliding scale of duties which would be imposed when the domestic price of wheat fell below a set amount. The high price caused by protection led to the formation of opposition groups, such as the Anti–Corn Law League in 1838, and to the founding of the *Economist* magazine in 1843. Pressure for repeal came from within Parliament by members of Parliament, such as Richard Cobden (elected in 1841), and from without by a number of factors: the well-organized public campaigning by the Anti–Corn Law League; the writings of classical economists, who were nearly universally in favor of free trade; the writings of popular authors such as Harriet Martineau, Jane Marcet, and Thomas Hodgskin; and the pressure of crop failures in Ireland in 1845. The Conservative prime minister Sir Robert Peel announced the repeal of the Corn Laws on 27 January 1846, to take effect on 1 February 1849 after a period of gradual reduction in the level of the duty. The act was passed by the House of Commons on 15 May and approved by the House of Lords on 25 June, thus bringing to an end centuries of agricultural protection in England.

LES ÉCONOMISTES (THE ECONOMISTS). Self-named group of liberal, free-trade political economists. The term "the economists" was applied to the eighteenth-century founders of political economy, such as the physiocrats and Adam Smith, as well as to the free-market political economists of the 1840s. The latter can be identified from their membership in or contributions to the following organizations: the Political Economy Society, *Le Journal des économistes,* and the Guillaumin publishing firm. Some of the leading figures in this group include the following: Charles Dunoyer (1786–1862), Pellegrino Rossi (1787–1848), Hippolyte Dussard (1791–1879), Hippolyte Passy (1793–1880), Horace Say (1794–1860), Eugène Daire (1798–1847), Louis Reybaud (1799–1879), Adolphe Blanqui (1798–1854), Frédéric Bastiat (1801–50), Gilbert Guillaumin (1801–64), Charles Coquelin (1802–52), Léon Faucher (1803–54), Ambroise Clément (1805–86), Michel Chevalier (1806–87), Louis Wolowski (1810–76), Adolphe Blaise (1811–86), Joseph Garnier (1813–81), Jean-Gustave Courcelle-Seneuil (1813–92), Maurice Block (1816–1901), Gustave de Molinari (1819–1912), and Henri Baudrillart (1821–92).

FEBRUARY REVOLUTION. See "Revolution of 1848," in this glossary.

FREE TRADE ASSOCIATION. See "Association pour la liberté des échanges," in this glossary.

GENERAL COUNCILS (CONSEILS GÉNÉRAUX DE DÉPARTEMENT). See appendix 2, "The French State and Politics."

GENERAL COUNCILS OF COMMERCE, MANUFACTURING, AND AGRICULTURE. See "General Councils of Commerce, Manufacturing, and Agriculture," in appendix 2, "The French State and Politics."

GOGUETTES, GOGUETTIERS. Social clubs where individuals could gather to drink and sing songs, often political or patriotic in nature. The poets who wrote these songs were called *goguettiers.* The members of these clubs were ordinary people, often from the lower or middle class, who would gather to talk politics when other forms of political association were forbidden or strictly limited. Bastiat quotes a number of *goguettiers* (e.g., Paul Émile Debraux and P.-J. Béranger), and this suggests that he knew their works quite well, perhaps even knowing some of their works by heart, which raises the intriguing possibility that he had attended meetings of the clubs.

IDEOLOGUES. Classical liberal republican group founded in the 1790s whose name refers to the four-volume work *Éléments d'idéologie* (1801–15) by Destutt de Tracy, who was one of the founders of the group. The theory of ideology had a specific meaning in the early nineteenth century. It referred to the ideas of Étienne Condillac (1715–80), who believed that all ideas were the result of sensations and wrote a pioneering treatise on economics, *Commerce and Government* (1776). The ideologues' belief in constitutional government and free markets incurred the wrath of Napoléon. Jefferson translated one of Destutt de Tracy's volumes on ideology into English, with the title *Treatise of Political Economy* (1817).

INTERNATIONAL CONGRESS OF THE FRIENDS OF PEACE (PARIS, AUGUST 1849). Third of seven congresses held between 1843 and 1853. The first International Congress of the Friends of Peace was held in London in 1843 on the initiative of the American Peace Society and Joseph Sturge. Some 340 delegates attended, the bulk of whom were British. The second, organized by Elihu Burritt and chaired by the Belgian lawyer Auguste Visschers, took place in Brussels in September 1848. At the third Congress, held in Paris 22–24 August 1849 and chaired by the novelist Victor Hugo, Bastiat gave a speech (see "Bastiat's Speech on 'Disarmament and Taxes' (August 1849)," pp. 514–20, in Addendum: Additional Material by Bastiat). The fourth was held in Frankfurt, 22–24 August 1850, with six hundred delegates, the fifth in London in July 1851, the sixth in Manchester in 1852, and the seventh in Edinburgh in 1853. The Congresses came to an end with the outbreak of the Crimean War in 1854.

IRISH FAMINE AND THE FAILURE OF FRENCH HARVESTS, 1846–47. The failure of the potato crop in Ireland, known as the Great Irish Famine of 1845–52, was caused by a disease which affected the potato crop (potato blight) and resulted in the deaths of 1 to 1.5 million people from famine and the emigration of a further million people out of a population of around seven million. In addition to the failure of the potato crop, there were other serious problems which were of concern, including the situation of tenant farmers unable to pay their rents, the continued export of food from Ireland during the famine, and restrictions on the free import of food from elsewhere in Europe. The famine gave impetus to the Anti–Corn Law League's efforts to dismantle British trade barriers which kept cheaper imported food from reaching Ireland. There were also crop failures in France in 1846–47 which led to price increases and hardship for many people.

The crop failures in 1846–1847 caused considerable hardship and a rise in food prices in 1847 across Europe. Some historians believe this was a contributing factor to the outbreak of revolution in 1848. The Economists believed that the hardship could have been alleviated if there had been international free trade in grain and other foodstuffs which would have allowed surpluses from some areas to be sold in areas where there were shortages. The repeal of the Corn Laws in Britain in May 1846 (but which did not take full effect until 1849) by Richard Cobden and the Anti–Corn Law League was a first step in this direction.

JACQUES BONHOMME. The name (literally "Jack Goodfellow") used by the French to refer to "everyman," sometimes with the connotation that he is the archetype of the wise French peasant. Bastiat uses the character of Jacques Bonhomme frequently in his constructed dialogues in *Economic Sophisms* as a foil to criticize protectionists and advocates of government regulation. In England at this time the phrase used to refer to the average Englishman was "John Bull"; in the late nineteenth and early twentieth centuries English judges used to refer to "the man on the Clapham Omnibus," meaning the average British citizen with common sense; a more colloquial contemporary American expression for the average man would be "Joe Six Pack."

The opposite of the clever Jacques Bonhomme figure was the stupid and slow-learning Gros-Jean (Big or Fat John). He was popularized by La Fontaine in his fable "The Milk Maid and the Pail." After daydreaming about how she will spend the money she has not yet earned at the markets, Perrette spills her pail of milk and ends up with nothing. She concludes the story by saying, "I am Gros-Jean, just like before."

The first time Bastiat used the character of Jacques Bonhomme was in the article "Salt, the Mail, and the Customs Service" in *JDE* (May 1846) which was later included in ES2 12. Here Jacques Bonhomme engages in a conversation with John Bull about the need for postal reform in France along the lines of the recent British reforms. He also appears in ES2 3 in "The Two Axes" (where Jacques Bonhomme is a carpenter who petitions the minister for trade M. Cunin-Gridaine for a law which would force carpenters to use blunt axes in order to increase the demand for carpentry work); ES2 10, in "The Tax Collector," where Jacques is a wine grower who argues with a tax collector, "Mr. Blockhead," about the nature of political representation and how his tax money is spent by the government; and ES2 13, in "Protection of the Three Municipal Magistrates" (where Jacques Bonhomme appears in the final scene of a small play to urge the oppressed people of Paris to throw off the yoke of economic regulations and the imposition of high city tolls). These three articles are undated but probably written in late 1847.

The main use of this character occurs in March and June 1848 in Bastiat's revolutionary magazines. He appeared briefly in March 12 in *La République française,* in two "petits fiches" (small posters) where, in ES3 21, "The Immediate Relief of the People," he appeals directly to the people not to be fooled by calls for the government to fund make-work programs such as the National Workshops, which were being set up at that time by Louis Blanc, and in ES3 22, "A Disastrous Remedy," where he warns the people about the folly of paying taxes with the one hand and receiving benefits from the state with the other hand. Both these short pieces were designed to be handed out as flyers on the streets or stuck on walls as posters for passers-by to read.

A more consistent use of the character Jacques Bonhomme was in June in another street magazine, this time called *Jacques Bonhomme,* in which Bastiat and his colleagues reported on the events taking place around them from the perspective of Jacques Bonhomme, in the hope that this would appeal more directly to the workers in the streets of Paris. The first issue (11 June 1848) began with a brief history of Jacques Bonhomme and his struggles against oppression and exploitation over the centuries. Bastiat is known to have written eight of the articles in the four issues which hit the streets, including what was an early version of his famous essay "The State."[1]

The final appearance of Jacques Bonhomme was in the last thing Bastiat ever wrote, *What Is Seen and What Is Not Seen* (July 1850), where he is used in five of the twelve chapters,[2] most notably in the first, "The Broken Window." It is the window of the shopkeeper Jacques Bonhomme which gets broken, thus producing a discussion about the opportunity costs of replacing it.

JULY MONARCHY (OF 1830). See "Revolution of 1848," in this glossary.

LUDDITES. Members of a movement in the early nineteenth century in England which protested the introduction of mechanized weaving machines, believing that they would put handloom weavers out of work. They were active between 1811 and 1813 before being suppressed by the government in a mass trial in 1813. They took their name from a weaver named Ned Ludd, who smashed weaving machines in 1779.

MIMEREL COMMITTEE. This was the shortened name for two protectionist bodies: "Comité pour la défense du travail national" (Committee for the Defense of National Employment), which was local, and the expanded "Association pour la défense du travail national" (Association for the Defense of National Employment), which was national. They were formed by the textile manufacturer Auguste Mimerel in 1842 in the northern manufacturing city of Roubaix in order to promote the interests of French industrial-

---

1. See "On Liberty" (11–15 June 1848) CW1, pp. 433–34; "Laissez-Faire" (11–15 June 1848) CW1, pp. 434–35; "The National Assembly" (11–15 June 1848) CW1, p. 451; "The State" (11–15 June 1848) CW2.8, pp. 105–6; "Taking Five and Returning Four Is Not Giving" (15–18 June 1848) CW4 (forthcoming); "A Hoax" (15–18 June 1848) CW4 (forthcoming); "A Dreadful Escalation" (20–23 June 1848) CW4 (forthcoming); "To Citizens Lamartine and Ledru-Rollin" (20–23 June 1848) CW1, pp. 444–45.

2. See WSWNS, 1. "The Broken Window," 3. "Taxes," 7. "Trade Restrictions," 8. "Machines," and 10. "Algeria."

ists in the face of growing interest in deregulation and liberalization on both sides of the channel and both sides of the border with Belgium. See also the entries for "Pierre Mimerel de Roubaix" and "Antoine Odier," in the Glossary of Persons, and the entry for "Association pour la défense du travail national," in this glossary.

NATIONAL WORKSHOPS (ATELIERS NATIONAUX). Established on 27 February 1848, in one of the very first legislative acts of the provisional government, to create government-funded jobs for unemployed workers. The workshops were engaged in a variety of public works schemes, and workers got 2 francs a day, which was soon reduced to 1 franc because of the tremendous increase in their numbers (29,000 on March 5; 118,000 on June 15). Workshops were set up in a number of regional centers, but the main workshop was in Paris. The workshops were regarded by socialists as a key part of the revolution and as a model for the future reform of French society. Much of the inspiration for them came from the writings of the socialist Louis Blanc, whose book *Organisation du travail* (1839) discussed the need for *ateliers sociaux* (social workshops) which would guarantee employment for all workers. The first director of the National Workshops was a young engineer, Émile Thomas, and Blanc was appointed head of the Luxembourg Commission, which had been set up to study the problems of labor and which gradually became a focal point for labor organizations and activity. In several of the sophisms Bastiat refers to the "Luxembourg Palace," where the Commission met, as shorthand for the socialist advocates of government wage control and subsidies.

Liberals like Bastiat regarded the workshops as expensive interventions by the government into the operation of the free market which were doomed to failure. He opposed them from the start, and he lobbied against them when he was vice president of the Finance Committee of the Assembly, but ironically he later vociferously defended workers' right to protest against the government and sought to protect them from being shot by the army. In May 1848 the Constituent Assembly formed a committee to discuss the matter, as the burden of paying for the National Workshops scheme was becoming too much for the government to bear. Bastiat was one of the speakers, and in his speech he distinguished between the right to work (*droit au travail,* where "work" is used as a noun and thus might be rendered as the "right to a job") and the "right to work" (*droit de travailler,* where "work" is used as a verb, meaning "the right to engage in work"). He was opposed to the former but supported the latter.

The increasing financial burden of the National Workshops led the Assembly to dissolve them on June 21, prompting some of the workers to riot in the streets of Paris during the so-called June Days, 23–26 June. The army under General Cavaignac was used to suppress the rioting, resulting in the death of about 1,500 people and the arrest of 15,000 (over 4,000 of whom were sentenced to transportation). The Assembly immediately declared a state of siege (martial law) in Paris and gave Cavaignac full executive power, which lasted until October. Publication of Bastiat's second revolutionary magazine, *Jacques Bonhomme,* was suspended because of the June Days (it appeared between 11 June and 13 July). In it appeared a draft of what was to become his pamphlet "The State." In the second-last issue, which was published the day before the National Workshops were closed by the government and rioting had broken out in the streets of Paris, Bastiat courageously published an article on the front page calling for their dissolution ("To Citizens Lamartine and Ledru-Rollin"). The magazine was forced to close because of the violence in the streets and the imposition of martial law. In a letter written to Julie Marsan on 29 June, Bastiat states that he became involved in the street fighting to attempt to disarm the fighters and to rescue some of the insurgents from being killed by the army (see CW1, pp. 156–57). In the crackdown which followed, Bastiat opposed the arrest and trial of Blanc for his participation in an earlier uprising in May and for being a figurehead of the June revolt.

NAVIGATION ACTS. Linchpin of the British policy of mercantilism from their introduction in 1651 to their abolition in 1849. The Navigation Act Bill was passed by Oliver Cromwell's government to prevent merchandise from being imported into Britain if it was not transported by British ships or ships from the producer countries. The first act applied to commerce within Europe and generated a war with Holland (1652–54). Extended to the colonies in 1660 and 1663, it generated a second war with Holland (1665–67). The Molasses Act of 1733 was designed to force the American colonists to buy more expensive sugar from the British West Indies and discourage trade with the French West Indies. The renewal of this act in 1764 as the Sugar Act was a major source of conflict which led to the American Revolution. The repeal of the Navigation Acts in 1849 was part of a concerted effort to introduce a policy of free trade in Britain and its empire during the 1840s. The repeal of the Corn Laws in 1846 was the other major platform of this effort.

PERFIDIOUS ALBION. "Faithless" or "deceitful England" was the disparaging name given to Britain by its French opponents. It probably dates from the 1790s, when the British monarchy subsidized the other monarchies of Europe in their struggle against the French Republic during the Revolution.

The phrase was also used during the 1840s as an attack on the policies of free trade which Britain was adopting, and those French supporters of free trade like Bastiat who were seen as "fifth columnists" for the British Empire. Bastiat made several trips to England to meet Richard Cobden and other members of the Anti–Corn Law League, and they in turn visited France. Bastiat was then in a way "importing" seditious and traitorous free-trade ideas into France. Bastiat makes fun of this name in "Protection, or the Three Municipal Magistrates" (ES2 13) by talking about "Perfidious Normandy," which sends its lower-cost butter to Paris, thus undermining the local butter industry in the same way that lower-cost English goods were competing with French-produced goods.

PHALANX. Self-sustaining community of the followers of the utopian socialist Charles Fourier. He envisaged that new communities of people would spring up in order to escape the injustices of free-market societies and industrialism. He borrowed the Greek word "phalanxes" for his new self-supporting communities, each of which would consist of about sixteen hundred people who would live in a specially designed building, called in French a *phalanstère,* or "phalanstery." A number of communities modeled on his ideas were set up in North America—in Texas, Ohio, New Jersey, and New York. Fourier's ideas had some influence in French politics during the Revolution of 1848 through the activities of Victor Considérant and his "right to work" movement.

PHYSIOCRATS. Group of French economists, bureaucrats, and legislators who came to prominence in the 1760s and included such figures as François Quesnay (1694–1774), Anne-Robert-Jacques Turgot (1727–81), Mercier de la Rivière (1720–94), Vincent de Gournay (1712–59), Mirabeau (1715–89), and Pierre Samuel du Pont de Nemours (1739–1817). They are best known for coining the expression "laissez-faire" as a summary statement of their policy prescriptions.

As the word *physiocracy* suggests (the rule of nature or natural law), the physiocrats believed that natural laws governed the operation of economic events and that rulers should acknowledge this fact in their legislation. They further believed that agricultural production was the source of wealth and that all barriers to its expansion and improvement (such as internal tariffs, government regulation, and high taxes) should be removed. The strategy of the physiocrats was to educate others through their scholarly and journalistic writings as well as to influence monarchs to adopt rational economic policies via a process of "enlightened despotism." This strategy met with very mixed results, as Turgot's failed effort to deregulate the French grain trade in the 1770s attests.

POLITICAL ECONOMY SOCIETY. See "Société d'économie politique," in this glossary.

REPRESENTATION. Throughout "The Tax Collector" (ES2 10), Bastiat uses numerous words and phrases to describe the way representative democracy works. In doing this he is pointing out the differences between two very different ways of conducting one's affairs. The first is private, namely the strict legal process of giving someone power of attorney to act on one's behalf, or the market process of making a contract with somebody to provide a service which is voluntarily paid for. For this Bastiat uses the words *placer une procuration* (to appoint someone to act with one's power of attorney) and *s'arranger directement* (to engage in an exchange directly with a supplier of a good or service). The second is political, namely voting for a politician who will represent one's interests in the Chamber of Deputies. For this Bastiat uses the words *nommer pour député* (nominate as one's representative) or *se faire représenter par quelqu'un* (to be represented by somebody). The tension in this chapter comes from the dissonance between the winemaker Jacques Bonhomme, who thinks of the word in the former sense and therefore thinks the person he voted for in the election will act in his interests and not those of the politician himself or those of powerful manufacturers and other vested interests, and the tax collector Mr. Blockhead, who uses euphemisms and language drawn from the private legal and economic world to describe the way in which representative politics works. He keeps referring to Bonhomme's political representatives as *votre chargé de pouvoirs* (the person you have appointed to exercise political powers), *votre fondé de pouvoirs* (the person you have set up to wield political power over you), and *votre chargé de procuration* (the person you have appointed with power of attorney over your affairs), which confuses and infuriates Bonhomme because he doesn't think he has done these things.

REVOLUTION OF 1848 (ALSO "FEBRUARY REVOLUTION"). Because France went through so many revolutions between 1789 and 1870, they are often distinguished by reference to the month in which they occurred. Thus we have the "July Monarchy" (of 1830), when the restored Bourbon monarchy of 1815 was overthrown in order to create a more liberal and constitutional monarchy under Louis-Philippe, 26–29 July 1830; the "February Revolution" (of 1848), when the July Monarchy of Louis-Philippe was overthrown and the Second Republic was formed, 23–26 February 1848; the "June Days" (23–26 June 1848), when a rebellion by some workers in Paris who were protesting the closure of the government-subsidized National Workshops work-relief program was bloodily put down by General Cavaignac; the "18th Brumaire of Louis-Napoléon," which refers to the coup d'état that brought Louis-Napoléon (Napoléon Bonaparte's nephew) to power on 2 December 1851 and that ushered in the creation of the Second Empire—the phrase was coined by Karl Marx and refers to another date, 18 Brumaire in the Republican calendar, or 9 November 1799, when Napoléon Bonaparte declared himself dictator in another coup d'état. Bastiat was an active participant in the 1848 Revolution, being elected to the Constituent Assembly on 23 April 1848 and then to the Legislative Assembly on 13 May 1849.

SOCIALIST SCHOOL. The rise of socialist ideas in the twenty-odd years before the 1848 Revolution is one of the targets of Bastiat's writings. Socialism arose out of a critique of the development of modern industrialization, especially of factory production. Socialists objected to wage labor, free-market prices, private ownership of production by large capitalists, and the making of profit, interest, and rent, which they thought occurred at the expense of the workers. Some of the leading figures of the French socialist school are the Comte de Saint-Simon (1760–1825), Charles Fourier (1772–1837), Étienne Cabet (1788–1856), Pierre Leroux (1798–1871), Victor Prosper Considérant (1808–93), Pierre Joseph Proudhon (1809–65), and Louis Blanc (1811–82). During the 1840s the work of Proudhon on property was a serious challenge to the economists (including *Qu'est-ce que la propriété?* [1840]), as were the writings and political activities of Louis Blanc on "the right to work" and the National Workshops. Bastiat spent much time criticizing the ideas of Proudhon on property, interest, and profit, and Louis Blanc's views on the right to work. Other issues which were challenged by the socialists included the morality of profits, interest, and rent; the private ownership of property (versus communal ownership); and the justice of the current system of land ownership.

SOCIÉTÉ D'ÉCONOMIE POLITIQUE (POLITICAL ECONOMY SOCIETY). Refounded in late 1842 after a false start in early 1842 and had its first monthly meeting at the Maison-Dorée restaurant on 15 November 1842. It was attended by Joseph Garnier, Adolphe Blaise, Eugène Daire, Gilbert-Urbain Guillaumin, and a fifth member who soon dropped out because he was a supporter of tariffs. Its first president was Charles Dunoyer, who served from 1845 to 1862, and Joseph Garnier was made permanent secretary in 1849. Its membership in 1847 was about fifty and grew to about eighty by the end of 1849. It is not known when Bastiat joined the society, but he is first mentioned in the minutes for August 1846, when the society hosted a banquet in honor of Richard Cobden, and Bastiat was one of several members of the society to make a formal toast to "the past and present defenders of free trade in the House of Lords and the House of Commons." A summary of its monthly meetings was published in *Le Journal des économistes.*

SOCIÉTÉ D'ENCOURAGEMENT POUR L'INDUSTRIE NATIONALE (SOCI-ETY TO PROMOTE NATIONAL INDUSTRY). Founded in 1801 and still in existence today. It was modeled on the Society for the Encouragement of Arts, Commerce, and Manufactures (founded in 1754 in London), which was seen as crucial in the spread of industrial and scientific ideas which lay behind British industrialization. The founding president of the French Society was the industrial chemist Jean Antoine Chaptal (1801–32).

SUPERIOR COUNCIL OF COMMERCE (CONSEIL SUPÉRIEUR DU COM-MERCE). The Ordinance of 1831 created within the Ministry of Commerce a "Conseil supérieur du commerce" (Superior Council of Commerce) which had the authority to conduct official inquiries into matters such as tariff policy. At the first such inquiry, held in October 1834, the largest and most politically well-connected manufacturers, landowners, and merchants closed ranks in their opposition to any tariff reform.

UTOPIAS. An important part of the classical liberal critique of socialism was its analysis of the utopian vision many socialists had of a future community where their ideals of common ownership of property, the equality of economic conditions, state-planned and state-funded education, and strictly regulated economic activity for the "common good" were practiced. Bastiat makes many references in his writings to the ideas and proposed communities of people like Fénelon, Saint-Simon, Fourier, and Owen. In an article titled "Utopie," by Hippolyte Passy, in the *Dictionnaire de L'Économie Politique,* which summed up the thinking of the liberal political economists on this topic just two years after Bastiat's death, Passy stated that Bastiat had provided the key insight into the differences between the socialists' and the economists' vision of the future of society: the socialist vision was a *factice,* or artificial one, with an order imposed by a ruling elite, party, or priesthood, while the liberal vision was a "natural" or spontaneous one that flowed "harmoniously" from the voluntary actions of individuals in the marketplace. Given the harshness of the economists' rejection of socialist utopian schemes, it is rather ironic that the classical liberals also had their utopian moments.

One could also mention here Condorcet's idea of the "Tenth Epoch" (1795), Charles Comte's and Charles Dunoyer's idea of the "industrial stage" of economic development (1820s), and Gustave de Molinari's vision of a fully privatized society where there was no role left for the state (1849).

Bibliographical Note on the Works Cited in This Volume

In the text, Bastiat cites or alludes to many literary, political, and economic works, especially those published during the debates about free trade and protection which took place between 1844 and 1850. We have listed these works with a full citation in the bibliography of primary sources. In the glossaries, if a work is cited, we have given only the title of the work and the date when it was first published, for example, Romanet, *Rapport fait au Comité central pour la défense du travail national* (1843).

In the bibliography of primary sources, we have tried, if possible, to cite editions published during Bastiat's lifetime. For example, Bastiat cited Jeremy Bentham quite frequently but used the French editions published by Éti-enne Dumont in the early nineteenth century and not the English-language editions. Thus we cite in the footnotes the 1816 edition of the "Traité des sophismes politiques," published in Geneva and not the Bowring English edition published in 1838–43.

Bastiat was sometimes quite cavalier in citing the sources he used, such as the plays of Molière, and did not provide act or scene numbers. He also quoted from memory and sometimes got the quotation slightly wrong, or changed the name of the character in order to make a contemporary political point. We have used editions of Molière which Bastiat most likely had access to, checked his quotations against the original, and have indicated in the footnotes where Bastiat strays from the original text.

For background information about key concepts and biographical details of political figures and authors, we have frequently consulted the *Dictionnaire de l'économie politique* (1852–53). Bastiat was closely connected to the group of classical liberal political economists in Paris during the 1840s: he was a member of the Société d'économie politique (founded 1842); he wrote many articles for *Le Journal des économistes* (founded 1841), including many of his economic sophisms before they were turned into books; he was even offered the job of editing the journal, which he turned down because he wanted to focus on his free trade campaign. The authors who wrote for the *Dictionnaire de l'économie politique* knew Bastiat personally and professionally, and their articles have provided a great deal of information about his life, ideas, and political activities.

In some cases Bastiat does not quote an author or authors directly but paraphrases their ideas in his own words. For example, in his newspaper articles he refers to speeches in the Chamber of Deputies given by protectionists and mentions pamphlets they have written. Wherever possible we have tried to track down these speeches and pamphlets, but we have not always been able to do so. For speeches and votes which Bastiat made in the Constituent and National Assemblies after the February Revolution of 1848, we have used the official *Compte rendu des séances de l'Assemblée Nationale Constituante (4 Mai 1848–27 Mai 1849)* and the *Compte rendu des séances de l'Assemblée Nationale Législative (28 Mai 1849–1 Déc. 1851)* to find information about Bastiat's legislative activities.

Since Bastiat makes so many references to the amounts the French government raised in taxes and spent on various programs, we have constructed a composite budget of French government finances for the years 1848 and 1849 when Bastiat was active in politics, most notably serving as vice president of the Finance Committee of the National Assembly. This can be found in appendix 4, "French Government's Budgets for Fiscal Years 1848–49." The data have been taken from *L'Annuaire de l'économie politique et de la statistique* and other sources (see appendix 4, pp. 496–503). Whenever Bastiat mentions a figure concerning government taxation or expenditure, we have checked this against the official data and have found him to be very accurate. Articles in the *Dictionnaire de l'économie politique* also provide considerable amounts of economic data on matters concerning government expenditure and policy. The details are discussed in the footnotes.

We have also consulted the 1835 edition of the *Dictionnaire de l'Académie française* in order to understand some of the nuances of the French language as it was used in Bastiat's day. This has been especially helpful in appreciating some of the many puns, jokes, and plays on words in which Bastiat liked to indulge.

Bibliography

PRIMARY SOURCES

WORKS BY BASTIAT

"Abondance." In *Dictionnaire de l'économie politique* (1852) 1:2–4.

Ce qu'on voit et ce qu'on ne voit pas: Choix de sophismes et de pamphlets économiques. Preface by Jacques Garello. 3rd ed. Paris: Romillat, 2004.

Ce qu'on voit et ce qu'on ne voit pas, ou l'Économie politique en une leçon. Par M. F. Bastiat, Représentant du peuple à l'Assemblée nationale, Membre correspondant de l'Institut. Paris: Guillaumin, 1850.

Ce qu'on voit et ce qu'on ne voit pas, ou l'Économie politique en une leçon. 4th ed. Paris: Guillaumin, 1869.

Ce qu'on voit et ce qu'on ne voit pas, ou l'Économie politique en une leçon, 5e édition précédée d'une notice biographique et augmentée de nombreuses notes par H. Bellaire. Paris: H. Bellaire, 1873.

Ce qu'on voit et ce qu'on ne voit pas, ou l'Économie politique en une leçon. 5th ed. Paris: Guillaumin, 1879.

Ce qu'on voit et ce qu'on ne voit pas: ou l'Économie politique en une leçon. L'État. Brussels: J. Lebègue, 1914.

Ce qu'on voit et ce qu'on ne voit pas, précédé d'une table ronde présidée par Alain Madelin, le 22 novembre 1993. Paris: Romillat, 1994.

Cobden et la ligue, ou l'Agitation anglaise pour la liberté du commerce. Paris: Guillaumin, 1845.

"De l'influence des tarifs français et anglais sur l'avenir des deux peoples." *Journal des économistes* 9 (October 1844): 244–71.

Economic Harmonies. Translated by W. Hayden Boyers. Edited by George B. de Huszar. Introduction by Dean Russell. Irvington-on-Hudson, N.Y.: Foundation for Economic Education, 1996. First edition, 1964.

Economic Sophisms. Translated from the fifth edition by Patrick James Stirling. Edinburgh: Oliver and Boyd, 1873.

Economic Sophisms. Translated and edited by Arthur Goddard. Irvington-on-Hudson, N.Y.: Foundation for Economic Education, 1964.

Economic Sophisms by Frédéric Bastiat. Translated by Patrick James Stirling with an introduction by H. H. Asquith. 1909. Reprint, London: T. F. Unwin, 1921.

Economic Sophisms; or, Fallacies of Protection. London: Published for the Cobden Club by T. F. Unwin, 1909.

Essays on Political Economy, by the Late M. Frédéric Bastiat. London: Cash, 1853. Part 2. That Which Is Seen, and That Which Is Not Seen, pp. 1–72.

Essays on Political Economy, by the Late M. Frédéric Bastiat. Translated from the Paris Edition of 1863. Preface by "H.W.," pp. iii–xvi. Chicago: The Western News Company, 1869.

L'État. In *Le Journal des débats,* 23 September 1848, 1–2.

Falske Sætninger i Statshusholdningslæren: Række 1–2. Translated by A. V. Laessøe. Copenhagen: C. A. Reitzel, 1848.

Free Trade, Peace and Goodwill: Being Selections from Bastiat's "Fallacies of Protection." London: Cobden Club, 1915.

Gratuité du crédit. Discussion entre M. Fr. Bastiat et M. Proudhon. Paris: Guillaumin, 1850.

Harmonies économiques. 2me édition. Augmentée des manuscrits laissés par l'auteur. Publiée par la Société des amis de Bastiat. Paris: Guillaumin, 1851.

Harmonies of Political Economy, trans. Patrick James Stirling. 2 vols. Santa Ana, Calif.: Register Pub., 1944–45.

Hvad man ser og hvad man ikke ser, kortfattet Statshusholdningslære. Copenhagen: C. A. Reitzel, 1852.

Jacques Bonhomme. L'éphémère journal de Frédéric Bastiat et Gustave de Molinari (11 juin–13 juillet 1848). Recueil de tous les articles, augmenté d'une introduction par Benoît Malbranque. Paris: Institut Coppet, 2014.

The Law. Irvington-on-Hudson, N.Y.: Foundation for Economic Education, 1950.

"The Law," "The State," and Other Political Writings, 1843–1850. The Collected Works of Frédéric Bastiat. Indianapolis: Liberty Fund, 2012.

Lettres d'un habitant des Landes, Frédéric Bastiat. Edited by Mme Cheuvreux. Paris: A. Quantin, 1877.

"La Loi," *DEP,* vol. 2, pp. 93–100.

The Man and the Statesman: The Correspondence and Articles on Politics. The Collected Works of Frédéric Bastiat. Indianapolis: Liberty Fund, 2011.

Œuvres choisies de Fr. Bastiat. 3 vols. Vol. 1, *Sophismes économiques. Petits pamphlets.* Vol. 2, *Sophismes économiques. Petits pamphlets.* Vol. 3, *Harmonies économiques* [described as the 4th edition]. Paris: Guillaumin, 1863.

Œuvres complètes de Frédéric Bastiat, mises en ordre, revues et annotées d'après les manuscrits de l'auteur. 6 vols. [Edited by Prosper Paillottet with the assistance of Roger de Fontenay, but they are not credited on the title page.] Paris: Guillaumin, 1854–55.

Œuvres complètes de Frédéric Bastiat, mises en ordre, revues et annotées d'après les manuscrits de l'auteur. Edited by Prosper Paillottet and with a "Notice sur la vie et les écrits de Frédéric Bastiat" by Roger de Fontenay. 2nd ed. 7 vols. Paris: Guillaumin, 1862–64. [This edition differs from the first with a new seventh volume of essays and correspondence.]

Œuvres complètes. Édition en 7 volumes, sous la direction de Jacques de Guenin. Vol. 1, *L'Homme.* Introduction by Jacques de Guenin; éloge funèbre by Gustave de Molinari; notes, chronology and glossary by Jean-Claude Paul-Dejean. Paris: Institut Charles Coquelin, 2009.

Œuvres économiques, textes présentés par Florin Aftalion. Paris: Presses universitaires de France, 1983.

"Opinion de M. Frédéric Bastiat." In *Le Droit au travail à l'Assemblée nationale: Recueil complet de tous les discours prononcés dans cette mémorable discussion par MM. Fresneau, Hubert-Delisle, Cazalès, Gaulthier de Rumilly, Pelletier, A. de Tocqueville, Ledru-Rollin, Duvergier de Hauranne, Crémieux, M. Barthe, Gaslonde, de Luppé, Arnaud (de l'Ariége), Thiers, Considérant, Bouhier de l'Ecluse, Martin-Bernard, Billault, Dufaure, Goudchaux, et Lagrange (textes revus par les orateurs), suivis de l'opinion de MM. Marrast, Proudhon, Louis Blanc, Ed. Laboulaye et Cormenin; avec des observations inédites par MM. Léon Faucher, Wolowski, Fréd. Bastiat, de Parieu, et une introduction et des notes par M. Joseph Garnier,* 373–76. Paris: Guillaumin, 1848.

Pamphlets. Preface by Michel Leter. Paris: Les Belles Lettres, 2009.

Popular Fallacies Regarding General Interests: Being a Translation of the "Sophismes économiques," by Frederic Bastiat. With notes by George Richardson Porter. London: J. Murray, 1846.

Popular Fallacies Regarding Trade and Foreign duties: Being the "Sophismes économiques" of Frédéric Bastiat; Adapted to the Present Time by Edward Robert Pearce Edgcumbe. London: Cassell, Petter Galpin for the Cobden Club, 1882.

Propriété et loi. L'État. Paris: Institut économique de Paris, 1983.

Selected Essays on Political Economy. Translated by Seymour Cain. Edited by George B. de Huszar. Irvington-on-Hudson, N.Y.: Foundation for Economic Education, 1968. First published 1964 by D. Van Nostrand Company.

"Situation économique de la Grande-Bretagne. Réformes financières. Agitation pour la liberté commerciale," *JDE,* June 1845, T. XI, no. 43, pp. 233–65.

Social Fallacies by Frederic Bastiat. Translated from the 5th French edition by Patrick James Stirling, with a foreword by Rose Wilder Lane. Santa Ana, Calif.: Register Publishing Co., 1944.

Sofismas económicos. Madrid: Colegio de sordos mudos y ciegos, 1847.

Sofismi economici. Translated by Antonio Contrucci and Antonio Scialoja. Florence: C. P. Onesti, 1847.

Sophismes économiques. Paris: Guillaumin, 1846. [The first edition of the First Series.]

Sophismes économiques. Preface by Michel Leter. Paris: Les Belles Lettres, 2005. (2nd. ed., 2009.)

Sophismes économiques; Suivis de Ce qu'on voit et ce qu'on ne voit pas. Paris: Arctic, 2006.

Sophismes économiques. 2e série. Paris: Guillaumin, 1848. [The first edition of the Second Series.]

Sophisms of the Protectionists. By the Late M. Frederic Bastiat. Part I. Sophisms of Protection—First series. Part II. Sophisms of Protection—Second series. Part III. Spoliation and Law. Part IV. Capital and Interest. Translated from the Paris edition of 1863 by Horace White and Mrs. L. S. McCord. New York: American Free Trade League, 1870.

Sophisms of the Protective Policy. Translated by Mrs. D. J. McCord, with an introductory letter by Dr. Francis Lieber. New York: George P. Putnam; Charleston, S.C.: John Russell, 1848.

Speech [on "Disarmament, Taxes, and the Influence of Political Economy on the Peace Movement"]. In *Report of the Proceedings of the Second General Peace Congress, held in Paris, on the 22nd, 23rd and 24th of August, 1849. Compiled from Authentic Documents, under the Superintendence of the Peace Congress Committee,* 49–52. London: Charles Gilpin, 1849. Shorter French version in *Congrès des amis de la paix universelle réuni à Paris en 1849: compte-rendu, séances des 22, 23, 24 Aout;—Résolutions adoptées; discours de Mm. Victor Hugo, Visschers, Rév. John Burnett; Rév. Asa Mahan, de l'Ohio; Henri Vincent, de Londres; Ath. Coquerel; Suringar, d'Amsterdam; Francisque Bouvet, Émile de Girardin; Ewart, membre du Parlement; Frédéric Bastiat; Richard Cobden, Elihu Burritt, Deguerry; Amasa Walker, de Massachussets; Ch. Hindley, membre du Parlement, etc., etc.; Compte-rendu d'une visite au Président de la République, de trois meetings en Angleterre; statistique des membres du congrès, etc.; précédé d'une Note historique sur le mouvement en faveur de la paix.* Edited by Joseph Garnier, 25–26. Paris: Guillaumin, 1850.

Staatshuishoudkundige drogredenen. Translated by Willem Richard Boer. Utrecht: C. van der Post Jr., 1847–48.

Things Seen and Not Seen. Translated by William Ballantyne Hodgson. Reprinted from the *Newcastle Weekly Chronicle.* London, 1879.

Die Trugschlüsse der Schutzzöllner gegenüber der gesunden Handels-politik. Translated by Carl August Noback. Berlin: A. von Schröter, 1847.

Die Trugschlüsse der Schutzzöllner gegenüber der gesunden Handels-politik; Staatshuishoudkundige drogredenen. Translated by Willem Richard Boer. Utrecht: C. van der Post Jr., 1847–48.

Was man sieht und was man nicht sieht, oder die politische Œkonomie in Einer Lection; Frieden und Freiheit oder das Budget; Der Krieg gegen die Lehrstühle der politischen Œkonomie. Leipzig, 1853.

Wat men ziet en wat men niet ziet. Dordrecht: P. K. Braat, 1850.

What Is Free Trade? An Adaptation of Frederick Bastiat's "Sophismes économiques."

Designed for the American reader. By Emile Walter, a worker [Alexander Del Mar]. New York: G. P. Putnam and Son, 1867.

What Is Seen and What Is Not Seen: Or Political Economy in One Lesson. Translated by William Ballantyne Hodgson. London: W. H. Smith and Son, 1859. Reprinted from the *Manchester Examiner and Times,* 1852.

What Is Seen and What Is Not Seen. In *Selected Essays on Political Economy,* translated by Seymour Cain, edited by George B. de Huszar, introduction by F. A. Hayek, 1–50. Irvington-on-Hudson, N.Y.: Foundation for Economic Education, 1995. http://oll.libertyfund.org/title/956/35425.

WORKS BY OTHER AUTHORS CITED IN THE TEXT, NOTES, AND GLOSSARIES

Actes officiels du gouvernement provisoire dans leur ordre chronologique, arrêtés, décrets, proclamations, etc., etc.: Revue des faits les plus remarquables précédés du récit des événements qui se sont accomplis les 22, 23 et 24 février 1848. Paris: Barba, Garnot, 1848.

Amé, Léon. *Étude économique sur les douanes.* 2nd ed. Paris: Guillaumin, 1860.

Annales de la Société d'Économie politique, publiées sous la direction de Alphonse Courtois fils, secrétaire perpetual. 15 vols. Paris: Guillaumin, 1846–86. Vol. 1, 1846–1853.

L'Annuaire de l'économie politique et de la statistique, par les rédacteurs du Journal des économists. 56 vols. Paris: Guillaumin, 1844–99. [*L'Annuaire* was a series which published a separate volume every year from 1844 to 1899.]

Anonymous. *Plus de conscription!* (Signé: Allyre Bureau, L'un des rédacteurs de "la Démocratie pacifique") (Paris: Impr. de Lange Lévy, 1848).

Arago, Benjamin Antier-Chevrillon, with Etienne Arago. *Mandrin. Melodrame en trois actes.* Paris: Bezou, 1827.

Arago, François. *Biographie de Marie-Jean-Antoine-Nicolas Caritat de Condorcet.* Paris: F. Didot frères, 1849.

———. *Études sur les fortifications de Paris, considérées politiquement et militairement.* Paris: Pagnerre, 1845.

———. *Sur les Fortifications de Paris.* Paris: Bachelier, 1841.

Association pour la défense du travail national, Examen des théories du libre-échange et des résultats du système protecteur. Imprimerie de A. Guyot, 1847.

"Bastiat." In *Dictionnaire des parlementaires français comprenant tous les Membres des Assemblées françaises et tous les Ministres français, depuis le 1er mai 1789 jusqu'au 1er mai 1889,* 1:192–93. Paris: Bourloton, 1889.

Beaumarchais, Pierre-Augustin Caron de. *Théâtre de Beaumarchais. Précédé d'une notice sur sa vie et ses ouvrages, par M. Auger.* Paris: Librairie de Firmin Didot frères, 1844.

Belloc, Alexis. *Les Postes françaises. Recherches historiques sur leur origine, leur développement, leur legislation*. Paris: Firmin-Didot, 1886.

Bentham, Jeremy. "Anarchical Fallacies: Being an Examination of the Declaration of Rights Issued during the French Revolution." In *The Works of Jeremy Bentham*, vol. 2. Edinburgh: William Tait, 1843. http://oll.libertyfund.org/titles /1921#lf0872-02_head_411.

———. "The Book of Fallacies: From Unfinished Papers of Jeremy Bentham." In *The Works of Jeremy Bentham*, vol. 2. Edinburgh: William Tait, 1843. http:// oll.libertyfund.org/titles/1921#lf0872-02_head_315.

———. *Handbook of Political Fallacies*. Revised and edited by Harold A. Larrabee. Introduction by Crane Brinton. New York: Harper, 1962.

———. "Lettres sur la Défense de l'usure." In *Mélanges d'économie politique II. Necker, Sur la législation et le commerce des grains. Galiani, Dialogues sur le commerce des blés. Montyon, Quelle influence ont les diverses espèces d'impôts sur la moralité, l'activité et l'industrie des peuples. J. Bentham, Lettres sur la Défense de l'usure. Précédés de notices historiques sur chaque auteur, et accompagnés de commentaires et de notes explicatives par M. Gust. de Molinari.* Collection des principaux économistes, vol. 15. Paris: Guillaumin, 1848.

———. *Principles of Judicial Procedure, with the Outlines of a Procedure Code*. In *The Works of Jeremy Bentham*, vol. 2. Edinburgh: William Tait, 1843. http:// oll.libertyfund.org/titles/1921#lf0872-02_head_001.

———. "Sophismes anarchiques." In *Tactique des assemblées législatives, suivie d'un traité des sophismes politiques; Ouvrage extrait des manuscrits de M. Jérémie Bentham, jusiconsulte anglois, par Ét. Dumont*, 2:271–392. Geneva: J. J. Paschoud, 1816.

———. *Théorie des peines et des recompenses, ouvrage extrait des manuscrits de M. Jérémie Bentham, jurisconsulte anglais. Par M. Et. Dumont*. 3rd ed. Paris: Bossange frères, 1826. (1st ed., London: Vogel et Schulze, 1811.)

———. "Traité des sophismes politiques." In *Tactique des assemblées législatives, suivie d'un traité des sophismes politiques; Ouvrage extrait des manuscrits de M. Jérémie Bentham, jurisconsulte anglois, par Ét. Dumont*, 2:1–267. Geneva: J. J. Paschoud, 1816.

———. *The Works of Jeremy Bentham*. Edited by John Bowring. 11 vols. Edinburgh: William Tait, 1838–43. http://oll.libertyfund.org/titles/1175.

Béranger, Pierre-Jean de. *Béranger's Songs of the Empire, the Peace, and the Restoration*. Translated into English verse by Robert B. Clough. London: Addey and Co., 1856.

———. *Chansons de Béranger*. New ed. Brussels: A. Wahlen, 1832.

———. *Choix de chansons nationales anciennes, nouvelles et inédites*. Edited by P.-J. Béranger, Casimir Lavigne, Emile Debraux, et al. Paris: Les Marchands de Nouveautés, 1831.

————. *Œuvres complètes de Béranger.* New edition illustrated by J. J. Grandville. Paris: H. Fournier, 1839.

————. *Œuvres complètes de P. J. de Béranger contenant les dix chanson nouvelles, avec un portrait gravé sur bois d'après Charlet.* Paris: Perrotin, 1855.

Bernard, A. "Résumé des budgets de la France de 1814 à 1847." In *L'Annuaire de l'économie politique et de la statistique,* 1849, 67–76.

Blanc, Louis. *Histoire de la Révolution française.* 12 vols. Paris: Langlois et Leelereq, 1847–69.

————. *Organisation du travail.* Paris: Prévot, 1840.

————. *Le Socialisme; droit au travail, réponse à M. Thiers.* Paris: M. Levy, 1848.

Boileau-Despréaux, Nicolas. *Œuvres de Boileau Despréaux, à l'usage des lycées et des écoles secondaires.* New ed. Lyon: Perisse frères, 1810.

Boissonade, Gustave. *La Fontaine, économiste: Conférence publique et gratuite faire à la Faculté de Droit de Paris, le dimanche 11 février 1872.* Paris: Guillaumin, 1872.

Bonaparte, Napoléon. *Mémoires de Napoléon Bonaparte: Manuscrit venu de Sainte-Hélène.* Paris: Baudouin, 1821.

————. *Mémoires pour servir à l'histoire de France, sous Napoleon, écrits à Sainte-Hélène, par les généraux qui ont partagé sa captivité, et publiés sur les manuscrits entièrement corrigés de la main du Napoléon.* Edited by Baron Gaspard Gourgaud and Charles-Tristan Montholon, comte de. 8 vols. Paris: Firmin Didot, père et fils, 1823.

Bourgat, Jean-François. *Code des douanes, ou Recueil des lois et règlements sur les douanes en vigueur au 1er janvier 1848.* 2nd ed. Paris: Guillaumin, 1848.

Bureau, Allyre. *Plus de conscription!* Paris: Impr. de Lange Lévy, 1848.

Cabet, Étienne. *Voyage et aventures de lord William Carisdall en Icarie.* Paris: H. Souverain, 1840.

Carrel, Armand. *Œuvres politiques et littéraires d'Armand Carrel, mises en ordre, annotées et précédées d'un notice biographique sur l'auteur.* Edited by M. Littré and M. Paulin. Paris: F. Chamerot, 1857.

Castille, Hippolyte. *Histoire de la seconde République française.* 4 vols. Paris: Victor Lecou, 1854–56.

————. *Portraits historiques au dix-neuvième siècle.* Paris: Ferdinand Sartorius, 1856.

Chateaubriand, François-René, vicomte de. "Conclusion. L'idée chrétienne est l'avenir du monde." In *Mémoires d'outre-tombe,* 11:491. Paris: Eugène et Victor Penaud, 1850.

Chevalier, Michel. *Cours d'Économie politique fait au Collège de France par Michel Chevalier.* Vol. 2, "Douzième leçon. Concours de l'armée française aux travaux des fortifications de Paris," Bruxelles: Meline, Cans, 1851, pp. 183–96. First ed. 1844.

————. *Les fortifications de Paris, lettre à M. Le Comte Molé.* Paris: Charles Gosselin, 1841.

————. "*Statistique des travaux publics, sous le Gouvernement de Juillet,*" Annuaire de l'économie politique et de la statistique pour 1849. Paris: Guillaumin, 1849, pp. 209–37.

Clément, A. "*Fonctionnaires,*" Dictionnaire de l'économie politique. Coquelin, Charles, and Gilbert-Urbain Guillaumin, eds. Paris: Librairie de Guillaumin et Cie., 1852–53. Vol. 1, pp. 787–89.

————. "*De la spoliation légale,*" *Journal des économistes,* 1 July 1848, Tome 20, no. 83, pp. 363–74.

Clément, Pierre. *Histoire du système protécteur en France depuis le ministère de Colbert jusqu'à la Révolution de 1848, suivie de pièces, mémoires et documents justificatifs.* Paris: Guillaumin, 1854.

Collin-Harleville, Jean François. *Œuvres de Collin-Harleville, contenant son théâtre et ses poésies fugitives, avec une notice sur sa vie et ses ouvrages.* Paris: Delong-champs, 1828.

Compte rendu des séances de l'Assemblée Nationale (4 mai 1848–27 mai 1849). Exposés des motifs et projets de lois présentés par le gouvernement; rapports de Mm. les Représentants. 10 vols. Paris: Imprimerie de l'Assemblée national, 1848–50.

Compte rendu des séances de l'Assemblée Nationale Législative (28 mai 1849–1 déc. 1851). Exposés des motifs et projets de lois présentés par le gouvernement; rapports de Mm. les Représentants. 17 vols. Paris: Imprimerie de l'Assemblée national, 1849–52.

Comte, Charles. *Histoire complète de la Garde nationale, depuis l'époque de sa fondation jusqu'à sa réorganisation définitive et la nomination de ses officiers, en vertu de la loi du 22 mars 1831, divisée en six époques; les cinqs premières par Charles Comte; et la sixième par Horace Raisson.* Paris: Philippe, Juillet, 1831.

————. *Traité de législation, ou exposition des lois générales suivant lesquelles les peuples prospèrent, dépérissent ou restent stationnaire.* 4 vols. Paris: A. Sautelet, 1827. (2nd ed., Paris: Chamerot, Ducollet, 1835; 3rd ed., Brussels: Hauman, Cattoir, 1837.)

————. *Traité de la propriété.* 2 vols. Paris: Chamerot, Ducollet, 1834. [Brussels edition, H. Tarlier, 1835. A second, revised edition was published in 1835 by Chamerot, Ducollet of Paris in 4 volumes to coincide with the publication of its sequel, *Traité de la propriété.* A revised and corrected third edition was published in 1837 by Hauman, Cattoir of Brussels.]

Condillac, Étienne Bonnot, abbé de. *Commerce and Government Considered in Their Mutual Relationship.* Translated by Shelagh Eltis, with an introduction to his life and contribution to economics by Shelagh Eltis and Walter Eltis. Indianapolis: Liberty Fund, 2008. http://oll.libertyfund.org/titles/2125.

————. *Le commerce et le gouvernement, considérés relativement l'un à l'autre. Ouvrage élémentaire.* Amsterdam and Paris: Jombert & Cellot, 1776.

————. "Le commerce et le gouvernement." In *Mélanges d'économie politique. D. Hume, Essais sur le commerce, le luxe, l'argent, l'intérêt de l'argent, les impôts, le crédit public, etc.* Forbonnais, *Principes économiques.* Condillac, *Le commerce et le gouvernement.* Condorcet, *Mélanges d'économie politique.* Lavoisier et Lagrange, *De la richesse territoriale du royaume de France. Essai d'arithmétique politique.* B. Franklin, *La science du bonhomme Richard, et autres opuscules. Précédés de notices historiques sur chaque auteur, et accompagnés de commentaires et de notes explicatives par MM. Eugène Daire et G. de Molinari.* Collection des principaux économistes, vols. 14 and 15. Paris: Guillaumin, 1847.

Condorcet, Jean-Antoine-Nicolas de Caritat, marquis de. *Œuvres de Condorcet.* Edited by A. Condorect O'Connor and François Arago. 12 vols. Paris: Didot, 1847–49.

Considerant, Victor Prosper. *Principes du socialisme. Manifeste de la démocratie au XIXe siècle.* 2nd ed. Paris: Librairie Phalanstérienne, 1847.

———. *Le socialisme devant le vieux monde, ou Le vivant devant les morts.* Paris: Librairie Phalanstérienne, 1848.

———. *Théorie du droit de propriété et du droit au travail.* Paris: Librairie phalanstérienne, 1848.

Coquelin, Charles. "Budget." In *DEP,* 1:224–35.

Courier, Paul-Louis. *Collection complète des pamphlets politiques et opuscules littéraires de Paul-Louis Courier, ancien canonnier à cheval.* Brussels: Chez tous les libraires, 1827.

———. *Pamphlet des pamphlets.* Paris: Chez les Marghands de Nouveautés, 1824.

Courtois, Alphonse. "Le budget de 1848." In *L'Annuaire de l'économie politique et de la statistique,* 1848, 29–51.

———. "Le budget de 1849." In *L'Annuaire de l'économie politique et de la statistique,* 1850, 18–28.

D'Amilaville, Étienne Noël. "Population." In *Encyclopédie, ou dictionnaire raisonné des sciences, des arts et des métiers,* edited by Denis Diderot, 13:88–103. Neuchatel: Samuel Faulche, 1765.

Désaugiers, Marc Antoine Madelaine. *M. Vautour, ou le propriétaire sous le scellé, vaudeville en un acte; par MM. Désaugiers, Tournay et George-Duval.* 2nd ed. Paris: Masson, 1805.

Destutt de Tracy, Antoine. *Commentaire sur l'esprit des lois.* Paris: Delaunay, 1819.

———. *Éléments d'idéologie.* 4 vols. Paris: Didot l'aîné, et al., 1801–15.

———. *Traité d'économie politique.* Paris: Bouguet et Lévi, 1823.

Dictionnaire de l'Académie française. 6th ed. Paris: Didot frères, 1835. Online at the ARTFL Project, Dictionnaires d'autrefois, http://portail.atilf.fr/dictionnaires/ACADEMIE/SIXIEME/sixieme.fr.html.

Dictionnaire de l'armée de terre: ou recherches historiques sur l'art et les usages militaires des anciens et des moderns, vol. 3. Edited by Étienne Alexandre Bardin and Oudinot de Reggio. Paris: Perrotin, 1841.

Dictionnaire de l'économie politique, contenant l'exposition des principes de la science, l'opinion des écrivains qui ont le plus contribué à sa fondation et à ses progrès, la bibliographie générale de l'économie politique par noms d'auteurs et par ordre de matières, avec des notices biographiques et une appréciation raisonnée des principaux ouvrages, publié sur la direction de MM Charles Coquelin et Guillaumin. 2 vols. Paris: Librairie de Guillaumin et cie., 1852–53. (2nd ed., 1854; 3rd ed., 1864; 4th ed., 1873.)

Dictionnaire des finances, publié sous la direction de M. Léon Say, par MM. Louis Foyot et A. Lanjalley. 2 vols. Paris: Berger-Levrault, 1889.

Dictionnaire général de la politique, par Maurice Block avec la collaboration d'hommes d'état, de publicistes et d'écrivains de tous les pays. New ed. 2 vols. Paris: O. Lorenz, 1873.

Dombasle, Christophe-Joseph-Alexandre Mathieu de. *Des impôts dans leurs rapports avec la production agricole.* Paris: Huzard, 1829.

———. *Du sucre indigène, de la situation actuelle de cette industrie en France, de son avenir et du droit dont on se propose de la charger.* Paris: Huzard, 1837.

———. *Œuvres diverses. Économie politique. Instruction publique, Haras et remonte.* Paris: Bruchard, Huzard, Audot, 1843.

Le Droit au travail à l'Assemblée Nationale: Recueil complet de tous les discours prononcés dans cette mémorable discussion par MM. Fresneau, Hubert-Delisle, Cazalès, Gaulthier de Rumilly, Pelletier, A. de Tocqueville, Ledru-Rollin, Duvergier de Hauranne, Crémieux, M. Barthe, Gaslonde, de Luppé, Arnaud (de l'Ariége), Thiers, Considérant, Bouhier de l'Ecluse, Martin-Bernard, Billault, Dufaure, Goudchaux, et Lagrange (textes revus par les orateurs), suivis de l'opinion de MM. Marrast, Proudhon, Louis Blanc, Ed. Laboulaye et Cormenin; avec des observations inédites par MM. Léon Faucher, Wolowski, Fréd. Bastiat, de Parieu, et une introduction et des notes par M. Joseph Garnier. Paris: Guillaumin, 1848.

Duchâtel, Charles Marie Tanneguy, comte. *Considérations d'économie politique sur la bienfaisance, ou De la charité dans ses rapports avec l'état moral et le bienêtre des classes inférieures de la société.* Paris: Guiraudet et Jouaust, 1836.

———. *De la charité dans ses rapports avec l'état moral et le bien-être des classes inférieures de la société.* Paris: Mesnier, 1829.

———. *Enquête relative à diverses prohibitions établies à l'entrée des produits étrangers, commencée le 8 octobre 1834, sous la présidence de T. Duchâtel, Ministre du commerce.* 3 vols. Paris: Imp. Royale, 1835.

Dunoyer, Charles. "*Esquisse historique des doctrines auxquelles on a donné le nom industrialisme, c'est-à-dire, des doctrines qui fondent la société sur l'Industrie,*" Revue encyclopédique, février 1827, vol. 33, pp. 368–94. Reprinted in *Notices d'économie politique,* vol. 3 of *Œuvres,* pp. 173–99.

———. *De la liberté du travail, ou simple exposé des conditions dans lesquelles les force humaines s'exercent avec le plus de puissance.* 3 vols. Paris: Guillaumin, 1845.

———. *L'Industrie et la morale considérées dans leurs rapports avec la liberté.* Paris: A. Sautelet, 1825.

———. *Nouveau traité d'économie sociale.* Paris: A. Sautelet, 1830.

———. *Œuvres de Dunoyer, revues sur les manuscrits de l'auteur.* 3 vols., ed. Anatole Dunoyer (Paris: Guillaumin, 1870, 1885, 1886). Avec une notice sur la vie et les travaux de l'auteur, par Mignet.

Dupin, Charles. *Le petit commerçant français.* Vol. 4 of *Le petit producteur français.* 7 vols. Paris: Bachelier, 1827.

Ferrier, François Louis Auguste. *Du gouvernement considéré dans ses rapports avec le commerce, ou de l'administration commerciale opposée aux économistes du dix-neuvième siècle.* Paris: Pélicier, 1804. (2nd ed., 1821; 3rd ed., 1822.)

Foë, Daniel de. *Robinson Crusoé, par Daniel de Foë.* Translated by Pétrus Borel. 2 vols. Paris: Francisque Borel et Alexandre Varenne, 1836.

Fonfrède, Henri. "Du système prohibitif." In *Œuvres de Henri Fonfrède, recueillies et mises en ordre par Ch.-Al. Campa, son collaborateur,* 7:243–404. Paris: Ledoyen, 1846.

Fontenay, Roger de. *Du revenu foncier.* Paris: Guillaumin, 1854.

Fonteyraud, Henri Alcide. *Mélanges d'économie politique. La Ligue anglaise pour la liberté du commerce. Notice historique sur la vie et les travaux de Ricardo.* Edited by J. Garnier. Paris: Guillaumin, 1853.

Fourier, François-Marie Charles. *La Fausse industrie morcelée répugnante et mensongère et l'antidote, l'industrie naturelle, combinée, attrayante, véridique donnant quadruple produit.* 2 vols. Paris: Bossange père, 1835–36.

———. *Le Nouveau monde industriel et sociétaire ou invention du procédé d'industrie attrayante et naturelle, distribuée en séries passionnées.* Paris: Bossange père, 1829.

———. *Le nouveau monde industriel et sociétaire.* Vol. 6 of *Œuvres complètes de Ch Fourier.* Paris: La Société pour la propagation et pour la réalisation de la théorie de Fourier, 1841.

Fox, William Johnson. *Anti–Corn Law Speeches, Chiefly Reprinted from the "League" Newspaper; and Occasional Speeches.* Vol. 4 of *Memorial Edition of the Collected Works of W. J. Fox.* London: Charles Fox and Trübner and Co., 1866.

Garnier, Joseph. *Du principe de population.* Paris: Guillaumin, 1857.

———. *Éléments de l'économie politique, exposé des notions fondamentales de cette science.* Paris: Guillaumin, 1846.

———. *Introduction à l'étude de l'économie politique.* Paris: Guillaumin, 1843.

———. *Richard Cobden, les ligueurs et la ligue.* Paris: Guillaumin, 1846.

———. *Traité d'économie politique: Exposé didactique des principes et des applications de cette science et de l'organisation économique de la société.* Paris: Guillaumin, 1860.

———. *Traité d'économie politique sociale ou industrielle; Exposé didactique des principes et des applications de cette science et de l'organisation économique de la société.* 6th ed. Paris: Garnier frères, 1868.

Gaulthier, Louis Madeleine Claire. *Protection du travail national. Congrès agricole des 7 départements du Nord, . . . réuni à Amiens. Extraits des "Procès-verbaux des séances du congrès du Nord, en ce qui concerne la question du libre-échange," les 6, 7 et 8 novembre 1846.* Paris: Guiraudet et Jouaust, 1846.

Girardin, Émile de. *Abolition de l'esclavage militaire. Les 52,* vol. 9. Bibliothèque démocratique. Paris: M. Lévy, 1849.

Hatin, Eugène. *Bibliographie historique et critique de la presse périodique française, ou Catalogue systématique et raisonné de tous les écrits périodiques de quelque valeur publiés ou ayant circulé en France depuis l'origine du journal jusqu'à nos jours, avec extraits, notes historiques, critiques et morales, indication des prix que les principaux journaux ont atteints dans les ventes publiques, etc. Précédé d'un essai historique et statistique sur la naissance et les progrès de la presse périodique dans les deux mondes.* Paris: Didot frères, fils, 1866.

Hill, Rowland. *Post Office Reform; Its Importance and Practicability.* London: Charles Knight and Co., 1837.

Horace. *Œuvres complètes d'Horace. Édition polyglotte publiée sous la direction de J. B. Monfalcon.* Paris: Cormon et Blanc, 1834.

———. *Satires, Epistles and Ars poetica.* With an English translation by H. Rushton Fairclough. The Loeb Classical Library. Cambridge, Mass.: Harvard University Press, 1942.

Hugo, Victor. *Hernani.* In *Œuvres complètes de Victor Hugo. Drame. III.* Paris: Eugène Renduel, 1836.

Joffres, Pierre-Didier. *Études sur le recrutement de l'armée; suivies d'un Projet de loi.* Paris: J. Dumaine, 1843.

Jomini, Antoine Henri. *Précis de l'art de la guerre, ou Nouveau tableau analytique des principales combinaisons de la stratégie, de la grande tactique et de la politique militaire.* Paris: Anselin, 1838.

———. *Traité de grande tactique, ou, Relation de la guerre de sept ans, extraite de Tempelhof, commentée et comparée aux principales opérations de la dernière guerre; avec un recueil des maximes les plus importantes de l'art militaire, justifiées par ces différents événements.* Paris: Giguet et Michaud, 1805.

Joubleau, Félix. *Études sur Colbert: ou Exposition du système d'économie politique suivi en France de 1661 à 1683.* 2 vols. Paris: Guillaumin, 1856.

Jouyne, Zéphirin. *Abolition du système prohibitif des douanes, grande extension du commerce extérieur, ou entretiens sur le commerce extérieur se rattachant au régime protecteur des douanes, à la liberté du commerce entre peuples, au crédit commercial et foncier, avec des observations sur les questions agitées entre les socialistes et les économistes.* Paris: Guillaumin, 1849.

———. *Grande extension du commerce extérieur de la France et de ses industries agricole et manufacturière par le retrait des prohibitions inscrites dans les tarifs des douanes, ou entretiens entre un économiste et un industriel sur le commerce extérieur, sur la législation des douanes et sur l'influence de cette législation dans l'économie sociale d'un pays.* Paris: Eugène Pick, 1857.

Kant, Immanuel. *Kant's Critique of Practical Reason and Other Works on the Theory of Ethics.* Translated by Thomas Kingsmill Abbott. 4th rev. ed. London: Longmans, Green and Co., 1889. http://oll.libertyfund.org/titles/360.

La Fontaine, Jean de. *Fables de La Fontaine.* Illustrated by J. J. Grandeville. New ed. Paris: H. Fournier ainé, 1838.

———. *Fables de La Fontaine. Nouvelle edition, revue et accompagnée de notes par C. A. Walckenaer.* Paris: Nepveu, 1826.

Lamartine, Alphonse de. "Sur la subvention du Théâtre-Italien (Discussion du budget) Assemblée National.—Séance du 16 avril 1850." In *La France parlementaire (1834–1851). Œuvres oratoires et écrits politiques. Précédés d'une étude sur la vie et les œuvres de Lamartine par Louis Ulbach. Troisième série: 1847–1851,* 6:160–66. Paris: A. Lacroix, Verboeckhoven, 1865.

Lestiboudois, Thémistocle. *Économie pratique des nations, ou système économique applicable aux différentes contrées, et spécialement à la France.* Paris: L. Colas, 1847.

Lobet, Jules. *"Chemins de fer," Annuaire de l'économie politique et de la statistique pour 1848.* Paris: Guillaumin, 1848, pp. 289–311.

MacGregor, John. *The Commercial and Financial Legislation of Europe and America, with a Pro-Forma Revision of the Taxation and the Customs Tariff of the United Kingdom.* London: Henry Hooper, 1841.

———. *Commercial Statistics. A Digest of the Productive Resources, Commercial Legislation, Customs Tariffs, Navigation, Port, and Quarantine Laws, and Charges, Shipping, Imports and Exports, and the Monies, Weights, and Measures of all Nations. Including all British Commercial Treaties with Foreign States.* 2 vols. London: Charles Nott, 1843.

———. *Commercial Tariffs and Regulations of the Several States of Europe and America, Together with the Commercial Treaties between England and Foreign Countries.* London: Charles Whiting, 1843.

Malebranche, Nicolas de. *Recherche de la vérité.* In *Œuvres de Malebranche, nouvelle édition, collationnée sur les meilleurs textes, et précédée d'une introduction, par M. Jules Simon. Deuxième Série.* Paris: Charpentier, 1842.

Malthus, Thomas Robert. *Essai sur le principe de population, par Malthus, traduit de l'anglais par MM. Pierre et Guillaume Prévost (de Genève). Précédé d'une introduction par P. Rossi, et d'une notice sur la vie et les ouvrages de l'auteur, par Charles Comte, avec les notes des traducteurs, et de nouvelles notes par M. Joseph Garnier.* Collection des principaux économistes, vols. 7 and 8. Paris: Guillaumin, 1845.

———. *Essai sur le principe de population par Malthus.* Traduit de l'anglais par Mm. Pierre et Guillaume Prévost (de Genève). Précédé d'une introduction par. P. Rossi, et d'une notice sur la vie et les ouvrages de l'auteur, par Charles Comte, avec les notes des traducteurs, et de nouvelle notes par M. Joseph Garnier. 2e édition. Paris: Guillaumin, 1852.

———. *An Essay on the Principle of Population.* London: J. Johnson, 1798. 3rd ed., London: J. Murray, 1826.

———. *An Essay on the Principle of Population, or a View of Its Past and Present Effects on Human Happiness; with an Inquiry into Our Prospects respecting the Future Removal or Mitigation of the Evils Which It Occasions.* 6th ed. 2 vols. London: John Murray. 1826. http://oll.libertyfund.org/titles/1944.

———. *Observations on the Effects of the Corn Laws.* London: J. Johnson, 1814.

———. *Principles of Political Economy.* London: J. Murray, 1820.

Marcet, Jane Haldimand. *Conversations on Political Economy; in which the elements of that science are familiarly explained.* 6th ed. London: Longman, Rees, Orme, Brown, and Green, 1827. http://oll.libertyfund.org/titles/2048.

———. *John Hopkins's Notions on Political Economy.* London: Longman, Rees, Orme, Brown, Green, and Longman, 1833. http://oll.libertyfund.org /titles/310.

Martineau, Harriet. *Illustrations of Political Economy.* 3rd ed. 9 vols. London: Charles Fox, 1832. http://oll.libertyfund.org/titles/1873.

Metastasio, Pietro. *Opere scelte di Pietro Metastasio, publicate da A. Buttura. Tomo primo.* Paris: Baudry, 1840.

Molière, J.-B. Poquelin de. *Le Misanthrope.* Translated by Curtis Hidden Page. New York: G. P. Putnam, 1913.

———. *Œuvres complètes de Molière, avec les notes de tous les commentateurs. Édition publiée par L. Aimé-Martin.* Paris: Lefèvre, 1826.

———. *Théâtre complet de J.-B. Poquelin de Molière, publié par D. Jouast en huit volumes avec la préface de 1682, annotée par G. Monval.* Paris: Librairie des bibliophiles, 1882–83.

Molinari, Gustave de. *Conversations familières sur le commerce des grains.* Paris: Guillaumin, 1855.

———. *Conversations sur le commerce des grains et al protection de l'agriculture.* Paris: Guillaumin, 1886.

———. *Cours d'économie politique, professé au Musée royal de l'industrie belge.* 2 vols. Brussels: Librairie polytechnique d'Aug. Decq, 1855.

———. *L'évolution économique du XIXe siècle: théorie du progrès.* Paris: C. Reinwald, 1880.

———. *L'évolution politique et la Révolution.* Paris: C. Reinwald, 1884.

———. "Frédéric Bastiat: Lettres d'un habitant des Landes" [review]. *Journal des économistes* 3 (July 1878): 60–70.

———. *Histoire du tarif.* 2 vols. Vol. 1, *Les Fers et les houilles.* Vol. 2, *Les Céréales.* Paris: Guillaumin, 1847.

———. *Les Révolutions et le despotisme envisagés au point de vue des intérêts matériel; précédé d'une lettre à M. le Comte J. Arrivabene, sur les dangers de la situation présente,* par M. G. de Molinari, professeur d'économie politique. Brussels: Meline, Cans et Cie, 1852.

———. *Les Soirées de la rue Saint-Lazare. Entretiens sur les lois économiques et défense de la propriété*. Paris: Guillaumin, 1849.

——— [signed "Le Rêveur"]. "L'Utopie de la liberté. Lettres aux socialistes." *Journal des économistes* 20 (15 June 1848): 328–32.

Montaigne, Michel de. "Le Profit d'un est dommage de l'autre." In *Essais de Montaigne, suivis de sa correspondance et de la servitude voluntaire d'Estienne de la Boëtie. Édition variorum, accompangné d'une notice biographique de notes historiques, philologiques, etc. et d'un index analytique par Charles Louandre*. 4 vols., chap. 21, 1:130–31. Paris: Charpentier, 1862.

Moreau de Jonnès, Alexandre. *Le Commerce au dix-neuvième siècle*. 2 vols. Paris: Renard, 1827.

———. *Éléments de statistique, comprenant les principes généraux de cette science, et un aperçu historique de ses progress*. Paris: Guillaumin, 1847.

———. *Recherches statistiques sur l'esclavage et sur les moyens de le supprimer*. Paris: Guillaumin, 1841.

———. *Statistique de l'agriculture de la France, contenant: la statistique des céréales, de la vigne, des cultures diverses, des pâturages, des bois et forêts et des animaux domestiques, avec leur production actuelle, comparée à celle des temps anciens et des principaux pays de l'Europe*. Paris: Guillaumin, 1848.

———. *Statistique de l'industrie de la France*. Paris: Guillaumin, 1856.

Nodier, Charles. *Vocabulaire de la langue française: Extrait de la dernière édition du Dictionnaire de l'Académie publié en 1835*. Edited by Charles Nodier and Paul Ackermann. Paris: Firmin-Didot, 1836.

Nouveau dictionnaire d'économie politique. Edited by Léon Say and Joseph Chailley. Paris: Guillaumin, 1891–92.

Parny, Évariste Désiré de Forges. *La Guerre des dieux, poème en dix chants, par Évariste Parny*. Paris: Debray, 1808.

———. *Œuvres choisies de Parny, augmentées des variantes de texte et de notes*. Paris: Lefèvre, 1827.

Pascal, Blaise. *The Thoughts of Blaise Pascal*. Translated from the text of M. Auguste Molinier by C. Kegan Paul. London: George Bell and Sons, 1901. http://oll.libertyfund.org/titles/2407.

Perrault, Charles. *Œuvres choisies de Ch. Perrault, de l'Académie française, avec les mémoires de l'auteur, et des recherches sur les contes des fees*. Edited by Collin de Plancy. Paris: Brissot-Thivars, 1826.

Plus de conscription! (Signé: Allyre Bureau, l'un des rédacteurs de "la Démocratie pacifique") Paris: Impr. de Lange Lévy, 1848.

Procès-verbaux des séances de la Chambre des députés: Session 1847. Paris: A. Henry, 1847.

Projet de loi pour la fixation des recettes et des dépenses de l'exercice 1850. Vol. 3, *Budget des dépenses du Ministère de la guerre. Budget des dépenses du Ministère de la marine et des colonies*. Paris: Imprimerie nationale, 1849.

Proudhon, Pierre-Joseph. *Qu'est-ce que la propriété? ou Recherches sur le principe du droit et du gouvernement. Premier mémoire.* Paris: Prévot, 1841.

———. *Système des contradictions économiques, ou Philosophie de la misère.* 2 vols. Paris: Guillaumin et cie, 1846.

Quesnay, François, et al. *Physiocrates. Quesnay, Dupont de Nemours, Mercier de la Rivière, l'Abbé Baudeau, Le Trosne, avec une introduction sur la doctrine des Physiocrates, des commentaires et des notices historiques, par Eugène Daire.* Collection des principaux économistes, vol. 2. Paris: Guillaumin, 1846.

Regnard, J. F. *Œuvres de Regnard.* Vol. 1. Paris: Martel Ardant frères, 1847.

Renouard, Augustin-Charles. "*Parasites,*" *Dictionnaire de l'économie politique.* Coquelin, Charles, and Gilbert-Urbain Guillaumin, eds. Paris: Librairie de Guillaumin et Cie., 1852–53. Vol. 2, pp. 323–29.

Reybaud, Louis. *Le Baron de Paturot à la recherche de la meilleure des monarchies, par un républicain du lendemain.* Paris, 1849.

———. *Études sur les réformateurs ou socialistes modernes. Saint-Simon, Charles Fourier, Robert Owen,* 6th ed. 2 vols. Paris: Guillaumin, 1849.

———. *Jérôme Paturot à la recherche de la meilleure des républiques.* 4 vols. Paris: Michel Lévy frères, 1848.

———. *Jérôme Paturot à la recherche d'une position sociale et politique. Édition illustrée par J. J. Grandville.* 2 vols. Paris: J. J. Dubochet, 1846.

———. *Quelques chapitres des mémoires de Jérôme Paturot, patenté, électeur et éligible, écrits par lui-même.* 2 vols. Brussels: Société Typographic Belge, A. Wahlen, 1843.

Ricardo, David. *Œuvres complètes de David Ricardo, traduites en français, par MM. Constancio et Alcide Fonteyraud, augmentées de notes de Jean-Baptiste Say, de nouvelles notes et de commentaires par Malthus, Sismondi, MM. Rossi, Blanqui, etc., et précédées d'une notice sur la vie et les travaux de l'auteur par M. Alcide Fonteyraud.* Collection des principaux économistes, vol. 13. Paris: Guillaumin, 1847.

———. *On the Principles of Political Economy and Taxation.* London: J. Murray, 1817.

———. *The Works and Correspondence of David Ricardo.* Edited by Piero Sraffa with the collaboration of M. H. Dobb. 11 vols. Cambridge: Cambridge University Press, 1951; Indianapolis: Liberty Fund, 2005. http://oll.libertyfund .org/titles/159.

Richelieu, Armand Jean du Plessis, cardinal-duc de. *Maximes d'état et fragments politiques de Cardinal de Richelieu, publiés par M. Gabriel Hanotaux.* Paris: Imprimérie Nationale, 1880.

Robert, Adolphe, et Gaston Cougny. *Dictionnaire des parlementaires français comprenant tous les Membres des Assemblées françaises et tous les Ministres français, depuis le 1er mai 1789 jusqu'au 1er mai 1889.* Vol. I. A-Cay, publié sous la direction de MM. Adolphe Robert et Gaston Cougny. Paris: Bourloton, 1889–91.

Romanet, Auguste, vicomte de. *De la protection en matière d'industrie et des réformes de Sir Robert Peel: Mémoire lu à l'Académie des sciences morales et politiques, le 15 mars 1845.* Paris: Chez Renard, 1845.

———. *Mémoire sur le principe de l'amélioration des races de chevaux, et sur la préférence qui doit être accordée, comme moyen d'encouragement, soit aux prix de course, soit aux primes locales, Suivant Le Sexe De L'animal. Lu à l'Académie des sciences le 19 juin 1843. Notice sur les travaux de M. le vte de Romanet. Membre du Conseil général de l'agriculture, du commerce et des manufactures, à l'appui de sa candidature à la place d'Académicien libre, vacante par le décès de M. le duc de Raguse.* Paris: Bouchard-Huzard, 1852.

———. *Notice sur les travaux de M. le vte de Romanet. Membre du Conseil général de l'agriculture, du commerce et des manufactures, à l'appui de sa candidature à la place d'Académicien libre, vacante par le décès de M. le duc de Raguse.* Paris: Bouchard-Huzard, 1852.

———. *Rapport fait au Comité central pour la défense du travail national.* Paris: Dauvin et Fontaine, 1843.

Rousseau, Jean-Jacques. *A Discourse on Inequality.* Translated with an introduction and notes by Maurice Cranston. Harmondsworth: Penguin, 1984.

———. *Du contrat social et autres œuvres politiques.* Introduction by Jean Ehrard. Paris: Garnier Frères, 1975.

———. *The Political Writings of Jean Jacques Rousseau, ed. from the original manuscripts and authentic editions.* With introductions and notes by C. E. Vaughan. 2 vols. Cambridge: Cambridge University Press, 1915. http://oll.libertyfund .org/titles/1880.

Saint-Chamans, Auguste, vicomte de. *Du système d'impôt fondé sur les principes de l'économie politique.* Paris: Le Normant, 1820.

———. *Nouvel essai sur la richesse des nations.* Paris: Le Normant, 1824.

———. *Traité d'économie publique, suivi d'un aperçu sur les finances de France.* 3 vols. Paris: Dentu, 1852.

Say, Horace. *Paris, son octroi et ses emprunts.* Paris: Guillaumin, 1847.

Say, Jean-Baptiste. *Cours complet d'économie politique pratique.* 6 vols. Paris: Rapilly, 1828–33.

———. *Cours complet d'économie politique pratique. Ouvrage destiné à mettre sous les yeux des hommes d'état, des propriétaires fonciers et des capitalistes, des savans, des agriculteurs, des manufacturiers, des négocians, et en général de tous les citoyens, l'économie des sociétés, par Jean-Baptiste Say, Seconde édition entièrement revue par l'auteur, publiée sur les manuscrits qu'il a laissés et augmentée de notes par Horace Say, son fils.* Collection des principaux économistes, vols. 10 and 11. Paris: Guillaumin, 1840.

———. *De l'Angleterre et des Anglais.* Paris: A. Bertrand, 1815.

———. *Œuvres complètes.* Edited by André Tiran et al. Paris: Economica, 2006.

———. *Œuvres diverses de J.-B. Say, contenant Catéchisme d'économie politique,*

Fragments et opuscules inédits, Correspondance générale, Olbie, Petit volume, Mélanges de morale et de littérature. Précédées d'une notice historique sur la vie et les travaux de l'auteur, avec des notes, par Ch. Comte, E. Daire et Horace Say. Collection des principaux économistes, vol. 12. Paris: Guillaumin, 1848.

———. *Traité d'économie politique.* Paris: Déterville, 1803.

———. *Traité d'économie politique, ou simple exposition de la manière dont se forme, se distribuent et se consomment les richesses. Par Jean-Baptiste Say. Sixième édition entièrement revue par l'auteur, et publiée sur les manuscrits qu'il a laissés, par Horace Say, son fils.* Collection des principaux économistes, vol. 9. Paris: Guillaumin, 1841.

———. *Traité d'économie politique, ou simple exposition de la manière dont se forment, se distribuent et se consomment les richesses.* First edition, Paris: Deterville, 1803; fourth edition, Paris: Deterville, 1819.

Simiot, Alexandre Étienne. *Gare du chemin de fer de Paris à Bordeaux.* Bordeaux: Durand, 1846.

Smith, Adam. *An Inquiry into the Nature and Causes of the Wealth of Nations.* Edited by R. H. Campbell and A. S. Skinner. 2 vols. Vol. 2 of *The Glasgow Edition of the Works and Correspondence of Adam Smith.* Indianapolis: Liberty Fund, 1982.

———. *An Inquiry into the Nature and Causes of the Wealth of Nations,* edited with an Introduction, Notes, Marginal Summary, and an Enlarged Index by Edwin Cannan (London: Methuen, 1904). 2 vols. http://oll.libertyfund.org /titles/171.

———. *Recherches sur la nature et les causes de la richesse des nations, par Adam Smith, traduction du Comte Germain Garnier entièrement revue et corrigée, et précédé d'une notice biographique par M. Blanqui, avec les commentaires de Buchanan, G. Garnier, Mac Culloch, Malthus, J. Mill, Ricardo, Sismondi; Augmentée de notes inédites de Jean-Baptiste Say, et d'éclaircissements historiques par M. Blanqui.* Collection des principaux économistes, vols. 5 and 6. Paris: Guillaumin, 1843.

Tabarin. *Œuvres complètes de Tabarin, avec les recontres, fantaisies et coq-à-l'âne facétieux du Baron de Gratelard. Et divers opuscules publiés séparément sous le nom ou à propos de Tabarin. Le tout précédé d'un introduction et d'une bibliographie tabarinque, par Gustave Aventin.* 2 vols. Paris: P. Jannet, 1858.

Table analytique par ordre alphabétique de matières et de noms de personnes du Compte rendu des séances de l'Assemblée nationale constituante (4 mai 1848–27 mai 1849) et des documents imprimés par son ordre. Rédigée aux Archives de l'Assemblée nationale. Paris: Henri et Charles Noblet, Imprimeurs de l'Assemblée nationale, 1850.

Table analytique par ordre alphabétique de matières et de noms de personnes du Compte rendu des séances de l'Assemblée nationale législative (28 mai 1849–2 décembre 1851) et des documents imprimés par son ordre. Rédigée aux Archives du Corps législatifs. Paris: Henri et Charles Noblet, Imprimeurs de l'Assemblée nationale, 1852.

Tastu, Amable. *Aventures de Robinson Crusoé, par Daniel de Foë, traduites par Mme A. Tastu, suivies d'une Notice sur Foé et sur le matelot Selkirk, par Louis Reybaud, et ornées de 50 gravures sur acier, d'après les dessins de M. de Sainson.* Paris: Didier, 1837.

Thiers, Adolphe. *De la propriété.* Paris: Paulin, Lheureux, 1848.

———. *Discours de M. Thiers sur le régime commercial de la France: Prononcés à l'Assemblée nationale les 27 et 28 juin 1851.* Paris: Paulin, Lheureux et cie, 1851.

Thompson, Thomas Perronet. *A Catechism on the Corn Laws; With a List of Fallacies and the Answers.* 18th ed. London: Robert Heward for the Westminster Review, 1834. (1st edition, 1827.)

———. *A Catechism on the Currency, by the author of the "Catechism on the Corn Laws."* 3rd ed. London: Effingham Wilson, 1848.

———. *Contre-enquête par l'homme aux quarante écus: Examen de l'enquête commerciale de 1834.* Brussels: Association belge pour la réforme douanière, 1835.

———. *Corn-Law Fallacies, with the Answers. Reprinted from The Sun Newspaper. With a Dedication to the Manchester Chamber of Commerce. By the author of the Catechism on the Corn Laws.* 2nd ed. London: Effingham Wilson, 1839.

———. *Exercises, Political and Others.* 6 vols. London: Effingham Wilson, 1842.

———. *Letters of a Representative to His Constituents, during the Session of 1836. To which is added, A running commentary on anti-commercial fallacies, reprinted from the Spectator of 1834. With additions and corrections.* London: Effingham Wilson, 1836.

Turgot, Anne-Robert-Jacques. *Œuvres de Turgot. Nouvelle édition, classée par ordre de matière. Les notes de Dupont de Nemours, augmentée de lettres inédites, des Questions sur le commerce, et d'observations et de notes nouvelles, par MM. Eugène Daire et Hippolyte Dussard, et précédée d'une notice sur la vie et les ouvrages de Turgot, par M. Eugène Daire.* Collection des principaux économistes, vols. 3 and 4. Paris: Guillaumin, 1844.

Twain, Mark. *Following the Equator: A Journey around the World.* Hartford, Conn.: The American Publishing Company, 1898.

Vesian, Gustave. *De la colonisation en Algérie.* Paris: Gabriel Roux, 1850.

Vidal, Auguste-Théodore. *Traité de pathologie externe et de médecine opératoire.* 2nd ed. 5 vols. Paris: J. B. Baillière, 1846.

Viennet, J. P. G. *Épitre aux chiffonniers sur les crimes de la presse.* Paris: Ambroise Dupont, 1827.

Virgil. *Virgil's Aeneid.* Translated by John Dryden with introductions and notes. New York: P. F. Collier and Son, 1909. http://oll.libertyfund.org/titles/1175/217545.

Vuitry, Adolphe. *Études sur le régime financier de la France avant la Révolution de 1789.* 3 vols. Paris: Guillaumin, 1878–83.

Whately, Richard. *Introductory Lectures on Political Economy, Delivered in Easter Term 1831.* 2nd ed. London: B. Fellowes, 1832.

SECONDARY SOURCES

Arblaster, Anthony. *The Rise and Decline of Western Liberalism.* Oxford: Basil Blackwell, 1984.

Baslé, Maurice, and Alain Génédan. "Frédéric Bastiat, théoricien et militant du libre-échange." In *L'Économie politique en France au XIXe siècle,* edited by Yves Breton and Michel Lutfalla, 83–110. Paris: Economica, 1991.

Bouchet, Thomas. "Le Droit au travail sous le 'masque des mots': Les économistes français au combat en 1848." *French Historical Studies* 29, no. 4 (2006): 595–619.

Boudreaux, Donald. "Comparative Advantage." In *The Concise Encyclopedia of Economics,* edited by David Henderson. Indianapolis: Liberty Fund, 2007. http://www.econlib.org/library/Enc/ComparativeAdvantage.html.

Bramsted, E. K., and K. J. Melhuish, eds. *Western Liberalism: A History in Documents from Locke to Croce.* London: Longman, 1978.

Breton, Yves. "The Société d'économie politique of Paris (1842–1914)." In *The Spread of Political Economy and the Professionalisation of Economists: Economic Societies in Europe, America and Japan in the Nineteenth Century,* edited by Massimo M. Augello and Marco E. L. Guidi, 53–69. London: Routledge, 2001.

———, and Michel Lutfalla, eds. *L'Économie politique en France au XIXe siècle.* Paris: Economica, 1991.

Demier, Francis. "Les Économistes libéraux et la crise de 1848." In *Les Traditions économiques françaises, 1848–1939,* edited by Pierre Dockès et al., 773–84. Paris: CNRS Editions, 2000.

Deschamps, Henry Thierry. *La Belgique devant la France de juillet: L'opinion et l'attitude françaises de 1839 à 1848.* Bibliothèque de la Faculté de philosophie & lettres de l'Université de Liège, 137. Paris: Les Belles lettres, 1956.

Ekelund, Robert B., and Robert F. Hébert. *A History of Economic Theory and Method.* London: McGraw-Hill, 1983.

Fernandes, Felipe Tâmega, and Antonio Tena-Junguito. "How Much Trade Liberalization Was There in the World before and after Cobden-Chevalier?" Paper presented at the Conference Tariffs in History, Madrid, May 13–14, 2010.

Garello, Jacques, ed. *Aimez-vous Bastiat?* Paris: Romillat, 2002.

Gide, Charles, and Charles Rist. *A History of Economic Doctrines from the Time of the Physiocrats to the Present Day.* Translated by R. Richards. London: George G. Harrap, 1961.

Girard, Louis. *Les libéraux français, 1814–1875.* Paris: Aubier Montaigne, 1985.

Hamowy, Ronald, et al. *The Encyclopedia of Libertarianism.* Los Angeles: Sage, 2008.

Hart, David M. *Class Analysis, Slavery and the Industrialist Theory of History in French Liberal Thought, 1814–1830: The Radical Liberalism of Charles Comte and Charles Dunoyer.* Unpublished PhD dissertation, King's College Cambridge, 1994. davidmhart.com/liberty/Papers/ComteDunoyer/CCCD-PhD /HTML-version/index.html.

Hayek, F. A. "Introduction." In *Selected Essays on Political Economy,* by Frédéric Bastiat. Translated by Seymour Cain. Edited by George B. de Huszar. Irvington-on-Hudson, N.Y.: Foundation for Economic Education, 1975.

———. "The Use of Knowledge in Society." *American Economic Review* 35, no. 4 (September 1945): 519–30. http://oll.libertyfund.org/titles/92.

Hazlitt, Henry. *Economics in One Lesson.* New York: Harper and Brothers, 1946.

———. *Economics in One Lesson.* New York: Manor Books, 1974.

Hülsmann, Jörg Guido. "Bastiat, Frédéric (1801–1850)." In *The Encyclopedia of Libertarianism,* edited by Ronald Hamowy et al., 25–27. Los Angeles: Sage, 2008.

———. "Bastiat's Legacy in Economics." *Quarterly Journal of Austrian Economics* 4, no. 4 (Winter 2001): 55–70.

Irwin, Douglas A. *Against the Tide: An Intellectual History of Free Trade.* Princeton: Princeton University Press, 1996.

Jardin, André. *Histoire du libéralisme politique de la crise de l'absolutisme à la constitution de 1875.* Paris: Hachette, 1985.

Journal des économistes et des études humaines 11, no. 2/3 (June 2001). Editor-in-Chief: Pierre Garello. Special issue devoted to papers given at the Bastiat bicentennial conference. http://www.degruyter.com/view/j/jeeh.2001.11.2 /issue-files/jeeh.2001.11.issue-2.xml.

Lalouette, Jacqueline. "La Politique religieuse de la Seconde République." *Revue d'histoire du XIXe siècle* (Société d'histoire de la révolution de 1848 et des révolutions du XIXe siècle) 28 (2004): 79–94.

Leroux, Robert. *Political Economy and Liberalism in France: The Contributions of Frédéric Bastiat.* London: Routledge, 2011. [This book contains the best bibliography on Bastiat to date.]

———, and David M. Hart, eds. *French Liberalism in the Nineteenth Century: An Anthology.* London: Routledge, 2012.

———. *L'Âge d'or du libéralisme français: Anthologie XIXe siècle.* Paris: Ellipses, 2014.

Leter, Michel. "Éléments pour une étude de l'École de Paris (1803–1852)." In *Histoire du libéralisme en Europe,* edited by Philippe Nemo and Jean Petitot, 429–509. Paris: Presses universitaires de France, 2006.

Le Van-Lemesle, A. L. "Guillaumin, éditeur d'économie politique, 1801–1864." *Revue d'économie politique* 95, no. 2 (1985): 134–49.

———. "La Promotion de l'économie politique en France au XIXe siècle 1815–1881." *Revue d'histoire moderne et contemporaine* 27 (April–June 1980): 270–94.

Liggio, Leonard. "Charles Dunoyer and French Classical Liberalism," *Journal of Libertarian Studies* 1, no. 1 (1977): 153–78.

Lutfalla, Michel. "Aux origines du libéralisme économique en France: 'Le Journal des économistes.'" *Revue d'histoire économique et sociale* 50, no. 4 (1972): 494–517.

Minart, Gérard. *Frédéric Bastiat (1801–1850). Le Croisé de libre-échange.* Paris: L'Harmattan, 2004.

———. *Gustave de Molinari (1819–1912). Pour un gouvernement à bon marché dans un milieu libre.* Paris: Éditions de l'Institut Charles Coquelin, 2012.

———. *Jean-Baptiste Say (1767–1832). Maître et pédagogue de l'école française d'économie politique libérale.* Paris: Institut Charles-Coquelin, 2005.

Nataf, Philippe. "La Vie et l'œuvre de Charles Coquelin (1802–1852)." In *Histoire du libéralisme en Europe,* edited by Philippe Nemo and Jean Petitot, 511–30. Paris: Presses universitaires de France, 2006.

Newman, Edgar Leon, and Robert Lawrence Simpson, eds. *Historical Dictionary of France from the 1815 Restoration to the Second Empire.* 2 vols. Westport, Conn.: Greenwood Press, 1987.

O'Brien, Patricia. "*L'Embastillement de Paris*: The Fortification of Paris during the July Monarchy," *French Historical Studies* 9, no. 1 (1975): 63–82.

Oncken, August. *Die Maxime Laissez faire et laissez passer: Ihr Ursprung, ihr Werden. Ein Beitrag zur Geschichte der Freihandelslehre.* Bern: K. J. Wyss, 1886.

Poitier, Jean-Pierre, and André Tiran, eds. *Jean-Baptiste Say: Nouveaux regards sur son œuvre.* Paris: Economica, 2003.

Raico, Ralph. "Classical Liberal Exploitation Theory: A Comment on Professor Liggio's Paper," *Journal of Libertarian Studies* 1, no. 3 (1979): 179–83.

———. "Classical Liberal Roots of the Marxist Doctrine of Classes." In *Requiem for Marx,* edited by Yuri N. Maltsev, 189–220. Auburn, Ala.: Ludwig von Mises Institute, 1992.

———. "The Centrality of French liberalism." In *Classical Liberalism and the Austrian School.* Foreword by Jörg Guido Hülsmann. Preface by David Gordon. Auburn, Ala.: Ludwig von Mises Institute, 2012, pp. 219–53.

Roche, George Charles, III. *Frédéric Bastiat: A Man Alone.* New Rochelle, N.Y.: Arlington House, 1971.

Rosanvallon, Pierre. *Le moment Guizot.* Paris: Gallimard, 1985.

Rothbard, Murray N. *An Austrian Perspective on the History of Economic Thought.* 2 vols. Vol. 1, *Economic Thought before Adam Smith.* Vol. 2, *Classical Economics.* Auburn, Ala.: Ludwig von Mises Institute, 2006.

Ruggiero, Guido de. *The History of European Liberalism.* Translated by R. G. Collingwood. Boston: Beacon Press, 1967.

Russell, Dean. *Frédéric Bastiat: Ideas and Influence.* Irvington-on-Hudson, N.Y.: Foundation for Economic Education, 1965.

Schatz, Albert. *L'Individualisme économique et social.* Paris: Armand Colin, 1907.

Schumpeter, Joseph A. *History of Economic Analysis.* Edited from a manuscript by Elizabeth Boody Schumpeter. New York: Oxford University Press, 1974.

Silberner, Edmund. *La Guerre et la paix dans l'histoire des doctrines économiques.* Paris: Sirey, 1957.

———. *The Problem of War in Nineteenth-Century Economic Thought.* Translated by Alexander H. Krappe. Princeton: Princeton University Press, 1946.

Simon, Walter, ed. *French Liberalism, 1789–1848.* New York: John Wiley and Sons, 1972.

Sowell, Thomas. *Economic Facts and Fallacies.* 2nd ed. New York: Basic Books, 2011.

Spitzer, Alan B. *The French Generation of 1820.* Princeton: Princeton University Press, 1987.

Staum, Martin S. "French Lecturers in Political Economy, 1815–1848: Varieties of Liberalism." *History of Political Economy* 30, no. 1 (1998): 95–120.

———. "The Institute Economists: From Physiocracy to Entrepreneurial Capitalism." *The History of Political Economy* 19, no. 4 (1987): 525–50.

Steiner, Philippe. "Say et le libéralisme économique." In *Histoire du libéralisme en Europe,* edited by Philippe Nemo and Jean Petitot, 381–403. Paris: Presses universitaires de France, 2006.

Swedberg, Richard. *Tocqueville's Political Economy.* Princeton: Princeton University Press, 2009.

Taussig, Frank. *The Tariff History of the United States.* 6th ed. New York: G. P. Putnam, 1914.

Tena-Junguito, Antonio. "Assessing the Protectionist Intensity of Tariffs in Nineteenth-Century European Trade Policy." In *Classical Trade Protectionism 1815–1914,* edited by Jean-Pierre Dormois and Pedro Lains, 99–120. London: Routledge, 2005.

Todd, David. *L'Identité économique de la France: Libre-échange et protectionnisme, 1814–1851.* Paris: Grasset, 2008.

Vanhaute, Eric, C. O'Grada, and R. Paping. "The European Subsistence Crisis of 1845–1850. A Comparative Perspective." In *When the Potato Failed: Causes and Effects of the "Last" European Subsistence Crisis, 1845–1850,* edited by E. Vanhaute, C. O'Grada, and R. Paping, 15–42. Turnhout: Brepols Publishers, 2007.

Waha, Raymond de. *Die Nationalökonomie in Frankreich.* 2 vols. Stuttgart: Ferdinand Enke, 1910.

Weil, Georges. *Histoire de parti républicain en France, 1814–1870.* Paris: F. Alcan, 1928.

Welch, Cheryl B. *Liberty and Utility: The French Idéologues and the Transformation of Liberalism.* New York: Columbia University Press, 1984.

Whatmore, Richard. *Republicanism and the French Revolution: An Intellectual History of Jean-Baptiste Say's Political Economy.* Oxford: Oxford University Press, 2000.

Index

Molinari, Gustave de (*continued*)
la Révolution, 482, 482n31, 554; "Frédéric
Bastiat: Lettres d'un habitant des Landes," 390n16; and *Jacques Bonhomme*,
lxx, 522, 568–69; and *Le Journal des
économistes*, 569; and labor exchanges,
441n1, 525n1; "The Law-Abiding Revolutionary," lxviiin40; *The Learned Ladies*
[Les Femmes savantes], 345n4; and *Le
Libre-échange*, 570; and Malthusian theory, 463; on Martineau's writing, 116n4,
552; and *La République française*, lxviii,
lxviiin40, 377n1, 387n8, 390n16, 524n1,
571; *Les Révolutions et le despotisme envisagés au point de vue des intérêts matériel*,
480n24, 482, 482n30; and Smithian
view of the state, 462n3; *Les Soirées de
la rue Saint-Lazare* [Conversations on
Saint Lazarus Street], 413n2, 462n3, 471,
531n5, 539, 554; supporter of Napoléon,
538; and theater, 413n2; and utopianism,
583; "L'Utopie de la liberté. Lettres aux
socialistes" [The Utopia of Liberty. Letters to the Socialists], 187n2; writings
of, 539
monarchists, 487–88
monarchy. *See also* July Monarchy; Restoration; constitutional, 464; in England,
328–29; during Restoration, 486
monasteries, 158n7
"Mondor" and "Tabarin." *See* Girard, Antoine and Philippe
money. *See also* currencies; "Damned
Money" (CW4), xxiii, lxxii, lxxiin49,
429n4, 444–45n2; defined, xxxii;
printing of, 437; terms for, xxv; types of,
437n2
moneylenders, 445n3
"Monita Secreta: The Secret Book of
Instructions" (ES3 20), lvi–lvii, 65n2,
371–77, 457
Le Moniteur (government journal), 199,
199n4, 491
Le Moniteur industriel (journal), 5, 5n6, 146,
148n8, 155n1, 166, 167, 199n4, 230–31,
245n11, 246, 259, 269n2, 271, 273, 297,

297n4, 305, 349–50, 358, 360–61, 363–
64, 406, 489, 570
monopoly: electoral monopoly, 392n23;
"The Physiology of Plunder" (ES2 1),
114–16, 115n3, 128–30; "The Specialists"
(ES3 11), 308; "To Artisans and Workers"
(ES2 6), 159; true vs. natural monopoly,
128n19
Montagnards, 223n15, 422n1, 488, 489
Montaigne, Michel Eyquem de, xlix, 11, 531,
554–55; *Essays*, 554; "Le Profit d'un est
dommage de l'autre" [One Man's Gain
is Another Man's Loss], xlix, 11, 11n7,
108n12, 179n1, 337n18, 555
Montesquieu, Charles Louis de Secondat,
Baron de, 531, 555; Destutt de Tracy on,
543
Moore, Edward, 333, 333n14
morality: anti-luxury nature of, 444, 449;
morally good, 78n1; and public interest,
446; "Two Moral Philosophies" (ES2 2),
xxii, lvi, lvii–lviii, lviiin22, lixn23, 131–38,
477n17, 483
Moreau de Jonnès, Alexandre, 62, 62n3, 555
"More Reciprocity" (ES1 15), 78–79
Morocco, 136n11
Morrill tariff of 1861, lxxix
Mugron (France), 305n2, 359n13, 366n4,
491–92, 566
mutual aid societies, 143, 143n2, 441, 441n5
mythology, 342; Minotaur, 265n8, 342; Pan
vs. Apollo in musical competition, 170n1

names, in original French, xxx
Napoléon Bonaparte, lxi, 223n15, 358, 420,
537–38; Bastiat as supporter of, 538; and
cantonniers system, 60n7; and Colonne
Vendôme, 180n5; and Continental
Blockade, 5n7, 22n7, 280n4, 503, 537,
538; defeat of, 120n10; and education,
494; *Mémoires*, 5n7, 420n5, 538; and
public works, 420, 420n5; and Roustam/
Roustan Raza, 358n11; and slavery, 366n2,
506; supporters of, 223n15, 488; on tariffs,
5, 5n7; tax administration under, 195n22,
501, 502

This book is set in Adobe Garamond, designed by Robert Slimbach in 1989. The face is based on the refined array of the typefaces of French punchcutter, type designer, and publisher Claude Garamond. These faces combine an unprecedented degree of balance and elegance and stand as a pinnacle of beauty and practicality in sixteenth-century typefounding.

Claude Garamond (ca. 1480–1561), a true Renaissance man, introduced the apostrophe, the accent, and the cedilla to the French language.

This book is printed on paper that is acid-free and meets the requirements of the American National Standard for Permanence of Paper for Printed Library Materials, Z39.48-1992. ∞

Book designed by Barbara E. Williams
BW&A Books, Inc.
Durham, North Carolina
Typography by Graphic Composition, Inc.
Athens/Bogart, Georgia
Printed and bound by Color House Graphics,
Grand Rapids, Michigan